CRITICAL SURVEY
OF
POETRY

CRITICAL SURVEY
OF
POETRY

English Language Series

Authors
Hoo–McK

4

Edited by
FRANK N. MAGILL

Academic Director
WALTON BEACHAM

SALEM PRESS
Englewood Cliffs, N. J.

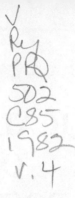

LIBRARY OF CONGRESS CATALOG CARD NUMBER: 82-62168
Complete Set: ISBN 0-89356-340-4
Volume 4: ISBN 0-89356-344-7

Second Printing

PRINTED IN THE UNITED STATES OF AMERICA

LIST OF AUTHORS IN VOLUME 4

CRITICAL SURVEY
OF
POETRY

THOMAS HOOD

Born: London, England; May 23, 1799
Died: London, England; May 3, 1845

Principal poems and collections
Odes and Addresses to Great People, 1825 (with John Hamilton Reynolds); *Whims and Oddities: In Prose and Verse*, 1826-1827; *The Plea of the Midsummer Fairies, Hero and Leander, Lycus the Centaur, and Other Poems*, 1827; *The Comic Annual*, 1830-1839, 1842 (poetry and prose); *The Epping Hunt*, 1829; *The Dream of Eugene Aram*, 1831; *Hood's Own: Or, Laughter from Year to Year*, 1839; *Whimsicalities: A Periodical Gathering*, 1844.

Other literary forms
As a journalist, Thomas Hood contributed prose as well as poetry to such periodicals as the *London Magazine*, *The New Monthly Magazine*, and *Hood's Magazine and Comic Miscellany*, while serving as their editor. He also wrote drama criticism for *The Atlas* for several months in 1826, before trying to write dramatic pieces of his own. In 1828, he wrote an ill-fated farce, *York and Lancaster: Or, A School Without Scholars*, for the theater manager Frederick Henry Yates, and followed this unsuccessful attempt with at least two more burlesques which have been lost in whole or in part. He wrote two closet dramas that were not published until after his death: *Lamia: A Romance* (published in 1852) based on Keats's poem of the same title, and *Guido and Marina: A Dramatic Sketch* (published in 1882), a romantic dialogue.

Hood did numerous etchings and drawings for his publications, and had others executed under his direction. His best-known engraving, "The Progress of Cant," a large Hogarthian-style work published in 1825, shows a rag-tag parade of Londoners bearing signs and banners to proclaim their favorite causes and philosophies, meanwhile exhibiting their contrary actions.

Encouraged by the early success of his first volumes of comic verse, Hood published a two-volume collection of short stories entitled *National Tales* in 1827; unfortunately, just as his attempts to write drama demonstrated his lack of dramatic skill, the stories exhibited that he had no real talent for prose fiction. Hood imitated the Italian *novella* form used by the Elizabethans, without writing a single story of literary value. He also wrote two novels— *Tylney Hall* (1834) and *Up the Rhine* (1840)—with somewhat better popular success, although the novels were nearly as lacking in literary merit. *Tylney Hall* went through numerous printings in England and America, but owed its success to the humorous portions; the serious plot and major characters are rather insipid, manifesting the same contrivance and shallowness that afflicted his short stores. *Up the Rhine* was a success in the bookstalls—in England, America, and, predictably, in Frankfurt. A travelogue-novel similar to Mark Twain's *Innocents Abroad* (1869), *Up the Rhine* draws upon Hood's "exile" years in Germany (1835 to 1839). It is light and enjoyable reading, but far from "quality" fiction. In both novels Hood gave free vent to his punning genius, which adds humor but detracts from the overall temper of both stories. Another novel, *Our Family*, remained incomplete at Hood's death, although several chapters were published serially in *Hood's Magazine* (it was eventually published in 1861). There is no evidence that Hood's aspirations to be a novelist would have produced a better book. His many letters, though often delightful and always sparkling with wit and humor, are difficult to read. Hood's main difficulty as a prose writer was his inability to sustain a smooth, readable text that is not chopped up by distracting word-play; in addition, he was simply not a good storyteller. Both problems greatly handicapped his ability to write long poetic narratives as well.

Achievements

Hood's position in the generally overlooked period between the end of the Romantic movement and the beginning of the Victorian era has caused his true importance to be greatly underestimated. Although he can scarcely be called one of the giants of English poetry, his achievements are far from insignificant. His primary contributions to English letters have been fourfold: the refinement of English poetic humor, the popularization of poetry, the sympathetic portrayal of common English domesticity, and the arousal of humanitarian sentiments on a popular level.

Hood's comic verse—of which the amount is greater than and the quality superior to the work of any other English or American poet—evolved into what J. C. Reid calls "a highly individual amalgam of the farcical and the sinister, the pathetic and the ghoulish, that has few ancestors but many heirs." Hood's peculiar style did not preclude his diverse experimentation, whereby he often imitated and improved upon earlier comic techniques. He remains without rival in the use of the pun. He left a legacy of humorous poetry so varied that it not only provides a smooth transition from the often acrimonious wit of the eighteenth century—with none of the acrimony—but also often anticipates comic techniques and themes that died with Hood until they were resurrected in the twentieth century, especially in the dark or grotesque humor of writers such as Franz Kafka.

Because Hood made poetry relevant to everyday life and wrote in a highly entertaining style, verse once more became something that the common people could enjoy. Since the death of William Shakespeare, who also catered in his drama to popular tastes, poetry had become an almost purely academic art form. The neoclassical movement isolated poetry from the common man to a great extent through various formulary restraints and elevated diction. The Romantic movement sought to reestablish the language of life as the language of poetry, but the philosophy and ideals of many Romantics were inaccessible to the masses. Hood popularized poetry by brilliantly expressing commonplace ideas in common words.

Writing for a popular audience meant being free to explore popular themes. Hood's treatment of domestic scenes merits special attention. Ordinary house-wives and mothers, with their squalling babes in arms, domestic servants, husband-wife or parent-child relations, all of the accoutrements of home and hearth (especially cookery) receive sympathetic treatment from the pen of this devoted family man. Hood takes the reader into mansions, but through the servant's entrance, and takes the butler's perspective or leaves the reader in the kitchen. What William Hogarth did with engraving, Hood did with poetry. Not afflicted by pretension or ambition, but sensitive to both, he remained the poet of the common man throughout his career.

In his later years, this sympathy for the proletariat led to some of the first and finest advocacy of basic human rights ever to be expressed in verse. Hood echoed the faint cries of social protest sounded by William Blake, amplified them, and added his own passionate appeals for reform. Never a revolution-ary, Hood sought to inspire the upper middle class to extend a hand of true charity and compassion to the needs of the poor, sought to influence indus-trialists to pay a decent wage, sought to influence a notoriously competitive society to reassess its values. Hood was a voice crying somewhat in vain in the wilderness, but those he inspired were able to induce many notable social reforms in the second half of the nineteenth century.

On a more mundane level, Hood served in various editorial and journalistic capacities from 1821, when he became a proofreader and contributor for the *London Magazine*, until 1845, when he was still producing material on his deathbed for the magazine he had founded, *Hood's Magazine*. In the years between, he was associated with *The Atlas* (as drama critic, 1826), *The New Monthly Magazine* (as editor, 1841-1843), and a number of annuals, including his own *Comic Annual*.

Biography

Thomas Hood's father, also named Thomas, was a partner in the book-selling and publishing firm of Vernor and Hood, which produced *Poetical Magazine*, *Lady's Monthly Museum*, and the *Monthly Mirror*. His mother, Elizabeth Sands, was the daughter of an engraver. Both occupations deter-mined the future career of Thomas Hood, one of six children in the Hood family to survive infancy. Hood's early education was at an Islington prepa-ratory school, then at the Alfred House Academy at Camberwell Green. The deaths of his father and elder brother in 1811 left Thomas the man of the family, so he took a job clerking to supplement the family income. Poor health forced him to move from clerking to engraving for his uncle, but because his constitution continued to suffer, he was sent in 1815 to live with relatives in Dundee, Scotland, where he continued his apprenticeship in the engraving trade. At Dundee Hood began writing seriously. His health improved, and he returned to London in the autumn of 1817, where he worked as an engraver until he was hired in 1821 by John Taylor, a former employee of Hood's father and then editor of the *London Magazine*. Within a few months his mother died, leaving Hood the responsibility of providing for four sisters, one of whom also died a short time later.

At the *London Magazine* Hood was plunged into the company of many of England's prominent writers—Charles Lamb, Allan Cunningham, T. G. Wainewright, and John Hamilton Reynolds. Hood's friendship with Reynolds brought him into close contact with the circle and work of the recently deceased John Keats, and Hood strove for several years to imitate the great Romantic's lush and effusive style. Indeed, he was thought by many (including Cunningham) to be the logical successor of Keats, but Hood's collaboration with Reynolds on a book of comic verse in 1825 did more to further his literary career than any of his attempts to imitate the Romantics. During the same year, Hood married Reynolds' sister Jane and settled into the domestic life that would later inspire much of his poetry. Since he had ceased to edit the *London Magazine* during the previous year, Hood was obliged to publish in earnest for an income.

Hood's first daughter was born and died in May, 1827, inspiring Lamb's famous elegy "On an Infant Dying as Soon as Born." Hood's repeated exposure to the death of those closest to him was having a profound impact on his poetry, in which death figures so prominently. The following year an attack of rheumatic fever left Hood in the weakened condition that plagued him for the rest of his life. Hood continued writing, even while ill, since it was his sole means of support. He produced the first of his *Comic Annuals* in 1830, the year that his daughter Frances Freeling was born. Although his comic verse was popular, the Hood family never advanced beyond a lower-middle-class life-style. In 1832, they moved into their own home—Lake House in Wanstead—but the failure in 1834 of an engraving firm in which Hood had heavily invested, together with his own financial mismanagement, forced them to relinquish the house and accept the more economical life of the Continent. After the birth of his only son, Tom, Hood moved his family to Coblentz, Germany, to begin an "exile" that lasted until 1840.

In 1841, Hood assumed the editorship of *The New Monthly Magazine*. In and out of illness, financially struggling, and changing residences almost annually, Hood began to write his poems of social conscience. In 1843, he ceased editing *The New Monthly Magazine* to found *Hood's Magazine*, which he edited until early in 1845, although he was seriously ill during the entire period. A Civil List pension was granted his wife in November, 1844, when Hood was confined to what would be his deathbed. He continued writing almost to the very end. He died in May, 1845, and is buried at Kensal Green, London. Perhaps the finest tribute to his poetry is found in a letter from Hood to Frederick Ward, written in the summer of 1844: "Though I may not have reflected any very great honour on our national literature, I have not disgraced it. . . ." Such humility was typical of Thomas Hood.

Analysis

Primarily because he lived to write and wrote to live, Thomas Hood managed to publish a staggering amount of poetry in a relatively short time. Unfortunately, the pressure to keep the creditors at bay and the bacon on his table rendered much of his poetry unworthy of regard; he often failed to edit poems for which he could hardly afford enough time to write. He was seldom more than a hack writer, churning out journalistic doggerel and meanwhile maintaining an apparently voluminous correspondence, editing his annuals and magazines, executing his engravings, and trying to establish a reputation as a novelist. The mystery of his life is that he accomplished all this as a frequently bedridden invalid.

As a consequence of his need to offer original and entertaining poetry to the public on a regular basis, Hood wandered widely through the realm of possibilities to produce a profusion of experiments in form and content, in theme, rhythm, and rhyme—perhaps covering a wider range than any other English poet. In Hood one can find examples of such peculiarities as initial rhyme, various metrical arrangements of anapests and dactyls, all the major English stanza forms, and imitations of numerous styles—from those of Geoffrey Chaucer, Edmund Spenser, John Milton, Alexander Pope, Percy Bysshe Shelley, Lord Byron, Keats, and Shakespeare, to a host of lesser lights. Hood's imitations are often well-executed; his originals are even better. Omitting what is merely topical, trivial, childish, or deplorable, one finds that the remainder of Hood's canon contains a considerable quantity of poetry, some of it brilliant.

Hood began writing poetry as a pastime about 1814, during the period when he supplemented the family income by working as a clerk. In "Literary Reminiscences" (1833), Hood recalls how he stole moments from his employer, uninformatively identified as "Bell & Co.," to "take stray dips in the Castalian pool." A year later, after removing to Dundee, Scotland, to improve his health, Hood started writing a satirical *Dundee Guide*, the manuscript of which was unfortunately lost by 1820, although enough lines survived in a letter to show that it was nothing brilliant. As early as 1816, however, Hood began making anonymous contributions to Dundee periodicals, and thus first began to see his work in print. This fired him with a thirst to sell himself to "that minor Mephistopheles, the Printer's Devil." Hood was at this time being influenced by William Wordsworth and Samuel Taylor Coleridge, Byron, and Shelley; to a lesser extent by Charles Lamb, George Crabbe, Robert Southey, and Leigh Hunt; and most of all by Sir Walter Scott, "The Great Unknown." The narrative manner of Byron's *Childe Harold's Pilgrimage* (1812-1818), *The*

Giaour (1813), *The Bride of Abydos* (1813), *The Corsair* (1814), and *Lara* (1814) tempered by the influence of Scott's *The Lay of the Last Minstrel* (1805), *Marmion* (1808), *The Lady of the Lake* (1810), *Waverley* (1814), and *Rokeby* (1815) combined to foster Hood's first major poem, *The Bandit*, probably written between 1815 and 1817 but not published until forty years after his death.

The Bandit is a relatively long poem (some 820 lines divided into three cantos), a narrative about Ulric, the Earl of Glenallen, who, as a result of treacherous circumstances, has been forced into the role of "Chieftain" to a band of outlaws. Although a cunning and brave leader, Glenallen secretly despises the mischievous deeds he has done, yet "Repeated wrongs had turned his breast to steel,/ And all but these he had forgot to feel." In the first canto, Glenallen discloses the plans of his final act as chief of the bandits, "To 'venge the wrongs he suffered from the world!" Heedlessly, he discloses to the outlaws his true identity as Earl of Glenallen, proclaimed a traitor to the throne of Scotland. All the bandits except Wolf, Glenallen's rival, depart with the chieftain to take revenge on Glenallen's former friend, Arden, at the latter's wedding to Glenallen's former betrothed, Adelaide. In the second canto, Glenallen disrupts the wedding and announces his intention of murdering Arden before he can consummate the marriage; but after the pitiful pleadings of "trembling Adelaide," he repents and orders his bandits to disperse. Just as this moment Wolf arrives with another band to take Glenallen for the reward on his head. In the ensuing swordplay, Arden makes several attempts to save the life of Glenallen, who is finally wounded into unconsciousness after killing Wolf. Before the bandits can deal with the wedding guests, however, the castle is mysteriously set afire. The bandits take up the unconscious Glenallen and flee. Canto three opens with Glenallen already in the custody of the authorities, locked away in a tower and awaiting execution. In his bitterness of soul, he eagerly awaits the release that death will bring him. The keeper enters and proves to be a former confederate: "Is it Donald! or a mocking dream?/ Are these things so, or do they only seem?/ Am I awake?" Donald, after failing to convince Glenallen to escape, and in haste for what seems to be the sound of an approaching guard escort, lends his dagger to the captive so that he might dispatch himself honorably. Glenallen perishes just as "Pardon! Pardon!" echoes on the walls and Arden rushes into the cell.

The puerility of the plot and the verse fails to disguise the influences of Romanticism. Glenallen is a typically Romantic hero, arraigned in a stock melodramatic situation, pausing at the appropriate times to brood over his cruel alienation from humanity and life, more ready to die than to live. His is the childish fantasy of "after I'm dead and gone, then they'll be sorry they hurt me," but, after all, it is the same childishness of vision that pervades much of Byron and Shelley. The significance of *The Bandit* lies in Hood's ability to use language well and to exercise a healthy imagination in verse that accommodates at least the superficial elements of Romanticism at a time before he has seriously devoted himself to writing poetry.

Although there were Romantic tendencies in Hood's own writing before Keats's death, one can find in his verse a pronounced identification with the style of Keats that extends about five or six years after 1821, beginning with Hood's introduction to the Reynolds family through his work at the *London Magazine* that same year. John Hamilton Reynolds and his sisters had enjoyed a close friendship with Keats, and entertained fond memories of the young Romantic. Hood entered an atmosphere in the Reynolds household suffused with intimacies from the life and work of the relatively unknown Keats. To this period belongs most of what is often called Hood's "serious" poetry. The Romantic movement had peaked and already begun to decline into the commonplace sentimentality and melodrama from which Robert Browning and Alfred, Lord Tennyson were destined to rescue it momentarily. Shelley and Byron's best works had already been published; indeed, Shelley died soon after Keats. Coleridge had graduated to philosophy, Wordsworth had defected to the establishment. Keats's final volume—*Lamia, Isabella, The Eve of St. Agnes, and Other Poems*—had appeared in 1820 (Hood's closet drama *Lamia*, based on Keats's poem, was written in 1824, but not published until after Hood's death). With friendly critics encouraging and applauding the growing likeness of Hood's poetry to that of Keats, it was an easy time for Hood to begin imagining himself to be Keats's successor.

Perhaps a sense of identification with Keats's illness and death led Hood to give death such a preeminent place in his serious and even in his comic verse. Hood seems to accord death a place of passive acceptance, at times even to embrace it. For example, "The Sea of Death," which appeared first in the *London Magazine* (March, 1822) and later in *Plea of the Midsummer Fairies*, makes the somewhat trite comparison of death to an "ocean-past" that erases the sand-tracks of life "like a pursuing grave." This idea, however, is developed into a passively beautiful scene, where "spring-faced cherubs" also are asleep in "the birth-night of their peace," For contrast, Hood adds "neighbour brows scarr'd by the brunts/ Of strife and sorrowing"; and with the dead, Time itself "Slept, as he sleeps upon the silent face/ Of a dark dial in a sunless place." It is a typically Romantic eschatology; death is a place of silence and repose, a dreamlike eternity. Although Hood's view of death acquired a more theologically sound dimension during the next twenty years, his attitude of resignation to the inevitable does not change. His awareness of the closeness of death permeates all of his poetry; death, dying, and corruption tinge nearly every poem with sobriety and cause his humor to wax dark. Living in continual ill health as he did, this could hardly be called a Romantic affectation.

Hood's important poems from this period include a number of sonnets, many deserving more attention than they have received. The sonnets also reflect the influence of the Romantic poets. "Midnight," the pair "On a Sleeping Child" (all three in the *London Magazine*, December, 1822), and the eulogistic "Sonnet: Written in Keats's 'Endymion'" (the *London Magazine*, May, 1823) are among his very best. Another, beginning "It is not death . . .," reveals not only Romantic, but also direct Shakespearean influence. It was included, along with most of his other "serious" poetry, in the volume *Plea of the Midsummer Fairies*.

Most of the poems in this book (twenty-two out of thirty-seven) had been previously published, many in the *London Magazine*. The book constitutes the evidence offered by many that Hood was a thwarted Romantic, so pervasive is the influence of Keats. The title poem consists of 126 Spenserian stanzas (except that the final lines are pentameters), celebrating, "by an allegory, that immortality which Shakspeare has conferred on the Fairy mythology by his Midsummer Night's Dream." Hood has previously written a fairly long Romantic allegory, *The Two Swans* (1824), and so had prepared himself to create what he no doubt hoped would be considered his masterpiece. Charles Lamb, to whom the poem was affectionately dedicated, likened the poem to "the songs of Apollo," but few others have felt it to be so. Although the poem abounds in the lush sensual imagery characteristic of Keats, it sags hopelessly throughout, mainly because the story is too skimpy and the monologues too substantial for a narrative of that length. The narrator, who happens upon a circle of accommodating but unhappy fairies (including Titania, Puck, Ariel, and Queen Mab), learns from Titania that they are unhappy because their "fairy lives/ Are leased upon the fickle faith of men." Her complaint lasts through nearly eight stanzas, after which the "melancholy Shape" of Time (Saturn, Mutability) appears with "hurtful scythe" to harvest the wee folk. After an argument between the fairies and Saturn that lasts seventy-five stanzas (nearly sixty percent of the poem), the ghost of Shakespeare arrives just in time to save the fairies, who express their affectionate gratitude by crowning the Bard with a halo "Such as erst crown'd the old Apostle's head." As an allegory defending the importance of imagination (Fancy) above Reason in poetry, the significance of human feeling, the allurements of Nature, and the mysterious, "Plea of the Midsummer Fairies" fails; seeking to establish the principles of the Romantic movement, Hood offended through employment of its excesses.

The second poem in the volume, *Hero and Leander*, while certainly not lagging as a narrative, nearly approaches *The Bandit* in its tendency toward melodrama. Written in the sestina form of Shakespeare's *Venus and Adonis* (1593), the poem has a loveliness of its own but it is not brilliant. By far the better is the third poem, *Lycus, the Centaur*, first published in 1822. Dedicated to Reynolds, it employs the strikingly unusual rhythm of anapestic tetrameter couplets that give the impression of fast-paced narrative; it is a galloping rhythm, suitable to horses and centaurs. The 430 lines of the poem are rich in sensuous detail, a feature that lies nearly dormant in poetry from Keats to A. C. Swinburne. *Lycus, the Centaur* must be read aloud to be thoroughly appreciated. Admittedly, Hood's poetry did not achieve anything near perfection. The poem has flaws, as when Lycus complains of his loneliness: "There were women! there men! but to me a third sex/ I saw them all dots— yet I loved them as specks"; or when several successive closed couplets begin to give the feel of "The Night Before Christmas," but *Lycus, the Centaur*, for all its faults and its Keatsian imagery, is original and beautiful.

Most critics agree that the best poems in *Plea of the Midsummer Fairies* are the lyrics, most of which are definitely Keatsian. Hood's "Ode: Autumn" at times provides an interesting contrast to Keats's "Ode to Autumn," but there is more to compare than to contrast. Two other short poems on autumn are included in the volume, as are three poems on the loss of innocence ("Retrospective Review," "Song, for Music," and "I Remember, I Remember"), a decent "Ode to Melancholy," and some of Hood's best sonnets. Pervasive throughout the book is the awareness, without terror, of death and corruption. Although the volume of serious poems caused some readers to see Hood as a worthy successor to Keats, *Plea of the Midsummer Fairies* met with a generally poor critical and public reception and failed to sell out even a single printing.

The apparent cause of this cool reception is that during the years immediately preceding its publication Hood had captured the public's attention as a writer of comic verse. In 1825 he produced *Odes and Addresses to Great People* (in collaboration with Reynolds), and in the following year the first series of *Whims and Oddities*. The time for humor in poetry had come—not the incisive, often caustic wit of the eighteenth century, but an inoffensive, wholesome humor to help people laugh their way through the oppressively industrial times at the beginning of the nineteenth century. The reading public wanted a humor that appealed to men of low estate without being vulgar. It found in the humorous verse of Thomas Hood exactly what it sought, and came to expect nothing more nor less than that from him.

The success of Hood's early comic publications depended heavily upon his skill as a punster, examples of which are so abundant that they need not be dwelt upon at length. Most commonly cited in this regard are the two ballads, "Faithless Sally Brown" and "Faithless Nelly Gray." In the first, two lovers go out for a walk that is interrupted by an impress gang from the Royal Navy: "And Sally she did faint away,/ While Ben he was brought to." After Ben's tour of duty is finished, he returns to find Sally is another man's sweetheart; he laments, "I've met with many a breeze before,/ But never such a blow." In the opening stanza of the second poem, "Ben Battle was a soldier bold,/ And used to war's alarms:/ But a cannon-ball took off his legs,/ So he laid down his arms!" Although these are not the best examples of his craft, there is no question that Hood was the best punster of his century (perhaps the best in English letters); most of his puns are exceptional. Unfortunately, much of Hood's humor is topical; many of his puns and jokes cannot be grasped by the modern reader without an understanding of the times and a knowledge of the idiom of the 1820's and 1830's. Even so, many of Hood's poems retain an appreciable humor for today because they present general observations on the human condition. The most notable include "An Address to the Steam Washing Company" in *Odes and Addresses*; "A Valentine," "The Fall of the Deer," "December and May," "She Is Far from the Land," "Remonstratory Ode: From the Elephant at Exeter Change. . . ," "The Sea-Spell," and the darkly humorous "The Last Man," all in *Whims and Oddities* (First Series); and "Bianca's Dream," "A Legend of Navarre," "The Demon-Ship," and "Tim Turpin" in *Whims and Oddities* (Second Series). In "The Demon-Ship" Hood does a masterful job of creating a terrifying situation that is reversed in the humor of the closing lines; in "The Last Man," the wry ending cannot shift a much longer poem into the comic mode, so that the overall effect is far from humorous. As a serious poem, "The Last Man" offers a brilliant description of a postapocalyptic world.

Hood continued writing "serious" poetry during the remainder of his life, but until the last few years his comic verse claimed the limelight. With the failure of the engraving firm in 1834, and the subsequent "exile" to Germany, however, financial and physical hardship weighed heavily upon Hood and his family, and his comic verses began to acquire a certain note of sobriety. There had always been a loosely didactic element, a flexible moralizing, in his humor. Without gross distastefulness, Hood amused his audience by good-naturedly ridiculing people and institutions that were newsworthy or offensive to the public—in a way that often seemed to "teach a lesson." One of the most consistent objects of his humor was human greed; another was impoverishment. Employee displacement caused by unjust laws or advancements in technological efficiency also provoked his satirical wit. Since Hood no longer entertained hopes of succeeding Keats, his "serious" poetry began to develop an originality and power of its own, as Hood became a voice of the people's protest against those institutions. Hypocrisy and ambition became primary targets of his comic verse, which also developed a morbid, often sadistic, grotesqueness. Poems such as "Death's Ramble," from *Whims and Oddities*, in which a morality play is effected through pun after pun, led to "Death in the Kitchen" (1828), in which the puns are ingenious but the philosophizing about death unhumorous; to "Gog and Magog" (1830), with its hints of judgment and violence; to "Ode to Mr. Malthus" (1839), wherein the double standard of the well-to-do is satirized; and, finally, to *Miss Kilmansegg and Her Precious Leg* (1840). Each poem outdoes the last in taking a more caustic, albeit humorous, view of humanity or some of its elements.

Beginning with *Miss Kilmansegg and Her Precious Leg*, the serious side of Hood sought to reassert itself again, this time with a vigor and force of wit that it had manifested only in comic verse, but with a simplicity of expression unencumbered by flowery Romantic or Elizabethan rhetoric. During the final years of his life, Hood produced his greatest impact on English poetry in the songs of social protest—*Miss Kilmansegg and Her Precious Leg*, "The Song of the Shirt," "The Bridge of Sighs," and others—and his artistic masterpiece, "The Haunted House," which alone said Edgar Allen Poe, "would have secured immortality for any poet of the nineteenth century."

Miss Kilmansegg and Her Precious Leg is a long satirical narrative of almost 2,400 lines. The central character is born into a family of great wealth

> When she saw the light—it was no mere ray
> Of that light so common—so everyday—
> That the sun each morning launches—
> But six wax tapers dazzled her eyes,
> From a thing—a gooseberry bush for size—
> With a golden stem and branches.

After separate passages dealing in detail with her pedigree, birth, christening, childhood, and education, the reader learns that one day, while riding, Miss Kilmansegg lost control of her horse, which bolted at the sight of a ragged beggar, and in the ensuing accident "Miss K." lost her leg. Because she had been educated to a life-style of conspicuous consumption and hatred for the ordinary, she insists fanatically on replacing her natural leg with a golden one: "All sterling metal—not half-and-half,/ The Goldsmith's mark was stamped on the calf." (The pun on "golden calf" is intentional.) After she receives the expensive leg, the poem pursues her through her career as a fashionable debutante, her courtship, and her subsequent marriage to a foreign Count of questionable origin. Their honeymoon is spent at a country estate, where she learns that her husband's sole interest is gambling. After several years of tumultuous living that exhausts all of "Miss K's" resources, the Count murders her in the night, using her expensive leg as a bludgeon. Hood concludes the poem with a moral reminiscent of the "Pardoner's Tale" from Chaucer: "Price of many a crime untold;/ Gold! Gold! Gold! Gold:/ Good or bad a thousand fold!" The poem is very funny throughout, but the humor is accompanied by an undercurrent of bitterness against the rich, and the moralizing stanza at the poem's conclusion seems to affirm its serious didactic intention.

Eight months later the *New Monthly Magazine* published Hood's *A Tale of a Trumpet*, another long satirical poem, this time about a deaf woman to whom the Devil supplies a trumpet through which she can hear all manner of scandalous gossip. Again, the poem ends in a moral against rumor-mongering. In November, 1843, *Punch* published Hood's "A Drop of Gin," a poem reminiscent of Hogarth's famous engraving "Gin Lane." The following month *Punch* published "The Pauper's Christmas Carol" and "The Song of the Shirt," poems of social protest which probably better express Hood's mind than any other poems of his last fifteen years.

"The Song of the Shirt," with its driving, mechanical rhythm, is based on the plight of a poor widowed woman with starving infants who was arrested while trying to pawn some of her employer's garments to obtain money for food (she was a seamstress for seven shillings a week). Touched by the newspaper accounts and always sensitive to the exploitation of the poor, Hood wrote what his wife considered to be his finest poem. In it, a woman sits sewing, and as she sews she sings the "Song of the Shirt": "Work! work! work!/ While the cock is crowing aloof!/ And work—work—work,/ Till the stars shine through the roof!" The poem calls to mind the protest movements, and revolutions which were soon to plague Europe in the wake of the Industrial Revolution—and the publication of Karl Marx's *Communist Manifesto* in 1848 and *Das Kapital* in 1850. The Woman's lament is a desperate appeal born of the most abject misery: "Oh! God! that bread should be so dear,/ And flesh and blood so cheap!"

"The Haunted House" (*Hood's Magazine*, January, 1844) over which Poe became ecstatic, is indeed a powerful artistic creation: a descriptive, camera-eye narrative that builds an atmosphere of terror—which dissipates in the absolute meaninglessness of the poem. The reader can learn nothing of the source of the mystery, other than that a murder has apparently been committed, and that the house is haunted. The conclusion of the poem could be transplanted to any other part of the poem without disrupting the internal logic. It is as if Hood had left "The Haunted House" unfinished, perhaps to add to the sense of mystery and terror, but more likely through a lack of inspiration.

The artistic achievement represented by this poem notwithstanding, Hood's heart in these last years was more concerned with the suffering of others. Having spent so many years in sickness and pain, laboring feverishly to meet endless deadlines, striving in spite of his own sufferings to make others laugh, he had acquired a true compassion for the poor and unfortunate that sought to be expressed in his verse. His last years of writing produced "The Lady's Dream" (February, 1844), a song of regret for a life not spent ministering to the needs of others; "The Workhouse Clock" (April, 1844), an "allegory" that fires its blistering sermon at a leisurely middle class: "Christian Charity, hang your head!"; and "The Lay of the Labourer" (November, 1844), a panegyric to the working class.

A final volume of comic verse—*Whimsicalities: A Periodical Gathering*—appeared in 1844, but besides "The Haunted House," Hood's most regarded publication of that year is "The Bridge of Sighs." Often anthologized or cited as an example of dactylic verse, it concerns a young woman who commits a desperate suicide by leaping from a city bridge. Journalistic, as most of Hood's verse was, "The Bridge of Sighs" is based on an actual case; whatever the circumstances of the original suicide were, however, Hood turns the incident to good use in expounding a favorite theme:

> Alas! for the rarity
> Of Christian charity
> Under the sun!
> Oh! it was pitiful!
> Near a whole city full,
> Home she had none!

Hood continued to write even as he lay upon his deathbed, where, among other poems and letters, he produced "Stanzas" (March, 1845): "Farewell, Life! My senses swim;/ And the world is growing dim;/ . . . Strong the earthy odour grows—/ I smell the Mould above the Rose!" Hood's farewell to life concludes with the same homely, cheerful philosophy that infused so much poetry written in pain, the same positive outlook that inspired him to ask for reform rather than revolution: "Welcome, Life! the Spirit strives!/ Strength returns, and hope revives;/ . . . I smell the Rose above the Mould!" The juxtaposition of the stanzas intimates that Hood's source of hope and strength was his willingness to embrace death without terror. Nine years after his death, a monument was erected over his grave, paid for by public subscription. Beneath the bust of Hood is engraved a simple coat-of-arms: on the shield is a heart pierced by a sewing needle; under it, the scroll reads, at Hood's request, "He sang the Song of the Shirt."

Major publications other than poetry
NOVELS: *Tylney Hall*, 1834; *Up the Rhine*, 1840.
SHORT FICTION: *National Tales*, 1827.
PLAYS: *York and Lancaster: Or, A School Without Scholars*, 1828 (written); *Lamia: A Romance*, 1852; *Guido and Marina*, 1882.
MISCELLANEOUS: *The Works of Thomas Hood*, 1869-1873 (Thomas Hood, Jr., and Mrs. Frances Freeling Broderip, editors, 10 volumes); 1882-1884 (11 volumes); 1972 (8 volumes).

Bibliography
Clubbe, John. *Victorian Forerunner: The Later Career of Thomas Hood*, 1968.
Elliot, Alexander. *Hood in Scotland*, 1885.
Jerrold, Walter. *Thomas Hood: His Life and Times*, 1907.
——————— . *Thomas Hood and Charles Lamb: The Story of a Friendship*, 1930.
Reid, J. C. *Thomas Hood*, 1963.

Larry David Barton

GERARD MANLEY HOPKINS

Born: Stratford, England; June 11, 1844
Died: Dublin, Ireland; June 8, 1889

Principal collections

Poems of Gerard Manley Hopkins, Now First Published, with Notes by Robert Bridges, 1918; *Complete Poems*, 1947; *The Poems of Gerard Manley Hopkins*, 1967.

Other literary forms

In addition to his poems, Gerard Manley Hopkins' letters and papers have been published in six volumes: *The Letters of Gerard Manley Hopkins to Robert Bridges* (1935, 1955, C. C. Abbott, editor), *The Correspondence of Gerard Manley Hopkins and Richard Watson Dixon* (1935, 1955, C. C. Abbott, editor), *Further Letters of Gerard Manley Hopkins* (1937, 1956, C. C. Abbott, editor), *Notebooks and Papers of Gerard Manley Hopkins* (1937, Humphry House, editor), *The Journals and Papers of Gerard Manley Hopkins* (1959, Humphry House and Graham Storey, editors), and *The Sermons and Devotional Writings of Gerard Manley Hopkins* (1959, Christopher Devlin, editor). As were the poems, these letters and papers were collected from manuscripts long after Hopkin's death. In addition to the published material, there are significant unpublished lecture notes and documents by Hopkins at the Bodleian Library and the Campion Hall Library at Oxford University.

Achievements

Although Hopkins saw almost none of his writings published in his lifetime, he is generally credited with being one of the founders of modern poetry and a major influence on the development of modernism in art. Many of his letters reflect a sense of failure and frustration. "The Wreck of the *Deutschland*," which he considered to be his most important poem, was rejected by the Jesuit magazine *The Month*. As a professor of classical languages and literature, he was not a productive, publishing scholar. As a priest, his sermons and theological writing did not find popular success. Yet in 1918, some thirty years after his death, his friend Robert Bridges published a collection of his poems. By 1930, when the second edition of this volume appeared, Hopkins began to attract the attention of major theoreticians of modernism: Herbert Read, William Empson, I. A. Richards, and F. R. Leavis. They acclaimed Hopkins as a powerful revolutionary force in poetry. Interest in his poetry led scholars to unearth his scattered letters and papers. Here, too, modern readers found revolutionary concepts: inscape, instress, sprung rhythm, underthought/overthought, counterpoint. Since about 1930 an enormous amount of scholarly analysis has combed through Hopkins' poetry and prose, establishing beyond doubt that he is one of the three or four most influential forces in modern English literature.

Biography

Gerard Manley Hopkins was the first of eight children born to Manley Hopkins, a successful marine insurance agent who wrote poetry and technical books. The family was closely knit and artistic. Two of Hopkins' brothers became professional artists, and Hopkins' papers contain many pencil sketches showing his own talent for drawing. He was devoted to his youngest sister Grace, who was an accomplished musician, and he tried to learn several musical instruments as well as counterpoint and musical composition. The family was devoutly Anglican in religion. When Hopkins was eight years old, they moved from the London suburb of Stratford (Essex) to the more fashionable and affluent Hampstead on the north edge of the city. From 1854 to 1863 Hopkins attended Highgate Grammar School. Richard Watson Dixon, a young teacher there, later became one of Hopkins' main literary associates. Hopkins studied Latin and Greek intensively, winning the Governor's Gold Medal for Latin Verse, as well as the Headmaster's Poetry Prize in 1860 for his English poem "The Escorial." His school years seem to have been somewhat stormy, marked by the bittersweet joy of schoolboy friendships and the excitement of a keen mind mastering the intricacies of Greek, Latin, and English poetry. He was such a brilliant student that he won the Balliol College Exhibition, or scholarship prize. Balliol was reputed to be the leading college for classical studies at Oxford University in the 1860's. Hopkins attended Balliol from April, 1863, until June, 1867, studying "Classical Greats," the philosophy, literature, and language of ancient Greece and Rome. The first year of this curriculum required rigorous study of the structure of the Latin and Greek languages. This linguistic study terminated with a very demanding examination called "Moderations." Hopkins earned a grade of "First" in his Moderations in December, 1864. The remaining years of "Classical Greats" involved the study of the philosophy and literature of ancient writers in their original tongues, concluding with the "Greats" or final honors examination. Hopkins concluded his B.A. (Hons.) with a "First in Greats" in June, 1867. A double first in Classical Greats is a remarkable accomplishment. Benjamin Jowett, the Master of Balliol and himself a famous classical scholar, called Hopkins "The Star of Balliol" and all who knew him at this period predicted a brilliant career for him. Hopkins loved Oxford—its landscapes and personalities, the life of culture and keen intellectual striving—and always looked back to his college days with nostalgia. His schoolmate there was Robert Bridges, who was to be his lifelong friend and correspondent.

These years were not peaceful, however, for the promising young scholar and poet. The colleges of Oxford University were then religious institutions. Only Anglicans could enroll as students or teach there. For some thirty years before Hopkins entered Balliol, Oxford University had been rocked by the "Oxford Movement." A number of its illustrious teachers had questioned the very basis of the Anglican Church, the way in which the Church of England could claim to be independent of the Roman Catholic Church. Many of the leading figures of the Oxford Movement had felt compelled to leave Oxford and the Church of England and to convert to Roman Catholicism. Among the converts was Cardinal John Henry Newman, whose *Apologia pro Vita Sua*, or history of his conversion from the Anglican to the Roman Church, was published in 1864, the year Hopkins was preparing for his Moderations at Balliol. To follow Newman's lead meant to give up hope of an academic career at Oxford, and perhaps even the hope of completing his B.A. Nevertheless, by 1866 Hopkins was convinced that the only true church was the Roman. In October, 1866, he was received into the Roman Catholic Church by Newman himself. It is hard for modern readers to imagine the pain and dislocation this decision caused Hopkins. His family letters reveal the anguish of his father, who believed that his son's immortal soul was lost, not merely his temporal career. Hopkins was estranged from his family to some degree ever after his momentous conversion. After he had completed his B.A. at Oxford, Hopkins taught in 1867 at Newman's Oratory School, a Roman Catholic grammar school near Birmingham. There he decided to enter a religious order. In May, 1868, he burned all manuscripts of his poems, thinking that poetry was not a fit occupation for a seriously religious person. Fortunately, some of his early writing survived in copies he had given to Robert Bridges. He wrote no further poetry until "The Wreck of the *Deutschland*" in 1875.

In the summer of 1867 he went on a walking tour of Switzerland. In that September he entered the Jesuit Novitiate, Manresa House, London, for the first two years of rigorous spiritual training to become a Jesuit priest. There he followed the regime of the Spiritual Exercises of St. Ignatius Loyola (1491-1556), making vows of poverty, chastity, and obedience. From 1870 to 1873 he studied philosophy at St. Mary's Hall, Stonyhurst, in the North of England. Although Hopkins had been a brilliant student of classical philosophy at Oxford, he seems not to have pleased his Jesuit superiors so well. Perhaps part of the problem was an independence of mind which could be disconcerting. At Stonyhurst he first read the medieval philosopher John Duns Scotus, who had an unusually strong influence on Hopkins' ideas. He then returned to Manresa House for a year as Professor of Rhetoric. From 1874 to 1878 he studied theology at St. Bueno's College in Wales. There he began to write poetry again when he heard of the wreck of a German ship, the *Deutschland*, and the death of five Catholic nuns aboard.

It is the custom in the Jesuit order to move priests from one location to another frequently and to try them out in a variety of posts. In the next few years, Hopkins tried many different kinds of religious work without remarkable success. He was assigned to preach in the fashionable Farm Street Church in London's West End, but he was not a charismatic or crowd-pleasing performer. Parish work in the Liverpool slums left him depressed and exhausted. When he was assigned temporarily to the Catholic parish church in Oxford, he seemed to have had trouble getting along with his superior. Finally, he was appointed Professor of Greek and Latin Literature at University College, Dublin, Ireland. He held this post until his death in 1889. The Catholic population of Ireland at that time was in near-revolt against English oppression. Hopkins felt a conflict between his English patriotism and his Catholic sympathies. Although he had been a brilliant student as a young man, the University College duties gave him little opportunity to do gratifying scholarly work. Much of his time was spent in the drudgery of external examinations, grading papers of hundreds of students he had never taught. His lectures were attended by only a handful of students. He projected massive books for himself to write, but never was able to put them together. In this period he wrote many sonnets which show spiritual desolation, unhappiness, and alienation. He died of typhoid in 1889 at the age of forty-five. Not until a generation later did the literary world recognize his genius.

Analysis

In 1875 a number of Roman Catholic religious people had been driven out of Germany by the Falck Laws. In the winter of that year, five exiled nuns took passage on the *Deutschland*, which ran aground in a snowstorm near the Kentish shore of England. The ship gradually broke up in the high seas and many lives were lost, including the nuns'. Their bodies were brought to England for solemn funeral ceremonies and the whole affair was widely reported in the newspapers. At this time Gerard Manley Hopkins was studying theology at St. Bueno's College in Wales. He read the reports in the press and many details in his poem reflect the newspapers' accounts. He seems especially to have noticed the report that, as passengers were being swept off the deck into the icy seas by towering waves, the tallest of the five nuns rose up above the others just before her death and cried out for Christ to come quickly to her. Hopkins discussed this fearful catastrophe with his rector, who suggested that someone should write a poem about it. Taking that hint as a command, Hopkins broke his self-imposed poetic silence and began to write again. What seems to have captured his imagination was the experience of the tall nun at her moment of death. How frightening and cruel it must have been to be on the deck of the shattered ship! Yet she was a faithful Catholic servant of God. How could God torment her so? What did she mean when she cried out for Christ to come to her as the fatal waves beat down on her?

"The Wreck of the *Deutschland*" is a very difficult poem. Unlike the smooth sentences of Tennyson's *In Memoriam* (1850), for example, Hopkins' elegy is contorted, broken, sometimes opaque. When Robert Bridges published the first volume of Hopkins' poems in 1918, he warned readers that "The Wreck of the *Deutschland*" was like a great dragon lying at the gate to discourage readers from going on to other, more accessible poems by Hopkins. The thread of the occasion, however, can be traced in the text. The dedication of the poem to the memory of five Franciscan nuns exiled by the Falck Laws drowned between midnight and morning of December 7, 1875, gives the reader a point of reference. If readers skip to stanza twelve, the story goes ahead, following newspaper accounts of the events reasonably clearly. Stanza twelve relates that some two hundred passengers sailed from Bremen bound for America, never guessing that a fourth of them would drown. Stanza thirteen explains how the *Deutschland* sailed into the wintry storm. Stanzas fourteen and fifteen tell how the ship hit a sandbank and people began to drown. Stanza sixteen depicts an act of heroism in which a sailor tries to rescue a woman, but is killed; his body dangles on a rope for hours before the eyes of the sufferers. Stanzas seventeen through twenty-three are about the tall nun. In stanza twenty-four the poet contrasts his own comfortable setting under a safe roof in Wales with that of the nuns who were in their death struggle on the stormy sea. He has no pain, no trial, but the tall nun is dying at that very moment. Rising up in the midst of death and destruction, she calls, "O Christ, Christ, come quickly." Stanzas twenty-five through thirty-five contemplate that scene and ask, "What did she mean?" when she called out. What was the total meaning of her agony and life? The poem therefore can be divided into three sections: Stanzas one to ten constitute a prologue or invocation, stanzas eleven through twenty-five depict the agony of the shipwreck and the tall nun, and stanzas twenty-five through thirty-five contemplate the meaning of that event. The middle section, describing the shipwreck and the tall nun's cry, is reasonably clear. Difficult details in this section are mostly explained in the notes to the revised fourth edition of *The Poems of Gerard Manley Hopkins*. There are some additional perspectives, however, which are helpful in grasping the total work.

"The Wreck of the *Deutschland*" is related to the Jesuit contemplative "composition of place" and "application of the senses." As a member of the Society of Jesus, Hopkins' daily life and devotions were shaped by the *Spiritual Exercises* (1548) of St. Ignatius Loyola. Moreover, at certain times in his career he withdrew from the world to perform the spiritual exercises in month-long retreats of an extremely rigorous nature. One objective of the spiritual exercises is to induce an immediate, overwhelming sense of the presence of Divinity in our world. To accomplish this end, the contemplative is directed by the *Spiritual Exercises* to employ the technique of "composition." For example, to get a sharper sense of the divine presence, one might contemplate the birth of Christ. First one must imagine, or compose, the scene of the Nativity in all possible detail and precision. When Christ was born, how large was the room; what animals were in the stable; where was the holy family;

were they seated or standing; what was the manger like? The imagination embodies or composes the scene. The contemplative then applies his five senses systematically to the composition. What did it look like, sound like, smell like, feel like, and taste like? Such a projection of the contemplative into the very situation induces a very powerful awareness of the religious experience. "The Wreck of the *Deutschland*" is similar to such a contemplative exercise. Hopkins is trying to experience the religious truth of the nuns' sacrifice. The middle of his poem is a composition of the scene where the tall nun died. It is constructed systematically to apply the five senses. Stanza twenty-eight depicts the struggle of the poet to put himself in the nun's place, to feel what she felt, to suffer as she suffered, to believe as she believed. At her death, she saw her Master, Christ, King. The poet tries to participate in her experience. "The Wreck of the *Deutschland*" should be read in comparison with other poems of the religious meditative tradition—for example, the poetry of George Herbert, Richard Crashaw, and Henry Vaughan. Louis L. Martz in *The Poetry of Meditation: A Study in English Religious Literature of the Seventeenth Century* (1962) is the best introduction to this important aspect of Hopkins' work.

In addition to the religious complexities of the poem, there are aesthetic complexities. Hopkins claimed to have discovered a new poetic form, "sprung rhythm," which he employed in "The Wreck of the *Deutschland*." Despite intense scholarly investigation of Hopkins' metrics, there is no clear agreement as to what he means by "sprung rhythm." We can sketch the general outline of his practice here. "The Wreck of the *Deutschland*" contains thirty-five stanzas, each with eight lines of varying length. If one counts the syllables in each line, or if one counts only the accented syllables in each line, there is a rough agreement in the length of a particular line in each of the stanzas. For example, line one has four or five syllables in almost all stanzas. Line eight is much longer than line one in all stanzas. What makes lines of varying length metrical?

It is sometimes thought that Hopkins was isolated in the Jesuit order and did not know what he was doing when he created unusual poetic forms. That is absurd, for he was a professor of classical literature and in correspondence with leading literary scholars. The best way to look at sprung rhythm is to see what Hopkins' associates thought about meter. Robert Bridges, his college friend and lifelong correspondent, studied the iambic pentameter of Milton and wrote a major book on the prosody of Milton. Bridges thought that Milton built his lines out of iambic feet, units of two syllables with the second syllable pronounced more loudly than the first. An iambic pentameter line therefore had five iambic feet, or ten syllables with the even-positioned syllables stressed more loudly than the odd-positioned ones. Lines in Miltonic pentameter which do not fit this pattern follow a few simple variations defined by Bridges. Bridges' study appears to be accurate for Milton, but clearly

Hopkins is not writing poetry of this sort. The number of unstressed syllables differs widely in his lines, a condition that Bridges shows never occurs in Milton.

Another of Hopkins' correspondents, Coventry Patmore, was a leading popular Catholic poet who wrote a study of English metrics based on time, similar to the prosody of hymns. Hopkins' sprung rhythm seems more consistent with such a musical time-based pattern than with the accentual-syllabic pattern of Milton as defined by Bridges. Hopkins, as a professor of classical languages, knew the advanced linquistic work going on in that area. Greek poetry was thought to be quantitative, based on the length of vowel sounds. As a schoolboy Hopkins had to practice translating an English passage first into Latin, then into Greek poetry, arranging the long and short vowels into acceptable feet. (Some of his Latin and Greek poetry is collected in *The Poems of Gerard Manley Hopkins.*) Modern readers are not often trained to understand these models in classical languages and so do not appreciate how important they are to Hopkins' patterns in English verse. In Hopkins' unpublished papers, there are lines of Greek poetry interlined by drafts of his English poems, sometimes with arrows and doodles matching up the English and Greek phrases. It seems possible that Hopkins based his distinctive rhythms on Greek models, especially the odes of Pindar, a topic that has been partially explored in Todd K. Bender's *Gerard Manley Hopkins: The Classical Background and Critical Reception of his Work* (1966). Essentially, however, the key to sprung rhythm remains to be discovered.

"The Wreck of the *Deutschland*" was submitted to the Jesuit magazine *The Month* and, after some delay, rejected for publication. Hopkins said that they "dared not" print it, although there is no need to imagine a dark conspiracy among the Jesuit authorities to silence Hopkins. It is likely that the editors of *The Month* simply found "The Wreck of the *Deutschland*" baffling in form and content. The rejection dramatizes, however, a peculiar condition in Hopkins' life. His unquestionable genius for poetry found almost no encouragement in his immediate surroundings as a Jesuit priest. His poetry is, of course, shaped by Roman Catholic imagery and is mainly devotional in nature. Without his Church and his priestly calling, he never could have written his poems. On the other hand, what he wrote was largely unappreciated by his closest associates. Ironically, this highly religious poet became famous in our century because of the praise of readers who were frequently anti-Roman Catholic. There was a central anguish in Hopkins life, a conflict between his priestly duties and his artistic creativity. Many scholars have tried to explain how Hopkins' poetry and his priesthood fit together. One of the best such studies is John Pick's *Gerard Manley Hopkins: Priest and Poet* (1942). Roman Catholic critics usually tend to say that the Catholic faith made Hopkins a great writer. Readers who are hostile to Catholicism tend to think that Hopkins was a serious writer in spite of extreme discouragements and restraints placed on him by his faith. The truth is probably somewhere in the middle. If Hopkins had not been severely troubled, he would have had little motivation to write. His poems show all the commonplaces of religious imagery found in much less powerful Catholic poets, such as his friend Coventry Patmore. Hopkins rises above the average religious versifier because of his original genius, yet this originality is what the Jesuit editors of *The Month* did not understand.

Stung by the criticism of his major poem, not only by the Jesuit editors but also by his friend Robert Bridges, Hopkins never again tried to write something so long and elaborate. He retreated into the most traditional form in English prosody, the sonnet. After "The Wreck of the *Deutschland*," Hopkins' most famous work is the sonnet "The Windhover." More has been written about these fourteen lines than about any other piece of poetry of comparable length in English. All of Hopkins' sonnets are related to the Petrarchan model, but he alters the tradition to fit his peculiar genius. The poem employs line-end rhymes abba abba cdcdcd. In addition to the repetition of sound at the end of each line, there is also thickly interwoven alliteration and assonance within each line. This internal rhyme is related to the *cynghanedd* or consonant chime of Welsh poetry. Hopkins tried to learn Welsh when he was a student at St. Bueno's College in Wales and he actually wrote a bit of Welsh poetry in the form called *cywydd*. The meter of "The Windhover" is the so-called sprung rhythm, allowing great variation in the length of lines. The Petrarchan sonnet uses its rhyme scheme to define two parts of the poem: abba abba is the octave or exposition in the opening eight lines, cdcdcd is the sestet or commentary in the concluding six lines. Hopkins explained in his letters that the essence of a sonnet is balance and proportion. The octave asserts a situation or condition and then a surprising commentary comes back in the sestet to reply to the octave. Since the sestet has only six lines, it must be correspondingly "sharper" or more forceful if it is to balance the initial statement. The key to the sonnet is this proportion. Hopkins wrote some sonnets longer than the usual fourteen lines and a few shorter, "curtail" or cut-short, sonnets. In all his sonnets, however, he maintains the proportion of octave to sestet, eight to six, and forces the shorter conclusion to a higher pitch of intensity.

In its octave, "The Windhover" describes the flight of a hawk of a kind commonly used in falconry or hunting circling against the dawn sky. The sestet begins with the description of the hawk diving, plummeting earthward, as it "buckles." The sure, steady circling of the hawk in the octave is astonishing, but the sudden buckling downward is even more thrilling. It is beautiful and breathtaking. In the sestet the increased beauty of the hawk as it dives is compared to a plough made to shine as it is driven through sandy soil, and to an ember coated with ashes that sparkles when it falls and breaks.

"The Windhover" illustrates one of the key terms in Hopkins' aesthetic vocabulary: "inscape," a word he coined for the inner nature of a thing which distinguishes it from everything else in creation. Hopkins' reading of Duns Scotus is pertinent to his concept of inscape. *Qualis* in Latin means *what*. When we look at the *qualities* of things, we examine *what* they have in common with other members of their class. The *qualities* of a good racing horse are those features that it has in common with other good horses. Duns Scotus imagines that there is an opposite to *quality*. *Haec* means *this* in Latin. Duns Scotus coins the word *haecceitas*, the "thisness" of a thing, which sets it apart from everything else, making it unique and different—the principle of individuation. Hopkins frequently celebrates the rare, unusual, or unique in nature. He turns away from the universal quality and toward the individual. The octave of "The Windhover" can be seen as the poet's description of a natural event: the flight and dive of a falcon. In that movement, he seeks to find the inscape, the innermost shape as evidence of God's presence in the created world. He tries to see into the form of the thing, to find what makes it original, unique, special, strange, striking. Like the sacrifice of the tall nun in "The Wreck of the *Deutschland*," the act of the hawk is "composed" so as to be the object for a religious meditation.

Paradoxically, the only way to grasp the unique inscape of a thing is to compare it with something else. The tension of this paradox is evident in the striking, surprising comparisons which Hopkins employs in "The Windhover," comparing the dive of a hawk with a plough shining in use and a burning coal sparkling as it collapses. The poem says that these three events are comparable or analogous in that in each case when the object *buckles* it becomes brighter and more glorious. When the hawk buckles in its dive, it is a thousandfold more lovely than in its stately circling. When the rusty plough buckles to its work, the abrasion of the sandy soil makes the ploughshare shine in use. When the ash crumbles or buckles, its inner brightness shows through the gray, outer ash-coating. Hopkins gave "The Windhover" the dedication, "To Christ Our Lord." The Jesuit order sees itself as the chivalry or the Knights of Christ. Ignatius advises the novice to buckle on the armor of Christ. To become a Jesuit, to buckle on the armor of a true Christian knight, is the proper and glorious activity of a man who would follow his nature, or unique calling. In like manner, a hawk follows its true nature, it *is* what it was *made to be*, when it sails in the wind and dives. A plough was made to work the earth, a coal to burn, and these things do what they were intended to do when they buckle. The activity of buckling may be painful or dangerous, but it produces glory, brilliance, grace, and beauty. The discipline of accepting the vows of the Jesuits may be painful in some earthly way, but it brings the glory of Christ's service. Christ, too, accepted the pain and duty of his earthly incarnation. He was buckled to the cross. He did what he had to do and so was brought to glory through pain and humiliation. The structure of "The Windhover" appears to be a set of analogies or comparisons all coming together in the word *buckle*. Such a structure is also to be found in the odes of the Greek poet Pindar, which Hopkins studied intensely in school. Pindar's poems praise a great athlete or hero by linking together a series of seeming digressions in one key image or figure, sometimes called a "constellation," such as the "golden lyre," a "beacon fire," a "horse," or a "tree." Hopkins' poetry unites the Christian tradition of anagogical interpretation of the created world and the Classical Greek tradition of the Pindaric ode.

Most of Hopkins' shorter poems are sonnets, yet within the confines of this form, Hopkins displays great originality in his metrical structure, his repetition of sound in alliteration and internal rhyme, and his changes in the length of the sonnet while maintaining the crucial eight-to-six proportion of the octave/ sestet division. Like the form of the sonnet, the subjects of most of Hopkins' poems are extremely traditional: (1) elation at the sight of some particular bit of nature; (2) personal dejection, desolation, and despair; (3) celebration of the inner worth of an outwardly ordinary human being. These three topics are commonplaces of Romantic and post-Romantic literature. Hopkins' originality lies in treating these subjects with unusual power and perception. Romantic poets such as William Wordsworth and Percy Bysshe Shelley often looked at nature and said that they felt their hearts leap up to behold the beauty of Spring or Autumn. For Hopkins, every little corner of Nature was evidence of the divine presence of God. His Christianity reinforces the romantic sentiment. The confluence of the romantic and the Christian tradition produces unusually powerful statements.

Consider, for example, the sonnet "Hurrahing in Harvest." Like "The Windhover," this poem is an Italian sonnet, rhymed abba abba cdcdcd. Note the unusual rhyme sound ending lines six and seven. "Saviour" rhymes with "gave you a 'r' . . ." so that the rhyme sound carries over the end of line six to include the "r" of "rapturous" in line eight. This extended rhyme is common in Hopkins and illustrates his predilection for unusual twists within the framework of rigid traditional expectations. The subjects of "The Windhover" and "Hurrahing in Harvest" are also similar. In both poems, the speaker looks up at the sky and finds nature breathtakingly beautiful. "Hurrahing in Harvest" declares that the summer is now ending. The *stooks*, or shocks of bundled grain, are now stacked in the fields. The technical and regional term *stooks* is characteristic of Hopkins' vocabulary. The word is not commonly known, but it is exact. The speaker looks up at the autumnal skies and sees the clouds. With the bold verbal comparisons which the poet prefers, he compares the skies to "wind-walks," like alleyways for the winds. The clouds are like "silk-sacks"; they are soft, dainty, and luxurious. The movement of the clouds across the sky is like "meal-drift" or flour pouring across the heavens. In that soft, flowing beauty, the speaker walks and lifts up his eyes. He sees the glory of the natural scene and then recognizes that beyond the heavens, behind all the created universe, there stands the Savior. He at first rejoices in the sheer beauty of nature, but such earthly beauty leads him to the unspeakable inner beauty of Christ's immediate presence in the natural world. In the sestet, the speaker sees the azure hills of autumn as strong as the shoulder of a stallion, majestic and sweet with flowers, like the shoulder of God bearing the creation in all its glory. The speaker realizes that all this is here for him to see and the realization makes his heart leap up as if it had wings; his spirit hurls heavenward.

Hopkins wrote many poems celebrating nature in sonnet form. "God's Grandeur" states in the octave that the grandeur of God's creating has been obscured by the industrial revolution, trade and toil. The sestet replies that there is a spark of freshness deep in nature which will spring up like the sun at dawn because God broods over the earth like a bird over its egg. "The Starlight Night" begins with a powerful octave describing the beauty of the stars in the night sky. The sestet replies that the stars are like a picket fence separating us from heaven through which we can glimpse a bit of what is on the other side. "Spring" typically gives an excited picture of the juice and joy of the earth stirring in springtime and compares it to the youthful, primal goodness of children, a hint of sinless Eden.

"Pied Beauty" is one of Hopkins' most important philosophical poems on nature. It reflects his study of Duns Scotus and his notion of inscape. The poem is a "curtail" or cut-short sonnet, only ten and a fraction lines long. Hopkins explained that this poem maintained the eight-to-six ratio, which he felt was the key to the sonnet form. The exposition, which occupies the first six lines, states that God is especially to be praised for the irregular, dappled, serviceable parts of creation. The sestet generalizes that whatever is contradictory, strange, or changeable originates in God. In Platonic thought, a material thing is beautiful insofar as it approaches its unchanging ideal. For example, a beautiful circle is one that approaches—as nearly as possible in our world—the perfection of an ideal circle. Because the things of our world are always struggling to become like their perfect forms, our material world is always changing. It is sometimes called the mutable world of "becoming." The ideal world cannot change, however, because when something is perfect, any change would make it imperfect. The world of Platonic ideals is therefore unchanging. It is sometimes called the world of permanent "being." "Pied Beauty" makes a striking statement about the nature of beauty. It asserts that things are not beautiful because they approach the perfect type, but because they are various, changing, contradictory. Hopkins seems to be praising the very aspect of the material world that Platonic philosophy connects with degeneration and decay. Somehow God, who is perfect and unchanging, has fathered a universe of imperfection, contradiction, and decay. Nevertheless, this created world reflects his praise: Duns Scotus maintained that God's perfection must be manifest somehow in the constant change and variety of his creation.

Hopkins' admiration for Duns Scotus is expressed in "Duns Scotus's Oxford," which combines the nature-sonnet and the celebration of a famous man. Its octave depicts the ancient university town of Oxford. The sestet comments that this was the very city that Duns Scotus knew when the subtle doctor taught there in the thirteenth century. Now Hopkins finds Scotus to have the best insight into philosophical problems, even more comforting to him than Greek philosophers such as Plato, or Italian philosophers such as St. Thomas Aquinas. All of the nature sonnets give an extremely sharp picture of some relatively common event or situation in nature: a hawk in flight, the landscape of Oxford, the rebirth of the countryside in springtime, the clouds and fields of autumn. The poet reflects on the source of all this beauty. The scene itself uplifts his spirits, but the awareness of God's creative force glimpsed behind the material world brings even more elation.

A second group of poems is in the tradition of the heroic sonnet. These poems examine a person's life and define what is noteworthy in an ordinary man's career. "The Lantern Out of Doors" is typical. The octave tells of seeing a lantern moving at night. There must be someone behind that light, but he is so far off that he passes in the darkness and all that can be seen is a little spark. We have trouble knowing other people, and death is soon upon us. The sestet replies that Christ knows every person; Christ is the first and last friend of every man. "Felix Randal," one of Hopkins' best sonnets, is about a blacksmith who fell ill and died. The once powerful man wasted away, but he finally came to accept Christ. Paradoxically, in the weakness of his death he became more blessed than in the pagan power he was so proud of in the days when he forged and fitted horseshoes with his fellow workers. "The Soldier," "Tom's Garland: Upon the Unemployed," and "Harry Ploughman" all fit into the category of poems celebrating the inner worth of ordinary people. Perhaps the pattern of this kind of sonnet is best displayed in "In Honour of St. Alphonsus Rodriguez: Laybrother of the Society of Jesus." Alphonsus Rodriguez performed no noble deeds. For forty years, however, he faithfully carried out his duty and filled his station as doorkeeper. It is not his exploits, but his humanity, that Hopkins celebrates. Humility, obedience, and simple faith have their reward. The poem is in the tradition of Milton's theme of the faithful Christians; "they also serve who only stand and wait."

The third major theme of Hopkins' sonnets is spiritual desolation and terror. These poems constitute the dark, opposite side of Hopkins' view of reality. In the nature poems, the poet looks at some part of the created universe and feels that God is in every corner of our world. His joy, already aroused by the pure beauty of nature, rises to an ecstatic pitch when he realizes that God is behind it all. The poems of desolation, sometimes called the "terrible sonnets," on the other hand, imagine a world without God—all joy, freshness, and promise withdrawn. They depict the dark night of the soul. Many readers think that these poems are directly autobiographical, indicating that Hopkins in the last years of his life was devastated by despair. This view is probably not sound. The sonnet is a highly dramatized form; sonnets are traditionally constructed like little plays. Thus the speaker of one of Shakespeare's sonnets is no more Shakespeare, the man himself, than is Macbeth or Hamlet, and the persona or mask through which a sonneteer speaks is not to be confused with the real author. The *Spiritual Exercises* of Saint Ignatius, moreover, follows a spiritual progression which every Jesuit would imitate in his retreats and private worship. In a long retreat, lasting about a month, the exercitant is called upon to drive himself gradually into a state of extreme desolation into which a renewed sense of God's presence finally bursts like Easter into the dormant world. The sonnets of terror may be as artificial as Elizabethan love sonnets. They may be, to some degree, virtuoso exercises in imagining a world devoid of spirituality and hope. The real feelings of Hopkins may be quite separate from the imagined feelings of the persona who speaks these sonnets. On the other hand, we can hardly imagine that Hopkins could write these poems unless there were some wrenching personal feelings motivating his creative act.

The sonnets of terror appeal to readers in our century because they mirror a cosmic despair or alienation. The feeling that modern man is a stranger in a strange land, that he is alienated from the profit of his own productivity, that he is caught in a meaningless or absurd activity like Sisyphus rolling his stone endlessly up a mountain in Hell, is extremely widespread in the twentieth century. It is doubtful that Hopkins felt alienated in exactly this way. His religious belief promised him a future life and salvation. When he speaks of despair, it is always hypothetical: think how unbearable life would be *if* there were not hope. "Carrion Comfort," among the best of Hopkins' dark sonnets, considers despair, which is itself a sin, depicting the struggle of the Christian with his own conscience. It begins a series of six sonnets of unusual power which treat the struggle of the soul. These poems should be read in sequence: (1) "Carrion Comfort," (2) "No Worst, There Is None," (3) "To Seem a Stranger Lies My Lot," (4) "I Wake and Feel the Fell of Dark, Not Day," (5) "Patience, Hard Thing," and (6) "My Own Heart Let Me Have More Pity On." Read in sequence, these sonnets constitute a short psychodrama or morality play. The Christian speaker confronts his own doubt, weakness, and unworth, and is terrified of God. In five scenes he is seen writhing and twisting in mental contortions of guilt and terror. At the conclusion of "My Own Heart Let Me Have More Pity On," the sestet provides the dramatic release, as God's smile breaks through, like sunlight on a mountain guiding the traveler. This sonnet sequence corresponds to the progress of the exercitant through the final stages of his spiritual exercises. The same progress of the mind, through terror to elation at the Resurrection, is outlined in "That Nature Is a Heraclitean Fire and of the Comfort of the Resurrection." The first segment of this poem looks at the changing natural world. Like a bonfire, everything around us is changing, decaying, being consumed. Man seems so pitifully weak and vulnerable among these flames. The only hope is Christ's promise of salvation, which comes to man like a beacon. Man will pass through the fire and, even when all else is destroyed, his soul will endure like an immortal diamond.

A striking characteristic of Hopkins' poetry is his rich vocabulary. As he sought to find the inscape or unique form in the created universe, he also attempted to find in language the original, spare, strange, exactly right word. He was one of the best trained linguists of his age, working at the research level in Latin and Greek, while studying Anglo-Saxon and Welsh. His notes and journals show him repeatedly developing elaborate etymologies of words. He belonged to a widespread movement in the Victorian era, spearheaded by Robert Bridges and his Society For Pure English, which glorified the archaic elements in modern English. He records in his notes dialect words, and the special words used by workers for their tools or by country people for plants and animals. This attention to the texture of language pours forth in his poetry in an unusually rich, eccentric vocabulary.

Despite the orthodoxy of his religious views, Hopkins is known as one of the founders of modernism in literature. He is frequently compared with Walt Whitman, Emily Dickinson, and the French Symbolist poets as a great revolutionary who rebelled against the sterile forms of Victorian verse and brought a new urgency, freshness, and seriousness to poetry. He revolutionized the very basis of English meter with his experiments in sprung rhythm. He revitalized the bold metaphor in the manner of the English metaphysical poets. He created a whole new lexicon, a poetic vocabulary constructed from dialect, archaic, technical, and coined words. The critics who initially praised his work in the 1920's and 1930's tended to see him as a cultural primitive, a man isolated from the corruption of society and so able to return to a state of nature and get to the core of language more easily than writers, such as Alfred, Lord Tennyson, who seemed corrupted by false traditions. Although Hopkins was undoubtedly a great innovator, he was certainly not a cultural primitive. He was a highly trained professor of Latin and Greek language and literature. In addition to his "Double First in Greats" from Oxford University, he undertook years of rigorous philosophical and theological training with the Society of Jesus. He was at the center of a group of correspondents who were as powerful intellectually as any group we can find in his era: Bridges, Dixon, Patmore, and other less frequent scholarly correspondents. Hopkins was not a naïve writer; on the contrary, he was an extremely sophisticated writer. His poetry is revolutionary, not because he was ignorant of tradition, but because he brought together many powerful threads of tradition: the contemplative practice of the *Spiritual Exercises*, with their "composition of place" and "application of the senses"; the conventions of the Petrarchan sonnet; the complicated metrical studies of Bridges, Patmore, and the classical scholars;

the classical philosophical background of Oxford University; and the medieval thought of the Jesuit schools, especially of John Duns Scotus. These traditions met, and sometimes conflicted sharply, in Hopkins. From that confluence of traditions he gave modern readers the unique gift of his poems.

Major publications other than poetry

NONFICTION: *The Letters of Gerard Manley Hopkins to Robert Bridges*, 1935, 1955 (C. C. Abbott, editor); *The Correspondence of Gerard Manley Hopkins and Richard Watson Dixon*, 1935, 1955 (C. C. Abbott, editor); *Further Letters of Gerard Manley Hopkins*, 1937, 1956 (C. C. Abbott, editor); *Notebooks and Papers of Gerard Manley Hopkins*, 1937 (Humphry House, editor); *The Journals and Papers of Gerard Manley Hopkins*, 1959 (Humphry House and Graham Storey, editors); *The Sermons and Devotional Writings of Gerard Manley Hopkins*, 1959 (Christopher Devlin, editor).

Bibliography

Bender, Todd K. *Gerard Manley Hopkins: The Classical Background and Critical Reception of His Work*, 1966.

Dilligan, Robert J., and Todd K. Bender. *A Concordance to the English Poetry of Gerard Manley Hopkins*, 1970.

Dunne, Tom. *Gerard Manley Hopkins: A Comprehensive Bibliography*, 1976.

Gardner, W. H. *Gerard Manley Hopkins, 1844-1889: A Study of Poetic Idiosyncracy in Relation to Poetic Tradition*, 1949.

Hartmann, Geoffrey H. *The Unmediated Vision: An Interpretation of Wordsworth, Hopkins, Rilke, and Valery*, 1954.

Kenyon Critics. *Gerard Manley Hopkins*, 1945.

MacKenzie, Norman H. *A Bibliography*, 1968.

Pick, John. *Gerard Manley Hopkins: Priest and Poet*, 1942.

Schneider, Elizabeth. *The Dragon in the Gate: Studies in the Poetry of G. M. Hopkins*, 1968.

Sulloway, Alison G. *Gerard Manley Hopkins and the Victorian Temper*, 1972.

Thornton, R. K. R. *All My Eyes See: The Visual World of Gerard Manley Hopkins*, 1975.

Todd K. Bender

A. E. HOUSMAN

Born: Fockbury, England; March 26, 1859
Died: Cambridge, England; April 30, 1936

Principal collections
A Shropshire Lad, 1896; *Last Poems*, 1922; *More Poems*, 1936; *Collected Poems*, 1939.

Other literary forms
A. E. Housman's only work of prose fiction is *A Morning with the Royal Family*, a youthful fantasy printed without his permission in 1882 in the *Bromsgrovian* and unpublished elsewhere. His translations total 102 lines from Aeschylus' *Septem Contra Thebas* (467 B.C., *Seven Against Thebes*), Sophocles' *Oedipus Coloneus* (401 B.C., *Oedipus at Colonus*), and Euripides' *Alcestis* (438 B.C.) and first appeared in A. W. Pollard's *Odes from the Greek Dramatists* in 1890. They have since been included in the *Collected Poems*. Henry Maas has collected more than eight hundred of Housman's letters, which, though not in the great tradition of English letter-writing, shed considerable light on the poet's enigmatic personality. The sensitive letters to Moses Jackson remain unpublished.

Achievements
Although Housman's fame today rests on a handful of poems, it was to classical scholarship that he devoted most of his life. For nearly fifty years he was a professor of Latin, first at University College, London, and later at Cambridge University. A profound and prolific scholar fluent in five languages, he published in that time approximately two hundred critical papers and reviews spanning the entire spectrum of classical literature from Aeschylus to Vergil. This work consists mainly of textual emendations of corrupt manuscripts and is highly technical, providing a stark contrast to the lucid simplicity of his poetry. Titles such as "Emendationes Propertianae," "The Codex Lipsiensis of Manilius" and "Adversaria Orthographica" abound in *The Classical Papers of A. E. Housman* (1972), collected and edited by J. Diggle and F. R. D. Goodyear in three volumes. In addition, Housman has left behind editions of Ovid, Juvenal, Lucan, and Manilius and several major lectures including *The Confines of Criticism* (1969) and *The Name and Nature of Poetry* (1933).

Housman held no illusions either about the power of classical knowledge to influence human character or the extent of its appeal, but he nevertheless placed the highest premium on learning for its own sake and was a relentless seeker after truth using the method of textual criticism, which he defined in *The Application of Thought to Textual Criticism* (1922) as "the science of discovering error in texts and the art of removing it." This was for him "an aristocratic affair, not communicable to all men, nor to most men." The one thing most necessary to be a textual critic "is to have a head, not a pumpkin, on your shoulders, and brains, not pudding, in your head." He applied to others the same rigorous standards of scholarship that he set for himself, and he had no sympathy for incompetence in any form. He was particularly annoyed by the practice of modern criticism of following one manuscript whenever possible instead of weighing the relative merits of alternative manuscripts, a practice, he writes in his Preface to Juvenal (1905), designed "to rescue incompetent editors alike from the toil of editing and from the shame of acknowledging that they cannot edit." His harshest words are reserved for self-complacent and insolent men masquerading as sane critics. His vituperative attacks on Elias Stoeber and Friedrich Jacob in his 1903 Preface to Manilius may be taken as typical: "Stoeber's mind, though that is no name to call it by, was one which turned as unswervingly to the false, the meaningless, the unmetrical, and the ungrammatical, as the needle to the pole," and "Not only had Jacob no sense for grammar, no sense for coherency, no sense for sense, but being himself possessed by a passion for the clumsy and the hispid he imputed this disgusting taste to all the authors whom he edited." The extent of Housman's learning and the unbridled candor of his judgments made him a respected and feared polemicist and perhaps the most formidable classicist of his age. W. H. Auden called him "The Latin Scholar of his generation."

Throughout his career Housman repeatedly denied having any talent for literary criticism, and he turned down the Clark Lectureship in English Literature at Trinity College, Cambridge, on the ground that he did not qualify as a literary critic, who, he wrote in *The Confines of Criticism*, is rarer than "the appearance of Halley's comet." When he was at University College, London, he delivered papers on various English poets including Matthew Arnold, A. C. Swinburne, and Alfred, Lord Tennyson, but he refused to allow them to be published and apparently resented the demands the Literary Society made on him, writing in his Preface to Arthur Platt's *Nine Essays* (1927) that "Studious men who might be settling *Hoti's* business and properly basing *Oun* are expected to provide amusing discourses on subjects of which they have no official knowledge and upon which they may not be entitled even to open their mouths." Nevertheless, Housman's several excursions into literary criticism reflect a great sensitivity to such central concerns as the integrity of literary texts and the debasement of language. In its emphasis on the numinous intractibility of great poetry, *The Name and Nature of Poetry* is an oblique repudiation of the intellectualism of T. S. Eliot and I. A. Richards. Housman's criticism shows the influence of Matthew Arnold, but the importance he attached to the undergirding of impressionistic judgments with sound scholarship goes beyond that Victorian sage.

As a poet, Housman was successful to the point of celebrity. *A Shropshire Lad* was initially slow to catch on with the reading public, but after Grant Richards took over as Housman's publisher, it became a great success on both sides of the Atlantic. Its moody *Weltschmerz* caught the fin de siècle mood, just as *Last Poems* captured the ennui of a war-weary generation. Today the inevitable reaction has set in and Housman's poetry is not as highly regarded as it once was. The melancholy of his poems too often seems uninformed by spiritual struggle, but the plaintive lyricism of his best work has a universal and enduring appeal.

Biography

Alfred Edward Housman was born on March 26, 1859, in Fockbury, Worcestershire, into an ancient family of preachers and farmers whose English roots extended back to the fourteenth century. His great-grandfather on his father's side, an evangelical preacher who lived out his life with a wife and eight children in genteel poverty, was shy and unassertive in manner but inwardly tough, capable of bearing up under the hardships of life with manly fortitude. Housman was able to observe at first hand that stoicism which informs so much of his mature poetry in his own mother, Sarah, whose prolonged suffering and death after bearing seven children was a model of quiet courage. In the words of George L. Watson, "With his grimly stoical demeanor, Housman often recalled some ancestral farmer, glowering at the inclement weather" (*A. E. Housman: A Divided Life*, 1957). No such family precedent exists for Housman's career as a scholar unless it be a distant cousin on his father's side who was a lecturer in Greek and Divinity at Chichester College, and still less exists for the poet's rejection of the Church within a year of his mother's death.

The death of Housman's mother on his twelfth birthday brought a traumatic end to his childhood and left him with a profound sense of loss from which he never fully recovered. He had adored the witty, intelligent woman who took pride in her descent from Sir Francis Drake, and her death created a vacuum which could not be filled by his father, Edward, a lackluster solicitor who took increasingly to drink during Sarah's illness and who two years after her death married his cousin Lucy and began a long slide into poverty, dying after many years of broken health in 1894. Alfred was never close to his father. He regarded his drunkenness and general improvidence as intolerable weaknesses and held him in barely concealed contempt. He was, however, close to his six brothers and sisters during his early life and, as the oldest, conducted literary parlour games for them, taking the lead in writing nonsense verse, a practice that continued during summer vacations through his college years.

Sarah's death was not permitted to interrupt for long Housman's studies at nearby Bromsgrove School, where he had enrolled on a scholarship in the fall of 1870. Bromsgrove was an old and reputable public school and provided an excellent foundation in the classics, English, and French. As a student, Housman was introspective and shy and was known as "Mouse" by his classmates. Throughout his childhood, he was afflicted with a nervous disorder and while a student at Bromsgrove he had violent seizures which the headmaster attributed to St. Vitus's dance (chorea). Later in life this nervous condition took the form of occasional facial contortions which might "incongruously reappear in the course of the most impersonal lectures, as he read aloud one of the odes of Horace, leaving his astonished students 'afraid the old fellow was going to cry,'" in the words of George L. Watson. His nervous affliction notwithstanding, Housman seemed to thrive on the rigorous eleven-hour-a-day regimen at Bromsgrove School. In 1874, he appeared for the first time in print with a poem in rhymed couplets about the death of Socrates for which he won the prize for composition in English verse and which he delivered on Commencement Speech Day. It was published in the *Bromsgrove Messenger* on August 8, 1874, much to his later chagrin. In adult life, Housman was always jealous of his reputation and forbade the publication of his juvenilia and occasional addresses, which he felt did not meet the high standards he set for himself.

Housman's career at Bromsgrove School ended in triumph as he won the Lord Lyttelton prize for Latin verse, the honorarium for Greek verse, and the Senior Wattell prize, along with a generous scholarship to St. John's College, Oxford. At least some of Housman's success at this time can be attributed to Herbert Millington, who became headmaster at Bromsgrove School in 1873. A man of keen intellect, Millington presented a formidable figure to the students, and Housman felt some hero-worship for him, referring to him much later as a good teacher for a clever boy. Millington was the most important role model of Housman's youth.

In the fall of 1877, Housman entered Oxford and within a few days was writing irreverently to his stepmother about the solemn Latin ceremony of matriculation. He joined the Oxford Union, and although he was inactive he was "an avowed member and staunch champion of the Conservative faction" (Watson). Generally, however, Housman remained uninvolved in the life of the University. He was unimpressed by its professors and attended only one lecture by the illustrious Benjamin Jowett. Housman came away disgusted by Jowett's disregard for the "niceties" of scholarship. A lecture by John Ruskin also left Housman unimpressed. Housman later wrote that "Oxford had not much effect on me." This was not entirely the case, for it was at Oxford that he began to develop in earnest his capacity for classical scholarship. Passively resisting the conventional curriculum, Housman early in his Oxford career decided to devote his energies to the text of the Latin poet Propertius, whose garbled works required extensive editorial attention. He continued to work on Propertius for the remainder of his time at Oxford.

George Watson writes that Housman was already "embarking on those problems of conjectural emendation which are the acme of classical learning." It was also at this time that Housman began keeping a commonplace book of his favorite quotations, which tended toward the sepulchral, as one might expect of a young man whose only adornments for his college rooms were Albrecht Dürer's "Melancholia" and "The Knight, Death and the Devil." Housman's favorite poem during his early Oxford years was Arnold's *Empedocles on Etna* (1852), which he said contained "all the law and the prophets." He was attracted to Thomas Hardy's early novels for their gloomy stoicism. For a time Housman flirted with the poetry of Swinburne and wrote an antiecclesiastical poem, "New-Year's Eve," modeled on Swinburne's style.

Clearly the most important thing that happened to Housman during these years was his friendship with Moses Jackson, which had a deep and lasting effect on him. Among the first people he met at Oxford were A. W. Pollard and Jackson. He liked them both, but he was especially attracted to the latter. Jackson was everything that Housman was not: sociable, handsome, athletic, charismatic. A brilliant student of engineering, he excelled with ease at everything he did. The three became fast friends, and in 1879, Housman won a first class in Moderations but his failure to win either the Hertford Classical Scholarship or the Newdigate Prize for English verse was an omen of worse to come. In his last year at Oxford, Housman shared rooms with Pollard and Jackson and according to Watson this "was to be the most perturbed and momentous period of his life." There is convincing evidence that at this time Housman developed a passionate attachment for Jackson, which he kept hidden from everyone at great psychic cost to himself. He became irritable and moody, but his friends apparently suspected nothing. He failed his examination in Greats, and in the summer of 1881, he returned to his family in disgrace. Andrew S. Gow in his *A. E. Housman: A Sketch* (1936) attributes Housman's failure to the nature of the curriculum, which emphasized history and philosophy at the expense of literature, but the weight of more recent opinion, including that of Watson and Maude M. Hawkins (*A. E. Housman: Man Behind a Mask*, 1958) places the blame on Housman's changed feelings for Jackson.

Housman returned to Oxford in the fall of 1881 to qualify for the lowly pass degree. He worked occasionally as a tutor in Greek and Latin at his old school and studied intensively for the Civil Service Examination. In December, 1882, he moved to London to share lodgings with Jackson and Jackson's younger brother, Adalbert, and went to work in the Patent Office, where he spent the next ten years registering trademarks. From this point until 1885, not one letter emerged from Housman and not even a brother and sister could gain access to him when they came to live in London. In 1886, Housman, seeking the peace of solitude, took private rooms in Highgate, and from this time on his "invariable mode of life," according to Watson, would be "monastic seclusion." Only the Jackson brothers were encouraged to intrude upon his privacy.

In 1888 Housman broke upon the scholarly world with an avalanche of brilliant critical articles that won for him an international reputation (and would secure for him the Chair in Latin at University College, London, in 1892). When one remembers that these early scholarly publications were researched in the evenings at the British Museum after a full day at the Patent Office, his accomplishment must be seen as nothing short of heroic. His *Introductory Lecture* (1937) was given on October 3, 1892, at University College and earned for him the lasting respect of his colleagues. Housman's scholarly writing continued unabated during his years there. He continued to work on the manuscripts of Propertius, edited works by Ovid and Juvenal, and in 1897 came out with a brilliant series of papers on the *Heroides*. In the meantime, Moses Jackson had gone to live in India and Adalbert had died, plunging Housman into near suicidal gloom which was to persist at intervals for the rest of his life and which could be relieved only by creative activity. In 1896, *A Shropshire Lad* appeared, published at his own expense, and 1899 saw the first paper on Manilius, the poet who was to become the object of Housman's most important work of scholarship. His edition of Manilius appeared in five books over a twenty-seven-year period, "a monument of incomparable skill and thankless labour."

The eventual success of *A Shropshire Lad* and Housman's recognized position as a scholar of the first rank made him something of a celebrity, and during his last ten years at University College, he would dine at the Cafe Royal with a select circle of friends that included his brother Laurence, his publisher Grant Richards, his faculty colleague Arthur Platt, and a few others. By now Housman was a connoisseur of fine food and wine and an accomplished dinner conversationalist. He remained aloof from the London literary scene, however, and had little appreciation for the serious writers of his day, including the poet William Butler Yeats. On a lesser level, he intensely disliked the novels of John Galsworthy, and when James Joyce's *Ulysses* (1922) was published, Housman sniffed, "I have scrambled and waded through and found one or two half-pages amusing." Nor did he display any interest in music or painting. About such composers as Vaughan Williams and Charles Butterworth, who set some of his poems to music, Housman remarked, "I never hear the music, so I do not suffer."

In October, 1911, Housman was elected Kennedy Professor of Latin at Cambridge University and a Fellow of Trinity College. His brilliant inaugural lecture on *The Confines of Criticism* remained unpublished during his lifetime because he was unable to verify a reference in it to Percy Bysshe Shelley. At the university, Housman became a member of a select group of the faculty known as "The Family," which met twice a month for dinner. At these ritual banquets Housman proved a good raconteur and was a well-accepted member of the group, but according to Gow, he held himself back from intimate friendships with his colleagues for fear of rejection or disappointment. He was equally distant toward his students; and his lectures, which he gave twice weekly in all three academic terms, were sparsely attended both because of the highly technical nature of his subject matter and the coldness of his demeanor on the platform. Throughout his twenty-five years at Cambridge, Housman continued to publish widely, directing his major efforts to the edition of Manilius. He was both respected as a great scholar and feared as a devastating polemicist. *Last Poems*, which appeared in 1922, was a great success. In the spring of 1933, Housman was prevailed upon to give the Leslie Stephen Lecture. He delivered *The Name and Nature of Poetry* on the twenty-second anniversary of his inaugural lecture as Kennedy Professor of Latin. In the summer of 1935, an ill Housman rallied enough strength for one last trip to France, where he had vacationed regularly since 1897. Weakened by heart disease, he died in Cambridge on April 30, 1936. In the words of Watson, he "wore in absolute repose a look of 'proud challenge.'"

Analysis

A. E. Housman once remarked with that scathing condescension of which he was a master that A. C. Swinburne "has now said not only all he has to say about everything, but all he has to say about nothing." Actually, when Housman was at Oxford he fell under Swinburne's powerful spell. His "New Year's Eve" (*Additional Poems*, XXI) written about 1879, celebrates the death of the gods in a labored imitation of the "Hymn to Proserpine": "Divinities disanointed/ And kings whose kingdom is done." The poem is interesting but uninspired and it is well that Housman early rejected Swinburne as a model. Still, one wishes that Housman had possessed more of the older poet's exuberance of imagination and richness of rhetoric, for it is in these qualities that his poetry is most deficient. Practically all of his poems are variations on the related themes of mortality and the miseries of the human condition; while a close reading reveals considerably more variety than at first appears, it is nevertheless true that the body of Housman's poetry is slighter than that of any other English poet of comparable reputation. The authorized canon consists of only three small volumes which were published separately: *A Shropshire Lad*, *Last Poems*, and the posthumous *More Poems*. The twenty-three *Additional Poems* and three verse translations have been added to the *Collected Poems* for a total of 175 original poems. All are short, some no more than a stanza in length. The predominant form is the lyric. The tone is characteristically mournful and the mood elegiac. It is useless to look for any kind of development, either of substance or technique, in these poems, for most of them were written in the 1890's when Housman was under great psychological stress. They are intensely autobiographical inasmuch as they spring from the deep well of Housman's psyche, but few refer to specific events in his life. Housman's passion for privacy was as great as Robert Browning's, and he was attracted to the lyric as a verse form largely because of its essential impersonality. The emotion of his poems is usually general, an undifferentiated *Weltschmerz*, and such dramatic elements as may occur as persona and setting are characteristically undefined. The extremely personal and revealing "The world goes none the lamer" (*More Poems*, XXI) and "Because I liked you better" (*More Poems*, XXXI) are exceptional.

In the world of Housman's poetry, which is more obviously consistent than that of more complex poets, youth fades into dust, lovers are unfaithful, nature is lovely but indifferent, and death is the serene end of everything. These great archetypal themes have given rise to some of the world's finest poetry, from Sir Walter Raleigh's "The Nymph's Reply to the Shepherd" to William Butler Yeats's "Sailing to Byzantium." What makes them interesting in Housman's poetry are the particular forms in which they are cast. "With rue my heart is laden" (*A Shropshire Lad*, LIV), a poem sometimes set to music, may be taken as exemplary of his lyricism:

> With rue my heart is laden
> For golden friends I had,
> For many a rose-lipt maiden
> And many a lightfoot lad.
> By brooks too broad for leaping
> The lightfoot boys are laid;
> The rose-lipt girls are sleeping
> In fields where roses fade.

In this lyric of studied simplicity there is a classical blending of form and substance. The simple and inventive diction; the Latinate syntax, parallelism, and balance; the alternating seven- and six-syllable lines restrain still further the already generalized emotion; and while the poem is cold and artificial, it has a kind of classical grace. A comparison with William Wordsworth's "A Slumber Did My Spirit Seal" will reveal the power of a great sensibility working through the constraints of classical form to convey a sense of profound personal feeling.

In too many of Housman's lyrical poems, including the well-known "When I was one-and-twenty" (*A Shropshire Lad*, XIII) and "When first my way to fair I took" (*Last Poems*, XXXV), the feeling is severely attenuated by a mannered flatness, and the passion that the poet undoubtedly experienced is swallowed up by the generalization of the emotion. At worst, the feeling degenerates into the bathos of "Could man be drunk for ever" (*Last Poems*, X) or the histrionic posturing of "Twice a week the winter thorough" (*A Shropshire Lad*, XVII), but at their best there is a genuine communication of feeling, as in "Yonder see the morning blink" (*Last Poems*, XI) and "From far, from eve and morning" (*A Shropshire Lad*, XXXII). There is a thin line between the expression of the poignancy of existence and sentimentality, and it is a tribute to Housman's tact that he so seldom crosses it.

Housman's poems work best when the emotion is crystallized by a dramatic context, as in some of the love pieces and the poems about soldiers in which the oracular pronouncements about the miseries of living which so easily lapse into an unacceptable didacticism are subordinated to more concrete situations. "Oh see how thick the goldcup flowers" (*A Shropshire Lad*, V) is a clever and humorous dialogue between a young blade and a girl who spurns his advances, but beneath the surface gaiety there is the slightest suggestion of the mortality and faithlessness of lovers. In "Delight it is" (*More Poems*, XVIII) the youthful speaker addresses the maiden in words of reckless honesty—"Oh maiden, let your distaff be/ And pace the flowery meads with me/ And I will tell you lies"—and one is to assume that he is a prototype of all young lovers.

In "Spring Morning" (*Last Poems*, XVI), the idyllic beauty of an April morning and the universal renewal of life in the spring place in ironic relief the "scorned unlucky lad" who "Mans his heart and deep and glad/ Drinks the valiant air of dawn" even though "the girl he loves the best/ Rouses from another's side." The speaker of "This time of year" (*A Shropshire Lad*, XXV) is more fortunate, but only because the former lover of his sweetheart has died. "Is my team ploughing" (*A Shropshire Lad*, XXVII) dramatizes a similar situation in which the surviving youth has taken his dead friend's girl. In a dialogue that extends beyond the grave, the living lover tells his dead friend: "I cheer a dead man's sweetheart/ Never ask me whose." One of the most effective of Housman's love poems is "Bredon Hill" (*A Shropshire Lad*, XXI), in which the sound of the church bells reminds the speaker of the untimely death of his sweetheart. The poem ends ambiguously with the distraught lover saying to the humming steeples: "Oh, noisy bells, be dumb/ I hear you, I will come." Also with death in mind is the speaker of "Along the field" (*A Shropshire Lad*, XXVI), who a year before had heard the aspen predict the death of his sweetheart. The prediction fulfilled, he now walks beside another girl, and under the aspen leaves he wonders if they "talk about a time at hand/ When I shall sleep with clover clad/ And she beside another lad."

In all of these poems love is doomed to transience by infidelity or death. This, they say, is the human condition. In virtually all of them, death has supplanted sex as the major ingredient, making them unique in English love poetry.

Death is also, less surprisingly, the main element in most of Housman's military poems. The poems about soldiers, with the exception of the frequently anthologized "Epitaph on an Army of Mercenaries" (*Last Poems*, XXXVII), are not as well known as some of Housman's other poetry. At first sight they may seem somewhat out of place, but it is not surprising that an introverted classical scholar of conservative convictions should glamorize the guardians of the Empire. The attitude toward the soldier is consistently one of compassion and respect and the poems convey a depth of sincerity not always felt elsewhere. The prospect of young men going to die in foreign lands in the service of the Queen takes on an added poignancy from the death of Housman's younger brother, Herbert, who was killed in the Boer War. On another level, a soldier's death is an honorable form of suicide and a way to attain lasting fame. "The Deserter" (*Last Poems*, XIII) and "The Recruit" (*A Shropshire Lad*, III) may be taken as typical. In the first, the lass, rejected by her lover so that he may rejoin his comrades, upbraids him and others like him for scouring "about the world a-wooing/ The bullet to their breast"; in the second, the lad is promised eternal fame either as a returning hero or as a slain comrade. In "Lancer" (*Last Poems*, VI), the speaker affirms his coming death with the ringing refrain of "*Oh who would not sleep with the brave?*" In these poems Housman succeeds in investing Thanatos, characteristically an enervated and sterile attitude, with a singular vitality. The placid stoicism of the soldiers makes these ultimately the least melancholy of all of Housman's poems.

The melancholy that permeates virtually every line of Housman's poetry is a matter of temperament more than of a well-wrought metaphysics. He affirms the existence of the soul in such poems as "The Immortal Part" (*A Shropshire Lad*, XLIII) and "Be still, my soul" (*A Shropshire Lad*, XLVIII) even as he denies its immortality, the agnostic "Easter Hymn" (*More Poems*, I) notwithstanding. Such monologues to the dead as "To an Athlete Dying Young" (*A Shropshire Lad*, XIX) and "Shot? so quick, so clean an ending?" (*A Shropshire Lad*, XLIV) are intended as no more than poetic license. Death is seen as the final, desirable release from the Sisyphean exhaustion of living. Thanatos ultimately leads to suicide, which in several of the poems is prescribed as the best antidote for the illness of life. Other strategies for coping with the suffocating consciousness of "our long fool's-errand to the grave" are hedonism and, more logically, stoicism.

In Housman's hedonistic poems, the traditional sexuality of the *carpe diem* theme has been eliminated. In his most rousing invitation to pleasure, "Think no more lad" (*A Shropshire Lad*, XLIX), the lad is told to "be jolly/ Why should men make haste to die?" Such pleasures as "jesting, dancing, drinking" stave off the darkness, since "'tis only thinking/ Lays lads underground." The other exercises in hedonism are more subdued. The speaker of "Loveliest of trees" (*A Shropshire Lad*, II), aware of his limited time, will go about the woodlands "To see the cherry hung with snow," and "The Lent Lily" (*A Shropshire Lad*, LXXIX) invites anyone who will listen to enjoy the spring and gather all the flowers that die on Easter day. In "Reveille" (*A Shropshire Lad*, IV), the lad is enjoined to rise and enjoy the morning, for "Breath's a ware that will not keep/ Up, lad: when the journey's over/ There'll be time enough to sleep." "Ho, everyone that thirsteth" (*More Poems*, XXII) makes an effective use of the living waters of Scripture as a metaphor of fulfillment. The poem concludes that "he that drinks in season/ Shall live before he dies," but the "lad that hopes for heaven/ Shall fill his mouth with mold."

Stoicism is a more satisfying way of coming to grips with the human condition, and it provides the basis for several of Housman's most rewarding poems, including "The Oracles" (*Last Poems*, XXV), "The Sage to the Young Man" (*More Poems*, IV), and "The chestnut casts his flambeaux" (*Last Poems*, IX). In this last poem, an embittered young man drinking in a tavern deplores the passing of another spring and curses "Whatever brute and blackguard made the world" for cheating his "sentenced" soul of all that it has ever craved. Then with dramatic suddenness, he sees that "the troubles of our proud and angry dust/ Are from eternity," and this leads to his stoic affirmation that "Bear them we can, and if we can we must." The idea here that human misery is both certain and universal is the central focus of such powerful poems as "The First of May" (*Last Poems*, XXXIV), "Westward on the high-hilled plains" (*A Shropshire Lad*, LV), and "Young is the blood" (*More Poems*, XXXIV). In "Young is the blood," the speaker identifies his own pain in a youth he espies whistling along the hillside highway and proclaims in the succession of the generations "that the sons of Adam/ Are not so evil-starred/ As they are hard." This is the heart of Housman's stoicism, and this is one of his more honest and successful poems.

In a number of Housman's poems, the universalization of the existential predicament embodies a vision of the remote past that suggests the ultimate insignificance of everything. The speaker of "When I watch the living meet" (*A Shropshire Lad*, XII) is reminded by the moving pageant filing through the street of the dead nations of the past where "revenges are forgot/ And the hater hates no more," just as the speaker of "On Wenlock Edge" (*A Shropshire Lad*, XXXI) is put in mind by a storm of "the old wind in the old anger" threshing the ancient Roman city of Uricon. He knows the storm will pass even as "the Roman and his trouble," both now "ashes under Uricon." The perspective shifts to the future in "I wake from dreams" (*More Poems*, XLIII) and "Smooth between sea and land" (*More Poems*, XLV), which present visions of apocalyptic dissolution.

The poetry of Housman is the poetry of negation. Most of it is shot through with a nameless melancholy and much of it is pessimistic. His lyrics invite comparison with Hardy's, with which they are often included in anthologies, but they reflect none of Hardy's moral depth. They are closer in spirit to those of Heinrich Heine, whom Housman mentioned as one of the three major influences on his work, along with the English ballads and the songs of William Shakespeare. Housman's *Weltschmerz* struck a deep chord in two generations of English readers, making *A Shropshire Lad* and *Last Poems* two of the most popular volumes of poetry of their period. Today, Housman's reputation is tempered by the knowledge that his poetry, though capable of creating haunting moods, neither expands nor deepens one's self-awareness nor one's awareness of life, despite his claim in "Terence, this is stupid stuff" (*A Shropshire Lad*, LXII) that it prepares one for life's rigors. For this reason Housman must be considered a minor poet.

Major publications other than poetry

NONFICTION: *The Application of Thought to Textual Criticism*, 1922; *The Name and Nature of Poetry*, 1933; *Introductory Lecture*, 1937; *Selected Prose*, 1961 (John Carter, editor); *The Confines of Criticism*, 1969; *The Letters of A. E. Housman*, 1971 (Henry Maas, editor); *The Classical Papers of A. E. Housman*, 1972 (J. Diggle and F. R. D. Goodyear, editors).

MISCELLANEOUS: *M. Manilii Astronomicon Liber Primus*, 1903 (edited); *Ivnii Ivvenalis Satvrae*, 1905 (edited); *M. Manilii Astronomicon Liber Secundus*, 1912 (edited); *M. Manilii Astronomicon Liber Tertius*, 1916 (edited); *M. Manilii Astronomicon Liber Quartus*, 1920 (edited); *M. Annaei Lvcani Belli Civilis Libri Decem*, 1926 (edited); *M. Manilii Astronomicon Liber Quintus*, 1930 (edited).

Bibliography

Ehrsam, Theodore G. *A Bibliography of Alfred Edward Housman*, 1941.
Gow, Andrew S. *A. E. Housman: A Sketch*, 1936.
Hawkins, Maude M. *A. E. Housman: Man Behind a Mask*, 1958.
Marlow, Norman. *A. E. Housman: Scholar and Poet*, 1958.
Watson, George L. *A. E. Housman: A Divided Life*, 1957.

Robert G. Blake

WILLIAM DEAN HOWELLS

Born: Martins Ferry, Ohio; March 1, 1837
Died: New York, New York; May 11, 1920

Principal collections

Poems of Two Friends, 1860 (with John J. Piatt); *Poems*, 1873; *Samson*, 1874; *Priscilla: A Comedy*, 1882; *A Sea Change: Or, Love's Stowaway*, 1884; *Poems*, 1886; *Stops of Various Quills*, 1895; *The Mother and the Father*, 1909.

Other literary forms

A professional writer almost from boyhood, William Dean Howells achieved a major reputation as novelist, editor, and critic, and, in addition to poetry, published well-received biographies, short stories, travel letters, social criticism, autobiographical sketches, and stage plays. His most important productions, however, were the novels in which he attacked sentimentality of thought and what he saw as falsification of moral and ethical belief. He based his novels on the actions of "ordinary" men and women, insisting that language and motivation be true to a particular time and place; he made himself, with Mark Twain and Henry James, one of the leading American spokesmen for realism in fiction. During most of his adult years he was, indeed, the arbiter of taste in American literary circles.

Achievements

Howells' early novels include works contrasting American and Italian characters, and depictions of life in New England and the Northeast. The best known of these, *Their Wedding Journey* (1872), is an episodic set of sketches showing a young couple's honeymoon trip to Niagara. Most of this early work may be classified as comedy of manners. In the 1880's, Howells began to publish the realistic works that were to bring him fame. The most considerable of these include *A Modern Instance* (1882), the story of the failed marriage of Marcia Gaylord to an unscrupulous newspaperman, and Howells' masterpiece, *The Rise of Silas Lapham* (1885), the story of a businessman who maintains his moral integrity at the cost of financial disaster. In the 1890's, Howells began to write of the problems of social justice that paralleled the rise of industry. *A Hazard of New Fortunes* (1890) portrays the repentance of a wealthy businessman who at first opposes the socialist ideas of the editor of a magazine he finances, then learns to accept them when his own son is killed during a strike. Some of his novels of this period deal with the problems of women while others sketch the experience of literary life in New York. Howells also wrote several character studies of Americans that constitute a return to the comedy of manners. The best-known works of his later years, however, are the Utopian stories *A Traveler from Altruria* (1894) and its sequel, *Through the Eye of the Needle* (1907). Other well-known books are the autobiographical *A Boy's Town* (1890) and *Years of My Youth* (1916). The literary criticism that helped make him the most imposing force in American letters in the last thirty years of his life is represented by *Criticism and Fiction* (1891), *My Literary Passions* (1895), and *Literature and Life* (1902).

Through his column in *Harper's New Monthly Magazine* and other critical writings, his example as a leading novelist of realism and his friendship with most of the prominent writers and editors of the time, Howells came to be a much honored spokesman. Among the younger writers whom he encouraged were Hjalmar Boyesen, Hamlin Garland, Stephen Crane, Frank Norris, and Robert Herrick. He gave his literary credo in *Criticism and Fiction*, declaring that the American state is built on "the affirmation of the essential equality of men," and that the resulting culture is characterized not by "distinction" of individuals and works but by "common" beauty, by a "quality of solidarity" that tends to "unite rather than sever" mankind. The only distinction worth achieving, he held, is that which gives "expression of American life in art." As a man of his age, Howells also asserted that art must serve morality and must picture "the smiling aspects" of experience, and that most novels should find their substance in the "passions" of ordinary men and women rather than in the "guilty love" that, he said, is rare in real life even though it is the chief topic of French novels.

One consequence of his distaste for the expression of extramarital love relationships was an inability to give more than limited approval to the work of Walt Whitman. Toward the end of Howells' long life, the younger generation was beginning to see him as spokesman not for the new but for the "Puritanism" that they considered themselves to be attacking. His clear, graceful style, intelligent civility, and accurate observation wear well, however, and his reputation has recovered. Though he may never again be thought of as well as he was in the 1890's, his work will no doubt outlive changes in fashion.

Biography

Like Mark Twain and Walt Whitman, William Dean Howells, a native of Ohio, had little formal schooling and began work as a printer while still in his boyhood. His father read verse aloud to the family, and the country newspapers he worked on during his father's moves about the state often printed poetry. From 1856 to 1861, Howells wrote for the *Ohio State Journal* in Columbus, studied languages, read widely from his father's library and any other collections he could find, and developed the ambition to be a poet that led to the publication (with his friend John J. Piatt) of *Poems of Two Friends*. He wrote the campaign biography of Abraham Lincoln in 1860 and was rewarded with an appointment as American consul in Venice. In Italy, he continued to write verse and to read widely, learning Italian, observing the contrasts in American and European character, and publishing sketches of life and travel in Europe, as well as a study of Italian poetry. In later years he occasionally used Italy as a setting for his novels. Returning to the United States in 1865, he worked for five years as subeditor of the *Atlantic Monthly* until becoming the editor-in-chief, a post he held from 1871 to 1881. Like his close personal and literary friend Twain, he retained affection for the Midwest of his boyhood, while appropriating some of the sophistication of the cosmopolitan literary man. His first novel, *Their Wedding Journey*, began the development of the comedy of manners that characterized his novels of the 1870's.

In 1881, Howells left the *Atlantic Monthly* and began to write principally for the *Century Illustrated Monthly* magazine and to publish realistic studies of characters facing ethical problems—notably among them *A Modern Instance* and *The Rise of Silas Lapham*. In what may be considered his third period, Howells moved to New York as an editor and critic for *Harper's New Monthly Magazine* and became passionately caught up in problems of the industrial age as he saw them represented in a New York traction strike, the Haymarket Riot, and the works of Leo Tolstoy and Henry George. This interest led to a series of novels showing the demoralizing effects of the economic system upon personal character, as in *A Hazard of New Fortunes*. He also published his utopian novels and, in his later years, returned from time to time to the comedy of manners. He continued to publish poetry, prose, and drama until his death in 1920.

Analysis

Oddly, it was his novelistic realism that assured William Dean Howells of remaining an idealist in verse. Having no taste for the role of transcendental bard assumed by Whitman, Howells continued through most of his career to follow the practices of such idealist poets of the day as Edmund Clarence Stedman, Richard Henry Stoddard, Bayard Taylor, and Thomas Bailey Aldrich. Only after coming to sympathize with the protests against economic oppression that workingmen and radicals of the 1880's and 1890's were mounting did he begin in the early 1900's to move away from the consolatory elegiac, toward the ironic stance that would be characteristic of poetic modernism.

When in 1910 Howells looked back at his career, he observed, in a tone both defiant and wistful, that "There is a mystic power in verse which utters in a measured line the passion and the aspiration which a whole unmetred volume cannot express." Howells grew up in a home where the father read poetry aloud to the family and in a culture that still valued poetry above fiction. When he began to write, he thought of himself as a poet until the difficulties of achieving publication of verse and the success of his essays caused him to turn to prose. Verse remained for him an honorable craft, an avocation wherein he could relax the discipline that kept excess of sentiment out of his novels. Yet poetry was perhaps also an opening to a more profound world, to a realm of possibility that he could not confirm by observation and therefore excluded from his prose. Late in his career, he began to move toward verse to express the uncertainties and disappointments of the industrialized world.

Howells' poetic sensibility originated in the sentimental genteel mode whose chief spokesman was Edmund Stedman. In 1861, Howells wrote to Stedman's mother, Mrs. W. B. Kinney: "I think Mr. Stedman the best of our young American poets." That this was not simply polite flattery is demonstrated by Howells' support of Stedman's position when that poet and critic derided Whitman's work as vulgar. Howells did later come to a not entirely whole-hearted recognition of Whitman, and he was perceptive enough to see the artistry in Herman Melville's poems, as he later welcomed the writing of Emily Dickinson and recognized the merit of Edwin Arlington Robinson and Robert Frost. Howells, however, certainly never thought of himself as a modernist.

Howells generally intended his lyric poetry to present a mood, a momentary feeling of melancholy, pathos, joy, wonder, or other similarly uncomplicated emotions. Whether lyric or narrative, the aim was to hold up a feeling, an impression, or an event for static contemplation, rather than to develop idea or character. The language is the ordinary—often, too ordinary—"good English" of the classroom and the editorial desk, with much use of the inversions of syntax and the special diction characteristic of romantic writing. His verse avoids "exaggeration" as carefully as his prose, a discipline acceptable in realism but nearly fatal to poetry. Most of his verse celebrates a world purged of the cantankerous and ugly, the malicious and dull. Even his occasional poems set in the Midwest or in Venice are intended to arouse sentimental responses rather than to develop new awareness. Only in his fifties, after setbacks in his career and his personal life, did Howells recognize that the blows delivered to romantic idealism by the forces summed up as Darwinism and industrialization might prove fatal.

Howells' first three books were in reality one. His first book appeared in the second half of the volume *Poems of Two Friends* (the first half of the book was filled with poems by John J. Piatt, a lifelong friend who became one of the best-known Midwestern poets of the day). Most of the poems from this first book reappear in *Poems* (1873). As was the publishing custom at the time, the pieces in this second book were in turn reprinted almost unchanged, except for four additions, in *Poems* (1886). The 1886 volume thus represents Howells' work from youth to middle age.

Prominent in the volume are several rather long narrative poems. In these, as in his lyrics, Howells' aim is to enable the reader to enjoy contemplation of an experience arousing melancholy, pathos, or any other "standard" emotion. In most of these poems Howells used a hexameter line that emphasizes the poet's artifice that what is conveyed is somewhat removed from ordinary existence.

Howells modeled his narrative poems on the domestic narrations of Henry Wadsworth Longfellow and Alfred Tennyson, not on their retellings or imitations of the classics. Three of his narrative poems are set in Ohio. "The Pilot's Story," perhaps the best known of his poems, was first published in the *Atlantic Monthly* in September, 1860. The pilot of a steamboat moving up the Ohio tells how a well-dressed white man once brought aboard a beautiful woman who, though white in appearance, had enough Negro blood to be held as a slave. The man, fleeced by gamblers, coldly told the woman that he had sold her to make good his losses. Stunned, she shrieked at him—he had broken a promise to set her free. Although the other passengers gathered around, her owner seized her; whereupon she broke away and leapt to her death, crushed by the paddlewheel. The narrator reports that "the odorous breath of the willows/ Smote with a mystical sense of infinite sorrow" upon the pilot's auditors. Pathos is thus the aim of the poem. The unusual setting and the implied nostalgia for the river as it was before it became an industrialized canal give the poem appeal, but it lacks the dramatic conflict necessary for tragedy. Modern readers may mistake it for an antislavery tract, but the fact that the woman is a slave is only an incidental necessity of the plot. Howells' aim was to arouse emotion, not to argue a social issue.

Another well-known hexameter narrative with an early Midwestern setting, "Louis Lebeau's Conversion," is also essentially static. The narrator is an American poet in Venice, where Howells served as American consul from 1861 to 1865. Howells wrote to his sister that the idea came to him after hearing his parents describe an oldtime camp meeting. The narrator recalls his "story of free, wild life in Ohio," reflecting on the beauties of the forest scene and praising the religious faith of the people. The event takes place on an evening in a clearing lit by pyres of wood (a setting much like the camp meeting scene in the 1916 novel *The Leatherwood God*). The title character in the poem is a "wild river man" who loves the daughter of the exhorter. The father has forbidden Lebeau to court the girl unless he undergoes conversion. The "wild" man sturdily resists a variety of tearful pleas but surrenders when the girl herself takes him by the hand and leads him to the altar to kneel with her. The motivating power is the "tender" love of the young woman, an entirely ethereal figure. Lebeau's conversion simply happens after Howells has accumulated a sufficient mass of sentimental appeal; therefore, the poem is a failure as an account of a dramatic happening.

Howells' best narrative poems, at least to modern taste, engage some complexity of thought and feeling. Both are set in Venice. "No Love Lost" is an epistolary poem concerning Americans in Europe. Philip, a young man, has been reported killed during the Civil War but, in fact, has only been taken prisoner. When he reappears, he hears from Bertha, his betrothed, that she has fallen in love with another man. When Philip sees Bertha in Venice, he renounces her. Some of the story is told in letters from Clara, a young woman who has meanwhile fallen wildly in love with Philip and accordingly sees his every action as heroic. The narrator ends with the half-humorous remark that "I don't exactly see where the heroism commences"—the best line in the poem both because it is given in natural English and because it suggests that the story is not quite so unusual and wonderful as the participants believe it to be. The line has the effect of upsetting expectations, enabling Howells to pose as a bit too sophisticated to believe entirely in the melodramatic story. The reader will note that Philip does not make a serious attempt to regain Bertha's love, presumably because in the nineteenth century the fact that she had involved herself with another man had made her "soiled goods."

The best of the narrative poems is "Pordenone." The narrator is a modern man who studies the peeling frescoes on the wall of a Venetian building that once was a monastery but is now a barracks for Austrian soldiers. He begins to imagine the time of the Renaissance when the artist Pordenone painted these walls, perhaps modeling some figures after the girl Violenta. An amusing participant in the imagined scene is an old friar who mistakes one biblical event for another. Pordenone thinks of his contemporary Titian as a rival, and at first rejects the greater artist's offer of friendship. This gives Titian an opening to make a long aesthetic and moral statement that artists are only "Pencils God paints with," and that it is "the delight of doing" that keeps an artist at his work. The narrator then returns to the present, never learning what happened to the characters. Inevitably, the reader will compare Howells with Robert Browning: the material would make a fine dramatic monologue, but Howells' conception is too lax for the craggy, taut treatment that his British contemporary would have given it.

The most unusual of the narratives almost succeeds in achieving the charm that Howells could never quite produce. "Bopeep: A Pastoral" is a tale set in a never-never land and is so openly sentimental and conforming that it almost works as a delightful story (or as a sly put-on). Out herding her sheep one day, Bopeep is "stung" by a snake and, as everyone has heard, loses the flock. Wandering about in a directionless way, she finds a bright little cabin in the forest inhabited by a handsome young hermit. He turns out to be the son of old King Cole, who rejoices to have his son return to the family castle with a charming young woman. Howells apes Tennyson's diction, but the tale is commonplace because even when imitating a master he cannot avoid flatness of language.

Themes of the narratives are love, death, nostalgia, and the sense of loss, which may come with such changes as maturity and the cycle of seasons. Most of the lyrics in *Poems* center on one or another of these matters, generally assembling clichés of idea and feeling in such inherited forms as the sonnet, couplets, and other rhymed patterns. The poems "Caprice," "Before the Gate," "Through the Meadow," and "The Sarcastic Fair" all portray women who are more clever than their men at perceiving the quality of a love relationship. Other love lyrics show a girl crying as her man rides away, a lover who feels jealousy, and (in "Forlorn") the not very convincing despair of a lover who "came too late" to find his sweetheart. The best of the poems, "Feurbilder," deals not with young love but with a marriage relationship. A couple sits before a fire with their young daughter. The child sees in the flames a young woman who loves a man her own age, but then sees her marrying an older man even as a funeral procession—presumably for the young man—passes by. The child's mother pales, but the father is pleased. The reader assumes that the child's vision is analogous to the parents' marriage. The poem "Clement" is, like "No Love Lost," interesting for the student of morality, for here the failure of love to result in marriage is clearly occasioned by the woman's having been married before.

Several of Howells' poems deal with death. Though this topic is of interest in every era, Victorian writers—as the critic Leslie Fiedler has observed—gave it the attention now reserved for sex. The most likely explanation of the interest in the funereal is that Americans were continuing the emphasis on pathos which they inherited from English writers of the sentimental movement, particularly from the poets of the "Graveyard School." When they bothered to defend their practice, writers asserted that they were intent on improving morality, a bit of cant no more self-delusive than twentieth century proclamations that lurid treatments of sex are "liberating." Whatever the reasons, Howells as a man of his time wrote several poems on death. "Pleasure-Pain"—an early piece sometimes printed in later books under the title "Summer Dead" and sometimes given in shortened versions—is in the mood of Heinrich Heine's "Das lyrische intermezzo" sequence; simpler, however, in both phrasing and thought, the poem presents a domesticated story with bobolinks, a rural village, and an old man telling a tale to a child.

The poems "Rapture," "Dead," "In August," and three pieces on the Civil War ("The Battle in the Clouds," "For One of the Killed," "The Two Wives") all present standard emotions in standard ways. The poorest of the poems on death is the hastily written "Elegy on John Butler Howells," a piece honoring Howells' younger brother, who died on April 27, 1864. The poem is datelined Venice, May 16, 1864, and apparently was dashed off just after Howells received the letter informing him of the death.

Poems on the theme of the loss of freshness as one matures are, like several on the sadness which may come with autumn, entirely ordinary. Four poems on nostalgia are also trite, especially the collection of worn notions entitled "The Empty House." Little more originality appears in two pieces which allude to the poet's old home in Ohio. The speaker of "The Song the Oriole Sings" hears in New England an oriole that reminds him of his Midwestern boyhood. The speaker of "The Mulberries" is in Venice, where, seeing fruit for sale on the Rialto bridge, he remembers the berries he ate in Ohio. The best-known of the poems of nostalgia, "The Movers," dated Ohio, 1859, gives a static scene intended, as usual, to arouse pathos. A young couple with children and dog pass in their wagon, toiling up the side of a valley and turning for a last look at their log cabin; their memories are held for a moment before they turn to resume their westward move. Nothing happens to make the moment dramatic. Howells again has assembled a poem out of a store-house of sentimental objects and emotions.

The poems in *Stops of Various Quills* (1895) show Howells facing up to the difficulties confronting the idealist in the last decade of the century. What these forty-three poems reveal, however, is not a new Howells but the old one thwarted. Still a romantic idealist, he continues evoking the standard sentiments, but he is aware that the received values are faltering. He criticizes not the values themselves but the human condition which cannot support them. Meanwhile, he enjoys the chance to stir the emotions by using criticism as a device for approaching from a new direction such conventional themes as the sadness of change, the persistence of "Care," the problems of why one is born and what happens after death, the aesthetic nobility of disillusion, and the existence of guilt, despair, and cruelty. The forms also remain traditional, most of the pieces being presented in couplet or in sonnet form, the rest in other conventional rhyme schemes.

Two poems suggest Howells' debt to Ralph Waldo Emerson. The ten couplets which make up "Statistics" conclude that evil and crime average out about the same from place to place, but men are on a "spiral" and "somewhere there is a God." Another set of couplets, this one entitled "Time," is reminiscent of the earnest moralism of Emerson's "Days." Time warns that once it passes it never returns, implying that one should take advantage of it while one can. The newest note in *Stops of Various Quills* is a touch of social criticism. This criticism is, however, based on the morality of romantic sentimentalism rather than the practical-minded recognition of social reality found in Howells' prose speculations on the need for social reform. In "Twelve P.M." the speaker gratefully concludes that to come home from a dinner party and become "one's sheer self again" is to drop the social façade and confront "the eternal Verity."

Two poems show a man discovering that his supposedly deserving fellow men may be deceptive or evil. In "Parable," a young man who follows Christ's admonition to give his goods to the poor discovers that his beneficiaries engage in crime. Like Andrew Carnegie and other contemporary stewards of wealth, he decides that hereafter he will keep "for some wise purpose" what Providence has bestowed on him and will give only to the "Deserving Poor." In "Materials of a Story," a friend tells the narrator how, upon the death of an ex-convict he had helped, the man's mother asked for the plate from his coffin and for the flowers—not out of love for her son, but in order to sell the items to buy liquor. The narrator does not moralize: he simply goes "on up town," accepting the story as one version of the way people are.

The poems with most appeal to present-day readers move into strong criticism of the way the economic system treats some workers. "Labor and Capital" suggests that the horse which draws a freight wagon and the man who drives it are on the same level: both are slaves of "the Company." "The King Dines" is a heavily ironic picture of a poor man on a cold park bench, gnawing on the bone his wife has brought him for lunch.

Though he ultimately settled for the received tradition, Howells was attempting to confront the new. The development may be traced not only in his lyric and meditative verse but also in the four verse plays among his thirty-six surviving dramas (at least several other plays have disappeared). Such theater critics as Walter J. Meserve and Arthur Hobson Quinn give Howells high marks for achievement in social comedy. His verse for the stage began, however, with an effort at tragedy. *Samson* (1874) is a fairly literal English rendition of *Sansone* by the Italian Hippolito D'Aste, a work elaborating on the Bible story. Howells' blank verse is uneven, but the play's production brought him to the attention of theater people.

Howells' first verse comedy is also a retelling of another writer's work. *Priscilla: A Comedy* (1882) is a dramatization of Longfellow's poem "The Courtship of Miles Standish" (1858). Howells received Longfellow's approval to undertake the play, but could not work as closely with him as he had intended because the poet died in 1882. Howells' version strengthens both the action and the characterization, replacing Longfellow's mood of dreamy contemplation with vigorous scenes of action and using much spare dialogue, adding minor characters to enliven the happenings, and building up the character of Standish. These improvements place the focus not on mood but on relationships among the characters.

The first of Howells' two completely original verse dramas is an early example of the form now known as musical comedy. Though *A Sea Change: Or, Love's Stowaway* (1884) has never been produced, it is a "Lyricated Farce"—as the subtitle terms it—that should have done well on the stage. Much of the verse is in the manner of W. S. Gilbert, but its most notable feature is the observation of the social role of upper-middle-class American women, a matter Howells studied often in his novels and prose plays. His skill in verse and his professionally adept stagecraft combine with his presentation of the coyness and determination of a young woman, the romantic foolishness of her young man, and the obtuseness of middle-aged parents to make an amusingly thoughtful entertainment. Howells' only serious verse comedy is *The Mother and the Father*, a set of three related blank verse dialogues on problems of birth and death, leading to the central characters' troubled hope that they can retain consoling faith in God and immortality despite the death of their daughter.

Much of the writing in *The Mother and the Father* shows that near the end of his career Howells was moving toward the spare line, natural diction, and thoughtfulness of Robinson and Frost. Given a touch of irony, he would have placed himself among those now seen as modernists. A similar development appears in "Black Cross Farm," printed as one of five poems interspersed among the prose sketches in the collection *The Daughters of the Storage* (1916). The other four poems in this work are genial, well-told stories of no special significance; the reader, indeed, might deduce from them that Howells had given up concern with the fading of idealism. In "Black Cross Farm," however, Howells gave one of his better treatment of the idealist's problem. The narrator and his friend go through the fields to visit an abandoned farm. The purpose of the walk is to see a large black cross someone had nailed to the barn. The friend tells the narrator that no one knows why the cross was placed there; there is no explanation for it, no legend concerning it. The narrator observes that the boards could not have crossed by chance and that in that area the farm's owner would not have been Catholic; he asks if the maker of the cross could have intended a secret expiation. The friend's answer, a suggestion that appeals to the narrator, is given in lines that in attitude and phrasing sound much like Robinson:

> Suppose
> That some one that had known the average woes
> Of human nature, finding that the load
> Was overheavy for him on life's road,
> Had wished to leave some token in this Cross,
> Of what had been his gain and been his loss,
> Of what had been his suffering and of what
> Had also been the solace of his lot?

The narrator decides that he likes this uncertainty better than a "more definite" and thereby "vulgarer" story. The pace is a bit slow, but in its suggestion of a resigned yet faintly buoyant idealism as a way of confronting the difficulties of existence, and in its use of pentameter couplets that are natural in phrasing, free from any special diction, the poem is comparable to the work of Frost as well as that of Robinson. If Howells had more frequently written such quality poetry as that found in "Black Cross Farm," he would hold a place in critical esteem as one who made a major attempt to deal with the aesthetic problems of his time. Because he seldom escaped well-worn forms and sentiments, however, he must be viewed as a potentially fine poet who only fitfully moved toward achievement.

Major publications other than poetry

NOVELS: *Their Wedding Journey*, 1872; *A Chance Acquaintance*, 1873; *A*

Foregone Conclusion, 1875; *The Lady of the Aroostook*, 1879; *The Undiscovered Country*, 1880; *A Modern Instance*, 1882; *A Woman's Reason*, 1883; *The Rise of Silas Lapham*, 1885; *Indian Summer*, 1886; *The Minister's Charge*, 1887; *April Hopes*, 1888; *Annie Kilburn*, 1889; *A Hazard of New Fortunes*, 1890; *The Quality of Mercy*, 1892; *An Imperative Duty*, 1892; *The World of Chance*, 1893; *The Coast of Bohemia*, 1893; *A Traveler from Altruria*, 1894; *The Day of Their Wedding*, 1896; *A Parting and a Meeting*, 1896; *An Open-Eyed Conspiracy*, 1897; *The Landlord at Lion's Head*, 1897; *Their Silver Wedding Journey*, 1899; *Ragged Lady*, 1899; *The Kentons*, 1902; *The Son of Royal Langbrith*, 1904; *Through the Eye of the Needle*, 1907; *New Leaf Mills*, 1913; *The Leatherwood God*, 1916.

SHORT FICTION: *A Fearful Responsibility and Other Stories*, 1881; *Christmas Every Day*, 1893; *Mrs. Farrell*, 1921.

PLAYS: *The Parlor Car*, 1876; *Out of the Question*, 1877; *A Counterfeit Presentment*, 1877; *The Register*, 1884; *A Sea-Change*, 1888; *The Albany Depot*, 1892; *A Letter of Introduction*, 1892; *The Unexpected Guest*, 1893; *A Previous Engagement*, 1897; *Room Forty-five*, 1900; *The Smoking Car*, 1900; *An Indian Giver*, 1900; *Parting Friends*, 1911; *The Complete Plays of W. D. Howells*, 1960 (Walter J. Meserve, editor).

NONFICTION: *Venetian Life*, 1866; *Italian Journeys*, 1867; *The Undiscovered Country*, 1880; *Tuscan Cities*, 1886; *Modern Italian Poets*, 1887; *A Boy's Town*, 1890; *Criticism and Fiction*, 1891; *My Year in a Log Cabin*, 1893; *My Literary Passions*, 1895; *Impressions and Experiences*, 1896; *Stories of Ohio*, 1897; *Literary Friends and Acquaintances*, 1900; *Heroines of Fiction*, 1901; *Literature and Life*, 1902; *Letters Home*, 1903; *London Films*, 1905; *Certain Delightful English Towns*, 1906; *Roman Holidays*, 1908; *Seven English Cities*, 1909; *Imaginary Interviews*, 1910; *My Mark Twain*, 1910; *Familiar Spanish Travels*, 1913; *New Leaf Mills*, 1913; *Years of My Youth*, 1916; *Eighty Years and After*, 1921; *The Life in Letters of William Dean Howells*, 1928.

Bibliography

Engel, Bernard F. "The Genteel Poetry of William Dean Howells," in *MidAmerica*. VI (1979), pp. 44-61.

_____ . "William Dean Howells and the Verse Drama," in *Essays in Literature*. VII (Spring, 1980), pp. 67-78.

Kirk, Clara M., and Rudolph Kirk, eds. "Introduction," in *William Dean Howells: Representative Selections*, 1950.

Bernard F. Engel

LANGSTON HUGHES

Born: Joplin, Missouri; February 1, 1902
Died: New York, New York; May 22, 1967

Principal collections

The Weary Blues, 1926; *Fine Clothes to the Jew*, 1927; *Dear Lovely Death*, 1931; *The Negro Mother*, 1931; *The Dream Keeper and Other Poems*, 1932; *Scottsboro Limited*, 1932; *A New Song*, 1938; *Shakespeare in Harlem*, 1942; *Jim Crow's Last Stand*, 1943; *Lament for Dark Peoples*, 1944; *Fields of Wonder*, 1947; *One Way Ticket*, 1949; *Montage of a Dream Deferred*, 1951; *Selected Poems of Langston Hughes*, 1959; *Ask Your Mama: Or, 12 Moods for Jazz*, 1961; *The Panther and the Lash: Or, Poems of Our Times*, 1967.

Other literary forms

In addition to his prolific production of poetry, Langston Hughes wrote, translated, edited and/or collaborated on works in a number of other genres. He wrote two novels, *Not Without Laughter* (1930) and *Tambourines to Glory* (1958), and produced several volumes of short stories, including *The Ways of White Folks* (1934), *Laughing to Keep from Crying* (1952), and *Something in Common and Other Stories* (1963). Hughes's short fiction also includes several collections of stories about his urban folk philosopher, Jesse B. Semple (Simple): *Simple Speaks His Mind* (1950); *Simple Takes a Wife* (1953); *Simple Stakes a Claim* (1957); *The Best of Simple* (1961); and *Simple's Uncle Sam* (1965).

Hughes published several works for young people, including the story *Popo and Fifina: Children of Haiti* (1932), with Arna Bontemps; biographies of black Americans in *Famous American Negroes* (1954), *Famous Negro Music Makers* (1955), and *Famous Negro Heroes of America* (1958); and a series of "first book" histories for young people, such as *The First Book of Negroes* (1952), *The First Book of Jazz* (1955), and *The First Book of Africa* (1960).

Hughes's histories for adult readers include *The Fight for Freedom: The Story of the NAACP* (1962) and two pictorial histories in collaboration with Milton Meltzer, *A Pictorial History of the Negro in America* (1956) and *Black Magic: A Pictorial History of the Negro in American Entertainment* (1967). Other experimental volumes of photo essays are *The Sweet Flypaper of Life* (1955), with photographs by Roy De Carava, and *Black Misery* (1969), with illustrations by Arouni.

Major translations by Hughes include *Cuba Libre* by Nicolás Guillén (1948), with Ben Carruthers; *Gypsy Ballads*, by Federico García Lorca (1951); and *Selected Poems of Gabriela Mistral* (1957).

Hughes was also productive as a playwright, although his plays did not enjoy much critical or financial success. They include *Mulatto* (1935); *Little*

Ham (1935); *Simply Heavenly* (1957), based on the characters in his Simple stories; and *Tambourines to Glory* (1963), adapted from his novel. The last play was billed as a "gospel song-play," and Hughes created four other plays in that category: *Black Nativity* (1961), *Gospel Glory* (1962), *Jericho-Jim Crow* (1963), and *The Prodigal Son* (1965). These productions are of interest mainly because they underscore Hughes's heartfelt sympathy with the black folk life of America, a love affair he carried on throughout his works.

Hughes wrote the libretti for several operas, a screenplay—*Way Down South* (1942), with Clarence Muse—radio scripts, and song lyrics. His most famous contribution to musical theater, however, was the lyrics he wrote for Kurt Weill and Elmer Rice's musical adaptation of Rice's *Street Scene* (1947).

Over the years, Hughes also wrote several nonfiction articles, mainly focused on his role as a poet and his love of black American music—jazz, gospel, and the blues. Perhaps his most important article was his first: "The Negro Artist and the Racial Mountain," published in *The Nation* on June 23, 1926, in defense of the idea of a black American literary style, voice, and subject matter.

Anthologies of Hughes's work include *The Langston Hughes Reader* (1958), and *Five Plays by Langston Hughes* (1963), edited by Walter Smalley. Hughes himself edited many volumes of work by black American writers, including *The Poetry of the Negro, 1746-1949* (1949), with Arna Bontemps; *The Book of Negro Folklore* (1958), also with Bontemps; *New Negro Poets: U.S.A.* (1964); *The Book of Negro Humor* (1966); and *The Best Short Stories by Negro Writers: An Anthology from 1899 to the Present* (1967).

Finally, there are the two volumes of autobiography, *The Big Sea: An Autobiography* (1940) and *I Wonder as I Wander: An Autobiographical Journey* (1956). A planned third volume was not completed.

Achievements

All of his works illustrate the depth of Hughes's commitment to a celebration of black American life in all its forms and make immediately evident the reason why he has been proclaimed "The Poet Laureate of Black America." As a young poet he won prizes in contests sponsored by *The Crisis* and *Opportunity*, and his first two volumes of poetry, *The Weary Blues* and *Fine Clothes to the Jew*, won critical acclaim. Hughes also won a Harmon Gold Award for his novel *Not Without Laughter*, as well as a Rosenwald Fund Fellowship in the early 1930's, which enabled him to make his first cross-country reading tour.

His stature as a humorist grew from his creation of Jesse B. Semple, also known as Simple, a Harlem barstool philosopher in the tradition of American folk humor ranging from Davy Crockett to Mr. Dooley. Hughes wrote about Simple in columns published in the *Chicago Defender*, begun in the 1940's and continuing into the 1960's. His Simple columns also appeared in the *New*

York Post between 1962 and 1965. Publication of his five books of Simple sketches increased the readership of that sage of Harlem with his views on life in white America.

Although Hughes never had any one big seller, his efforts in so many fields of literary endeavor earned for him the admiration and respect of readers in all walks of life. Certainly, too, Hughes is a major poetic figure of his time and perhaps the best black American poet.

Biography

James Mercer Langston Hughes (the first two names were soon dropped) was born in Joplin, Missouri, on February 1, 1902. His parents, James Nathaniel and Carrie Mercer Langston Hughes, separated when Hughes was young; by the time he was twelve, he had lived in several cities: Buffalo, Cleveland, Lawrence and Topeka, Kansas, Colorado Springs, and Mexico City (where his father lived). Until 1914, however, Hughes lived mainly with his maternal grandmother in Lawrence.

Hughes began writing poetry during his grammar school days in Lincoln, Illinois. While attending Cleveland's Central High School (1916-1920), Hughes wrote his first short story, "Mary Winosky," and published poems in the school's literary publications. The first national publication of his work came in 1921, when *The Crisis* published "The Negro Speaks of Rivers." The poem had been written while Hughes was taking a train on his way to see his father in Mexico City, a visit that the young man dreaded making. His hatred for his father, fueled by his father's contempt for poor people who could not make anything of themselves, actually led to Hughes's being hospitalized briefly in 1919.

Hughes's father did, however, send his son to Columbia University in 1921. Although Hughes did not stay at Columbia, his experiences in Harlem laid the groundwork for his later love affair with the city within a city. Equally important to Hughes's later work was the time he spent at sea and abroad during this period of his life. His exposure to American blues and jazz players in Paris nightclubs and his experiences in Europe, especially in Africa, although brief, provided a rich source of material that he used over the next decades in his writing.

The years between 1919 and 1929 have been variously referred to as the Harlem Renaissance, the New Negro Renaissance, and the Harlem Awakening. Whatever they are called, they were years of rich productivity within the black artistic community, and Hughes was an important element in that Renaissance. While working as a busboy in the Wardman Park Hotel in Washington, D.C., in 1925, Hughes showed some of his poems—"Jazzonia," "Negro Dancers," and "The Weary Blues"—to Vachel Lindsay, who read them during one of his performances that same evening. The next day, Hughes was presented to the local press as "the busboy poet." With that introduction, and with the aid of people such as writer Carl Van Vechten and Walter White (of the NAACP), Hughes's popularity began to grow. He published *The Weary Blues* in 1926 and entered Lincoln University in Pennsylvania, where he completed his college education. The 1920's also saw the publication of his second volume of poems, *Fine Clothes to the Jew*, and the completion of his first novel, *Not Without Laughter*.

During much of the early 1930's, Hughes traveled abroad. He went to Cuba and Haiti during 1931-1932 and joined a group of young writers and students from Harlem on a film-making trip to Russia in 1932-1933. Publishing articles in Russian journals enabled him to extend his own travels in the Far East; he also began to write short stories during that time. By 1934, he had written the fourteen stories that he included in *The Ways of White Folks*.

During the mid-1930's, several of Hughes's plays were produced: *Mulatto* (1931), and *Little Ham* were among them. In the course of having these plays performed, Hughes started the Harlem Suitcase Theatre in 1938, the New Negro Theatre in Los Angeles (1939), and the Skyloft Players of Chicago (1941).

After the publication of his first autobiographical volume, *The Big Sea*, Hughes spent time in Chicago with the group he had founded there. When America entered World War II, Hughes produced material for the war effort, ranging from "Defense Bond Blues" to articles on black American participation in the war. In addition, during the 1940's, he began work on his translations of the poetry of Nicolás Guillén, wrote essays for such diverse magazines as the *Saturday Review of Literature* and *Negro Digest*, wrote the lyrics for *Street Scene*, and published three volumes of poetry: *Shakespeare in Harlem*, *Fields of Wonder*, and *One Way Ticket*.

Also in the 1940's, Hughes "discovered" Jesse B. Semple. Drawing inspiration from a conversation he had in a bar with a worker from a New Jersey war plant—during which the man complained to his nagging girl friend, "You know white folks don't tell colored folks what cranks crank"—Hughes developed the framework for his Simple stories. He combined his own authorial voice, the voice of Simple's learned interrogator (eventually named Boyd), and the voice of Simple himself to weave a mixture of folk humor that has direct ties back to the "old southwest" humor of Mark Twain and his contemporaries.

The next decades saw continued production of poetry and other writing by Hughes. He wrote his pictorial histories and his "first books" for children. He continued his public readings, often accompanied by piano and/or jazz orchestra—a prototype of the Beat poets. His second volume of autobiography, *I Wonder as I Wander*, was published in 1956, and *The Langston Hughes Reader*, an extensive collection of his work in several genres, appeared two years later. The last two volumes of his poetry, *Ask Your Mama* and *The Panther and the Lash*, continued his experimentation with incorporating jazz and folk elements in his poetry.

Hughes spent the last years of his life living and working in Harlem. He encouraged younger black writers, publishing several stories by newcomers in his *The Best Short Stories by Negro Writers*, as well as including works by established older writers such as Ralph Ellison and Richard Wright. Hughes died on May 22, 1967, in Harlem, the city that so inspired and informed his best work. No one caught the magic that Harlem represented during his lifetime in quite the way that Hughes did.

Analysis

Langston Hughes often referred to three poets as his major influences: Paul Laurence Dunbar, Carl Sandburg, and Walt Whitman. If one were to assay which qualities of Hughes's poetry show the influence of which poet, one might say that Hughes got his love of the folk and his lyric simplicity from Dunbar, his attraction to the power of the people—especially urban dwellers—and his straightforward descriptive power from Sandburg, and his fascination with sensual people—people of the body rather than the mind—and his clear sense of rhythm from Whitman. No one would draw such a clear delineation, but the elements described are essential elements of Hughes's poetry. His work explores the humor and the pathos, the exhilaration and the despair, of black American life in ways that are sometimes conventional and sometimes unique. He explored the blues as a poetic form, and he peopled his poems with Harlem dancers, as well as with a black mother trying to explain her life to her son. He worked with images of dreams and of "dreams deferred"; he looked at life in the middle of America's busiest black city and at the life of the sea and of exploration and discovery. Always, too, Hughes examined the paradox of being black in mostly white America, of being not quite free in the land of freedom.

Hughes's first collection of poetry, *The Weary Blues*, contains samples of many of the poetic styles and themes of his poetry in general. The collection begins with a celebration of blackness ("Proem") and ends with an affirmation of the black American's growing sense of purpose and equality ("Epilogue: I, Too, Sing America"). In between, there are poems that sing of Harlem cabaret life and poems that sing the blues. Some of the nonblues poems also sing of a troubled life, as well as an occasional burst of joy. Here, too, are the sea poems drawn from Hughes's traveling experiences. All in all, the sparkle of a love of life in these poems was that which caught the attention of many early reviewers.

The titles of some of the poems about cabaret life suggest their subject: "Jazzonia," "Negro Dancers," "The Cat and the Saxaphone (2 a.m.)," and "Harlem Night Club." "The Cat and the Saxaphone (2 a.m.)" is especially intriguing because it intersperses a conversation between two "jive" lovers with the first chorus of "Everybody Loves My Baby," producing the effect of a jazz chorus within the song's rhythmic framework.

Part of the controversy which flared in the black community during the Harlem Renaissance involved whether an artist should present the "low-life" elements or the more conventional middle-class elements in black American life. Hughes definitely leaned toward the former as the richer, more exciting to portray in his poetry.

Because the blues tradition is more tied to the common folk than to the middle-class, Hughes's interest in the possibilities of using the blues style in his poetry is not surprising. He took the standard three-line blues stanza and made it a six-line stanza to develop a more familiar poetic form; the repetition common in the first and second lines in the blues becomes a repetition of the first/second and third/fourth lines in Hughes's poems. As in the traditional blues, Hughes varies the wording in the repeated lines—adding, deleting, or changing words. For example, here is a stanza from "Blues Fantasy":

> My man's done left me,
> Chile, he's gone away.
> My good man's left me,
> Babe, he's gone away.
> Now the cryin' blues
> Haunts me night and day.

Often exclamation points are added to suggest more nearly the effect of the sung blues.

There are not as many blues poems in this first collection as there are in later ones such as *Fine Clothes to the Jew* and *Shakespeare in Harlem*. (The latter contains a marvelous seven-poem effort entitled "Seven Moments of Love," which Hughes subtitled "An Un-Sonnet Sequence in Blues.") The title poem of this first collection, "The Weary Blues," is an interesting variation, because it has a frame for the blues which sets up the song sung by a bluesmaker. The poet recalls the performance of a blues singer/pianist "on Lenox Avenue the other night" and describes the man's playing and singing. Later, the singer goes home to bed, "while the Weary Blues echoed through his head." Over the years, Hughes wrote a substantial number of blues poems and poems dealing with jazz, reflecting clearly his love for the music that is at the heart of the black American experience.

Some of the poems in *The Weary Blues* are simple lyrics. They are tinged with sadness ("A Black Pierrot") and with traditional poetic declarations of the beauty of a loved one ("Ardella"). The sea poems are also, by and large, more traditional than experimental. Again, their titles reflect their subject matter: "Water-Front Streets," "Port Town," "Sea Calm," "Caribbean Sunset," and "Seascape."

A few of these early poems reflect the gentle but insistent protest that runs through Hughes's poems; they question the treatment of black Americans and search for a connection with the motherland, Africa. The last section of the book is entitled "Our Land," and the first poem in the section, "Our Land: Poem for a Decorative Panel," explores the idea that the black American should live in a land of warmth and joy instead of in a land where "life is cold" and "birds are grey." Other poems in the section include "Lament for Dark Peoples," "Disillusion," and "Danse Africaine." Perhaps the most poignant poem in the book is also in this last section: "Mother to Son." The poem is a monologue in dialect in which a mother encourages her son to continue the struggle she has carried on, which she likens to climbing a rough, twisting staircase: "Life for me ain't been no crystal stair./ It's had tacks in it . . . And places with no carpet on the floor—/ Bare." The collection's final poem, "Epilogue" ("I, Too, Sing America"), raises the hope that some day equality will truly be reached in America for the "darker brother" who is forced "to eat in the kitchen/ When company comes." Taken together, the poems of *The Weary Blues* make an extraordinary first volume of poetry and reveal the range of Hughes's style and subject matter.

The next two principal volumes of poetry, *Fine Clothes to the Jew* and *The Dream Keeper and Other Poems*, present more of Hughes's blues poems (the latter volume is primarily in that genre) and more poems centering on Harlem's night life. The final two volumes, *Ask your Mama* and *The Panther and the Lash*, continue the experiment of combining musical elements with poetry and offer some of Hughes's strongest protest poetry.

Ask Your Mama is dedicated to "Louis Armstrong—the greatest horn blower of them all." In an introductory note, Hughes explains that "the traditional folk melody of the 'Hesitation Blues' is the leitmotif for this poem." The collection was designed to be read or sung with jazz accompaniment, "with room for spontaneous jazz improvisation, particularly between verses, when the voice pauses." Hughes includes suggestions for music to accompany the poetry. Sometimes the instructions are open ("delicate lieder on piano"), and sometimes they are more direct ("suddenly the drums roll like thunder as the music ends sonorously"). There are also suggestions for specific songs to be used, including "Dixie" ("impishly"), "When the Saints Go Marchin' In" and "The Battle Hymn of the Republic." As a final aid, Hughes includes at the end of his collection "Liner Notes" for, as he says, "the Poetically Unhep."

Throughout, the poems in *Ask Your Mama* runs the current of protest against "the shadow" of racism that falls over the lives of the earth's darker peoples. Shadows frequently occur as images and symbols, suggesting the fear and the sense of vague existence created by living in oppression. "Show Fare, Please" summarizes the essence of the poet's feeling of being left out because he has not got "show fare," but it also suggests that "the show" may be all illusion anyway. Not all of the poems are so stark; the humor of Hughes's earlier work is still very much in evidence. In "Is It True," for example,

Hughes notes that "everybody thinks that Negroes have the *most* fun, but, of course, secretly hopes they do not—although curious to find out if they do."

The Panther and the Lash, the final collection of Hughes's poetry, published the year he died, also contains some of his most direct protest poetry, although he never gives vent to the anger which permeated the work of his younger contemporaries. The collection is dedicated "To Rosa Parks of Montgomery who started it all . . ." in 1955 by refusing to move to the back of a bus. The panther of the title refers to a "Black Panther" who "in his boldness/ Wears no disguise,/ Motivated by the truest/ Of the oldest/ Lies"; the lash refers to the white backlash of the times (in "The Backlash Blues").

The book has seven sections, each dealing with a particular part of the subject. "Words on Fire" has poems on the coming of the Third World revolution, while "American Heartbreak" deals with the consequences of "the great mistake/ That Jamestown made/ Long ago"; that is, slavery. The final section, "Daybreak in Alabama," does, however, offer hope. In spite of past and existing conditions, the poet hopes for a time when he can compose a song about "daybreak in Alabama" that will touch everybody "with kind fingers."

The poetry of Langston Hughes is charged with life and love, even when it cries out against the injustice of the world. He was a poet who loved life and loved his heritage. More than any other black American writer, he captured the essence of the complexity of a life that mixes laughter and tears, joy and frustration, and still manages to sing and dance with the spirit of humanity.

Major publications other than poetry

NOVELS: *Not Without Laughter*, 1930; *Tambourines to Glory*, 1958.

SHORT FICTION: *The Ways of White Folks*, 1934; *Simple Speaks His Mind*, 1950; *Laughing to Keep from Crying*, 1952; *Simple Takes a Wife*, 1953; *Simple Stakes a Claim*, 1957; *The Best of Simple*, 1961; *Something in Common and Other Stories*, 1963; *Simple's Uncle Sam*, 1965.

PLAYS: *Mulatto*, 1935; *Little Ham*, 1935; *Simply Heavenly*, 1957; *Black Nativity*, 1961; *Jericho-Jim Crow*, 1963; *Tambourines to Glory*, 1963.

NONFICTION: *The Big Sea: An Autobiography*, 1940; *I Wonder as I Wander: An Autobiographical Journey*, 1956.

MISCELLANEOUS: *Troubled Island*, c. 1930 (opera libretto); *The Poetry of the Negro*, 1746-1949 (with Arna Bontemps), 1949; *The Book of Negro Folklore*, 1959 (with Arna Bontemps); *Simply Heavenly*, c. 1959 (opera libretto); *New Negro Poets: U.S.A.*, 1964; *The Book of Negro Humor*, 1966; *The Best Short Stories by Negro Writers: An Anthology from 1899 to the Present*, 1967.

Bibliography
Barksdale, Richard K. *Langston Hughes: The Poet and His Critics*, 1971.
Dickinson, Donald C. *A Bio-Bibliography of Langston Hughes, 1902-1967*, 1972.
Emanuel, James A. *Langston Hughes*, 1967.
O'Daniel, Therman B., ed. *Langston Hughes: Black Genius*, 1972.
Meltzer, Milton. *Langston Hughes: A Biography*, 1972.
Waldron, Edward E. "The Blues Poetry of Langston Hughes," in *Negro American Literature Forum*. V (Winter, 1971), pp. 140-149.

Edward E. Waldron

TED HUGHES

Born: Mytholmroyd, England; August 17, 1930

Principal poems and collections
The Hawk in the Rain, 1957; *Lupercal*, 1960; *Selected Poems*, 1962; *The Burning of the Brothel*, 1966; *Recklings*, 1967; *Scapegoats and Rabies*, 1967; *Wodwo*, 1967; *Crow: From the Life and Songs of the Crow*, 1970; *Poetry Is*, 1970; *Selected Poems, 1957-1967*, 1972; *Season Songs*, 1975; *Gaudete*, 1977; *Cave Birds: An Alchemical Cave Drama*, 1979; *Remains of Elmet: A Pennine Sequence*, 1979; *Moortown*, 1979; *Under the North Star*, 1981.

Other literary forms
Ted Hughes is a prolific poet, but he has been equally productive in other forms of writing as well. He has written numerous poems, short stories, and plays for children, which have been collected in the following: *Meet My Folks!* (1961), *How the Whale Became* (1963), *The Earth-Owl and Other Moon People* (1963), *Nessie the Mannerless Monster* (1964), *The Iron Man* (1968), and *The Coming of the Kings and Other Plays* (1970). He has edited and introduced the work of Keith Douglas, Emily Dickinson, Sylvia Plath, and William Shakespeare. His *Poetry in the Making* (1967), which brings into a single volume a series of BBC lectures by Hughes, defines his own stance as a poet and discusses the nature of poetry in general; as an introduction to poetry, it is one of the finest of its kind. Hughes has written several radio plays, a version of Seneca's *Oedipus* in 1968, as well as essays and reviews for periodicals such as *The Nation, New Statesman, The Observer, The Guardian*, and *The New York Review of Books*. Several of his poems and talks are on records available through the British Broadcasting Corporation and in libraries throughout the world.

Achievements
In 1956, the Poetry Center of the Young Men's and Young Women's Hebrew Association of New York held a competition for a first book of poems in English. The prize was publication by Harper and Row of the winning manuscript. Out of 287 entries, the judges chose Hughes's *The Hawk in the Rain*. Marianne Moore, one of the three judges (with W. H. Auden and Stephen Spender), in her Introduction to the American edition of the book, wrote: "Hughes's talent is unmistakable, the work has focus, is aglow with feeling, with conscience; sensibility is awake, embodied in appropriate diction."
Beginning with the enthusiastic reviews which *The Hawk in the Rain* received when it appeared in 1957, Hughes's reputation as a major English poet has steadily increased. Today he is considered the most important single

figure to emerge on the British poetic scene since World War II.

Hughes's early work is reminiscent of Gerard Manley Hopkins, D. H. Lawrence, William Butler Yeats, Dylan Thomas, Theodore Roethke, and John Crowe Ransom, while his later work brings to mind the symbolic poetry of William Blake, T. S. Eliot, and Vasko Popa. His poetry is concerned with the most significant and human of themes: man's relation to the impersonal and nonhuman powers of the universe; his place in nature, time, and history. He draws upon religion, folklore, and mythology, using these for his own purposes in a language that brings shocks of recognition—an open, hard-edged, concentrated language that is well aware of its responsibilities. Hughes's native Yorkshire has contributed toward the making of this new language. As Keith Sagar has noted, the West Riding dialect has remained his "staple speech, concrete, emphatic, terse, yet powerfully, economically, eloquent." It is a language which as ably explores the many implications of the suffering that is peculiar to the state of being human—and, to that extent, powerless before the impersonal natural energies—as it states in a clear and uncompromising voice the actual state of things. Despite the fact that Hughes's poetry is concerned with the cause and nature of human suffering and pain, it is full of irony, wit, and humor, some of the best instances of which are found in parts of *Crow*.

Hughes's poetry has been translated into many languages and his poems have appeared in anthologies throughout the English-speaking world.

Biography

Edward James Hughes was the youngest of the three children of William Hughes, a carpenter who fought at the Dardanelles in World War I. The Calder Valley in Yorkshire, where the earliest years of Hughes's life were spent, was bordered by the industrial townships of South Lancashire and West Riding. His fascination with animals can be traced to his life there. The valley was full of animals of all kinds, and Hughes used to accompany his brother, a gamekeeper, on the latter's shooting "expeditions."

The valley, however, had a shut-in character, which encouraged the young Hughes to dream of the sad and desolate moors. Hughes recalls how the "most impressive early companion" of his childhood was a certain dark cliff which pressed its shape and various moods into [his] brain." The high moors were for him an exciting destination; their mood was exultant. Perhaps the energy that much of his early poetry displays has its source in this moorland.

In 1937, the Hughes family moved to Mexborough, in South Yorkshire, where they lived until 1952. Hughes wrote his first poems when he was fifteen and a student at Mexborough Grammar School. During the next two years he did National Service as a ground wireless mechanic in the Royal Air Force, at the end of which he went to Pembroke College, Cambridge. Although he disliked the highly intellectual atmosphere at Cambridge, the fine training in archaeology and anthropology that he received there was to prove immensely fruitful in his later poetic career. After being graduated in 1954, he spent the next two years as a rose gardener, a night watchman, a zoo attendant, a schoolteacher, and a reader at a film studio.

Early in 1956, Hughes and a few others launched a magazine of poetry called *St. Botolph's Review*, which did not survive beyond its first issue. At the party held to inaugurate the journal, Hughes met Sylvia Plath, who was a student at Newnham College on a Fulbright Scholarship. They married in June of that year. The following summer the couple moved to the United States, where they held teaching positions at Smith College (Northampton, Massachusetts) and the University of Massachusetts, respectively. They soon gave up those assignments, however, to devote their time to writing.

In December, 1959, they returned to England, living first in Heptonstall and later in a cottage in Devon (where Ted Hughes still lives). Their first child, Frieda, was born in April, 1960, and the second, Nicholas, was born in January, 1962. Although at this time they were creatively very productive, with Sylvia completing her autobiographical novel *The Bell Jar* and starting to write her famous *Ariel* poems and Hughes writing most of the poems which later appeared in *Wodwo*, their marriage was failing. In August, 1962, they separated; the following February Sylvia Plath committed suicide.

There followed a nearly blank creative period for Hughes that lasted until 1966. Since then he has written fairly consistently, producing as many as seven major collections of poetry. His next book, to be called *Foxes*, is awaiting publication.

Analysis

Ted Hughes has been called "our first poet of the will to live" (Calvin Bedient). He has written poetry that, in a curiously implicit way, points to the "life force" that Hughes sees as reigning over the world. His poetry celebrates this powerful force, which he has discovered in the wild world of animals; he has been called, very aptly, "a worshipper of the claw." He has realized the large limitations of man, his helplessness in the face of death as well as of life. The animals, however, are much stronger; they are the heroes of Hughes's world. Being free from the hesitations, the self-consciousness, and the moral and psychological conflicts that trouble human beings, animals embody the purest kind of energy.

Hughes's poetry shows a fusion of two primary influences: his childhood love for animals, and his love for the philosophy of Arthur Schopenhauer. The poet's interest in animals, however, has little to do with the "animal joy" of his younger days; it has to do with animal power. Schopenhauer has influenced his poetry not only because his is a philosophy of nihilism, but also because his nihilism has indirectly pointed the way toward the superiority of animals over men, of brute strength and raw unthinking energy over mere ratiocination. As Hughes has said, in an interview with Ekbert Faas for the *London Magazine*, his poetry is "the record of just how the forces of the Universe try to redress some balance disturbed by human error." His hawk is "a diamond point of will"; his animals display "the arrogance of blood and bone" with "an energy too strong for death."

If his animals achieve what human beings only dream of achieving, then Hughes's poetry achieves something that earlier kinds of poetry had failed to do. His poetry passionately asserts action, although it does not exclude contemplation. Its world is primarily physical. It represents a positive reaction against what his friend the poet A. Alvarez called "the disease so often found in English culture: gentility." It is frank, unpretentious, and alive with a power that is rarely to be found in English poetry before him. Critical readings of Hughes's poetry, therefore, should not be confined to what his poems ostensibly describe; they must take appropriate account of the prophetic role that he seems to have assigned to them. Hughes even thinks of the poem as "a sort of animal": it is as much pure instinct as in an animal, and as involuntary and inspired in its action as is that of an animal. The poet deals with his words in much the way that an animal deals with his prey; each has his nibbling habits.

Images of animals, especially images relating to animal hunting, appear repeatedly in his poetry and prose. In *Poetry in the Making*, he compares the act of writing poetry with the act of capturing animals:

> The special kind of excitement, the slightly mesmerized and quite involuntary concentration with which you make out the stirrings of a new poem in your mind, then the outline, the mass and colour and final form of it, the unique living reality of it in the midst of the general lifelessness. . . . This is hunting and the poem is a new species of creature, a new specimen of the life outside your own.

Hughes's many "animal poems" are excellent examples of empathic contemplation. Animals leap off his pages with all their primal energy and vigor; they assert the endlessness of life in the very face of death and destruction. They can be destroyed, but because the life force breathes through them they cannot be tamed. A look at the titles of Hughes's best-known poems shows his multifaceted nonhuman universe: "The Hawk in the Rain," "The Jaguar," "The Horses," "The Thought-Fox," "Crow Hill," "Hawk Roosting," "An Otter," "Pike," "Ghost Crabs," "The Bear," "Skylarks," "Wodwo," *Crow*, *Cave Birds*.

Any analysis of Hughes's poetry must take into consideration the subtle interplay of its dramatic and narrative elements. "The Thought-Fox" and "Hawk Roosting" are excellent embodiments of his major themes and techniques. "The Thought-Fox," as Keith Sagar writes, is "both a description . . . and a splendid example" of the magic process of poetic composition. Although the fox in the poem is a "thought-fox"—a metaphorical being who steals into the landscape of the poet-speaker's mind—its presence in the poem is much more than metaphorical. Hughes's strong visual imagination, coupled with his highly evocative language, treats the fox in such a way that the reader can see it, smell it, listen to its paws on the snow, and even touch it. The poem is part inspiration, part the subtle technique that brings a thought to life, and part the thought itself. Unlike "Hawk Roosting," in which the details of description do not seem to cohere easily, here the line of movement is as clear, smooth, and sure as the fox who is responsible for drawing it across the speaker's "blank page."

In the poem's opening line, the speaker declares something that would have been true even without such a declaration: "I imagine this midnight moment's forest." The reader realizes at once that the landscape is both symbolic and real. The forest and the "midnight moment," it would seem, were there even before the speaker consciously imagined their being there. That first line does something else too: it makes the "midnight moment" and the "forest" inseparable parts of a thinking mind which belongs to them as much as they belong to it. The narrator's mind, the "moment," and the "forest" belong to one another and together create a perfectly dramatic landscape. Every abstraction, every feeling is perceived in a disturbingly *physical* way, as though each had a body and a personality of its own.

The "something else" of which the speaker is so strongly aware is at once near and far away from him, at once near his "clock's loneliness" and the "blank page where his fingers move" and far away inside the depths of the forest; it is "something more near/ Though deeper within darkness" than the stars that the speaker cannot see. The mysterious being, unnamed until this moment, and unrecognized, is "entering the loneliness." The loneliness is not confined to the immediate surroundings of the speaker; it extends far beyond what the eyes cannot see. It is not the speaker's loneliness into which the fox enters, but a loneliness that is much less personal. The use of "the" (instead of "my") before "loneliness" makes the condition a part of an unlocalized and nonpersonal process.

The "thing" enters the loneliness as though the latter were a house with its doors wide open to receive a nightly guest; it appears that the "blank page" is kept open for the important guest's all-important signature. The first eight lines of the poem create an atmosphere of mystery and magic within which anything might happen; they keep the reader anxious about the things to come, about a nighttime consciousness. Into this dark world comes a small, faintly seen unit of light—the fox. Then there is a long unbroken movement until one reaches the poem's end. The fox comes nearer and nearer until it leaps into the "dark hole of the head." The end has almost arrived; what happens thereafter is something which is impossible to realize or explain: "The page is printed."

The rhythm of the lines perfectly captures the rhythm of the fox's slow and delicate movement. The metaphor, slowly and imperceptibly, *becomes* the animal. The fox's nose touches "twig, leaf"; the eyes (so very often an important constituent of Hughes's animal imagery) "serve" a movement that must take place in spite of everything. The forest of the mind's dark night is being unavoidably invaded by the predator of thought, who sets his neat prints into the soft snow "now/ And again now, and now, and now." He knows how to move on the snowy clearings, "Between trees"; he knows his way. With every "now" he comes a step nearer to the "blank page." The imitatively rhythmic repetitions, together with the pauses between them, make the fox's movement spread over an entire landscape. He is everywhere, an all-pervasive presence. His shadow takes care of the possible dangers ("Warily a lame/ Shadow lags by stump and in hollow") while the body pre-pares to come "Across clearings."

The fox, however, is not a "body" but an "eye"—a body whose intentions have been concentrated in its seeing through the dark, a body which remains admirably undisturbed by anything outside itself. Even the eye is not really an eye, but "a widening deepening greenness"—an eye that magically turns every aspect of the nightly landscape into its own image, that spreads its own color over mind and matter. All this has been happening from the speaker's standpoint too. The "something alive" of the first stanza has become the one "eye" whose "greenness" deepens and widens as it comes "Brilliantly, con-centratedly . . . about its own business" and invades the speaker's waiting mind. Suddenly, coming as if from nowhere, "with a sudden sharp hot stink of fox" it enters the "dark hole" of the speaker's head. The starless window and the ticking clock are still there, but the loneliness has been replaced by a friendly message. The "blank page" is no longer blank; it has received the strong marks of the all-seeing and all-knowing fox's feet.

There is something urgent and inevitable about the sequence of events, something that could not have been avoided however the speaker tried. Even as the poem records the events leading to the slow final coming to form of the "poem" within it, Hughes's page is being "printed." The moment of the fox's entry into the "dark hole of the head" coincides with the moment of the poem-within-the-poem's completion in both space and time.

Hughes uses a variety of poetic devices to achieve his purpose: alliteration (lame/lags, sudden/sharp/stink), tentative rhythms ("Something else is alive," "Something more near"), a blend of slow-moving and fast-moving lines. Although the poem is about the process of poetic composition (which is like the fox's surreptitious invasion), it is difficult to ignore the fox as a concrete participant. The poem makes—as many of Hughes's best poems do—an abstraction too tangible to be taken only metaphorically. The "thought-fox," remaining a "thought-fox," has also become the "thing-fox."

At least two inferences about Hughes's poetry can be drawn from a reading of "The Thought-Fox": first, the uncontestable nature of the "action" with which it deals—what M. L. Rosenthal would call its "rightness"; and second, the absolute stillness within which that "action" takes place. Even the "sudden sharp hot" foxy stink is supposed to disappear within a moment's reflection, so that before one becomes aware of what has happened, the page is already "printed."

These two characteristics appear again in "Hawk Roosting." The roosting hawk is both the protagonist and the first-person narrator of the poem, displaying, in an eminently self-conscious and egotistic fashion, his own savage achievements and intentions. His view of the world has nothing uncertain or tentative about it. He knows exactly where he is—at the very center of the created world, sitting on one of its trees, still, unmoving, like a giant organic rock. He is most unlike any *human* creature in that he does not have any dreams; his very existence presupposes fulfillment.

The poem is the hawk's internal monologue, and it presents the reader with not merely *a* hawk, but the very spirit or consciousness of the hawk—fierce and cruel in its arrogance, radiating animal pride. He is the still center around which moves the created world—the sun, the trees, the earth itself—as though the one end and purpose of creation were to keep him strong and "going." Every other creature has meaning only as his prey, whom he watches with an eye that "has permitted no change" and shall not permit any in the future. Like his ugly black friend in Hughes's sequence *Crow*, the hawk is "Clothed in his conviction." He is just there, to be endured and admired by an amazed humanity.

As one reads the poem's first few lines, one begins to doubt the appropriateness of the seemingly innocent title of the poem; after all, it is not the hawk "roosting," but displaying, in an unapologetic way, his own character. The short, abrupt lines, and the half-sentences point to the nature of the speaker: there is nothing sophisticated about his thought or language, as there is nothing polished about his outward bearing. The lines also display Hughes's economical and suggestive use of language, his acute sense of the evocative power of single words.

The roosting hawk is concretely characterized by the word "Inaction." He is resting, with his eyes closed, but there is no "falsifying dream" between his "hooked head and hooked feet"—between his brain which thinks and his feet which act. If he is doing anything, it is only the "rehearsal," in sleep, of what he has already achieved—"the perfect kills." The "high trees" have made themselves "convenient" to him in his attacks on his prey; the air has made itself "buoyant" for him to ride on; the sun's rays have provided him with the necessary warmth and light; and the earth lies, with its "face upward," for his "inspection." His strong feet are "locked upon the rough bark." He is holding creation in his feet, the creation which took a long time to produce his "each feather." The process of evolution culminates in him; there cannot be any further development.

Flying high up into the sky, the hawk slowly "revolves" the earth and sweeps down on what he likes, "because it is all mine." There is nothing civilized or refined about his "manners," which are "tearing off heads" and "allotment of death." Nothing can come between him and his victim. No explanation, no legal, moral, or philosophical argument support his "right." Backed by the magnificent, angelic power of the sun ("The sun is behind me"), he does not seek any other form of support. His autocratic, tyrannical self has never allowed any "change," and he is going to maintain the status quo ("I am going to keep things like this").

Although a first reading of the poem might not point to anything more than a vainglorious hawk shouting out his dreams, subsequent readings point to a highly symbolic situation. Hughes's hawk is ancient in his origin. The ancient Egyptians considered it as "the pre-eminent divine being"—perhaps touched by evil but nevertheless divine. Hughes places his hawk in a preeminently twentieth century context. The predator brings to the reader's mind the figure of the modern tyrant, shamelessly asserting his absolute right over the world and its people. Hughes, however, opposes this reading. He says in the *London Magazine* interview with Faas: "That bird is accused of being a fascist. . . . Actually what I had in mind was that in this hawk Nature is thinking. Simply Nature."

While the almost fabular reading of the bird as the symbol of totalitarian dictatorship may not be accepted, the bird quite certainly points to certain dominant tendencies of the human race—those which are a peculiar result of man's getting more "civilized," tendencies which are closely associated with the recent scientific and technological discoveries and inventions and with the power which these have placed in man's hands. By presenting a picture of the devilish hawk, Hughes indirectly refers to those positive values to which men have chosen to remain blind and insensitive; while he celebrates the energy that the hawk so unmistakably has, he rejects the end to which such energy is directed. Seen in this light, the poem requires an ironic rereading. As M. L. Rosenthal says, here as elsewhere in his poetry, Hughes is "humanly free to dissociate himself from the vision of terror whose literal acceptance would constitute a form of madness," and, consequently, "the bias of the poetry lies in another direction."

The lines do not follow any regular metrical pattern and, with the exception of "feet" and "eat" of the third and fourth lines, the poem is without rhyme. The vocabulary is also limited. Even so, the poem gives an impression of compactness and force. The lines, unequal in length, follow normal speech patterns, and although the poem is divided into four-line stanzas, the lines break conventional syntactic patterns and move forward with a force that appropriately expresses the bird's arrogant assertiveness. The simple collo-quial language ("It is all mine," "The sun is behind me, "I am going to keep things like this"), while it raises the hawk's vainly egotistic reflections to a new level of prominence, undercuts it by indirectly referring to the ultimate meaninglessness of such thoughts.

The language of Hughes's best poems is "characterized by its faithfulness to the facts . . . a language spiced with great relish for experience" (Keith Sagar). In them "observation and imagination are so subtly merged . . . [that] their beauty is equally objective image and feeling" (Calvin Bedient). Hughes's own words about why he made the Crow the hero of his sequence are revealing, inasmuch as they record, among other things, the real and intimate nature of his own experience with that bird: "The idea was originally just to write . . . the songs that Crow would sing. In other words, songs with no music whatsoever, in a super-simple and a super-ugly language which would in a way shed everything except just what he wanted to say without any other consideration."

The poems in *Crow* move, at one and the same time, among the literal bird, the "black bird" of folktale and myth, the trickster working in opposition to the loving creator, and the twentieth century symbol of nihilism. The reader's attention, however, is insistently directed to the *bird*, starkly real and familiar despite everything. The Crow's adventures are at one time heroic and imaginative, while at other times almost comical. He survives every known disaster with a strength that is stronger than death. In the *Crow* poems, as later in the *Cave Birds* poems, Hughes explores what Leonard Baskin— his artist-friend and collaborator on these and other books—calls the "vision of aggressive predatory tyranny." In *Crow* and in *Cave Birds*, Hughes has created, in a language which is both simple and sensuous, a highly engaging bird drama that continuously refers to the human world.

Hughes's recent books, especially *Gaudete* and *Remains of Elmet*, show a development which, remaining close to the tradition he created with his first book, also suggests very different intentions. As the Argument which prefaces it declares, *Gaudete* is the half-mythic, half-symbolic story of an Anglican priest, the Reverend Nicholas Lumb, who is taken away by elemental spirits into the "other world." These spirits create an exact duplicate of Lumb out of an oak log. Since the new priest is created out of a log, he behaves like a "changeling." He interprets his role of administering the gospel of love by organizing the women of his parish into a "love-society" whose purpose is "the birth of a Messiah to be fathered by Lumb." At this point in the story the changeling "begins to feel a nostalgia for independent, ordinary human life, free of his peculiar destiny," but the spirits who created him decide to "cancel" him. The narrative recounts the final day of the changeling's life. The original Lumb, now a transformed man, having gone through his strange experiences in the "other world," reappears in the West of Ireland, where he roams about composing hymns and psalms to a nameless goddess. The poem, which was originally intended as a film scenario, has been called "the most important poetic work in English in our time" (Sagar). Like T. S. Eliot's *The*

Waste Land (1922), with which it has been compared, it deals with death, fertility, rebirth, and atonement.

With *Remains of Elmet* Hughes returns to his native Calder Valley. The poems in this volume were a result of his nostalgic reaction to a set of photographs taken by Fay Godwin involving the valley and appearing in the book. The poems in *Remains of Elmet* are exquisitely delicate compositions and are very much unlike anything else Hughes has written. They seem to predict a very different kind of poetry from Hughes in the years to come.

Hughes's poetry is concerned with significant concepts and lasting issues, but it refuses to be brought within the limits of any particular, definable philosophy. By making the reader deeply conscious of the large and varied possibilities that life offers and sensitive enough to respond to life's mysteries, he has done what Lawrence did half a century ago. At times when men are too weak in body and in spirit to continue their ancient struggle with the nonhuman forces of the universe, Hughes's poetry has been able to offer them much-needed strength of heart.

Major publications other than poetry

PLAYS: *The House of Aries*, 1960 (radio play); *A Houseful of Women*, 1961 (radio play); *The Wound*, 1962 (radio play); *Difficulties of a Bridegroom*, 1963 (radio play); *Dogs*, 1964 (radio play); *Seneca's Oedipus*, 1968 (translation).

NONFICTION: *Poetry in the Making*, 1967.

CHILDREN'S LITERATURE: *Meet My Folks!*, 1961; *How the Whale Became*, 1963; *The Earth-Owl and Other Moon People*, 1963; *Nessie the Mannerless Monster*, 1964; *The Iron Man*, 1968; *The Coming of the Kings and Other Plays*, 1970.

Bibliography

Bedient, Calvin. *Eight Contemporary Poets*, 1974.
Gifford, Terry, and Philip Roberts. *Ted Hughes: A Critical Study*, 1981.
Rosenthal, M. L. *The New Poets: American and British Poetry Since World War II*, 1967.
Sagar, Keith. *The Art of Ted Hughes*, 1978.

Bibhu Padhi

RICHARD HUGO

Born: Seattle, Washington; December 21, 1923

Principal collections

A Run of Jacks, 1961; *Death of the Kapowsin Tavern*, 1965; *Good Luck in Cracked Italian*, 1969; *The Lady in Kicking Horse Reservoir*, 1973; *What Thou Lovest Well, Remains American*, 1975; *31 Letters and 13 Dreams*, 1977; *White Center*, 1980; *The Right Madness on Skye*, 1980.

Other literary forms

Richard Hugo's fiction and essays share the basic concerns of his poetry. *Death and the Good Life* (1981), a detective novel in the Dashiell Hammett-Raymond Chandler tradition, re-creates the familiar landscapes and character types of Hugo's West. Combining psychic exploration and social commentary, Hugo compensates for a somewhat melodramatic plot with an active sense of humor tinged with self-parody. Many of the vignettes in *Death and the Good Life* reveal an affinity with the method of poetic composition described in *The Triggering Town: Lectures and Essays on Poetry and Writing* (1979). The collection serves as both an excellent practical guide to teaching creative writing and an introduction to Hugo's own poetry. Emphasizing sound as a means of overcoming psychological blocks and discovering meaning, Hugo discusses his method of imaginatively reconstructing particular scenes. Hugo has also published several segments of an autobiography tentatively entitled *West Marginal Way*. Several recordings of his exceptional public readings are available.

Achievements

Hugo's importance derives from his ability to uncover the rich diversity of human experience generated by the alternately barren and breathtaking landscape of the American West. For many younger Western writers, Hugo occupies a position similar to that of William Faulkner in the South. Like Faulkner, Hugo confirms his region's unique identity, exploits the hidden poetry of its idiom, and commands the attention of the national literary community. His regional importance was recognized in 1966 when he won the Northwest Writers Award. Since then he has received a Rockefeller Foundation grant (1967) and a Guggenheim Fellowship (1977-1978). Two of his collections, *The Lady in Kicking Horse Reservoir* and *What Thou Lovest Well, Remains American*, have been National Book Award finalists. The latter volume also received the Theodore Roethke Memorial Poetry Prize in 1976.

Hugo's poetry incorporates modes developed by writers associated with highly diverse forms. Responding to the call of Walt Whitman and William

Carlos Williams for a specifically American poetic language, Hugo's distinctive personal voice also echoes the music of Theodore Roethke and Wallace Stevens. Though a much less philosophical poet than Stevens, Hugo shares his sense of the multiplicity of possible perceptions of any given scene. Hugo's choice of scenes and development of possibilities, however, accords with the emphasis of the Whitman-Carl Sandburg strain of populist poetry. The resulting voice attains a balance of social and aesthetic intensity which establishes Hugo's claim to recognition as one of the leading poets of his generation. Never dogmatic in politics or aesthetics, Hugo communicates his vision of the emotional complexity of ordinary life with a directness and integrity accessible to both academic and nonacademic readers.

Biography

Richard Franklin Hugo's parents separated when he was twenty months old. His mother, who was about eighteen at the time, had no means to support the child, so left him with her parents, who reared him in the working-class neighborhood of White Center just outside Seattle, Washington. Born Richard Hogan, his mother remarried in 1927, and he began using the name he is known by when he entered the eighth grade in 1936. Growing up during the Depression, Hugo was surrounded by the poverty which set White Center apart from the more affluent nearby neighborhoods of West Seattle. After serving in the United States Army Air Corps as a bombadier during World War II, Hugo attended the University of Washington, earning his B.A. degree in 1948 and his M.A. in 1952. During these years, he was taught by Theodore Roethke, who exerted a strong influence on Hugo. Following graduation, Hugo worked at the Boeing Aircraft Corporation in Seattle for thirteen years and married for the first time.

Publishing his first volumes while still at Boeing, Hugo left Seattle, spent a year in Italy, then joined the faculty at the University of Montana in 1964. He has subsequently taught at Colorado University, the University of Iowa, and the University of Arkansas at Little Rock. While at Iowa in 1970-1971, he suffered the near-breakdown which provides the background of *31 Letters and 13 Dreams*. Although he has spent most of his life in the American West, Hugo has also spent several periods abroad. The poems of *Good Luck in Cracked Italian*, the "Scotland" sections of *The Lady in Kicking Horse Reservoir*, and *The Right Madness on Skye* draw on these travels. Now living in Missoula with his second wife Ripley, Hugo has encouraged the development of many young writers, including Native Americans such as James Welch, while directing the creative writing program at the University of Montana. In 1977, he was appointed editor of the Yale Series of Younger Poets.

Analysis

Richard Hugo's poetry centers on two types of madness: a "wrong madness" of isolation, and a "right madness" of community. Paradoxically, the experience of dispossession provides the foundation for both types. Those who perceive their dispossession—economic, sexual, or psychological—as purely individual can only talk to themselves or remain silent. Only by recognizing dispossession as a shared experience can they form a community with a language capable of expressing either rage or compassion. Identifying closely with the dispossessed, Hugo seeks to develop a voice embodying his vision of emotionally intense connections with other people, with the land, with his own past, and with the language which allows him to escape the wrong madness of inarticulate disintegration. The origins, though not the boundaries, of this vision are in the American West. Concentrating on specific places and scenes, Hugo emphasizes that their meaning derives as much from the observer's state of mind as from intrinsic elements. Though the scenes themselves, especially in his early poetry, are Western, the states of mind recur throughout the world. Ultimately, Hugo seeks a voice like that of Gilleasbuig Aotram in "The Semi-Lunatics of Kilmuir," a poem set on the island of Skye. Himself "crazy like a dolphin," Aotram leads a band of "lunatics" rejecting the insane economic system where "You pay and pay and own nothing." Encountering a "real crazy" capable only of raving, Aotram addresses him in a voice which connects psychological orientation with social salvation: "'Had you the right madness bread would be secure.'" Directly addressing the reader (whose madness, like that of the "crazy," provides the potential base for an expanded community), the concluding lines reiterate the saving power of place and affirm Hugo's populist faith: "Have the right madness. This land has always passed on/ and, like you, is still here." Connection with the land offers hope, however mad it may seem, for an enduring social and psychological security.

Hugo's distinctive stylistic signatures reflect this emphasis on place, concern with shared experience, and struggle to overcome the wrong madness in the individual. Although many poems vary from the details of the pattern, a typical Hugo lyric describes a specific scene, frequently the social landscape of a town, to an implied audience who may be someone familiar with the scene, an aspect of the persona, or a potential reader such as the one addressed at the end of "The Semi-Lunatics of Kilmuir." Investing the scene with an initial emotional meaning, often derived from some disquieting realistic detail, he explores its psychological implications, frequently leading to a transformation of the original emotional tone. Hugo typically writes in a loosely iambic four- or five-stress line organized into verse paragraphs around shifts in time, scene, or tone. Rarely employing end-rhyme, he uses numerous internal rhymes and sound echoes both to establish prosodic coherence and to reveal emotional possibilities. In his early poems Hugo in fact pledged himself to repeating "interesting" sounds within eight syllables, thereby creating a richness of sound texture which remains in his later work. By concentrating on sound rather than meaning as such, Hugo argues in *The Triggering Town*, he was able to discover emotional connections which had been consciously repressed. This connection between sound and psychological release recurs frequently in Hugo's poetry, where transformed perceptions of the original scene occur in connection with new clusters of sounds.

This basic pattern can be seen clearly in "Degrees of Gray in Philipsburg," perhaps Hugo's finest, and certainly his most widely anthologized single poem. The first line, "You might come here Sunday on a whim," places the persona in Philipsburg and addresses the listener. The next sentence, "Say your life broke down," establishes both the initial tone attached to the scene and the importance of the "you" in relation to the thematic and emotional impact of the poem. This second person exists on two levels, one psychological (as an aspect of the persona) and one social (as a person with whom the persona ultimately shares the experience). Only by coming to terms with the psychological "you" can the persona free himself to react to the red-haired waitress of the final stanza and to communicate with the social "you." Hugo structures the poem around this movement toward increased freedom, especially as it interacts with the persona's changing perception of his immediate surroundings.

Initially, the persona creates a Philipsburg reinforcing the sense of emotional breakdown that he projects onto the second person. Assuming a stance of total dispossession ("The last good kiss you had was years ago"), he perceives only manifestations of the wrong madness. Walking "streets/ laid out by the insane," he imagines only one human inhabitant, a prisoner in jail "not knowing what he's done." Emblems of social isolation are everywhere; two "dead kilns" overlook the town. The persona contemplates a "defeat/ so accurate, the church bell simply seems/ a pure announcement: ring and no one comes." The acceptance of this defeat, simultaneously sexual and social ("no one comes"), culminates in the final stanza in the old man who threatens to "go to sleep and not wake up." Confronted with death as the ultimate price of resignation, however, the persona rebels against this madness which he now sees in himself: "You tell him no. You're talking to yourself." The negation paradoxically effects a transition to an affirmative vision. Where previously the persona encountered only a gray ghost town where "the best liked girls/ . . . leave each year for Butte," he now recognizes the redemptive presence of the slender girl whose "red hair lights the wall." Previously blinded by his memory of sexual dispossession ("the ancient kiss still burning out your eyes"), the persona now sees the sexually charged potential of his surroundings.

Before reaching this epiphany, however, he must come to terms with his own responsibility for the emotional grayness of his initial perception. At first he attempts to evade this responsibility by refusing to identify clearly the broken down "you" with himself and by focusing only on the aspects of the landscape which indulge his depression. Gazing out at the inaccessible pastures which contrast sharply with "the various grays/ the mountain sends," the persona accepts "rage" as "the principal supporting business of Philipsburg" and "hatred" of the mill that no longer provides economic sustenance but "won't fall finally down." His perception of economic dispossession is accurate but his resignation to isolation is only one of the possible "degrees of gray." Hugo emphasizes the hopelessness of the response with a texture of sound in the second stanza which reinforces the quiescent tone. An almost unbroken flow of extended vowel sounds (rage, hatred, grays, gaze, green, eat, town, down) is accompanied by soothing consonants. Particularly prominent are "l" (mill, bill, repeal, liked, girls, leave), "w" (now, mountain, wipe, known, town, down) and "m" (mountain, mill, mines, memory). The only contrasting sounds occur when the persona describes the 1907 silver boom with a cluster of "b," "v," and "z" sounds. The boom, however, remains in the irrecoverable past. The syntax of the description breaks down—no verb follows the apparent subject "boom"—and the persona's memory "resolves itself in gaze," returning to the dominant sound texture of the stanza. The interlude introduces the sounds which will spur the regeneration of the final stanza, but Hugo leaves them dormant. The sequence of end-rhymes and slant-rhymes of the stanza (now, out, town, down) works in conjunction with the other sounds to emphasize the passive acceptance of dispossession. At no point does the sound pattern allow a break from the flow of depressed perceptions or encourage an emotionally intense response to dispossession.

The persona's movement toward renewed intensity begins with his moment of total despair at the beginning of the third stanza. Seeing nothing but external desolation, he embraces internal isolation and longs for blindness: "Isn't this your life? That ancient kiss/ still burning out your eyes?" The question, despite its attempt to distance the agony by projecting it onto the ambiguous "you," introduces the new pattern of sound and rhythm which reawakens the persona's sense of emotional and sexual possibility. The kiss that existed only "years ago" at the start of the poem similarly assumes a new emotional presence. In essence, the key to this renewal is the persona's discovery of a new voice, one capable of directly expressing the rage which seemed abstract and distant in the second stanza.

In the third stanza, dispossession no longer *sounds* inevitable. The transformed language frees the persona for a clearer perception of psychological and social connections. Consisting of five questions, the stanza phrases each in terms of negation: "Isn't this your life," "Isn't this defeat," "Don't empty houses." Even those not beginning with negatives include negative phrases: "no one comes," "never let you have." Rather than implying deeper resignation, these anticipate the affirmative negations of the final stanza: "Say no to yourself," "You tell him no." In addition, Hugo carefully controls the rhythm of the questions (four, eight, eighteen, four, and thirty-six words long), building from an implied acceptance of "the ancient kiss" to the explicit outrage of: "Are magnesium/ and scorn sufficient to support a town,/ not just Philipsburg, but towns/ of towering blondes, good jazz and booze/ the world will never let you have/ until the town you came from dies inside?" The sound texture of the questions extends that of the preceeding stanza, particularly with the consonants "m" (simply, seems, comes, empty, magnesium) and "w" (town, towns, towering, world, will, town). In order to effect the psychological transition, however, Hugo introduces new patterns of shorter vowels (which allow the tempo to speed up) and sharper consonants, particularly "f" (life, defeat, sufficient, Philipsburg), "s" (this, kiss, isn't, so, simply, seems, scorn, sufficient, dies, inside) and, most important, the thematically crucial "z's." Thinking of "jazz" and "booze," the persona realizes that the "world," the source of his dispossession, ultimately demands total psychic and social isolation. The powerful rhythm combines with the difficult syntax of the question to create a sense of emotional urgency centering on the persona's relationship with his own psychological and social past ("the town you came from").

The climactic negations, therefore, take on an intricate complex of meanings. The determination to "say no" spurs the persona's recognition of the internal level of his conversation/soliloquy: "You're talking to yourself." Rejecting the social madness which offers "magnesium and scorn" as the basis of community, he simultaneously rejects the wrong madness of the old man/ prisoner's resignation to death. These refusals generate a new vision of the landscape he had previously seen as entirely gray. Seeing the "silver" of his money (significantly, the first bright color is also a degree of "gray") and the "red hair" of the girl, the persona achieves new economic and personal awareness. By accepting the isolated "you" as himself, he provides an image of the process of regeneration which paradoxically expands the "you" to include all readers sharing the initial feeling of dispossession.

This complex interdependence of internal and external realities is a *leitmotiv* of Hugo's poetry. Feelings of psychological alienation and social isolation frequently reinforce one another, as in "Helena, Where Homes Go Mad," "Port Townsend," and "Montana Ranch Abandoned." Conversely, psychological recovery, usually based on a deeper confrontation with the past, is normally accompanied by an expanded vision of community, as in "What Thou Lovest Well, Remains American," and "Missoula Softball Tournament." Hugo's two most recent volumes, *White Center* and *The Right Madness on Skye* (both published in 1980), exemplify the pattern. *White Center* marks Hugo's return to "the town he came from," his refusal to let his experience die. *The Right Madness on Skye* demonstrates his vision of a community extending beyond the bars and softball fields of the West. Of course it would be too simple to say that one volume is internal, the other external. *White Center* returns to Hugo's social, as well as his psychological, roots. The vision of community in *The Right Madness on Skye* clearly has its foundation in

Hugo's personal perception. Together the two volumes provide a complex gloss on Hugo's basic insight that "All cause is local, all effect" ("A Snapshot of Uig in Montana"). Far from being limiting, Hugo's regionalism becomes the source of his encompassing vision. Grounding himself firmly in the local causes of dispossession, he develops a vocabulary capable of revealing the immediate dispossession as a bond with communities everywhere.

This continuing struggle for a common vocabulary can be seen in the contrast between "A Map of Montana in Italy" in *The Lady in Kicking Horse Reservoir* and "A Snapshot of Uig in Montana" and "A Map of Skye" in *The Right Madness on Skye*. Hugo's fascination with representations, particularly maps and photos, testifies to a certain interest in the nature of perception and the relationship between art and reality. Rather than concentrating on the self-reflexive aspects of the question, however, Hugo meditates on the relationship between individual attitude and social context. Where "A Map of Montana in Italy" emphasizes the difficulty of overcoming the social constraints on individual recovery, the later poems present a more hopeful vision of renewed social connection.

"A Map of Montana in Italy" explores the roots of the Western sense of dispossession in a mythology of violence which threatens to engulf the larger community; even the relatively gentle Italians cheer the movie violence at the poem's conclusion. Although he begins with images of coldness and violence, Hugo stresses that Montana is colored white "on *this* map" (emphasis added). Intimating an awareness of other possibilities, he explicitly recognizes that the emotional implications of the map are projected rather than intrinsic: "Glacier Park's green with my envy." Similarly, he maintains an awareness of potential freedom, of maps of places where "antelope sail/ between strands of barbed wire and never/ get hurt." Spatially removed from Montana, Hugo continues to share the Western sense of psychic dispossession: "It's white here too." Rather than resigning himself, however, he attempts to find freedom from paralysis, reinterpreting the whiteness of the map as a call for a desperate compassion: "This map is white, meaning winter, ice/ where you are, helping children who may be already frozen." The only hope lies in reaching those who may already be lost.

Although the Montana weather provides his physical image, Hugo clearly identifies the American mystiques of monetary success and macho toughness as the real sources of the emotional dispossession. He characterizes Montana's "successful" towns as narrow-minded and dull, dedicated to making money. Conversely, the "interesting" towns "have the good sense to fail." Throughout the state, the immature macho stance represses any admission of vulnerability: "There's too much/ schoolboy in bars—I'm tougher than you—/ and too much talk about money." With no foundation for human connection, the tensions are internalized in dreams of "jails and police." These in turn are denied through projection onto a mythical "Poland." Again the American myth precludes recognition of shared dispossession; only Eastern Europeans live in communist-imposed chains. Like the jail of "Degrees of Gray in Philipsburg," however, the prison is more internal than external. Unable to free themselves, the psychic prisoners become social jailers, working against the possibility of the community which might liberate them: "With so few Negroes and Jews we've been reduced/ to hating each other, dumping our crud/ in our rivers, mistreating the Indians." The "whiteness" of the Montana map assumes racial and cultural dimensions, reinforcing the refusal to admit connection with other communities of the dispossessed (and ultimately with the landscape itself). Trapped by insufficient myths reflecting the wrong madness of American culture, the Western community remains ignorant of the existence of alternative maps.

Where "A Map of Montana in Italy" reconsiders realities Hugo had previously experienced, both "A Snapshot of Uig in Montana" and "A Map of Skye" project possibilities onto a largely unknown landscape. As their titles imply, they "revise" the earlier poem. The new statements reflect Hugo's increasing concentration on specific forms of the right madness. "A Snapshot of Uig in Montana" begins with a relatively optimistic, though by no means facile, restatement of an image from "A Map of Montana in Italy": "Children take longer to die there." Speaking in a "we" voice implying connection and community, Hugo identifies a "music all moan dispossessed." This music unites the "failed" Montanans lasting out yet another white winter ("April and our snow hangs on") with the crofters on Skye whose island has been ravaged by historical invasions. In "A Map of Skye," Hugo pursues this sense of connection which involves new communities, new landscapes, and new languages.

Fascinated by the Nordic and Gaelic place names on Skye (much as he is fascinated by the Indian place names in the West), Hugo connects them with the history of dispossession: "It is all here/ in the names, the sound of broken bone and blood." This connection in turn sparks a vision of "slow recovery" generating "a continuum of song." Like the moan of the dispossessed, this continuum of song implies a community based on the acceptance of past pain, whether social or individual. The specific sources of dispossession will inevitably differ: "All cause is local, all effect" ("A Snapshot of Uig in Montana"). The resulting expressions, however, will share a vocabulary. By recognizing this connection, the dispossessed can discover new passages, internal and external. Contrasting sharply with the roads which were "red veins full of rage" on the map of Montana, the roads on the map of Skye promise connection with a "wider world beyond." The transformation testifies not to an essential difference between Montana and Skye but to Hugo's increased determination to provide new emotional maps.

Hugo develops the search for new connections and community most comprehensively in *31 Letters and 13 Dreams*, presenting a full cycle of personal and social disintegration and recovery. Written in Hugo's typical four- to five-stress line but unusually elusive in image and voice, the dream poems concentrate on the experience of an unnamed "you." The letter poems, written mostly in seven-stress Whitmanesque lines, focus directly on Hugo's relationship with specific people and places. The volume was arranged by Ruth Whitman, who brilliantly revealed the underlying unity evident in the thematic and Imagistic connections within sequences of dreams and letters. The early poems, for example, reflect a wrong madness shared by Hugo and the "you" of the dreams. Letters concerning Hugo's flight from Iowa City and his war experiences are juxtaposed with "In Your Fugitive Dream" and "In Your War Dream." Gradually, the volume progresses to the warmth of "Letter to Kathy from Wisdom," the reassurance of "Letter to Oberg from Pony," and the right madness of the concluding "In Your Good Dream." Ultimately *31 Letters and 13 Dreams* develops a vocabulary of dispossession in response to a "country where a wealthy handful/ of people tear down anything you could possibly love,/ break your affectionate connections with yourself by whim/ for profit" ("Letter to Oberg from Pony"). Only by recognizing the shared isolation of self and others can individuals rebuild these connections.

The stylistic tension between the dreams and the letters mirrors this thematic tension. While the dreams exist in a world of shifting Stevenesque images, the letters draw their vitality from shared social experience. If the dreams are "poetic" in the traditional sense, the letters are somewhat prosaic. The prosaic quality, however, is like that of the catalogs in "Song of Myself." Out of the unshaped experiences with which each letter begins, Hugo derives an intensity of perception which enables him to reforge the shattered connections between internal and external reality. The poetic intensity wells up out of ordinary details—concerning food, car trouble, weather—for Hugo's aesthetic is based on revealing the emotional intensity of everyday experience. "Letter to Peterson from Pike Place Market" exemplifies this process:

> Sorry. Got carried away. But you know, Bob, how
> in the smoky recess of bars all over the world, a man
> will suddenly dance because music, a juke box, a Greek taverna band, moves him, and
>   how when he dances we
> applaud and cry go. That's nobility of blood, a recognition
> by those who matter that in special moments
> we are together facing the brute descent of the sun
> and that cold brittle star we know already burned out.

Just as the bar scene becomes an emblem of human connection, Hugo's colloquial language ("Got carried away") rises suddenly to the poetic power of the speeding rhythm and the repeated sounds, particularly "b" (blood, brute, brittle, burned) and "t" (moments, brute, descent, brittle, out). Typically the letters return to the colloquial diction, implying the reintegration of poetic insight into the ordinary social context. In contrast, the dreams begin with intensely charged details such as the "seven ultra-masculine men" explaining "the bars of your cage are silver/ in honor of our emperor" ("In Your Bad Dream"). Developed emotionally rather than logically, the images maintain their intensity throughout, reflecting the manner in which the mind obsessively reworks external experience—in this case involving sexual and political dispossession—and establishes the basis for the perception of subsequent experience.

For Hugo, style—whether elusive or direct—involves an intensity of experience which is not limited to writing. In "Letter to Mantsch from Havre," he emphasizes the importance of style in all aspects of life: "So few of us are good at what we do, and what we do,/ well done or not, seems futile. I'm trying to find Monty Holden's barber shop. I want to tell him style in anything,/ pitching, hitting, cutting hair, is worth our trying even if we fail." The prosaic segments of the letter-poems link the poetic intensity with the actual experience of "those who matter," providing the barbers and pitchers with access to the world of Hugo's "Good Dream."

What Hugo offers this populist community is esssentially an outline of the process of finding the right madness. First, he traces individual alienation to a nearly unconscious acceptance of the social madness which devalues individuals in order to advance commercial and material interests. Second, he implies that resisting these forces demands recognition of the connections between isolated individuals and acceptance of the primacy of local truth. Finally, he insists that these local truths be shared.

The early letters in *31 Letters and 13 Dreams* concentrate almost entirely on Hugo's sense of isolation and, significantly, are relatively lacking in the poetic intensity which reflects shared experience. Only with the "Letter to Simic from Boulder" does his social vision begin to take shape. In this poem Hugo perceives himself, a bombardier, and Simic, a potential target on the ground, as victims of the same "mindless hate." The war, the social embodiment of mindless hatred, establishes the base for a common vocabulary even while rendering direct communication impossible:

> And what did your mind
> do with the terrible how of bombs? What is Serb for 'fear'?
> It must be the same as in English, one long primitive wail
> of dying children, one child fixed forever in a dead stare.

Hugo attributes his wartime actions to a "willing confusion" which he traces back to a belief in "Heroics," recalling the corrupt white myths in "A Map of Montana in Italy." This belief is even more clearly revealed as corrupt in the "Letter to Matthews from Barton Street Flats," which concentrates on the internment of Japanese-Americans during the war.

Rejecting the generalized heroics of the war, Hugo turns to the more legitimate, because more local, heroic figure of softball player Mike Mantsch. Comparing his own poetry with Mantsch's hitting, Hugo restates the parallel between various types of experience:

> The ball jumps
> from your bat over and over. I want my poems to jump
> like that. All poems. I want to say once to a world that feels
> with reason it has little chance, well done. That's the lie
> I cannot shout loud as this local truth: Well done, Mike.

Significantly, Mantsch resembles the figure of Buss in the "Dream on the Eve of Success," the psychological turning point of the volume. Buss, also a softball star, speaks with the "you" while the "president" speaks an incomprehensible gibberish which no longer distorts the persona's self-image: "You cannot understand his claim." Again, the local emphasis helps to counter the isolating social forces. Hugo deliberately turns away from the grand, the universal truth, which, however well-intentioned, can only be a "lie." In the face of massive social pressure, he affirms only that which is within his experience. The local poetry, the solid hit, and the dance in the bar carry far more importance than any generalized expression of "Heroic" bravado in the light of a "brute descending sun."

Building on this awareness, Hugo probes for the precise nature of "local truth." Increasingly, he focuses on the difficulties of personal identification with other dispossessed and alienated individuals, such as the mentally retarded Kenny in "Letter to Wagoner from Port Townsend." Although he used to fish with Kenny when they were young, Hugo eventually came to see him as "subnormal," repressing his knowledge of shared experience: "finally we saw each other/ in passing in White Center and didn't speak." Accepting the social definition of "normality" enforces separations. Not yet able to establish a realistic connection with Kenny, Hugo projects the impulse onto the tide which is "washing the remains of crippled fish back deep to the source,/ renewing the driftwood supply and the promise of all night/ fires on the beach, stars and dreams of girls, and that's/ as rich as I'll ever get. We are called human." Turning from the social to the personal definition of "richness," Hugo recognizes that the crippled Kenny shares his origin and his dreams, his humanity. The imaginative act assumes populist significance.

Perhaps the most powerful poem in the volume, "Letter to Levertov from Butte" emphasizes the profound social consequences of the wrong madness. It's intense outrage immediately precedes "In Your Dream on the Eve of Success," which includes the imaginative destruction of the "president" who stands apart from the dispossessed. In Butte, "where you choose sides/ to die on, company or man, and both are losers," Hugo contemplates his own "inadequate" labor, rejecting the materialistic identification of "salary or title" with human worth. This sense of shared isolation leads to a clearer perception of the difficulty of communicating with precisely those who most need connection: "the wife who has turned/ forever to the wall, the husband sobbing at the kitchen/ table and the unwashed children taking it in and in and in/ until they are the wall, the table." This emphasis on the dehumanizing impact of industrial forces makes it clear that Hugo is not romanticizing poverty. As in the "Letter to Simic from Boulder," he stresses that the unresisting individual ultimately merges with the dehumanizing machinery which enforces the wrong madness: "hate takes over, hippie, nigger, Indian, anyone you can lump/ like garbage in a pit, including women." This ability both to accept his connection with the poverty of Walkerville and to understand the extent to which this poverty further isolates the impoverished underlies Hugo's resolve to shape a communal vocabulary of dispossession. Hugo clearly perceives this vocabulary as necessary for his internal as well as his social survival: "And I want my life/ inside to go on long as I do, though I only populate bare/ landscape with surrogate suffering, with lame men/ crippled by more than disease, and create finally/ a simple grief I can deal with, a pain the indigent can find/ acceptable." Ultimately, Hugo commits himself to creating a poetry of the man dancing in the darkness of the bars, the lost friend crippled by a social structure that denies his humanity, the women and children becoming the wall.

This resolve is far more than a poetic pose. The style of Hugo's poetry, as well as its content, attests to his desire to reach "the people who matter," to realize the populist ideal of direct communication. Seeking a renewed sense of connections, Hugo refuses to separate himself from his past, his people, or his poetry. In "Letter to Kathy from Wisdom," he insists that "old towns we loved in matter, lovers matter, playmates, toys/ and we take from our lives those days when everything moved,/ tree, cloud, water, sun, blue between two clouds, and moon,/ days that we danced, vibrating days, chance poem." Overcoming his sense of isolation, Hugo extends himself to his community. "Letter to Oberg from Pony," one of the greatest of American populist poems, rings with the right madness of Hugo's hard-won local truth:

> This is only to assure you, Art,
> that in a nation that is no longer one but only an
> amorphous collection of failed dreams, where we have been told
> too often by contractors, corporations and prudes that
> our lives don't matter, there still is a place where the soul
> doesn't recognize laws like gravity, where boys catch trout
> and that's important, where girls come laughing down the dirt road
> to the forlorn store for candy.

Major publications other than poetry
NOVEL: *Death and the Good Life*, 1981.

NONFICTION: *The Triggering Town: Lectures and Essays on Poetry and Writing*, 1979.

Bibliography
Allen, Michael S. *We Are Called Human: The Poetry of Richard Hugo*, 1982.
Garber, Frederick. "Fat Man at the Margin: The Poetry of Richard Hugo," in *Iowa Review*. III, no. 4 (1972), pp. 58-69.
_____. "Large Man at the Mountains: The Recent Work of Richard Hugo," in *Western American Literature*. X (November, 1975), pp. 205-218.
Holden, Jonathan. *The Rhetoric of the Contemporary Lyric*, 1980.
Howard, Richard. *Alone with America: Essays on the Art of Poetry in the United States Since 1950*, 1969.

Craig Werner

LEIGH HUNT

Born: Southgate, England; October 19, 1784
Died: Putney, England; August 28, 1859

Principal poems and collections
Juvenilia, 1801; *The Feast of the Poets*, 1814; *The Story of Rimini*, 1816; *Foliage*, 1818; *Hero and Leander, and, Bacchus and Ariadne*, 1819; *The Poetical Works of Leigh Hunt*, 1923 (H. S. Milford, editor).

Other literary forms
Leigh Hunt was a poet, familiar essayist, critic, political commentator, playwright, and translator. While he wrote well in all of these genres and with occasional brilliance in some, his reputation as an essayist has best endured. The critical essays reveal a keen sense for what is good in literature; they quote extensively from the works being considered. The familiar essays are famous for their quiet good humor. They are seldom as polished as the essays of Charles Lamb or as perceptive as those of William Hazlitt; still, a few—such as "Getting Up on Cold Mornings" and "Deaths of Little Children"—continue to be anthologized as classics.

Achievements
In his own time, the general reading public respected Hunt as an important literary figure, one whose opinions on literature and the political scene were both valid and influential. His role as editor of several periodicals afforded him an effective means of voicing those opinions to a great many readers, far more than expensive books could reach. Thus Hunt was the great popularizer of the Romantic movement in England. Later critics, however, concluded that several of his contemporaries, though then of less influence and popularity, were actually better artists and more profound thinkers. The common twentieth century attitude has tended to ignore Hunt's individual achievements, rather viewing him as the comparatively less important hub of an illustrious literary circle: John Keats, Percy Bysshe Shelley, Lord Byron, Charles Lamb, and William Hazlitt, in particular. More recently, critics have again begun to assess Hunt's own achievements, and while few would allow that he was as fine a poet as Keats, as graceful an essayist as Lamb, or as profound a critic as Hazlitt, still his work does not merit oblivion. His translations are among the finest in English, and he must be credited with increasing the English-speaking world's awareness of Italian literature. His countless journalistic pieces reflect wide reading and high standards of scholarship, and he deserves recognition for his contribution to the quality of popular journalism. A fair assessment of Hunt's literary achievement would have to include his positive influence on the several young poets who went on to surpass their

mentor, but that assessment should also not overlook the quality of his own work as a journalist and translator.

Biography

Leigh Hunt was the son of a Philadelphia lawyer who had returned to England at the time of the American Revolution. The father was a highly principled if rather impractical man who changed his profession from lawyer to Unitarian minister and occasional tutor. At seven years of age, young Hunt was sent to school at Christ's Hospital, where Charles Lamb and Samuel Taylor Coleridge had also been students. Hunt's *Autobiography* (1850) reveals that from his earliest years he was instilled with a hatred of all that is evil. He detested violence, was shocked by profane language, and opposed tyranny by defending his weaker schoolmates with passive resistance of schoolyard bullies. Hunt stayed at Christ's Hospital until he was fifteen. At seventeen he published a volume of juvenile verse.

In 1808, Hunt became the editor of a journal, *The Examiner*, owned by his brother John. *The Examiner* championed a number of liberal causes: abolition of slavery, freedom of the press, an end to imprisonment for debt. In their catalog of social evils the Hunts did not hesitate to include even the Prince Regent of England. Their description of the Prince as "a violator of his word, a libertine over head and ears in debt and disgrace, a despiser of domestic ties, the companion of gamblers" resulted in a libel case and two years' imprisonment for both brothers. Prison was not very hard on Leigh Hunt. He had a decent room, which he decorated with flowered wallpaper, and in which he received such notable visitors as Byron, Shelley, and Hazlitt. After his release, Hunt published his major poem, *The Story of Rimini*, and became the literary mentor to young Keats. The Tory critics, however, could not forgive the slanderer of the Prince and viciously attacked Hunt. In 1817, *Blackwood's Magazine* coined the term "cockney school" to describe Hunt's frequently colloquial style, and the appellation was to plague him for many years.

In 1822 Hunt and family arrived in Italy. Shelley invited him to assume editorship of *The Liberal*, a periodical conceived by Byron and Shelley as a vehicle for their own writings. Shelley was drowned soon thereafter, and when Byron, upon whom the Hunts had depended for financial support, left Italy, the family was stranded until 1825, when Hunt borrowed enough money to return to England. He naturally felt that Byron had done him an injustice and in 1828 he published *Lord Byron and Some of His Contemporaries*, presenting a most unfavorable picture of Byron's personal fears and dishonesties. Hunt maintained in the face of widespread adverse criticism that he had included nothing which he did not believe to be entirely true. True or not, few considered it proper to write so about a man who had recently gone to a heroic death.

With the exception of the embarrassment resulting from his identification with the character Harold Skimpole in Charles Dickens' *Bleak House* (1852) (Dickens insisted that any similarity was unintentional), the remainder of Hunt's life was rather uneventful. He wrote voluminously in all literary forms and on countless topics. The *Cambridge Bibliography of English Literature* (1966) estimates that a complete edition of his prose works alone would fill forty volumes. He lived to see his liberal ideas become the popular thought of the day and himself a respected figure in the literary community. Hunt's productive life ended peacefully in 1859 while he was visiting one of his oldest friends, the printer Charles Reynell, in Putney.

Analysis

Leigh Hunt's three-volume *Autobiography* has remained the single most important source of information on both the facts of his life and those personal attributes which influenced his writings. There is, in fact, comparatively little in the *Autobiography* dealing exclusively with Hunt; it is more a series of recollections and examinations of his many literary friends. This fact is of some importance in understanding Hunt the man, for it reflects a total lack of selfishness and a genuine sympathetic concern for the many fortunate people who won his friendship. These friendships were treasured by Hunt, and in the accounts of his youthful infatuations is reflected the simple kind-heartedness and romantic idealism which were noted by his contemporaries and by later critics. The *Autobiography* does not follow a strict chronology but is rather a series of units. For example, he describes his parents' lives until their deaths before he discusses his own early years. In fact, Hunt's father lived to see his son a successful editor. This organizational method may well be a result of Hunt's reliance on personal taste. His taste of course was selective; he extracted from his experience what he considered excellent and showed little regard for the organizational coherence of the whole. His literary criticism, indeed even his poetry displays the same fondness for selection found in his autobiography.

Most critics agree that Hunt's greatest contribution to poetry was not the poetry he himself wrote but his fine criticism of the poetry of others. Again, Hunt's criticism is based on his own excellent taste, but his taste was far more useful in recognizing good literature than in distinguishing what was specifically bad and forming a thoughtful critical opinion as to the nature of the faults. In practice, Hunt the critic was a selector; he chose those passages from a work which especially appealed to his taste and quoted them at length. Thus he assumed that the works would speak for themselves. He did not conceive of a critic as one who thinks for the reader and locks literature into a single interpretation. If Hunt has survived as a critic, it is because his personal taste was so good. At the same time, his natural sensitivity to what is fine in literature may be said to have worked against his ever achieving a place among the very greatest critics. He had no need for detailed analysis to tell him what was fine in art, and he created no aesthetic concepts approaching the sophistication of some of his contemporaries, notably Coleridge. Thus, Hunt cannot be numbered among the important literary theoreticians. His reputation as a quite respectable critic is dependent on the fact that he was perhaps the greatest appreciator of literature in the history of English letters.

The same quality of taste that enabled Hunt to select what was best in the writings of others also influenced his own poetic compositions. That selective talent, however, did not serve Hunt the poet quite so well. In the composition of his own verse, he was inclined to combine lines and passages reflective of specific poetic principles without a view to the appropriateness of the principle in relation to the poem as a whole. For example, Hunt as the great popularizer of Romantic literary ideas did more than William Wordsworth to bring home to the nineteenth century reader the notion that poetry should reflect the language really used by people. Another aim of the Romantics was to make a place in literature for the experiences of the lower classes, comprising that whole stratum of society that neoclassical writers generally ignored. Hunt's conviction that it was the business of poetry to do these things led him, much more than Wordsworth, Coleridge, and his other illustrious contemporaries who shared these ideas, to overlook yet another major principle of composition that had so concerned the neoclassicists: decorum.

Decorum demanded that all of the various elements of a work of art contribute to the unified effect of the work as a whole. Thus, diction must be appropriate to character and action; a king suffering tragedy should not speak like the common man in the street. Decorum made the poet responsible to the propriety of the particular work. Hunt too often forced the work to comply with principle, and while the principle of natural poetic language suited certain poems, lines such as "The two divinest things this world has got,/ A lovely woman in a rural spot" are jarring. The many critics who have viewed Hunt's poetry with disfavor have really played variations on a single theme: the unevenness of the work. The tone is inappropriate for the subject; good writing is not maintained throughout; the central idea is lost for the digressions. These are all pitfalls into which a reliance on personal taste might lead one, and though Hunt is guilty of all this, it must also finally be acknowledged that this same disregard for uniformity resulted in an important contribution to English poetry of the nineteenth century.

The unfortunate couplet just quoted is from *The Story of Rimini*, a retelling of Dante's tragic story of Paolo and Francesca and Hunt's most ambitious poetic effort. At the time of its composition, Hunt found John Dryden "The most delightful name to me in English literature." In the *Autobiography* he confesses that while *The Story of Rimini* was intended to reflect the vigor and music of Dryden's natural style, his personal taste produced some variations, such as a more simple diction and less vigorous versification. Obviously the results of these liberties were not always happy. The effect of *The Story of Rimini* on English poetry, however, was certainly positive. The poem contributed greatly to the breakup of the highly polished closed couplet perfected by Alexander Pope; Hunt called for a less rigid couplet structure making use of run-on lines and feminine endings. The poem had a marked influence on the styles of several of his contemporaries. Some of Keats's most important early pieces, such as "I Stood Tip-toe Upon a Little Hill" and "Sleep and Poetry," show the influence of Hunt's couplet. Indeed, the motto for "I Stood Tip-toe" was borrowed from *The Story of Rimini.*

Still, the vicious political critics from *Blackwood's Magazine* and the *Quarterly* who dubbed Hunt the leader of the so-called Cockney School of poetry were not completely wrong in their identification of the poem's faults. The freer couplet form resulted in an easy, almost conversational tone which was only aggravated by colloquial diction. Hunt simply did not recognize that some of the ingredients he selected to mix in this noble experiment were not appropriate to the dignity of the subject. Regardless of particular theories of poetic composition or the unique tastes of any age, a character such as Francesca deserves better than "She had strict notions on the marrying score."

Despite its several flaws, *The Story of Rimini* does contain passages of natural grace and elegance. Clearly Dryden's lesson was not completely lost on Hunt. Moreover, the canon of Hunt's poetry includes some astonishingly pure gems that prove the truth of the judgment of *The Cambridge History of English Literature* (1916) that Hunt's best poetry is better than his best prose. These best efforts are short—sonnets and brief narratives. The rigid structure of the sonnet seems to have provided the direction that Hunt was likely to lose sight of in his longer experiments, and brief narratives prevented those digressions which he was likely to engage in for their own sake and at the expense of the clarity of his theme. The sonnet on "The Nile" is an example of Hunt at his best. Critics have generally praised it over the sonnets on the same topic by Keats and Shelley. Here, Hunt achieves smooth versification with natural rhymes and diction reflective of the tranquil progress of the river through an ancient and glorious landscape. Very unobtrusively, in only the last one and a half lines, meditation on the river is allowed to slide gracefully into a metaphor for meditation on human experience. Had Hunt more often shown the sense of dignity and decorum obvious in "The Nile," his place as an important English poet would be secure.

The best of the brief narratives is also Hunt's most famous poem. "Abou Ben Adhem" first appeared in Hall's *Amulet* (1835) and is certainly one of the most frequently anthologized poems in the English language. The poet relates a simple tale, and while an incident of angelic visitation might seem to demand the most heroic language, Hunt wisely understood that the point of the tale is not so much the magnificence of the angel as it is the intimacy that exists between a good person and the divine. The character of Abou, then, is most important; that character had to be made to appeal to human readers. Thus, Abou, secure in his knowledge of what he is, is not intimidated by the angel. His address is respectful but relaxed and touched by humor. He does not disagree with the angel's omission of his name from the list of those who love God but politely suggests an alternative: "I pray thee then/ Write me as one that loves his fellow-men." In this poem of only eighteen lines, Hunt successfully drew a quite sophisticated character and suggested a relationship between God and man more subtle than the implied message that God loves people who love their neighbors. In the hands of a lesser poet, "Abou Ben Adhem" might have been an undistinguished exercise in lofty language and baroque figures; the theme would allow such an approach. Indeed, in the hands of Hunt it might have been a hodgepodge of styles and words at war with themes, but in this poem and several others he managed to keep his eye on the poem itself rather than on assorted notions about poetry.

In his *Essay on Criticism* (1711), Alexander Pope describes two kinds of literary genius: the genius to create the material of poetry, the rhetorical figures, the variety of styles, and the genius to know how to arrange the material into a unified whole. In this latter respect Hunt too often showed himself deficient. When he managed to overcome that deficiency, as he often did, he showed himself the worthy companion of Keats, Shelley, and the many immortal Romantics who loved him so well.

Major publications other than poetry
PLAY: *A Legend of Florence*, 1840.
NONFICTION: *Lord Byron and Some of His Contemporaries*, 1828; *Imagination and Fancy*, 1844; *Wit and Humour*, 1846; *Men, Women and Books*, 1847; *Autobiography*, 1850; *Leigh Hunt's Dramatic Criticism, 1808-1831*, 1949 (Carolyn W. Houtchens and Lawrence H. Houtchens, editors); *Leigh Hunt's Literary Criticism*, 1956 (Carolyn W. Houtchens and Lawrence H. Houtchens, editors).

Bibliography
Blunden, Edmund. *Leigh Hunt and His Circle*, 1930.
Johnson, Brimley R. *Leigh Hunt*, 1970.
Landré, Louis. *Leigh Hunt (1784-1859)*, 1935-1936.
Lowell, Amy. *John Keats*, 1925.
Marshall, William H. *Byron, Shelley, Hunt and "The Liberal"*, 1960.
Stout, George D. *The Political History of Leigh Hunt's Examiner*, 1949.

William J. Heim

DAVID IGNATOW

Born: Brooklyn, New York; February 7, 1914

Principal collections

Poems, 1948; *The Gentle Weight Lifter*, 1955; *Say Pardon*, 1961; *Figures of the Human*, 1964; *Rescue the Dead*, 1968; *Earth Hard: Selected Poems*, 1968; *Poems 1934-1969*, 1970; *Selected Poems*, 1975 (Robert Bly, editor); *Facing the Tree*, 1975; *Tread the Dark*, 1978; *Sunlight: A Sequence for My Daughter*, 1979; *Whisper to the Earth*, 1981.

Other literary forms

In 1973, *The Notebooks of David Ignatow* was published by the Swallow Press, and in 1980 the University of Michigan Press brought out David Ignatow's *Open Between Us* as a volume in its "Poets on Poetry" series, a collection of lectures, interviews, book reviews, and personal essays. Ignatow also wrote a substantial number of short stories for various small magazines in the 1940's and 1950's.

Achievements

Because of his deliberate eschewal of traditional poetic techniques, including rhyme and meter, and his firm insistence upon the "plain style" in contradiction to prevailing modes of the day, Ignatow has endured a long period of public and academic neglect, not unlike that endured by his idol and warm supporter, William Carlos Williams. Also like Williams, he was an early victim of T. S. Eliot's extraordinary success, which has tended to cast much modern American poetry in a convoluted Donne-shadowed mold, despite Eliot's own sympathetic openness to free verse.

Ignatow's first two collections, *Poems* and *The Gentle Weight Lifter*, were decidedly the work of a poet at odds with the dominant mandarin sensibility of the period. The first collection occasioned an enthusiastic review by Williams in *The New York Times* (November 21, 1948), a review that led to a friendship between the two men. Although conversational in style, the poems' simplicity of diction and syntax, their almost clumsy rejection of conventional lyricism, and their steadfast metaphoric sparseness placed them outside the mainstream of contemporary aesthetics, causing more than one critic to label their author a "naif" or "primitive." Randall Jarrell's more accurate review of *The Gentle Weight Lifter* in the *Yale Review* (Autumn, 1955) characterized Ignatow's poetry as "humane, unaffected, and unexciting," noting that he lacked Williams' "heights and depths."

From the beginning, Ignatow has proclaimed himself "a man with a small song," identifying most strongly with Walt Whitman and Williams in terms of wanting to articulate the travails and tragedies of the ordinary citizen in his own language. A strong chord of social and political protest inevitably accompanied such a program, and not a little of Ignatow's value resides in his willingness to confront the inequities he has seen all around him.

Yet, it must have become increasingly evident to Ignatow that very few of the poems in his first two books were clear successes, for all their integrity of purpose and manner, and that something more was needed if he hoped to achieve the same sort of understated suggestiveness that Ernest Hemingway, an admired fellow writer, had achieved in his best short stories. He had to find a method that could weld Hemingway's lean but loaded sentences to the plain style learned from Williams and the kind of parabolic structures encountered in the Bible (an important source); that is, he needed to use narrative as metaphor but he needed to free it from the innate limitations of a prose mode by more direct confrontations with unconscious forces. Allegory was an obvious answer, as in Stephen Crane's neglected verse, but the specific modernist approach was found in the nightmare revelations of the surrealists, which seemed to complement perfectly readings in Charles Baudelaire and Arthur Rimbaud.

Consequently, beginning with *Say Pardon*, Ignatow's deceptively modest story-poems started to illuminate deeper, darker undercurrents, started to probe Freudian streams with relentless innocence. In "The Dream" a stranger approaches "to fall down at your feet/ and pound his head upon the sidewalk" until "your life takes on his desperation," even after waking. Like Baudelaire, Ignatow remained a poet of urban landscapes, committed to a moral exploration of man's most ambitious and ambiguous invention, yet he has never lost his spiritual roots in a Jewish past in his search for godhead and ideal certitudes. In the book's title poem, for example, he advises, "Say pardon/ and follow your own will," but two poems later, "The Complex" addresses the dilemma of a father whose "madness is to own himself/ for what he gives is taken," while another poem, "And I Said," envisions "God" behind "my enemy."

The tension energizing his strongest poems, an ethical and psychological matrix of contending defiance and guilt, often entails a transformation of public material into family dramas, spotlighting an ambivalent father figure, a wronged wife, a victimized son. A prolific writer intent upon processing every vagrant bit of daily experience, however trivial, Ignatow has published more poems than he should, far too frequently lapsing into sententious whimsy or belaboring the obvious. This has contributed, no doubt, to his dismissal by many academics. It was not until the 1970's and the publication of *Poems 1934-1969* and the *Selected Poems* that the true extent of his contribution to American literature was appreciated, climaxing in the award of the prestigious Bollingen Prize and reconfirming the truism that risk-taking and pratfalls are ever the hallmarks of the serious artist.

Fellow poets have been more ready to concede and celebrate the sly art beneath Ignatow's rough surfaces—at least poets who share his concern for establishing an alternative aesthetic closer to the Whitman-Williams line of descent, ranging from Charles Reznikoff to the "deep image" school of Robert Bly, James Wright, and Diane Wakoski. They have helped bring Ignatow's verses to the forefront of contemporary American poetry—Bly in particular, through his choices for the *Selected Poems.*

In recent years, belying his age, Ignatow has continued to evolve, another sign of genuine talent, and has relaxed enough, at last, to appreciate poetic stances at the opposite end of the scale, including a growing comprehension of Eliot's technical radicalism and intelligence. If *Tread the Dark* exhibited symptoms of possible fatigue, compulsive reiteration of death threats and near self-parodies, these have since been denied in the moving *Sunlight: A Sequence for My Daughter* and *Whisper to the Earth*, in which the concluding "With Horace" epitomizes Ignatow's determination to dig for rocks, to strike off "his fire upon stone."

Ignatow has received the National Institute of Arts and Letters Award (1964), two Guggenheim Fellowships (1965 and 1973), the Shelley Memorial Award (1965), and the Bollingen Prize (1977).

Biography

Born February 7, 1914, in Brooklyn, New York, the son of Russian immigrant parents, Max and Yetta (née Reinbach) Ignatow, David Ignatow had the misfortune to graduate from New Utrecht High School in 1932: "I stepped out of high school into the worst economic, social, and political disaster of our times, the Great Depression." He did enroll at Brooklyn College but lasted only half a semester, subsequently schooling himself in literary matters by reading Hemingway, Whitman, Friedrich Nietzsche, Arthur Schopenhauer, Søren Kierkegaard, the Russian novelists, the French poets of the previous century, and the Bible. He worked in his father's commercial pamphlet bindery, running a machine or delivering the finished pamphlets by hand-truck, and wrote stories and poems in his spare hours. Oppressed by the tedious labor, and by an ambivalent, often heated relationship with a hard-driving father, Ignatow envisioned literature as an escape. With his mother's aid, he managed to secure an appointment as a reporter for the WPA Newspaper Project. The year before, his short story "I Can't Stop It" had appeared in *The New Talent* magazine, earning a place on Edward J. O'Brien's Honor List in his *The Best American Short Stories* annual in 1933.

Ignatow was finally able to leave the family business and home in 1935, when he found a cheap apartment in Manhattan's East Village, where he became a part of the literary scene and met artist Rose Graubart, whom he married two years later. Their son David was born in 1937. Financial difficulties harassed the young couple, and in the period from 1939 to 1948 Ignatow was forced to work at a series of low-paying jobs, as night clerk at the Sanitation Department, as a Health Department clerk, as an apprentice handyman in the lathe workshop at the Kearny Shipyards in New Jersey, and, for five years, as night admitting clerk at Beth Israel Hospital in New York. It was during his last year at Beth Israel that his first collection, *Poems*, appeared and garnered an enthusiastic review from William Carlos Williams. Williams, in fact, emerged as a friend, as did Charles Reznikoff, and these two poets probably exerted the most enduring influence upon Ignatow's career.

The year 1955 proved to be crucial in Ignatow's life. *The Gentle Weight Lifter* was published; he was asked to edit the Whitman Centennial issue of the *Beloit Poetry Journal*; and his son began to exhibit the signs of mental illness that would eventually result in his being institutionalized. A daughter, Yaedi, was born the next year, and Ignatow became closely associated with *Chelsea* magazine. In 1961, his third volume of poetry, *Say Pardon*, was published by Wesleyan University Press—destined to remain his publisher for almost two decades—but money was still a pressing problem, and Ignatow worked as a paper salesman in the years between 1962 and 1964, also serving as an auto messenger for Western Union on the weekends. During the same interval, he spent a year as poetry editor of *Nation* and gave a poetry workshop at the New School for Social Research.

The publication of *Figures of the Human* helped to earn him an award from the National Institute of Arts and Letters in 1964, his first significant token of recognition. This was followed by a Guggenheim Fellowship a year later. In 1965 he also won the Shelley Memorial Award and was Visiting Lecturer at the University of Kentucky. Other academic posts came his way: at the University of Kansas in 1966 and at Vassar College from 1967 to 1969. He then accepted positions as Poet-in-Residence at York College (CUNY) and as adjunct professor at Columbia University, where he has remained. Editorial assignments included extended stints with *Beloit Poetry Journal* and *Chelsea*, and in 1972 he was among the first associate editors connected with the founding of the *American Poetry Review*, a connection that was dissolved near the decade's end when he and a group of fellow editors resigned in protest over what they perceived as implicit unfairness in the magazine's attitude toward women and minority groups.

In 1973 Ignatow was granted a second Guggenheim Fellowship, but the award that had the most to do with bringing his name before a broader audience was the Bollingen Prize of 1977. The publication of *The Notebooks of David Ignatow*, selections from his journals which the poet hoped, in vain, would result in a wider readership for his poetry, had made clear the terrible cost of being a writer, particularly an antiestablishment writer, in America, while also demonstrating with high principle, brutal candor, and almost claustrophobic narcissism, the ultimate advantages and limitations of constantly translating self into *res*. Ignatow's career achieved ironic completeness with his election to the presidency of the Poetry Society of America in 1980.

Analysis

In his poetry written in the 1930's and 1940's, later gathered in the first section of *Poems 1934-1969*, David Ignatow projected an abiding concern for both the well-made poem, however occasionally denuded of conventional lyric devices, and a reformer's vision of realistic life, in the city, in the streets, in the homes of the poor and outcast, who are romantically linked with the artist's difficult lot. The subjects were traditional—marriage, murder, sex, love's complexities, adolescence, the death of Franklin D. Roosevelt—but their treatment exhibited a diverting ability to make sudden leaps from the banal to the profound, always in language direct enough to disarm. "Autumn Leaves," for example, moves skillfully from an ordinary image of the leaves as Depression victims to a vivid figure of God sprawling beneath a tree, gaunt in giving, "like a shriveled nut where plumpness/ and the fruit have fed the worm." This kind of dramatic shift epitomizes Ignatow's focus on social injustice and his often bitter struggle with a religious heritage and the questionable place of deity in a scheme of things so geared to grind down human hopes.

Surprisingly, many of the early poems betray a professional smoothness and a reliance on metaphor and balanced lines that one might not expect from a disciple of Williams; there is scant sense in these poems of a language straining for experimental intensities. "The Murderer," an undeniable failure, marked by simplistic psychology but true to its author's identification with the underclass, can only express love for "those who cart me off to jail" in easy prose: "I love them too/ for the grief and anger/ I have given." More relevant, the murderer had killed with a knife, that most intimate of weapons, which reappears again and again in the Ignatow canon, a reflection of the menace and death lurking behind every scene of ordinary existence, as well as symbolic reminder of murderous impulses and contrary fears of castration by the father and his capitalistic society.

In *Poems*, which is a bundle of furies, rage against America's hunger for money, "our masterpiece" (according to a poem of that title), and frustration at being caught in its fatal web—"Keep me from doing what I want/ and I shall harm someone,/ including myself"—the obsession with creating a "small song" rarely escapes self-imposed boundaries. Occasionally, as in "At the Zoo," a quiet pathos gives modest dimensions their proper subject; an elephant trapped and separated from his real self, like the poet of course, in "stingy space and concrete setting." Repeatedly, however, as in "Come!" and "The Poet Is a Hospital Clerk," Ignatow underestimates his audience, wherein lies the innate danger of such songs, and settles for either blatant self-abasement—"I have said it before, I am no good"—or political invective:

"Come, let us blow up the whole business;/ the city is insane." At his best, he can produce "Europe and America," merging anger against world ills with ambivalence toward his father, the knife resurfacing in a climax of fused violences:

> My father comes of a small hell
> where bread and man have been kneaded and baked together.
> You have heard the scream as the knife fell;
> while I have slept
> as guns pounded offshore.

Working with a larger canvas and a surer touch, *The Gentle Weight Lifter* evinces a growing dependence on narrative means and on verbal portraits and mirrors of the people who define Ignatow's imagination. The collection is not unlike an urbanized *Spoon River Anthology* (1915), albeit brightened by exotic historic additions and splashes of darker Kafkaesque tones. In its quest for parrallel lives and allegorical configurations, the collection ranges back in time to ancient Greece, to Oedipus at Colonnus in "Lives II"—tellingly centered on the father, not Antigone, his head in her lap as "he thought surely some cover/ could be found for him"—to Nicias in "The Men Sang," a parable about the poet's generic function, and to the Old Testament in "The Pardon of Cain," which captures Cain in the "joy" of having freed himself from death's insidious allure.

Though not yet prevalent, surrealistic perspectives, when they do appear, tend to be founded upon absurd juxtapositions of mythic and modernist elements, as in "News Report," where "a thing" arises from a sewer to run amok among urban females—primeval sexuality rampant in a city field. Each victim describes her special view, "one giving the shaggy fur, the next the shank bone/ of a beast." In the end, the creature is an obvious refugee from Greek mythology, "the red teeth marks sunk into the thigh/ and the smell of a goat clinging tenaciously." Throughout the book, there is a stubborn quest for philosophic truths at variance with contemporary culture, and the governing voice, confounding Ignatow's own aesthetic, often resounds with a pedant's dense lexicon, as in "The Painter," a sensitive inquiry into a particular artist's world, which has a fourth stanza beginning: "These are not dreams, and the brush stroke is the agent./ At the hour of appropriate exhaustion, leaving the field/ of canvas, she ravens on the transient bread and cheese."

This is far from streamlined narrative terseness, far from the language of the man in the street, and it points up *The Gentle Weight Lifter*'s uneasy transitional quality, despite several remarkable poems, and its abrupt swings between simple allegorical spareness and thicker meditative measures. In *Say Pardon*, much of the uncertainty has disappeared, carrying Ignatow's main voice and means closer to the spare slyness that distinguishes his final style. In *Babel to Byzantium* (1968), James Dickey salutes the collection's "strange, myth-dreaming vision of city life" and isolates, with acute accuracy, its basic modus operandi as "an inspired and brilliantly successful metaphysical reportage." Since it announces a greater willingness to accept a surrealistic path to unconscious resources, without jettisoning conversational immediacy and treasured social and moral concerns, one of the key poems is "How Come?" A naked, unpretentious self funnels the experience into Everyman's tale: "I'm in New York covered by a layer of soap foam." The conceit, whimsey in service of darker designs, is logically developed, radio newscasts informing him of the foam's spread to San Francisco, Canada, and the Mexican border, climaxing with "God help the many/ who will die of soap foam." Light fantasy has suggested the paradox of drowning in cleanliness, next to American godliness, the pollution of scientific and commercial advances against nature.

The relaxed speech is matter-of-fact, contrasting scaffolding for a surreal flight, not quite as jagged as it will later become in Ignatow's continued effort to simulate urban realities, and the situation adeptly yokes "what if" fantasy to persistent reformist despair. More touching, though no less characteristic, are two poems about the author's institutionalized son, "In Limbo" and "Sunday at the State Hospital," the former a brief statement of grief, insisting that "there is no wisdom/ without a child in the house," and the latter recounting a visit in which the son cannot eat the sandwich his father has brought him:

> My past is sitting in front of me
> filled with itself
> and trying with almost no success
> to bring the present to its mouth.

A poem called simply "Guilt" lays bare the emotional core of these and other family verses: "Guilt is my one attachment to reality."

Jewish guilt, the anxiety bred of childhood training in a context that conditions love to obedience, outsider status, and unresolved Oedipus complexes, must forever seek release not only in the past, but in a specific religious ethos as well. Thus, the last section of *Say Pardon* is a procession of spiritual selves that assumes a living godhead, who proffers salvation (from guilt, rage, hatred) through the act of loving fatherhood, the "Lord" claiming "you will win your life/ out of my hands/ by taking up your child." These lines are from "I Felt," second in the series of twelve poems, after "The Mountain Is Stripped," where the poet had conceded, "I have been made frail with righteousness:/ with two voices. I am but one person." Because of its inveterate opposition to his rational espousal of liberal dogma and experimental openness, this conservative streak in Ignatow's consciousness, which helps to fuel his moral indignation, generates the lion's share of the tension in some of his strongest poetry. It also explains how such a cosmopolitan individual could, as revealed in *The Notebooks of David Ignatow*, react with abhorrence to homosexuality, viewing it as a degeneration into self-love.

"And I Stand," third in the series, ostensibly a declaration, has the impact of a prayer in its speaker's avowal not to kill his enemy, standing and gazing, instead, past "my enemy at Him." Noah, Samson, and Job, three personifications of a volatile man-god fulcrum, are considered for antithetical urges, their stories rephrased, until the final poem, "The Rightful One," confronts a divine visitation, a New Testament Christ to replace the Old Testament's paternal fierceness, full of forgiveness, "his hair long, face exhausted, eyes sad," with pardon again based on selfless parenthood: "Bless your son . . . / . . . And the Rightful One/ was gone and left a power to feel free." Redemption is not the reader's, however, ideal or otherwise, since boredom is the normal response when any dramatic conflict flattens out into a species of George Santayana's "animal faith," intimating that belief, in this case, is either forced or without sufficient doubt.

Figures of the Human is free of such overt metaphysical gestures toward mental entropy, and more potent as a result. Its first section concentrates on those human figures whose crimes and tragedies populate the daily tabloids; it is tuned to the violence, urban and sudden, that Ignatow deems typical of modern life. A victim, for example, of a random, fatal assault in his own home is elegized in "And That Night." The poem's attitude is one of primitive awe: "You bring up a family in three small rooms,/ this crazy man comes along/ to finish it off." Note how the language refuses mandarin remoteness, and savors instead the vernacular tongue of victim and reporter. Another victim, a nine-year-old girl raped and thrown off a tenement roof, is the voice in "Play Again," which enables Ignatow to grant her (at the brink of poor taste) a sacrificial mission:

> The living
> share me among them. They taste
> me on the ground, they taste me
> in the air descending.

Salvation comes, saving the poem, with a beautiful death plea, as the child and author ask readers to play again "and love me/ until I really die, when you are old/ on a flight of stairs." A poem called "Two Voices," echoing Alfred, Lord Tennyson, underscores the almost schizophrenic division in self of which the poet is always aware; the retreat into "Baudelaire, Whitman, Eliot" versus the need for active involvement in a present tense is translated into a suicidal leap into a winter lake, which is daring, if deadly, because it challenges "the weather," nature itself.

The rest of *Figures of the Human*, three further sections, varies its approach with frequent recourse to personal days and ways—"My mind is green with anxiety/ about money"—and surreal fantasies, one of which, the brief "Earth Hard," has a delicious Blakean air:

Earth hard to my heels
bear me up like a child
standing on its mother's belly.
I am a surprised guest to the air.

Childhood is an issue in the title poem also, questing after "the childhood spirit" of a maddened beloved for the impulse that impels art as well: "Then are we loved, hand drawing swiftly/ figures of the human struggling awake." This is mission and theme combined, dream explicating experience, and a reply to the savage urge that brings back the "knife" in other poems.

Whatever else it accomplishes, *Figures of the Human* demonstrates the firm command Ignatow had obtained over his unique aesthetic, culminating, four years later, in *Rescue the Dead*, his finest, most consistently effective volume of verse, which is, at times, his most autobiographical. As the title avers, the major goal of the book is to revive the past, the personal dead and strangers and the dead in spirit. A handful of its poems have already been recognized for the virtuoso performances they are, among them "The Boss" and "The Bagel," first and last in the initial section, which is introduced by a "Prologue" that offers up parents "who had small/ comfort from one another." The larger arrangement of the section, which evolves from a bitter portrait of a sinning father into the playful absurdity of a man turning into a rolling bagel, has the additional weight of a small sequence about the father: five poems, beginning with the "Prologue" and concluding with his "Epitaph," which prays: "Forgive me, father,/ as I have forgiven you/ my sins."

The Freudian chain has thus been broken, at least for the moment, at least within the limits of the poem, and "Nourish the Crops," the next poem, can proceed to the other father, God, realizing self as the "product of you to whom all life/ is equal." The proposition here is the same frightening one, minus deity, facing Albert Camus and Jean-Paul Sartre in the 1950's, modern man's existential dilemma vis-à-vis an indifferent cosmos. In spite of conflict-ing religious restraints, for Ignatow the pivotal answer must be imagination, ceaseless reworkings of the Romantic heritage he had forsworn, and an alter ego in pursuit of a bagel, sounding like Williams and Wright, tumbling head over heels, "one complete somersault/ after another like a bagel/ and strangely happy with myself." In the title poem, the climb to redemption is pitted against paradox—"Not to love is to live"—and has the poet conceding his incapacity to choose love over life (survival, materialist wants) and asking that you "who are free/ rescue the dead." A powerful poem at the end of the second section, "The Room," reconfirms the crucial role of imagination in the battle against loneliness, emotional and physical, again seeking, with fluid lyricism, escape from loss of self and others—his bed constructed from "the fallen hairs/ of my love, naked, her head dry"—through a magical transfor-mation, the persona flying around his dark room like a bat or angel.

The fourth section of *Rescue the Dead* is the weakest by far, its lapses made glaring by the general excellence of section three, which focuses on rituals of survival in breathless contrast to the violence of the real world (inner and outer), circling from the murder of innocence in England to a derelict, who returns, like "a grey-haired foetus," to his mother while asleep, and two ignored children in the "East Bronx," sharpening their "knives against the curb." The failure of the section stems from a stubborn determination to fashion vehicles of protest, blunt weapons to combat what is perceived as massive public wrongs, such as the Vietnam War and the Medgar Evers incident, and even contains a poem about "Christ" and dares add the coda of "In My Childhood," a facile memory of a yellow canary and a boy with an air gun. Returning to more complex private visions to tap a wellspring, the fifth section recoups some of the lost poetic energy, humming apprecia-tions, never without saving shadows, of a put-upon wife, a foraging bum, an old love, and so on. It peaks with "Omen,"a sentimental grab for love from sylvan nature that beats false, but provides a smooth thematic entry to the sixth and final section of eleven poems about poetry, three of which are dedicated to admired fellow craftsmen, Denise Levertov, Marianne Moore, and Williams.

Like Stanley Kunitz, whom he closely resembles in his search for paternal, mystical salvation amid alien corn, Ignatow summons up Dante for validation in "Anew," commencing, "Dante forgot to say,/ Thank you, Lord, for sending me/ to hell." The apex of the sequence is "Walk There," an allegorical walk in a dark wood, full of fear, before a heaven is glimpsed: "Ahead, is that too the sky/ or a clearing?/ Walk there." The desire is credible and is honestly earned by prior struggles with private and public demons, but the poetry that inevitably concludes an Ignatow collection, mirroring Dante's *Paradiso*, never equals in intensity and metaphoric convolutions the engrossing journey through infernal regions that got him there.

Facing the Tree is more of a mixed bag than its predecessors, sure of its technique and confident in voice, and including a growing fondness for prose poems, that most dangerous invitation to self-indulgence. The voice of "Read-ing the Headlines" mates, typically, personal and social anguish: "I have a burial ground in me where I place the bodies/ without fuss or emotion." Whimsy alternates with stark tragedy as the naïve but shrewd narrator reacts to an evil world by laboring to extract some psychological and spiritual truths from its surface madness, filtered, always, through the mesh of a receptive self. The poems that work efficiently, such as "Letter to a Friend," "My Own Line," "The Refuse Man," "Autumn," "In Season," and several untitled prose poems, are those which remember to keep near the taut edge of the parabolic methodology that Ignatow has perfected, avoiding the glibness and rhetorical excess that ruin so many others in the book, notably where they are attached to political frames, such as "My President Weeps" and "Now

Celebrate Life and Death."

Tread the Dark is similarly confident in style and speech, but its obsession with death and the absence of adequate counter-moods numb the reader to its occasional brilliance and successes, such as "The Abandoned Animal," "Death of a Lawn Mower," "The Dead Sea," "The Forest Warden," "An Account in the Present Tense. . . ," "Midnight," and two untitled pieces, numbered 46 and 80. All the poems are numbered, stressing their author's conception of them as a series structured upon the *leitmotiv* of death. In treading the dark, fighting off oblivion with imagination, the poet too often treads familiar waters, flounders into pretentiousness and embarrassing archness, appropriately reaching a nadir in "Epilogue," a short coda that has the persona, aware of being watched by trees ("tall gods") in his study, bow over his typewriter and start "the ceremony/ of a prayer." A year later, the publication of the highly charged *Sunlight* sequence demonstrated that the decline signaled by *Tread the Dark* was temporary.

Although not equal to Ignatow's strongest volumes, *Figures of the Human* and *Rescue the Dead*, *Whisper to the Earth* is ripe with readiness, open to new modes, and at peace with the softer hues of twilight and autumn and the death they prefigure. Divided into five sections, the collection's first group of poems, with a single exception, approach nature directly, forsaking urbanscapes in favor of garden meditations upon apples and trees and stones, a strategy for resolving death fears, so that entering the grave will "be like entering my own house." In a poem for his daughter, "For Yaedi" Ignatow claims that when he dies he wants it said, "that I wasted/ hours in feeling absolutely useless/ and enjoyed it, sensing my life/ more strongly than when I worked at it." Elegies fittingly dominate the next two sections, but the ones for his father and mother—"Kaddish," "The Bread Itself," "A Requiem," and "1905"—can be counted among the most evocative poems he has ever written, regardless of their mellow reordering of the past to concentrate upon his parents' genuine gifts to him. The father is forgiven by way of a comprehension of his own harsh youth in Russia, and the mother is celebrated as the "bread" that sustained him. Tension here is less important than the positive electricity of love heightening the language out of itself and its narrative solidity.

Section four, "Four Conversations," is the weakest series in the book, a sequence of dialogues that seems to lead toward Wallace Stevens, but its experimental boldness reflects credit upon Ignatow's resolve not to surrender to old age's penchant for self-parody and safe repetitions. In the final section, the prose poem holds sway, at its tightest in "I Love to Fly," which uses a dream to good effect. The climax is in "With Horace," an identification with the Roman poet that accepts the Sabine Farm wisdom of his retreat from the city to use the experience of his late years as a new tool for penetrating nature's rock hardness.

Major publications other than poetry
NONFICTION: *The Notebooks of David Ignatow*, 1973; *Open Between Us*, 1980.

Bibliography
Bly, Robert. "Some Thoughts on *Rescue the Dead*," in *Tennessee Poetry Journal*. III (Winter, 1970), pp. 17-21.
Lavenstein, Richard. "A Man with a Small Song," in *Parnassus*. IV (1975), pp. 211-222.
Mazzaro, Jerome. "The Poetry of David Ignatow," in *Boundary*. IV (1975), pp. 289-297.
Wagner, Linda W. "On David Ignatow," in *Tennessee Poetry Journal*. III (Winter, 1970), pp. 41-45.
Zweig, Paul. "David Ignatow," in *American Poetry Review*. V (January-February, 1976), pp. 29-30.

Edward Butscher

RANDALL JARRELL

Born: Nashville, Tennessee; May 6, 1914
Died: Chapel Hill, North Carolina; October 14, 1965

Principal collections

"The Rage for the Lost Penny," in *Five Young American Poets*, 1940; *Blood for a Stranger*, 1942; *Little Friend, Little Friend*, 1945; *Losses*, 1948; *The Seven-League Crutches*, 1951; *Selected Poems*, 1955; *The Woman at the Washington Zoo*, 1960; *The Lost World*, 1965; *The Complete Poems*, 1969.

Other literary forms

An important critic and teacher of literature as well as a poet, Randall Jarrell published critical essays, translations, children's books, and a novel. His first book of criticism, *Poetry and the Age* (1953), examines the function of the poet in modern society, the nature of criticism, and the work of John Crowe Ransom, Wallace Stevens, Marianne Moore, and William Carlos Williams. Direct, witty, and sometimes harsh commentary in these essays aims at expanding the appreciative faculty in its broadest sense. The next collection, *A Sad Heart at the Supermarket* (1962), examines values and literature, including the American obsession with consumption. *The Third Book of Criticism* (1970), collected posthumously, includes discussions of Wallace Stevens, Robert Graves, W. H. Auden, Robert Frost, Russian novels, and American poetry since 1900. Close reading, Freudian analysis, myth interpretation, and religious considerations are features of Jarrell's method. His translations include *The Golden Bird and Other Fairy Tales of the Brothers Grimm* (1962) and *Faust, Part I* (1976), as well as other works for children and adults. Jarrell's novel, *Pictures from an Institution* (1954), presents life in an academic community from a satirical point of view. His children's books are *The Gingerbread Rabbit* (1963), *The Bat Poet* (1964), and *The Animal Family* (1965).

Achievements

Jarrell's reputation as an artist and critic spans a writing career of thirty-three years. Initially recognized as a poet of World War II, Jarrell received a Guggenheim Post-Service Award in 1946. He also served as literary editor of the *Nation*, visiting lecturer at the Salzburg Seminar, and visiting fellow in creative writing at Princeton. Awarded a second Guggenheim Fellowship in 1963, he served as a chancellor of the Academy of American Poets and a member of the National Institute of Art and Letters. One of his collections of poetry and translations, *The Woman at the Washington Zoo*, won the National Book Award in 1960.

Jarrell's chief contribution to the poetry of the twentieth century is his insistence that the experience of ordinary people is worth exploring to discover truth. His work reflects a determination to communicate everyday experience in a language and a form that speak to the general reader as well as to the literary scholar.

Biography

Randall Jarrell spent his youth in Tennessee and California, living with his grandparents in Hollywood for a time when his parents separated. Although his family expected him to go into his uncle's candy business, Jarrell enrolled in psychology at Vanderbilt University, where he met the poet and critic John Crowe Ransom and, through him, other members of the waning Fugitive movement, including Robert Penn Warren, Allen Tate, and Donald Davidson. In 1937, Jarrell and his associate Peter Taylor followed Ransom to Kenyon College, where Jarrell began a lifelong association with Robert Lowell. During this period, Jarrell also completed work for his M.A. degree in literature, including a critical thesis on A. E. Housman under the direction of Donald Davidson.

Jarrell began his career as a professor at the University of Texas in Austin, where he met Mackie Langham, who became his wife in 1940. He enlisted in a ferry-pilot training program soon after Pearl Harbor, but actually began his military career as a private in the Army Air Corps. He served as a Celestial Navigation tower operator at Chanute Field in Illinois and Davis-Monthan Field in Arizona. After the war he taught at Sarah Lawrence College and then at the Women's College of the University of North Carolina in Greensboro. In the summer of 1948, Jarrell traveled to Europe, teaching American Civilization at the Salzburg Summer Seminar. In 1951 Randall and Mackie Jarrell separated, and in 1952 they were divorced. Jarrell married Mary von Schrader late in 1952.

Jarrell was hospitalized briefly for a nervous disorder in 1965. He continued to teach at the University of North Carolina in Greensboro until October of that year, when he was struck and killed by an automobile in Chapel Hill, North Carolina.

Analysis

Randall Jarrell's poetry speaks with intelligence and humanity about the problem of change as it affects men and women in the twentieth century. Often using the motif of a dreamer awakening in an unfamiliar world, Jarrell probes the experience of each speaker to discover enduring truths, however bleak they may be. Although the speakers in his poems learn that the difference between innocence and experience is often bewilderment and pain, they also express a sense of dignity and affirmation. Whether the focus is on a soldier facing death, a mother relinquishing her son, or a lonely woman wandering in a zoo, Jarrell's poems achieve a balance between the common experience of humanity and the suffering of the individual.

From the beginning of his career, Jarrell confronts the necessity that opposes human desires. In early works such as "For an Emigrant" and "The Refugees," he acknowledges the enormous isolation that engulfs hopeful arrivals gaining their freedom only to endure without identity in their new homeland. On a larger scale, Jarrell also anticipates the self-destructive force of mankind in poems such as "The Automaton" and "The See-er of Cities," in which archetypal death figures hover on the horizons of civilization. Jarrell's lasting concern, however, is the individual's search for meaning in a world of change and death. In "90 North," a poem following the pattern of the dreamer awakening to the world of experience, a child secure in bed at night dreams of discovering the North Pole. Envisioning himself as an adult explorer, the lone survivor of his party, the child reaches his goal only to find darkness and cold. This experience of emptiness and death becomes for him the truth he sought: "Nothing comes from nothing . . ./ Pain comes from the darkness/ And we call it wisdom. It is pain." Next, the child's dream is juxtaposed with an adult's dream in which North has no meaning, for the adult realizes that the dark world of dream is the final reality of man's experience, the meaninglessness acceptable only to the unconscious and terrifying to the conscious explorer of existence. A deep-sea diver makes a similar journey in "The Iceberg," finding ultimate annihilation in the "sick ambiguous wisdom of the sea" and surfacing to observe the many faces of the great berg melting as he loses consciousness.

In his second collection, *Little Friend, Little Friend*, Jarrell's presentation of those affected by World War II reflects the same concern with the extremes of psychological experience, whether at firsthand or vicariously. In the war poems, specific characters and settings provide a structural basis and blank verse provides the medium for the voices. In "2nd Air Force," a mother visiting her son at an air base senses the necessary detachment of the young soldiers preparing their bombers, "hopeful cells/ heavy with someone else's death." She knows that her son, like the others, may as easily be a victim, and she ponders whether all her years of hope and care "meant this?" In the course of her meditation, she sees in her imagination the crash of her son in a burning plane; the distress call "little friend," Jarrell's title for the book, is repeated without hope of the young pilot's survival. "Losses," one of the most famous poems in the collection, voices the confusion of young soldiers for whom death has yet no personal meaning. They are amazed when members of their group disappear during training, since ordinary accidents lack the heroism expected in wartime. In their view, "it was not dying: everybody died," and surely they expected more of the experience than to die "like aunts or pets or foreigners." Even in battle over the unfamiliar cities of the enemy, the youths still fail to comprehend the meaning of their end. The problem, as Jarrell's simple, colloquial speaker addresses it, is that "When we left high school nothing else had died/ For us to figure we had died like." Their dream of life failed to allow for personal experience of death; the cities they bomb are no more to them than names studied in geography class at school.

Jarrell's awareness of the child within each fighting man appears also in "The State" and "The Death of the Ball Turret Gunner," often anthologized for their dramatic appeal. The speaker of the first understands the power of government through the loss of his family. He begins, "When they killed my mother it made me nervous," continuing to lament the loss of his sister, and finally his cat; their disappearance causes the death of his consciousness, underscored by the simple frantic expression of a child. The speaker of "The Death of the Ball Turret Gunner" endures a cycle of birth to death in the course of his service to the "State." Awakening to discover himself in the rotating turret of a fighting plane "six miles from earth, loosed from its dream of life," his nightmare of reality ends violently as it began, but his voice persists: "When I died they washed me out of the turret with a hose." A poem recording a similar awakening with greater detail and tension, "A Pilot from the Carrier," describes a flier's escape from his burning plane and his lengthy parachute descent. Imagery of fire and ice effectively captures the intensity of his struggle to free himself from the "blazing wheel" of the cockpit. As the ball turret gunner falls into the belly of the State, so the pilot descends toward the warmth of earth, its sunlight and stillness contrasting with his frenzied escape. As he hangs suspended over the sea, his new perceptions, "the great flowering of his life," create a sense of detachment and calm. The brilliant gleam of his burning plane as it reaches the water reveals his location to an enemy plane so that he recognizes the approach of death as clearly as if he were "reading a child's first scrawl." In his last moments he learns the lesson of his own vulnerability in the unreasoning natural world. As a bombardier realizes in "Siegfried," death simply comes: "It happens as it does because it does."

The difficulty of reconciling a moral perspective with the life of war is the subject of "Eighth Air Force," one of Jarrell's best-known poems. Civilian life and battle merge for the men of this force that bombed continental targets from bases in Britain. Having the opportunity for some domestic comforts, the men groom themselves, keep pets, and even cut flowers. As they lounge, playing cards and counting up their missions, are they murderers because they have fulfilled their duty the day before? The persona delivers no harsh judgment on these whom he observes, for he has been one of them and has survived. As Pilate offered Christ, so he offers these figures for whom he has suffered and lied in his dreams. As he sees it, the guilt must be widely shared: "Men wash their hands, in blood, as best they can." Actor and victim become arbitrary designations once the process of war begins. In this view, to "behold the man" carries complex contradictory associations. The men are saviors of Europe, sinners against their own consciences, and scapegoats for others' blame. As the speaker shares their role, the reader must evaluate the speaker's final judgment that he "finds no fault in this just man," a composite symbol for the Eighth Air Force and humanity itself.

Jarrell also deals with the problems of accepting violence and death as a part of life in "Burning the Letters," portraying the wife of a pilot killed in the Pacific. Her husband died a fiery death, and now, several years later, she burns his letters as a sign of relinquishment. Jarrell notes that she was once a Christian, and, in her meditation, imagery of her husband's death mingles continually with imagery of Christ as she struggles to reconcile the paradox of life exchanged for death. In the context of her loss, Christ appears as a flame and a bird of prey seeking the hidden lives of those who dwell in darkness; then they turn on him, drawing from his life both bread and blood. Entering her dream, the woman sees herself as an aging child, clutching at the Christ figure who devours his own body before flickering away in the darkness. In addition to identifying the death of her husband with the death of Christ, she also recalls the sea burial of her husband in terms of the secretive burial of Christ's body. Like those who buried Christ, and those who bury the dead at sea, she attempts to bury her dead in flames. Although she chooses life for herself, her final prayer is addressed to the grave. Her acceptance of the death of her husband points toward a final emptiness and negation; in this nightmare of experience she acknowledges the same end discovered by the dreaming child in "90 North."

If human experience converges ultimately in isolation, emptiness, and darkness, where is the life men expect to have lived? Dreams also carry out this function in Jarrell's poems. "Absent with Official Leave" records the dreamlife of a soldier who finds his only protection from painful experience in sleep. There he achieves identity beyond his number and enjoys relationships not controlled by authority. After the lights dim, he enters the larger world "where civilians die/ Inefficiently, in their spare time, for nothing." Curved roads, contrasting sharply with the grids of army life, lead into a pastoral atmosphere where hunters seek birds in sporting fashion. In a cottage, the soldier visualizes the careful work of loving women "tending slow small fires." Their presence signals a transition to the "charmed" world of a fairy tale, where the soldier becomes a bear sheltered by Snow White and Rose Red as snow falls in the form of gentle blossoms. Negative forces appear, also, in the shape of accusing eyes and "grave mysterious beings" from his past, who represent the causes that justify war. Although they mourn his fate hypocritically at best, in his dream they grant him justification, signifying the love that he longs to experience. The poem reflects Jarrell's interest in the fairy tale and myth as a means of wish-fulfillment connected with the unconscious. The dreamer awakes, however, to the darkness of his fellow soldiers. A fuller development of the conflict between the fairy-tale world of dream and the painful nature of reality is "The Marchen," dramatizing men's desires to live and rule over an obstacle-filled environment.

While many critics believe that Jarrell found his most effective subject in the turmoil of war, his interest in the folktale stimulated a series of meditative poems in the collection *The Seven-League Crutches*. In the well-known poem "A Girl in a Library," Jarrell considers the outlook of a modern young coed napping in the library. Although she is no intellectual (her subjects are home economics and physical education), she too is a dreamer, with the simplicity of a kitten. Unaware of the power that the library offers in terms of art or science, she rests secure in the method of her modern studies of function and technique. The speaker who observes her, however, recognizes her potential as a woman of virtue and intelligence such as Alexander Pushkin's Tatyana Larina, if she should ever awake from her "sleep of life." Her courses in food preparation and exercise will surely not arouse the soul within her, which "has no assignments/ neither cooks/ Nor referees." The mythic self locked within her, however, balances the speaker's judgment of her superficial dreams and pursuits. Two earlier poems that reflect similar needs among young students are "Children Selecting Books in a Library" and "The Carnegie Library, Juvenile Division." In these poems, children seek intellectual transformation, unknowingly, in the imaginative world of myth and fairy tale, in contrast with the older girl, who will never be significantly changed by anything in the library. She will, however, carry out the rituals of love and suffering that the speaker anticipates in his allusions to the Corn King and Spring Queen of the ancient myths.

Jarrell's interest in the psychology of the fairy tale also appears in several reworkings of well-known works. "A Quilt Pattern" incorporates the plot of "Hansel and Gretel" in a child's dream that forms the narrative line of the poem, enriched with allusions to the Fall of Genesis. Hansel and Gretel are renamed "Good Me and Bad Me" to underscore the psychological aspects of the story. Similarly, Jarrell's version of "Cinderella" portrays her as an ash girl rejecting the world in favor of an "imaginary playmate," the godmother. This Cinderella indulges herself in fantasies that are destructive in the end. She moves from the fireside of her childhood to the furniture of marriage and family life, then finally into the fires of Hell, where she is again happy in isolation from reality. In like manner, Jarrell deals with the other side of fairy tales in "The Sleeping Beauty: Variation of the Prince" and "La Belle au Bois Dormant." In the first reworking of the tale, Jarrell proposes a new ending in which the prince does not awaken the princess with his kiss, but determines to sleep on eternally with her, thus achieving a truly permanent union. The story also embodies a death wish—the desire for an unbroken peace—and a rejection of sexual fulfillment. In "La Belle au Bois Dormant," Jarrell uses the sleeping beauty story in a perverse way to present a woman who has been murdered and dismembered by her lover. The poems are characteristic of Jarrell in the theme of a lonely death without transcendence or hope, but the characters lack the grounding in a human context that enhances Jarrell's best work.

"The Woman at the Washington Zoo," one of Jarrell's most powerful treatments of human loneliness, reflects the intensity of experience typical of his poetry. An aging woman finds herself envying the caged specimens she observes for the attention they receive, while she remains invisible among the sightseers. Women pass her in brightly colored saris corresponding to the dramatic clothing of the leopard in his cage. The navy print she wears, however, receives no attention, no complaints, and entraps her as surely as iron bars imprison an animal body. The tall columns of Washington serve the same function, in fact, separating the lonely woman from the other workers whom she passes. Her inner cries burst out in frustration at the world's indifference to her suffering. In desperation she covets the experience of violence she sees as the animals devour their meat. Identifying with the offal rejected by all but the vulture, the old woman imagines the hope of a magical transformation and release. Calling out to this ugliest of birds, she visualizes herself among the animal kingdom with man as the ruler: "You know what I was,/ You see what I am: change me, change me!" In the impossibility of her outward renewal is the necessity that frustrates hope; in the expression of her need is release and affirmation of self. Jarrell's poem gives utterance to the suffering of the woman as a type and as an individual, providing a wider recognition of her existence and of the human need for inner change and transformation through love.

Jarrell's last volume of poetry, *The Lost World*, emphasizes the themes of his maturity: aging, loneliness, loss, and the dreamworld where every man is a child. "Next Day," for example, is narrated by a lonely middle-class woman who has suddenly recognized her passage into old age. Her material and social success far surpass that of the woman at the zoo, but she is equally unhappy. The title of the poem refers to the woman's vision of herself in the mirror the day after attending the funeral of a friend her age. In plain language and a contemporary American setting Jarrell presents ordinary experience with great psychological intensity.

The poems of the final collection also treat the experiences of pain and loss with an affirmative note, for especially in these poems Jarrell develops the power of the dreamworld as real, if only in a metaphorical sense. In "The Lost Children," "The Lost World," and "Thinking of the Lost World," the experience of reality attains for some a magical, mythical quality in its own right. "The Lost Children" originated as a dream recorded by Jarrell's wife and develops a wish-fulfillment sequence found in "They" by Rudyard Kipling. While Kipling's story involves the recovery of a man's beloved child among several who have returned to earth after death, Jarrell's poem uses this dream as a background for a mother's contemplation of the possession and loss of a child as it matures. Each stanza then presents a stage in the process of separation and maturity. Eventually the parent exchanges the parental bond for friendship with the child as an adult, but the initial relationship lives on in the mother's consciousness. The mother compares the persistence of memory to a hide-and-seek game that the little girls still require her to play. The thought of them brings sadness at their separation, but the richness of the association remains.

"The Lost World" recovers portions of Jarrell's own past, using sensory impressions as Marcel Proust uses them in *Le temps retrouvé* (1927, *The Past Recaptured*). The poem is Jarrell's own, however, although it may have been stimulated by his interest in Proust's *À la recherche du temps perdu* (1913-1927, *Remembrance of Things Past*). Jarrell employs the effective strategies of his thirty years' writing experience to create impressions of his life in Hollywood in the 1920's, combining the world of his neighborhood with the world of art and filmmaking. Although the poem is narrated in the present tense, a sense of the struggle of re-creating time appears periodically as a conflict. Images of Hollywood, boyhood fantasies, and intense moments of pleasure or fear interweave in a journey undertaken to establish relationships between the past and the meaning of the present. "Thinking of the Lost World" considers the importance of the quest for the lost world of childhood. In keeping with the meditative intent of the poem, Jarrell returns from the formalistic use of terza rima that structures "The Lost World" to the conversational free verse characteristic of his later work. The flavor of chocolate tapioca evokes memories for the speaker of the poem as did the taste of the madeleine in Proust's great work of memory, but Jarrell's narrator finds the way into the past more difficult. "The sunshine of the Land/ Of Sunshine is a gray mist now," he admits, and the atmosphere is as polluted as that of an area given up to industry. In the realm of memory he constructs a compensating fantasy, an "undiscovered/ Country between California and Arizona," where his past resides. He longs, too, for the objects of the past: his "Mama's dark blue Buick" or "Lucky's electric" surely could transport him back. His late aunt reappears to him often in the guise of other women, and in this regard his past sustains itself in awakening memory.

The changes in his own body also testify to some remarkable ongoing process that persists despite the attempts of his memory to conserve the lost world of childhood and maturity. For the speaker as for the mother in "The Lost Children," the paradox is that while nothing remains, all of the past belongs to the rememberer. As he says, "My soul has memorized world after world," and in this memory he finds not merely an acceptable end, but happiness. For him, an awareness of the loss is assurance of some existence in the past that transcends time and death. The awareness itself is a "reward," a way of coming to terms with change in human experience, perhaps the central concern of Jarrell's poetry.

Tremendous sensitivity, critical insight, and human concern characterize the work of Jarrell throughout his career. The vigor of his last poems suggests that his work had not reached its end, although much of his talent had fulfilled itself in his last books. Jarrell wrote poetry with a human focus, poetry that is lasting and influential in its attempt to communicate the nature of experience in the modern world.

Major publications other than poetry

NOVEL: *Pictures from an Institution*, 1954.

SHORT FICTION: *The Golden Bird and Other Fairy Tales of the Brothers Grimm*, 1962 (translation).

PLAY: *Faust, Part I*, 1976 (translation).

NONFICTION: *Poetry and the Age*, 1953; *A Sad Heart at the Supermarket*, 1962; *The Third Book of Criticism*, 1970.

CHILDREN'S LITERATURE: *The Gingerbread Rabbit*, 1963; *The Bat Poet*, 1964; *The Animal Family*, 1965.

Bibliography

Ciardi, John, ed. *Mid-Century American Poets*, 1950.

Ferguson, Suzanne. *The Poetry of Randall Jarrell*, 1971.

Humphrey, Robert. "Randall Jarrell's Poetry," in *Themes and Directions in American Literature*, 1969. Edited by Ray B. Browne and Donald Pizer.

Lowell, Robert, Peter Taylor, and Robert Penn Warren, eds. *Randall Jarrell, 1914-1965*, 1967.

Quinn, Sister M. Bernetta. *The Metamorphic Tradition in Modern Poetry*, 1966.

Chapel Louise Petty

ROBINSON JEFFERS

Born: Pittsburgh, Pennsylvania; January 10, 1887
Died: Carmel, California; January 20, 1962

Principal collections

Flagons and Apples, 1912; *Californians*, 1916; *Tamar and Other Poems*, 1924; *Roan Stallion, Tamar, and Other Poems*, 1925; *The Women at Point Sur*, 1927; *Cawdor and Other Poems*, 1928; *Dear Judas and Other Poems*, 1929; *Descent to the Dead: Poems Written in Ireland and Great Britain*, 1931; *Thurso's Landing and Other Poems*, 1932; *Give Your Heart to the Hawks and Other Poems*, 1933; *Solstice and Other Poems*, 1935; *Such Counsels You Gave to Me and Other Poems*, 1937; *Poems Known and Unknown*, 1938; *The Selected Poetry of Robinson Jeffers*, 1938; *Be Angry at the Sun and Other Poems*, 1941; *Medea*, 1946 (verse drama, translation); *The Double Axe and Other Poems*, 1948; *Hungerfield and Other Poems*, 1954; *The Beginning and the End*, 1963; *Selected Poems*, 1965; *The Alpine Christ and Other Poems*, 1973; *Brides of the South Wind*, 1974.

Other literary forms

Robinson Jeffers explained his own work and expressed his ideas on society and art in some detail in the forewords to the Modern Library edition (1935) of his *Roan Stallion, Tamar, and Other Poems* and his *Selected Poetry of Robinson Jeffers* (1938). Other important prose statements are "Poetry, Gongorism and a Thousand Years," *The New York Times Book Review*, Jan. 18, 1948, pp. 16, 26; *Themes in My Poems* (1956); and *The Selected Letters of Robinson Jeffers, 1897-1962* (1968, Ann N. Ridgeway, editor).

In addition, the poet William Everson has collected, from various forgotten pages, two volumes of poetry that Jeffers had discarded. These volumes reconstitute the work of the transitional period from 1916 to 1922. They are *The Alpine Christ and Other Poems* (1973) and *Brides of the South Wind* (1974).

Achievements

More than twenty years after his death, Jeffers remains probably the most controversial American poet, with the exception of Edgar Allan Poe, who has ever been termed "major." A number of important writers and critics have ranked him with Walt Whitman and invoked the Greek tragedians in trying to suggest his somber power. In the early years of his fame his books typically went into several editions, and he was the subject of a *Time* magazine cover story. In 1947 his free translation of *Medea* for the New York stage brought him new acclaim as a dramatic poet. Since the early years of his fame, however, some critics, few but influential, were hostile, and others found Jeffers merely uninteresting as the subject of critical examination. The deep division over Jeffers' importance as a poet is seen today in college anthologies: he is given generous space in some, and omitted entirely from others. The weight of criticism, however, has been consistently on the positive side. In relatively recent years, a number of serious studies have been published which, while strongly favorable, avoid the extravagant praise of some of Jeffers' early admirers. All but the most hostile critics are agreed that Jeffers had an unmistakably original voice, strong dramatic talents, and great descriptive ability. He is the only American poet of note since Edwin Arlington Robinson—who praised him highly—to write a large quantity of narrative poetry. Some of Jeffers' short lyrics, moreover, notably "Hurt Hawks," "The Eye," "The Purse-Seine," and "Shine, Perishing Republic," seem destined to become classics. In addition to his poetic gifts, and indeed inseparable from them, is the force of a world view that is unusual, coherent, and challenging, a set of reasoned attitudes that justifies classifying him as a philosophical poet of unusual interest. Jeffers' radical skepticism about the human race, embodied in his doctrine that man should "uncenter himself" from the universe, is expressed in poetry that draws on considerable scientific and historical study, on thorough knowledge of religious and classical literature, and on deep resources of myth and ritual. It is the combination of poetic power and philosophical stance that argues strongly for Jeffers' place in a twentieth century pantheon of American poets.

Biography
     John Robinson Jeffers' life, milieu, and work are of one piece. From early adulthood, one can see him choosing a place of living and a way of life that are strongly reflected in his poetry and also in his occasional prose statements about his work.
     When Jeffers was born in Pittsburgh in 1887 his father was forty-nine, his mother twenty-seven. His father's occupation as well as his age set the boy apart; the senior Jeffers had been a Presbyterian minister and was Professor of Old Testament Literature and Exegesis at Western Theological Seminary. Young Robin was an only child for seven years, and he spent much of his time in solitary wandering or reading on the relatively isolated family property. He was later educated in Switzerland for nearly four years, in schools in which the language of instruction was either French or German. His father had introduced him to Greek at the age of five, and he also acquired Latin and some Italian. After his parents moved to Los Angeles, he entered Occidental College, where he continued his classical and literary education and supplemented his childhood religious training with courses in biblical literature and theology.
     Although popular with his fellow students, Jeffers already was establishing the pattern of his life through his interest in camping and mountain climbing

on the one hand, and in reading and writing on the other. Graduating at eighteen, he then pursued medical studies at the University of Southern California, and later studied forestry, hoping to find a way to support himself amid nature that would permit him time for poetry. A small legacy, however, enabled him to settle, with his bride Una Call Custer, in Carmel, California, in 1914. The whole area, then uncrowded, had a dramatic beauty, and Jeffers called it his "inevitable place." He was profoundly affected by its massive simplicity of elements: huge, treeless mountains plunging directly into the Pacific, broken by occasional narrow canyons in which grew at that time little groves of redwoods; the constant pound and swirl of the sea against bare granite shore-rocks; hawks soaring above the cattle-pasturing headlands. In this setting, Jeffers helped masons to construct a simple stone house on Carmel Point, looking directly seaward; and, later, he built with his own hands, using boulders that he laboriously rolled up from the shore, his famous "Hawk Tower." Evoking with its name the fierce independence of the birds that were one of his favorite subjects, the tower became symbolically for him a place beyond time, a psychological vantage point for his often apocalyptic and prophetic stance in the world.

With his wife, to whom he was devoted, Jeffers reared twin sons (a daughter, born first, lived only a day), and lived quietly in Carmel, departing only for vacations in Taos, New Mexico, and for rare trips to the East Coast or the British Isles. With a very few exceptions, he did not participate in the round of readings, book reviews, or campus appearances that characterizes the life of so many American poets. He won a number of important awards, including the Academy of American Poets prize, but he was never given the Pulitzer Prize, even though Edna St. Vincent Millay and Louis Untermeyer, among others, repeatedly pressed his case.

When Jeffers died in 1962, it was in the seaward bedroom of his own house. There, in the poem "The Bed by the Window," he had many years earlier envisioned the day when a ghostly figure would appear, rap with his staff, and say, "Come, Jeffers."

Analysis

Robinson Jeffers' central concept of the universe and of mankind's place in it, all-important in understanding his poetry, is grounded in his respect for scientific thought and in his own historical observations, but strongly colored in its expression by emotion. From science, he took a cool, analytical view of the human race as one species that evolved in one stage of an ever-evolving, dynamic universe—a mere "fly-speck" in the scheme of things. Perhaps because of his interest in astronomy (his younger brother, Hamilton, was for many years a scientist at the Lick Observatory in California), he took an extraterrestrial view even of the earth. The first photograph taken by the astronauts of the earth from the vicinity of the moon represented a view that

Jeffers had achieved in his imagination long before: "It is only a little planet/ But how beautiful it is. . . ." In "The Double Axe," Jeffers paid tribute to one of the scientists who helped him to achieve this view, Copernicus, hailing him as the first who "pushed man/ Out of his insane self-importance. . . ."

A second factor which influenced Jeffers' outlook was his study of history. From the British archaeologist Flinders Petrie and the Italian philosopher Giovanni Battista Vico, Jeffers drew the concept of cultural cycles and the conviction that cultural or national groupings are inherently unstable and social progress temporary. This view, again, was bolstered by his observations of the inevitable cycles of growth, flowering, and decay in nature. It was given special force by Jeffers' belief, influenced by Oswald Spengler, that Western civilization was already on the downgrade.

Many scientists share Jeffers' objective view of the world but not the intensity of his feeling for the insignificance of humanity or the "beauty of things," his often-used phrase for natural loveliness. The roots of Jeffers' feeling seem to be in the Calvinistic teachings of his father's religion, which proclaimed the glory of God and the nothingness of man. Rejecting his father's Christian God, Jeffers transferred his religious feeling to a new object, a universe whose parts are all "expressions of the same energy," a dynamic universe, ever in strain and struggle, and ever in that process discovering its own nature. In a letter outlining his views, Jeffers wrote, "This whole is in all its parts so beautiful, and is felt by me to be so intensely in earnest, that I am compelled to love it, and to think of it as divine." He went on to say that he felt there was "peace, freedom, I might say a kind of salvation, in turning one's affections toward this one God, rather than inward on one's self, or on humanity, or on human imagination and abstractions. . . ." Jeffers' sole admission of the possibility that humans could have a positive effect was to say that one may "contribute (ever so slightly) to the beauty of things by making one's own life and environment beautiful. . . ." While he granted that such action could include moral beauty, which he called one of the qualities of humanity, for the most part the weight of his emotions was on the side of sad resignation where the human race was concerned, or actual disgust with its frequent moral ugliness.

Jeffers' intensity of feeling for natural beauty and especially for the dynamism of nature was profoundly affected by his lifelong residence on the spectacular Carmel coast. The area is not only ruggedly beautiful, but is also wracked by periodic events reminding one of the awesome power of nature and of man's uncertain tenure on earth: brush fires that sweep the dry hills in late summer and sometimes destroy farms and homes; earthquakes that shudder along the San Andreas fault; fierce winds that torture the picturesque Monterey cypresses; drenching rains that bring floods and dangerous mudslides. These natural events, recalling the fire, earthquake, wind, and deluge of the biblical apocalypse, appear as major instruments of destruction in many of the narratives, and are centrally important, too, in some of the lyrics. Most important, probably, was the sheer beauty of the surroundings, beauty which Jeffers identified as one of the six major themes in his poems in a talk given in 1941 at the Library of Congress. It is possible to imagine Jeffers living on the coast of Ireland, or in the Scottish Hebrides, or on a mountainside, but not in a quiet New England meadow or an industrial city. He chose his landscape, his "inevitable place," and it in turn formed him and became a major actor in his dramas. Today the Carmel/Big Sur area is known as "Jeffers country."

The expression of his basic attitudes, to which Jeffers eventually gave the name "Inhumanism," took three major forms in poetry: dramatic, narrative, and, loosely considered, lyric. The dramatic poetry includes not only a play primarily intended for stage production, Euripedes' *Medea*, but also dramas primarily intended to be read, a Japanese Noh play, and a masque. The narratives and dramas range in length to well above one hundred pages. The lyrics include some poems that are of substantial length—several pages or more. Some poems are mixtures of elements and defy classification.

The narratives and dramas reveal metaphorically—and occasionally through interposed comments—Jeffers' preoccupation with the self-concern and solipsism of the human race. At the same time, they express the poet's sense of the historical cycles of human behavior and of the larger cycle of death and rebirth that Jeffers called, in "Cawdor," the "great Life." To embody these attitudes, Jeffers chose a number of often shocking subjects: incest, murder, rape, self-mutilation because of guilt, suicide, and the sexual feelings of a woman for a horse.

One of the best of the long narratives, the one which caused the greatest initial sensation when it was published with other poems in 1924, is *Tamar*. The setting is an isolated part of the California coast, where the Cauldwell family lives. Circumstances lead the daughter, Tamar, and her brother, Lee, into incest. Later, Tamar learns that her father had committed the same sin with his sister, now long dead. In one strange scene on the beach at night Tamar is possessed sexually by the ghosts of the Indians who once occupied the area; the scene is a kind of descent into death, and after it Tamar is a "flame," self-destructive and demonic, feeling herself doomed because of her breaking of natural laws. She then tempts her father sexually, as if to prove her depravity, although she commits no sexual act with him. Finally, the entire family is consumed in a fire from which they could have saved themselves had not Tamar, her brother, and her suitor, Will Andrews, been acting out the climax of fierce sexual jealousy.

This seemingly fantastic and occasionally lurid drama was based on one or both of the two biblical Tamar stories, and on Percy Bysshe Shelley's *The Cenci* (1820), all of which include incest. These tales in turn, however, are undershadowed by the Greek myth of the creation of the human race: the incest of Heaven and Earth to produce Titan, and Titan's ensuing incest with his mother, Earth, to produce a child. Thus Jeffers has created a modern story based on layers of myth, reminding readers of the powerful libidinal forces that have been repressed by millennia of taboos but never, as Sophocles and Sigmund Freud noted, eliminated from human nightmares. Further, the isolated home of the Cauldwells on Point Lobos allegorically suggests the entire world, and the initial incest has strong overtones of Adam's fall. Thus man's failure to relate himself humbly to his environment, obeying natural laws such as the ban on incest is comparable to Adam and Eve ignoring God's command to know their place in the scheme of things. The expulsion of Adam and Eve from Paradise is comparable to the troubles visited on the little world of the House of Cauldwell. The story, moreover, is a chapter of apocalypse, with fire—persistently invoked throughout as an agent of cleansing destruction—accomplishing the destruction of Judgment Day. It is prophecy inasmuch as it warns against man's self-concern. It is also persistently evocative, as Robert J. Brophy has pointed out (*Robinson Jeffers: Myth, Ritual, and Symbol in His Narrative Poems*, 1973), of the monomyth of the seasonal cycle of death and rebirth. Yet only in relatively recent years have critics paid systematic attention to the complexity of *Tamar* and Jeffers' other narratives.

Those other narratives similarly explore recurrent patterns of human conduct as expressed in folklore, myth, or religion. "Roan Stallion," the poet's most powerful short narrative, is a modern version of the myth of God uniting with a human. This pattern is seen not only in the Christian story of the fatherhood of Jesus, but also in myths from various cultures, especially the Greek tales of Zeus and his sexual encounters—with Leda, when he took the form of a swan; with Antiope, as a satyr; with Europa, as a bull; and others. "The Tower Beyond Tragedy," one of Jeffers' most successful long poems, is a free adaptation of the first two plays of Aeschylus' *Oresteia* (458 B.C.). In "Cawdor," the poet reworks the Hippolytus story of Euripides, adding an element—self-mutilation—from Sophocles' *Oedipus the King* (429-401 B.C.). "The Loving Shepherdess," another relatively early narrative that was well received, is imaginatively based on the Scottish legend of "Feckless Fannie." "Such Counsels You Gave to Me" is built on suggestions from the Scottish ballad "Edward, Edward," which in turn, like all true ballads, invokes deep folk memories. Other narratives explore age-old problems. "Give Your Heart to the Hawks" explores the question of who should administer justice; "Thurso's Landing" considers when, if ever, it is right to take another's life out of pity.

In one of his early long poems—the longest, in fact, at 175 pages—Jeffers did not base his story on myth or folklore, but created a poem that has become itself a kind of literary legend of magnificent failure: *The Women at Point Sur*. It is a violent, brilliant, chaotic, and difficult-to-comprehend story of a mad minister who collects disciples by telling them that there are no more moral rules and that they can do as their hearts, or bodies, desire. The poem did not generally achieve one of its main purposes, which, as Jeffers put it, was to show "the danger of that 'Roan Stallion' idea of 'breaking out of humanity,' misinterpreted in the mind of a fool or a lunatic." The prologue and other parts are impressive, nevertheless, and the poem has a curiously prescient character. Barclay, who commits an incestuous rape to prove that he is beyond good and evil himself, leads his followers into sex orgies. Not very many years later, the Big Sur area of the poem was the scene of sometimes tragic experimentation in sexual behavior amid some of the more extreme communes and "sensitivity institutes." Further, Barclay's corrupting influence on those around him prefigured the monstrous sway that Charles Manson held over the young women who went out from his remote California hideaway to do murder at his bidding.

The nature of the narratives and dramas changed somewhat through the years. In Jeffers' first mature period (his youthful work, when he produced two volumes of conventional verse, is of interest only to specialists), the concentration was on writing modern versions of myths, such as *Tamar*. In the second period, ranging from the late 1920's to about 1935, the narratives were realistic, though still based on older stories. Such scenes as the violation of Tamar by ghostly Indians were no longer written. "Cawdor," "Thurso's Landing," and "Give Your Heart to the Hawks" were in this vein, while "Dear Judas," chronologically a part of the period, a play in the Japanese Noh form, was based on myth and religion. In the late 1930's, Jeffers again concentrated on myth. In two of his least successful narratives, "Solstice" and "Such Counsels You Gave to Me," he focused on what Frederick I. Carpenter (*Robinson Jeffers*, 1962) has called "case histories in abnormal psychology." In the same period Jeffers wrote, "At the Birth of an Age," a philosophical poem, partly in dramatic form, which has as a central figure a self-torturing Hanged God of the universe. One of the most interesting of Jeffers' poems, it is also one of the most complex and difficult, often appealing primarily to the mind, and having some of the same virtues and faults as Shelley's *Prometheus Unbound* (1820).

Jeffers again ventured into the mythic and the supernatural in "The Double Axe," a two-part poem published in 1948. In the first part, "The Love and the Hate," he took an idea from his earlier "Resurrection," a short narrative (1932) about a World War I soldier returned miraculously from the grave. In "The Love and the Hate," Hoult Gore has similarly returned from death in World War II. His denunciation of war and his presentation of the facts about who actually suffers for the pride of patriots and politicians, are sometimes eloquent, but the ghoulishness of the central figure, the walking corpse, is so naturally repellent that it is difficult for the reader to sympathize with the hero emotionally, much less to identify with him. Additionally, there are moments when the writing comes close to unintentional humor, as when

Gore's widow, first seeing him, says he looks "dreadful." The violence of the action, even though it is meant to be cleansing, is not properly prepared for by the buildup of emotions, so that it seems exaggerated and gratuitous. The second half of the poem, "The Inhumanist," is much more successful. In this poem Jeffers creates a new mythical hero, an old man armed with Zeus's double-bitted axe, which is a symbol both of divine destruction and procreation. This Inhumanist has various adventures in the course of a complex and sometimes supernatural story. Despite its flaws, which include prosy passages of bitter political ranting, it is one of the essential poems for anyone wishing to achieve a full knowledge of Jeffers' thought.

"The Double Axe," which dealt a heavy blow to Jeffers' reputation, was succeeded by one other major narrative, another excursion into the supernatural, but this time a generally successful one—"Hungerfield." Written after the crushing blow of Una Jeffers' death, "Hungerfield" tells the story of a man who wrestled with death to save his mother from cancer. This violation of natural laws causes all kinds of other natural disasters to occur, recalling the way that the "miracle drugs" and chemical sprays with which people and farmlands are treated cause unforeseen and often disastrous side effects. The Hungerfield story, which also has mythic references (Hungerfield is a Hercules figure), is framed by Jeffers' personal meditation on the death of his wife, and ends with his reconciliation with it. These framing passages lack the compactness and intense poetic power of Jeffers' best lyrics, but their directness, tenderness, and simplicity carry them past the danger of sentimentality and make them moving and effective.

The lyric poems, which are here taken to include all the shorter poems that are not basically narratives or dramas, celebrate the same things and denounce the same things as the narratives. Being mostly meditations on one subject, they are more intense and unified, and are free of the problems of multilayered poems such as *The Women at Point Sur*. Typically, a Jeffers lyric describes an experience and comments upon it; and it does this in the simple, declarative voice that stamped every poem with his unique signature.

"The Place for No Story," although exceptionally short, is an excellent example. Jeffers opens with a simple description: "The coast hills at Sovranes Creek:/ No trees, but dark scant pasture drawn thin/ Over rock shaped like flame." Then he describes the "old ocean at the land's foot, the vast/ Gray extension beyond the long white violence." He describes a herd of cattle on the slope above the sea, and above that "the gray air haunted with hawks. . . ." Ending this section with a colon, he draws, figuratively and spiritually, a deep breath and simply states:

> This place is the noblest thing I have ever seen
> No imaginable
> Human presence here could do anything
> But dilute the lonely self-watchful passion.

There are many qualities to notice in this simple poem, qualities that will stand for those of scores of other lyrics, meditations, mixed-mode poems, and sections of the narratives and dramas. First, there is the voice. It is simple and colloquial, as characteristically attuned to the rhythms of everyday American speech as anything by Robert Frost. The word order is natural. The diction is simple and dignified, but not formal. It reflects Jeffers' conscious decision to focus on things that will endure. It would have been easily comprehensible in sixteenth century England, and will almost certainly be so for centuries to come. The poem is written in the typical style of the mature Jeffers: no rhyme, no regular metrical pattern. As Jeffers explained, however, he had a sense of pattern that made him disagree with those who called his lines free verse. His feeling, he once wrote, was for the number of beats to the line and also for the quantitative element of long and short syllables. Most of his poems break up into recurring patterns of beats per line—ten and five, six and four, five and three alternations being common. In this poem, less regular than many, there is still a recurrence of four-beat lines, culminating in a pair at the end to make a couplet effect. The longer lines run mostly to six stresses, depending on how the poem is read. Binding the whole together is a subtle pattern of alliteration, a device that Jeffers used with full consciousness of his debt to the strong-stress lines of Anglo-Saxon verse. In the first few lines, for example, the hard "c" of "coast" is repeated in "Creek" (and picked up much later in another stressed word, "cows"); the "s" in "Sovranes" reappears in "scant" and "shaped"; the "d" in "dark" reappears in "drawn"; the "f" of "flame," in "foot"; the "v" of "vast" in "violence"; the "h" in "hills" appears five lines later in "herd," six lines later in "hardly," seven lines later in "haunted" and "hawks." A notable assonance is "old ocean," which works to slow down its line with its long syllables.

In this short lyric, too, are embodied some of Jeffers' key ideas. The ocean's "violence" reminds the reader of the struggle ever-present in the natural world. The contrast between rock, a symbol of endurance, and flame, a symbol of violent change, suggests that even rocks undergo change from the same process of oxidation that produces flame. Above, the hawks are Jeffers' preferred symbol of independence and of the inexorable violence of nature. The poem simply and unaffectedly celebrates beauty, and at the end reminds the reader of the insignificance of human beings in a universe still discovering itself in the "passion" of its dynamic life.

The qualities found in this short lyric are found in abundance in many other poems of varying length. Among the most notable of the short poems not already cited are "To the Stone-Cutters," "Night," "Boats in a Fog," "Noon," "Rock and Hawk," "Love the Wild Swan," "Return," "All the Little Hoofprints," "Original Sin," "The Deer Lay Down Their Bones," and "For Una."

Among the longer lyrics, several are important for a full understanding of the poet. Chief among these is *Apology for Bad Dreams*, Jeffers' *ars poetica*. "Meditation on Saviors" and "De Rerum Virtute" are also important philosophical poems, as is "Margrave," a short narrative framed by an approximately equal amount of meditative lyric. Two large sections of "Cawdor" contain particularly powerful lyric sections. These, "The Caged Eagle's Death-Dream" and "The Old Man's Dream After He Died," have been reprinted in *The Selected Poetry of Robinson Jeffers* (1938).

After passing through a period (1938-1948) during which many of his poems were bitter political harangues, Jeffers achieved a quieter tone in the poems that were posthumously printed in *The Beginning and the End* (1963). They lack the close texture and the intensity, however, of his better poems from earlier years, and tend to become prosy. At the same time, in their increasing concern with astrophysics, the origins of human life, and the terrible prospect that all may end in a nuclear catastrophe, they explore new territory and provide a fitting, relatively serene end to an enormously productive career.

In seeking to place Jeffers in the continuum of American poets, one is drawn to generalizations that often apply surprisingly well to Walt Whitman, who was temperamentally and sometimes philosophically Jeffers' polar opposite. Like Whitman, Jeffers was a technical innovator, developing a typically long, colloquial line and a voice that can be mistaken for no other. Like Whitman, he was often charged, with some justification, with using inflated rhetoric and exaggeration to achieve his effects, and with repetitiveness. Like Whitman, he was a poet of extremes, and for that reason perhaps he will be best appreciated when some of the political and social passions which he stirred have been forgotten. Like Whitman, too, Jeffers had a well-developed set of attitudes toward society and the world. These views put both men in the prophetic stance at times. Like Whitman, Jeffers was deeply religious in a pantheistic way, and so profoundly conscious of the cycle of birth and regeneration that he thought of death as a redeemer.

Many of these characteristics are those of a public poet, a person in a dialogue with his nation and the world about its life and the right way of living. Beyond these qualities, Jeffers had other attributes of the public poet. He was not only prophetic, admonishing and seeking reform in attitudes and behavior, but also apocalyptic, standing apart and reminding his readers of the immanence and possible imminence of worldly destruction. He was historical, reminding them that cultures and nations had risen and fallen before them. He was an early environmentalist, reminding Americans that they were part of a complex cycle of life, and castigating them for their sins against the earth. He was an explorer of the depths probed by Freud and Carl G. Jung—and thus a psychological poet. He was also a mystical poet—the "Caged Eagle's Death-Dream" constituting a supreme illustration.

The process of sifting out and properly appraising the poems in which Jeffers succeeded in his various roles has begun. No single long narrative has been acclaimed by all favorable critics as entirely successful, but it is certain that at least half a dozen, probably led by "Roan Stallion," will survive. Many lyrics and shorter mixed-mode poems, however, are generally esteemed, and it is these poems that already have assured Jeffers a place among the honored writers of the century. Finally, the quality that seems most likely to ensure Jeffers' future stature is his very lack of timeliness. His references are not to ephemera but to rock, hawk, sea, and mountain—things that will be with the world as long as humans are there to perceive their beauty and their significance.

Major publications other than poetry
PLAYS: *Medea*, 1946 (translation); *The Cretan Woman*, 1954.
NONFICTION: *Themes in My Poems*, 1956; *The Selected Letters of Robinson Jeffers, 1897-1962*, 1968 (Ann N. Ridgeway, editor).

Bibliography
Bennett, Melba Berry. *The Stone Mason of Tor House*, 1966.
Brophy, Robert. *Robinson Jeffers: Myth, Ritual and Symbol in His Narrative Poems*, 1973.
Carpenter, Frederick I. *Robinson Jeffers*, 1962.
Coffin, Arthur B. *Robinson Jeffers, Poet of Inhumanism*, 1971.
Everson, William (Brother Antoninus). *Robinson Jeffers: Fragments of An Older Fury*, 1968.
Nolte, William H. *Rock and Hawk: Robinson Jeffers and the Romantic Agony*, 1978.
Powell, Lawrence Clark. *Robinson Jeffers: The Man and His Work*, 1940.
Squires, Radcliffe. *The Loyalties of Robinson Jeffers*, 1956.
Vardamis, Alex A. *The Critical Reputation of Robinson Jeffers*, 1972.

Edward A. Nickerson

SAMUEL JOHNSON

Born: Lichfield, England; September 18, 1709
Died: London, England; December 13, 1784

Principal poems and collection
London, 1738; *The Vanity of Human Wishes*, 1749. *Poems: The Yale Edition of the Works of Samuel Johnson*, 1965 (E. L. McAdam, Jr., and George Milne, editors, volume 6).

Other literary forms
Samuel Johnson was a journalist, essayist, critic, scholar, lexicographer, biographer, and satirist. Early in his career, he wrote reports on the debates in Parliament for *The Gentleman's Magazine*. Until 1762, when he received a pension from the British government, Johnson was a professional writer and wrote what publishers would buy. The most important results of his efforts, in addition to his poetry, were his *Dictionary of the English Language* (1755), *The Rambler* (1750-1752), *The Idler* (1758-1760), and *The History of Rasselas, Prince of Abyssinia* (1759). The *Dictionary* remains one of the outstanding achievements in the study of language. Johnson contracted in 1746 with a group of publishers to write the first comprehensive dictionary of the English language. Nine years later, with the help of only six assistants, he produced a work that is notable for its scholarship and wit. Although scholars fault its etymological notes, its definitions are generally apt and often colored by Johnson's wit, biases, and sound understanding of English usage. *The Rambler* and *The Idler* are composed of periodical essays, which, when combined with those that Johnson wrote for *The Adventurer* (1753), number more than three hundred. The essays discuss literature, religion, politics, and society. They were much admired in Johnson's day, but are less so in the modern era. They are often grave, but rarely dull, and represent some of the finest prose in English. Another important prose work, *Rasselas*, is Johnson's major contribution to fiction. Like Voltaire's *Candide: Or Optimism* (1759), *Rasselas* features a naïve young protagonist whose adventures gradually strip away his illusions. Johnson's work is the less harsh of the two, but is similar in tone.

Johnson's work as a biographer and scholar began early. In 1740, he wrote biographies of Admiral Robert Blake, Sir Francis Drake, and Jean-Philippe Barretier. These works are unoriginal in content. In 1744, he published *Life of Richard Savage*, which was later included in *Lives of the Poets* (1781), although it was often published separately. Savage was a bitter and angry man; Johnson emphasized with dramatic narrative the wrongs society had visited on him. Many years after the *Life of Richard Savage*, Johnson agreed to write a series of prefaces to the works of English poets for a group of booksellers. The result was *Lives of the Poets* (four volumes in 1779 and an additional six volumes in 1781). These essays are marked by Johnson's critical insight and immense knowledge of literature; many are still standard references. Johnson was also an editor, and produced an important edition of Shakespeare with commentary. Some critics have denigrated Johnson's lack of appreciation of Shakespeare's poetry, but his appraisal of the plays is well considered, and his defense of the plays against dogmatic neoclassical criticism is notable for its good sense.

Among Johnson's other significant writings are the political essays *Thoughts on Falkland's Islands* (1771) and *Taxation No Tyranny* (1775), and the account of his travels in Scotland with his young Scottish friend, James Boswell, entitled *Journey to the Western Islands of Scotland* (1775). In these works Johnson displays his hatred of war and political profiteering and his acuteness of observation.

Achievements

The diversity of Johnson's writings can be daunting; he was a novelist, playwright, essayist, journalist, editor, critic, scholar, biographer, lexicographer, etymologist, moralist, social and political commentator, philosopher, and poet. His poem *London* (1738) was published at least twenty-three times during his lifetime, and the popularity of his poetry contributed much to his reputation as the quintessential *man of letters*. In his era, no one had read more of the world's literature than he, and few equaled his literary achievements. In retrospect, Johnson seems to have so dominated the literary life of England that the period from 1750 to 1784 is often called the Age of Johnson.

"Poet" was a term of honor in eighteenth century England. The poet was at the apex of literature, and Johnson took pleasure in being referred to as one. After his death, his reputation as a poet fell from the high esteem of his contemporaries to a level of near disregard. His best-known poetry is the product of intellectual work, not inspiration. The Romantics and their nineteenth century descendants valued emotional and inspirational verse. Johnson's verse is well organized, often satirical, filled with social commentary and moralizing, and more realistically observational than metaphorical; his poetry is well within the Augustan style. In the twentieth century, readers have begun to rediscover Augustan satire, and interest in Johnson's poetry is growing.

He was among the best poets of his day, his verse being dynamic and rich in thought. He believed that poetry should emphasize the contemporary language of the poet; it should be accessible to the poet's contemporary readers. In this belief he is in the same tradition as John Donne, John Dryden, Alexander Pope, and even poets as recent as Karl Shapiro. The language of Johnson's verse is still accessible to readers; it is distinctive in its combination of precision, nearly explosive anger and contempt, and acute observation of the human condition.

Biography

Many writers have suffered, and many more have pretended to suffer, for their art. Samuel Johnson's own suffering in fact made his art necessary. He was born on September 18, 1709 to Michael Johnson, a bookseller, and Sarah (née Ford), who was then forty years old. The labor had been difficult, and Samuel Johnson was, by his own account, born nearly dead. While he was a child he contracted scrofula and smallpox; he was horribly scarred by the diseases and became deaf in one ear and partially blind in one eye. Although his father was a respectable citizen and even gained a small degree of prominence in 1709 as Sheriff of Lichfield, Johnson's ancestors were of humble background. His parents were unhappy with each other, and their mild mutual hostility contributed to the miseries of their son's life.

In spite of his ugliness, poor background, and unhappy family life, Johnson became a leader among his schoolmates. He was not an ideal student; he would neglect his studies, then in great bursts of energy apply himself to learning. Later in life he would write much as he had studied; for example, *Life of Richard Savage* was written in as little as thirty-six hours, and it has been claimed that *Rasselas* was completed in a week. He aspired to be almost anything but a writer. With a small savings he paid for more than a year at Oxford, October, 1728 to December, 1729, but lack of money forced him to leave the school. After his father's death in 1731, he tried teaching. He was temperamentally unsuited for teaching; he gesticulated wildly when lecturing, and his bizarre antics confused his students. David Garrick, the actor, was among his pupils, and later helped Johnson have the verse play *Irene: A Tragedy* (1749) produced. Johnson's next ambition was to become a lawyer, but his poverty and physical infirmities inhibited his studies and his ability to pursue strenuous professions. He turned to writing in order to support himself and his wife.

He married Elizabeth Jervis, the widow of Harry Porter, in 1735. She was nineteen years his senior, but provided him with love, a home, and companionship that helped to stabilize his passionate and explosive personality. Acutely aware of his responsibilities as a husband, Johnson took work where he could find it. He moved to London and persuaded the publisher of *The Gentleman's Magazine*, Edward Cave, to allow him to write for the periodical. During this period of his life he wrote and sold the poem *London*, and tried to interest theater owners in a rough version of *Irene*. As a professional writer who sought to meet the needs of publishers, Johnson wrote essays, reports, poetry, and biographies—whatever would earn him money. *London* was a success and greatly advanced his reputation, but he sold the copyright and profited little from it. His literary labors earned enough for food and a place to live, but he endured bitter poverty.

A group of London publishers contracted with him in 1746 for the *Dictionary of the English Language*, which he completed its compilation seven years later and which was published in 1755. The loyal support of the syndicate of publishers provided him with some small financial security, although his life remained hard. While writing the dictionary with the help of six secretaries, Johnson wrote *The Rambler*, which was published twice weekly from 1750 to 1752. The periodical's reputation was great, but its sales were small. Such was the reputation of the dictionary and *The Rambler* that Johnson became known as "Dictionary Johnson" and "Author of *The Rambler*." In 1749, the poem *The Vanity of Human Wishes* was published. Today it is probably the best known of Johnson's poetic works. Also in that year, David Garrick, Johnson's onetime pupil, by then a famous actor, produced *Irene* at the Drury Lane Theatre. The play lasted for nine nights, a respectable run, and Johnson earned almost two hundred pounds from the production. Subject to depressions in the best of times, Johnson was greatly saddened by the death of his wife in 1752.

From 1755 to 1762, Johnson's most important literary efforts were *The Idler*, which was published from 1758 to 1760 in the *Universal Chronicle*, and *Rasselas*. In 1759, Johnson's mother died. Perhaps her illness and death inspired Johnson to contemplate his youth and its disillusionments. The evident result was *Rasselas*. Some biographers assert that *Rasselas* was written to pay for his mother's funeral, but most scholars disagree. In 1762, Johnson was awarded an annual pension of three hundred pounds, enough to free him from the necessity of labor.

In 1763, Johnson met James Boswell, a young Scot who would become a favorite companion. It is because of Boswell's *Life of Samuel Johnson LL.D.* (1791) that scholars know more about the last twenty years of Johnson's life than they know of the previous fifty-five. Free from financial cares, and afflicted by a variety of physical complaints, Johnson did not write at the prodigious rate that he had when he was younger. His principal literary efforts were *Lives of the Poets*, a series of prefaces to English poets written for a consortium of booksellers, and *Journey to the Western Islands of Scotland*, an account of a tour in 1773 with Boswell. Johnson's poetry during his last years consisted primarily of parodies and burlesques written for friends, and Latin verse, composed mostly for his own contemplation. Always a moody and introspective man, his poetry became private and contemplative in his last years. In public, of course, he sought companionship and good conversation, relishing his status as England's leading man of letters. In private, he had an almost morbid dread of death. He believed that people should, at the peril of their souls, fulfill all of their talents; he was acutely aware of his own superior intellectual powers, and believed that he had not properly made use of them. Once in February, 1784, the dropsy that afflicted him disappeared while he prayed, and he took the relief to be a sign from God and spent the last months of his life in spiritual peace. He died on December 13, 1784, and was buried on December 20 in Westminster Abbey, as befitted a poet.

Analysis

Samuel Johnson wrote two major poetic works: *London* and *The Vanity of Human Wishes*. The remaining verse divides into the play *Irene*, poems in Latin, miscellaneous verse in English, and translations from Greek and Latin. *London* was the most popular of Johnson's poems during his life, and it remains the most accessible to modern audiences. Its language is clear and its images straightforward. Like *London, The Vanity of Human Wishes* is an imitation of the satires of Juvenal, a Latin poet of the first and second centuries. It is widely regarded as Johnson's poetic masterpiece and is Johnson's effort to convey the essence of the Christian ethos through verse and imagery. The density of its images and ideas makes *The Vanity of Human Wishes* difficult to interpret even for experienced critics. *Irene*, on the other hand, yields readily to interpretation through its strong plot, although its verse, while competent, is unremarkable.

Johnson customarily composed his poems mentally before committing them to paper. *London* was composed in this manner; it was written on large sheets of paper in two columns—the left being for the first draft and the right for revisions. Johnson's poetry is firmly in the Augustan tradition, typified in the eighteenth century by the works of Alexander Pope, Jonathan Swift, and Joseph Addison; *London* is characteristically Augustan in its dependence on a Latin model, in this case Juvenal's third satire. When the poem was published, the passages that were derived from Juvenal were accompanied by Juvenal's original lines, which were included at Johnson's request—a common practice at the time. A good edition of *London* will include the relevant Juvenalian passages.

Juvenal's third satire, Johnson's model for *London*, focuses on Rome. In general, Juvenal's satires attack what he perceived to be the immorality of Roman society. In his third satire he cites particulars in the city of Rome itself. Johnson focuses his poem on the city of London and, like Juvenal, cites particulars. He also includes translations from Juvenal's poem and updated versions of some of Juvenal's sentiments. As the accompanying Latin verse shows, Johnson's borrowings are only part of the whole and tend to illustrate the universality of some of the poem's ideas. Too much of *London* is original for it to be simply a translation. For example, Juvenal writes from the point of view of a conservative Roman who believed that his countrymen had grown soft from lack of war and sacrifice, while Johnson writes from the point of view of an eighteenth century Christian who believed that the vices of his age stemmed from his countrymen's failure to recognize the importance of the soul. Johnson was a man of ideas, and his ideas make *London* his own work—

a statement of his views of the city when he was a young man of twenty-eight.

London is written in rhyming iambic pentameter couplets. Johnson believed that blank verse could be sustained only by strong images; otherwise, verse needed clear structure and rhyme. His best poetry exemplifies his ideas about prosody; *London*'s heroic couplets follow the model established by Pope. The poem's language is lively and its ideas flow rapidly. Johnson's condemnations are sharply expressed:

> By numbers here from shame or censure free,
> All crimes are safe, but hated poverty.
> This, only this, the rigid law pursues,
> This, only this, provokes the snarling muse.

The city is portrayed as rife with crime, folly, and injustice. King George II is said to be more interested in Hanover than England and London; learning is said to be unrewarded (a favorite theme of Juvenal); government is said to be grasping while the nation sinks; and the city is characterized as architecturally in bad taste. The satire makes London seem bleak and ugly, but the language is exuberant and makes London's faults seem exciting.

The poem's persona (the speaker) is named Thales, who intends to leave London for Cambria (Wales); he craves solitude and peace. Some scholars have identified Thales as the personification of Richard Savage, who had suffered poverty and indignities in London; he left London in 1739 for Wales. Other scholars maintain that Johnson had not yet met Savage, and that *London* was, after all, published in 1738, a year before Savage's migration. This dispute over seeming minutiae represents a major problem that infects much criticism of Johnson's works. Those who support the notion that Savage is the original for Thales sometimes cite Johnson's assertion that anyone who is tired of London is tired of life. They maintain that the poem's point of view is not representative of Johnson but of Savage. Even some critics who do not assert that Savage was the model for Thales dismiss *London* as insincere—as an exercise that does not reflect Johnson's true love for the city.

Students new to the study of Johnson should be wary of reasoning based on Johnson's views in Boswell's *The Life of Samuel Johnson, LL.D.* Boswell's work is monumental; it has helped to shape the modern view of eighteenth century England. Johnson's opinions as reported by Boswell are forcefully expressed and seemingly permanently set, and even knowledgeable scholars have sometimes read into Johnson's early works the views he held when he was a conservative old man. In fact, like most writers who have been fortunate enough to have long careers, Johnson changed his views as he matured, as he read new works, and as he gained new experiences. As a young man, Johnson was rebellious and angry. He was learned and poor; he disliked the Hanoverian monarchy; and the architecture of London in 1738 could be not only ugly but downright dangerous—poorly built walls sometimes collapsed into the streets. The crowding, poverty, and crime of London would probably have shocked any young person from the country who was experiencing it for the first time; Johnson arrived in London in 1737, and the poem appeared in 1738.

The Vanity of Human Wishes, on the other hand, was written when Johnson was in his middle years. Juvenal's satires still interested him, as they did, according to Boswell, in his late years; and *The Vanity of Human Wishes* is an imitation of Juvenal's tenth satire. In this satire, Juvenal shows that people are unable to perceive their own best interests. Some people wish to be eloquent, even though Cicero was doomed by his own eloquence; others seek power, even though Alexander the Great was undone by power. Wise people, Juvenal says, would let the gods choose what is best for them. Typical of the Latin poet, the tenth satire expresses a conservative Roman's disgust with the foolishness of society in the Empire. The dominant themes in the satire would have appealed to Johnson: anger at a people who neglect the ideals that made them great, dismay at the successes of fools at the expense of supposedly intelligent people, and the notion that society's values were distorted, with learning and wisdom ranking below ignorance and vice.

The ethos of *The Vanity of Human Wishes* is Christian. Johnson replaces Juvenal's notion that people do not choose to do what will do them good with the idea that people choose vainly when they choose material and worldly success. Johnson also replaces Juvenal's notion that wise people let the gods choose for them with the idea that wise people put their lives in God's hands. The tenth satire of Juvenal was popular during the Middle Ages because preachers could convert its criticisms of vice into homilies on the dangers of materialism, and it provides ready material for Johnson's portrait of human life gone astray. Nearly 350 lines of his poem are devoted to discussing how people who seek wealth, power, or other earthly pleasures and rewards, fail to find happiness. The poem is thick with images and requires close reading; it is in large part depressingly negative. Much of human life seems hopeless. Even so, Johnson's scope is remarkable; he reaches beyond the range of *London* and beyond the range of Juvenal's satire; he discusses all human beings, everywhere. He cites Thomas Wolsey's power and wealth, Charles XII of Sweden's ambition, the miserable fates of John Churchill Marlborough, who was debilitated by strokes, and Jonathan Swift, who suffered from a disease similar to senile dementia. Neither power, wealth, ambition, honor, nor intellect mean much in the great scheme of life, and none are proof against misery and humiliation.

Johnson leaps back and forth through time, and from one part of the world to another, in his effort to convey the vastness of his topic and universality of his theme. He asserts:

> Unnumber'd suppliants crowd Preferment's gate,

> Athirst for wealth, and burning to be great,
> Delusive Fortune hears th' incessant call,
> They mount, they shine, evaporate, and fall.

A host of examples are mustered to support Johnson's contention that all earthly human wishes are vain; a reader can feel overwhelmed by the images and arguments that Johnson presents. If one does not read the poem carefully, one might interpret it as a despairing depiction of human endeavors and of lives without hope. Some critics call the poem "stoic," as if the only response to the hopelessness of life as depicted by Johnson were withdrawal and endurance. Such a reading misses the poem's fundamental point and fails to recognize Johnson's rejection of stoicism: "Must helpless man, in ignorance sedate,/ Roll darkling down the torrent of his fate?" No, Johnson answers, because "petitions yet remain,/ Which heav'n may hear, nor deem religion vain." God is the solution to the vanities of humanity. Stoicism demands a retreat into one's self; Johnson advocates that one reach outside himself. An important teaching of Christianity in Johnson's day was that one needed to seek beyond the material world for happiness—that unselfishness would bring enduring rewards. Johnson notes the "goods for man the laws of heav'n ordain," "love," "patience," and "faith." He says, "With these celestial wisdom calms the mind." Just as folly is universal, so too is the answer to folly. God responds to anyone who is devoted to Him.

The Vanity of Human Wishes is grim; the poem reflects Johnson's personality and his concerns, and his unhappy view of the disorder of an unfair world is expressed in relentless images. He was also a Christian, holding out hope for himself and the rest of humanity. His poetic skill is revealed in his shift from a lengthy account of the failures of even the best of people to the simple assertion of God's ability to ease the misery of anyone. He uses the heroic couplet, as in *London*, to give his poem a clear structure. Within that structure he maneuvers ideas with seeming ease and resolves the complex problem of the vanity of human wishes with the poetically elegant answer of the Christian ethos.

Johnson's play *Irene* was begun while he was still a teacher, before he moved to London in 1737, and he continued to work on it sporadically until 1749, when David Garrick produced it under the title *Mahomet and Irene*. The primary source for the play was the *Generall Historie of the Turkes* (1603), by Richard Knolles. The story is filled with intrigue: Mahomet, the Turkish Sultan, falls in love with a Greek Christian, Irene. He offers her wealth, power, and marriage, if she will renounce Christianity and convert to Islam. His followers are unhappy that their leader, who has conquered Constantinople, would fall for a conquered infidel, and they plot his overthrow. Greeks join in the plotting as well. After some soul-searching and passionate scenes, Irene yields to Mahomet and becomes a victim of the play's intrigues. The plot of *Irene* is surprisingly good, given its neglect by modern readers. Its weakness is in its blank verse, which, as Donald Greene notes in *Samuel Johnson* (1970), has a "sledgehammer monotony." Although the play made money during its run as Garrick's production and was reprinted three times while Johnson lived, it was not a critical success. Its verse is unimaginative and dull, unequal to the strengths of both plot and characters. Johnson reveals insight into his characters, particularly the spirutally struggling Irene, and an ability to present an interesting story.

Although *London* and *The Vanity of Human Wishes* are justifiably rated by critics as his best poems, much of Johnson's lesser verse is rewarding. His *Prologue Spoken at the Opening of the Theater in Drury-Lane* (1747), for example, discusses the merits of drama. In addition to writing prologues that are superior to most others, Johnson was a master of the epitaph and elegy. His "Epitaph on Hogarth" is representative of his ability to evoke pathos in a short poem with such lines as: "Here death has clos'd the curious eyes/ That saw the manners in the face." The poem on William Hogarth, the painter, was something of an exercise for Johnson, written as it was in response to Garrick's request for advice on an epitaph requested by Mrs. Hogarth. His "On the Death of Dr. Robert Levet" comes more from his heart. The elegy was written in 1782 after the death of the friend and surgeon who had been living in Johnson's home. The poem presents a picture of a man who was "Officious, innocent, sincere,/ Of ev'ry friendless name the friend." Johnson makes the poem a comment on life in general, both its sorrows and glories, and makes the seemingly humble Levet a representative of the best virtues: sacrifice for others, modesty in material desires, and selfless working to improve the lot of humanity. The poem is united by metaphor ("mine" and "caverns") and theme.

The somber themes of the elegy and epitaph and the weighty themes of the prologues and major poems might suggest that Johnson's verse is devoted exclusively to the unhappy aspects of life. Such a view, however, would be unbalanced. Even in the bitterness of *London* there is witty wordplay; and Johnson had a remarkable taste for stinging humor. He sent to Mrs. Thrale in 1780 a poem about her scapegrace nephew, John Lade, entitled "A Short Song of Congratulation." Lade had recently come into his inheritance, and Johnson lists the various ways that the young man could waste his money. The wit is pointed and accurate; Lade wasted his fortune. Most of Johnson's light verse is extemporaneous, being meant for his friends, rather than for the public, lacking the careful structure of Johnson's other poetry. His Latin poetry, on the other hand, is usually very well-constructed.

Johnson's stature as a poet has varied according to critical fashion. The critics of the Romantic and Victorian periods often dismissed his work as heavy-handed; they favored spontaneity and image over calculation and idea. Johnson was a man of ideas; he thrived on them and loved to toy with them, but his work was also emotional. The critics of the nineteenth century favored lyric poetry over satire and often missed the merits of the poetic tradition in which Johnson's best verse belongs. Twentieth century critics have, in general, rediscovered the virtues of Johnson's prosody. At his best, he fashions his verse with persuasive naturalness. His poetry conveys a powerful vision of the universality of the human condition. *The Vanity of Human Wishes* rightly ranks as one of the best and most important poems of world literature; with *London* and some of the minor poems, taken as a group, it argues powerfully for Johnson's status as a significant poet.

Major publications other than poetry

NOVEL: *The History of Rasselas, Prince of Abyssinia*, 1759.

SHORT FICTION: *The Rambler*, 1750-1752; *The Adventurer*, 1753-1754; *The Idler*, 1758-1760.

PLAY: *Irene: A Tragedy*, 1749.

NONFICTION: *Voyage to Abyssinia*, 1735 (translation); *Commentary* on Pope's *Essay on Man*, 1738-1739 (translation); *Marmer Norfolciense*, 1739; *A Compleat Vindication of the Licensers of the Stage*, 1739; *Life of Richard Savage*, 1744; *Miscellaneous Observations on the Tragedy of Macbeth*, 1745; *Dictionary of the English Language*, 1755; *The Plays of William Shakespeare*, 1765; *The False Alarm*, 1770; *Thoughts on Falkland's Islands*, 1771; *The Patriot*, 1774; *Taxation No Tyrany*, 1775; *Journey to the Western Islands of Scotland*, 1775; *Lives of the Poets*, 1779-1781.

MISCELLANEOUS: *The Works of Samuel Johnson*, 1787-1789.

Bibliography

Amis, George T. "The Style of *The Vanity of Human Wishes*," in *Modern Language Quarterly*. XXXV (1974), pp. 16-29.

Bate, Walter Jackson. *Samuel Johnson*, 1977.

Boswell, James. *The Life of Samuel Johnson, LL.D.*, 1791.

Boulton, James T. *Johnson: The Critical Heritage*, 1971.

Bronson, Bertrand H. *Johnson Agonistes and Other Essays*, 1946.

Eliot, T. S. "Johnson as Critic and Poet," in *On Poetry and Poets*, 1957.

Greene, Donald. *Samuel Johnson*, 1970.

Krutch, Joseph Wood. *Samuel Johnson*, 1944.

Kupersmith, William. "'More like an Orator than a Philosopher': Rhetorical Structure in *The Vanity of Human Wishes*," in *Studies in Philology*. LXXII (1975), pp. 454-472.

Voitle, Robert. *Samuel Johnson the Moralist*, 1961.

Wiesenthal, Alan J. "On the Literary Value of Samuel Johnson's Latin Verse," in *Humanistica Lovaniensia*. XXVIII (1979), pp. 294-301.

Kirk H. Beetz

BEN JONSON

Born: Westminster(?), England; June 11, 1573(?)
Died: Westminster, England; August 6, 1637

Principal collections

Works, 1616 (includes *Epigrams* and *The Forest*, two sections of non-dramatic verse); *Works*, 1640-1641 (includes *Underwoods*, a section of non-dramatic verse); *Ben Jonson*, 1925-1952 (C. H. Hereford, Percy Simpson, and Evelyn Simpson, editors, includes *Ungathered Verse*).

Other literary forms

Ben Jonson's fame has rested mainly on his comic drama, especially on the masterpieces of his maturity, *Volpone* (1605), *Epicœne: Or, The Silent Woman* (1609), *The Alchemist* (1610), and *Bartholomew Fair* (1614). Surviving earlier comedies are *The Case Is Altered* (1597?), *Every Man in His Humour* (1598), *Every Man out of His Humour* (1599), *Cynthia's Revels* (1600), *Poetaster* (1601), and *Eastward Ho!* (1605, with George Chapman and John Marston). Later comedies are *The Devil Is an Ass* (1616), *The Staple of News* (1626), *The New Inn* (1629), *The Magnetic Lady* (1632), and *A Tale of a Tub* (1633). Jonson wrote two tragedies, *Sejanus* (1603) and *Catiline* (1611). Two uncompleted works date apparently from the end of his life: the pastoral *The Sad Shepherd* and the tragedy *Mortimer His Fall* (only a few pages).

Jonson's court masques and entertainments may conservatively be said to number about thirty, differing tallies being possible depending on whether minor entertainments of various kinds are counted. Important titles include *The Masque of Blackness* (1605), *The Golden Age Restored* (1616), and *The Gypsies Metamorphosed* (1621). Besides plays, masques, and original non-dramatic verse, Jonson wrote and translated a few other works which help to place him in the Renaissance humanistic tradition; all were first published in the 1640-1641 *Works*. As a vernacular humanist, Jonson wrote *The English Grammar* (1640); he translated Horace's *Ars Poetica* (*The Art of Poetry*) in 1640; finally, he compiled and translated extracts from classical and modern authors, mostly having to do with ethics, education, and rhetoric; the collection is entitled *Discoveries* (1641).

Achievements

Jonson's achievement as a writer of verse can best be summarized by saying that he founded English neoclassicism. Jonson, of course, wrote several decades before what is usually thought of as the neoclassic age, but his work clearly foreshadows that of John Dryden and Alexander Pope. His, like theirs, was a mode of poetry generally imitative of ancient Roman forms, concerned, as important Roman writers had been, with behavior on a specifically human stage of action, and sometimes heroic, often satirical, in tone and stance.

Biography

Benjamin Jonson's father, a minister, died a month before his son's birth. Ben's mother remarried, apparently fairly soon thereafter, the stepfather being a master bricklayer of Westminster. "A friend" enrolled Jonson at Westminster School, but (as he told William Drummond) he was "taken from" school at about the age of sixteen and "put to" a "Craft," presumably brick-laying. Unable to "endure" this occupation, Jonson escaped briefly into the wars with The Netherlands. The next few years (roughly, his early twenties) are the most obscure of Jonson's life. At some point during this time he married and began having children, although practically nothing is known about his wife or family.

Jonson reappears in the late 1590's in theatrical records as an actor and part-time playwright. In these years Jonson was repeatedly at odds with the law, usually because of his involvement with satirical or political drama. He also attracted the authorities' hostility through his conversion to Roman Catholicism. (Eventually he returned to the Church of England, and later in life expressed, above all, distaste for those who claimed complete theological certainty.) In the series of comedies of "humours" beginning with *Every Man in His Humour*, Jonson coined an original form of satirical comedy based on the caricature of psychological types. In 1600 to 1601 he temporarily aban-doned the open-air "public" playhouses to present his "comical satires" at the more fashionable indoor "private" theater at Blackfriars. The move was part of the provocation of the "stage quarrel" or "war of the theaters," in which Jonson, Thomas Dekker, and John Marston traded plays lampooning one another. Jonson's earliest datable nondramatic poetry also belongs to these years. From the first, Jonson wrote occasional and panegyric verse addressed to the aristocracy, invoking their patronage.

The first decade and a half of the seventeenth century were the years of Jonson's superb creativity and greatest popularity as a playwright. During those years he was in social contact with fellow playwrights such as William Shakespeare, and also with scholars such as William Camden and John Selden. Jonson's associations, however, were not limited to the theatrical and the learned; he was steadily employed as the writer of court masques throughout the reign of James I. Both the King and the aristocrats at the court responded to Jonson's work for many years with notable offers of support. The years from 1616 through 1624 probably marked the height of his prestige. In 1616 he published his *Works* in folio. A royal pension came in the same year and, in 1619, an honorary degree from Oxford. Also gratifying was the gathering around Jonson of the "Tribe of Ben," a circle of poetic "Sons," including Thomas Carew and Robert Herrick, who adopted him as their mentor.

The accession of Charles I to the throne in 1625 ended Jonson's tenure as regular writer of masques for the court, and in other respects also the last dozen years of Jonson's life contrast with the preceding successful decades. At some points during these last years, he was clearly in financial need, and in 1628 he suffered a stroke. He was writing comedies again for the popular stage, but none of them won much acclaim. Against such bleak circumstances, however, stands a persistence of poetic energy, embodied in much outstanding verse attributable to these years. Jonson held the regard of his "Sons" until his death in 1637, and beyond: one of them, Sir Kenelm Digby, finally assembled and published Jonson's later, along with his earlier, *Works* in 1640-1641.

Analysis

Until the last few decades, attention to Ben Jonson's poetry focused largely on the famous songs and the moving epitaphs on children. Such choices were not ill-advised, but they are unrepresentative. The works in these modes certainly rank among Jonson's most successful, but they differ in tone from Jonson's norm.

Songs such as "Kiss me, sweet: the wary lover" and "Drink to me only with thine eyes" evoke emotions beyond the world of reason or fact, partly through reference to extravagant gestures and implausible experiences: hundreds and thousands of kisses, a wreath that will not die after the beloved has breathed on it. Through rhythms that are stronger and less interrupted than Jonson usually created, the songs activate the capacity to respond sensually and irrationally to language. Some of them create magical secret worlds where sense and emotion are to be experienced in disregard of troubling or qualifying context (the "silent summer nights/ When youths ply their stol'n delights" in "Kiss me, sweet: the wary lover"). Exactly such worlds are created, but also subjected to critique, in *Volpone* and *The Alchemist*.

The epitaphs, particularly those on Jonson's own children ("On my First Son," "On my First Daughter") are so effective because in them subjective emotions strain against rational conviction. Jonson's statement in each of these poems is doctrinal and exemplary, involving resignation to the will of God, but part of the power of the affirmation of belief arises from Jonson's undertone of grief over which faith has won out. Regret and despair have not been reasoned away but are being rationally controlled; consolation is not easy.

Such richly concentrated poems obviously deserve attention; that they should have received exposure to the virtual exclusion of Jonson's less lyrical or emotive verse, however, perhaps represents a holdover from Romantic or Victorian taste for rhapsodic expressions of feeling and imaginative vision in poetry. In fact, the renewal of contact with the Metaphysical sensibility achieved by T. S. Eliot and other critics in the 1920's and 1930's, which brought about the displacement of Victorian approaches to a number of seventeenth century writers, did not do so, immediately or directly, in the case of Jonson as a nondramatic poet. Some of Jonson's works are recognizably close to the secular reaches of John Donne's writing, but the speaker's psychological self-discovery through metaphor, so often the business of a Donne poem, is only occasionally Jonson's way. The contrast is especially clear between Jonson's poetic range and the realm of the meditative, intense, often all-but-private Metaphysical religious lyric. Jonson wrote very few strictly devotional poems; the ode "To Heaven" is probably the only strikingly successful work that could bear that label. In poems such as the ode to Sir Lucius Cary and Sir Henry Morison and the funeral elegies, where the afterlife is mentioned, the relation of humanity as such to divinity is not the real focus of attention. The poems involve tensions mainly between diverse human levels, between more ordinary experience on the one hand and, on the other, an excellence or superiority of nature which Cary, Morison, Lady Jane Pawlet, and the other exemplary figures achieve.

At most, only on the peripheries of Jonson's nondramatic verse can it be seen to approximate pure emotive lyricism, or can be cast in Metaphysical terms. Only very recently has criticism achieved a modern reunderstanding of Jonson's achievement, involving a strongly positive evaluation of his central, typical poetic work. Jonson emerges in this recent criticism as decisively a neoclassic artist, the intellectual background of whose poetry is Renaissance humanism.

Jonson appears as a humanistic thinker in his *Discoveries*, and his career reflected humanistic motivations and aspirations. Fundamentally, Jonson conceived of learning, thought, and language as phases of the active life of man. Humanists conceived of education as the initiation of patterns of wise and effective behavior in the student's life. Humanistic education was largely linguistic, because of the traditional importance of the persuasive linguistic act, the centrality of oratory (or, for the Renaissance, the counseling of the prince and nobles) in the repertory of practical, political skills. Patterns both of moral behavior in general and of speech specifically were normally learned through imitation of the deeds and words of figures from the past; for most humanists, and very definitely for Jonson, this did not mean that modern men were supposed to become mere apes of their predecessors, but rather that, through first following models, men should exercise and organize their own capacities to a point where they could emulate and rival the ancients, becoming effective on their own terms as the ancients were on theirs.

As a nonaristocratic humanist in a stratified society, Jonson essentially followed a pattern marked out since the time of Thomas More and Thomas Elyot early in the preceding century when he attached himself to noble households and the court. Debarred by birth from directly wielding the largest measure of power in his society, he engaged in action obliquely by speaking to the powerful, counseling and offering praise to encourage the elite in the wise conduct of life and authority. This was the light in which Jonson saw his masques, not only as celebrations but also as reminders of ideals such as justice which should inform the court's activity. A great many of Jonson's moralizing poems addressed to noblemen and others also clearly exhibited actual hortatory intent.

Jonson's thought includes, as one might expect, special factors that set it off somewhat from humanism as it appears in other contexts. For one thing, while Jonson was not an unbeliever, it is certainly true that his humanism does not merge clearly and continuously into moralistic, pastoral Christianity, as had that of Desiderius Erasmus a hundred years before. The ethical universe of *Discoveries* is one of Roman, not obtrusively Christian virtues; if anything, Jonson looks forward toward later secular rationalism. Another characteristic of Jonson's humanism is the traces of influence from Seneca and Roman Stoicism, apparent in his writing, as elsewhere in early seventeenth century English expression. A main effect of Senecan influence on Jonson seems to have been to encourage a concern with and regard for what can best be called integrity; that is, the correlation of an individual's behavior with his inner nature rather than with outward circumstance. Such concern naturally belonged with the Senecan concept of specifically linguistic behavior which *Discoveries* expresses—a heightened awareness of style as emerging from and conveying an image of the "inmost" self.

Jonson's neoclassic verse is the poetic cognate of his quite secular, somewhat Senecan version of humanism. Splitting the relation into separate aspects only for the sake of analysis, one can say that in form Jonson's poems are above all linguistic acts, the talk of a persona to an implied (often, a designated) human audience. In content, the poems are orderings of levels or modes of human behavior.

Jonson's "An Epistle answering to One that asked to be Sealed of the Tribe of Ben" is identified by its title in terms of the act of communication that it imitates, the letter. Relatively few of Jonson's titles actually include the word "epistle," but many of them involve, or even simply consist of, the designation of an addressee—"To Katherine Lady Aubigny," "To Sir Robert Wroth," and so on. Thus the reader is asked to be aware of many of Jonson's poems not primarily in terms of any myths they may relate or images they may invoke, but as linguistic action, the linguistic behavior of a human speaker toward a human audience.

The fiction of speaker and audience is not an inert element but has an impact on the poem's other aspects. Many qualities of style are conditioned by the character of the addressee and his relation to the speaker. In the "Epistle to Master John Selden," the speaker states that he feels free to use a curt, "obscure," at times almost telegraphic style because "I know to whom I write": he knows that Selden is not only intelligent but is also at home with the speaker's ways of thinking. Generally, the grandiloquence, expansiveness, and elaborate structure of public oratory will rarely be appropriate for an epistle or other poem addressed by one person to another.

Jonson's style in "An Epistle answering to One that asked to be Sealed of the Tribe of Ben" is fairly typical of that in a number of his poems. His diction is generally colloquial; Edmund Bolton's characterization of Jonson's "vital, judicious and practicable language" (in Bolton's *Hypercritica*, c. 1618) is an excellent general description of the style. Syntactic units in Jonson's poems are by and large brief and stopped abruptly so that one jumps (or stumbles) from clause to clause rather than making easy transitions. Units are typically not paired or otherwise arranged symmetrically in relation to one another. The effect in "An Epistle answering to One that asked to be Sealed of the Tribe of Ben" is one of rather blurting, unpremeditated speech, propelled by some emotional pressure. Structurally, too, the poem seems unpremeditated, beginning with appropriate introductory comments to the would-be disciple to whom Ben is writing, then falling away into contemptuous griping about phony elements in Jonson's society, circling down into what reads like underlying anxiety about Jonson's personal situation—and coming through this human situation to a now almost heroic assertion of what it means to be Ben or one sealed of his tribe.

In other poems, the style varies, within a generally informal range. Jonson's meaning can in fact be obscure when the syntax is very broken or a great deal of meaning is concentrated in one phrase; the effect is often that of a rather impatient intelligence, not using more words than it needs to communicate meaning to its immediate addressee. In extreme cases, the reader may feel like an outsider reading a communication not meant for him (see, for example, the "Epistle to Sir Edward Sackville"). Such privacy, immured by style, sets Jonson off somewhat from Augustan neoclassic writers such as Alexander Pope, who usually engage in smoother and more public address.

Entitling the poem an "Epistle," besides drawing attention to its character as a linguistic act, also of course associates it with a generic tradition. Seneca was the most influential classical practitioner of the moral epistle as a prose form, Horace of the form in verse. Jonson's epistles and many of his other poems evoke these authors' works in content and style, sometimes through specific allusion. Clearly related to classical tradition, yet utterly topical and personal (with its references to the politics of "Spain or France" and to Jonson's employment as a writer of masques), "An Epistle answering to One that asked to be Sealed of the Tribe of Ben" is a successful act of humanistic imitation. Overt reference to tradition reveals the moral statement of Jonson's poetry in relation to the whole body of classical moral wisdom—and implies that Jonson is not afraid of the juxtaposition.

The particular wisdom of this poem is conveyed most clearly in the description of the course of conduct Jonson has "decreed" for himself, which comes after the middle of the poem's descriptions of a social environment of indulgence of appetite, empty talk, and illusory "Motions." Jonson's resolve is to

"Live to that point . . . for which I am man/ And dwell as in my Center as I can." The image is one of withdrawal from concern for meaningless external situations; it is also a picture of a life standing in relation to some firm, definite principle, as opposed to the poem's earlier images of unfounded judgments and groundless chatter.

The ideas of withdrawal and of a "Center" within the personality are clearly reminiscent of Seneca and Horace. The most characteristic aspect of the poem's meaning is that it consists of definitions not so much of the ideal principle itself as of the behavior which is or is not oriented to it. Jonson is not much concerned with describing the Center except as such, as a point from which surrounding space takes orientation. He is concerned with describing centeredness, and distinguishing it from shapeless and unfocused conditions; or, to return from geometry to humanity, with describing what it is like to operate on a firm moral basis, and distinguishing this from the "wild Anarchy" in which those outside the Tribe of Ben live.

The focus on behavior which is or is not guided, rather than on the available guiding transcendent principle, corresponds to the specifically secular emphasis of Jonson's humanism. There is an almost (though certainly not quite) agnostic quality in Jonson's almost interchangeable references to the "point," the "Center," "heaven," and "reason" as the source of his wisdom and strength. Clearly it is the exemplification of those qualities in life that interests him. Such an interest makes Jonson stand out as strikingly modern against the backdrop, for example, of the highly articulated ideal world of Edmund Spenser; it links Jonson forward to the essence of English neoclassicism, such as in Pope's ethically oriented satires and moral essays.

It should be noted that the movement toward the Center involves choice and effort: Jonson must decree it to himself, and even those who have been once sealed to the tribe of Ben have still to fear the shame of possibly stumbling in reason's sight. For good or evil, no destiny holds Jonson's human beings in place. The ideal principle is not only vaguely defined, but it is merely an available, not a controlling factor.

Like the epistles and other more or less epistolary longer poems, Jonson's epigrams are, in form, primarily linguistic acts. They are comments "on" or "to" someone. They are self-consciously brief remarks, aiming to capture or essentialize a character—sometimes, implicitly, to reduce an object to its true dimensions (many of Jonson's epigrams are satirical).

The epigrammatic mode is closely related to the epistolary in Jonson's practice and in the tradition out of which he writes. Martial, the Roman epigrammatist whom Jonson regularly imitated, conceived of his works as epistles in brief. Jonson's style has the same constituents. The broken syntax sometimes seems part of epigrammatic compression; sometimes it promotes a casualness which is part of Jonson's reduction and dismissal of a satirized personality, as in Epigram 21 ("On Reformed Gamester").

The pentameter couplets in which Jonson writes not only the epigrams but the great bulk of his neoclassic verse are derived partly from normal English practice for nonlyric poetry going back through Geoffrey Chaucer. They are also, however, influenced by a classical form, the elegiac distich . . . a prosodic vehicle used by, among others, Martial. Readily recognizable and essentially symmetrical, the form tends to stand as a strong balancing, controlling, ordering presence in the poetry in which it appears. Part of its potential is as a structure for concentrated, gnomic, almost proverbial utterance, easy for the reader to carry away in his mind; this potential is best realized when the couplet is a tightly closed unit, as is normally the case in Pope.

Jonson uses the form in the several ways just mentioned. Couplet order underscores orderly, almost (for Jonson) patterned, praise of a firmly centered man in Epigram 128 ("To William Roe"). Some epigrams consist of single gnomic couplets (Epigram 34, "Of Death"), and others are memorable for neat, closed-couplet wit (Epigram 31, "On Banck the Usurer"). Both Jonson's prestige and his virtuoso skill in testing the couplet's range of uses were important in establishing it as the standard neoclassic prosodic structure. Jonson's most characteristic way of exploiting the couplet, however, was not simply to employ, but simultaneously to violate, its order, to write across the prosodic structure as if in disregard of it. Actually, more often than not, in Jonson's verse, syntactic and phrasal breaks do not come at such points within a line as to facilitate the prosodic caesura, nor are they matched with line endings or even the ends of the couplets themselves (see for example Epigram 46, "To Sir Luckless Woo-all"). The couplet may be opposed by meaning, along with grammar: antitheses and other logical and rhetorical structures work at cross purposes with the prosody (Epigram 11, "On Some-Thing, that Walks Some-Where").

In such circumstances, the couplet does not cease to be an obtrusive form. Jonson maintains the reader's awareness of it, precisely as a structure that is not managing to control or limit the autonomy of his grammar, rhetoric, and logic. The latter, of course, are the elements of the oratorical presence in the poetry—of Jonson's voice or speech. The net effect is to enhance the sense of the independent liveliness of the speaking persona, his freedom to move about, to understand and to explain in his own way, on his own terms. Jonson's handling of the couplet implies through form a quite radical version of secular humanism, a sense of the detachment of linguistic action (and of man the linguistic actor) from any containing structure.

Many of the same kinds of content are present in the epigrams as in the epistolary writings. The epigrammatic image of William Roe's stable personality, mentioned earlier, is obviously cognate with Ben's self-image in "An Epistle answering to One that asked to be Sealed of the Tribe of Ben," as are such portrayals as those of Sir Henry Nevil (Epigram 109), William, Earl of Pembroke (102), and Sir Thomas Roe (98). (The latter contains one of

Jonson's more gnomic statements of the concept of the inner-directed and self-sufficient man: "Be always to thy gathered self the same/ And study conscience, more than thou would'st fame.") Satire, often a phase in the epistles, can fill entire epigrams. Something, that Walks Somewhere, Sir Voluptuous Beast (Epigrams 35 and 36) and Don Surly (Epigram 38) are incisively but fully realized satiric characters, clearly inhabitants of the same world as the "humour" characters Corbaccio and Epicure Mammon in Jonson's plays. Something, that Walks Somewhere, the lord who walks in "clothes brave enough," "buried in flesh, and blood," unwilling to do and afraid to dare, is one of Jonson's most powerful pictures of pointless, disorganized life—almost of disorganized protoplasm. Jonson suggested in many indirect ways that he regarded Horace as his mentor, and his work certainly has many Horatian traits, but his satire sometimes seems to belong less in the Horatian than in the harsher Juvenalian category.

"To Penshurst," one of Jonson's most famous poems, celebrates a different kind of relatedness from the internal centering discussed so far. Here human life is benign because it stands within what men have recently learned to call an ecosystem: a web of connections between elements that feed and feed off one another and through interaction perpetuate one another's well-being. At Penshurst, the Sidney family's country estate, nature freely delivers its supply into the Sidneys' hands; fish and birds "officiously" serve themselves up; but here and even more in the very similar poem "To Sir Robert Wroth," one feels that the humans could have a harvesting function, culling what sometimes seems almost like a glut of natural abundance. In any case, the human lords of Penshurst themselves stand as the basis of further relations, providing a social center to which neighbors from a whole community and guests from farther away "come in." The neighbors bring even more food, and the "provisions" of Penshurst's "liberal board" flow back to them. The system yields more than it can use, and the superflux passes to the unenvied guest and is there, ready to be offered to the king, the regulator of a larger system and community, when he happens into this particular sphere. The system, though nature flows through it, is not mindless. From Penshurst's lady's "huswifery" up through "The mysteries of manners, arms and arts" which the house's children are learning, specifically human roles and human activities have their place in this strong and ample natural and human network; in fact, the sophisticated culture of an ancestral figure of the house, Sir Philip Sidney, can be alluded to without seeming out of place here.

A close modern analog to "To Penshurst" is W. H. Auden's "In Praise of Limestone," where man also meshes with landscape in a perfect way; Auden's description of the limestone system, however, is interrupted by accounts of less pleasing, more technological adjustments of the relation. In "To Penshurst," on the other hand, contrasting satiric pictures or references have less share than in almost any of Jonson's works. Only a few lines, mainly at the poem's beginning and end, succinctly insert Jonson's usual distinctions. Penshurst is Edenic. One is left with the uneasy feeling that the poem's being so much anthologized may be bound up with its being, for Jonson, atypically untroubled.

Jonson's ode "To the Immortal Memory and Friendship of that Noble Pair, Sir Lucius Cary and Sir H. Morison" stands near the beginning of the history of English efforts to imitate Pindar's odes. It has a complex and stately stanzaic structure. Nevertheless, many traits are carried over from Jonson's epigrammatic and epistolary style, in particular the tendency toward syntax that is at odds with prosodic divisions, of which the poem contains egregious examples: for instance, a stanza break comes in the middle of the name "Ben/ Jonson." An epic, "Heroologia," which Jonson planned, would probably have represented another extension to a new genre of his characteristic manner and ethical matter. The epic was to be in couplets and was to deal with "the Worthies of his country, roused by fame" (reports William Drummond). Like Pope, Jonson actually wrote a mock-epic rather than the serious one; Jonson's work is the "merdurinous" "On the Famous Voyage" (Epigram 133).

The ode to Cary and Morison is extreme in imagery as well as in syntactic-prosodic tension. It opens with a notorious image, that of the "infant of Saguntum" who retreated back to the womb before it was "half got out," appalled by the horror and devastation of wartime scenes into which it was being born. Jonson goes on to surprise conventional taste even further by suggesting that this vaginal peripety represents a "summ'd" "circle . . . of deepest lore, could we the Center find." References to circle and center of course bring along a whole train of important imagery and structure in Jonson, as well as alluding to the structure of the whole poem, with its repeated peripeteia of "Turn," "Counter-Turn," and "Stand."

The will to shock, or at least to write in uncompromisingly extraordinary ways, may indirectly express the speaker's grief and sense of loss (the poem's occasion is Morison's death). It is certainly connected with a larger demand to see life in an unconventional way, which is the poem's essential consoling strategy. (Jonson speaks of the "holy rage" with which Morison "leap'd the present age"; readers are asked to do the same thing, in the same mood.) The distinction that Jonson insists on is between visions of life as "space" and as "act." In terms of the former—sheer duration—Morison's life was indeed lamentably cut off: he lived barely into his twenties. In terms of "act," Morison's life was perfect:

> A Soldier to the last right end
> A perfect Patriot, and a noble friend,
> But most a virtuous Son.
> All Offices were done
> By him, so ample, full and round,
> In weight, in measure, number, sound

As, though his age imperfect might appear,
His life was of Humanity the Sphere.

This is, notably, purely secular consolation. There are later references to a "bright eternal day," but it has less to do with Christian Paradise than with a pagan heaven of commemoration, in which Morison (and Cary) may persist as an "Asterism," a constellation. The poem's contrast with "Lycidas" marks the distance between John Milton's more old-fashioned Christian humanism and Jonson's untheological mind.

Jubilation, rather than lamentation, over Morison's perfection of "act" is, like most of Jonson's higher choices, not easy to maintain. The speaker's own "tongue" "falls" into mourning at one point. Cary, Morison's great friend who survives him and to whom the poem is at least in part addressed, is exhorted to "call . . . for wine/ And let thy looks with gladness shine"—and to maintain connection. Like the centered men of the epigrams and epistles, and like the Sidneys of Penshurst, Cary is to act in relation, to "shine" on earth in conjunction with Morison's now heavenly light. The function of the poem vis-à-vis Cary is to establish this relation for him, and the broken but single name of Ben Jonson bridges over precisely the two stanzas where the relation of the two friends is most fully discussed.

The poem includes a satirical picture. Contrasting with the vital life of act, the vacuous life of space is personified as a futile careerist, "buoy'd . . . up" in the end only by the "Cork of Title." More than by alternation of satiric and positive images, however, the poem works by a tension constant throughout: the tension between the naturalistic sense of death as an end, which is never really lost, and the other vision which Jonson is insisting upon. The poem is a celebration of secular heroism. It depicts that quality in its subjects ("Nothing perfect done/ But as a Cary, or a Morison"), enacts it in its language, and demands it of its readers. The tension and energy which the poem displays are the reasons for reading Jonson's verse.

Major publications other than poetry

PLAYS: *The Case Is Altered*, 1597?; *Every Man in His Humour*, 1598; *Every Man out of His Humour*, 1599; *Cynthia's Revels*, 1600; *Poetaster*, 1601; *Sejanus*, 1603; *The King's Entertainment in Passing to his Coronation*, 1603 (masque); *The Masque of Blackness*, 1605; *Volpone*, 1605; *Eastward Ho!*, 1605 (with George Chapman and John Marston); *The Masque of Beauty*, 1608; *The Masque of Queens*, 1609; *Epicœne: Or, The Silent Woman*, 1609; *The Alchemist*, 1610; *Catiline*, 1611; *Oberon, the Fairy Prince*, 1611 (masque); *Bartholomew Fair*, 1614; *The Devil Is an Ass*, 1616; *The Golden Age Restored*, 1616 (masque); *Pleasure Reconciled to Virtue*, 1618 (masque); *The Gypsies Metamorphosed*, 1621 (masque); *The Staple of News*, 1626; *The New Inn*, 1629; *Chloridia*, 1630 (masque); *The Magnetic Lady*, 1632; *A Tale of a Tub*,

1633.

NONFICTION: *The English Grammar*, 1640; *Ars Poetica*, 1640 (*The Art of Poetry*, translation); *Discoveries*, 1641 (compiler and translator).

Bibliography
Barish, Jonas A. *Ben Jonson and the Language of Prose Comedy*, 1960.
Greene, Thomas M. "Ben Jonson and the Centered Self," in *Studies in English Literature*. X (1970), pp. 325-348.
Herford, C. H., Percy Simpson, and Evelyn Simpson, eds. *Ben Jonson*, 1925-1952.
McEuen, Kathryn Anderson. *Classical Influence on the Tribe of Ben*, 1939.
McLean, Hugh. "Ben Jonson's Poems: Notes on the Ordered Society," in *Essays in English Literature from the Renaissance to the Victorian Age. Presented to A. S. P. Woodhouse*, 1964.
Miner, Earl. *The Cavalier Mode from Jonson to Cotton*, 1971.
Orgel, Stephen. *The Jonsonian Masque*, 1965.
Parfitt, George. *Ben Jonson: Public Poet and Private Man*, 1976.
Peterson, Richard S. *Imitation and Praise in the Poems of Ben Jonson*, 1981.
Piper, William Bowman. *The Heroic Couplet*, 1969.
Spanos, William V. "The Real Toad in the Jonsonian Garden: Resonance in the Nondramatic Poetry," in *Journal of English and Germanic Philology*. LXVIII (1969), pp. 1-23.
Summers, Joseph H. *The Heirs of Donne and Jonson*, 1970.

John F. McDiarmid

JAMES JOYCE

Born: Rathgar, Dublin, Ireland; February 2, 1882
Died: Zurich, Switzerland; January 13, 1941

Principal poems and collections
Chamber Music, 1907; *Pomes Penyeach*, 1927; "Ecce Puer," 1932.

Other literary forms
Although James Joyce published poetry throughout his career (*Chamber Music*, a group of thirty-six related poems, was in fact his first published book), it is for his novels and short stories that he is primarily known. These works include *Dubliners* (1914), a volume of short stories describing what Joyce saw as the moral paralysis of his countrymen: *A Portrait of the Artist as a Young Man* (1916), a heavily autobiographical account of the growing up of a writer in Ireland at the end of the nineteenth century and the beginning of the twentieth; *Ulysses* (1922), a novel set in Dublin in 1904, recounting the day-long adventures of Leopold Bloom, a modern-day Odysseus who is both advertising man and cuckold, Stephen Dedalus, the young artist of *A Portrait of the Artist as a Young Man* now grown somewhat older, and Molly Bloom, Leopold's earthy wife; and *Finnegans Wake* (1939), Joyce's last published work, not a novel at all in the conventional sense, but a world in itself, built of many languages and inhabited by the paradigmatic Earwicker family.

Achievements
Joyce's prose works established his reputation as the most influential writer of fiction of his generation and led English prose fiction from Victorianism into modernism and beyond. To this body of work, Joyce's poetry is an addendum of less interest in itself than it is in relationship to the other, more important, work. At the same time, in the analysis of Joyce's achievement it is impossible to ignore anything that he wrote, and the poetry, for which Joyce reserved some of his most personal utterances, has its place along with the play *Exiles* (1918)—now seen as more important than it once was—and the essays, letters, and notebooks.

Biography
The life of James Joyce is interwoven so inextricably with his work that to consider one requires considering the other. The definitive biography of Joyce, by Richard Ellmann, is as strong in its interpretation of Joyce's work as it is of his life. If Joyce, as Ellmann suggests in that biography, tended to see things through words, readers must try to see him through *his* words—the words of his work—as well as through the facts of his life.

Joyce was born into a family whose fortunes were in decline, the first child to live in the match of a man who drank too much and accumulated too many debts and a woman whose family the Joyces considered beneath them. John Joyce, James's father, became the model for Stephen's father both in *A Portrait of the Artist as a Young Man* and in *Ulysses*, where he is one of the most memorable characters, and also a model for H. C. Earwicker in *Finnegans Wake*. If Joyce's father seemed not to understand his son's work or even to show much interest in it during his lifetime, that work has become a surer form of immortality for him than anything he ever did himself.

Joyce was educated at Clongowes Wood College, a Jesuit school not far from Dublin which he memorialized in *A Portrait of the Artist as a Young Man*, and then later at Belvedere College, also Jesuit, in Dublin. In 1898, upon his graduation from Belvedere, he entered University College, Dublin. At this point in his life, increasingly rebellious against the values of his home and society, Joyce did his first writing for publication. He was graduated from the university with a degree in modern languages in 1902 and then left Dublin for Paris to study medicine. That, however, quickly gave way to Joyce's real desire to write, and he entered a difficult period in which he turned to teaching to earn a living. The problems of the father had become the problems of the son, but during this period Joyce wrote some of his best earlier poems, including what is now the final piece in the *Chamber Music* sequence. With the death of his mother imminent in April, 1903, Joyce returned to Dublin, where, the following winter, he began to write the first draft of *A Portrait of the Artist as a Young Man* (known as *Stephen Hero*).

By far the most important event after Joyce's return to Ireland, however, was his meeting in June, 1904, with the woman who was to become his mate for the rest of his life, Nora Barnacle, whose roots (like those of the family Joyce) were in Galway, the westernmost county in Ireland. If Joyce's mother's family had seemed too low for the Joyces, Nora's family was even lower on the social scale, but Joyce, like Stephen Dedalus, was to escape the net of convention and take the woman he loved away from Ireland to live in a succession of temporary residences on the Continent while he established himself as a major writer. The model, at least in part, for Molly Bloom and also for Anna Livia Plurabelle, Nora, not Joyce's legal wife until 1931, was the mother of their two children—Giorgio, born in 1905, and Lucia, born in 1907—and Joyce's main emotional support for almost four decades.

From the time Joyce and Nora moved to the Continent until the outbreak of World War I, they lived chiefly in Trieste, a port city in northeastern Italy which in appearance seemed more Austrian than Italian; there Joyce taught English in a Berlitz School, and wrote; he returned to Ireland only twice, in 1909 and again in 1912, for what turned out to be his last visit. With the outbreak of the war, Joyce and his family moved to Zurich, which was neutral ground, and in 1920—after a brief sojourn once again in Trieste—moved to Paris, where they were to remain until the fall of France twenty years later.

Paris in the 1920's, Ernest Hemingway was to write years later, was a "moveable feast," but Joyce, as always, was a selective diner, an integral part of the literary life of Paris at that time, yet aloof from it, imaginatively dwelling in the Dublin of 1904, the year he had met Nora. Having published *Chamber Music*, *Dubliners*, *A Portrait of the Artist as a Young Man*, and *Exiles*, Joyce had embarked on his most ambitious project to date—a treatment in detail of one day in Dublin—June 16, 1904—and the adventures of a modern-day Odysseus, Leopold Bloom, ultimately to be his greatest single achievement in characterization. The serialization of *Ulysses* had begun in 1918; its publication in book form waited until Joyce's fortieth birthday, on February 2, 1922. Because of publication difficulties resulting from censorship, Joyce did not realize much financially from the book until later in his life, and remained dependent upon a succession of patrons and subscribers not only for its initial publication but also for his livelihood. With its publication, however—difficult though it was to achieve—came the recognition of Joyce as the greatest living novelist in English, a master stylist who had managed (as such major figures as T. S. Eliot and Ezra Pound were quick to see) to give the modern experience a historical dimension which so many realistic novels had lacked.

As recognition of *Ulysses* came, Joyce characteristically moved on to something different (in a sense, in his published work he almost never repeated himself, in style or in form, though he dealt continuously with certain themes), publishing in 1924 the first portion of what for years was termed "Work in Progress" and then ultimately became *Finnegans Wake*. This novel broke new ground in the same way *Ulysses* did, in its rendering of unconscious universal experiences and in its use of language; but it took much longer for it to achieve general recognition as a masterpiece. Plagued throughout his lifetime by financial problems, health problems (especially with his eyes), and family problems (his daughter's mental health was always fragile, and she has lived most of her life in a sanatorium), Joyce remains the prime example of the artist as exile.

Analysis

Chamber Music appeared in 1907, but James Joyce had been working on the poems which comprise the volume for some time before that date. As early as 1905 he had worked out a plan for the poems, different from the one finally devised for the 1907 version but perhaps more revealing of the thematic content of the poetry. With the addition of several poems not in the 1905 scheme, *Chamber Music* came to thirty-six poems of varying lengths and forms, the work of a young man who had already largely abandoned poetry in favor of prose fiction.

In many ways the poems of *Chamber Music* are typical of the period in which they were written. The poetry of the late nineteenth century in English has a hothouse quality; like the French Symbolist, who—next to the English

Romantics—provided the chief inspiration throughout this period, the poets of the *fin-de-siècle* eschewed ordinary life in favor of an aesthetic ideal. This was in fact the final flowering of the ideal of art for art's sake so important to nineteenth century literature and art, an attitude which the young Joyce flirted with and ultimately abandoned, satirizing it in the pages of *A Portrait of the Artist as a Young Man*. In the poems of *Chamber Music*, however, the satire is less easy to detect, and fin-de-siècle themes provide the basis of many of the poems in the sequence. The dominant note of the poetry of the fin-de-siècle is one of weariness or sadness, the favorite time dusk or night, the favorite stance one of retreat; in Joyce's *Chamber Music* poems, as later in *A Portrait of the Artist as a Young Man*, such favorite attitudes are questioned but not totally rejected. If the final note is one of anger or bitterness rather than simply of sadness or despair, there is still a strong enough taste of the latter to mark the poems—even the celebrated number XXXVI—as the work of a young man who has grown up in the last important moment of aestheticism. Even so, the experience of the young man who is the principal speaker of the sequence of poems seems ultimately to toughen him in a way more typical of Joyce than of the poetry of the fin-de-siècle.

In Joyce's 1905 sequence, the personae of the poems are more easily perceived, the themes developed in them clearer, as William York Tindall was first to point out at length in his 1954 edition of *Chamber Music*. In that sequence there are thirty-four poems, designated first in the following list, with the numbers from the 1907 edition in Roman numerals in parentheses immediately after: 1 (XXI), 2 (I), 3 (III), 4 (II), 5 (IV), 6 (V), 7 (VIII), 8 (VII), 9 (IX), 10 (XVII), 11 (XVIII), 12 (VI), 13 (X), 14 (XX), 15 (XIII), 16 (XI), 17 (XIV), 18 (XIX), 19 (XV), 20 (XXIII), 21 (XXIV), 22 (XVI), 23 (XXXI), 24 (XXII), 25 (XXVI), 26 (XII), 27 (XXVII), 28 (XXVIII), 29 (XXV), 30 (XXIX), 31 (XXXII), 32 (XXX), 33 (XXXIII), and 34 (XXXIV).

This sequence has certain important features. Poem 1 (XXI) introduces the young man of the sequence, a sort of romantic rebel in the tradition of the Shelleyan hero, a "high unconsortable one" more in love with himself than with anyone else. This them of aloofness and narcissim is struck in several poems following this one—in 2 (I), 3 (III), and 4 (II)—but by 5 (IV) the young man has not only become the speaker of the poem, but he has also found someone to love. Poem 6 (V) gives her a name—"Goldenhair"—and establishes the theme of the next group of poems: the young man in pursuit of Goldenhair, in the traditional rites of courtship. In 7 (VIII) he pursues her through the "green wood" and in 8 (VII) he sees her among the apple trees, vernal settings for these ancient rites. In 9 (IX), however, he cannot find her, and 10 (XVII) explains why: here the third persona of the sequence is introduced—the rival who is a friend of the young man and who, at the same time, is threatening his relationship with Goldenhair: "He is a stranger to me now/ Who was my friend." Poem 11 (XVIII), addressed both to Goldenhair and to the rival, complains of the failure of friends and suggests that another woman may well give the young man succor. As the poems proceed, this other woman takes on a variety of connotations, until finally, in 17 (XIV) the young man imagines his union with her in terms suggesting that she has combined characteristics, in Tindall's words, "of church, mother, muse, nation, and soul." After 17, the poems do variations on the themes of separation and lost love, ending in 33 (XXXIII) and 34 (XXXIV) on a decidedly wintry note: "The voice of the winter/ Is heard at the door./ O sleep, for the winter/ Is crying, 'Sleep no more.'"

This pattern of love challenged by a rival and ending in bitter or mixed feelings occurs elsewhere in Joyce's work, most notably in *A Portrait of the Artist as a Young Man* and in the play *Exiles*, where, as a test of a relationship, it provides the major theme. *Chamber Music* thus becomes an early working out of this theme, though Joyce ultimately agreed to an ordering of the poems (devised by his brother Stanislaus) different from the one of 1905—allowing for an ending on a much stronger note with poem XXXVI, beginning "I hear an army charging upon the land," which was not part of the 1905 sequence at all and which suggests an attitude that is more than simply passive or accepting on the part of the young man. These little poems, while carrying the weight of themes developed more completely in Joyce's later work, are also lyrics light and fresh enough to serve as the basis of songs. Joyce himself set a number of them to music, and over the years they have been set by many other composers as well.

Poem 16 (XI) illustrates the technique of the lyrics of *Chamber Music*. The diction is simple but frequently archaic—note the use of "thee" and "thy," "hast" and "doth," in keeping with much of the lyric poetry of the 1890's— and the tone light and songlike, with touches of irony apparent only in the last few lines of the second stanza. This irony is heralded in line 9 by the verb "unzone," which stands out in a poem of otherwise simple diction. Like many such words in these poems, "unzone" is unusual for the accuracy with which it is used (compare, for example, "innumerous" in poem 19 [XV]), Joyce returning to its original meaning of "encircle" or "surround," derived by way of the Latin *zone* from Greek *zona*, or "girdle." What is frequently most distinctive about Joyce's choice of words, in prose as well as in poetry, is their accuracy. In this context, the contrast between the formality of "unzone" and the "girlish bosom" of the next line, reinforced by the irony in other poems of the series dealing with the wooing of Goldenhair, makes the reader question her innocence if not the young man's intentions.

The repetition of the opening lines of 16 is another notable feature of the series. In 12 (VI) one can see the same quality on a somewhat larger scale, the final line pointing back to the beginning of the poem. If the poems of *Chamber Music* are relatively simply lyrics, they have their own complexities and ambiguities, as this poem shows. The "bosom" of the first stanza is conceivably Goldenhair's, but may also be interpreted as that of mother or church. "Austerities," like "bosom" used twice in the poem, in particular leads the reader to think so, the bosom or heart leading to an ascetic, not hedonistic, form of satisfaction for the young man. In this poem the young man flees from the relationship with Goldenhair and seeks other means of satisfaction. The language of the poem creates irony through repetition, forcing the reader to reexamine the premises of the relationship described. If this technique is much simpler than the one Joyce employed in his prose masterpieces, it is certainly a technique of the same order.

In 1927, Joyce published a second volume of poetry with the unassuming title *Pomes Penyeach*. The occasion for the volume was largely negative; stung by criticism of "Work in Progress" from people such as Ezra Pound, who had been so supportive of *Ulysses*, Joyce wished to show that he could also produce a relatively simple volume of lyrics. Unfortunately, for the taste of the time the lyrics were too simple and the volume went largely ignored; Pound himself suggested that Joyce should have reserved the poems for the Bible or the family album. This criticism now seems unfair, or at least out of proportion. The thirteen poems of *Pomes Penyeach* do not in any sense break new ground in English poetry, but they provide a kind of personal comment on Joyce's private life which is not easy to find in the prose works, and some of them are also simply good lyrics in the manner of *Chamber Music*.

The poems represent work of a period of approximately twenty years, beginning with "Tilly," composed in 1903 just after Joyce's mother's death, and ending with "A Prayer" of 1923, though stylistically they are of a piece. In this poetry Joyce favored a diction and tone which seemed archaic by the late 1920's, and did so without any of the irony apparent or at least incipient in certain poems of *Chamber Music*. If the mood of these poems did not suit the times in which they appeared, neither did it seem to suit the style of the supreme punster of "Work in Progress." They provide the single instance in Joyce's published work of an anachronism—a work which looks back in style and tone, in this case to the poetry of Joyce's youth and young manhood, rather than forward in time—and this accounts in part for their unenthusiastic reception.

In *Pomes Penyeach* the poems occur in roughly chronological order, in the order of their composition, and may be grouped according to subject matter. Some celebrate Joyce's feelings toward his children, as in "A Flower Given to My Daughter" or "On the Beach at Fontana," while others refer to feelings provoked in him by women he fancied himself to be in love with, either in the Trieste period or in Zurich during World War I. Some poems suggest certain of the prose works, such as "She Weeps over Rahoon" with its echoes of the long story "The Dead," written some five years before the poem. The final poem of the group, "A Prayer," returns to the mood of the darker poems in *Chamber Music* and to the image of woman as vampire which occurs so frequently in the poetry and art of the fin-de-siècle. It also suggests the strain of masochism which shows itself so often in Joyce's work in connection with sensuous pleasure. All in all, these lyrics provide an engaging record of various moods of Joyce as he passed into middle age, tempered by the public reputation he had acquired by that time.

"A Flower Given to My Daughter" and "A Prayer" illustrate the extremity of mood and variety of technique of these poems. In the first, the inverted word order and quaint diction of the poem—"sere" is the best example of the latter—do not keep the last line from being extremely touching, in part because it is so realistic a description. Joyce manages in the best of *Pomes Penyeach* to find just such a strong line with which to end, establishing a kind of contrast between the somewhat antique technique of the poem and conclusions remarkable for their simplicity and strength. "A Prayer" is far more dramatic in tone, but here the long lines and the rolling words ("remembering" followed by "pitying") also carry the reader into the joy become anguish of the final lines. In these poems as in others of the group, Joyce seems to be using the style and tone of another time with sometimes deadly effect—a conscious archaism rather than the more distanced irony of some of the poems of *Chamber Music*.

In 1932, Joyce published his last poem, "Ecce Puer," a touching commemoration of two occasions—the death of his father and the birth of his grandson and namesake Stephen James Joyce, the son of Giorgio and his wife Helen. "Tilly," the first item of *Pomes Penyeach*, was written on the occasion of the death of his mother and is in many ways the strongest of the group; "Ecce Puer"—written just after the death of John Joyce—is even stronger. For felt emotion conveyed, it has no equal among Joyce's works in this form, and its concluding stanza is all the more touching for its echoes of the theme of paternity so important to *Ulysses*—"A child is sleeping:/ An old man gone./ O, father forsaken,/ Forgive your son!" In fact, the poem was completed not many days after the tenth anniversary of the publication of *Ulysses*, which provides yet a third occasion for its composition.

In addition to *Chamber Music*, *Pomes Penyeach*, and "Ecce Puer," Joyce also published occasional broadsides—satiric poems to express his unhappiness over various literary matters. These include "The Holy Office" (1904) (now the rarest of all the published works of Joyce), an attack on the Irish literary movement by a young writer who already knew that his work was to be essentially different from theirs, and "Gas from a Burner" (1912), an attack on the Dublin publisher who ultimately burned the proofs of *Dubliners* rather than print what he considered an indecent book.

Finally, in *A Portrait of the Artist as a Young Man*, one of the crucial moments occurs (in the final part of the book) when Stephen Dedalus composes a poem in the form of a villanelle. This poem, while technically not Joyce's, represents as sure a comment as Joyce ever made on the aestheticism of the 1890's, and thus stands in contrast with *Pomes Penyeach* which echoes the themes and tones of that time.

Joyce's poetry was ultimately expressed most fully in his prose works, where the traditional distinctions between poetry and prose are effectively blurred. Perhaps in the end his lyric poetry is best viewed as a minor expression— almost a form of relaxation—of a master stylist in prose.

Major publications other than poetry

NOVELS: *A Portrait of the Artist as a Young Man*, 1916; *Ulysses*, 1922; *Finnegans Wake*, 1939; *Stephen Hero*, 1944.

SHORT FICTION: *Dubliners*, 1914.

PLAY: *Exiles*, 1918.

NONFICTION: *Letters of James Joyce*, 1957 (Stuart Gilbert, editor); *Selected Letters of James Joyce*, 1975 (Richard Ellmann, editor).

Bibliography

Bowen, Zack R. *Musical Allusions in the Works of James Joyce: Early Poetry Through Ulysses*, 1974.

Doyle, Paul A., ed. *A Concordance of the Collected Poems of James Joyce*, 1966.

Howarth, Herbert. "*Chamber Music* and Its Place in the Joyce Canon," in *James Joyce Today: Essays on the Major Works*, 1966. Edited by Thomas F. Staley.

Moseley, Virginia D. *Joyce and the Bible*, 1967.

Read, Forrest, ed. *Pound/Joyce: The Letters of Ezra Pound to James Joyce*, 1967.

Ryan, John, ed. *A Bash in the Tunnel: James Joyce by the Irish*, 1970.

Sisson, C. H. "The Verse of James Joyce," in *English Poetry 1900-1950: An Assessment*, 1971.

Tindall, William York. "Joyce's Chambermade Music," in *Poetry*. LXXX (May, 1952), pp. 105-116.

Warner, Francis. "The Poetry of James Joyce," in *James Joyce: An International Perspective*, 1982. Edited by Suheil Badi Bushrui and Bernard Benstock.

Archie K. Loss

DONALD JUSTICE

Born: Miami, Florida; August 12, 1925

Principal collections

The Summer Anniversaries, 1960, 1981; *Night Light*, 1967, 1981; *New Poetry of Mexico*, 1970 (includes ten poems translated by Justice, Mark Strand, editor); *Departures*, 1973; *Selected Poems*, 1979.

Other literary forms

Best known for his poetry, Donald Justice has also written plays, short stories, critical essays, reviews, and the libretto for Edward J. Miller's opera *The Young God*. His stories "The Lady" and "Vineland's Burning," first published in *The Western Review*, were included in the O. Henry Awards *Prize Stories* of 1950 and 1954. Both portray characters who are locked inside themselves; like a number of Justice's poems, these stories discover the humanity of people who might be overlooked as uninteresting or dismissed as insane. Justice has recently returned to writing short fiction. His reviews demonstrate the concern for craftsmanship that characterizes his own work.

Achievements

Justice is a consummate craftsman. His carefully polished work demonstrates the power and beauty of the appropriate form. He deals with his major themes, change and loss, by fashioning poems which allow him and the reader to contemplate things that cannot stay. He is a literary, some would say academic, poet. If his range is limited, he does not overextend or repeat himself. His voice is quiet, nostalgic but not sentimental, and sometimes ironic. Whether he is writing about artistic activity or more ordinary experiences and people, his personae and other characters are "real," humanly significant. Instead of saying, "This is the way I feel," he conveys that "This is how things go."

His first book was the Lamont Poetry Selection for 1959, and his *Selected Poems* was awarded the Pulitzer Prize in 1980. Among his other awards are the Harriet Monroe Memorial Prize, grants in poetry from the Rockefeller and Guggenheim Foundations, and a grant in theater from the Ford Foundation. His work is respected by fellow poets.

Biography

Born and reared in Miami, Donald Justice was graduated from the University of Miami in 1945. He received an M.A. degree from the University of North Carolina in 1947 and a Ph.D. from the University of Iowa in 1954. From 1948 to 1949, he attended Stanford University to study with Yvor Winters. Among his other teachers were Karl Shapiro, Robert Lowell, and John Berryman.

Justice has taught at various universities, including Syracuse, the University of California at Irvine, Princeton, and the Universities of Iowa and Virginia. He is now at the University of Florida in Gainesville. He married Jean Ross in 1947 and has one son.

Analysis

The character of Donald Justice's work is most clearly seen against the background of major developments in contemporary poetry. Like most American poets of the 1950's, he worked within the formalist tradition. In the next decade he became involved in the translation of contemporary French and Mexican poets. Following this immersion in the "new surrealism," he began to use suggestive images and freer forms. He has not, however, reacted against T. S. Eliot's ideal of the impersonal poet, nor has he repudiated meter, rhyme, and other traditional artifices; he values them because they provide aesthetic distance during the composing process and an intelligible, satisfying shape for the completed poem.

Justice has observed that "one of the motives for writing is surely to recover and hold what would otherwise be lost totally—memory or experience." He regards the poem not as an expression of the writer's personality but as an artifact which registers a significant perception ("The Effacement of Self: An Interview with Donald Justice," in *Ohio Review*, XVI, no. 3, 1975). In "Meters and Memory" he argues that it is technical skill that makes a subject "accessible to memory, repeatedly accessible, because it exists finally in a form that can be perused at leisure, like a snapshot in an album" (*The Structure of Verse*, 1979, Harvey Gross, editor). Artifice, then, is not incompatible with genuine expression; it is one of the "fixatives" that constitute art—indeed, that make it possible.

Justice's mastery of literary forms and commitment to pattern are evident in *The Summer Anniversaries*, which includes syllabic and accentual poems, sestinas, and sonnets. More than a third of the poems in this collection are rhymed, and most of the others use repetition, assonance, or consonance in place of end-rhyme. No slave to convention, Justice varies traditional forms as he explores his major themes: childhood, loss, and memory. "Sonnet to My Father" pays respects to the Italian sonnet, but Justice substitutes repetition for rhyme. It is fitting that the second, third, sixth, and seventh lines end with "mine," for the poem is about the speaker's participation in his father's dying. The end-words of lines nine through eleven—"die," "place," and "there,"—are mirrored at the ends of the poem's final lines—"there," "place," "die." This repetition represents the son's identification with the father, made explicit in the last line: "while I live, you cannot wholly die." As in most of Justice's early work, the diction, while not elevated, is elegant.

The poem is a carefully controlled expression of emotion.

Justice uses archaic diction in the remarkable "Tales from a Family Album," a syllabic poem of five nine-line stanzas. The speaker feels constrained to speak of his family's "doom," the effect, or cause, of their "acquaintance/ Not casual and not recent with a monster." Although their ancestral tree might be represented by an ordinary Georgia chinaberry, they have known uncommon tragedy. Even now there lives a cousin with a paw print on his forehead, and the speaker vividly recalls the fate of another "kinsman" who attempted to write the family history: he "perished,/ Calling for water and the holy wafer,/ Who had, ere that, resisted much persuasion." With characteristic gentle irony, Justice uses old-fashioned vocabulary and syntax to portray an imaginative Southerner who longs to be respected as a gentleman.

"In Bertram's Garden," a poem concerned with a young woman's loss of innocence best illustrates Justice's use of convention and allusion. As Michael Rewa has shown in "'Rich Echoes Reverberating': The Power of Poetic Convention" (*Modern Language Studies*, IX, no. 1, 1978-1979), the poet examines Jane's fall ironically but not unsympathetically by alluding to Ben Jonson's celebration of chastity in "Queen and Huntress, chaste and fair." (Justice's poem uses the same rhyme scheme as Jonson's and, in the third stanza, the same meter.) Jane's seducer, Bertram, reminiscent of the cynical lover in William Shakespeare's *All's Well That Ends Well* (1602-1604), is also associated with corruption and Cupid, the antitheses of chastity. By placing his poem within a tradition, Justice provides a moral basis for assessing the seduction. As is true of many of his works, "In Bertram's Garden" will be most appreciated by a highly literate audience, but even the reader unaware of its references to Jonson, Shakespeare, Alfred, Lord Tennyson, and perhaps Andrew Marvell will understand why Jane is to "lie down with others soon/ Naked to the naked moon." Toyed with and cast aside, she can no more recover her belief in love than she can retrieve her virginity.

During the 1960's, a number of American poets were making statements on public issues and writing about personal tragedies. *Night Light*, Justice's second collection, includes a few poems critical of the pragmatism, conformity, and latent authoritarianism he saw in mid-century America. "Memo from the Desk of X" and "For a Freshman Reader" anticipate a not-too-distant time when poetry will become extinct, to be replaced by "more precise" statement. The undergraduate is advised not to "bother with odes," not to risk "singing": "The day will come when once more/ Lists will be nailed to the door/ And numbers stamped on the chest/ Of anyone who says No" ("For a Freshman Reader"). "To the Hawks," dated February, 1965, sees the escalation of American involvement in Southeast Asia as the beginning of the end of the world. The poet's vision of dawning horror is held in place by sixteen pairs of five-syllable lines. Only the title and dedication ("*McNamara, Rusk, Bundy*") mark the poem as an occasional piece: it might have been written yesterday.

While Robert Lowell, John Berryman (both had been Justice's teachers), and other "confessional poets" probed their traumas and anxieties, Justice wrote guardedly and ironically about the self. "A Local Storm" mocks the ego that takes a storm as a personal threat. In "Heart," Reason speaks to Passion: after urging that "we" should behave maturely, "more becomingly," the speaker finally admits that self-indulgence is irresistible. "We will take thought for our good name"—after one more revel. "Early Poems" comments on Justice's work: "How fashionably sad my early poems are!" he exclaims. "The rhymes, the meters, how they paralyze." Such manicured structures attract "no one" now; it is time for renewal. After a "long silence" comes "the beginning again." Written at (and about) a time when many poets were avoiding rhyme, meter, and logical structure, "Early Poems" is neatly rhymed and carefully ordered. Although responsive to contemporary developments, Justice is not a trend-setter or camp-follower. "Early Poems" is followed by two blank pages and then "The Thin Man," thirty syllables spoken by a persona who relishes "rich refusals"; Justice, beginning again, departed from the beautiful intricacies of formalism and developed a plainer style.

There are no sonnets or sestinas in *Night Light*; there are two prose poems. Rhyming infrequently, Justice experiments with varying line lengths and minimal punctuation. "Dreams of Water" consists of three short lyrics linked by subject and mood; reluctant to relinquish the unifying power of symmetry, Justice gives each poem the same shape: three three-line stanzas followed by a single line.

Most of *Night Light* is concerned with neither the self nor poetry but with obscure people—an anonymous servant and artist who lived centuries ago; the man at the corner who might be a salesman, a tourist, or an assassin; people in bus stops; the stranger whose lights are burning at 3:00 A.M.; men turning forty; a woman whose letters are sold at auction. Imagining what their lives might be like, Justice conveys a sense of their humanity and, in some cases, their otherness. "The Man Closing Up," free verse "improvisations on themes from Guillevic," is unified by images of decay and enclosure. Cutting off all outside influences, the title character climbs up into himself like someone ascending the stairs of a lighthouse. Still more unreachable and mysterious are the suicides, once regarded as friends, who refused to show themselves in life and now must always be strangers ("For the Suicides of 1962").

Night Light, written in the early and middle 1960's, is a transitional book. Still committed to the polish and detachment favored by T. S. Eliot and the New Critics, Justice did not reject, as some contemporaries did, the patterned regularity of meter and rhyme, but he more frequently allowed his forms to "make themselves up as the poems get written."

The aptly named *Departures* deals with endings, partings, and other moments when one realizes the futility of trying to defect time. Several of Justice's speakers and characters are weary or broken. "A Letter" sketches the desperation of a woman in an asylum. Depressed, disoriented, and troubled by painful memories, she thinks of exposing her "wounds" and her bosom to "the young doctor/ Who has the power to sign prescriptions, passes." Reading her letter, the speaker in the poem understands that she cannot escape her sadness. If she is released, she will return to the city (itself a sanatorium, Justice suggests) to resume her former habits—and find herself "suddenly/ Ten years older, tamed now, less mad, less beautiful." In "A Dancer's Life," neither neurosis nor sex obscures a celebrated dancer's vision of the emptiness of her life. Although she is still famous and beautiful enough to attract young men, she realizes that she has already passed her peak and thinks, *"How disgusting it always must be to grow old."*

The title *Departures* also reflects a change in Justice's style. There are few signs of formalism. Some pieces are fragments, bits from a notebook. Two consist entirely of questions, two of riddles. Justice uses occasional rhyme, assonance, consonance, and other means of structuring his poems. "Absences," an evocation of subtle, evanescent things and experiences, is composed of related images. The dreamlike companion poem "Presences" uses repetition and association to convey the paradoxical constancy of loss and change. Most of the key words and end-words in "Presences" are repeated; departures, disappearances, and transitions are dreams and drifting clouds, "going away in the night again and again," yet they persist in the mind as they do in the poem. Justice's statement that he likes a poem "to be organized," "to have an apprehensible structure," is not surprising. His typical poem is not contained by, but *is*, its structure. Often it further defines itself in relation to other works of art.

By identifying various sources (including Rafael Alberti, Eugene Guillevic, César Vallejo, and Ingmar Bergman) and noting that some of his poems "come, in part, from chance methods," he asks the reader to consider the way in which the individual poem develops and its relation to other compositions. For this unromantic writer, poetry is a tradition and a craft, not just the pronouncement of a personal vision. Justice presents even first-person narratives as things composed, not manifestations of his unique sensibility. A poem based on the premise that "Donald Justice is dead" and buried under "the black marl of Miami" is entitled "Variations on a Text by Vallejo." Poets, human beings—not just "I"—find ways to deal with mortality. Justice has explained his use of chance methods as "a further means of keeping [himself] distant" from his materials. By shuffling cards on which he had written sentences and words that interested him, then exercising "esthetic choice," he formed some lines and images that he was able to develop into poems (*Ohio Review*, XVI).

A third of the poems in *Departures* are concerned with artists and art, especially with poetry. "Self-Portrait as Still Life" distinguishes two kinds of artists: those who wish to come, singing and playing guitars, "into the picture," and those who say, "Myself, I'm not about to/ Disturb the composition." Two other poems assess contemporary poetry and Justice's relation to it. The "I" of "The Telephone Number of the Muse" dryly but with some regret chronicles the end of his affair with the mistress who now wishes to be "only friends." He still calls her sometimes, long distance, "And she still knows my voice, but I can hear,/ Always beyond the music of her phonograph,/ The laughter of the young men with their keys." Youths who barge unprepared and uninvited into the muse's presence are satirized in "Sonatina in Green" (*"for my students"*). The young anticipate ecstasy; they do not think of work. The ironic poet, an experienced teacher of writing and literature, also looks askance at "[The] few with the old instruments,/ Obstinate, sounding the one string"— limiting themselves to the music of another time instead of responding to the requirements of the present. The poem argues that there is too much performance, too much publication, too little craftsmanship: "There has been traffic enough/ In the boudoir of the muse." Justice himself is a relatively reticent poet, publishing only ninety-eight titles (some poems have two or more parts) in his first three books.

Selected Poems includes seventy-six poems from the previous collections, arranged, as he puts it, "in fair chronological order." He revised many poems as he prepared this book. A group of sixteen previously uncollected titles, also arranged chronologically, once again demonstrates his stylistic virtuosity. As Dana Gioia has observed, *Selected Poems* "reads almost like an anthology of the possibilities of contemporary poetry" (*Southern Review*, XVII, Summer, 1981). The earliest poem is a Shakespearean sonnet; there are several free-verse poems, while other compositions, including some recent ones, are rhymed.

In the middle and late 1970's Justice continued to observe ordinary people and seemingly insignificant incidents and places, sometimes drawing upon memory, as he had done at the beginning of his career. "Childhood," set in Miami in the 1930's, is narrated in the present tense. Justice represents the texture of the child's "long days": the Sunday boredom, his delight in the starry ceiling of the Olympia Theater, the exhilarating crime of using a drinking fountain for "colored" people. This personal poem is placed, as Justice tends to do, in relation to tradition: there is an epigraph from Arthur Rimbaud, and the work is dedicated to William Wordsworth, Rimbaud, Hart Crane, and Rafael Alberti, "the poets of a mythical childhood."

"First Death," a narrative in tetrameter couplets, uses concrete details to re-create the child's loneliness, restlessness, and fear in the three days following his grandmother's death. Justice comments on the poem's subject and form in *Fifty Contemporary Poets: The Creative Process* (1977). This essay elucidates what might be called his philosophy of composition. As he recalls,

"First Death," began with his writing couplets about "nothing" until an image activated boyhood memories. Writing in a tight form about the child he was in 1933 provided "the illusion of distance" that makes him a craftsman. Although the poem is easily paraphrased, Justice remarks, its form—the shaping and cadences and rhymes that *"fix* the poem, as the right solution fixes the snapshot"—gave its maker the pleasure of finding an appropriate form and enable the reader to experience the child's misery. Justice concludes that he likes the poem "because it records something otherwise lost."

All of Justice's poems are attempts "to keep memorable what deserves to be remembered." He captures the essence of a fantasy, experience, or memory in a vivid detail or image—funeral flowers "sweating in their vases," the "clean blue willowware" prayed over in Depression Miami, the pianist rapt in his finger exercises, Death's extended hand "a little cage of bone"—and "fixes" it with an appropriate form, using free verse, metrics, syllabics, rhyme, or any device or convention that helps to make it durable. Much of his work develops by alluding to or departing from other poems or art forms, European and Latin American as well as Anglo-American. For Justice, the choice to make craft, not the self, his chief concern has meant freedom to develop his individual talent.

Major publications other than poetry
ANTHOLOGIES: *The Collected Poems of Welden Kees*, 1960, 1975; *Contemporary French Poetry*, 1965 (with Alexander Aspel).

Bibliography
Ehrenpreis, Irvin. "Boysenberry Sherbert," in *New York Review of Books*. XXII (October 16, 1975), pp. 3-4.
Howard, Richard. *Alone with America: Essays on the Art of Poetry in the United States Since 1950*, 1969.
Swiss, Thomas. "The Principle of Apprenticeship: Donald Justice's Poetry," in *Modern Poetry Studies*. X (1980), pp. 44-58.

Mary De Jong

PATRICK KAVANAGH

Born: Inniskeen, Ireland; October 21, 1904
Died: Dublin, Ireland; November 30, 1967

Principal poems and collections

Ploughman and Other Poems, 1936; *The Great Hunger*, 1942; *A Soul for Sale*, 1947; *Recent Poems*, 1958; *Come Dance with Kitty Stobling and Other Poems*, 1960; *Collected Poems*, 1964; *Complete Poems*, 1972 (Peter Kavanagh, editor).

Other literary forms

Three fictional autobiographies—*The Green Fool* (1938), a collection of short stories and sketches and the novels *Tarry Flynn* (1948), and *By Night Unstarred* (1977)—are based on Patrick Kavanagh's early years in County Monaghan. The latter part of *By Night Unstarred* pursues his life into Dublin. Various prose essays and occasional pieces can be found in *Collected Pruse* (1967) and *November Haggard* (1971). *Kavanagh's Weekly*, a magazine which published thirteen issues between April 12 and July 15, 1952, contains a variety of fiction, commentary, and verse which was written under various pseudonyms but is almost all Kavanagh's own work (reprinted, 1981). *Lapped Furrows* (1969) and *Love's Tortured Headland* (1978) reprint correspondence and other documents between 1933 and 1967. Since the poet's death, his brother Peter has been editing and publishing his work, and Peter's biography, *Patrick Kavanagh: Sacred Keeper* (1979), contains a number of previously unpublished or unreprinted documents. Despite the claims of various titles, Kavanagh's work remains uncollected. A poem ("The Gambler") was adapted for ballet in 1961, and *Tarry Flynn* was dramatized in 1966; each was performed at the Abbey Theatre.

Achievements

Despite handicaps of poverty, physical drudgery, and isolation, Kavanagh became the leading figure in the "second generation" of the Irish Literary Revival. He practically reinvented the literary language in which rural Ireland was to be portrayed. Bypassing William Butler Yeats, J. M. Synge, and Lady Gregory, he returned for a literary model to a fellow Ulsterman, William Carleton, and to his own experience of country life as a subject. He invested his fiction and poetry with fresh regional humor which did not sentimentalize or condescend to its characters. His vision is fundamentally religious, imbued with a Catholic sacramental view of nature. His various criticisms of Irish life and institutions arise from an unrefined but genuine spirituality. The quality of Kavanagh's work is uneven, and his public attitudes inconsistent. Even so, the sincerity of his best work, its confidence in its own natural springs, its apparent artlessness, its celebration of local character, place, and mode of expression, make him the most widely felt literary influence on the poets of contemporary Ireland, most significantly on those with similar backgrounds, such as John Montague and Seamus Heaney.

Biography

Patrick Kavanagh was the fourth of the ten children of James Kavanagh, a shoemaker, and his wife Bridget. The Kavanagh home is in Mucker, a townland of Inniskeen, County Monaghan, near the Armagh (and now Northern Ireland) border. The boy attended Kednaminsha National School until he was thirteen, when he was apprenticed to his father's trade. Later, he worked a small farm purchased in the nearby townland of Shancoduff. His first literary influences were the school anthologies which featured Henry Wadsworth Longfellow, Charles Kingsley, William Allingham, Alfred, Lord Tennyson, Robert Louis Stevenson, and Thomas Moore, and his earliest poems were written in school notebooks. As he worked on his small farm, he nurtured his taste on magazines picked up at fairs in the town of Dundalk. His keen observations of country life, its customs, characters, and speech patterns, together with his growing awareness of his sensitivity which set him apart from his peers, are well set forth in his account of his early life, *The Green Fool*. Many of his early poems appeared in the 1930's in *The Irish Statesman*, whose editor, Æ (George William Russell) was the first to recognize and cultivate the peasant poet. Æ Russell introduced him to modern world literature, providing him with books, advice, payment, and introductions to the Irish literary establishment. Of the books given him by Russell, *Gil Blas of Santillane* (1715, 1724, 1735), *Ulysses* (1922), and *Moby Dick* (1851) remained the classics most revered by Kavanagh.

After he moved to Dublin in 1939, he supported himself as a journalist. Throughout the 1940's he wrote book and film reviews, a range of critical and human interest pieces, city diaries, and various pieces for *The Irish Press* (as "Piers Plowman"), *The Standard*, *The Irish Times*, and *Envoy*. During that time, the long poem *The Great Hunger*, his second poetry collection, *A Soul for Sale*, and the novel *Tarry Flynn* appeared, so that following the deaths of Yeats (1939) and James Joyce (1941), he emerged as the central figure in Irish literary life. His most ambitious journalistic venture was in 1952 when, with his brother's financial and managerial assistance, he produced *Kavanagh's Weekly*, which ran for thirteen issues (April 12-July 5). This production comprises the fullest expression of Kavanagh's "savage indignation" at the mediocrity of Irish life and letters. It is useful as a document of the Dublin ethos in the early 1950's and in reading Kavanagh's poetry of the same period. In October, 1952, *The Leader* responded—in a spirit typical of the infamous factionalism of Dublin's literary politics—with a malicious "Profile," which prompted Kavanagh to file suit for libel. Following a celebrated trial, which

Kavanagh lost, he fell dangerously ill with lung cancer.

He made a dramatic physical recovery, however, which in turn revivified his creative powers. This second birth resulted in a group of poems—mainly sonnets—written in 1955 and 1956—set in and around the Rialto Hospital and by the Grand Canal, Dublin, and published in *Recent Poems* and *Come Dance with Kitty Stobling and Other Poems*. Thereafter he went into a slow decline, physically and creatively. In April, 1967, he married Katherine Moloney, but he died the following November. He is buried in Inniskeen.

His brother Peter (twelve years his junior) was Kavanagh's constant correspondent, financier, confidant, critic, and promoter. He has edited and published many works arising from this fraternal collaboration, including *Lapped Furrows*; *November Haggard*; *Complete Poems*, which supersedes and corrects *Collected Poems*; a bibliography, *Garden of the Golden Apples* (1972); and a documentary biography, *Patrick Kavanagh: Sacred Keeper*. Despite its title, *Collected Pruse* contains only a sampling of Kavanagh's prose works.

Analysis

Although he frequently and vehemently denied it, Patrick Kavanagh was a distinctively Irish poet. He had already formed his own voice by the time he discovered—or was discovered by—the Revival and became a leading figure in the "second generation." Kavanagh was not a Celtic mythologizer such as W. B. Yeats, a conscious dialectician such as J. M. Synge, a folklorist such as Lady Gregory, an etymologist such as James Joyce, or a Gaelic revivalist such as Douglas Hyde. He felt and wrote with less historical or political consciousness than his progenitors. His gifts and temperament made him an outsider in Inniskeen, his lack of formal education and social grooming excluded him from Dublin's middle-class literary coteries, and his moral sensibility excluded him from Bohemia. Yet in retrospect, he emerges as the dominant Irish literary personality between 1940 and 1960. Although he admired each of the Revival's pioneers for particular qualities, he regarded the Irish Literary Revival in the main as an English-inspired hoax. The romanticized peasant, for example, he considered the product of Protestant condescension, and he felt that too many writers of little talent had misunderstood the nature of Yeats's and Joyce's genius and achievements, so that the quality of "Irishness" replaced sincerity.

Against a pastiche of literary fashions which misrepresented the peasant, attempted the revival of the Irish language, promoted nationalism in letters and in politics, Kavanagh posited his own belief in himself, in his powers of observation, and his intimate knowledge of the actual lives of country people. Kavanagh's subsequent popular success in Ireland and his influence on the "third generation" are attributable to several distinct characteristics: his parochialism, which he defined as "confidence in the social and artistic validity of his own parish"; his directness, the apparent off-handedness of his work, and his freedom from literary posing; his deep Catholicism, which went beyond sentimentality and dogma; his imaginative sympathy for the ordinary experiences of country people; his comedy; his repose; his contemplative appreciation of the world as revelation; and his sincerity, his approval of feelings arising only from a depth of spirit. Although he has often been admired for one or more of these virtues, and although his manner often masked these qualities, they must be taken as a whole in accounting for his character as a poet. He disdained the epithet "Irish poet," yet shares with each of the pioneers of the Revival one or more signally "Irish" characteristics.

Kavanagh's creative development followed three stages: first, the works of intimacy with and disengagement from the "stony grey soil" of parochial Monaghan; second, the works which show his involvements with Dublin or national cultural issues; and third, his "rebirth" in the post-1955 reconciliation of public and private selves, when rural parish and national capital find mutual repose.

His two most successful fictional works, *The Green Fool*, and *Tarry Flynn*, provide a rich lode of documentation of their author's country background and the growth of his sensibility. Some of his finest lyrics come from this period, along with his *magnum opus*, *The Great Hunger*. All of these works are set in the same few townlands, and the theme is the revelation of grace in ordinary things and tasks. Through these poems, and from *The Green Fool* to *Tarry Flynn*, the poet's confidence in his own visionary gifts progressively deepens, even though the expression is often uncertain. In a handful of lyrics, however, such as "Ploughman," "Inniskeen Road: July Evening," "A Christmas Childhood," "Spraying the Potatoes," "Shancoduff," and "Epic," Kavanagh's technique realizes his intentions. In each of these, the chance appearances belie the deft design, and the natural voice of the countryman is heard for the first time since Carleton in Irish literature.

"Shancoduff" (*Complete Poems*) is one of Kavanagh's most successful expressions of his parochial voice and is a representative early poem. The small farmer's pride in his bare holding is seemingly disquieted by a casual comment from passing strangers: "By heavens he must be poor." Until this uninvited, materialistic contrast with other places intrudes, this little world, although uncomfortable, has been endurable. Now it may not be so.

Before the cattle drovers assess the farm, the readers have seen it through the eyes of its owner, and they do not need to be told that he is a poet. With him they have first observed these hills' exemplary, incomparable introspection (lines 1-7). Even as his readers are being invited to contemplate the hills' ontological self-sufficiency, however, the poet, by necessity a maker of comparisons, introduces mythological and geographical allusions from the larger world. Even though these references—to Lot's wife, the Alps, and the Matterhorn—ostensibly imply his sympathy with his property's self-justification, their very statement admits some kind of comparison and betrays the principle it proposes. This and the irony in "fondle" arrange the scene for the dour pragmatism of the jobbers. Shancoduff is very poor land, poets do make poor farmers, or farmers make poor poets, and the eavesdropping owner-farmer-poet seems disconcerted. The question in line 16 is slyly rhetorical, however; the poet's evident disdain for the jobbers implies that his heart may not be quite so "badly shaken."

The poem operates by a set of contrasts which set the cold, wet, dark, ungainly native places against apparently more positive reflections from the outside. Earth and water oppose air and fire; St. Patrick's see of Armagh (and/or ancient Ulster's adjacent capital of Emhain Macha) is a counterattraction to the foreign cities of dubious renown—Sodom, Rome, London, even perhaps Tokyo. The gauche place-names of Kavanagh's parish do not seem to invite tourists, yet they combine in shaping the poet's attitude to these humble townlands and the design of the poem (see also "Old Black Pocket"; "Glassdrummond," "Streamy/Green Little Hill"; "Featherna," "Streamy"; with the "Big Forth" they compose an ancient, native estate).

The poem uses seasonal, biblical, and religious images to suggest his parochial independence from urban cultures, while foreshadowing several motifs which run through Kavanagh's later works: his distrust of cities and critics, his investment of local dialect or commonplace phrases with larger, often mystical, reference, his disdain for positivist assessments, and his cutting irony. Yet, despite the representative nature of its content, it must be admitted that by its total coherence and clarity this poem stands out from most of his work.

The Great Hunger is Kavanagh's most ambitious poem and is one of signal importance in the literature of modern Ireland. First published in 1942, it is 756 lines long, in fourteen sections. It narrates the life of Patrick Maguire, a peasant farmer whose life is thwarted by physical poverty, Jansenism, and the lack of imagination. The poem is Kavanagh's most extensive rebuke to the idealization of the peasant: a report "from the other side of the ditch," it has great reportorial force. For just as it describes the degradation of the rural poor, it also projects Maguire sympathetically as a figure of keen self-awareness and spiritual potential. Maguire's anguish is muffled and extended by his procrastination, the dull round of gossip, gambling, and masturbation. The Church distorts his natural religious sensibilities into patterns of guilt, which, together with his mother's hold on the farm, conspire to justify his pusillanimity. Woman is the embodiment of life's potentialities, and Maguire's failure to marry is thus the social expression of his spiritual retardation.

The title recalls the potato famine of 1845 to 1847, when starvation and disease ravaged the population and caused long-term psychological and social harm. The mood of the people turned pessimistic as they accepted the disaster as a judgment from an angry deity, and they turned penurious and late-marrying. This historical catastrophe had a deeply depressing effect on rural life, enlarged the power of the Church, reduced national self-confidence, and led to the disuse of the native language and the loss of the gaiety and spontaneity for which the Irish had been renowned. Kavanagh's poem reflects several of these effects with unflinching honesty.

The poem is a *tour de force* of descriptive writing, technical variation, and complex tonal control. In the modernist mode, it utilizes the rhythms and idioms of jazz, nursery rhymes, ballads, the Hiberno-English dialect, the Bible, the pastoral, and the theater, with only occasional lapses in momentum. The poet stands at very little distance from his subject; the tone is somber to bitter. Kavanagh shows compassion rather than condescension toward his protagonist; the humor is grim and restrained. *The Great Hunger* suffers by its occasional stridency, but its urgency and commitment do not diminish it as much as its author would have readers think when he later disowned it as "lacking the nobility and repose of poetry" (*Self-Portrait*).

By the time Kavanagh had made that statement, he had gone through some important changes in spirit. Even though *The Great Hunger* established his reputation in Dublin's literary life, he suffered from lack of patronage and managed to survive only by journalism. That activity he undertook with zest and courage—witness *Kavanagh's Weekly*—but it brought to the fore some of his insecurities which found expression in flailing abuse of his rivals and in sententious dogma on a range of public issues. As the objects of his satirical verses changed, the central vision began to disintegrate. The bitter libel suit against *The Leader* was a personal disaster. His bout with lung cancer took him close to death, and his creative energies had reached their nadir. His remarkable physical recovery, however, led to a spiritual revivification on the banks of the Grand Canal, Dublin, in the year following the summer of 1955.

This reinvigoration of spirit is reflected in a group of sonnets published in *Recent Poems*, and *Come Dance with Kitty Stobling*, notably the title poem of the latter, along with "Canal Bank Walk," "The Hospital," and "Lines Written on a Seat on the Grand Canal." As his various accounts (notably in *Self-Portrait*) of this experience testify, Kavanagh rediscovered his original capacities to see, accept, and celebrate the ordinary. In these poems, the original innocence of the Monaghan fields graces his experience of Dublin, mediated by his hospitalization and the repose offered by the environment of the Grand Canal. Kavanagh purged these poems of many defects which had marred his previous work—contentiousness, self-pity, shrill engagement in passing events, messianic compulsions—all of which arose from relative shallows. In "Lines Written on a Seat on the Grand Canal," for example, there is a nicely balanced irony in the mock-heroic view of self, which is deftly subsumed by the natural grace observed in the setting. The artificial roar is drowned by the seasonal silence. The well-tempered voice of the poet commands original simplicities with easeful assurance. The poet's memorial, "just a canal-bank seat for the passer-by," summarizes Kavanagh's testament: his acknowledgement of Yeats, his self-definition as observer, namer, and diviner, and his humility as no more than a "part of nature." The countryman, the poet, the visionary, the Irishman, and the citizen are finally reconciled to one another. Although the poem appears to mirror the persona's affection of indifference, its taut conclusion indicates that casualness has not been easily won.

The accomplishment of these late poems notwithstanding, Kavanagh retained a sense of defeat to the end of his career. He never overcame a defensiveness arising from his deprived youth. He rarely reconciled his feelings for his Monaghan sources and his need for a Dublin audience. His *Complete Poems* show how small a proportion of his total production is truly successful. Nevertheless, his impact on Irish cultural life is large, and this is attributable to the color of his personality, the humor of his prose, and his unsentimental social criticism, as much as to his poetic oeuvre.

Major publications other than poetry
NOVELS: *Tarry Flynn*, 1948; *By Night Unstarred*, 1977.
SHORT FICTION: *The Green Fool*, 1938.
NONFICTION: *Lapped Furrows*, 1969 (Peter Kavanagh, editor); *Love's Tortured Headland*, 1978.
MISCELLANEOUS: *Kavanagh's Weekly*, 1952, 1981; *Self-Portrait*, 1964, 1975; *Collected Pruse*, 1967; *November Haggard*, 1971 (Peter Kavanagh, editor).

Bibliography
Kavanagh, Peter, ed. *Garden of the Golden Apples*, 1972.
Nemo, John, ed. "A Bibliography of Writings by and about Patrick Kavanagh," in *Irish University Review*. III (Spring, 1973), pp. 80-106.

Cóilín Owens

JOHN KEATS

Born: Moorfields, London, England; October 29 (or 31), 1795
Died: Rome, Italy; February 23, 1821

Principal poems and collections

Poems, 1817; *Endymion*, 1818; *Lamia, Isabella, The Eve of St. Agnes, and Other Poems*, 1820. The standard edition of Keats's poetry is *The Poems of John Keats* (1978, Jack Stillinger, editor). Poetry citations are to that text.

Other literary forms

In *The Use of Poetry* (1933), T. S. Eliot referred to the letters of John Keats as "the most notable and the most important ever written by any English poet," primarily because "there is hardly one statement of Keats about poetry, which . . . will not be found to be true." The letters also offer an important gloss on specific poems and have thus become important for understanding Keats. Besides many passing comments of brilliance, the central concept of the letters is "negative capability." As defined by Keats, it is the capability to remain "in uncertainties, Mysteries, doubts, without any irritable reaching after fact & reason" (I, 193), which implies a disinterestedness that permits even competing ideas full play to reach their potential. In his letters, Keats often carried an idea to its extreme with extraordinary intellectual flexibility; another day, its opposite will surface to be worked out, as all things "end in speculation" (I, 387). The concept is also taken to include Keats's understanding of the poetical character, or the ability to surrender one's personal self to create characters and objects with independent life. Keats believed that the artist's first responsibility was to create beauty, which implies that the artist's personally held ideas and beliefs should be temporarily suspended or treated only partially so as to realize fully the work's aesthetic potential. Through the use of sympathetic imagination, Keats attempted to become the thing he was creating, to intensely identify with its life, not to find his personal life reflected in it. The standard edition of Keats's letters is *The Letters of John Keats* (1958, Hyder Edward Rollins, editor, 2 volumes). Text citations are to that edition.

Achievements

Without being facetious, one could identify Keats's greatest achievement as becoming one of the greatest poets of the English language in twenty-five years, three months, and twenty-two days of life, for Keats died before the age of twenty-six. Douglas Bush has said that no other English poet would rank as high as Keats if he had died as young—not William Shakespeare, John Milton, or Keats's greatest contemporary, William Wordsworth. Whereas other poets, especially his Romantic contemporaries, have gone in and out of critical fashion, Keats's reputation has endured since shortly after his death.

Keats followed the Shakespearean model of impersonality in art; that is, the surrendering of self to the fullest development of character and object, and it is this impersonality, coupled with intensity, that makes his poetry readily accessible to a wide range of modern readers. The reader does not have to re-create Keats's time, empathize with Romantic norms and beliefs, or identify with the poet's unique biographical experiences, to appreciate his poetry fully. Keats is sane, honest, and open; his art is varied, intense, and rich in texture and experience. As he said of his poetic model, Shakespeare, Keats was as little of an egotist as it was possible to be, in the Romantic period, at least, in the creation of art.

Biography

Though the events of John Keats's life are meager, his biography has fascinated many. Keats did not have a single physical, social, familial, or educational advantage in life, nothing to prepare for or enhance the development of his genius. Internally, however, he was afire with ambition and the love of beauty. Even at that, he did not discover his poetic vocation until late, given the fact that he died at the age of twenty-five and spent the last eighteen months of his life in a tubercular decline. His career lasted from 1816, when Keats renounced the practice of medicine, to the fall of 1819, when he stopped working on his last great, though incomplete, poem, *The Fall of Hyperion: A Dream* (1856). One almost has to count the months, they are so few and precious. In fact, in a single month, May, 1819, he wrote four of his great odes—"Ode to a Nightingale," "Ode on a Grecian Urn," "Ode on Melancholy," and ironically, "Ode on Indolence."

This remarkable and courageous poet, the oldest of four children, was born to keepers of a London livery stable. His father was killed in a fall from a horse when John was eight; his mother died from tuberculosis when he was fourteen. His relatives arranged for schooling and apothecary training so that he might make a living, but the year he received his certificate, 1816, he began to devote himself to poetry. He wrote some good, but mostly bad, poetry, or at least poetry that does not add much to his reputation, until the summer of 1818. His reward was a brutal review of his major early work, *Endymion*, in a leading magazine of the day. Keats was criticized so severely that Percy Bysshe Shelley speculated that the review began Keats's physical decline.

Actually, the truth was much worse. Keats was nursing his brother Tom, who was dying from tuberculosis, when the reviews came out. Though he was too strong in character to be deeply affected by criticism, especially when he was a more astute critic of his poetry than his readers, a contagious illness could hardly be thwarted with character. In the fall of 1818, Keats also fell deeply in love with Fanny Brawne. They intended to marry, but his illness

soon made their future together impossible. Sadly, the futility of their love
and passion offered important inspiration to Keats's poetry. By late fall, 1819,
in the same year that he had written "The Eve of St. Agnes," the odes,
Lamia, and *The Fall of Hyperion*, his illness was severe enough to arouse his
deep concern. In July, 1820, his influential volume *Lamia, Isabella, The Eve
of St. Agnes and Other Poems* was published. Keats, however, now separated
from Fanny, ill, in desperate need of money, and unable to achieve his major
ambition of writing a "few fine Plays" in the manner of Shakespeare, was
utterly despondent. He later spent a few months under the care of the
Brawnes, but left England for Italy in September, 1820, in an attempt to save
his life in the milder Italian weather. Joseph Severn, a dear friend, nursed
him until his death in Rome in February, 1821.

Forever thinking aloud in his letters about the central concerns of existence,
Keats once found purpose in this earthly life as "a vale of soul-making"; that
is, while every human being perhaps contains a spark of divinity called soul,
one does not attain an identity until that soul, through the medium of intelligence and emotions, experiences the circumstances of a lifetime. Thus the
world has its use not as a vale of tears, but, more positively, as a vale of
becoming through those tears. Keats's soul flourished as rapidly as his genius,
and the poetry is evidence of both.

Analysis

Lieben und arbeiten—to love and to work—are, psychologists say, the
principal concerns of early adulthood. In John Keats's case, they became, as
well, the dominant themes of his most important poetry. The work theme
includes both the effort and the love of creating beauty and the immortality
Keats longed for as recompense. Once, perhaps exaggerating, Keats wrote
that "the mere yearning and fondness" he had "for the Beautiful" would keep
him writing "even if [his] night's labours should be burnt every morning and
no eye ever shine upon them." Not passing, however, was the tenacity of his
ambition: "I would sooner fail than not to be among the greatest." Keats's
quest for immortality takes several forms: it appears openly, especially in the
sonnets and in "Ode on Indolence" and "Ode to Psyche" as the anxieties of
ambition—being afforded the time, maintaining the will and energy, and, not
least, determining the topic, or territory, for achievement. It includes a metamorphosis fantasy, whereby the young poet, whether immortal as in *Hyperion:
A Fragment* or mortal as in the revised *The Fall of Hyperion*, becomes deified
or capable of immortal poetry through absorption of divinely granted knowledge. The ambition/work theme also takes a self-conscious turn in *The Fall
of Hyperion*, questioning the value to a suffering mankind of the dreamer-
poet's life and work.

The love theme explores dreams of heterosexual bliss, but it also moves
into the appropriate relationships to be had with art and nature. The imag-

ination is the ally of love's desires; reality and reason are their nemeses. In "The Eve of St. Agnes," a better lover, in *Lamia*, a better place, are dreams which dissipate in the light of reality and reason. "Ode to a Nightingale" attempts a flight from reality through identification with beautiful song rather than through dream, but the result is an intensification of distress. "Ode on Melancholy," "To Autumn," and "Ode on a Grecian Urn," however, suggest perspectives on the human condition, nature, and art that can be maintained with honesty and deeply valued without recourse to dream. One could say that Keats's love theme moves toward the understanding and acceptance of what is.

Concomitant with the maturation of theme and perspective is Keats's stylistic development. Like most poets, Keats went through phases of imitation during which he adapted the styles and themes he loved to his own work and ambitions. Leigh Hunt, Edmund Spenser, John Milton, and always Shakespeare, provided inspiration, stylistic direction, and a community of tradition. Regardless of origin, the principal traits of Keats's style are these: a line very rich with sound pattern (as in "with brede/ of marble men and maidens overwrought," which also includes puns on "brede" ("breed") and "overwrought" (as "delicately formed on" and as "overly excited"); synaesthetic imagery, or imagery that mingles the senses ("soft incense," "smoothest silence"); deeply empathic imagery ("warmed jewels," "all their limbs/ Locked up like veins of metal, crampt and screwed"); stationing or positioning of characters to represent their dramatic condition (so Saturn after losing his realm, "Upon the sodden ground/ His old right hand lay nerveless, listless, dead,/ Unsceptered; and his realmless eyes were closed"); the use of the past participle in epithets ("purple-stained mouth," "green-recessed woods"); and, of course, as with every great writer, that quality which one can only describe as *Je ne sais quoi*—I know not what—as in the lines from the sonnet "Bright Star": "The moving waters at their priest-like task/ Of pure ablution round earth's human shores."

Themes of ambition and accomplishment inform many of Keats's sonnets. The claiming of territory for achievement is the focus of "How Many Bards Gild the Lapses of Time," "On First Looking into Chapman's Homer," "Great Spirits Now on Earth Are Sojourning," and the great "Ode to Psyche." In "On First Looking into Chapman's Homer," for example, Keats recounts the discovery of Homer's "demesne." The extended metaphor of the sonnet is narrator-reader as traveler, poet as ruler, poem as place. The narrator, much-traveled "in the realms of gold," has heard that Homer rules over "one wide expanse," yet he has never "breath[ed] its pure serene." During the oration of Chapman's translation, however, he is as taken as an astronomer "When a new planet swims into his ken" or as an explorer, such as "stout Cortez," when "He stared at the Pacific—and all his men/ Looked at each other with a wild surmise—/ Silent, upon a peak in Darien." The complementary images of the distant planet and the immense ocean suggest both the distance the narrator is from Homeric achievement and its epic proportions. His reaction, though, represented through the response of Cortez, is heartening: while lesser beings look to each other for cues on what to think, how to react, the greater explorer stares at the challenge, with "eagle eyes," to measure the farthest reaches of this new standard for achievement.

Following the lead of his contemporary William Wordsworth, though with a completely original emphasis, Keats's territory for development and conquest became the interior world of mental landscape and its imaginings. Wordsworth had defined his territory in "Prospectus" to *The Recluse* (1798) as "the Mind of Man—/ My haunt, and the main region of my song." Whereas Wordsworth believed that mind, "When wedded to this goodly universe/ In love and holy passion," could create a vision of a new heaven and a new earth, Keats initially sought to transcend reality, rather than to transform it, with the power of the imagination to dream. "Ode to Psyche" explores Keats's region and its goddess, who was conceived too late in antiquity for fervid belief. While Wordsworth asserts in "Lines Composed a Few Miles Above Tintern Abbey" (1798) that "something far more deeply interfused" could sanctify our experience with nature, Keats locates days of "holy . . . haunted forest boughs" back in a past that precedes even his goddess of mind. The only region left for her worship must be imagined, interior. As priest, not to nature, but to mind, the poet says he will be Psyche's "choir" to "make delicious moan/ Upon the midnight hours," her voice, lute, pipe, incense, shrine, grove, oracle, her "heat/ Of pale-mouthed prophet" dreaming in "some untrodden region of [his] mind." In the "wide quietness" of this sacred microcosm, "branchèd thoughts, . . ./ Instead of pines shall murmur in the wind"; a "wreathed trellis of working brain" will dress "its rosy sanctuary"; the goddess' "soft delight" will be all that "shadowy thought can win." In keeping with the legend of Cupid as lover of Psyche, a casement will remain open at night "To let the warm Love in!" Keats's topic becomes, then, how the mind is stimulated by desire to create imagined worlds, or dreams, rather than, as in Wordsworth's case, how the mind is moved by love to re-create its perception of the real world.

Besides finding his territory for achievement, Keats struggled as well with the existential issues of the artist's life—developing the talent and maintaining the heart to live up to immense ambitions. It is to be doubted whether poets will ever be able to look to Shakespeare or to Milton as models without living in distress that deepens with every passing work. The "writing of a few fine Plays," meaning Shakespearean drama, remained Keats's greatest ambition to the end. Yet the achievement of *Paradise Lost* (1667) haunted him as well, and the first *Hyperion* was an attempt in its mold. Keats became more critical of Milton's achievement during the course of composing *Hyperion*, however, for it was, "though so fine in itself," a "curruption [sic] of our Language," too much in "the vein of art," rather than the "true voice of feeling." In fact, Keats gave up *Hyperion* because Milton's influence weighed so heavily that he could not distinguish the poem's excessively self-conscious artistry from its true beauty derived from accurate feeling.

Aesthetic considerations aside, a recurring theme in Keats's works of epic scope was the fantasy of poetic metamorphosis. The sonnet "On Sitting Down to Read King Lear Once Again" introduces the wish for transformation that will enable the poet to reach Shakespearean achievement. The metaphor is consumption and rebirth through fire, as adapted from the Egyptian legend of the phoenix bird, which was said to immolate itself on a burning pile of aromatic wood every five hundred years to engender a new phoenix from its ashes. The narrator-poet lays down his pen for a day so that he might "burn through" Shakespeare's "fierce dispute/ Betwixt damnation and impassion'd clay." To "burn through" must be read two ways in the light of the phoenix metaphor—as reading passionately through the work and as being burned through that reading. He prays to Shakespeare and the "clouds of Albion" not to let him "wander in a barren dream" when his long romance, *Endymion*, is concluded, but that "when . . . consumed in the fire" of reading *King Lear*, he may be given "new phœnix wings to fly at [his] desire." Out of the self-immolating achievement of reading will arise a poet better empowered to reach his quest.

The transformation theme of *Hyperion* exceeds the passionate wishfulness of "On Sitting Down to Read King Lear Once Again" by stressing the need for "knowledge enormous," as befits the poem's epic ambitions. *Hyperion* is a tale of succession in which the Titans are supplanted by the Olympians as the reigning monarchs of the universe, with focus upon Hyperion the sun god being replaced by Apollo, the new god of poetry and light. It has been suggested that *Hyperion* becomes Keats's allegory for his own relationship with his poetic contemporaries, especially Wordsworth. Keats had said that Wordsworth was Milton's superior in understanding, but this was not owing to "individual greatness of Mind" as much as to "the general and gregarious advance of intellect." *Hyperion* embodies this hypothesis of progress in its succession and transformation themes.

The poem opens with Saturn, that was the supreme god of the Titans, in a position of perfect stasis—the stationing we referred to above—stupefied by his loss of power—"His old right hand lay nerveless, listless, dead,/ Unsceptered." Thea, the bewildered wife of the as-yet-undeposed Hyperion, visits to commiserate. She informs Saturn that the new gods are wholly incompetent; Saturn's "sharp lightning in unpracticed hands/ Scorches and burns our once serene domain." The question is: Why, with the world running perfectly, was there a need for change? Saturn, an image of pomposity and egotism, perhaps inspired by Wordsworth's character, knows only of his personal loss:

> I have left
> My strong identity, my real self,
> Somewhere between the throne, and where I sit
> Here on this spot of earth.

"Thea, Thea! Thea!" he moans, "where is Saturn?" Meanwhile, Hyperion is pacing his domain in the region of the sun, wondering: "Saturn is fallen, am I too to fall?" In his anxiety he overreacts, attempting to wield more power than he ever possessed by making the sun rise early. "He might not," which dismays him tremendously. The first book of this unfinished three-book epic ends with Hyperion sailing to earth to be with his fallen peers.

At the same time, Saturn and Thea also reach those "regions of laborious breath" where the gods sit

> Dungeoned in opaque element, . . .
> Without a motion, save of their big hearts
> Heaving in pain, and horribly convulsed
> With . . . boiling gurge of pulse.

The Titans receive their deposed king with mixed response—some groan, some jump to their feet out of old respect, some wail, some weep. Saturn, being unable to satisfy their need to know why and how they have fallen, calls upon Oceanus, the former god of the sea, for not only does he "Ponderest high and deep," he also looks content! Oceanus then reveals a law of succession particularly appropriate for the early nineteenth century: "We fall," he says, "by course of Nature's law, not force/ Of thunder, or of Jove." Blinded by sheer supremacy, Saturn has not realized that, as he was not the first ruler, so he will not be the last. Nature's law is the law of beauty. Just as heaven and earth are more beautiful than chaos and darkness, and the Titans superior in shape and will to heaven and earth, so the new gods signal another significant advance in being; "a fresh perfection treads,/ A power more strong in beauty, born of us/ And fated to excel us," Oceanus explains, "as we pass/ In glory that old Darkness." In short, the eternal law is that "first in beauty should be first in might."

On Apollo's isle the important transformation is about to begin. Apollo, as a good Keatsean poet, can make stars throb brighter when he empathizes with their glory in his poetry; yet he is inexplicably sad. Mnemosyne the muse seeks to assist her favorite child, who aches with ignorance. She emits what he needs to know and he flushes with

> Names, deeds, gray legends, dire events, rebellions,
> Majesties, sovran voices, agonies
> Creations and destroyings, all at once
> Pour[ing] into the wide hollows of [his] brain.

Apollo shouts, "knowledge enormous makes a God of me" and "wild commotions shook him, and made flush/ All the immortal fairness of his limbs." It is like a death pang, but it is the reverse, a dying into life and immortal power. The poem ends incomplete with Apollo shrieking, Mnemosyne arms in air, and the truncated line—"and lo! from all his limbs/ Celestial * * *." No one has been able to conjecture to the satisfaction of anyone else where the poem might have gone from there, although the result of Apollo's transformation seems inevitable. He would replace Hyperion, effortlessly, in this pre-Darwinian, pre-Freudian, universe where sons, like evolving species, acquire power over the earth without conscious competition with their fathers. As Oceanus indicates, the Titans are like the

> forest-trees, and our fair boughs
> Have bred forth . . .
> . . . eagles golden-feathered, who do tower
> Above us in their beauty, and must reign
> In right thereof.

However timorously, it would follow that Keats, bred on Spenser, Shakespeare, Milton, and Wordsworth, would have to live up to, if not exceed, their accomplishments.

This myth of progress would necessarily still require the superior poem to be written to support its prophetic validity. Keats knew that he needed deeper knowledge to surpass Wordsworth, but there was not much he could do about it. Though it was an attractive imagining, no god was likely to pour knowledge into the wide hollows of his brain. "I am . . . young writing at random—straining at particles of light in the midst of a great darkness," he wrote with characteristic honesty, "without knowing the bearing of any one assertion of any one opinion." Ironically, his dilemma brought out the strength his modern readers prize most highly, his courageous battling with, to use his favorite phrase of Wordsworth's, "the Burthen of the mystery." Caught in this impasse between noble ambition and youthful limitation, Keats's spirit understandably failed in weaker moments. His self-questioning was exacerbated when he reflected upon the frailty of earthly achievement. Such is the torment in "On Seeing the Elgin Marbles," the Grecian ruins brought to England by Lord Elgin.

The narrator opens feeling "Like a sick eagle looking at the sky" in the face of the magnificent architectural ruins. Ironically, they are only the "shadow of a magnitude" that once was, an insubstantial image emphasizing how much has been lost rather than how much was once achieved. Human achievement wasted by time brings the narrator a "most dizzy pain" born of tension between body and soul over committing one's life to mortal achievement. In "Ode on Indolence," Keats enjoys a temporary respite from his demons—love, ambition, and poetry—in a state of torpor in which the body temporarily overpowers spirit. One morning the shadows come to him: love the "fair Maid"; "Ambition, pale of cheek,/ And ever watchful with fatiguèd eye"; and, "the demon Poesy." At first he burns to follow and aches for wings, but body prevails: even poetry "has not a joy—/ . . . so sweet as drowsy noons,/ And evenings steeped in honeyed indolence." The victory is transitory outside the poem; within it, a respite from ambition, love, and work is accepted.

All of these issues—the quest for immortality; the region of quest as dream; the transformation essential to achieve the quest; the spiritual weakness inevitably felt in the face of the challenge to be immortal; and, beyond all these, an altruism that seeks to distinguish between the relative value of humanitarian works and poetry in behalf of suffering humanity—are melded in Keats's second quest for epic achievement, *The Fall of Hyperion*. Following a brief introduction, the poem moves to a dream arbor reserved for the dreamer, who "venoms all his days,/ Bearing more woe than all his sins deserve." Remnants of a feast strew the ground; the narrator eats, partakes of a draught of cool juice and is transported through sleep and reawakening to a second dream kingdom. He finds himself this time amid remnants of an ancient religious festival. These dream regions represent Keats's aspirations to romance and epic respectively. Off in the west, he sees a huge image being ministered to by a woman. The image is Saturn; the minister is Moneta, Mnemosyne's surrogate. Moneta's face is curtained to conceal the immense knowledge her eyes can reveal to those worthy of receiving her immortal knowledge. She challenges the narrator to prove himself so worthy by climbing the altar stairs to immortality, or dying on the spot. Cold death begins to mount through his body; in numbness he strives to reach the lowest step— "Slow, heavy, deadly was my pace: the cold/ Grew stifling, suffocating, at the heart;/ And when I clasped my hands I felt them not." At the last moment, he is saved; his "iced feet" touch the lowest step and "life seemed/ To pour in at the toes." He learns that he has been saved because he has felt for the suffering of the world, though he is only a dreamer, without hope for himself or of value to others. True poets, Moneta tells him, pour balm upon the world; dreamers increase the vexation of mankind.

Although in his letters Keats gave precedence to "fine doing" over "fine writing" as "the top thing in the world," the poem does not clarify whether humanitarians are above the poets of mankind, though both are unquestionably above the dreamers. The poem then moves to the metamorphosis that will make the dreamer a poet through the acquisition of knowledge. Moneta's bright-blanched face reveals the immortal sorrow she has endured for aeons; her eyes hold the narrator enthralled with the promise of the "high tragedy" they contain, for their light and the sorrowful touch of her voice reveal deep knowledge. He begs to know and she relates the fall of the Titans. The revelation begins the narrator's transformation: "Whereon there grew/ A power within me of enormous ken./ To see as a God sees." His vision opens with the "long awful time" Saturn sat motionless with Thea at his feet. In anguish the narrator sits on a tree awaiting action, but the pain must be endured, for knowledge does not come easily or quickly, not even in a dream. The narrator curses his prolonged existence, praying that death release him from the vale, until Saturn moves to speak and the narrator witnesses scenes of the beginning of things from *Hyperion*. The poem continues but this version also ends incomplete, with Hyperion flaring to earth.

It is a poignant fact that Keats never believed that his poetry, his work, had come to anything, his epic endeavors left incomplete, no "few fine Plays" written. Writing to Fanny Brawne in February, 1820, he said that he had frequently regretted not producing one immortal work to make friends proud of his memory. Now frighteningly ill, the thought of this failure and his love for Fanny were the sole two thoughts of his long, anxious nights. Quoting Milton's lines on fame from, "Lycidas," Keats wrote to her: "Now you divide with this (may *I* say it) 'last infirmity of noble minds' all my reflection."

Their love had earlier spawned his most important love poems, though he refused his created lovers the bliss of unreflecting love. It would seem unfortunate that dreams do not outlast the act of dreaming, but Keats's romances, "The Eve of St. Agnes" and *Lamia*, approach wish-fulfillment more critically. "The Eve of St. Agnes" permits a love dream to become flesh to provoke a dreamer's response to the contrast between dream and reality, though they are, in person, the same; *Lamia* permits a too-ordinary mortal to enter the love dream of a lovely immortal to elicit the likely response of the nondreamer to the experience of continuous, in this case, carnal, perfection. Together the poems serve to show that lovers cannot have it either way: either reality will not be good enough for the dreamer, or the dream will not satisfy the extra-romantic desires of the nondreamer.

"The Eve of St. Agnes" presents an array of wish-fulfilling mechanisms that seek to alter, control, or purify reality—praying, suffering, drinking, music, ritual, dance, and, at the center, dreaming. This poem with a medieval setting opens with a holy beadsman, "meagre, barefoot, wan," praying to the Virgin in the castle's icy chapel. Though he is fleetingly tempted to walk toward the music dancing down the hall from a party within, he turns to sit among "rough ashes" in recompense for his and others' sins. Among others praying this frigid night is Madeline, who follows the ritual of St. Agnes: if a maiden refrains from eating, drinking, speaking, listening, looking anywhere, except up to heaven, and lies supine when she retires, she will be rewarded with the vision of her future husband. The irony of the patron saint of virgins inspiring a heterosexual vision is lost on the young girl, panting as she prays for all "the bliss to be before to-morrow morn." Meanwhile, Porphyro, her love, is in reality racing across the moors to worship his Madeline. As Madeline works on her dream, Porphyro will act on his desired reality—

getting into Madeline's bedroom closet where "he might see her beauty unespied,/ And win perhaps that night a peerless bride."

The lovers' stratagems provide a weird culmination, though they move in complementary pattern. While Madeline is undergoing her ritualistic deprivations, Porphyro is gathering, through the assistance of her wily old nurse, Angela, a banquet of delights to fulfill deliciously her sensual needs; while she undresses, he gazes, of course, unseen; while she silently sleeps, he pipes in her ear "La belle dame sans merci." When she awakens to find the man of her dream at her side, however, the seemingly perfect solution is shattered. Madeline's dream of Porphyro was better than Porphyro and she tells him so: "How changed thou art! how pallid, chill, and drear!" She implores that he return to her as the dream. Porphyro arises, "Beyond a mortal man impassioned far/ At these voluptuous accents" and

> like a throbbing star
> . . . .
> Into her dream he melted, as the rose
> Blendeth its odor with the violet—
> Solution sweet.

The moon of St. Agnes, which has been languishing throughout the poem, sets as Madeline loses her virginity. Madeline, however, comes out of the experience confused; she wanted a dream, not reality, and apparently she could not distinguish between them at their climax. Now bewildered, and feeling betrayed and vulnerable to abandonment, she chides Porphyro for taking advantage. He assures her of his undying devotion and the two flee the sleeping castle into the storm, for he has prepared a home for her in the southern moors. The drunken revelers from the party lie benightmared; Angela soon dies "palsy-twitched"; and the loveless beadsman, after thousands of Aves, sleeps forever among his ashes.

A skeptical reading of the poem has found Porphyro a voyeur and (perhaps) a rapist, Madeline a silly conjurer whose machinations have backfired; an optimistic reading has Madeline and Porphyro ascending to heaven's bourn. The language, imagery, and structure allow both interpretations, which is the way of complex ironic honesty. The dream experience, for example, has two parts: the first when Madeline awakens to find Porphyro disappointingly imperfect; the second when the two blend into "solution sweet." It would seem that dream and reality have unified in the second part, but the first part is not thereby negated. Rather, the lovers are lost in sensory intensity, which, according to Keats, makes "all disagreeables evaporate." Whether the moment of intensity is worth the necessary conjuration before or the inevitable disillusionment afterwards is a judgment on the nature of romance itself, down to this very day.

Lamia provides the nondreamer, Lycius, with much more than the two ordinary lovers of "The Eve of St. Agnes" are permitted; but the question is whether more is better. T. S. Eliot wrote that mankind cannot stand very much reality; Keats suggests in *Lamia* that neither can we bear very much dreaming. Lamia, as imagination incarnate, provides her lover Lycius with a realized dream of carnal perfection that extends continuously until he tires of her adoration. When Lamia, once bound in serpent form, was capable of sending her imagination abroad to mingle among the mortals of Corinth, she saw Lycius in a chariot race and fell in love. After being released from her serpent prison house by another immortal, Hermes, in an exchange of wish-fulfillments, she assumes a glorious woman's body to attract Lycius. She is successful, but a series of compromises must be made to win him and satisfy his desires. Those compromises are the record of imagination's degeneration. Because Lycius is so overwhelmed by her beauty, he believes she must be immortal and loses his confidence. She "throws the goddess off" to encourage his masculinity. When he tires of the carnal pleasure she provides in the "purple-lined palace of sweet sin," she begs on her knees that he might preserve the privacy of their dream, for she knows of her vulnerability to reason. The sight of her begging brings out the sadist in Lycius, who "takes delight in her sorrows, soft and new." His passion grown cruel, Lamia plays the complementary masochist, burning, loving the tyranny. She grants his wish that they should be married before all of Corinth, and creates a feast and a vision of palatial splendor for the "gossip rout." The philosopher Apollonious, tutor to Lycius, crashes the party to destroy the dream with his "keen, cruel, perceant, stinging" eye. Apollonious is reason to Lamia's imagination, and in the confrontation between them, Lamia dissipates; Lycius the scholar-lover dies because he is incapable of balancing reason and imagination; and Apollonious is left with a Pyrrhic victory, for he has lost his pupil whom he intended to save.

Ironically, the loss of the dream, the dreamers, and the battle is not even tragic because not one was worthy of salvation. Lycius risks his dream so that his friends will look with admiration, but his friends choke over his good fortune; Lamia concedes to this foolish vanity; and Apollonious, the brilliant sophist, mistakes the whole situation, feeling that Lycius has become the prey of Lamia. More than saying that dreams cannot mix with reality, *Lamia* warns that imagination cannot be prostituted to the pleasure principle. Dreams are pure and sensitive constructs inspired by love, created for the psyche by the imagination. The eye of self-consciousness; participation with others, including loved ones; the dictates of forces less pure than love—all cause dissolution of the ephemeral dream.

"Ode to a Nightingale" leaves the medium of the dream for empathic identification with a natural being that seems to promise transcendence of the human condition. Again, a transcendence of self is fleetingly achieved, leaving the poet, *in propria persona*, more isolated and bewildered thereafter. He opens the poem having returned from identification with the bird's "happiness" that causes and permits it to sing "of summer in full-throated ease." The poet, however, is now drowsy and numb, so far has he sunk from that high experience of unself-conscious joy. He wishes for any wine, human or divine, that might effect a dissolution of consciousness and a return to the bird; for among men, "but to think is to be full of sorrow/ And leaden-eyed despairs." The transience of the physical splendor of beauty, of the psychological heights of love; the tragedy of early death, the indignity of aging to death; participation in human misery—all have thwarted any love or hope he might feel for the human condition.

In the fourth stanza the poet seems to join the bird, but ambiguously. After exhorting his imagination and/or the bird to fly "Away! away!" where he will reach it on "the viewless wings of Poesy," he seems to achieve the connection: "Already with thee! tender is the night." The eighth and final stanza supports the interpretation of his extended identification, for it has the poet being tolled back from the bird "to my sole self." Before the identification in stanza four, however, he has qualified the power of those viewless wings to keep him in stable flight, for "the dull brain perplexes and retards." Consequently, throughout the poem, he is neither entirely with the bird, nor entirely in his metaphysical agony, but rather in a state of mixed or split consciousness that leads to the poem's concluding questions: "Was it vision, or a waking dream?/ Fled is that music:—Do I wake or sleep?" In the sixth stanza, for example, as he sits in his "embalmèd darkness" in the arbor, he says, "Darkling I listen; and, for many a time/ I have been half in love with easeful Death." Shortly, he seems to be lost in the ecstasy of the bird's song. Yet immediately he retracts, for common sense tells him that, if he were dead, his ears would be in vain, and "To thy high requiem" of the bird, he would "become a sod."

The seventh stanza distinguishes the immortality of the bird's song from the mortality of the poet, and for another passing moment he seems to experience identification as he slips into empathy with those through time who have also heard the immortal song, especially Ruth of the Old Testament: "Perhaps the self-same song that found a path/ Through the sad heart of Ruth, when, sick for home,/ She stood in tears amid the alien corn." This song that flows through time sparks both the poet's identification with it and his empathy for fellow beings. He is not as explicit as Walt Whitman would be in defining immortality as empathy for all beings and experiences of all times, but his revealed feeling for others is the eternal human counterpart to the song that eternally elicits the feeling. Still, the great divider between the bird and poet is the poet's self-consiousness. The bird, unaware of its individuality and coming death, is more a medium of the song of its species than a being in its own right. The poet withdraws completely in the final stanza to his "sole self." The imagination cannot support the identification with a dissimilar being for very long. The bird's song fades until it is metaphorically dead to the poet, "buried deep/ In the next valley glades." The stimulus for experience now fled, the poet recognizes the division he has undergone between empathy and identity, being in and out of self, with neither strain coming to resolution. The bewilderment of the conclusion reflects perfectly the imperfect resolution of his experience.

The "Ode on Melancholy" offers perhaps the most positive perspective possible to one who appreciates this tragedy of the human condition. Its psychology is a variant of Satan's from *Paradise Lost*: "Evil, be thou my good." The poet advises that when the "melancholy fit shall fall," as fall it must, one should not seek to escape with "poisonous wine," "nightshade," or other agents that would "drown the wakeful anguish of the soul," for that very anguish is the catalyst for more intensely valuing transient beauty, joy, and love. Even the anger of a loved one will reach a value transcending relationship, if we "Emprison her soft hand, and let her rave,/ And feed deep, deep upon her peerless eyes." The glow fired by her passion, the beauty, joy, and pleasure that accompany love, all must dwindle, die, depart, sour; but if one holds an awareness of their end while indulging in their prime, the triumph of deep inclusive response will reward the sensitive soul with ultimate mortal value. It will be among Melancholy's "cloudy trophies hung," which is to say, the "sadness of her might" will hold him forever sensitive to the richness of transience.

In like manner, "To Autumn" offers a pespective on nature in the ultimate richness of its condition. It has always been difficult for poets to look upon nature without moralizing its landscape for human edification. The Romantic period especially sought its morality from nature and its processes. Keats, however, describes nature without pressing metaphor out of it; his goal is to offer it as worthy in itself so that we might love it for itself. If there are analogues between human nature and nature, they are not the subject, concern, nor purpose of the poem. As several critics have noted, the stanzas move from the late growth of summer to the fulfillment of autumn to the harvested landscape; correspondingly, the imagery moves from tactile to visual to auditory in an ascension from the most grossly physical to the most nonphysical. The sun and the season are in league to load and bless the vines with fruit, and in a string of energetic infinitives, the push of life's fulfillment is represented: "To bend with apples the mossed cottage trees," to "fill all fruit with ripeness to the core," "To swell the gourd, and plump the hazel shells," "to set budding more,/ And still more, later flowers for the bees." An image of surfeited bees, who think summer will never end, their "clammy cells" are so "o'er-brimmed," concludes the first stanza.

Stanza two presents the personification of autumn "sitting careless on a granary floor;" sound asleep "Drowsed with the fume of poppies" in the fields; "by a cyder press, with patient look," watching the "last oozings hours by hours." The harvested stubble plains of stanza three provoke the poet's question, "Where are the songs of spring?" Even so, the question is raised more to dismiss it as irrelevant than to honor its inevitability. Autumn has its own music and the poem softly presents it: as the stubble plains are covered with the rosy hue of the dying day, the "small gnats mourn," "full-grown lambs loud bleat," "Hedge crickets sing," "with treble soft/ The red-breast whistles from a garden-croft," and "gathering swallows twitter in the skies." The suggestion of animate life singing unconsciously in its joy, while just as unconsciously readying for winter, signals the end of the natural year. Unlike Shelley, however, who in "Ode to the West Wind" looks through the fall and coming winter to spring as an analogue of rebirth for mankind, Keats allows not more than a suggestion of what is to follow, and that only because it belongs to the sound and action of the season. Autumn is accepted for itself, not as an image, sign, or omen of spiritual value. Ripeness is all.

As "Ode on Melancholy" and "To Autumn" established perspectives on the human condition and nature, so "Ode on a Grecian Urn" establishes a relationship with art. This ode begins and ends by addressing the urn as object, but the subject-object duality is dissolved in the third of the five stanzas. The experiential movement of the poem is from ignorance through identification to understanding. The poet addresses the urn as a "bride of quietness," "still unravished" by passing generations. It is a "foster child of silence and slow time." Once the child of the artist and his time, the urn belongs not to eternity, for it is vulnerable to destruction, but to the timeless existence of what endures. It is a sylvan historian, containing a narrative relief of the beings and scenes of its surface. The poet asks questions of it as historian; what gods, music, bacchanalian frenzy it images. All is silent; but that is best, we learn, for "Heard melodies are sweet, but those unheard/ Are sweeter," free to become as flawless as imagination can wish. The second stanza finds the poet moving close, addressing the urn's individuals. The "Fair youth" who pipes the song so softly that only the spirit hears, the "Bold lover" who has neared the lips of his maiden, both arouse the poet-lover's empathy.

In the third stanza, the poet participates fully in the urn's existence as he inspires scenery and youths with imaginative fervor. The "happy, happy boughs! that cannot shed/ [their] leaves, nor ever bid the spring adieu"; the "happy melodist, unwearied,/ Forever piping songs forever new"; and, above all, "more happy love! more happy, happy love!/ Forever warm and still to be enjoyed,/ Forever panting, and forever young"—none of it can pass. Nature, art, and love remain in the glow of their promise. The love on the urn arouses a special contrast with "breathing human passion . . ./ That leaves a heart high-sorrowful and cloyed,/ A burning forehead, and a parching tongue." The fourth stanza begins to pull out of intense identification, with questions on the urn's religious scene: "Who are these coming to the sacrifice?" To what "green altar" does the priest lead his sacrificial heifer? What town do they come from that will be emptied of its inhabitants forever? Stanza five again addresses the urn as object, but with increased understanding over stanza one. She is now "Attic shape! Fair Attitude! with brede/ Of marble men and maidens overwrought." The bride, though unravished and wed to quietness, has her breed of beings, themselves passionately in pursuit of experience. She is a "silent form" that "dost tease us out of thought/ As doth eternity: Cold Pastoral!" If her silence provokes participation so that viewers lose self-consciousness in her form, then truly they are teased out of thought, as the poet was in stanza three. Why, though, is she a "Cold Pastoral!"

Critics have taken this to be the poet's criticism of the urn in her relationship with those who contemplate her; perhaps it is best, however, that the urn remain cold, if she is to encourage and reward the viewers' empathy. Stanza three criticized human passion for its torrid intensity in contrast with the urn's image of love "Forever *warm* and [thus] still to be enjoyed." The urn remains a cold object until it is kindled by the viewers' passion. When the mortals of the present generation have been wasted by time, the urn will continue to exist for others, "a friend to man," to whom it (or the poet) has this to say: "Beauty is truth, truth beauty—that is all/ Ye know on earth, and all ye need to know."

Much ink has been spilled over these final lines of the "Ode on a Grecian Urn" and the technicalities of this famous problem for criticism must be at least briefly addressed. The difficulty is in determining who is saying what to whom; the issue has a mundane origin in punctuation. According to the text of the *Lamia* volume, the lines should be punctuated with the quotation marks enclosing only the beauty-truth statement: "'Beauty is truth, truth beauty'— that is all. . . ." If the lines are punctuated thus, the urn makes the beauty-truth statement, and the poet himself offers the evaluation of it, either to the urn, to the figures on the urn, or to the reader. Many scholars, however, see the matter differently; they would place the entire aphorism within quotations, based upon manuscript authority: "Beauty is truth . . . need to know." With this punctuation, the urn is talking to man. Both choices lead to problematic interpretations. In the former case, it does not make much sense for the poet to speak to the urn or to its images about "all ye know on earth," as if there were someplace else for the urn to know something. There might be an afterlife where things can be known, but not for the urn. On the other hand, it would be odd for the poet to speak to the reader in that way, too. The inconsistency in tone would be especially awkward. Several lines earlier, he had joined his reader in saying to the urn: "Thou . . . dost tease us out of thought." To refer now to "us" as *ye*, as in "that is all/ Ye know on earth," is out of tone. On the other hand, the argument against the urn speaking the entire aphorism is directed against its sufficiency. It has been argued that human beings need to know a great deal more than "Beauty is truth, truth beauty," no matter how one tries to stretch the meanings of the terms to make them appear all-inclusive. There is no way to resolve this critical problem with confidence, though trying to think through it will provide an exercise in Keatsean speculation at its best.

To agree that the experience the poet undergoes is entirely satisfactory might be enough, though there is not critical unanimity about this, either. Lovers about to kiss, rather than kissing; trees in their springtime promise, rather than in fruition; a song that has to be imagined; a sacrifice still to be made, rather than offered—all can suggest experience short of perfection. Yet, like Keats's dreams which surpass reality, these figures are safely in their imaginative prime. The kiss, after all, may not be as sweet as anticipated; the fruit may be blighted; the song may be tiresome or soon grow so; the sacrifice may be unacceptable.

In fact, a reader comes to Keats's poetry as the poet himself came to the urn. Like all great art, Keats's poetry is evocative; it leads its readers' emotions and thoughts into and then out of its formal beauty to teach and delight. One can stand back and examine its formal perfection; one can ask questions of it about human nature and its desires for being and loving. Yet only through the experience of it can one learn what it has to teach; only after one goes through the empathy of Keats's narrator in stanza three can one speak with confidence of its meaning.

Major publication other than poetry

NONFICTION: *The Letters of John Keats*, 1958 (Hyder Edward Rollins, editor, 2 volumes).

Bibliography

Bate, Walter Jackson. *John Keats*, 1963.
_____ , ed. *Keats: A Collection of Critical Essays*, 1964.
Bush, Douglas. *John Keats*, 1966.
Mellor, Anne K. *English Romantic Irony*, 1980.
Sperry, Stuart M. *Keats the Poet*, 1973.
Stillinger, Jack. *The Hoodwinking of Madeline and Other Essays on Keats's Poems*, 1971.
_____ , ed. *Keats's Odes: A Collection of Critical Essays*, 1968.
Wasserman, Earl R. *The Finer Tone: Keats's Major Poems*, 1953.

Richard E. Matlak

WELDON KEES

Born: Beatrice, Nebraska; February 24, 1914
Died: San Francisco, California; July 18, 1955

Principal collections

The Last Man, 1943; *The Fall of the Magicians*, 1947; *Poems, 1947-1954*, 1954; *Collected Poems of Weldon Kees*, 1975 (revised).

Other literary forms

While the poetry of Weldon Kees eventually dominated his literary career, he began by publishing more than three dozen short stories in little magazines, such as *The Prairie Schooner*, that were scattered throughout the Midwest. From his first published story in 1934 (while still an undergraduate) to his last one in 1940 ("The Life of the Mind"), Kees's reputation grew steadily and impressively. He was frequently cited in annual anthologies such as those published by New Directions. Edward J. O'Brien designated twenty of his stories as "distinctive" in his *Best Short Stories*, an annual distillation from thousands of stories published in English; indeed, O'Brien's 1941 volume was dedicated to Kees. Kees's commitment to short fiction, however, had already waned by then.

In addition to Kees's short stories, he also published a number of reviews in prestigious periodicals such as *Poetry*, *The Nation*, and *The New York Times Book Review*. His interests were astonishingly diverse, and he reviewed books of poetry, fiction, music, art, criticism, and psychology. In 1950, Kees served as art critic for *The Nation*, publishing an important series of articles on the "abstract expressionists." He also wrote the essay "Muskrat Ramble: Popular and Unpopular Music," based on his study of jazz, which was anthologized for its insights into popular culture. Kees also tried his hand at writing plays, and he left behind an experimental, off-Broadway sort of play, *The Waiting Room*, that remains unpublished despite its commendation by; Kenneth Rexroth.

Besides writing, Kees managed to make, or help to make, several short "art films" that are representative of American expressionist cinematography of the period. Notable are *The Adventures of Jimmy*, for which he wrote a jazz score, and *Hotel Apex*, his own psychological study of urban disintegration. His filmmaking extended to studies in child and group psychology that led to an association with the psychiatrists Gregory Bateson and Jurgen Ruesch; with the latter, Kees coauthored *Nonverbal Communication: Notes on the Visual Perception of Human Relations* (1956), which contains a stunning series of still photographs taken by Kees himself. Published after his disappearance in 1955, this volume and *The Collected Poems* are essential for an understanding of Kees's poetry.

Achievements

While Kees was fairly well-known and critically acclaimed by reviewers such as Rexroth in his own time, his work is now all but forgotten. A thorough assessment of his place in American poetry remains to be done, yet one senses that Kees has been influential and important in unacknowledged quarters of contemporary poetry. The inclusion of Kees in *The Norton Anthology of Modern Poetry* (1973) should expand his audience. His editor, Donald Justice, has seen fit to revise *The Collected Poems* fifteen years after initial publication. Larry Levis, whose first three books have each won a major national award, includes the eulogy "My Only Photograph of Weldon Kees" in his most recent book *The Dollmaker's Ghose* (1981).

If, as Rexroth has suggested, Kees was "launched" into poetry by Conrad Aiken, T. S. Eliot, and W. H. Auden, he also assimilated the objectivist viewpoint of William Carlos Williams, the incremental method of Ezra Pound, the prose rhythms of Kenneth Fearing, and the proletarian realism of James T. Farrell, in moving far beyond those early influences. Kees may, indeed, yet be seen as an important figure in the transition from modernist poetics to the postmodern sensibility, with its preoccupation with loss, fictions of the self, and parody of older forms.

More than as an unknown link in the history of poetics or as an artist of amazing versatility, Kees's achievement is a poetry that is singularly voiced in its blunt honesty and articulate despair over the loss of Walt Whitman's American idealism. There is no poet in all of American literature more bitter than Kees; yet that "permanent and hopeless apocalypse" (Rexroth) in which he lived does not hinder his eloquence, nor does it erode an eerie serenity that constantly seems to accept certain doom. Kees even seems to anticipate the now-familiar despair of the nuclear age in his poem "Travels in North America," in which he declares that "the sky is soiled" by the "University of California's atom bomb." Had he been publishing in the 1960's or the 1970's, Kees might be read widely. As Rexroth has concluded, the poems of Kees may simply have been "just a few years too early."

Biography

Weldon Kees remained in his birthplace, the small town of Beatrice in rural Nebraska, until he attended the University of Nebraska. His childhood and adolescence appear typical of the era and place. By the time Kees had been graduated from a liberal arts curriculum in 1935, he had made a sufficient impression on Professor L. C. Wimberly to become a regular contributor and reviewer for *The Prairie Schooner*. After serving as an editor for the Federal Writers' Project in Lincoln, Kees moved to Denver in 1937 to work as a librarian, eventually becoming director of the Bibliographical Center of Research for the Rocky Mountain Region. His first published poem, "Sub-title," appeared that year in an obscure little magazine called *Signatures*; from then on, Kees turned increasingly toward poetry for the expression of his artistic vision.

By 1943, Kees had moved to New York where he worked as a journalist for *Time* and became involved in documentary film-making. That year also saw the publication of his first book of poems, *The Last Man*, by the Colt Press in San Francisco. Midway through the 1940's, Kees took up painting, choosing to identify himself with what was to be known as the abstract expressionist movement. He exhibited his work in one-man shows at the Peridot Gallery; at least once, his paintings were shown with those of Hans Hofmann, William de Kooning, Jackson Pollock, and Robert Motherwell—the major artists of the movement. Kees also found time to continue writing poems, and they appeared in *Poetry*, *The New Yorker*, and *Harper's*, among other leading journals. His second collection of poems, *The Fall of the Magicians*, was published in 1947.

Kees abandoned New York for San Francisco sometime in 1951. There he began serious study of jazz piano and jazz composition. He continued his work in cinematography and made several movies himself. Kees also began exploring nonverbal signs with Jergen Ruesch and interpersonal cues with Gregory Bateson in an attempt to grasp the commonplace, to exploit it, and to express it immediately and directly by a method that was "spare, rigorous, and clinical." Meanwhile, he continued to paint and write; in 1954, his last book, *Poems, 1947-1954*, was published in San Francisco.

Aside from Kees's far-ranging activities and multitalented pursuits, his life to this point, in the words of Justice, seems to have been "a fairly typical career for any writer reaching manhood in the depression and passing through a time of political crisis and war." On July 18, 1955, however, Kees's car was found abandoned on the approach to the Golden Gate Bridge. In a review that appeared that same day in *The New Republic*, Kees had written of "our present atmosphere of distrust, violence, and irrationality" that led to "so many human beings murdering themselves—either literally or symbolically. . . ." Justice reports that in the weeks before his car was found, Kees had spoken to friends both of suicide and of going away to Mexico to begin a new life. His disappearance, it seems, was not an act of sudden or impulsive desperation, but rather the culmination of nearly two decades in which his poetry shows an increasing despair that grew deeper with his avid scrutiny of humanity in contemporary society and his insistent denial of those superficial values by which human beings sought to order their lives. Whether Kees did commit suicide or whether he simply fled from any previous social context in his life, his disappearance was the ultimate symbolic act against what he perceived to be an indifferent society seized by the doldrums of pervasive mediocrity.

Analysis

Perhaps the neglect that Weldon Kees's poetry has suffered results from the lack of a single, brilliant "masterpiece." There is no long poem, no ambitious project or sequence like those on which many modern and contemporary poets have founded their reputations. There is no pretentious, gaudy innovation of form that would assure him a place in debates on "technical craft." Many of Kees's poems suffer from flaws such as awkward allusions or tedious repetitions, but despite all such deficiencies his work is original for its soft voice that expresses a tone of hard bitterness. That voice is not especially pleasing in its barrage of satiric details, yet it retains a unique capacity to haunt the memory of anyone who has read his poems. Donald Justice is surely correct in asserting that Kees's poetry "makes its deepest impression when read as a body of work rather than a collection of isolated moments of brilliance," for "there is a cumulative power to the work as a whole to which even the weaker poems contribute."

In Kees's early poems such as "The Speakers," one detects the unmistakable echoes of T. S. Eliot, while a poem such as "Variations on a Theme by Joyce" employs a Joycean "war in the words." Even in those first poems, however, Kees comes quickly to his own sense of rhythm and tone. While he played with formalism by using the villanelle and the sestina, and while he experimented with form in such poems as "Fuge" and "Round," Kees settled in to a rhythmic prose line that was more flexible than traditional meter and more restrictive than free verse. Possessing a naturally good ear, Kees successfully wed form and content by starting with facts and things and then consummated them by placing the right words in the right order—in short, a wholly natural proselike but lyrical style. The consequent unobtrusive tone of the poems is the very heart of Kees's poetic vision.

Kees chose as an epigraph to his final book a passage from Nathaniel Hawthorne's *The Marble Faun* (1860) that reveals much about Kees's own perspective in his poetry. His quest was to enter "those dark caverns into which all men must descend, if they would know anything beneath the surface and illusive pleasures of existence." Hawthorne's novel itself is a study of ambivalent meaning in a world scattered among the fragments of tradition and the incomprehensible debris that is left to the artist. Seeing himself in a similar world, but facing an even more painful disintegration than Hawthorne had perceived, Kees sought to enter his own "dark caverns" by explicating and disclosing the ironies of the "surface" and satrizing the "pleasures of existence." Whatever hope marks that quest—and it does not appear with any frequency—can be found in the intense scrutiny of both personal and public experience, capable not only of recognizing and accepting continuous despair, but also of remaining detached from its implications. Kees proposes a self-protective hope, simple, isolated, solitary, and stationary, out of which, with absolute denial, the self can create a system of values by which it can survive—honestly and naturally—with perhaps its greatest pleasure being in art itself.

The pervasive anguish and bitterness that runs through Kees's poetry like grain through wood appeared in his earliest work. In the early poem "For My Daughter," as the speaker gazes into his "daughter's eyes," he perceives "hintings of death" which he knows "she does not heed." Continuing his contemplation of the destruction of her youth, he fears that she will be subjected to the "Parched years that I have seen" and intensifies his dread by assuming that she will be ravished by "lingering/ Death in certain war." Worse yet, the speaker bemoans the possibility—even probability—that his daughter will be "fed on hate" and learn to relish "the sting/ Of other's agony" in which the masochism of self-destruction overwhelms the tenderness of love. In the midst of such bleak projection, Kees undermines the speaker's fearful uncertainties. "These speculations," says the speaker, "sour in the sun." Just as the reader begins to applaud the father for coming to his senses and rejecting his indulgent morbidity, Kees delivers an excruciating shock in the last line: "I have no daughter. I desire none." The reader now realizes that the despair is even greater than he had supposed; the speaker has already chosen not to have children, because he sees nothing but betrayal and suffering in his vision of the future. He chooses to withhold his own "procreative urge," viewing it as his own inevitable complicity in the suffocation of the unborn generations.

That rather private sense of futility gives way in other poems to a dramatic rendering of an equally futile sense in interpersonal relationships. In "The Conversation in the Drawing Room," Kees creates a dialogue between Hobart, a young man aghast at a "spot of blood" that is "spreading" on the room's wall, and Cousin Agatha, who; refuses to acknowledge his hysteria as anything but the result of reading *The Turn of the Screw* (Henry James, 1898) before bedtime. Agatha sees herself as compassionate and progressive; she remarks that the "weather is ideal" and ruminates on joining "a new theosophist group"as Hobart announces that the spot is "growing brighter." When he urges her to examine it, she dismisses it as an "aberration of the wallpaper" and suggests that he suffers from indigestion. When Hobart points out that the spot has become "a moving thing/ That spreads and reaches from the wall," Agatha's response denies even his presence: "I cannot listen to you any more just now." After treating her lily with "another aspirin" and finding her own "barbital," Agatha leaves Hobart twitching, "rather feebly," in the aftermath of a convulsion "on the floor," while speculating that his "youthful animal spirits" and "a decided taste for the macabre" have been responsible for his disconcerting "gasping and screaming." Declaring that it is "a beautiful afternoon," Agatha anticipates her evening dinner party and rejoices smugly that "everything is blissfully quiet now" so that she can depart for her routine afternoon nap. Quite apart from her perception of herself, Kees portrays a drastic indifference on Agatha's part that is the result of her mundane, trivial allegiance to and affirmation of the social and spiritual contexts that she unquestionably accepts as her own. Her unexamined, callous optimism has, in fact, destroyed not only her cousin Hobart, but also her own ability to see beyond the surface of a superficial value system. Agatha has not the slightest notion of the presence of evil in the world. Her refusal to acknowledge it is her constant contribution to its growth.

Kees was later to extend his satirical attack on the shallow values of society in a more mature series of poems that center on Robinson, an archetypal ordinary man who has little idea who he is, what he is doing, or where he has been. In the Robinson poems, however, Kees offers sympathy with ridicule, compassion with condemnation, and self-irony with parody. These poems, "Robinson," "Aspects of Robinson," "Robinson at Home" and "Relating to Robinson," show a curious use of the persona in that Robinson is usually absent or nearly absent from the poems. Kees writes primarily of the things or places that once affirmed his existence: the remnants of his life and actions are all that remain of him. When Robinson is present, he is isolated by a room, a hallway or a stairway, or he is insulated from the world to which he attempts to relate by a deep and troubled sleep. When Robinson looks into a "mirror from Mexico," he finds that it "reflects nothing at all." The pages in his books are blank. He attempts to telephone himself at his own empty house. His existence consists solely of traces of himself that he can no longer discern. Throughout the poems, Robinson speaks only once—and then out of a nightmare: "There is something in this madhouse that I symbolize—/ This city—nightmare—black. . . ." Hardly capable of such a statement in his waking state, Robinson speaks here as much for Kees as for himself. What Kees has sought to use as a device, the persona of absence, has resulted, because of his empathy with that persona, in the presence of his own voice. Kees's satire has become self-irony. The shallow life that he had wished to parody has become all too much a part of his own life.

By the final poem in the series, "Relating to Robinson," Kees's pretense of the persona itself has dissolved: "We were alone there, he and I,/ Inhabiting the empty street." The speaker confesses freely that Robinson is a fiction of himself: "His voice/ Came at me like an echo in the dark." As the creator of the persona, the poet must now accept those aspects of himself that he has sought to keep at a distance by his use of the device. Consequently, he must now accept the paradox that he himself is as much the creation of Robinson as Robinson is the product of his art, for he has now "no certainty,/ There in the dark, that it was Robinson/ Or someone else." In his exploration of "surfaces" and his analysis of "illusive pleasures," Kees has successfully overcome the phenomenological alienation between subject and object, but the intensity of his involvement in doing so has left hilm hopelessly entangled in the very shallowness he had hoped to overturn. His success is his failure.

In the wake of this tendency to undermine his own quest (his villanelles and sestinas fail precisely because they cannot contain his blunt confrontation with experience without seeming stillborn themselves), Kees developed a poetic technique that embodies his denial of false values, perhaps best illustrated in "A Salvo for Hans Hofmann," which reveals a good deal more about Kees than it does about the painter. Kees's antagonistic method intends to enter "the slashed world traced and traced again" so that by his entry it is "enriched, enlarged, caught in a burning scrutiny" which will illuminate "like fog-lamps on a rotten night" the decay and debris of contemporary civilization. He sifts through the surfaces, "the scraps of living," that continuously "shift and change," with the hope that by that very act, those fragments can be "shaped to a new identity" for both the self and the world. He seeks a path through the rubble where "the dark hall/ Finds a door" and, purging the pain, "the wind comes in." The search itself, however, remains suspect; the last line of the poem comments on the momentary fragility of any new identity: "A rainbow sleeps and wakes against the wall." If a splendid, euphoric new identity has been rekindled from the debris, then in all probability it too will be contained by experience and thus contaminated just as it has been before. The greater terror, however, is that the "rainbow" itself, while apparently new in its radiant beauty, may not be even a new identity of elusive quality but merely one more delusion grounded in the shallow pleasure of a two-dimensional painting. Once again, Kees finds himself turned back upon himself, just as he did in the Robinson poems.

It is this insistent turning back upon itself of the poem (and the poet) that crushes the faint hope of the self-protecting solipsism such as that found in "The Turtle." In this poem, probably written in the late 1940's, Kees seems to cling to a hope that serene detachment can shelter him from his excavations of despair. As he watches a turtle "beside the road," he is also aware of the "smells/ Of autumn closing in." His sense of dormancy, decay, and death, however, are not merely those associated with seasonal change, for there is little that would foreshadow rebirth in spring. The ominous smells are qualified by the din of "night traffic roaring by" on the superhighway that marks a civilization moving too fast to keep up with itself. His inner response is to feel "a husk . . . inside me, torpid, dry," like stale air "from a long-closed room" that "drifts through an opening door" into a tentative, fragile freedom from the indifferent rush of the world. His hope, at best, is to move "as a turtle moves/ Into the covering grass"; that is, Kees seeks a Whitman-like union with the earth that offers little distinction between life and death. The tenuous, plodding movement away from both the psychological turmoil and the speeding reality of "night traffic" is a denial both of the artifacts of civilization and of the human beings who have allowed such disintegration to occur. That denial undermines even an illusion of hope, for it implies the further denial of one's own life and art.

The slow retreat of the hard-shelled self seen in "The Turtle" into a place "far in the woods, at night" could not be sustained when the creature and its creations began to consume themselves. Kees fell prey to his own methods and convictions, for they carried him to a point of moral dilemma beyond which he could not return. His only choice, then, would seem to have been either the ultimate denial of suicide, or a purgative flight from the self-entangled surfaces to a possibility of a new identity. Many suicides by American poets seem ironically to have confirmed their stature in a world that they rejected. The very ambiguity of Kees's disappearance withholds the rather twisted fascination of the "poet and his suicide" from the shallowness of a society that he denied. Kees's art contains the prophecy that art must move beyond itself to some form of pure action. That was to mean for Kees that he would leave his readers with a mystery that would "cleanse/ What ever it is that a wound remembers/ After the healing ends."

Major publications other than poetry

SHORT FICTION: *Best Short Stories of 1941*, 1941 (Edward J. O'Brien, editor; contains twenty of Kees's stories).

PLAY: *The Waiting Room*, unpublished.

NONFICTION: *Nonverbal Communication: Notes on the Visual Perception of Human Relations*, 1956 (with Jurgen Ruesch; includes photographs by Kees).

Bibliography

Knoll, Robert E. "Weldon Kees: Solipsist as Poet," in *The Prairie Schooner*. XXXV (Spring, 1961), pp. 33-41.

Michael Loudon

X. J. KENNEDY

Born: Dover, New Jersey; August 21, 1929

Principal collections

Nude Descending a Staircase, 1961; *Growing into Love*, 1969; *Bulsh*, 1970; *Breaking and Entering*, 1971; *Emily Dickinson in Southern California*, 1974; *Celebrations After the Death of John Brennan*, 1974; *Three Tenors, One Vehicle*, 1975 (song lyrics in sections by Kennedy, James Camp, and Keith Waldrop); *One Winter Night in August and Other Nonsense Jingles*, 1975 (juvenile); *The Phantom Ice Cream Man: More Nonsense Verse*, 1979 (juvenile).

Other literary forms

Although X. J. Kennedy is best known for his poetry, he has also written reviews, several highly successful textbooks, and one novel for children, *The Owlstone Crown* (1982). Kennedy established himself as a witty and discriminating judge of contemporary poetry through a series of book reviews published in *Poetry* magazine from 1961 through 1966. The lively and lucid style developed in these essays played an important part in the success of his various textbooks and anthologies, which include *Mark Twain's Frontier* (1963, edited with James Camp), *An Introduction to Poetry* (1966, 1982), *Pegasus Descending: A Book of the Best Bad Verse* (1971, edited with James Camp and Keith Waldrop), *Messages: A Thematic Anthology of Poetry* (1973), *An Introduction to Fiction* (1976, 1979), *Literature* (1976, 1979), *Tygers of Wrath: poems of hate, anger and invective* (1981), and *The Bedford Reader* (1982, edited with Dorothy Kennedy).

Achievements

Kennedy's literary reputation rests almost exclusively on three volumes of poetry: *Nude Descending a Staircase*, *Growing into Love*, and *Emily Dickinson in Southern California*. Of his other published volumes, *Bulsh* has been unpopular and difficult to find in libraries; the title poem (reprinted in *Breaking and Entering*) is an entertaining but unimportant satire skewering a modern pretender to sainthood. Most of the poems in *Breaking and Entering* are reprinted from Kennedy's other volumes, although a few (notably "Consumer's Report" and "Drivers of Diaper Service Trucks Are Sad") are unavailable elsewhere. *Celebrations After the Death of John Brennan* is a series of memorial verses inspired by the death of one of Kennedy's former students; it was published in a very limited edition. *Three Tenors, One Vehicle* includes only a few song lyrics by Kennedy, most of which are available in his major collections.

The remaining volumes, *One Winter Night in August* and *The Phantom Ice Cream Man* are intended for children. Over the years, Kennedy has always remained interested in the challenge of composition for an audience that demands nothing more than clarity, wit, and fun. Indeed, he once described children's verse as a form of escape for poets "suffering psychic hangovers from excess doses of Kierkegaard and Freud" and longing to return to "a cosmos where what matters is whether a rabbit can find its red balloon again."

Although Kennedy has written a juvenile novel (*The Owlstone Crown*) and two volumes of nonsense verse, his literary achievement is measured only in terms of his serious poetry. The poems in *Nude Descending a Staircase* won for him both the Lamont Award from the Academy of American Poets and the Bess Hokin Prize from *Poetry* magazine. The publication of *Growing into Love* brought him the Shelley Memorial Award for 1970; and *Emily Dickinson in Southern California* and *Celebrations After the Death of John Brennan* in 1974 brought the Golden Rose from the New England Poetry Club. He has been a Bread Loaf Fellow in poetry (1960), a winner of a National Council on the Arts grant (1967-1968), and a Guggenheim Fellow (1973-1974).

Although Kennedy is often dismissed as a witty minor poet—a self-described "whittler of little boats in bottles"—he may in time be awarded higher stature. He has published sparingly and slowly. More prolific contemporary poets naturally tend to attract more frequent attention and thus are more likely to attain a loftier status in the hierarchy of living poets. Kennedy's verse, however, is of astonishing technical proficiency. Most likely, a large percentage of the poems in his volumes will withstand the test of time. Indeed, they have had to wear well before Kennedy himself would consent to their publication in book form; their appeal to other readers is demonstrated by their frequent inclusion in anthologies.

Kennedy has lived by his "Prayer to an Angry God" that in rereading his own words he should "Not spare,/ But smite." If there is justice in heaven or value in such textbook advice, he should eventually reap his reward.

Biography

The only child of a Roman Catholic father and a Methodist mother, Joseph Charles Kennedy must have sensed early in childhood the atmosphere of spiritual tension and uncertainty that is the most distinguishing and thought-provoking aspect of his poetry. A probable self-portrait of the youthful Kennedy occurs in "Poets," a brilliant and ironic sketch of the sensitive, dithering, bespectacled youths who, like stupid swans trapped in ice, can sometimes be freed to soar in dazzling glory. When only twelve, Kennedy published mimeographed science-fiction fan magazines entitled *Vampire* and *Terrifying Test-Tube Tales*.

He was graduated from Seton Hall University (1950) and took a master's degree from Columbia University (1951) before enlisting in the Navy. After his tour of duty, he spent a year studying in Paris, where he received a *certificat* in 1956. From 1956 to 1962 he pursued doctoral studies at the University of Michigan and came into contact with an elite coterie of young poets from the Detroit-Ann Arbor area. Among his friends of the period were Keith Waldrop, James Camp, Donald Hall, John Frederick Nims, and W. D. Snodgrass. He left Ann Arbor without completing work for his degree, spent one year teaching at the Woman's College of the University of North Carolina, and then joined the faculty of Tufts University, where he eventually rose to be a full professor. Since 1979 he has been a free-lance writer, living in Bedford, Massachusetts, with his wife Dorothy and their five children.

From 1961 to 1964 Kennedy was the poetry editor of the *Paris Review*. In 1971 he and his wife founded *Counter/Measures, a Magazine of Rime, Meter, and Song*, to counter the trend toward poetry in "open forms"—the kind of free verse that Kennedy has satirically described as "Disposable stuff, word-Kleenex." The last issue of the magazine appeared in 1974, and Kennedy's recent verse has itself occasionally been written in open forms.

Analysis

During a memorable exchange of opinions in the *Saturday Review*, John Ciardi insisted to X. J. Kennedy that poets writing in traditional forms strive to create artifacts for posterity and must therefore believe that there *will be* some posterity. In contrast, those writing casual, formless free verse "reject the idea of the artifact" as a result of a belief "that there is no world to follow, or none worth addressing." Kennedy disagreed. Not only did he contend that a poet such as Gary Snyder, who writes in open forms, manifestly believes in an Oriental concept of human continuity, but he also argued that the effort to create a permanent artifact in traditional poetic form does not necessarily imply a belief in any posterity to enjoy that artifact. Instead, he insisted that, "Even if it all goes blooey tomorrow, the act of trying to write a poem as well as possible is a good way of living until then."

The exchange illuminates the ethical as well as the artistic views of X. J. Kennedy. Recognizing the unsettling changes in art and life, and looking ruefully upon the weakening social and literary conventions, Kennedy continually seeks to resolve the tension between the traditional and the trendy, reactionary and radical. Through the course of his three major books of poetry, his world view shifts from a militant traditionalism (implying belief in God, in ever-renewing life, and in conventional verse forms) into a tolerant uncertainty. His recent poems display a lack of faith in traditional values, combined with a lack of trust in the new. Thus, he seems to stand on shifting ground, offering brilliant satirical insights into the modern world, but little advice about how best to live in that world. Indeed, he no longer seems as certain as he once was that traditional values offer "a good way of living until then."

A number of poems in Kennedy's first book, *Nude Descending a Staircase*, express his belief that the time is out of joint. In its very title, for example, "B Negative" suggests the dehumanizing effect of modern urban life. The poem's protagonist is given no name. Instead, he is identified only by his blood type and by an abbreviated description of his characteristics: "M/ 60/ 5 FT. 4/ W PROT." His monologue depicts the sterile environment of the city, where he discovers that it is spring by the increased litter of coughdrop boxes and "underthings cast off," rather than by daisies in the grass. Spring makes little mark on the city, "No bud from branches of concrete." The city is an unnatural, artificial place where pigeons too fat to stand peck shoelaces and eat sacks of corn as if they "grew on a stalk." It is a place so costly that grown men sleep on subways "tucked in funny sheets" taken from the daily newspaper. It is so dense that the sun cannot penetrate to the street level, and so frigid that spring has no "abiding heat." Here a man's virility can wither to impotence after years pronging litter, or shabbily sustained through steamy musings over the gaudy pages of a movie magazine. In the city the seasons have scant significance, and human life, stripped of its own seasonal qualities, becomes scanty too. The city blocks and cubic rooms create human integers that "wake one day to find [themselves] abstract." In cementing over human roots and rhythms, modern urban life generates abnormal beings who become either suicidal or sadistic.

The poem's diction and imagery are especially effective in suggesting the violence inherent in city surroundings. The daisies, for example, are described as "white eyeballs in the grass." The pick with which the speaker prongs litter is called a "stabpole." The subway riders are observed by "guards." The radio is turned off with a "squawk as if your hand/ Had shut some human windpipe with a twist." In this menacing environment the "routed spirit flees" or looks around "for a foothold—in despair." What comfort life is capable of offering lingers only as a memory of the past. In lines futilely addressed to a lost lover, the speaker laments that he can no longer remember "the twist that brought me to your street," nor can he summon up her face or recall her "outline on the sheet." At least for this speaker, the warmth of the past is irretrievable and the future offers only an increasingly frigid isolation.

Elsewhere in this first book of verse, however, Kennedy is confident that survival and sanity can be maintained in the changing modern world. Procreation can assure survival and continuity between past and future, while religion can provide the same sort of guidelines for a sane life that the rules of rhyme and meter provide for a sane poetry. Thus, after surveying various signs of foreboding (slips in the hangman's knot and the price of stocks, movement of mountains, proliferating madness), the poem "All-Knowing Rabbit" concludes with consolation. The rabbit, who eats voraciously to feed the offspring growing in her womb, smugly ponders "All secrets of tomorrow, of the Nile . . . And munches on, with giaconda smile." The rabbit, the Nile, and the giaconda smile are symbols of fecundity. At this stage in his career, it does not occur to Kennedy that exceptional fertility is itself one of the dangers of the mad world he inhabits. Furthermore, in this book Kennedy perceives only dimly the chinks in the armor of conventional religious faith. His poem "In Faith of Rising" sounds more like Gerard Manley Hopkins or George Herbert than the work of a man reared in an era when one catchphrase was, "God is dead." Kennedy's poem is a pious statement of trust that after death God will "cast down again/ Or recollect my dust."

The confident reverence of "In Faith of Rising" is, however, atypical even in Kennedy's early poetry. "First Confession" is much more representative of his general approach, in both content and style. The first confession inspires awe in the child who perceives the priest as a "robed repositor of truth," burns in his guilt while awaiting penance, and later kneels to take communion in "seraphic light." From the more experienced retrospective of the adult, however, the events take on comic overtones. He sees ludicrous elements coexisting with sanctity. The child "scuffed,/ Steps stubborn" to the confessional. His list of sins included the "sip snitched" from his father's beer and a bribe paid his girl friend to pull down her pants. He zealously said his penance twice to "double-scrub" his soul.

Kennedy emphasizes the disjunction between the holy and the humorous by deliberate incongruity in his choice of words. Formal language exuding a dusty odor of sanctity mingles with the stale stench of street speech. The "curtained portal," the "robed repositor of truth," and the dignified priest's "cratered dome" are somewhat sullied by contact with a diminutive sinner who snitches from his "old man's beer" and who bribes his girl "to pee." The priest himself becomes the object of mirth when he doles out penance "as one feeds birds." Even the sacrament of communion is trivialized at the end when the child sticks out his tongue at the priest: "A fresh roost for the Holy Ghost."

The mood that unfolds through "First Confession" is less skeptical than satirical. Modern humans—both priest and penitent—seem out of place within the ancient traditions of the Roman Catholic Church, just as the poem's use of contemporary slang seems to desecrate its setting. This sense of disjunction, of times out of joint, is characteristic of Kennedy's subsequent poetry.

By the time *Growing into Love* appeared in 1969, Kennedy's faith in the traditions of Roman Catholicism had weakened to the point where he could write in "West Somerville, Mass.": "My faith copped out. Who was it pulled that heist?" Here again one sees the bizarre verbal incongruity that had characterized "First Confession," but Kennedy has moved from satire of tottering traditions to outright skepticism and agnosticism. Nevertheless, he clearly feels a loss in abandoning his faith. A number of poems in the volume show his longing for the solidity of the past and his loathing of the impermanence of the present.

In "Cross Ties," for example, the speaker, walking along a railroad track "where nothing travels now but rust and grass," says, "I could take stock in something . . . Bearing down Hell-bent from behind my back." Figuratively, the speaker's situation is also Kennedy's. Uncomfortable in the present, Kennedy walks a track deserted by others. His poems rhyme and scan and he is predisposed toward tradition. In one sense, then, the speaker, like Kennedy, longs for a return to the past when trains served functions now taken over by semitrucks, superhighways, and motels. Both Kennedy and the speaker also long to believe in their lost religious faith with its freight of forces for good and evil. The speaker hears this phantom train's whistle in the "curfew's wail," sees its headbeam in the full moon, and hears the screech of "steel wrenched taut till severed" (the train's brakes?) in the hawk's cry. He explains the fact that no Hell-bent force strikes him down by hypothesizing that he is "Out of reach/ Or else beneath desiring," and he concludes by observing that when he spills the salt he throws some to the devil and he still allows the priest to bless his child.

The superficial appearance of faith in God and Satan is undercut, however, by closer analysis. The speaker begins by saying that he "could take stock in" this malign force. A statement beginning "I could take stock in . . ." normally continues with a conditional clause: for example, "I could take stock in purple people-eaters if someone could show me their lairs." The absence of the expected conditional clause implies that the speaker cannot state the conditions that must be met before he really *believes*. Moreover, it is clear that the speaker willfully imagines the malign force behind his back. He knows that the tracks are deserted, and he knows too that the curfew's wail, the moon's headbeam, and the hawk's cry are wholly natural phenomena. He uses these aspects of everyday reality in an attempt to scare himself into a faith in Satanic evil, for if there is a devil to fear there must also be a deity to love. He is, however, unsuccessful. As he walks along, "tensed for a leap" and trying to imagine some evil behind him, he declares himself "unreconciled/ To a dark void all kindness." This neatly ambiguous phrase could mean that he is unreconciled to an indifferent universe, a malign universe, or a Godless universe, but, whatever it means, it falls far short of positive faith in God. It is a phrase, then, that hedges its bets just as the speaker does with a pinch of salt and a mist of holy water.

The poem's title, "Cross Ties," has a similar multiplicity of meanings. In a naturalistic sense, the poem is about walking on railroad ties, and the title reflects that subject. Yet the poet's central interest is in the ties of emotion between the longing for the past years when engines rode the tracks and the longing for the faith in God that typified those years. Indeed, the poem's title, by suggesting the form of the crucifix, itself links the literal, historical, and religious implications of the poem.

Kennedy's consciousness of the disjunction caused by changes in the modern world finds expression in several poems in *Growing into Love* that deal with the American landscape. In "Main Road West," the television set in a motel room suddenly goes dead, and the speaker, left with "No magazines, no book but the Good Book," is forced to observe and reflect. He finds himself in a denatured environment. Although trees with leaves are few and "The wind's turned off," a sign for used cars burns brightly, keeping out the starlight, "As though stars will be foresworn, or stared down." Thus, the traveler sees that natural resources are being displaced by mechanical artifice.

"Driving Cross-country" makes the parallel point that imaginative resources are also being destroyed through mass-produced mediocrity. The poem begins with a series of baffling and discontinuous allusions to twentieth century counterparts of fairy-tale figures (Jack the Giant-killer, Cinderella, Sleeping Beauty). Collectively, these allusions illustrate how meager is the spirit of the present in comparison with the traditional legends of the past. The Jack the Giant-killers of today sing to cornstalks in Keokuk, and contemporary Cinderellas (with names like Ella Ashhauler) try to scrounge free meals in the Stoplight Lounge. The only magic of the age is that which has filled the nation with identical motel rooms—each deloused and designed by computer to offend no one. Victims of "Some hag's black broth," Americans hurtle down endless highways knowing that "We had a home. It was somewhere./ We were there once upon a time."

In these poems, as in "Cross Ties," there is a longing for a return to a better past—where nature reigned unchained and where natural man indulged in fantasy and belief. Similar points are made in "Peace and Plenty." Pine-clad hills lie stunned and bound by chains of motels; the river is so choked with debris that it cannot choose its course; the new-fallen snow must "Lay bare her body to the Presto-Blo"; and the blown rose finds her "quietus . . . inside the in-sink waste-disposer." By personifying and feminizing the hills, river, snow, and rose, Kennedy creates an image of nature ravished by the vile artificial constructions of man—the motels, engines, chemical wastes, snowblowers, and disposals.

Kennedy's rejection of mechanized and plasticized society is, however, refreshingly apolitical and unpredictable. In 1961, in apparent reaction to the space flights of Yuri Gagarin and Alan Shepard, Kennedy published "The Man in the Manmade Moon," a scathing satire on space flight and those who seek to promote it. Yet by 1969 his views had begun to change. In "Space," he reflects on man's increasing power over nature, a power bemoaned in "Main Road West," "Driving Cross-country," and "Peace and Plenty." He finds that the ability to escape from earth and let the unweighted heart beat freely has appeal, and the whole process of sending massive projectiles careening through the heavens at the flick of a switch makes Kennedy wonder what life will be like after this power spreads and increases: "Who will need long to savor his desire . . . when acts, once dreamt, transpire?" Will man return to the womb? Indeed, is the fetal crouch of the astronauts on takeoff and the fixation with landing on the moon (a traditional symbol of femininity) a disguised attempt to return to the womb? Kennedy explores these questions with sensitivity. Ultimately, he finds that he shares the same desires for escape that have moved men with slide rules to "Render our lusts and madnesses concrete." In a bar or at the wheel of a car, he too attempts to "shrug the world's dull weight" and is surprised to find himself, "Out after what I had long thought I'd hate."

Similarly, in "The Medium Is the Message" Kennedy contemplates the music-oriented youth of America, "transistors at their brains,/ Steps locked to rock." He concludes that "The rude beast slouches"—that Yeats's second coming is at hand and that "words in lines" will soon be obsolete. The modern age rejects the traditional iambic rhythms of the heart and insists instead on a rock music that beats to the "rush-hour traffic's fits and starts." So much is vintage Kennedy—rejecting contemporary changes in favor of the traditional past—but he surprises the reader when he admits that he would drop out only if he could pack along his own high-technology conveniences: "my hi-fi set,/ Electric light, a crate of books, canned beer. . . ."

Kennedy continues to explore his sense of disjunction between past values and present vicissitudes in *Emily Dickinson in Southern California* (1974), but the acute sense of impending disaster that had prompted earlier allusions to Yeats's "The Second Coming" is here replaced by his bemused transplantation of Emily Dickinson into Southern California. Although the title series of poems, like so much of Kennedy's verse, develops in part through incongruity, here the incongruities are more amusing than upsetting. The whole idea of observing the laid-back, let-it-all-hang-out California scene from the perspective of a wry and reclusive nineteenth century spinster is itself incongruous and delightful. Unfortunately, Kennedy does relatively little with this idea. Seven of the nine poems in the series are simple imitations of Dickinson's style and make no effort to force her approach into a confrontation with the modern world.

Kennedy's "Two Views of Rime and Meter" are written in free verse, a form that Kennedy rarely used in his earlier volumes. The first poem compares meter with the repetitious thud of a carpetbeater, and rhyme with the glittering dust. The second compares meter with the rhythm of copulation, and rhyme with the pleasure of simultaneous orgasm. The implications of the first metaphor are that meter and rhyme are monotonous, routine, and stale, while the implications of the second are that both devices are human, primal, delightful, and creative. The two views are incompatible and incongruous; as elsewhere, Kennedy's own position remains unresolved.

To the extent, however, that the debate about meter and rhyme is part of the larger debate about tradition and change, other aspects of the volume suggest Kennedy's increasing sympathy with the twentieth century. There is, for example, the fact that eight of the seventeen pieces in the volume can be classified as free verse. Furthermore, "Categories," a poem that specifically examines modern changes, concludes that one must come to understand transformations and adapt to circumstances. Although species collide, styles expire, and the century clots or collapses, man can begin to understand if "through the tip of his tongue he hear bright red." If this incongruous and paradoxical advice means anything at all, it certainly demands breaking free of perceptual limitations in the effort to grasp a new reality. Similarly, the poem's very last lines show that one must break free of the limitations of tradition. A novice Buddhist monk, "a scrubber of pots," is capable of teaching his master that, having "hatched from names" and lacking clean plates, one can "Serve cake on a shut fan." Thus, the old must learn from the young and the tradition-bound mind must hatch into a new freedom in order to adapt to difficulties.

Appropriately, the poem starts out with six lines of fairly standard iambic pentameter but becomes increasingly free from formal metrical constraints as it proceeds. If anything, this poem is even more sensitive to the rhythms and sounds of poetic language than many of Kennedy's rigorously metrical compositions. Fifteen of the poem's twenty lines can be classified as loose iambic pentameter, but Kennedy repeatedly alters the iambic rhythm to correspond with his rhetorical emphases. Thus, three of the poem's first four syllables are stressed in making the point that "Nothing stays put." An extra accented syllable is packed into the third line, making the description of the "too-close-following cars" onomatopoeic. The century's collapse through the "mind's pained hour-glass" throbs more forcefully because of the series of strong stresses, as does the need to "hear bright red." Perhaps, however, the last line of the poem is the finest example of Kennedy's liberation. Not only is the assertion that one can "Serve cake on a shut fan" an apt imagistic summary of the change in Kennedy's views and the point of the whole poem, but it is also impossible to scan. It has two stresses, two rests, and two more stresses. What could be more rhythmical and yet further from traditional meter?

This change in Kennedy's attitudes toward traditional thinking and traditional poetics is also reflected in a changed view of the American landscape. Perhaps man's creations do litter the land, but Kennedy has moved far from the depressed mood of the collector of debris in "B Negative" and the discouraged travelers of "Main Road West" and "Driving Cross-country." Now he is capable of writing a poem entitled "Salute Sweet Deceptions," in which he observes that in certain lights bare bricks turn amber, beer cans resemble stars, and raindrops clinging to telephone wires look like a "seedpearl necklace."

Kennedy's poetry, as it always has been, is dominated by incongruity, but the intense longing for tradition has been replaced by a mellow toleration of the times, and the intense commitment to meter and rhyme has been replaced by a growing interest in exploring the many forms of modern poetry. Kennedy has been quoted as saying, "Writing in rhythm and rhyme, a poet is involved in an enormous, meaningful game not under his ego's control. He is a mere mouse in the lion's den of the language—but with any luck, at times he can get the lion to come out." One hopes that in the future Kennedy will continue to coax the lion out any way he can. Readers can be just as moved by the natural agility and ferocity of the untamed lion as by brilliant circus tricks in rhyme and meter.

Major publications other than poetry
CHILDREN'S LITERATURE: *The Owlstone Crown*, 1982.
ANTHOLOGIES: *Pegasus Descending: A Book of the Best Bad Verse*, 1971 (with James Camp and Keith Waldrop); *Messages: A Thematic Anthology of Poetry*, 1973; *The Bedford Reader*, 1982 (with Dorothy Kennedy).
MISCELLANEOUS: *Mark Twain's Frontier*, 1963 (edited with James Camp); *An Introduction to Poetry*, 1966, 1982; *An Introduction to Fiction*, 1976, 1979; *Literature*, 1976, 1979; *Tygers of Wrath: poems of hate, anger and invective*, 1981.

Bibliography
Ciardi, John. "Counter/Measures: X. J. Kennedy on Form, Meter, and Rime," in *Saturday Review*. IV (May 20, 1972), pp. 14-15.
"Kennedy, Joseph Charles," in *Contemporary Authors*. IV, pp. 341-342, new revision series.
Kennedy, X. J. "The Poet in the Playpen," in *Poetry*. CV (December, 1964), pp. 190-193.
Rosenthal, M. L. "Poetic Power—Free the Swan," in *Shenandoah*. XXIV (Fall, 1972), pp. 89-91.
Williams, Miller, ed. "X. J. Kennedy," in *Contemporary Poetry in America*, 1973.

Jeffrey D. Hoeper

HENRY KING

Born: Worminghall, England; 1592
Died: Chichester, England; 1669

Principal collection
Poems, Elegies, Paradoxes, and Sonnets, 1657.

Other literary forms

Henry King's significant literary remains other than poetry are his Latin verses and his surviving sermons, which span almost a half-century and provide an excellent record of his ministerial concerns. They have not, however, been collected.

Achievements

A full assessment of King's poetic stature has been slow to evolve. It appears that among his contemporaries King was renowned less as a poet than as a churchman, as an eminent preacher and respected Bishop of Chichester, and there is no evidence to suggest that King would have preferred to be viewed in any other way. It was only in the period during which for political reasons he was forcibly denied his bishopric that King, at a rather advanced age, published his poetry, and his output is relatively modest—by the reckoning of his most modern editor, Margaret Crum (*The Poems of Bishop Henry King*, 1965), only eighty-six poems, exclusive of his little-read and little-esteemed metrical transcriptions of the Psalms. Though the widespread appearance of a number of King's poems in various manuscripts both during his life and for several decades after his death would attest to some popularity, King's poetic achievement as a whole was left to rest in oblivion throughout the eighteenth and much of the nineteenth centuries.

Newly edited and republished in 1843, King's poems attracted some of the attention paid in the late nineteenth and early twentieth centuries to England's poetic antiquities and seventeenth century divines, and when King's good friend and religious associate John Donne came to be "rediscovered" and reacclaimed as one of England's great poets, King's poetic canon began to receive its first sustained critical study. Comparisons with Donne's verse have been inevitable and not wholly to King's advantage. King's personal association with Donne and a general resemblance between the cerebral and sometimes recondite imagery that King employs and the ingeniously involved "conceits" made famous by Donne have led to King's being labeled one of the lesser disciples of Donne's "school," or what Samuel Johnson dubbed the "metaphysical" mode of poetry. That King's imagery is less "knotty" and philosophically adventurous than Donne's and that King's verse lacks the dramatic impact so conspicuous in Donne's have made it easy to confuse difference with inferiority and to view King, not as a poet with his own concerns and idiom, but simply as Donne's unsuccessful imitator. Moreover, the high percentage of his verse which is "occasional," that is, which was prompted by and composed for a particular event, may suggest that his poetry lacks the spontaneity and originality the modern reader demands of poetry.

With closer scrutiny, however, has come the recognition not only that King may owe as much to Ben Jonson as he does to Donne, but also, and more important, that, far from being anyone's servile imitator, King studied and emulated the example of older contemporaries such as Donne and Jonson while fashioning a poetic style through which he spoke with his own distinctive, ever thoughtful, frequently meditative, voice. In the evolution of poetic techniques and tastes in the seventeenth century, King's volume of published verse is a valuable document, encompassing as it does a period of forty-five years (1612-1657), and at once reflecting the poetic practices of the Elizabethan period and presaging those of the Restoration and neoclassicism. To the epigrammatic plainness and conciseness of Jonson's iambic pentameter and tetrameter rhymed couplets, King brings a refinement of expression that heralds the lapidary smoothness cultivated by practitioners of the rhymed couplet form in the middle and later decades of the century, and if some of King's images recall the kind of imagery brought into vogue by Donne near the beginning of the century, the polished trenchancy of some of King's more satiric and polemical pieces foreshadows the great heroic verse satires of John Dryden near the end of the century.

Above all, King's poetry is of immense interest as a lucid record of a poet's response to a most turbulent and critical period in English history, a period which brought fundamental changes to England's political, social, and religious institutions, and which challenged the perceptive poet to examine the purposes and value of his art. Like the actors Hamlet so esteemed, King's poems are "the abstract and brief chronicles of the time," and King himself a diligent poetic chronicler of the significant literary-historical events of his lifetime: the deaths of great poets, the births and deaths of princes and heirs to the throne, the travails and deaths of monarchs. To these subjects King brought the unifying perspective of a poet nurtured in the Renaissance view of the cosmos and disposed to see in the events of the world—no matter how great or small—the workings of a divinely ordered universe. Thus, side by side in King's poetic "Kalendar" stand poems on affairs of state and affairs of the heart; and in the upheavals of the body politic and the death of a king, as in personal disruptions and the death of a wife, King is prepared to read the hints of a greater disorder and the portents of a world with, in Donne's words, "all cohaerance gone." It is in its power to illuminate these correspondences between the "greater" and "lesser" worlds, and between the poet's private self and his public role, that the signal achievement of King's poetry lies.

Biography

Even a cursory examination of the poet's background will suffice to show that Henry King's art is very much a reflection of the life that produced it. Born in 1592, King was the eldest of five sons of John King, scion of an aristocratic family and renowned Anglican divine and eventual Bishop of London. Since John King intended each of his sons to enter the ministry, Henry received an education befitting a man of learning. As a youngster, he attended the Westminster School, where Ben Jonson, among many other notables, had studied, and where, as part of his classical training, he became practiced in the techniques of versification. After he left Westminster he proceeded to Oxford, where he took his B.A. degree in 1611, his M.A. in 1614, and his B.D. and D.D. in 1625.

The oldest son of an influential clergyman, King came into contact as a child and young man with some of the most distinguished churchmen and courtiers of the time, among whom was John Donne. Donne was a good friend of John King and, according to Donne's early biographer, Izaak Walton, grew to be no less fond of Henry. In 1616, as a young student of divinity, King was named to the clerical office of Prebendary of St. Paul's Church, where several years later Donne would become Dean. Their relationship remained close, and shortly before his death in 1631, Donne made King his legal executor. King's final service for Donne came in the form of the funeral elegy he composed, "Upon the Death of my ever Desired friend Dr. Donne Deane of Pauls."

From the example of his father, from his formal education, and, not improbably, from his acquaintance with Donne would emerge the intellectual cast of mind and the religious and political propensities that would permanently shape King's life, his career, and, no less so, his poetry. From all that is known of it, King's life appears to have been a genuinely religious one, predicated on a belief that God's ordinances were embodied in two temporal institutions: the Church and the Crown. Thus, religious orthodoxy and political conservatism were the mainstays of his thought and colored almost everything he wrote. No personal loss—not even the death of his young wife in 1624—could overturn his religious convictions, and, while in his verse he acknowledges the pain of loss most frankly, as he does in the celebrated elegy he wrote for his wife, "An Exequy to his Matchlesse never to be forgotten Freind," his affirmation of the triumph of the immortal soul over death is nonetheless assured.

Nor did the tribulations of the civil tumult weaken his adherence to either Church or monarch, despite the considerable privations his loyalty cost him. In 1643, a victory of the forces representing the Parliamentary and Puritan factions over the Royalist army led to the ejection of King from the bishopric of Chichester to which he had been elevated only a year before. Stripped of almost all of his property and personal papers, King existed on rather modest means—apparently not without some harassment—for the next seventeen years, until, with the Restoration of the monarchy in the person of Charles II, King returned to his church in Chichester. In the years immediately following his ejection, King wrote his most staunchly partisan and pro-Royalist verse, culminating in by far his longest and most passionate pieces, the elegies written just after the execution of Charles I in 1648, "A Deepe Groane, fetch'd at the Funerall of that incomparable and Glorious Monarch," and "An elegy upon the most Incomparable King Charls the First."

Yet, as strong as King's personal convictions were, his best verse is curiously undogmatic. The depth of King's learning and belief manifests itself not in a welter of information to be presented as absolute truth, but in a self-assured spirit of inquiry. If King shares anything with Donne, it is the pleasure he takes in exploring an idea through the play of language and metaphor. Like Donne, King seems often to be probing, discovering the essential likenesses in things that have ostensibly little in common, between an emotional state or religious point, for example, and the physical properties of the universe. Thus, when King takes a position on an issue he does not presume its correctness, but demonstrates it carefully and seriously, yet imaginatively. It is the depth of both his convictions and intelligence that leaves the reader with the sense of having shared or worked through with the poet the experience he presents in his verse. King's poetic corpus may be relatively small, but a survey of his poems gives one the impression of having learned a good deal about their author precisely because King shows so much, not only of what he thinks, but how he thinks as well.

Analysis

Like most of the technically accomplished poets of his era, Henry King was proficient in a wide range of forms and styles. Yet the form which seems to have been most congenial to his poetic temper, and in which he wrote his most memorable pieces, was the elegy. Constituting a significant part of his rather compact volume, elegies punctuate King's entire poetic career, accounting for his first datable poem, "An Elegy Upon Prince Henryes Death" (1612), and his last, "An Elegy Upon my Best Friend L. K. C." (Lady Katherine Cholmondeley, 1657). Indeed—though it is unlikely that King himself would have coveted this distinction—the list of notable personages memorialized so eloquently in his funeral poems might well give King claim to the title of elegiac poet laureate of the seventeenth century.

That what King calls the "Elegiack Knell" peals so resonantly in his verse is in part a measure of the "occasional" and "public" character much of his poetry assumed. For King, as for many of his contemporaries, private experience and public events were not inimical as poetic subjects, but complementary; in both lay hints of universal significance for the discerning poet to interpret and elucidate. Thus, a poem called forth by a particular "occasion"—

the birth of a child or the death of a celebrated war hero—could serve as a vehicle for recording, for solemnizing, the significance of an event for both the poet and the world at large. No "occasion," though, fulfills this purpose more ably than that of death, for no event is at once so private and so public, and when, in turn, death deprives the world of an individual of especial importance, a "Matchlesse" wife, or a "most Incomparable" monarch, for example, the scope of the loss is all the more conspicuous, its implications all the more universal. The "weeping verse" and funeral rites invoked in King's elegies are in part, then, a literary convention by means of which King affirms and reaffirms the common basis of experience that he as a poet shares with the public about whom and for whom he writes.

Still, to suggest that the elegiac strain in King's verse is in some sense "conventional" is not to impugn or belittle what it may reveal about the innermost concerns of King's poetic psyche. In her seminal discussion of "The Laureate Hearse" in *Studies in Seventeenth Century Poetic* (1948), Ruth Wallerstein has persuasively argued that the response to death in the elegiac poems of the seventeenth century crystallized the deepest spiritual and poetic preoccupations of the era, a thesis to which King's elegies prove no exception. For King the "occasion" of death subjected the aspirations of life and art to their most intense scrutiny. In metaphoric terms, King conceived of death as a literary text, the "Killing rhetorick" and "Grammer" of which contained lessons about human experience that King seems never to have tired of reading.

Just how tireless this reading was is suggested not only by the sheer frequency with which elegiac themes appear in King's verse but also by their appearance in poems that are not explicitly funereal pieces and have little ostensibly to do with the issues of death and mourning. A conspicuous example is the poem King wrote in honor of the newly born Prince Charles, entitled "By Occasion of the young Prince his happy birth. May 29-1630." No subject, one would think, has less to do with death than does birth, and, in an ethos in which the divine right of kings was a respected principle, no birth would be a source of as much public rejoicing as would that of a prince and heir apparent. Yet, at the outset of the poem, the reader finds King laboring, not to express his joy but to explain why he has hesitated to write, why at first, in fact, he "held it some Allegiance not to write." What has tempered King's celebrative mood is the recognition that everything that makes the arrival of Prince Charles a welcome event entails a sobering reflection about his father, King Charles. In the advent of a child abides the hope of immortality, along, unfortunately, with the acknowledgement of mortality. Hence, even a newly born child is a *memento mori*, and in that book of harsh lessons by which King metaphorically conceived of death, children form "The Smiling Preface to our Funerall." The arrival of a prince, connoting as it does the hope of a smooth succession and continuity in the royal line, underscores the inevitability of the death of the monarch; to acclaim the birth of Charles the Prince is, King fears, to anticipate and make seem all the more imminent the passing away of Charles the King.

Such insights bring King to something of a dilemma. As a loyal Englishman he would like to use his poetic gifts to frame a compliment to the Crown. Yet his poetic vision enables, obliges, him to see the infant prince both for what he is and for what he represents. The apprehension of mortality and the rhetoric of death force King to see and say things inappropriate to the ostensibly complimentary occasion; but to excise his elegiac concerns, King implies, is to render his compliment hollow and poetically false.

King's solution, both in this poem and in many others, is to reconcile his elegiac presentiments with his religious convictions and to turn the occasion of paying a compliment into an opportunity for teaching a salutary lesson. True, the birth of an heir is a tacit intimation of mortality, but mortality itself is but a milestone on the soul's journey to immortality, and but the last instance of finitude before all time is transformed into the infinitude of life everlasting. To pretend to ignore death, to be obsessed with prolonging life on earth, is to repudiate a fundamental article of faith: "And wee in vaine were Christians, should wee/ In this world dreame of Perpetuitye." Rather deftly, King pays the royal father the ultimate compliment of eschewing flattery and appealing, instead, to wisdom and Christian humility to accept a wholesome truth: "Decay is Nature's Kalendar; nor can/ It hurt the King to think He is a Man." With these reflections articulated, and with the fullest implications of the Prince's birth understood, King can with more genuine enthusiasm acclaim the happy event and even look forward to that time when young Charles will "lead Succession's goulden Teame" and ascend to his father's throne.

The poem on "the young Prince" exemplifies the pattern of argumentation that King pursues in much of his verse, wherein, with varying degrees of success and conviction, he strives to achieve a synthesis in which elegiac sadness and pessimism over the transience of this world is answered by religious belief in the permanence of the next. Nowhere, perhaps, is this religious elegiac vision more moving and more triumphant than in King's most frequently anthologized piece, the poem he wrote upon the death of his young wife Anne, "An Exequy To his Matchlesse never to be forgotten Freind." What at first seems peculiar about this poem, which deals with so emotionally charged an experience, and which ultimately manages to be so moving, is that it at first appears so distanced, so oddly impersonal. Little is learned about Anne herself, and one wonders at first whether King is merely making use of the death of his wife as a pretext for a philosophical discourse. One has only to read a little way into the poem to discover that it is delivered as a meditation in which Anne is a rather abstracted presence. The title of the poem may promise that it is addressed "*To* his Matchlesse never to be forgotten Freind" [italics added], but the poem opens with the poet apostrophizing a burial monument, "Thou Shrine of my Dead Saint." To the extent that Anne herself is addressed at all within the first ten lines of the piece, it is not as a person but as "Deare Losse," It is this "Losse" which consumes all of the poet's emotional energy, but that energy has been subsumed in study, in a commitment to do nothing but "meditate" on the loss itself. It is the "Deare Losse" which forms "the Book,/ The Library whereon I look."

Although the poet at first seems to be distanced from Anne, it is precisely this distancing that establishes the emotional tension and intensity within the poem. The poet must turn to the study of his loss because that is all that is left him; all that remains of Anne, after all, is the "Lov'd Clay" lying in the tomb. In the discipline of meditation, then, the poet finds a method of coping with death and a means by which he may explore the psychology of grief and "compute the weary howres/ With Sighes dissolved into Showres."

Initially, at least, meditation enables the poet, not so much to allay his grief, as to define its scope. The emotional void left by the death of Anne makes existence as a whole a desolation because it was Anne who gave existence its meaning. Here the influence of Donne upon King becomes readily apparent, for in attempting to define the impact of his wife's loss, King employs the kind of imagery used by Donne to illustrate the experiences of separation and loss in poems such as "A Valediction: Forbidding Mourning" and "A Nocturnal upon Saint Lucy's Day." The extinction of Anne's life is like the extinction of the sun, since it was she who brought "Light and Motion" to the poet's now darkened "Hemispheare." Yet this is a "straunge Ecclipse," one "As ne're was read in Almanake," because it was not caused by the obstruction of the moon but by the earth itself, which in reclaiming Anne's "Lov'd Clay" has "interposed" itself between the poet and his sun.

What makes this "Ecclipse" especially "straunge" is not merely its provenance but its duration. Unlike a "normal" solar eclipse, this one is not transitory, but will endure as long as the earth endures. The eclipse of the poet's world is not an extraordinary phenomenon but a systemic and all too ordinary condition. With the recognition of this fact comes the realization of the immensity of the poet's loss. In depriving the poet of his wife, mortality has made earthly existence at once a void and a barrier to their reunion that can only be surmounted by the extinction of existence itself.

Still, implanted in the depths of King's sorrow are the very seeds of his remission, although King's recognition and articulation of this truth proceed as much from the promptings of his faith as from the workings of his intellect. If by dying Anne has succumbed to the mortality inherent in her earthly nature, it follows that all things earthly, including the earth itself, must inevitably succumb as well. Thus, the onerous sentence of King's grief bears with it the promise of a terminus, and King can look forward to that apocalyptic "Day" when "a fierce Feaver must calcine/ The Body of this World," even as a more localized fever has already consumed the body of Anne, "My Little World."

The expectation of the world's dissolution would not be much of a source of comfort to the poet were it not coupled with his unqualified belief in a universal Resurrection. On this premise turns the argument—and the mood— of the latter parts of the poem. Death becomes, then, less a boundless condition than a transitional event: the death of the body brings about the liberation of the soul, while the death of earthly existence is the purificatory and regenerative mechanism by which "our Bodyes shall aspire/ To our Soules blisse." So it is that no hint of equivocation mars the confidence with which the poet envisions that endless day on which "wee shall rise,/ And view our selves with cleerer eyes/ In that calme Region, where no Night/ Can hide us from each other's sight." Moreover, that the poet begins to use pronouns such as "wee" and "us" suggests that the reunion with Anne to be attained in the general Resurrection is already under way, and that the gulf created by death which had so tormented the poet at the outset of the piece has already been bridged by the poetic process of meditation. Death becomes less an insuperable foe than a functionary accountable to a higher power. Anne's tomb is less a devourer of her flesh than a temporary custodian whose duty will be to return on the day of the Resurrection an accurate "reck'ning" of "Each Grane and Atome of this Dust." Nothing has been, or will be, lost.

At the same time, it is a measure of the complexity and artistry of King's vision that no matter how assured his faith leads him to be about the ultimate implications of death, its immediate reality remains no less horrid. Although King's quickened religious insight may enable him to think of Anne now, not as someone gone forever, but as his temporarily sleeping bride, there is something chillingly reminiscent of Juliet's entombment in the Capulets' charnel house in the picture of King's young wife, enfolded with "Black Curtaines," lying on "Thy cold bed/ Never to be disquieted." Death seems no less importunate, no less an interloper, and when the poet poignantly takes "My last Goodnight" he forcibly acknowledges that he is still very much wedded to the things of this world, "to that Dust/ It so much loves." Indeed, the poet's resounding triumph in the conclusion of the poem takes the form of a paradox: the more fully he affirms his mortality the more clearly he beholds the date of his transcendence, the very rapidity with which mortality encroaches setting the pace by which immortality approaches. It is this image of mortality fused with immortality in one relentless motion that resonates in the cadences of King's parting assurance to his wife that "My pulse, like a soft Drum/ Beates my Approach, Tells Thee I come," while the resolute stroke of eight monosyllabic words underscores the poet's final promise that "I shall at last sitt downe by Thee."

Elegiac sadness for the human condition merges with religious conviction in King's poem to his wife to produce an illusion of poise and inner assurance which make the poem one of the great elegies of the language and, not surprisingly, his most highly esteemed work. In other poems, King's vision is more darkly elegiac, his remorse over the fragility of human existence less evenly tempered by the consolation of faith. One striking instance is the twelve-line epigram entitled, "Sic Vita," a poem very much in the *memento mori* tradition, the very compression and conciseness of which give dramatic immediacy to its familiarly elegiac theme that existence is transitory and all too peremptorily brief. In the first six lines of the poem, King presents a series of six exquisite and ephemeral natural phenomena whose exquisiteness, in fact, arises from their ephemeral character and from the teasing hope they engender that somehow they can be preserved, frozen in time. The space is very small, but King manages to select examples that are representative of the diverse operations of the natural world, both great and small: a falling star, a soaring eagle, the fecundity of spring, a gust of wind on the sea, some dew drops, some bubbles on the surface of water. All of these are introduced as terms of one extended simile, and in the seventh and eighth lines one discovers that what draws them together, besides their ephemeral attractiveness, is that they are emblems of man. Man is but one more image of transience, and, like the other entities of nature, he too has a life and "Light" that are "borrow'd" and will be "streight Call'd in, and Pay'd to Night."

If it took only one eight-line sentence to establish the common bond between man and the other elements of his universe, it takes only one four-line sentence to make the implications of this bond briskly and brusquely clear. Swept up in the annihilative rush of time, mortality, and King's swiftly paced iambic tetrameter verse are all the things of nature, including man and, worse, all traces of man's life: "The Dew dryes up: The Starr is shott:/ The Flight is past: And Man Forgott."

For King, the brevity of existence is, however, often only a catalyst for other, even more somber, ruminations about the human condition. Indeed, the importunity of death would hold little but terror for King did he not see it as the culmination of the sorrows that afflict and waste a man's life. "What is th' Existence of Man's Life?" King asks rhetorically at the outset of "The Dirge," only to answer the question immediately: "open Warr, or Slumber'd Strife," from which "Death's cold hand" alone provides a reprieve. What makes this "strife" most pernicious is that it arises from the disorders that original sin has wrought upon the human soul and psyche, effectively making man his own implacable foe, in whom "each loud Passion of the Mind/ Is like a furious gust of Wind."

It is this perception that makes King, at his most pessimistic, a satirist in the vein of the writer of Ecclesiastes, a scourge of vanity, of the delusions and emptiness that are the inveterate accessories of one's existence. Such is certainly the stance King assumes in "The Dirge," in which he concludes by employing one of William Shakespeare's recurrent metaphors, likening man's existence to a play, "a weary Enterlude," the acts of which are consumed by man's "vaine Hope and vary'd Feares," and the only fitting "Epilogue" to which is "Death." Even more stridently contemptuous is the assessment of man and his aspirations that King offers in "An Elegy Occasioned by Sicknesse." Here illness becomes a meditative device to turn one's attention inward and "Make Man into his proper Opticks look,/ And so become the Student and the Book." What this self-inventory reveals is rather deflating. From conception and birth man is ordained to emerge as little else but "complicated Sin." At the height of his pretensions he is merely "Poore walking Clay," fated to be "a short-liv'd Vapour upward wrought,/ And by Corruption unto nothing brought."

In the face of these dour appraisals of man's worth, the value and role that King allots in his poetry to meditation and the self-scrutiny entailed in meditation become clear. Central to King's excoriation of human vanity is the premise that man's intellect is a casualty of his spiritual defects, that vanity prevents man, for all his apparent intellectual attainments, from knowing himself and what conduces to his own good. Thus, the meditative strain so recurrent in King's poems has, in part, a hortatory function and invites man to lay aside the studies of the external world with which he is so preoccupied in order to study himself, his "proper Opticks," the better to confront and dispel, if possible, the mists impairing his vision.

Such is the challenge posed in "The Labyrinth," which opens with the proposition that "Life is a crooked Labyrinth" in which man is "dayly lost" and then proceeds to draw the reader into a scrutiny of the conundrums that lie at the heart of human conduct. How can it be that man can know what is good, resolve to do the good, and then lapse and relapse into wrong, ever erring, never extricating himself from the labyrinth his will has created? "Why is the clearest and best judging Mind/ In her own Ill's prevention dark and blind?" What contrition can possibly be effective when the mind has become so practiced at begging forgiveness while rationalizing the commission of sin, when, like the usurper King Claudius in Hamlet, the sinner cannot in good conscience seek to undo what he has done since he knows that he would do it again? The more thoughtfully the reader ponders these questions, the more surely he is drawn into the labyrinth the poet is describing, for in posing these questions the poet has been appealing to the reader's intellect; and the more the reader acknowledges the intellectual validity of the questions, the more deeply he identifies himself as an intellectual and implicates himself in the cycle of rationalization and recrimination that the labyrinth comprises.

Are there answers to these questions? None, King implies, that can be provided by human intellection, even as there are no strategies the intellect can devise on its own for coping with the experience of death. The intellect is part of the problem, and, unaided, it cannot provide a solution to what King calls "this home-bred tyranny." Instead, King can only abjure his intellectual pretensions and appeal to God for the insight which the human mind lacks. With a nod to Ezekiel (11:19), King calls upon God in his redemptive power to soften man's heart and "imprint" upon his "breast of flint" the marks of true contrition, for it is only through the genuine conversion of the heart that the mists clouding the mind will be dispersed. For King, as for his contemporaries, there was no inherent dichotomy between the mind and the emotions, the affections of the mind following directly from the disposition of the heart and soul. Thus, God is beseeched to provide not merely emotional reassurance but intellectual clarity, or "thy Grace's Clew," with which King, like some latter-day, Christianized Theseus, may aspire to thread his way through "this Labyrinth of Sinne/ My wild Affects and Actions wander in."

The skepticism with which King regards the powers of the human intellect very much affects the attitude he brings to the intellectual activity of writing poetry. If the intellect is impaired by its own frail mortality, then the verse that the intellect produces will be similarly inept, incapable of dealing satisfactorily with the experiences and paradoxes of the human condition. Indeed, in depicting the phenomenon of death, for example, as a text, as a book with its own lessons to impart, King explicitly calls attention to the deficiencies of his own text, his verse. Thus, in his early "Elegy Upon Prince Henrye's Death," King not only laments the passing of the young prince, but wonders how his own verse can ever do justice to the occasion or presume to vie in eloquence with the succinctly "Killing rhetorick" of death, which manages to embody "Woe's superlative" in only two words: "Henry's dead." Again and again, King's poetry runs a poor second either to the experience to which it responds or to the emotion it is intended to express. "And think not," he hastens to assure his deceased friend in "The Departure: An Elegy," that "I only mourne in Poetry and Ink." Rather, the "melancholy Plummets" of his pen "sink/ So lowe, they dive where th'hid Affections sitt." So impatient does King ultimately profess to become with the inadequacy of his verse that in his last datable poem, "An Elegy Upon my Best Friend, L. K. C." (Lady Katherine Cholmondeley, 1657), King announces his "long Farewell" from his poetry, "That Art, where with our Crosses we beguile/ And make them in Harmonious numbers smile"—a valediction in which King strives for that elusive fusion of art and life by burying his verse with his friend.

It is not to impugn King's sincerity to suggest that his insistence upon the deficiencies of his poetry owes a good deal to convention. As an apt student of poetry and poetic tradition, King would have been quite aware of the innumerable writers of and before his time who displayed their eloquence by lamenting their ineloquence, who emblazoned the depth of their passion or sense of loss by artfully expressing their inability to express their passion or loss. With King, however, the convention acquires something of the force of a personal signature. Loath to divorce his poetic craft for his life, he was even less willing to excise his verse from the principles and beliefs that gave his life its purpose. Convinced of the contingency and vulnerability of human existence, King could not consider his poetic exercises as anything but reflections of his own limitations. King would not have minded very much the gentle irony that the very powers he denigrated in his verse helped to ensure the continued survival and appeal of that verse.

Bibliography
Berman, Ronald. *Henry King and the Seventeenth Century*, 1964.
Fuller, Thomas. *The Worthies of England*, 1952. Edited by J. Freeman.
Mason, Lawrence. "The Life and Works of Henry King, D.D.," in *Transactions of the Connecticut Academy of Arts and Sciences*. XVIII (November, 1913), pp. 227-289.
Tuve, Rosamund. *Elizabethan and Metaphysical Imagery*, 1947.

Thomas Moisan

GALWAY KINNELL

Born: Providence, Rhode Island; February 1, 1927

Principal poems and collections
What a Kingdom It Was, 1960; *Flower Herding on Mount Monadnock*, 1964; *The Poems of François Villon*, 1965 (translation); *On the Motion and Immobility of Douve*, 1968 (translation); *Poems of Night*, 1968; *Body Rags*, 1968; *Lackawanna Elegy*, 1970 (translation); *First Poems 1946-1954*, 1971; *The Book of Nightmares*, 1971; *The Avenue Bearing the Initial of Christ into the New World: Poems 1946-1964*, 1974; *Mortal Acts, Mortal Words*, 1980; *Selected Poems*, 1982.

Other literary forms
Galway Kinnell has published a novel, *Black Light* (1965, revised 1980), a short story, "The Permanence of Love" (*New World Writing*, 1968), and various translations—including René Hardy's novel *Bitter Victory* (1965). Kinnell also has written theoretical essays, among them "The Poetics of the Physical World," in *Iowa Review*. He has also published *Walking Down the Stairs: Selections from Interviews* (1978).

Achievements
Kinnell has created one of the most eclectic yet distinct American voices in contemporary poetry. His extensive journeying and sojourning in the country's varied regions have helped him develop this unique voice, which modulates between the northeastern *savoir faire* of "The Avenue Bearing the Initial of Christ into the New World" (*What a Kingdom It Was*) and the southwestern savvy of "The Last River" (*Body Rags*). Kinnell, in the tenor of Walt Whitman and Robert Frost, vividly evokes the locales he describes.

Kinnell's achievement also lies in his perfecting both the lyric and the narrative poem. From the tender melody of "First Song" (*What a Kingdom It Was*) that wakes a boy's heart "to the darkness and into the sadness of joy" to the more jarring "The Milk Bottle" (*Mortal Acts, Mortal Words*), "where a sea eagle rings its glass voice," the three decades of Kinnell's lyrics illustrate the progression of modern music from harmony to resolved discord. Kinnell's longer poems are artfully structured, the sections discrete yet one evolving into the next. *The Book of Nightmares* is the most exemplary; it is a ten-part poem with each part in a sense shaped as a contemporary ode composed of seven sections.

In reviewing *Body Rags*, Laurence Lieberman described Kinnell's recurring themes, explaining that his "generosity of spirit and . . . empathy for the mutilated souls of the crushed, the beaten, the solitary proud victims of back alleys and backwoods, give all of his work the rare quality of that which has been profoundly seen, witnessed, lived to the bones." In addition to the powerful images, themes, and language, and to the sense of immediacy conveyed by the first-person narrator, Kinnell's poetry is ultimately one of optimism. Even the most haunted poems, "The Avenue Bearing the Initial of Christ into the New World" and *The Book of Nightmares*, end literally with laughter.

Kinnell has received a Ford grant and a Fulbright (1955) and two Guggenheim Fellowships (1962, 1974), a National Institute of Arts and Letters Award (1962), a Longview Foundation Award (1962), a Rockefeller Foundation grant (1968), a National Endowment for the Arts grant (1969-1970), and numerous poetry prizes, including *Poetry* magazine's Bess Hokin (1965) and Eunice Tietjens Memorial Prize (1966), the Cecil Hemley Prize (1968), the Poetry Society of America's Shelley Memorial Award (1972), the National Institute of Arts and Letters Award of Merit Medal (1975), and the Landon Translation Prize (1979). Kinnell's poetry appeals not only to the purely literary, intellectual audience but also to the popular, as the journals and books in which he has published indicate: *Poetry*, *Atlantic Monthly*, *The New Yorker*, *Nation*, *Paris Review*, *Ladies' Home Journal*, and the *Pocket Book of Modern Verse*. Few poets have traveled as extensively to present readings of their poems; few have attracted such responsive audiences or promoted more enthusiasm for poetry.

Biography

Galway Kinnell was born in Providence, Rhode Island, on February 1, 1927. He grew up in Pawtucket, Rhode Island; his hometown and the surrounding New England countryside provided materials for much of his poetry. The Ten Mile River of Hornpout, for example, appears in "The Last River" (*Body Rags*), and "The Hen Flower" (*The Book of Nightmares*) reflects an understanding of chickens learned in the family henhouse in the backyard. In *Walking Down the Stairs*, Kinnell recounts that at the age of twelve writing poetry was what he wanted to do even though he did not begin writing seriously until he was eighteen.

Kinnell attended Princeton University for one semester in 1944, joined the Navy, and six months later returned to the university on the G.I. Bill of Rights. He left the Navy in 1946 and was graduated from Princeton *Summa Cum Laude* in 1948 with a B.A. degree. At Princeton, Kinnell was a student of the poet Charles Bell, author of *Songs for a New America* (1953), who encouraged Kinnell in his writing. Sharing an interest in the pioneer spirit of America, the two men began a professional relationship and a lifelong friendship. Though he was at Princeton with the poets R. P. Blackmur and John Berryman, Kinnell did not study with them. He did share his poems with another student, however; this was the poet W. S. Merwin, who also introduced him to the poetry of William Butler Yeats. Yeats, along with Walt Whitman—whom Kinnell did not discover until his early twenties—was to have the most profound influence on the young Kinnell. Kinnell lists his earliest influences, however, as Edgar Allan Poe, Emily Dickinson, Percy Bysshe Shelley, William Wordsworth, Rudyard Kipling, A. E. Housman, and even James Whitcomb Riley and Robert W. Service.

Kinnell received his M.A. in English in 1949 at the University of Rochester. He then taught and traveled extensively in the United States and abroad. Kinnell was an Instructor of English at Alfred University from 1949 to 1951 and the Director of the Liberal Arts Program at the Downtown Center of the University of Chicago from 1951 to 1955. In 1955, he went to France and translated the poetry of François Villon on a Fulbright Fellowship, serving as a *lectuer americain* at the University of Grenoble in 1956-1957 and at the University of Nice in 1957. Kinnell then returned to the United States as an Adjunct Assistant Professor for the Division of General Education at New York University. In the 1950's, he taught correspondence courses for the University of Chicago, an activity which inspired "The Correspondence School Instructor Says Goodbye to His Poetry Students" (*Body Rags*). In 1957, Kinnell suffered the tragic loss of his thirty-two-year-old brother Derry, for whom he wrote the elegy "Freedom, New Hampshire" (*What a Kingdom It Was*). In the late 1950's, he also met Inés Delgado de Torres, a native of Spain, whom he married in 1965. She read and translated Spanish poetry for him, introducing him to the poems of Pablo Neruda.

In 1960, Houghton Mifflin published Kinnell's first book of poems, *What a Kingdom It Was*. That same year Kinnell went to the University of Teheran in Iran on a Fulbright Fellowship and journeyed extensively through the Middle East. His experiences in Iran inspired the novel *Black Light* (published in 1966). In 1963, Kinnell was a field worker for the Congress of Racial Equality, registering blacks to vote in Louisiana. In conjunction with this work, he was jailed briefly, which inspired him to write about his experiences in "The Last River." In the early 1960's, Kinnell lived in the same building in New York City as the poet Denise Levertov; they shared poems, and from her comments Kinnell learned much about such matters as line breaks and verbal economy.

In 1964, *Flower Herding on Mount Monadnock*, Kinnell's second book of poetry, was published. From 1964 to 1970, Kinnell was Poet-in-Residence at Juniata College, Reed College, the State University of Colorado, the University of Washington, the University of California at Irvine, and the University of Iowa. The 1960's also saw the publication of *Body Rags* in 1967 and the birth of Kinnell's daughter Maud in 1966 and of his son Fergus in 1968; the names of both were inspired by his Irish ancestry and the Irish lore of Yeats. These two births served as the framework for *The Book of Nightmares* published in 1971. From 1969 to 1970, Kinnell was a resident writer at Deya

Institute, Mallorca. In the 1970's, he was a visiting professor at Queens College, the Pittsburgh Poetry Forum, Skidmore College, and the University of Delaware; he was an adjunct professor at Columbia University; a visiting poet at Sarah Lawrence College, Princeton University, and the University of Hawaii; a visiting professor of poetry at Brandeis University; and a Poet-in-Residence at Holy Cross College. In 1978, Kinnell returned to the University of Nice as a Fulbright lecturer and for the next three years was a Citizens' Professor at the University of Hawaii, spending one semester as a visiting writer at Macquarie University in Sydney, Australia.

In 1980, *Mortal Acts, Mortal Words* was published, largely reflecting Kinnell's family life. The death of his mother in 1974 is the subject of "Goodbye" and "The Last Hiding Places of Snow," and the experiences of his son open the collection with "Fergus Falling" and "After Making Love We Hear Footsteps." In 1979, Kinnell became Director of the Squaw Valley Community of Writers, and in 1981 he became Professor of English and Director of the Creative Writing Program at New York University, two positions which he currently holds. He makes his home in Sheffield, Vermont.

Analysis

The predominant themes of Galway Kinnell's poetry have been identified variously as pain, alienation, death, the mystery of time, the violence of twentieth century America, and, most recently, domestic life. Yet all of these motifs are in truth *leitmotivs* for Kinnell's major theme of mortality in all its nuances—the world, humanity, and death. Kinnell creates his poems from the real elements of the earth. "When stones come into a poem," he says in *Walking Down the Stairs*, "they usually are actual stones. Part of poetry's usefulness in the world is that it pays some of our huge unpaid tribute to the things and creatures that share the earth with us." Poetry readings are like skywriting, Kinnell says, as he insists on the power of the physical world and on the poem's power to represent it. Thus he stresses humanity's "sympathetic feelings, our capacity to know the life of another creature by imagining it." This banishing and vanishing of the ego echoes John Keats's notion that the poet has no single identity, that "if a Sparrow come before my Window I take part in its existence and pick about the Gravel." In his essay "The Poetics of the Physical World," Kinnell espouses "the glory of the ordinary," an outlook similar to that of William Wordsworth. Kinnell, though, makes the idea starkly modern, describing images as "those lowly touches of physical reality which remain shining."

Kinnell renders his obsession with the physical world in vivid imagery, in earthy language, and in metaphors of nature. Kinnell is an acute observer of the world around him, and in his poetry he *becomes* that world. Thus, for example, he can identify with animals that humanity ordinarily fears or loathes; he internalizes their essences, and presents them as fellow mortals.

"The Porcupine" and "The Bear" in *Body Rags* are two extraordinary examples, in Kinnell's words, of loving the things and creatures that surround us: "the capacity to go out to them so that they enter us, so that they are transformed within us, and so that our own inner life finds expression through them." Through this process of observation, internalization, and expression, the creature becomes at once a physical and a spiritual reality. In "The Porcupine," for example, Kinnell writes:

> In my time I have
> crouched, quills erected,
> Saint
> Sebastian of the
> sacred heart, and been
> beat dead with a locust club
> on the bare snout

The vividness and particularity of the porcupine with "quills erected," "beat dead," "locust club," and "bare snout" are evoked with simple, concrete words, first-person voice, and a conversational tone reminiscent of Frost. The extended symbol of the porcupine as Saint Sebastian visually recalls the martyr's being left for dead with arrows in his body and later clubbed to death for professing Christianity. Kinnell's reinterpretation of traditional symbols offers his reader a fresh view of the world, as in the lyric "How Many Nights" (*Body Rags*), which concludes with "a wild crow crying '*yaw yaw yaw*'/ from a branch nothing cried from ever in my life." This crow, no longer the traditional symbol of ill omen, breaks the terror of the night with its yea-saying call.

Kinnell's love for particularity and his identification with nature allow him to depict varying locales in startling detail. For example, in "The Last River" the essence of Louisiana is evoked as the reader encounters the ferry boats and the levee, the crepe myrtle tree, a passion flower, the "little tugs and sticklighters," "the courthouse in Amite," and the sonorous Louisiana names Ponchatoula, Plaquemine, Point Coupee. From the richness of the indigenous detail, the poem, like the river it describes, widens and deepens to establish relationships between North and South, black and white, man and man, man and nature. Kinnell magnifies the power of the Mississippi River, "The Mystic River" (the poem's original title), as he associates it with other American rivers—the Ten Mile of Hornpout in Rhode Island, the Passumpsic in Vermont, the East River in New York, and the Tangipahoa in Louisiana. In this way, Kinnell's voice becomes uniquely American.

Although the formal concerns of Kinnell's work have changed markedly since his juvenilia, his poems represent the physical world in the rich sounds of the words and in the thickly textured lines. In his early poems, Kinnell adhered to fixed forms, using traditional rhymes and meters, which he varied and eventually broke away from in order to write free verse. Stressing that form deals with the inner shape of a poem as well as the outer, Kinnell explains in "The Poetics of the Physical World" that "Whitman gave up the attempt to be a poet like the others and followed, rather, his own intimations of a wilder, freer poetry which could not be contained in the old forms." Kinnell does the same, and his poetry resounds with echoes of the physical world. "First Song" displays rich internal rhymes that compose a song in themselves: "in Illin*ois*, the small b*oy*/ *After* an *after*noon of carting d*ung*/ H*ung* on the fence rail" (italics added). In "Poems of Night," Kinnell illustrates the mystery of language with the line "Zygoma, maxillary, turbinate." In "Another Night in the Ruins," the modulations of the vowel "o" lead the reader through the poem and echo the haunting theme:

> I hear nothing. Only
> the cow, the cow
> of nothingness, mooing
> down the bones.

The play with the words in "The Hotel of Lost Light" from *The Book of Nightmares*—"post for him/ his final postcards to posterity"—is typical of the whimsical play with language and sound that Kinnell uses to capture the physical world in his verse, to illustrate the magical powers of language, and to illuminate the humorous facets of a dark world. "Blackberry Eating" and "Lava" in *Mortal Acts, Mortal Words* stand as two recent examples.

The Avenue Bearing the Initial of Christ into the New World is a collection which includes *First Poems 1946-1954*, *What a Kingdom It Was*, and *Flower Herding on Mount Monadnock*. Kinnell's early poems are of historical interest for the influences they reflect. "Two Seasons," for example, in *First Poems 1946-1954*, echoes Yeats's "Adam's Curse." The vivid imagery and powerful yet simple language that Kinnell assimilates and makes his own is most apparent in "The Comfort of Darkness," in which "Only the comfort of darkness/ Could melt the cries into silence,/ Your bright hands into mine," and in "The Feast," in which "The sand turns cold" and the two lovers rise and leave their "two shapes dying in each other's arms." "A Bird Comes Back" in *Flower Herding on Mount Monadnock* (like "The Fly" in *Body Rags*) is a direct response to Emily Dickinson's "These are the days when Birds come back" (130) and "I heard a Fly buzz—when I died" (465). In "The Descent," with an image and an insight worthy of Dickinson, Kinnell writes:

> No one
> Had told me heaven is overhead.
> I only knew people look down
> When they pray.

"The Middle of the Way," with its use of simple allegory, shows the influence of William Blake:

> In the heart of a man
> There sleeps a green worm
> That has spun the heart about itself,
> And that shall dream itself black wings.

Perhaps the greatest influence on Kinnell was Whitman, for critics have called Kinnell "the most American of our poets," a title Whitman enjoyed as author of *Leaves of Grass* (1855), typified by the lyric "I Hear America Singing." The twentieth century Kinnell hears a discordant America, as he records in "Vapor Trail Reflected in the Frog Pond" (*Body Rags*): "And I hear,/ coming over the hills, America singing, her varied carols I hear:/ crack of deputies' rifles . . . sput of cattleprod . . . TV groaning . . . curses of the soldier."

In *What a Kingdom It Was*, Kinnell's first major collection, the poet finds his own voice—so eloquent in the lyric "First Song," in which a boy harmoninzes with the sounds and creatures of nature—but most powerfully evoked in the longer poem "The Avenue Bearing the Initial of Christ into the New World." Regarding this longer poem, the reviewers agreed with Selden Rodman, who wrote in *The New York Times Book Review*: "I do not hesitate to call this the freshest, most exciting, and by far most readable poem of a bleak decade." "The Avenue Bearing the Initial of Christ into the New World" opens with the sounds and sights of Avenue C in New York City. It resounds with "pcheeks," clacks, swishes, "tics," squeaks, clanks, shrieks, clangs, and *oi weihs* from baby birds piping to be fed, to pushcarts and brooms, to black gospelers, to the laments of aged Jews. Residents, vendors, and transients people Avenue C; bakeries, fishmarkets, vegetable stands, and junkhouses display their wares.

As Ralph Mills writes,

> The poem evokes, through myriad impressions of the particulars of daily experience interspersed with the poet's imaginative projection into individual lives and his allusive imagery, provocative ironies, a comprehensive vision of people existing under circumstances of destitution . . . in a country that supposedly extends promises of refuge.

The poem is divided into fourteen sections, "the fourteen stations of the cross, down the fourteen intersections of Avenue C. . . . It is Israel in exile—the Jews, Negroes, Puerto Ricans who have become God's chosen people because they are [the] despised and rejected of men—bearing, like the Avenue itself, the initial suffering of man," writes Sherman Hawkins. "The Avenue Bearing the Initial of Christ into the New World" is one of Kinnell's most well-received poems, sometimes compared to T. S. Eliot's *The Waste Land* (1922). James Atlas wrote that Kinnell's poem builds "its immense rhetorical power from the materials of several dialects, litanies of place, and a profound sense of the spiritual disintegration that Eliot divined in modern urban life." Atlas concludes that the chaotic forces of survival preside over the latent terror in civilization.

Kinnell's next volume of poetry, *Flower Herding on Mount Monadnock*, is most distinguished by its title-poem. "Flower Herding on Mount Monadnock" opens much as "The Avenue Bearing the Initial of Christ into the New World" does—with birds heralding the dawn; but the reader is transported to the New Hampshire countryside, where the whippoorwill has hushed and the peabody bird and the mourning dove sing. Kinnell portrays not the decay of the city but rather the lushness of the country: "Grasshoppers splash up where I step,/ The mountain laurel crashes at my thighs." Despite the change in scenery, the poet must nevertheless face mortality, and he creates images of transience and death:

> I know
> The birds fly off
> But the hug of the earth wraps
> With moss their graves and the giant boulders.

As in "The Avenue Bearing the Initial of Christ into the New World," Kinnell invokes the four elements of earth, air, fire, and water, but "Flower Herding on Mount Monadnock" does not evoke the world of the holocaust—of human sacrifice and worldly decay—but reveals instead the world of nature, its self-sacrifice on the altar of a mountain. The final section of the poem is the most perfectly crafted. An ode in miniature, it alternates between one-line and three-line stanzas, as Kinnell describes his vision, physical and spiritual, of a flame-colored flower: "The invisible life of the thing/ Goes up in flames that are invisible,/ Like cellophane burning in the sunlight." In this mystical vision, Kinnell hears the flower "uttering itself in place of itself," its action of dying being its only life. The flower, at once partaking of all four elements, floats in the Empyrean and is a "wrathful presence" on earth. Kinnell frames his expanding symbol with spare but striking imagery, demystifying the flower to emphasize its mortality. This final section opens: "In the forest I discover a flower." It closes simply but poignantly: "It is a flower. On this mountainside it is dying."

One of Kinnell's best collections, *Body Rags* helped to foster his reputation as a superior lyric poet. The opening poem, "Another Night in the Ruins," recalls the theme of "Flower Herding on Mount Monadnock," but the poem focuses on the human being rather than on the flower. The speaker must learn, as he says in the concluding section, that he is not a phoenix,

> that for a man
> as he goes up in flames, his one work

is
to open himself, to *be*
the flames.

This process of self-knowledge and purification invites the "poetics of empathy" that allows the poet to create a poem such as "The Bear," one of Kinnell's most often anthologized shorter poems.

"The Bear," the concluding piece of *Body Rags*, takes its energy from the immediacy of its first-person narration, the present tense, the vivid actions, and the sensual imagery. Kinnell imagines himself as an Eskimo hunting a bear, planting a sharpened bone in blubber that will pierce the bear's organs, tracking the animal by its spilled blood which he eats for survival, feasting on its fallen body, shrouding himself in its skins, and dreaming of himself as a bear. The language is simple, precise, and effective. The verbs are colorful and active. The poem moves quickly and passionately—driven by the repetition of the conjunction "and," and by the startling imagery of sight, sound, and motion. "The Bear" ends with an affirmation of life: geese appear on the flyway, the dam-bear licks her cubs—"lumps of smeared fur/ and drizzly eyes into shapes," and the poet becomes the bear, "wandering: wondering/ what, anyway,/ was that sticky infusion, that rank flavor of blood, that poetry, by which I lived?" The poem can be read as an allegory of creation (the hunt lasts seven days), as a tale of a shaman who draws his magic from the animal he becomes, or as a simple tale of hunting; but most certainly, as the last lines suggest, "The Bear" is about writing poetry. Though the uninitiated reader may consider poetry as static and intellectual, Kinnell shows that for him poetry is dynamic and visceral, a matter of life and death. Kinnell transforms the physical action of "wandering" to the mental action of "wondering." He becomes the bear, and through incantation the reader becomes Kinnell becoming the bear.

The Book of Nightmares transforms the rags of the body to the shrouds of the mind. It is one of Kinnell's most powerful works and nearly defies description. Four years in the writing, the poem established Kinnell as one of America's best contemporary poets. Of the book, the poet M. L. Rosenthal wrote that it leaves its readers with "a true voice, a true song, memorably human." Donald Hall, another contemporary poet, wrote of "the presences of the poem: children, hotels, war, a sheriff, an airplane, the henyard, stars," explaining that "We do not enter *The Book of Nightmares*; it fills us up."

Here Kinnell's vision is at once real and surreal: it is a collage of images, precisely rendered, yet presenting subconscious mental activities. The poem is divided into ten parts, each of seven sections. As Katha Pollitt noted in *Nation*, the poem is written "in a Whitmanesque language at once flexible and charged, slangy and highly literary—that explores the interconnectedness of death and cruelty and violence with life and human love." The poem's first part, about the birth of the poet's daughter, Maud, and the last part, about the birth of his son, Fergus, serve as a frame for the poem. The opening image in part I, "Under the Maud Moon," merges the four elements of the universe, as the speaker lights a fire in the rain: "On the path,/ by this wet site/ of old fires . . . for her,/ whose face I held in my hands . . . I light/ a small fire in the rain." The next eight sections offer the dark vision of *The Book of Nightmares*—a vision of death, desolation, possession, war—but hope, like the small fire that keeps its flames through the final section, prevails.

The eight middle sections are richly varied. Part II, "The Hen Flower," takes as its subject the essence and mystery of hens. Part III, "The Shoes of Wandering," portrays the speaker possessed by the shoes of a previous owner now dead. Here is the culmination of Kinnell's identification with and internalization of the life surrounding him. The poet imagines himself as neither a flower nor a hen nor a bear, but literally puts himself in the shoes of another human being, follows in his footsteps, and dreams his nightmare. In Part VI, "The Dead Shall Be Raised Incorruptible," Kinnell invokes the horror of war: "*Lieutenant!/ This corpse will not stop burning!*" The vision is at once a literal abomination and a symbol of the twentieth century—"of my iron will, my fear of love, my itch for money, and my madness." These surrealistic visions and possessions, like waking nightmares, are terrifyingly realistic.

Kinnell himself emphasizes the poem's theme of mortality when he asserts that from one perspective *The Book of Nightmares* "is nothing but an effort to face death and to live with death." In *Walking Down the Stairs*, he explains that death has two aspects—"the extinction, which we fear, and the flowing away into the universe, which we desire—there is a conflict within us that I want to deal with." The poem closes where it began, and Part X, "Lastness," opens with the fire lighted in Part I: "Somewhere/ behind me/ a small fire goes on flaring in the rain." The bear presented in Section 2 of Part I reappears in Section 2 of Part X. In Part I, the speaker watches the bear eat a few flowers and trudge away, his fur glistening in the rain; in the final section, this bear watches another bear "eat a few flowers, trudge away,/ all his fur glistening/ in the rain." The observer and the observed, like the hunter and the hunted, become one. Part I, "Lastness," despite its title—or perhaps because of it—includes (as did "Under the Maud Moon") the birth of a child. Kinnell imagines birth as flaming into fire and song, inspired perhaps by the descent of the Holy Spirit in tongues of flame. He has described his daughter in her birth turning "blue as a coal" until at last "she sucks/ air, screams/ her first song—and turns rose." Birth and death form a continuum.

"Lastness" is a deluge, a confluence of the images from earlier sections:

> Here, between answer
> and nothing, I stand, in the old shoes
> flowed over by rainbows of hen-oil

. . . .
> On the river the world floats by holding one corpse.
> Stop.
> Stop here.
> Living brings you to death, there is no other road.

Kinnell asserts that not only does life bring the inevitability of death but it also brings individuality—an impenetrable singleness—and loneliness. Thus, in this his tenth and last poem, Kinnell envisions one and zero walking off the pages of his poem together: "one creature/ walking away side by side with the emptiness." Though Kinnell asserts that one must come to terms with death, he concludes that this reconciliation leads not to despair but to happiness, for "'*The wages of dying is love*'"—mortality is redeemed by love. *The Book of Nightmares* concludes:

> On the body
> on the blued flesh, when it is
> laid out, see if you can find
> the one flea which is laughing.

This lone flea in all its parasitic nastiness, by the very fact of its personified transformation through laughter, shows how Kinnell shatters the stereotypes of human perceptions. The laughing flea represents Kinnell's genuine optimism.

Mortal Acts, Mortal Words, Kinnell's most recent work, deals largely with the daily rounds of domestic life. As Margaret Gibson notes: "He gives us a distillation of his understanding of what it means to be son and father, husband and friend, lover." The critic Harold Bloom, writing in *The New York Times Book Review*, noted that Kinnell speaks straight out of the self and that his predominant metaphor is the flame of the Pentecost. The most effective poems here deal directly with death—death of a mother, father, brother, lover. "Goodbye" is a poem about endings and death, specifically about the death of the speaker's mother. Kinnell concludes his poem with a piece of wordplay illustrating a previous theme—"*the wages of dying is love*": "It is written in our hearts, the emptiness is all./ That is how we have learned, the embrace is all." "Emptiness" becomes transformed in the "e," "m," "p," and "s" to the "e," "m," "b," "s" of "embrace." The metaphor of the embrace—whether between man and woman or parent and child—has always been a central one for Kinnell. Central in "To a Child in Calcutta" and "Under the Maud Moon," the embrace is preserved vividly in "The Burn": "yesterday my/ arms/ died around you like old snakeskins."

Love—particularly the physical union of love—is a pervasive theme in Kinnell's poetry. "Love," the poet writes in "Flying Home," "is its own power,/ which continually must make its way forward, from night/ into day, from transcending union always forward into difficult day." Ironically, in

Mortal Acts, Mortal Words it is the waking day of worldly and commonplace existence that creates the nightmares and not the phantasmagoria of *The Book of Nightmares*. For Kinnell, love is a partaking of eternity. In "Pont Neuf at Nightfall," the speaker envisions the last portion of the light of the world as a very dim light in a hotel, a "past-light" as he calls it, one already part of memory, hovering over the lovemaking of a young couple who by their act "give themselves/ into time, and memory, which affirms time." Thus this light of the world, as Christ called himself on earth, is re-illumined by earthly love. Instants of finite time form the infinite time of memory.

From his earliest lyrics through "The Avenue Bearing the Initial of Christ into the New World" and "Flower Herding on Mount Monadnock," to the later poems "The Bear," *The Book of Nightmares*, and *Mortal Acts, Mortal Words*, Kinnell takes up again and again the subject of mortality—the brevity and dearness of life—human, animal, plant; Jew and Christian; black and white; flower, hen, and bear. He demonstrates the power of love to break the bonds of prejudice, of emptiness and time. In the penultimate stanza of *The Book of Nightmares*, Kinnell describes his poem as

> this earthward gesture
> of the sky-diver, the worms
> on his back still spinning forth
> and already gnawing away
> the silks of his loves, who could have saved him,
> this free floating of one
> opening his arms into the attitude
> of flight, as he obeys the necessity and falls. . . .

The metaphor here creates a paradox, for the silks of love that comfort people on earth are spun by the same worms that sever people from these loves and feed on their corpses. For Kinnell, the poem is a Christ-like gesture of falling to earth, arms open, offering the salvation of love—in Blake's words, "Eternity in an Hour."

Major publications other than poetry
NOVELS: *Black Light*, 1965, 1980; *Bitter Victory*, 1965 (translation).
SHORT FICTION: "The Permanence of Love," 1968.
NONFICTION: "The Poetics of the Physical World," 1971; *Walking Down the Stairs: Selections from Interviews*, 1978.

Bibliography
Atlas, James. "Autobiography of the Present," in *Poetry*. CXXV (February, 1975), pp. 295-302.
Hawkins, Sherman. "Galway Kinnell: Moments of Transcendence," in *The Princeton University Library Chronicle*. XXV (Autumn, 1963), pp. 56-70.

Howard, Richard. "Galway Kinnell," in *Alone with America: Essays on the Art of Poetry in the United States Since 1950*, 1969.

"Kinnell's 'First Song,'" in *The Explicator*. Melvin Walker La Follette, XIV (April, 1956), item 48; Gene H. Koretz, XV (April, 1957), item 43; James R. Hurt, XX (November, 1961), item 23.

Logan, John. "The Bear in the Poet and the Poet in the Bear," in *Nation*. CCVII (September 16, 1968), pp. 244-245.

Mills, Ralph J. "A Reading of Galway Kinnell," in *Iowa Review*. I (Winter, 1970), pp. 66-86, and I (Spring, 1970), pp. 102-122.

Nancy Wicker

RUDYARD KIPLING

Born: Bombay, India; December 30, 1865
Died: London, England; January 18, 1936

Principal collections

Schoolboy Lyrics, 1881; *Echoes*, 1884 (with Alice Kipling); *Departmental Ditties and Other Verses*, 1886; *Barrack-Room Ballads*, 1892; *The Seven Seas*, 1896; *An Almanac of Twelve Sports*, 1898; *Recessional and Other Poems*, 1899; *The Five Nations*, 1903; *Collected Verse*, 1907; *A History of England*, 1911 (with C. R. L. Fletcher); *Songs from Books*, 1912; *Sea Warfare*, 1916; *Twenty Poems*, 1918; *The Years Between*, 1919; *Rudyard Kipling's Verse: 1885-1918*, 1919; *Q. Horatii Flacci Carminum Librer Quintus*, 1920 (with Charles L. Graves, A. D. Godley, A. B. Ramsay, and R. A. Knox); *Songs for Youth*, 1924; *Sea and Sussex from Rudyard Kipling's Verse*, 1926; *Songs of the Sea*, 1927; *Rudyard Kipling's Verse: 1885-1926*, 1927; *Poems 1886-1929*, 1929; *Selected Poems*, 1931; *Rudyard Kipling's Verse: 1885-1932*, 1933; *The Sussex Edition*, 1937-1939; *Rudyard Kipling's Verse: Definitive Edition*, 1940.

Other literary forms

Rudyard Kipling is best known for his short stories. His *Just So Stories* (1902), *The Jungle Book* (1894), and *The Second Jungle Book* (1895), are favorites with children and are among the most widely read collections of stories in the world. His novel *Kim* (1901) also ranks among the world's most popular books. Kipling's fiction, however, presents a critic with most of the problems that his verse presents, making it difficult to discuss one without the other. The fiction is often thought to be barbaric in content and representative of a discredited imperialistic point of view; too often, critics discuss Kipling's political views (which are often misrepresented) rather than his literary merits. Kipling's contempt for intellectualism makes him unfashionable in most critical circles, and those who admit to having admired him seem to be ashamed of their affection. Not all critics, however, have been ambiguous in their admiration of Kipling's work; especially since the 1960's, critics have made the short stories objects of serious study. In any case, Kipling's fiction has remained immensely popular from the late Victorian era to the present. It has been made into no fewer than thirteen motion pictures, including *Captains Courageous* (1937) and *The Jungle Book* (1942 and 1967). Kipling's fiction has the vigor and passion that appeal to the popular imagination, and a subtlety and brilliant prose style that are worthy of careful study.

Achievements

Henry James called Kipling a genius; T. S. Eliot called him a writer of verse who sometimes ascended to poetry. His *Departmental Ditties and Other*

Verses brought him extravagant praise and fame. Some scholars assert that he was the world's best-known author from the 1890's to his death. Yet, even his admirers have been uncertain of his achievement, particularly in poetry. Kipling often sang his poems while he composed them; they are often ballads or hymns, and all feature clear rhythms that urge a reader to read them aloud. Their surface themes are usually easy to understand; the language is clear and accessible to even casual readers.

Perhaps the accessibility of Kipling's verse is the source of the confusion; twentieth century critics have all too often regarded poetry that is popular among the great unwashed as automatically bad; obscurity has been the hallmark of much of the best of twentieth century poetry. Kipling's verse is informed by the Victorian masters, such as Alfred Tennyson and Algernon Charles Swinburne. It is out of step with the Modernist school, which may be why many readers think of Kipling as Victorian, even though he actively wrote and published into the 1930's; his autobiography appeared in 1937, the year after his death. His harsh views of ordinary people, his angry polemics, political conservatism, and lack of faith in so-called utopian societies, and the Cassandra-like prophecies of war which fill much of his verse, repel many aesthetes and political liberals. Kipling has been portrayed as a philistine. The truth is that he did not understand much of the social change of his lifetime, but he understood people, and in his verse he preserves the thoughts, emotions, hopes, and despairs of people usually ignored by poets. If one approaches his verse with an open mind, one will likely find brilliant prosody, excellent phrasing, surprising metaphors, and a poetic ethos that transcends literary and political fashion.

Kipling won the Nobel Prize for Literature in 1907. The award was, in part, a recognition of Kipling's worldwide appeal to readers; he touched more hearts and minds than anyone else of his generation. His work added phrases to the English language; few today realize that they paraphrase Kipling when they assert that "the female is deadlier than the male," or that "East is East and West is West."

Biography

Joseph Rudyard Kipling was born in Bombay, India, on December 30, 1865. His parents were John Lockwood Kipling and Alice (née Macdonald) Kipling. His father was then a sculptor and designer, and was Principal and Professor of Architectural Sculpture of the School of Art at Bombay, and he later became Curator of the Museum at Lahore. His mother came from a family of accomplished women. John Lockwood Kipling set many of the high standards for literary skill that Rudyard endeavored to match in both fiction and poetry. Both parents encouraged their son's literary efforts and took pride in his achievements.

Except for a brief visit to England, Rudyard Kipling spent his first five years in India. In 1871 he was taken with his sister Alice to England and left with Captain and Mrs. Holloway of Lorne Lodge in Southsea. After several unhappy years in the ungentle care of Mrs. Holloway, he left Lorne Lodge in 1877. In 1878, he was sent to United Services College in Devon. In 1882, he traveled to Lahore, where his father had found him a job as a reporter for the *Civil and Military Gazette*. He had seen little of his parents since 1871. Somewhat to his annoyance, he discovered that his parents had gathered the verses from his letters to them and had them published as *Schoolboy Lyrics* in 1881. In 1887, he joined the staff of the *Pioneer* of Allahabad, which he left in 1889. His experiences in England figure in many of his stories; his experiences as a journalist in India are reflected not only in his fiction, but also in much of his best verse.

In 1888, Emile Edouard Moreau began The Indian Library, primarily to help Kipling and to capitalize on the young writer's talents. The first six volumes of the series consisted of Kipling's work. In 1889 Kipling traveled to Singapore, Hong Kong, Japan, through the United States, and to England. His *Departmental Ditties and Other Verses* was printed in England in 1890, and the response to his poetry moved him from the status of a promising young writer to the forefront not only of English letters, but also of world literature. His writing from 1890 onward brought him wealth and lasting popularity. The initial praise of his work was extraordinary—in 1892, Henry James wrote to his brother William, "Kipling strikes me as personally the most complete man of genius (as distinct from fine intelligence) that I have ever known"—but by the 1900's he would suffer extraordinary abuse at the hands of the critics. Kipling married Caroline Starr Balestier in 1892 and moved to Brattleboro, Vermont, where her relatives lived. While living in the United States he had two daughters. Although he liked his home in Vermont, Kipling left the United States when his enmity with his brother-in-law became public and created a scandal. After some traveling, he returned to visit his mother-in-law; during a stay in New York he and his family fell ill; his wife, younger daughter, Elsie, and baby son, recovered quickly, but he nearly died and his elder daughter, Josephine, did die.

He settled at Rottingdean in England in 1897. His wife took charge of much of his family and social affairs, and A. P. Watt, a literary agent, handled his literary and business affairs. His life in Rottingdean was productive, but isolated; as the years passed, he saw less and less of his literary friends. In 1907, to the chagrin of his detractors, he won the Nobel Prize for Literature. His poetry at the time warned England of impending war and of England's unpreparedness. When war began in 1914, his son, with his father's help, enlisted in the army. In late 1915, John Kipling was killed in a British attack during the Battle of Loos. From the end of World War I to his death, Kipling worked to perfect his literary art and vigorously expressed his opinions on politics and society. At the end of his life he wrote his autobiography and helped prepare the Sussex Edition of his works. He died January 18, 1936, while embarking on a vacation. His ashes were buried in Westminster Abbey's Poets' Corner.

Analysis

Rudyard Kipling's poetry is such a part of the culture of English-speaking people that one is hard put to approach his work without preconceived notions of its quality and content. In his own day, Kipling's poetry outraged many critics and provided handy epithets for politicians of many political leanings. Even today, scholars can be excited by his so-called racial and imperialistic topics. Myths thus abound. Kipling's verse is called racist; in fact, Kipling's verse repeatedly emphasizes that no one can rightfully be regarded superior to another on the basis of race or origin. "The White Man's Burden," he wrote, was to "Fill full the mouth of Famine/ And bid the sickness cease." Although imperialistic, the poem emphasizes not race, but the obligations of Europeans and Americans to the oppressed peoples of the world.

Kipling is said to glorify warfare by devoting much of his poetry to descriptions of the lives of soldiers; in fact, he shows war to be ugly and stupid. In "The Last of the Light Brigade," he portrays veterans of the Crimean War as destitute: "We leave to the streets and the workhouse the charge of the Light Brigade!" In the poem, Kipling calls attention to the differences between Tennyson's poetic description of the ill-fated charge and the degradation that characterized the soldiers' lives. Another myth is that Kipling's poetry is coarse and crude. The subject matter is, indeed, sometimes crude, but not the prosody. Even T. S. Eliot, who admired Kipling's work, asserted that Kipling wrote good verse that occasionally ascended to poetry, but that in general Kipling did not write poetry. Some of the sources of misconceptions about Kipling's poetic achievement seem obvious: casual or careless readings might glean only the surface remarks of subtle poems; Kipling's political poetry was and remains unpalatable to many people who condemn it on no other grounds than political distastefulness; his aggressive dislike of academics and admiration for men of action alienate many of those who would be likeliest to write about his poetry. Some of the negative myths are Kipling's fault. If one writes on the politics of the moment, one invites political interpretations of one's work.

Nevertheless, too much of the criticism of Kipling's poetry is clearly biased. Many rationales for denigrating the poetry seem contrived, as if covering reasons that would not bear exposure. After all, portraits of the hard lives of working people, as well as soldiers, dominate novels from Zola to the present; such novels are often praised for their realism. One of the most highly regarded Anglo-American poets of the twentieth century, Ezra Pound, was a Fascist who made propaganda radio broadcasts from Italy during World War II. His avowed racism is well-known and is as unpalatable to well-informed and compassionate people as anything to be found in the work of Kipling. Indeed, Kipling deplored Nazi Germany and dictatorships in general. Yet Pound was fashionable; Kipling was not.

Kipling's unfashionableness has its origins in two important aspects of his poetry: his versification was clear and usually unadorned, and his subjects were usually plain, working-class people. He began his career in the Victorian era, and his lyrical and narrative poetry has more in common with the styles of Tennyson, Robert Browning, and Swinburne, than it has with the styles that have been predominant in the twentieth century. One of the important aspects of Modernism in poetry was the emphasis on metaphor; metaphors were used to make such works as Eliot's *The Waste Land* (1922) hauntingly remote from casual reading. Critics came to expect good poetry to demand close and sometimes prolonged reading in order for one to understand even the most basic meanings of the verse.

Kipling's approach to his poetry was neither better nor worse than that of his later contemporaries; it was merely different, because he aimed for an audience other than the literary elite. Poetry had been a genre for popular reading; Kipling kept it such. His best poetry will reward close reading by perceptive readers; it will also reward the unskilled or casual reader with a basic surface meaning. For example, "Loot" provides a basic discussion of techniques for looting; the persona—the poem's speaker—says, "always work in pairs—/ It 'alves the gain, but safer you will find." A quick reading elicits the picture of a lowly soldier providing a description of an ugly but realistic aspect of war (and provides ammunition against Kipling for anyone who is determined to misread the poem as somehow glorifying looting). A close reading of the poem, however, reveals a careful use of language; Kipling uses his knowledge of soldiers and their ballads to give his persona an authentic voice. One will also discover a picture of the mindless violence and degradation of war at the level of the common foot soldier. Kipling's style was out of step with the literary movement of his day; it was judged by the wrong standards and often still is.

Poetry has traditionally been regarded as the elite of literary genres. The term *poet* was reserved in the sixteenth, seventeenth, and eighteenth centuries for those who had excelled in literature; it was a term of honor to which writers aspired. Poetry has been thought of as appropriate to high aspirations and great ideas; it has been considered "elevating." The Victorians added the notion that poetry was morally uplifting and that a poet was obliged to discuss high topics in grand language; thus, biblical phrasing and high-sounding archaisms such as "thee" and "thou" lingered in nineteenth century poetry. No matter how much they were involved with the literary revolutions of their time, Kipling's contemporaries were children of the Victorians. Many of the most admired poems of the first three decades of the twentieth century focused on the Arthurian legends or revived Latin poetic traditions.

Kipling's poetry, in contrast, focuses on common people, the active people whose raw manner of dealing with the world most interested him. Soldiers, as the frequent vanguard of the British Empire and the products of the laboring classes, were often subjects of Kipling's poetry; laborers themselves were also often the subject of his verse. Kipling gave these people voices; his keen insight made his language strikingly acute. It is coarse, harsh, and elemental. In addition, the poetry by which he is best known is in the ballad form. The ballad is a lyrical folk song that grows and changes with use and custom; it is heard in bars, at country fairs, and in the barracks of soldiers. Kipling's use of the ballad explains in part Eliot's judgment that Kipling is a verse-writer instead of a poet; the form is believed by some scholars to be beneath poetry.

Thus, elitism has had much to do with negative responses to Kipling; critics seem to believe that Kipling has degraded verse. Even though he was a conservative with some Victorian notions of poetry, Kipling was ahead of his time. Egalitarianism has been one of the significant movements in the twentieth century; literacy has burgeoned, as has access to literature. Kipling wrote for the broad literate mass of people; he gave voices to people who were generally left out of poetry, and he did not romanticize them. A soldier's achievement is to survive one more day; a laborer's achievement is to feed himself one more day. Their contempt for those who are not physically active fits well with Kipling's own disgust with aesthetes who are out of touch with much that is thought and done by those who provide the foundations for civilization.

Kipling's verse is highly crafted poetry. It uses metaphors and prosody in unusual ways, but this is a strength, not a weakness. Kipling's mastery of metaphor is apparent, for example, in "The Way Through the Woods," which describes an eroded road that was closed some seventy years before. On its surface, the poem offers a wistful description of the encroachment by the wilderness on a road no longer used. It is more than that, however; there is an eeriness in its description of "coppice and heath," "ring-dove broods," and "trout-ringed pools," which all utterly hide a road that makes its presence felt only in echoes of the past. The lost road and the woods that have covered it are metaphors for the passage of time and the transitoriness of human works. The theme of the fragility of human achievements is an important one in poetry; in "The Way Through the Woods," Kipling makes the theme mystical and haunting.

The near futility of human endeavors when confronting time is a common motif of Kipling's work. Although "The Way Through the Woods" is remote in tone and metaphor, Kipling is perfectly willing to be blunt—and still metaphorical. In "Cities and Thrones and Powers" he uses flowers as metaphors:

Cities and Thrones and Powers

> Stand in Time's eye,
> Almost as long as flowers,
> Which daily die:

The poem continues and turns tragedy into triumph:

> But, as new buds put forth
> To glad new men,
> Out of the spent and unconsidered Earth
> The Cities rise again.

Few readers would have trouble understanding the basic metaphor: flowers die but leave seeds that grow into new flowers, and cities do the same. Even Kipling's eccentric phrase "Almost as long as flowers" is within easy reach of the unsophisticated reader: in the vastness of time, cities exist only briefly. The surface meanings of the central metaphor do not preclude subtlety. The transitoriness of "Cities and Thrones and Powers" is a melancholy topic, one that other poets have used to show the vanity of human achievements. Percy Bysshe Shelley's "Ozymandias" is the archetypal expression of the theme; a pedestal alone in the desert bears an almost meaningless inscription: "My name is Ozymandias, king of kings:/ Look on my works, ye Mighty, and despair!" Shelley adds: "Nothing beside remains." A city and civilization are reduced to desert. Kipling takes the same sad theme, attaches it to flowers, making the frail plants bear the weight of civilization, and in flowers he reveals that seeming transitoriness is in fact a cycle of renewal. "Time," he says, "Ordains . . . That in our very death,/ And burial sure,/ Shadow to shadow, well persuaded, saith,/ See how our works endure!" In the deaths of human works are the seeds of new works: one civilization begets another.

Kipling's interest in the passing and survival of civilizations also extended to current events. In "The Dykes" of 1902, he ponders the dangers to Britain posed by the militancy of Europe. "These are the dykes our fathers made: we have never known a breach," he says. The people of Britain have built protections against their enemies, but through neglect the "dykes" might be broken. "An evil ember bedded in ash—a spark blown west by the wind . . ./ We are surrendered to night and the sea—the gale and the tide behind!" Kipling the prophet uses metaphor to warn of war. "The Dykes" is dynamic and threatening; history has shown its warning to be apt.

Kipling's narrative poetry is probably his best-known. It includes "Gunga Din" and "The Ballad of East and West," both of which discuss British imperialism and cultural differences and are thus unfashionable. "Gunga Din" is as well-known a poem as exists in English. In it Gunga Din, a water-bearer for British soldiers in India, faithfully serves his masters and saves the life of the poem's narrator—giving up his own life in the process. Kipling uses the rhythm of the ballad form to create strikingly memorable phrases, including the last lines:

> You Lazarushian-leather Gunga Din!
> Though I've belted you and flayed you,
> By the livin' Gawd that made you,
> You're a better man than I am, Gunga Din!

The language is raw and the verse melodic; the combination is powerful. Gunga Din's life is shown to be miserable, and his masters are shown as beastly, but Gunga Din is revealed as having a noble quality that Kipling valued; Gunga Din cares enough for his fellow men to die for them. Thus, the last line summarizes the central theme of the poem; Gunga Din is the better man.

In a similar vein, "The Ballad of East and West" shows that all men can understand one another in the fundamental test of courage:

> Oh, East is East and West is West, and never the twain shall meet,
> Till Earth and Sky stand presently at God's great Judgment Seat;
> But there is neither East nor West, Border, nor Breed, nor Birth,
> When two strong men stand face to face, though they come from the ends of the earth!

Kipling admired men of action and physical courage. He asserted that men can communicate on fundamental levels that transcend the veneer of culture. In "The Ballad of East and West" two strong men are brought face to face, their differences seemingly beyond hope of peaceful resolution. They discover that they are alike and not as different as others would believe. Beginning as enemies, they part as friends.

Kipling dealt with large metaphysical ideas, with the cycles of civilizations and the threats to Western civilization, yet for all his great themes, Kipling was at home with subjects no more lofty than the ordinary person's hope for a better future. In "The Absent-Minded Beggar," for example, Kipling reminds his readers of the hard lot of the dependents of the soldiers who fought in the Boer War. "When you've finished killing Kruger with your mouth,/ Will you kindly drop a shilling in my little tamborine/ For a gentleman in khaki order South?" The poem was written to help raise money for the needs of the families of the soldiers. The tone is sympathetic but honest. The British soldier has "left a lot of little things behind him!" The "little things" include children—not necessarily legitimate—wives, lovers, girl friends, and debts. The families will "live on half o' nothing . . . 'Cause the man that earns the wage is ordered out." The soldier is "an absent-minded beggar, but he heard his country call." Kipling's language demonstrates his understanding of his subject. The poem reveals the fundamental Kipling—not imperialist, not prophet, not poet playing with great poetic conceits—but a poet who understands people and cares about them. Few writers can be honestly said to have cared more about their subjects than Kipling.

Long after the politics of his day are forgotten and his polemics have become of interest only to literary historians, Kipling's essential efforts will still have meaning. Readers who approach Kipling's verse with a love for poetry can still declare as did David Masson to his students at Edinburgh in 1890, while holding a copy of "Danny Deever," "Here's Literature! Here's Literature at last!"

Major publications other than poetry

NOVELS: *The Light That Failed*, 1890; *The Naulahka: A Story of West and East*, 1892 (with Wolcott Balestier); *Captains Courageous: A Story of the Grand Banks*, 1897; *Kim*, 1901.

SHORT FICTION: *Quartette*, 1885 (with John Lockwood Kipling, Alice Macdonald Kipling, and Alice Kipling); *Plain Tales from the Hills*, 1888; *Soldiers Three: A Collection of Stories*, 1888; *The Story of the Gadsbys: A Tale Without a Plot*, 1888; *In Black and White*, 1888; *Under the Deodars*, 1888; *The Phantom Rickshaw and Other Tales*, 1888; *Wee Willie Winkie and Other Child Stories*, 1888; *The Courting of Dinah Shadd and Other Stories*, 1890; *The City of Dreadful Night and Other Places*, 1890; *Mine Own People*, 1891; *Life's Handicap*, 1891; *Many Inventions*, 1893; *The Jungle Book*, 1894; *The Second Jungle Book*, 1895; *Soldier Tales*, 1896; *The Day's Work*, 1898; *Stalky & Co.*, 1899; *Just So Stories*, 1902; *Traffics and Discoveries*, 1904; *Puck of Pook's Hill*, 1906; *Actions and Reactions*, 1909; *Rewards and Fairies*, 1910; *A Diversity of Creatures*, 1917; *Land and Sea Tales for Scouts and Guides*, 1923; *"They" and the Brushwood Boy*, 1925; *Debits and Credits*, 1926; *Thy Servant a Dog*, 1930; *Humorous Tales*, 1931; *Animal Stories*, 1932; *Limits and Renewals*, 1932; *Collected Dog Stories*, 1934.

NONFICTION: *Letters of Marque*, 1891; *A Fleet in Being: Notes of Two Trips with the Channel Squadron*, 1898; *From Sea to Sea: Letters of Travel*, 1899; *Letters to the Family*, 1908; *The New Army in Training*, 1915; *Sea Warfare*, 1916; *Letters of Travel, 1892-1913*, 1920; *The Irish Guards in the Great War*, 1923; *A Book of Words*, 1928; *Souvenirs of France*, 1933; *Something of Myself: For My Friends Known and Unknown*, 1937.

Bibliography

Birkenhead, Lord. *Rudyard Kipling*, 1978.
Carrington, Charles. *Rudyard Kipling: His Life and Work*, 1955.
Chandler, Lloyd H. *A Summary of the Work of Rudyard Kipling: Including Items Ascribed to Him*, 1930.
Gilbert, Elliot L., ed. *Kipling and the Critics*, 1965.
Green, Roger Lancelyn, ed. *Kipling: The Critical Heritage*, 1971.
Mason, Philip. *Kipling: The Glass, the Shadow and the Fire*, 1975.
Rutherford, Andrew, ed. *Kipling's Mind and Art*, 1964.

Stewart, J. I. M. *Rudyard Kipling*, 1966.
Wilson, Angus. *The Strange Ride of Rudyard Kipling: His Life and Works*, 1977.

Kirk H. Beetz

CAROLYN KIZER

Born: Spokane, Washington; December 10, 1925

Principal collections

The Ungrateful Garden, 1962; *Knock Upon Silence*, 1965; *Midnight Was My Cry: New and Selected Poems*, 1971.

Other literary forms

While continuing to publish poetry regularly in both major periodicals and small press magazines, Carolyn Kizer's record of prose publication is also noteworthy. Her critical essays and reviews of contemporary poetry have appeared in major publications for more than three decades. Her essays on modern women poets such as Eve Triem, Elinor Wylie, and Louise Bogan, as well as reviews of new work by contemporaries, have contributed to her reputation as a feminist critic.

A short story, "A Slight Mechanical Failure," appeared in *The Quarterly Review of Literature* in 1978. She has written two autobiographical memoirs, "A Muse," and "Notes for a Study Club Paper," concerning her mother and father, respectively.

Achievements

Ever since the appearance of *The Ungrateful Garden*, Kizer's first book, her polyphonic poetic voice has been praised by critics who have discovered in her virtuosity a sophistication they respect. Most reviewers have also referred to her poetic voice in terms of gender—whether as "feminine," "womanly," or "classic chic." "Pro Femina," in *Knock Upon Silence*, was immediately recognized for its feminist content, and it is now a standard offering in college courses on women's poetry.

Kizer's "imitations" from the Chinese and her translations of poetry from other languages form a distinct vein of her achievement. She has provided a number of original translations of the eighth century Chinese poet Tu Fu. Her renditions—"imitations," as she calls them—from Arthur Waley's translations include the "Tzu-Yeh" songs which have been praised by at least one Chinese scholar for their subtle nuances, which are close to the original. With Aijaz Ahmad, she has translated the work of the Urdu poet Faiz Ahmad Faiz, and she has worked with the Yugoslavian poet Bogomil Gjuzel in translating his poetry from the Macedonian.

Like Sylvia Plath and Adrienne Rich, poets roughly of her generation, Kizer began her career emulating male models. Many of her poems demonstrate the formal elegance of W. H. Auden and the musical expressionism of Theodore Roethke. Unlike many of her contemporaries, however, she has not thrown out traditional poetic forms or traditional mythologies about the poetic process. She employs a variety of conventional forms, from the "tempting tic of pentameter" to Japanese haiku, from meters reminiscent of Beowulf to modernist syllabics. One of the distinguishing features of her achievement over three decades is that she has not settled into a single voice or style but has added voices and styles as appropriate for various rhetorical occasions and purposes. Her adaptation of a well-practised ironic voice to feminist material echoes the subversive strategies used by precursors such as Emily Dickinson, while also attesting to the difficulty experienced by the contemporary woman who desires an authoritative voice within the literary tradition she inherits.

While her poetry treats the contradictions between femaleness and literary vocation explicitly, Kizer has not used the double bind to trace a death dance in the pulses of her art. Thus far, her strategies have been less psychologically spectacular than those of Sylvia Plath or Anne Sexton, and often more politically engaged. A devotion to formalism carefully qualifies her themes; wit, rhetorical interests, and faith and delight in immediate sensation ally her more with Muriel Rukeyser than with Sylvia Plath.

Biography

As yet there are no biographical studies of Carolyn Kizer, although her memoirs reveal a life of extraordinary variety and interest. An only child of parents with powerful and engaging personalities, Kizer confesses that she had a "spoilt childhood." Her mother, Mabel Ashley, brought qualifications to maternity which were unusual for her day: a doctorate degree in biology from Stanford University, administrative experience in the first federally funded drug clinic in New York, a history of I.W.W. activism, teaching, and years of independence. She steered her daughter toward creativity at an early age, proudly exhibiting her four-year-old's arbitrary scrawl of the letters "A, R, T" as her "first word." Benjamin Hamilton Kizer, the poet's father, was a well-known lawyer and regional planner. At home he was a self-contained and authoritarian personality as well as a constant reader, whose heroes were Benjamin Franklin and Oliver Wendell Holmes.

Kizer left Spokane to attend Sarah Lawrence College. After graduation, she traveled to China on a fellowship in comparative literature. Still in her twenties, she married, settled in Seattle, Washington, and gave birth to three children—Ashley, Scott, and Jill, alluded to in some of her poems. In her memoir, Kizer dates the onset of her "serious life" as a poet after she had turned thirty, having published only a few poems before then. In fact, her professional life has incorporated arts administration, teaching at poetry writing workshops, lecturing at numerous universities, and editing and writing reviews, as well as producing poems. She served as the first Director of Literary Programs for the National Endowment for the Arts, and has been in residence at the University of Iowa Writers' Workshop, Columbia University, and the University of Cincinnati, among others. The breadth of her experience has contributed to her reputation as a woman of letters, and to the authority of that image as it appears in her poems, which contain many literary allusions and display a knowledge and appreciation of traditional forms from Eastern as well as Western poetry.

Bibliographers and anthologists have often linked Kizer's work to the Pacific Coast region, and the association is valid to a limited extent. Her poems occasionally allude to regional place names, and hint at ecological concerns; she makes use of themes and forms from Oriental poetry, a characteristic often linked to the developing Northwest tradition. As founder and editor of *Poetry Northwest* in Seattle until 1965, Kizer was a part of a circle of poets at the University of Washington which included Theodore Roethke, David Wagoner, and Richard Hugo, although Kizer has described the group as having shared a camaraderie rather than a consistent style.

Analysis

Carolyn Kizer's poetry elaborates the psychosexual context in which women writers traditionally have worked toward literary self-invention. She does so using multiple voices and dramatis personae, often appropriating irony, paradox, and satire for rebellious purposes. Her techniques recall the subversive strategies of eighteenth and nineteenth century poets such as Emily Dickinson, who similarly revolted against the exclusion of women from the paradigms of authorship by telling the truth, but "telling it slant." Kizer's reaction thus does not always take a unique form, but her unique blending of thematic materials—the uses and abuses of the feminine and the feminist—forces a reconsideration of the boundaries which join the separate life and art, self-discovery and self-mythologizing.

Of the poems written during the 1960's, "Pro Femina" is perhaps the most familiar to Kizer's readers, having been anthologized in several important collections of women's poetry since its appearance in *Knock Upon Silence*. A witty, epigrammatic satire in verse, the poem is based on the Tenth Satire of Juvenal, in which women were held up to scorn for their vanity, and it borrows its prosody from the hexameters of the Roman rhetorician. The poem exemplifies a reaction against the conflict between femininity and literary vocation for a particular social and historical context: academic, shadowed by the 1950's, locked into male-defined paradigms. The poem enacts the struggle of a contemporary "woman of letters" to achieve an autonomous and powerful voice, while keeping a safe distance from the undesirable images of women she finds reflected in literature, philosophy, psychology, and history. Inasmuch as the poem alludes to misogynist attitudes from Catullus to Sigmund Freud, it demonstrates that the problem of female "poetic identity" is bound up with the very language in which women have been discussed. The fact that the speaker addresses two different audiences in the poem, one made up of women who write ("you," "we") and one of men who prevent them ("Jack") complicates its rhetoric. Seeking to change the stereotypes which afflict literary women from within the forms that legitimize them, the voice in the poem undergoes sudden, rapid shifts in direction and purpose as it works toward a satirical statement that is distinctly female, angry, determined.

The intellectual complexity of "Pro Femina" as well as of other early poems, such as "Streets of Pearl and Gold" (modeled after Andrew Marvell's "Upon Appleton House"), is reminiscent of the high value placed on paradox by the New Criticism, as well as by the phenomenology of Simone de Beauvoir's *The Second Sex* (1949). In a recent interview, Kizer stated that she had read *The Second Sex* during the 1950's, finding in it "confirmation" of what she had "instinctively felt" and had come upon through her own experience as well as through other reading, which had included works by Carl Jung and Joseph Campbell. Both *The Second Sex* and Jungian theory, whether or not they are conscious influences on "Pro Femina," are useful in understanding the psychological complexity which Kizer brings to her criticism of patriarchy in that poem. Whereas de Beauvoir emphasized that men in a patriarchal culture have defined women as "object" and "other" in order to constitute their active, determining, and sovereign selves, Kizer's poem reveals that creative women have had to struggle not only with literal oppression at home and at work but also with warring, internalized self-images—in Jungian terms, "shadows." These same-sex but opposing figures set up an internal drama between the woman's desire for active, creative subjectivity and the false, debilitating images of women as angelic or demonic which she inherits through the metaphors of the very tradition that nourishes her poetic sensibilities. In "Pro Femina," as in nineteenth century poetry by women, the conflict is fraught with aesthetic consequences: fragmentation, camouflage, repetition. The difference between the problem of poetic identity as explored in Dickinson's poems and in Kizer's is that Kizer treats the problem of internalization more explicitly. By making poetic identity into a discursive subject, as in "Pro Femina," she finds a way of acknowledging the difficulty at the same time that she works through it.

In each of the three sections of "Pro Femina," the speaker explores a different dimension of the problem of poetic identity, the problem of achieving a strong central self conducive to writing. Section one is organized around images of thwarted female speech; section two around fashion, literal and metaphorical styles which have been used to mask female body language; section three around undercover strategies which literary women have used to "sabotage" a tradition in which they have been expected to "write like a man" or be "despised" by "posterity." The language of the poem indicates the degree of hypertension which the subject engenders—lines densely packed with adjectives and intensifiers, syllables exploding with friction and cacophony, outbursts of exclamation. A closer examination of the movement within each section is important for understanding the terms in which Kizer paces off this difficult terrain, and for providing a context for the evolution of poetic identity in later poems.

Beginning with an allusion to the "noose" or albatross necktie" "hung" around the neck of the poet "unwomanly" enough to speak up, the speaker in the first section catalogs negative stereotypes of female speech and shows how—in contemporary jargon—these have "hung up" the creative woman. Allusions to the classics reverberate: women have "howled" for free will: like Charles Dickens' Mme. Defarges they have raged silently, "stabbing" the names of their "ancient/ Oppressors" into their texts; still others, like Jane Austen's heroines, have been mutely acquiescent. The most complex metaphor of female speech, the "hyena" voice of the woman of letters, appears as a coda to the first of three stanzas in section one: "We *are* hyenas. Yes, we admit it." On the surface, "Yes, we admit it" would seem to parody deliberately the acquiescence which the speaker seeks to revise through the perversity of her argument. In the context of Kizer's indictment of cultural misogyny, however, the hyena has at least two other uses in the poem: an outcast even on the outposts of civilization, the hyena is an appropriate figure for the exclusion of female authorship and authentic female experience from history. Yet another level of meaning is buried in the semiotics of the hyena's cry: because the hyena is known for its uncanny ability to mimic the human voice in such a way as to make the listener uneasy by the combination of resemblance and dissonance, the hyena's voice is an emblem of the ironic and angry voice of the woman poet, a voice that impersonates Juvenalian tones in order to make Juvenal's modern disciples overhear themselves more critically. Such a strategy, akin to Dickinson's "slanted truth," also avoids backlash from an audience presumed to be hostile. The double emphasis—"Yes, we admit it"—expresses the speaker's ambivalence toward her subject matter and her gender, while putting the subversive strategy she inherits from her literary foremothers to good use.

Donning the mask of the Juvenalian oppressor in order to take the sting out of his biting sarcasm is tricky business, however: it requires extraordinary energy and control, and it implies considerable self-sacrifice for the sake of art. Perhaps because such strategy depends upon the exploitation of inner divisions in order to create, the pattern in each section of the poem is that of a progressive dislocation of the poet from her haunting shadow-selves, and of ordinary women who acquiesce and who "choke" on their words from "real women," who are defiant and ambitious. The linguistic evidence for this unique kind of dissociation, angry rather than pathological, is the doubling and repetition of sounds and images, a simultaneous compulsion toward self-expression, alternating with compulsion against female freakishness. For example, in the first section the sequence of metaphors linking female speech to animal sounds reaches an anticlimax in the image of the acquiescent woman as inarticulate "cabbage . . . neutered by labour." In the second stanza the "choking violent writer" has as her opposite mirror image and shadow-self an exaggerated portrait of the compulsive shopper, "hobbled and swathed in whimsey." Various solutions are thrown out: diffusion ("observe our creative chaos") or male impersonality ("a formal, hard-fibered/ assurance"), yet because these spring from a structure of either/or alternatives, they replicate the writer's experience of being caught up in extremes, in a case where both/ and solutions are needed. Whereas in "Pro Femina" there is an integration of the psychological and political materials of poetic identity, the possibility of escape from ironic self-reflection is often closed off by the perverse imperatives of the satirical form itself, and by the ideology of Juvenal it consistently reflects. The poem closes with mock advice to the contemporary woman poet: "stand up and be hated . . . submerge self-pity in disciplined industry," and follows this up with an invocation to the family of the future, ultimately an argument for innovation from within the tradition.

In a recent interview, Kizer characterized the predominate "voice" in "Pro Femina" as "satiric-hysterical polyphony." In one sense, this term perfectly describes the innovativeness of the poem, which lies in the expression of female anger against a male-dominated tradition that has been internalized, but which does not provide models for straightforward, self-assertive speech except through male impersonation. The continued exploration of the possibilities of the voice that tells the truth but escapes the "sobriquets" of criticism explains the irony in poems such as "Singing Aloud," where the speaker begins by admitting that "trying to write poems" is one of her "faults." Irony barely conceals an undercurrent of rage in "Plaint of the Poet in an Ignorant Age," in which the speaker longs for a "flower-boy" so that she can "sit in a rockery by a pot of cold coffee/ Noodling in a notebook" while shouting imperiously to her muse. The flower boy is an obvious caricature of the muse figure who, as an idealized version of nature, provides unmediated intuitions of proper names. The implied contrast between the conditions under which the speaker works (her "bottle-cap king" knows "no name") and those under which creative men have labored, assisted by wives, mothers, and other helpmates, adds a literal dimension to the complaint. In more frankly auto-biographical vein, in "Running Away from Home," there is another satirical blend of voices. This time a combination of glee, naughtiness, and frustration works toward exorcising the repressive demons of a small-town girlhood which retains their awful, godly, paternal power to silence speech—"It's never over, the old church of our claustrophobia!"

When Kizer borrows Blakean energies from the Romantic tradition, as in "Tying One on in Vienna," after Heinrich Heine, satire and irony often give way to glee for its own sake. "Tying One on in Vienna" is particularly significant to the theme of poetic identity because it begins as a conscious imitation of the poet's drinking song, a traditional occasion for invoking the muse through the ritual toast to the anatomy of the poet's absent mistress. Kizer projects a female persona upon the incidents in Heine's poem, and the ironic consequences of the impersonation are apparent at once: she mischievously compares her lover's navel to that of a statue, his brain to that of an angel, reversing the "eternal feminine" of nineteenth century sentiments in order to reveal their slightly ridiculous underside. As the drinking progresses, poet and landlord become caricatures of the traditions they emulate, "weeping in an excess of feeling" over lost love and glory. The drunken spree culminates in a mock-apocalyptic vision as the pair stumble to the rooftop of the beer cellar for what becomes a transcendent and transcending vision of the props of their Romanticism, finding the "angels of Heine and Rilke" drunk, too, all singing "Hallelujah and Yippie." It is the irreverence of this exclamation that breaks up irony; as the couple laugh at themselves and at the often foolish monuments to the past, the reader is forced by the rollicking rhythms of the poem to laugh with them.

Although the development of the female satyr is one of Kizer's distinctive achievements, she works in other voices, too, from the tender solicitude offered to the absent lover in her Chinese "imitations" to the more straightforward and exhuberant gypsylike song of "For Jan, in Bar Maria," a poem which invokes the muse of a sisterhood passionate and powerful enough to generate wonder rather than sanction, in spite of the "shocking" public demonstration of liberty and *jouissance* that the open revelry of two young women in a small town represents. It is a mark of Kizer's development as a poet that she continues to explore the effects of various frames of reference on her voice, using mythological, autobiographical, and historical contexts to bring out various timbres. The path of these explorations can be traced through poems in which the persona of a goddess becomes a disguise for revealing power relations, and poems in which autobiographical details become a lens for framing an immediate sense of identity. Finally, Kizer has written a number of poems which place in the foreground the publicly political, such as "Seasons of Lovers and Assassins" and "A Muse of Water," but which also integrate the politics of personal relationships.

Kizer has stated that her Chinese "imitations" were inspired by her reading of Arthur Waley's translations and by a desire to "develop the poet's intention" rather than to "borrow poems to insert my own intention." In several of these imitations, she assumes the solitary voice of the oriental maiden of the "Tzu-Yeh" songs in order to develop the inherent drama in the situation of the woman who is ignored, abandoned, or separated from a more powerful but distant lover. In both "Hiding Our Love" and "Summer Near the River," the dramatic situation turns on the female speaker's appropriation of a man's dressing gown, in order to recover symbolically his presence or to gain access to the power he represents, as well as to the world beyond him. In "Hiding

Our Love," Kizer brings out the latent implications of the metaphor of the overlong sash on the man's gown, which "wraps twice" around the maiden's waist, suggesting internal as well as external constraint. The Chinese imitations belong to a unique cultural context which should be treated in its own right, but inasmuch as they contribute to Kizer's repertoire of dramatic voices and situations, as well as to the seductions and betrayals associated with male impersonation, they contribute to her ongoing fable of poetic identity.

In the mythologically inspired poems "Hera, Hung from the Sky," "Persephone Pauses," and "Columns and Caryatids," Kizer's female personae are trapped between archetypally and politically opposed realms of mother and father, male and female, procreativity and creativity, in predicaments which suggest an irresolvable distance between desire and actuality, aspiration and achievement. As the wife of Zeus, whose power she equaled in every way but in prophecy, where his power exceeded hers, Hera is an appropriate figure for a housewife as well as an aspiring, self-mythologizing poet. Following the myth, Kizer has Hera hanging by her heels, head first out of heaven, but with gold bracelets on her wrists, like the paradoxically privileged but imprisoned wife in "The Suburbans," whose nerves have grown "transparent" from "goldfish gazes." Gold in both poems is associated with being caught up in the terrifying but attractive reflections of the sun, a traditional symbol for masculine creativity and potency. Hera's crime is couched in metaphors of poetic vision: she has dared to "dream" and has become absorbed "by the gaze/ of self into self." The further association of Hera with Lucifer ("I have lost the war of air") adds to the implication that the speech of the powerfully creative woman is also demonic, her creative fire a kind of Satanic utterance in the eyes of the gods.

In "Persephone Pauses," a mythological goddess personifies the struggle for identity when the poet is a daughter, "pausing" on the threshold of her creative potential as well as her sexual maturity, and poised between two dominant but mutually exclusive fates, symbolized by the opposing realms of the parents, the daylight and the night-time worlds. Within the twenty-four-hour cycle of the poem, Persephone inherits her mother's dominance at nightfall, so she is loathe to reenter Hell's "sensual abyss." Because Persephone is a reader (the sun casts an ominous shadow on a letter from a friend at the beginning of the poem) and Neptune a sinister author—"grim tragedian" who "bedizens" her in the latest fashion and introduces her to the meters of ballroom dancing—the seduction scene is at the same time a seduction of the literary women into the perils of potential authorship, where she may be trapped by distorted, anxiety-provoking images of herself, her identity effaced, her nerves "dissolving in the gleam of night's/ theatrical desire."

In a number of childhood poems, the inner sources of creativity and self-definition are approached through more literal female figures—another poet, in "For Sappho/After Sappho," the poet's mother in "The Intruder" and "The

Great Blue Heron," and her own daughter in "The Blessing." The attitude
toward the mother figure, from whom the daughter inherits domination as
well as strategic wisdom and knowledge of her own nature, is sometimes
ambivalent. In "The Intruder," for example, the mother's initial sympathy for
a wounded bat dragged into the house by a cat turns into an initiation scene
which has implications for the daughter's identity. By example, the mother
figure teaches the daughter, whose gender also intrudes upon this scene, an
"intuitive love" of nature, but knowledge of nature also proves to be an
initiation into the "whole wild, lost, betrayed and secret life" of suffering
which encompasses the daughter's femaleness. When the bat is discovered to
be lice-infested, its body a host for "cozily sucked" parasites, the mother
"washes pity" for the creature from her hands, a gesture which symbolically
denies the bond of "dark blood" she and her daughter share, while passing
on the implication of guilt by association. Through this initiation the daughter,
too, becomes a guilty Eve.

For the daughter who is a poet, however, the mother's absense can stimulate
the desire to re-create herself in her own words, to clothe herself in metaphor.
Such a drive toward a separate identity by means of art is at issue in "The
Great Blue Heron," where a daughter's epiphanic vision of a heron on the
beach, "Shadow without a shadow,/ Hung on invisible wires," is both inspiring
and terrifying. The mother in the poem brings all her sinister knowledge of
the origins of life and death to the scene, recognizing in the bird a symbol
of mortality she and her daughter share ("she knew who he was"). In the last
stanza the poet looks back upon this symbol of death-in-life and upon her
mother's death from the distance measured by the burning of her own creative
fires into age and artistic achievement, signified by the fireworks, burning
paper, and conflagration of the summer house. The poem ends on the kind
of paradox Kizer is fond of developing: the mother's absence serves as inspiration for the daughter's poem, which is dedicated to her, yet because the
daughter shares this bond of sameness with the mother, the spectral bird still
haunts the poem, now both ghost and premonition of the daughter's death.

Whereas in earlier poems the mother-daughter relationship is typically used
to discover paradoxical self-reflections, in "The Blessing," a recent long poem
dedicated to the poet's daughter, Ashley, the perspective afforded by three
generations of mother-daughter bonding and bondage is used to unlock the
paradoxes of female identity. The opening paradox is that the daughter fills
her mother's unsatisfied desires at the expense of her own nature ("Holding
me together at your expense/ has made you burn cool"). The daughter proves
to be a mirror through which the poet can gain a clearer picture of her own
mothering: "So did I in childhood:/ nursed her old hurts and doubts." In the
course of investigating props in the family closet, the poet uncovers her father's
self-protectiveness, symbolized by his "overshoes," and unravels its implications for the family constellation. Finally, because the perspective across

three generations helps her to understand the original models for her shadow-selves, the poet can exorcise the demons of the "hysterical tongue" by offering an openhearted blessing to her daughter to "keep" a "wise heart and head." Like the beneficent crone who imparts ancient knowledge for an innocent girl's safekeeping in fairy tales, the mother blesses the daughter with an older meaning of the word *hysteria*, purged of its negative connotations and redefined as life-affirming, distinctly female wisdom.

The movement toward an integration from within by redefining the female shadow-selves is apparent in recent poems, but the need for such an integration is anticipated in earlier poems, such as "A Muse of Water," in which psychological, political, and prophetic materials are unified. In the first eight stanzas, the use of the female muse to inspire male authorship and the pollution of streams by "masters of civlization" are understood as parallel symptoms of a common malaise: men have appropriated female creativity in the construction of their designs by making women muses, goddesses, queens, laborers, wives—"poultice for his flesh" and "water for his fire." Through a sequence of metaphors linking the reclamation of land and the revitalizing of streams to the recovery of the lost female voices, Kizer charts a course for herself and for other poets—to "rejoice" in the "faint music" rising from the ruined tide pools and marshes, and to be mindful of hidden silences and buried casualties, "Lost murmur! Subterranean moan!" Kizer's most recent poetry continues to work toward this goal, in a spirit and method of inclusiveness. There are revisions of earlier female voices—the voice of the poet as mother—and there are also buried voices, such as that of "Fanny," the wife of Robert Louis Stevenson, whose creative identity Kizer explores in a long poem which encompasses the rise and fall of colonial imperialism. The continued exercise of the full range and capacity of her own voice nourishes and sustains a creative tension, which has been essential to Kizer's art.

Major publication other than poetry
SHORT STORY: "A Slight Mechanical Failure," 1978.

Bibliography

Cheung, Dominic. "Carolyn Kizer and Her Chinese Imitations," in *New Asia Bulletin*, 1978.

Davidson, Cathy, and E. M. Broner. *The Lost Tradition: Mothers and Daughters in Literature*, 1980.

Gilbert, Sandra M., and Susan Gubar, eds. *Shakespeare's Sisters: Feminist Essays on Women Poets*, 1979.

_____ . *The Madwoman in the Attic: The Woman Writer and the Nineteenth-Century Literary Imagination*, 1979.

Homans, Margaret. *Women Writers and Poetic Identity: Dorothy Wordsworth, Emily Brontë, and Emily Dickinson*, 1980.

Juhasz, Suzanne. *Naked and Fiery Forms: Modern American Poetry by Women: A New Tradition*, 1976.

Lee, L. L., and Lewis Merrill. *Women, Women Writers, and the West*, 1979.

Anita Helle

KENNETH KOCH

Born: Cincinnati, Ohio; February 27, 1925

Principal poems and collections

Poems, 1953; *Ko: Or, A Season on Earth*, 1960; *Permanently*, 1960; *Thank You and Other Poems*, 1962; *When the Sun Tries to Go On*, 1969; *Sleeping with Women*, 1969; *The Pleasures of Peace*, 1969; *The Art of Love*, 1975; *The Duplications*, 1977; *The Burning Mystery of Anna in 1951*, 1979.

Other literary forms

In addition to poetry, Kenneth Koch has published one novel, *The Red Robins* (1975), and two books of dramatic pieces: *Bertha and Other Plays* (1966), and *A Change of Hearts: Plays, Films and Other Dramatic Works 1951-1971* (1973). Both Koch's novel and his works for the stage are imaginative and improvisatory in their consistent portrayal of the comic drama of life.

The plays achieve their comic repercussions primarily through the juxtaposition of incongruous situations, and by means of rapid, often unpredictable changes of language, character, and scene. The plays echo and imitate older dramatic forms such as the Elizabethan chronical and the court masque, frequently appropriating the earlier dramatic conventions for comic purposes. *E. Kology* (1973), for example, a five-act play in rhymed verse is as much masque as play. In it, the main character, E. Kology, persuades various polluters of air and water to abandon their destructive habits. An additional masque element is provided by a troop of young men and women who assist E. Kology, performing a series of celebratory dances as part of the play's action. An even more masquelike play is *The Moon Balloon*, performed in New York's Central Park on New Year's Eve, 1969. *The Moon Balloon* is an entertainment in rhymed verse that makes use of spectacle, celebration, and metamorphosis.

History forms the basis for humor and metamorphosis in Koch's two historical plays, *Bertha* (1959), a historical pageant, and *George Washington Crossing the Delaware* (1962), a chronicle play. Bertha is a Norwegian queen who saves her people from the barbarian menace. She performs this feat regularly, whenever she becomes bored with routine rule. The humor of the play resides in the use of formal Elizabethan language to describe Bertha's idiosyncratic behavior, and in strangely concatenated literary allusions such as the linked references to *Antony and Cleopatra* (1606-1607) and *Alice in Wonderland* (1865), Bertha being related to both the tragic queen of Egypt and the mad queen of Wonderland.

George Washington Crossing the Delaware, perhaps Koch's best play, is part myth, part chronicle, part comedy. Its comic incongruities, its colloquial deflation of a more stately heroic language, and its juxtaposition of low comedy and high seriousness serve to make it a surprising and inventive theatrical entertainment.

Achievements

At his best, Koch is a good comic poet and a fine parodist. A poet of limited tonal range yet of a wide and resourceful imagination, Koch's random structures, open forms, and loose meters give his poetry freedom and surprise that occasionally astonish and often delight. Just as often, however, the formlessness of Koch's poems results in slackness and self-indulgence. The tension that one expects in good poetry, deriving largely from exigencies of form, is missing in Koch's poems.

In *The King of the Cats* (1965), F. W. Dupee compared Koch to Marianne Moore. Dupee notes that while both Koch and Moore make poetry out of "poetry-resistant stuff," Koch lacks Moore's patient scrutiny and careful, sustained observation. Preferring to participate imaginatively rather than to observe carefully, Koch often seems more interested in where he can go with an observation, with what his imagination can make of it, than in what it is in itself. At his best, Koch's imaginative facility translates into poetic felicity; at his worst, Koch's freedom of imagination obscures the clarity and lucidity of the poems, frequently testing the reader's patience.

Perhaps the most trenchant and perceptive criticism of Koch's work has been that of Richard Howard in his book on contemporary poetry, *Alone with America* (1950). Howard suggests that the central poetic problem for Koch is to sustain the interest of the instant, to hold onto the momentary imaginative phrase or the surprising conjunction of dichotomous ideas, experiences, and details. The result is that Koch frequently hurries beyond moments of imaginative vitality and verbal splendor; rather than sustaining or developing them, he abandons them. At his best, however, such abandonments lead to other moments that are equally splendid, culminating in convincingly coherent poems.

Some of Koch's most distinctive and successful poems are parodies. His parody of Robert Frost, "Mending Sump," in which he alludes to and satirizes the style and situation of both "Mending Wall" and "The Death of the Hired Man," is one of his most famous. A modestly successful parody, "Mending Sump" does not compare with Koch's brilliant and witty parody of William Carlos Williams' brief conversational poem, "This Is Just to Say." Koch entitles his parody "Variations of a Theme by William Carlos Williams." In four brief stanzas, Koch parodies the occasion, structure, rhythm, and tone of a poet whose work has powerfully influenced his own.

Although in his nonparodistic poetry Koch may not often attempt to imitate Williams, he does try to accomplish what Williams achieved in his best work:

the astonishment of the moment; the astonishment of something seen, heard, felt, or understood; the magic and the beauty of the commonplace. Koch, too, can astonish—but not by acts of attention like those of Williams nor by his power of feeling. Koch astonishes by his outrageous dislocations of sense and logic, his exuberant and risk-taking amalgamation of utterly disparate experiences. His achievement, finally, consists of small surprises, delights of image and allusion, phrase and idea; his poems rarely possess the power to move or instruct, but they do entertain.

Biography

Kenneth Koch was born in Cincinnati, Ohio, on February 27, 1925. Although he wrote his first poem when he was five, he did not begin writing seriously until he was seventeen, when he read the novels of John Dos Passos and was thereby stimulated to imitate their particular style of stream-of-consciousness. Koch served as a rifleman in the U.S. Army during World War II. After the war, he earned a B.A. degree from Harvard University in 1948, and a doctorate from Columbia in 1959. At Harvard, Koch was a friend of John Ashbery and Frank O'Hara, poets who held similar views about the nature of poetry. Later, when they had settled in New York, Ashbery, O'Hara, and Koch came to be thought of as principal poets of the New York School.

Koch spent three important years in Europe, mostly in Italy and France. During that time, he was influenced by the humorous, surrealistic verse of Jacques Prévert. In a brief autobiographical account that appeared in *The New American Poetry* (1960, Donald Allen, editor), Koch noted that French poetry "had a huge effect" on his own work. Moreover, he acknowledged that he tried to get into his own writing "the same incomprehensible excitement" that he found in French poetry.

Koch has taught at Brooklyn College, Rutgers University, and The New School for Social Research. Currently a Professor of English at Columbia, he has been a recipient of Fulbright, Guggenheim, and Ingram Merrill fellowships, and he has been awarded a grant from the National Endowment for the Arts. He lives in New York City.

During the late 1960's and early 1970's Koch began teaching poetry writing at P.S. 61, a grammar school in New York City, and at a neighborhood museum in Brooklyn. A few years later he taught similar classes at a New York nursing home. Out of these experiences came a series of books about the teaching of poetry to children and the aged. The first of these, *Wishes, Lies and Dreams: Teaching Young Children to Write Poetry* (1970), is perhaps the best known. A companion volume, *Rose Where Did You Get That Red?*, followed in 1973. Both are noteworthy for their inventive approach to teaching poetry, especially for the imaginative ways they keep reading and writing poetry together. An additional value of the books, and of two later volumes as well (*I Never Told Anybody: Teaching Poetry in a Nursing Home*, 1977, and *Sleeping on the Wing: An Anthology of Modern Poetry with Essays on Reading and Writing*, 1981), is that all of them reveal something about Koch's poetic temperament and inclinations. The qualities that Koch encourages in his students' writing animate his own poems. Open forms, loose meter, memory and feeling, joy and humor, colloquial language, imaginative freedom— these reflect Koch's view that "there is no insurmountable barrier between ordinary speech and poetry."

Analysis

Kenneth Koch has published three long poems: *Ko: Or, A Season on Earth*, a mock-heroic epic in ottava rima about a Japanese baseball player, a poem with a variety of story lines; *The Duplications*, a comic epic about sex that employs trappings of Greek mythology and that in its second part becomes a self-reflexive poem concerned with the poetic vocation; and *When the Sun Tries to Go On*, a poem that goes on for 100 twenty-four-line stanzas, in large part because Koch wanted to see how long he could go on with what was originally a seventy-two-line poem. All three long poems are characterized by Koch's infectious humor, his far-fetched analogies, and his digressive impulse.

More interesting and more consistently successful are Koch's shorter poems, ranging in length from a dozen lines to a dozen pages. In the poems included in Koch's best collections, *The Art of Love* and *The Pleasures of Peace*, one encounters Koch at his most graceful and disarming. In the best poems from these volumes (and there are many engaging ones), Koch exhibits his characteristic playfulness, deliberate formlessness, and almost surrealistic allusiveness. The poems are humorous yet serious in both their invitations and their admonitions.

Koch's major poetic preoccupations find abundant exemplifications in his volume *The Pleasures of Peace*. The title poem is divided loosely into fourteen sections, each section describing different kinds of pleasures: of writing, of peace, of pain, of pleasure itself, of fantasy, of reality, of memory, of autonomy, of poetry, and of living. The poem is both a catalog and a celebration of the rich pleasures of simply being alive. Its self-reflexiveness coexists with its Whitmanesque embrace of the range, diversity, and variability of life's pleasures. Another stylistic hallmark evident in this poem is a playful use of literary allusion. In addition to evoking Walt Whitman, Koch alludes directly to William Butler Yeats ("The Lake Isle of Innisfree"), Andrew Marvell ("To His Coy Mistress"), Robert Herrick, Percy Bysshe Shelley, and William Wordsworth. The allusions are surprising: Koch's lines modify and alter the words of the earlier poets as they situate them in the context of a radically different poem.

These observations about "The Pleasures of Peace" fail to account for what is perhaps its most distinctive identifying quality: a wild, surrealistic concatenation of details (pink mint chewing gum with "the whole rude gallery of war"; Dutch-speaking cowboys; the pleasures of agoraphobia with the pleasures of blasphemy; the pleasures of breasts, bread, and poodles; the pleasures of stars and of plaster). Moreover, amidst the litany of the poem's pleasures occur several notes of desperation—for the horrors of war and suffering. Koch seems to find it necessary to remind his readers of the peaceful pleasures of life largely because the horrors of war and the futility of modern life allow them to be forgotten.

Although Sigmund Freud is an obvious influence on Koch's "The Interpretation of Dreams," a zany poem that imitates the syntax of dream in its associative structure, in its dislocations and disruptions of continuity, and in its oddly mismatched characters, Whitman is the dominant voice and force behind most of the other poems in the volume. Whitman's influence is discernible in "Hearing," a rambling play on sounds in which Koch makes music out of the disparate noises of waterfalls and trumpets, throbbing hearts and falling leaves, rain and thunder, bluebirds singing and dresses ripping. The poem, concluding with the words "the song is finished," owes something also to the other American poets it invokes: Ezra Pound, William Carlos Williams, and Wallace Stevens.

It is Whitman, however, who stands behind Koch's "Poem of the Forty-Eight States," especially the Whitman of "On Journeys Through the States"; and it is Whitman who hovers over the incantatory litany of Koch's "Sleeping with Women," especially the Whitman of "The Sleepers" and "Beautiful Women." Perhaps the most successful of Koch's Whitmanesque poems is "Faces," which, while less uniform in tone than "Sleeping with Women," with its hypnotic, anaphoric incantation, and while not as close to Whitman's own tone, nevertheless carries something of Whitman's power of suggestion in its implication that the variety of faces called up in the poem (Popeye and Agamemnon, Herbert Hoover and the poor of the Depression) reflect the life of the speaker of the poem. By implication, Koch seems to suggest that each reader could create a similar yet highly individual and personal collage of faces that, taken together, reflect the range and variety of his experience and that, in a concentrated yet variegated image, sum up his or her life.

Koch's other important volume, *The Art of Love*, while retaining something of the humorous tone of *The Pleasures of Peace* as well as something of its imaginative wit, reaches more deeply in feeling and ranges more widely in thought. Many of the poems are cast in an admonitory mode; others are ironic, while still others include both irony and admonition. "The Art of Poetry" alternates between ironic posture and serious gesture in its descriptions of poetic attitudes, ideals, and practices. The speaker advises poets to stay young even while growing and developing, something that Koch has consistently tried to do. He suggests that a poet should imitate other poets, try on other styles, and try out other voices in an effort to form, paradoxically, his own style. After addressing the problems of beginning a poem, sustaining and ending it (and also revising it), the speaker reminds the poet to absorb himself totally in poetry, for only such a total immersion will enable the poet to see poetry as "the mediation of life." Such is Koch's poetic credo.

This poetic creed notwithstanding, perhaps the most unusual and the most useful advice in "The Art of Poetry" is given in a set of questions and answers that further reveal the direction and impulse of Koch's own poetry: Is the poem astonishing? Is it wise? Is it original? Does it employ cheap effects, tricks, or gimmicks? Does it engage heart and mind? Would the poet envy another's having written it? If the answer is "yes" to all but the fourth question, the poem qualifies, if not for greatness, at least for honesty and integrity, qualities and standards certainly deserving of respect and admiration. In his "The Art of Poetry" Koch seems to have achieved them.

Although not overtly about the art of poetry, "Some General Instructions" can be taken as describing Koch's poems even as it gives more explicit advice about living. One statement in particular suggests the connection between poetry and life: "Things have a way of working out/ Which is nonsensical, and one should try to see/ How the process works." This implies that nonsense ultimately makes sense, that beneath the apparent confusion lies order, purpose, and meaning. The statement provides a helpful gloss on the best of Koch's poems, which often go by way of nonsense to make a final and useful kind of sense.

"Some General Instructions" alternates between aphorism and meditative commentary. Like any set of aphorisms, it bristles with contradictions. Even so, it shines with joy and radiates humor. Koch seems to enjoy juxtaposing serious moral and ethical advice with comic yet practical admonition. He advises, for example, that his readers be glad, that they savor life, love, pleasure, and virtue, and that they not eat too many bananas.

Although a similar tone mixing playful humor with thoughtful advice permeates Koch's lovely and beautiful "On Beauty," a rather different note is struck by two other poems in the volume. In "The Circus," a nostalgic reminiscence about the time he wrote an earlier poem with the same title, Koch wonders about the value of the earlier poem, and then, by extension, about the value of any of his poems, about the value of his poetic vocation. Moving out of a concern with poetry, "The Circus" becomes more somber, turning into a meditation on time, death, and loss, especially the loss of friends. In "The Art of Love," a how-to manual of eroticism, the speaker describes a set of outrageous sadomasochistic procedures. The practical nature of the advice ranges from how to meet and greet a girl, to how to get her to do the things described in the poem. "The Art of Love" ends with a catalog of questions about love, some serious, some humorous. Ludicrous answers are provided to each question. Full of high spirits, erotic fantasies, hyperbole, and insult, the poem needs to be taken ironically if it is not to be considered an offense against decency. Even then, its specificity of reference and particularity of detail make it seem less an ironic poem about the art of love than a degrading if witty description of perverse fantasies.

Koch's talent is amply manifested in both *The Pleasures of Peace* and *The Art of Love*. While the poems do not range widely in style, theme, and technique, they do offer a distinctive set of pleasures for the accepting and patient reader, the pleasures of engaging an unusual and unpredictable poetic imagination as it reveals itself in a colloquially inflected idiom which is, by turns, earnest and ironic. Moreover, the deliberate dislocations of logical organization, the profusion of incongruities in image and idea, the exaggeration and far-fetched analogies, are all part of Koch's effort to avoid the predictable, the stodgy, and the dull. They are all part of his effort to create a poetry full of fun and surprise, a poetry which, even though it only infrequently ends in wisdom, nevertheless very often sustains the delight with which it begins.

Major publications other than poetry
NOVEL: *The Red Robins*, 1975.
PLAYS: *Bertha*, 1959; *George Washington Crossing the Delaware*, 1962; *Bertha and Other Plays*, 1966; *The Moon Balloon*, 1969; *A Change of Hearts: Plays, Films and Other Dramatic Works 1951-1971*, 1973.
NONFICTION: *Wishes, Lies and Dreams: Teaching Young Children to Write Poetry*, 1970; *Rose Where Did You Get That Red?*, 1973; *I Never Told Anybody: Teaching Poetry in a Nursing Home*, 1977; *Sleeping on the Wing: An Anthology of Modern Poetry with Essays on Reading and Writing*, 1981.

Bibliography
Dupee, F. W. *The King of the Cats*, 1965.
Gilbert, Sandra M. "A Platoon of Poets," in *Poetry*. CXXIII (August, 1976), pp. 292-294.
Howard, Richard. *Alone with America*. 1950.
Koch, Kenneth. "How Poetry Gets to Be Written," in *Comparative Literature Studies*. XVII (June, 1980), pp. 206-223.
O'Hara, Frank. "Another Word on Kenneth Koch," in *Poetry*. LXXXV (March, 1955), pp. 349-351.
Poulin, A., Ed. *Contemporary American Poetry*, 1971.

Robert DiYanni

CHARLES LAMB

Born: London, England; February 10, 1775
Died: Edmonton, England; December 27, 1834

Principal poem and collections

Blank Verse, 1798 (with Charles Lloyd); *Poetry for Children*, 1809 (with Mary Lamb); *The Works of Charles Lamb*, 1818; *Album Verses*, 1830; *Satan in Search of a Wife*, 1831; *The Poetical Works of Charles Lamb*, 1836.

Other literary forms

Charles Lamb began his literary career writing poetry and continued to write verse his entire life. He tried his hand at other genres, however, and is remembered primarily for his familiar essays. These essays, originally published in the *London Magazine*, were collected in *Essays of Elia* (1823) with another collection appearing ten years later, *Last Essays of Elia* (1833). In addition to his poetry and essays, Lamb wrote fiction, drama, children's literature, and criticism. He wrote one novel, *A Tale of Rosamund Gray and Old Blind Margaret* (1798). In 1802, he published his first play, *John Woodvil: A Tragedy*, which was followed shortly by another attempt at drama: *Mr. H.: A Farce in Two Acts* (1806). In addition to several prologues and epilogues, he published two other dramas: *The Pawnbroker's Daughter: A Farce* (1825) and *The Wife's Trial* (1827). In addition, he wrote (largely in collaboration with his sister Mary) several children's books: *The King and Queen of Hearts* (1806), *Tales from Shakespeare* (1807), *Adventures of Ulysses* (1808), *Mrs. Leicester's School* (1809), and *Prince Dorus* (1811). Lamb's criticism appeared in various periodicals but was never systematically collected and published during his lifetime. He did publish copious critical notes to accompany his voluminous extracts from Elizabethan plays, *Specimens of English Dramatic Poets, Who Lived About the Time of Shakespeare, with Notes* (1808).

Achievements

Much of Lamb's literary career was spent in search of an appropriate genre for his particular genius. He wrote poetry, drama, fiction, and criticism, but of these he truly distinguished himself only in criticism. When he happened upon the persona of Elia and the familiar essay, however, these early efforts contributed to his success. As if he had been in training for years preparing to create the *Essays of Elia*, Lamb applied what he had learned from each of the earlier literary forms in which he had worked. Incorporating his knowledge of the importance of rhythm, dramatic context, characterization, dialogue, tone, and point of view, he placed it into the *Essays of Elia* collections and created masterpieces.

Today's literary critics value the essays of Lamb because they embody and reflect in prose the Romantic predisposition found in the great poetry of the day. These familiar essays have a biographical impulse, organic form, symbolic representation, syntactic flexibility, and occasional subject matter. The popularity of Lamb's essays, however, does not depend upon their historical or theoretical relevance. The *Essays of Elia* collections were as celebrated in Lamb's day as they are in modern times and for the same reason: the character of Elia that Lamb creates is one of the most endearing personae in English literature. Elia's whimsical reminiscences may border upon the trivial, but that is insignificant, because the character of the speaker preempts the content of his speech. The personality of Elia becomes the focal point of the essay. His sentimentality, tempered by irony, elevates these pieces to the status of art, conferring upon them their timeless appeal.

Just as the character of Elia is essential to the success of the essays, Lamb's personality overwhelmed his accomplishments in his own day. No discussion of Lamb's achievements would be complete without mention of his many friends, who provided the essential ingredient for his famous nights at home and his fascinating correspondence. A list of his friends is a roster of the major figures of English Romanticism: Samuel Taylor Coleridge, Robert Southey, William Wordsworth, William Godwin, William Hazlitt, Thomas De Quincey, George Dyer, and Benjamin Robert Haydon. His mid-week parties from 1801 through 1827 assembled writers, artists, actors, and critics for both frivolous and serious discussion. Port, mutton, cards, and tobacco made the following work day the longest of the week for Lamb. What the success of his weekly gatherings suggests, his correspondence corroborates: Lamb was an honest critic, a sensitive friend, and a sympathetic confidant. When he mentioned his many friends, he assumed his usual tone of self-deprecation, claiming that they were "for the most part, persons of an uncertain fortune." When talking of Lamb, his friends were less diffident. Henry Crabb Robinson epitomizes the opinion of Lamb's friends when he characterized Lamb as "of all the men of genius I ever knew, the one the most intensely and universally to be loved."

Biography

Charles Lamb was born in London to poor parents. His father was a servant and clerk to Samuel Salt, Esquire, of the Inner Temple, and his mother was Salt's housekeeper. Like his older brother John, Lamb went to Christ's Hospital School when he was seven, sponsored by Salt. There he met Coleridge, who was to become his friend for life. Because of a stutter, Lamb did not follow Coleridge to Cambridge on scholarship. Instead, at the age of fourteen, with his education complete, he went to work. His first two apprenticeships came to nothing. In 1792, however, he took a position as an accountant in the East India House, where he remained until his retirement in 1825. Lamb often complained about his position at the East India House, claiming that the work was boring and unimaginative. In fact, the routine about which he complained was a settling and stabilizing influence that his temperament needed and his art exploited. Lamb received an adequate income for a modicum of work, and, though not rich, he was comfortable by the standards of his day. Two other events in his life, however, diminished the happiness offered by this financial security.

Among celebrated bachelors, Lamb is one of the most famous. His unmarried status, however, was not of his own choosing. Sometime around 1792, he fell in love with Ann Simmons, a Hertfordshire neighbor of his maternal grandmother Field. Mrs. Field is said to have discouraged the relationship by pointing out that there was insanity in the Lamb family, and Ann married a London pawnbroker and silversmith named Barton. Lamb's poetry, letters, and essays testify to the sorrow he felt over his loss. Thirty years later in "Dream Children," Elia would fantasize about the woman he never married and the children he never fathered, who instead "call Bartram father." Mrs. Fields's warning may have been a self-fulfilling prophecy. At the end of 1795, in despair over "another Person," Lamb committed himself to Hoxton Asylum for six weeks. In a letter to Coleridge dated May 27, 1796, he explains his condition: "I am got somewhat rational now, & *don't bite any one*. But *mad I was*—& many a vagary my imagination played with me."

The second unhappy event that crucially influenced Lamb's life was also related to madness. On September 22, 1796, his sister Mary went mad and fatally stabbed their mother with a kitchen knife. She was tried in the courts, found insane, and remanded to Lamb's custody for life, at his request. Because of his devotion to Mary, his life was altered permanently. Lamb and Mary had always been close, but now they became inseparable, except, that is, when Mary felt her madness coming on. Then the two could be seen walking hand in hand—crying and carrying Mary's straitjacket—to Hoxton Asylum where she would stay until she was well again. To make up for the family that neither of them had, they both cultivated a great number of friends. Stories abound concerning Lamb's remarkable personality, his charming wit, quick sallies, pointed puns, and clever ripostes. It was this engaging personality that Lamb managed to translate into his depiction of Elia. Elia first appeared in the *London Magazine* in August, 1820, with the essay "Recollections of the South-Sea House." Elia is, of course, a mask, but a mask sharing many of Lamb's traits and experiences.

In 1825, Lamb sent his last Elia essay to the *London Magazine*, and in that year he retired from the East India House. His retirement, eagerly awaited, proved disappointing. He missed the routine, the motivation, the camaraderie of the office. Worse was the frequent illness of Mary that left him alone more and more often. Lamb was not a man able to cope with loneliness, and his drinking increased. With the death of Coleridge in July of 1834, Lamb seemed to lose interest in life. On Saturday, December 27, 1834, he died in his home at the age of fifty-nine. He is buried in Edmonton churchyard, outside of London.

Analysis

Charles Lamb's attitude toward poetry evolved as he matured. As a young man, he considered himself an aspiring poet. He experimented with rhythms, modeled his diction after Sir Philip Sidney and his sentiment after William Lisle Bowles, discussed theory with Samuel Taylor Coleridge, and took pleasure in criticizing his own and others' work. In his early verse, there is little of the humor, irony, or modesty that typify his later writing. Lamb is not only serious but also self-consciously so, dealing with weighty topics in an elevated style. His early poems are heavy with melancholy and despair, even before Mary killed their mother. The poems are also personal and confessional and suggest an adolescent indulgence in emotion. Writing to Coleridge in 1796, Lamb explained, "I love my sonnets because they are the reflected images of my own feelings at different times."

Following Mary's disaster, Lamb's reality became as tragic as he had previously imagined. He wrote to Coleridge, "Mention nothing of poetry. I have destroyed every vestige of past vanities of that kind." This was the first of several renunciations of poetry made by Lamb throughout his life, but—like similar renunciations of liquor and tobacco—it was temporary. In a few months, he was sending Coleridge new verses, but the subject matter was altered. Lamb turned to poetry for solace and consolation, composing religious verse. His interest in poetry had revived, but the sensational occurrences that influenced the rest of his life encouraged him to become one of the least sensational of poets. From this new perspective, he counseled Coleridge to "cultivate simplicity," anticipating William Wordsworth's "Preface" to *Lyrical Ballads* (1798). In his next letter to Coleridge, he praised Bowles and Philip Massinger and said he favored "an uncomplaining melancholy, a delicious regret for the past." Lamb's early sentimentality had been displaced by real tragedy, and his poetry changed accordingly.

With the healing passage of time, Lamb's literary interests shifted. In the years 1800 and 1805, he wrote several poems, but for the most part these middle years of his literary career were spent as a journalist. Around 1820, Lamb again began to write poetry, but of a completely different sort. The last period of his poetic production had been spent writing album verse and other occasional poems. As he matured, Lamb outgrew his earlier confessional mode and turned to people and events around him for subjects. He used his imagination to a greater degree, coloring reality, creating fictions, and distancing himself from his subject. His poetry changed with him, and it came to reflect a fictitious personality similar to the Elia of the essays. Like the Elian essays, Lamb's later poetry contains many autobiographical elements, but they are cloaked and decorous. In place of self-indulgent confessions is a distance and control not found in the early verse.

Lamb wrote and published most of his serious verse—that which today is most often anthologized—in the period between 1795 and 1800. His best and worst poems are among these efforts, which are autobiographical and despondent. They mourn the loss of love, of bygone days, and of happier times. They vary greatly in form, as Lamb experimented with different meters and structures. He was most successful in tight and traditional verse forms, and least successful in blank verse. In fact, his blank verse is bad, a surprising situation since his strength in more structured forms is in the control and variation of meter and rhythm.

A favorite form of Lamb's throughout his life was the sonnet, which he began writing early in his career. Appropriately enough, two of his earliest and best poems are English sonnets, published in Coleridge's *Poems on Various Subjects* (1796). This first significant publication by Lamb shows the influence of the Elizabethans on his poetry. His syntax, imagery, and diction suggest the practice of two centuries earlier. One of these sonnets, "Was it some sweet device of Faery," mourns a lost love "Anna" and is clearly a response to the loss of Ann Simmons. The poem's sophisticated rhythm, with frequent enjambment and medial stops, transcends its commonplace subject. Here, as often in Lamb's poetry, the handling of rhythm turns what might be a mediocre effort into an admirable poem. His use of rhetorical questions in this sonnet is skillful, too. Unlike the stilted tone that such questions often provide, in this sonnet the questions actually help to create a sense of sincerity. Another sonnet from the same volume, "O, I could laugh to hear the midnight wind," also treats the subject of lost love. The poem is nicely unified by the images of wind and wave, and it reflects the Romantic idea of the unity of man and cosmos. It also presents another Romantic concept, the value of the imagination and the powerful influence of memory. This poem is a reminder that much of Wordsworthian theory was not unique to Wordsworth. The ideas that the poem considers may be Romantic, but the style is that of an earlier day. The diction is antique, the imagery tightly unified, and the sonnet form itself conventionally developed. Lamb's prosody is pleasant but not novel.

In 1797, Coleridge's book of poetry went into a second edition, but with an amended title, ". . . to which are now added Poems by Charles Lamb." Lamb had already contributed four poems to the earlier edition, but now there appeared fourteen of his poems. The additional ones are, on the whole, inferior to the initial four; seven are sonnets written about the same time as those that Coleridge had already published. Of interest is one addressed to Mary and written before her tragedy, "If from my lips some angry accents fell." The closing lines give a sense of the personal nature of these verses:

> Thou to me didst ever shew
> Kindest affection; and would oft times lend

> An ear to the desponding love-sick lay,
> Weeping with sorrows with me, who repay
> But ill the mighty debt of love I owe,
> Mary, to thee, my sister and my friend.

The other poem of note in this volume was published in a Supplement at the end of the edition. Lamb was signaling its inferiority, and his judgment was correct. "A Vision of Repentance" is an experiment in Spenserian stanza. It opens with a vision, "I saw a famous fountain, in my dream." The fountain turns out to be the waters of redemption that have attracted "Psyche" as well as the speaker. A dialogue between the two ensues, and Psyche reports that she has forsaken Jesus and given "to a treacherous WORLD my heart." After some further conversation, the speaker leaves Psyche with the wish, "Christ restore thee soon." The poem is one of several by Lamb that deal with Christianity. Like his other religious verse, it is flawed: didactic, prolix, and unrhythmical.

Lamb's failure with the Spenserian stanza is paralleled by his experiments in blank verse. In 1798, he and Charles Lloyd published a volume entitled *Blank Verse*. Lacking the direction given by a tight form or a controlling convention, Lamb's blank verse is verbose, clumsy, and unsure. His autobiographical subject matter and confessional intent are uncomfortably couched in an elevated style reminiscent of John Milton. The two are not compatible. The volume, however, does contain one work by Lamb worthy of his talent. "The Old Familiar Faces," though not in blank verse, is Lamb's best-known poem. The subject is typical of this period in Lamb's career; it is a lamenting revelation of intense personal grief and loss. Its power, however, lies not in its subject matter, but in the skillful way in which Lamb manipulates the prosody. The poem evokes man's essential isolation and loneliness in the dolorous tolling repetition of the phrase, "All, all are gone, the old familiar faces." The form of the poem creates the effect. Rather than blank verse or the thumping rhymed verse of which he was too fond, Lamb chose a three-line stanza that replaced rhyme with the repetition of the title line. In this way, he gained form without the convoluted syntax of the padded line that rhyme often demanded. The rhythm of the line is that used by Coleridge in "Christabel," and it is agreeable to think that it was Lamb who suggested this meter to his friend. The poem is justly often anthologized; its rhythm is perfectly suited to the subject. Ian Jack in the *Oxford History of English Literature* (1963) suggests that the success of the meter conflicts with the other poems in the volume. He concludes, "It is hard to say how far the effect of the poem is due to metrical sophistication, and how far to a felicitous awkwardness."

By 1800, the self-indulgent moroseness of Lamb's early verse was beginning to be displaced by a greater sense of reserve and control. These years saw less poetic activity by Lamb, but the poems he wrote are, on the whole, more able. An excellent example of the newfound discipline displayed by Lamb occurs in "Hester." The poem again deals with the subjects of loss, death, and despair, but he handles them with a new and previously uncharacteristic restraint. The tight rhyme scheme and the concluding hypermetrical iambic dimeter line provide Lamb with a form he uses well: a short line, a varied rhythm, and a regular stanza:

> A springy motion in her gait,
> A rising step, did indicate
> Of pride and joy no common rate
> That flush'd her spirit

"Hester" is not one of the immortal poems in the English language, but it is a solid achievement worthy of a young poet. Ian Jack has compared it favorably with the lyrical ballads of Wordsworth.

Another poem from this period breaks the morbidity of Lamb's previous verse and prefigures the wit and urbanity found in *Essays of Elia*. Lamb wrote "A Farewell to Tobacco" in what he called "a stammering verse" because he used tobacco to retard his own stammering. Once again he turned to the short line, in this case an irregular eight-syllable trochaic line with rhyming couplets, and it well served his comic intent. Gone is the gross subjectivity; instead, the poem humorously indicts tobacco, while admitting that the habit is unbreakable. Good-natured word play and clever burlesque make the poem one of Lamb's most enjoyable. The comic tone established in "A Farewell to Tobacco" appears again in 1812 when Lamb composed one of his few political poems. "The Triumph of the Whale" gently ridicules the Prince Regent by comparing George with a leviathan. He satirizes the Regent's girth, appetite, retinue, and failed constancy. The poem exists mainly, however, for the pun on which it ends: "the PRINCE of WHALES."

The last noteworthy poem of this period is a sonnet that illustrates Lamb's mature, relaxed, and personal style. "Written at Cambridge" is an autobiographical whimsy that details how the poet feels as he walks around the university. A note of disappointment begins the poem because the speaker regrets that he had been unable to attend such an institution. This sense of loss disappears, however, with the speaker's slightly foolish but nevertheless touching portrait of his imaginative usurpation of Cantabrigian wisdom while strolling its grounds. This poem is worthy of "gentle Charles."

Of the original poems published in the posthumous collection, *The Poetical Works of Charles Lamb*, almost half are from his last period, 1820 to 1834. Most of these are "album verse," a popular form in the 1820's. These occasional verses—written at the request of and about the album's owner—are humorous and light, built around epigrams, puns, and acrostics. Most of this album verse, while representative of the genre, is hardly memorable, with two exceptions. "On the Arrival in England of Lord Byron's Remains" is a good example of Lamb's mature tone, and it reveals his opinion of Byron: "lordly Juan, damned to lasting fame,/ Went out a pickle, and came back the same." A more serious work which arrives at unpleasant conclusions is "In My Own Album," a poignant comparison of life to an album. The poem returns to the theme of self-reproach that colored so much of Lamb's early verse, but there exists a distance and a universality that was not at work before. Rhymed tercets provide Lamb the form in which he worked best, and his iambic hexameters are smooth and graceful. The music of his verse complements his rhythm and meter.

Two of Lamb's best poems, both products of this late period, nicely exemplify his mature serious and comic styles. Both were written after Lamb had won recognition as an essayist, when he no longer felt he had to prove himself as a poet. Freed from the necessity of competing with Edmund Spenser, John Donne, and Milton (not to mention Coleridge, Robert Burns, and Robert Southey), Lamb discovered his own rhythm and voice. These, his finest verses, are the products of his natural strengths, and not those borrowed from another time or another artist. Relaxed and self-assured, Lamb mastered the short line and the comic effect of rhyme. He cultivated forms that worked for him and his voice. "On an Infant Dying as Soon as Born" deals with loss and death in a poignant and moving way. The maudlin, pathetic tone is gone. In its place is an elegant lament for the state of all men, an elegy that transcends the single occasion, a threnody whose language and figures are worthy of Andrew Marvell or Henry Vaughan. The dead child, addressed as "Riddle of destiny," presents to the speaker an insoluble problem, the suffering of innocent men. The speaker concludes that "the economy of Heaven is dark" and that even the "wisest clerks" are unable to explain why an infant dies while

> shrivel'd crones
> Stiffen with age to stocks and stones;
> And crabbed use the conscience sears
> In sinners of an hundred years.

The poem closes with a traditional, but guarded, optimism.

Lamb's longest and last poem published during his life, *Satan in Search of a Wife* (1831), consists of two books of thirty verses each. It is usually said that Lamb never valued this poem because he wrote his publisher not to mention that the "damn'd 'Devil's Wedding'" was written by the author of the *Essays of Elia*. Nevertheless, he thought highly enough of the poem to have it published. The ballad is Lamb at his best: light, jocular, ironic, punning, occasional, and personal. It begins with an echo of Lord Byron's *The Vision of Judgment* (1822) in reverse. Instead of St. Peter grown bored, the devil is out of sorts:

The Devil was sick and queasy of late,
  And his sleep and his appetite fail'd him;
His ears they hung down and his tail it was clapp'd
Between his poor hoofs, like a dog that's been rapp'd—
  None knew what the devil ail'd him.

The tale continues, telling of the Devil's love for a tailor's daughter, his successful wooing of her, and the joyful wedding. Lamb's autobiographical propensity shows up even here, for lurking behind all the fun are serious complaints about bachelorhood, about women as lovers, women as mothers, and even women who murder, with the speaker concluding that "a living Fiend/ Was better than a dead Parent." The poem is, however, anything but maudlin. It is an energetic and fancy-filled romp which spoofs the devil, marriage, foreigners, and the Christian idea of hell. It is vintage Lamb: genteel, a bit cynical, but kind and sincere. The essays of Lamb will continue to earn him fame, but poems such as *Satan in Search of a Wife* have been too long neglected.

Major publications other than poetry

NOVEL: *A Tale of Rosamund Gray and Old Blind Margaret*, 1798.

PLAYS: *John Woodvil: A Tragedy*, 1802; *Mr. H.: A Farce in Two Acts*, 1813 (performed 1806); *The Pawnbroker's Daughter: A Farce*, 1825; *The Wife's Trial*, 1827.

NONFICTION: *Specimens of English Dramatic Poets, Who Lived About the Time of Shakespeare, with Notes*, 1808; *Essays of Elia*, 1823; *Last Essays of Elia*, 1833.

CHILDREN'S LITERATURE: *The King and Queen of Hearts*, 1806; *Tales from Shakespeare*, 1807 (with Mary Lamb); *Adventures of Ulysses*, 1808; *Mrs. Leicester's School*, 1809 (with Mary Lamb); *Prince Dorus*, 1811.

Bibliography

Barnett, George L. *Charles Lamb*, 1976.
Brogan, Howard. "Satire and Humor in Lamb's Verse," in *The Charles Lamb Society Bulletin*. VIII (October, 1974), pp. 153-157.
Lucas, E. V. *The Life of Charles Lamb*, 1921.
_____ ed. *The Works of Charles and Mary Lamb*, 1903-1905.
Marrs, Edwin W., ed. *The Letters of Charles and Mary Anne Lamb*, 1975.
Seymour, William Kean. "Charles Lamb as a Poet," in *Essays by Divers Hands*. XXVI (March, 1954), pp. 103-126.

John F. Schell

WALTER SAVAGE LANDOR

Born: Warwick, England; January 30, 1775
Died: Florence, Italy; September 17, 1864

Principal poems and collections

The Poems of Walter Savage Landor, 1795; *Gebir: A Poem, in Seven Books*, 1798; *Poems from the Arabic and Persian*, 1800; *Poetry by the Author of Gebir*, 1800; *Gebirus, Poema*, 1803; *Count Julian* (a verse drama), 1812; *Idyllia Nova Quinque Heroum atque Heroidum*, 1815; *Idyllia Heroica*, 1820; *Andrea of Hungary*, 1839 (verse drama); *Giovanna of Naples*, 1839 (verse drama); *Fra Rupert: The Last Part of a Trilogy*, 1840 (verse drama); *The Siege of Ancona*, 1846 (verse drama); *The Hellenics Enlarged and Completed*, 1847; *Poemata et Inscriptiones*, 1847; *Italics of Walter Savage Landor*, 1848; *The Last Fruit off an Old Tree*, 1853; *Heroic Idyls, with additional poems*, 1863; *The Poetical Works of Walter Savage Landor*, 1937 (Stephen Wheeler, editor).

Other literary forms

Walter Savage Landor's reputation rests primarily on his poetry, but he was a skilled writer of prose as well. His political writings are notable for their anger and his criticism for its insight into the mechanics of writing. All of his prose is witty; it is frequently satirical. As with his poetry, Landor's prose works are carefully phrased and sometimes more perfect in their parts than their wholes. Ranking as one of the most important practitioners of nonfiction prose in the nineteenth century, he is viewed by critics as one of the outstanding prose stylists of the English language.

Achievements

Landor's poetry has never had a wide readership. Much of its appeal is in its near-perfect phrasing and versification; such an appeal of skill almost inevitably attracts admirers among other poets, the fellow practitioners of a demanding art. Landor remains admired for the variety of poetic forms that he mastered and for the clarity of his phrasing; he is often faulted for the detached tone of his work—for the lack of emotional response to his subjects. His poetry often seems crystalline and fragile, as if unable to withstand the burden of a large audience. Fine prosody and marvelously apt phrasing when combined with the distant tone of much of his verse makes ranking him among poets a difficult task. Compounding the difficulty are his poetry's classical characteristics, which seem in conflict with the Romantic and Victorian eras during which he wrote. His poetry lacks the emotional vigor of Percy Bysshe Shelley's work but compares well with the beauty of John Keats's odes and is superior to Lord Byron's verse in ingenuity. He cannot match William Wordsworth in importance to the history of poetry, although many poets have valued his contributions to the understanding of prosody. Taken by itself, apart from its era and influence, Landor's poetry is equal in melodic beauty and economy of phrasing to much of the best in English poetry. As a poet, Landor might fairly be ranked behind Wordsworth and Robert Browning in overall achievement and behind Keats in imagery; he is second to none in phrasing and prosody.

Biography

Walter Savage Landor was a man given to fierce passions; he could burst out in either anger or generosity almost without warning. He was egotistical and given to romantic notions about life; this combination caused him much unhappiness and yet underlies much of his best writing. He was born on January 30, 1775, in Warwick. In 1780, he began his schooling at Knowle; in 1783, he was sent to study at Rugby. After eight years of annoying his teachers and antagonizing others with his satirical sense of humor, he was sent home. Landor, however, remembered Rugby fondly; while there, he developed his taste for poetry and demonstrated a precocious skill in composing verse. Reverend William Langley, of Ashbourne, Derbyshire, became Landor's tutor in 1792. The next year, Landor entered Trinity College, Oxford. While at Oxford he punctuated a political dispute by shooting at a neighbor's shutters; suspended from college for two terms, he left Oxford in 1794, never to return. He moved to London and had his poetry published under a grand title for a mere twenty-year-old, *The Poems of Walter Savage Landor* (1795). The volume brought him a small but loyal following among other writers and readers who had a taste for fine literature.

When his father died, Landor inherited a large fortune. This he spent on a large estate in Wales and on outfitting his own regiment to fight in Spain against the French. After the French left Spain, Landor's regiment disappeared, and he hastened home. In Wales, he tried to improve the lives of the peasants and to introduce enlightened methods of managing an estate. No one seemed to appreciate his efforts, and after losing much money, he abandoned the effort.

In 1811, in one of his grand gestures, he married an attractive woman who was beneath him in both wealth and social station. Far from being grateful, his bride, Julia Thuillier, repeatedly cuckolded Landor and made his life unpleasant. She did not appreciate her husband's generous nature, his intellect, or his interests. Although she is often portrayed as a nasty and cruel woman, she and Landor seem to have had enough truces to produce a daughter and three sons. In 1814, Landor toured the Continent, where he was eventually joined by his wife. From 1816 to 1818, he stayed in Como, Italy, and in 1818 his first son was born. His daughter followed in 1820, while he was in Pisa. From 1821 to 1828, he lived in Florence, where his second and third sons were born in 1822 and 1825. By 1835, his family life was unbearable;

his wife dedicated herself to embarrassing him publicly and committing adultery privately. Landor had doted on his children and spoiled them; nevertheless, when he left his wife and returned to England, they chose to remain with her, although in the 1840's his two eldest sons and his daughter visited him for months at a time. During the years of unhappy marriage, Landor continued to write, building a loyal following of admiring friends, including Ralph Waldo Emerson and John Forster.

Landor's trenchant wit and attacks on the misdeeds of public officials frequently involved him in trouble. In 1857, old but still fiery, he published attacks on a Mrs. Yescombe, whom he saw as a villainess because of an injustice visited on a young woman. Convicted of libel in 1858, he left England in 1859 to seek refuge from litigation in Fiesole, where he had maintained his family since 1835. Rejected by his family, he wandered to nearby Florence, where Robert Browning offered him a home. He died on September 17, 1864. He had wanted to be buried near Bath in England but was interred instead at Florence. He had wanted an epitaph that mentioned his closest friends but instead received one that mentions his wife and children.

Analysis

The poems of Walter Savage Landor are like fragile crystals, the clarity of which disguises their masterfully crafted form. The meaning of Landor's verse often seems transparent; he believed in clarity as a poetic virtue. The seeming ease with which his verse can be understood belies the strenuous efforts Landor made to pare down his phrases and to present his ideas with near-perfect economy. Much of his success in economical phrasing comes from his mastery of a host of meters and poetic subgenres, chief among which were the verse drama, the dramatic scene, the heroic poem, and the Hellenic poem. Landor had a restless mind, requiring activity; he had a voracious appetite for ideas. Writing poetry provided him with relief from such intellectual demands. Poetry was thus more of a hobby than a career; Landor wrote verse for recreation, and the complexity of his prosody and the pureness of his language originate in part from this recreational aspect of his versifying. His poetry represented an effort to find peace of mind, to discharge some of his extraordinary intellectual energy. The literature of ancient Greece and Rome had a long history of amateur scholarly study and had inspired and informed the neoclassical period in England that was just ending when Landor was born, and he found ready materials for such agreeable study in a host of commentaries on form and style. The Greeks supplied him with ideas about life and human relationships; the Latin poets supplied him with high standards for poetic composition and style. He sometimes wrote in Latin, perhaps to capture the elegance and sense of sweet phrasing that typifies much of the best of the poetry of the classical Romans.

Landor's use of classical materials has long created problems for literary historians. His life spans the Romantic era and ends when the Victorian era was well under way. Although some Romantic poets—notably Percy Bysshe Shelley—used classical myths as subjects, they rarely employed classical forms. A classicist can be identified by his use of the standards of the ancient poets: an emphasis on phrasing, good sense, and logical order. A classicist restrains his emotions in favor of clarity of expression and tends to use classical works as models for his own. The Romantics, on the other hand, reacted to the preceding neoclassical age by emphasizing mysticism, nature, and traditional English poetic forms such as blank verse and the sonnet.

In his tastes and models, Landor was every inch a classicist and had more in common with Alexander Pope and Samuel Johnson than with Wordsworth or Shelley, but in his subjects he turned to nature as an ideal, somewhat as Wordsworth did and even more as did the Renaissance poet Sir Philip Sidney, and he wrote blank verse with a facility that had been alien to many of his neoclassical forebears. He had in common with his contemporaries a vast enthusiasm for poetry, but, whereas his contemporaries lived for their art, Landor's art was his servant. Emotional outbursts were reined in, uncontrolled poetic fervor was not for Landor. His spirit was as restless as Lord Byron's, but where Byron turned his restlessness into a poetic ideal, Landor used poetry to subdue his own restlessness. Thus, the determined and hard self-control evident in Landor's verse sets him apart from the poets of his time. Some critics call him a Romantic, though seemingly more for the age in which he lived than for the qualities of his work. He actually was the son of the neoclassical age; he followed a poetic path that was a logical extension of what the neoclassicists had achieved, while Wordsworth and the Romantics followed a poetic path that was a logical reaction against the neoclassicists. Landor was a classicist in a Romantic age.

As a good student of the classical authors, Landor believed in poetic simplicity. His verse dramas reveal at once the strengths and weaknesses of the simplicity that gives his poetry its crystalline character. Although not the best of his dramatic efforts, perhaps the best known of his dramas is the tragedy of *Count Julian* (1812). The play resembles a child's perception of tragedy— all loud voices and grim visages. The characters exclaim instead of converse; each word seems meant for the ages. The welter of "Ohs!" and other short exclamations are sometimes more risible than dramatic. Even so, the subject of *Count Julian* has much potential for good drama. A Spanish warrior who has driven the Moors from Spain avenges the rape of his daughter by his king by leading the Moors back into his country, with disastrous consequences. The play's blank verse is austere, remote from the characters and their emotions. Landor had hoped that *Count Julian* might be performed, but its poetry is more important than its drama; it is now regarded strictly as a closet drama. *Andrea of Hungary* (1839) and its sequels *Giovanna of Naples* (1839) and *Fra Rupert: The Last Part of a Trilogy* (1840) are dramatically and poetically more successful. Blank verse and character blend well in these plays; the scenes between Andrea and Giovanna in the first of them are relaxed, revealing two interesting personalities. Landor cared little for plot, which he called "trick"; thus, the sequence of events in his trilogy of plays is predictable and has few twists. Andrea is murdered, probably at the instigation of the ambitious Fra Rupert; Giovanna remains a paragon of virtue through three marriages and is eventually murdered; Fra Rupert commits suicide and his villainy is revealed. Landor uses the plot as a vehicle for some of his notions about power and politics and his blend of apt phrase, characterization, and good verse is often moving.

Landor's dramatic scenes also feature blank verse, though they are only short conversations. In "Essex and Bacon," for example, Landor shows the Earl of Essex meeting with Francis Bacon after the Earl's condemnation to death for treason. Landor's interest in ambition and the abuse of power provides the scene's depth. Essex sees himself as greater than Bacon because he took a glorious chance by opposing Queen Elizabeth, and he cannot understand how his friend can call him "lower than bergess or than churl." Essex declares, "To servile souls how abject seem the fallen!/ Benchers and message-bearers stride o'er Essex." He dismisses Bacon with contempt. When alone, Bacon is allowed the last word, which, in summary, says that ambition is often mistakenly thought to be great by those who allow it to run their lives, when, in fact, it is arrogance. The dramatic scenes generally reflect Landor's concern with the abuse of power; "Ippolito di Este" perhaps makes Landor's feelings clearest. This short drama introduces the audience to the brothers Ferrante, Giulio, and the Cardinal Ippolito di Este. Ferrante has the misfortune to have his eyes admired by a woman whom his brother the Cardinal desires; the Cardinal has Ferrante's eyes removed. The dramatic scene is truly horrible, even if Ferrante is too saintly to be palatable.

Of Landor's heroic poems, his first (and his first important poem, written when he was perhaps twenty years of age), *Gebir* (1798), is probably the best known. Gebir is king of Gades (Cadiz); he conquers Egypt and the heart of Queen Charoba, then is assassinated. The poem takes him through heroic adventures, including a trip to the underworld. *Gebir* reveals Landor's extensive scholarship, based as it is on Arabian history. The verse is spare, already featuring Landor's emphasis on succinct phrasing; its scenes are dramatic and resemble the tragedies in structure. Unfortunately, its language is too remote for successful characterization; Gebir, who is a strong, dynamic young man, talks like an ancient Greek god. His love, Charoba, is more accessible to readers, although she, too, often merely declaims. *Gebir* displays much fine poetry; it may not always succeed, but it is good enough by itself to establish Landor's claim to poetic importance. Admired by contemporary critics and poets, including Robert Southey, the poem established Landor as a significant poet.

Landor's so-called Hellenics are poems that are informed by ancient Greek myths and history. They encompass blank verse, lyrics, sonnets, and conversations. The best of these, such as "Coresos and Callirhöe," "The Altar of Modesty," "Acon and Rhodope," "Pan," and "The Marriage of Helena and Menelaos," are exquisite gems of the poet's art. Each is representative of Landor's classical principles; the poems are simple in form, their clarity of language being the result of much revision, and they reflect intelligent observation. They focus on characters and generally deliver homilies on love and life. In "Pan and Pitys," for instance, Pitys is loud in her derogation of Boreas, her suitor. Boreas hears her, and he drops a large rock on her. The exchanges between Pan and Pitys are loud and boisterous; her foolishness and insensitivity are also loud; perhaps she should have spoken more kindly of her suitor. In "Acon and Rhodope," a man loses sight of what is important in his life and loses all he cares for. The verse is thick with colors and odors that represent a mixture of life and death; apple trees have "freckled leaves" and oleanders have "light-hair'd progeny." The effect of the Hellenic poems is one of another world that is somehow part of the common one. The characters have thoughts, emotions, and problems, much like those that are common to humanity, but their world is richer, more intense than common experience. Such intensity is well evoked in "The Marriage of Helena and Menelaos," in which the sixteen-year-old Helena faces her husband-to-be and the prospect of adulthood for the first time. The gibes of siblings, the fears of appearing foolish, the sense of losing youth too soon, condense into a poignant, short series of events. "The Marriage of Helena and Menelaos" is a product of the mature Landor; it is alive with ideas, focused on a dramatic moment, and deceptively simple on its surface.

Although Landor strove to use elevated language and to create clear, often austere, verse, his poetry contains much variety and life. Works such as "Homer, Laertes, Agatha" and "Penelope and Pheido" not only feature Landor's classicism but feature high poetry and are lively as well. Landor brings humanity to his poetry; he focuses on the difficulties people have when faced with problems larger than themselves. As with other poets who lived long lives, Landor's verse changed over the years; it began by being brash and noisy, as in *Gebir* and *Count Julian*, grew to reflect his thoughts on politics and power, as in *Fra Rupert*, and attained a blend of erudition and humanity that bring sensitivity to "The Marriage of Helena and Menelaos," written when Landor was eighty-nine. Among his most sensitive and interesting works is the verse drama *The Siege of Ancona* (1846). Typical of Landor's work, it is known to only a few critics and admirers of poetry. Its verse is clear and its tone is heroic, without the declamatory faults of *Count Julian*; its psychology is subtle and its values those of a classicist who was nevertheless a part of the Romantic period. The Consul of Ancona asserts that "the air/ Is life alike to all, the sun is warmth,/ The earth, its fruits and flocks, are nutriment,/ Children and wives are comforts; all partake/ (Or may partake) in these" (III, ii, lines 48-52). Like Wordsworth, Landor found a universal metaphor in nature; unlike Wordsworth, he made his natural world Arcadian in the manner of English Renaissance poets. He labored at the classical ideal of spare verse and detached tone; he yielded to the Romantic desire to express his innermost spirit. At its best, his poetry is clear and crystalline, maintaining a warmth and sensitive empathy for the common joys, miseries, and confusions that people face in their daily lives.

Major publications other than poetry
NOVEL: *The Pentameron and Pentalogia*, 1837.
SHORT FICTION: *Dry Sticks Fagoted*, 1858.
PLAYS: *Count Julian*, 1812; *Andrea of Hungary*, 1839; *Giovanna of Naples*, 1839; *Fra Rupert: The Last Part of a Trilogy*, 1840; *The Siege of Ancona*, 1846.
NONFICTION: *Imaginary Conversations of Literary Men and Statesmen*, 1824-1829 (5 volumes); *Citation and Examination of William Shakespeare*, 1834.

Bibliography
Aldington, Richard. "Landor's 'Hellenics,'" in *Literary Studies and Reviews*, 1924.
Brumbaugh, Thomas B. "Walter Savage Landor as Romantic Classicist," in *Topic*. XXIII (1972), pp. 14-21.
Colvin, Sidney. *Landor*, 1881.
Dilworth, Ernest. *Walter Savage Landor*, 1971.
Elwin, Malcom. *Landor, a Replevin*, 1958.
Kelly, Andrea. "The Latin Poetry of Walter Savage Landor," in *The Latin Poetry of English Poets*, 1974. Edited by J. W. Binns.
Pinsky, Robert. *Landor's Poetry*, 1968.
Richter, Helene. "Walter Savage Landor," in *Anglia*. L (1926), pp. 123-152, 317-344; and LI (1927), pp. 1-30.
Super, Robert H. *Walter Savage Landor: A Biography*, 1954.
Swinburne, Algernon Charles. "Landor," in *Swinburne as Critic*, 1972. Edited by Clyde K. Hyder.
Vitaux, Pierre. *L'Oeuvre de Walter Savage Landor*, 1964.

Kirk H. Beetz

WILLIAM LANGLAND

Born: Cleobury Mortimer (?), Shropshire, England; c. 1332
Died: London(?), England; c. 1400

Principal poems

The Vision of William, Concerning Piers the Plowman, (A Text) 1362, (B Text) c. 1377, (C Text) c. 1393; *Richard the Redeless*, c. 1395 (attributed).

Other literary forms

William Langland wrote only poetry.

Achievements

Apparently, in its own day, *The Vision of William, Concerning Piers the Plowman* was a very popular work. More than fifty manuscripts of the poem in its various versions still exist. The poem's four printings before 1561 are evidence of its continued popularity well into the sixteenth century. The audience of *Piers Plowman* was not, as it was for most poems of the alliterative revival, a small group of provincial nobles; rather, as J. A. Burrow has shown, the poem would have been read by a broadly based national public of parish priests or local clergy whose tastes favored purely didactic literature. In addition, Burrow connects the poem with a growing lay public of the rising bourgeoisie, whose tastes were still conservative and generally religious. The didactic content of the poem, then, was its chief appeal in its own time.

By the sixteenth century, however, with the rise of Protestantism, William Langland's poem became acclaimed for its aspects of social satire. This strain in the poem had been underlined even in the fourteenth century, when John Ball, in a letter to the peasants of Essex during the revolt of 1381, mentioned Piers the Plowman. Possibly because of this mention, the very orthodox Catholic Langland came, ironically, to be associated with Lollardy, and to be looked upon as a bitter critic of the Roman Church and a precursor of Protestantism.

By the late sixteenth century, Langland's western Midland dialect had become too difficult for any but the most ardent reader, and so no new edition of *Piers Plowman* appeared until 1813. Though nineteenth century readers deplored Langland's allegory, they could still, like the readers before them, admire *Piers Plowman* as social satire, and, in addition, they could appreciate and admire the stark realism in such scenes as the confession of the seven deadly sins in Passus V (B Text). Their chief interest in Langland was historical: they viewed the poem as a firsthand commentary on the fourteenth century.

Modern criticism has begun to concentrate, for the first time, on the artistry of the poem. Elizabeth Salter has pointed out how, with the return of so many modern poets to the free accentual verse similar to Langland's, readers are now more able to respond to the verse of *Piers Plowman*. Further, with the contemporary conviction that everyday themes and language are valid subjects for poetry, readers have become more sympathetic to some of Langland's finest passages, which treat everyday experiences in the vocabulary of the common man.

Yet it seems, ultimately, that the first readers of *Piers Plowman* were most correct: the poem's basic intent is didactic, and, for Langland, all artistry was secondary to the message he was trying to convey. Perhaps his greatest achievement is the theme itself, which is at once as simple and as complex as any in literature. Beginning as the Dreamer's simple question in Passus II (B Text), "How may I save my soul?," the theme turns into a multilayered search for individual salvation, for the perfection of contemporary society, for a mystical union with God, and for a way to put mystical vision to practical use in perfecting society. These searches are set against varied landscapes ranging from the contemporary world to the inner world of the soul, across biblical history, through hell to Armageddon. For contemporary critics concerned largely with structure in literature, Langland's most remarkable feat is his ability, in spite of real or apparent digressions and inconsistencies, to put a poem of the encyclopedic range and depth of *Piers Plowman* together into a structured whole.

Biography

Virtually nothing is known of the poet who wrote *Piers Plowman*. At one time, in fact, there was some debate about whether a single author or perhaps as many as five were responsible for the three separate versions of the poem. That controversy has since ended, and scholarship has established a single author for all three versions.

That author's name was almost certainly William Langland. Two fifteenth century manuscript notes attribute the poem to Langland, and there is a line in the B Text which seems to be intended as a cryptogram of the poet's name: "'I haue lyued in londe', quod [I], 'my name is longe wille.'" One manuscript declares that Langland was the son of a certain Stacey (Eustace) de Rokayle, who later held land under the Lord Despenser at Shipton-under-Wychwood in Oxfordshire; in all likelihood, Langland's father was a franklin. It has been conjectured that Langland was illegitimate, but the difference in surname is no real reason to assume this, such differences being common in the fourteenth century. Langland was not born in Oxfordshire but rather in Shropshire, at Cleobury Mortimer, some eight miles from the Malvern Hills which serve as the setting for the first two visions in *Piers Plowman*. Because the B Text is dated with some accuracy at 1377, and because the poet in the B Text declares himself to be forty-five years old, the date of Langland's birth has been set at about 1332.

Whatever else is "known" about the author's life is conjectured from passages in the poem which describe the narrator's life, and is based on the assumption that the narrator, "Will," and the poet Langland are one and the same. In the C Text, the poet speaks of having gone to school, and most likely he was educated at the priory of Great Malvern in Worcestershire. He would have gone through the usual training for the priesthood, but, according to evidence in the poem, the deaths of his father and friends left him without a benefactor and forced him to abandon his studies before taking holy orders. He would have been unable to advance in the Church, having left school with only minor orders, partly because of his incomplete education and because, as the poet writes, he was married—a right permitted only to clerks in orders below subdeacon.

Because of these apparent facts, E. Talbot Donaldson assumes that Langland was an acolyte, one of the poor, unbeneficed clergy who had no official way of making a living within the Church hierarchy. Certainly he was poor, but he seems to have claimed exemption from manual labor by virtue of his being a tonsured clerk. W. W. Skeat conjectures that Langland may have earned some money as a scribe, copying out legal documents, since the poem displays a close knowledge of the form of such documents. Perhaps he was able to pick up odd clerical jobs here and there in the city of London, where, according to an apparently autobiographical account in the C Text, he went to live at Cornhill with his wife, Kitte, and daughter, Callote. According to this passage, Langland seems to have earned money by going about singing the office of the dead, or other prayers for the living, and making regular monthly rounds to the homes of his wealthy patrons.

Langland describes himself, though perhaps with some ironic hyperbole, as a singular character, apparently very tall and lean (his nickname is "Long Will"), wandering about dressed as a beggar, showing little respect for the wealthy who liked to parade their own importance, and spending time scribbling verses. Some considered him mad. Certainly it is true that he spent a good deal of time writing and rewriting *Piers Plowman*. He seems to have labored some thirty years, refining the poem, and perhaps was still revising it at his death: the last two passus of the C version show little change from those of the B Text, suggesting that Langland may have died before he finished the last revision. To be sure, the date of Langland's death is even less certain than that of his birth; it is unlikely that the poet survived his century. If, as has often been disputed, Langland was the author of the poem *Richard the Redeless*, he was still alive in 1399.

Analysis

Piers Plowman is a difficult poem. One is not likely to find a more complex poem, nor one which poses quite so many problems. An entrance to the poem might best be achieved by an examination of those problems—problems of text, of form, of structure, and of interpretation—one at a time.

First, the poem exists in three totally different versions. The earliest version, known as the A Text, must have been written, or at least begun, about 1362, since it alludes to such things as the plague of 1361 and a certain great wind storm known to have occurred in January, 1362. This first version is a poem of some 2,500 lines, consisting of a prologue and eleven books or "passus." In the second, or B Text, William Langland revised his poem and added nine new passus, expanding *Piers Plowman* to more than 7,200 lines. This version must have been written about 1377, since the fable of the cat and mice in the prologue seems to allude to events which occurred in the parliament of 1376-1377. Langland thoroughly revised the poem one more time, increasing its length by another hundred or so lines, and this final version is known as the C Text. It contains no prologue but twenty-three passus. W. W. Skeat dated the C Text about 1393, believing that it reflected the differences which began in 1392 between the citizens of London and the king. An earlier date may be more accurate, however, since Thomas Usk seems to refer to the C version of *Piers Plowman* in his *Testament of Love* (1387), and Usk died in 1388. In the C version the poet often attempts to clarify ambiguities, and at times eliminates some of the social criticisms. He also eliminates some of the more dramatic scenes in B, such as Piers's tearing of Truth's pardon in Passus VII. Although the C Text may represent the author's ultimate intent, and although recent accurate critical texts of the C Text have made it more universally available, the vast majority of scholars and readers have preferred the B version, and so all references to the poem in this analysis are to George Kane and E. Talbot Donaldson's edition of the B Text.

Having established the B version as the poem, however, one is not at all sure what sort of poem it is. *Piers Plowman* falls simultaneously into several categories, none of which defines it completely. It is, first, a poem of the alliterative revival. Poetry in English had originally been alliterative, and followed strict metrical rules. When English verse began to appear once more in the west and north in the mid-fourteenth century, poets attempted to follow this native tradition. The Middle English alliterative line, however, was much freer than it had been in Old English: lines had no fixed syllabic content, the number of stressed syllables was not always four, as in classic alliterative verse, but might be three, five, or six, and the alliterated sound was not always governed by the third stressed syllable, as in classic alliterative verse. The alliterative poets did, however, tend to rely on a special poetic diction and to decorate their poetry with elaborate rhetorical figures recommended by the poetic manuals of the time, such as that of Geoffrey of Vinsauf. Langland, however, differed markedly from other alliterative poets. Possibly because his audience was not the aristocracy, he had no interest in elaborate rhetoric or poetic diction, but rather used simple vocabulary and employed only those figures of speech which involved repetition, since his goal was to get his message across clearly. Langland did, however, continue and even furthered the trend toward a freer alliterative line, employing various rhythmic patterns as they suited the tone of his poem, sometimes alliterating a different sound in the second half-line than he had in the first, sometimes not alliterating at all, and often tossing in Latin quotations as nonalliterating half-lines. The overall tendency of Langland's verse, despite the Latin, is toward a naturalness of vocabulary and rhythm.

Piers Plowman also has a great deal in common with sermon literature. G. R. Owst saw Langland as drawing primarily from the pulpits of England his message of social reform, justice for the poor, condemnation for those who pervert the great institution of the Church, and a recommendation of love and work as opposed to revolution. Elizabeth Salter sees Langland's emphasis on teaching rather than fine writing, and his use of metaphors and imagery in a purely functional manner to illustrate his material, as consistent with sermon literature; however, *Piers Plowman*, in scope and complexity, goes far beyond even the most elaborate sermons, so again the label "sermon in verse" is inadequate.

The poem also takes the form of a dream vision. For the Middle Ages, influenced as they were by the biblical stories of Joseph and Daniel and by Macrobius' famous commentary on the *Dream of Scipio*, dreams were profoundly important, and could often take on oracular significance. Thus, beginning with Jean de Meung's thirteenth century *Romance of the Rose*, there arose a genre of poetry containing a dreamer-narrator who relates his vision, which may be full of signs which the reader must interpret. Once again, however, *Piers Plowman* transcends the bounds of the form, for Langland writes not of one vision but of many. There are, in fact, ten separate visions in the poem, two of which are represented as dreams within dreams. Moreover, in contrast with the more typical medieval love visions, Langland seriously presents the visions as divine revelations. Perhaps Morton Bloomfield is more accurate, then, in describing *Piers Plowman* as an *apocalypse*: a literary work in the form of a vision revealing a divine message and deeply criticizing contemporary society.

A knowledge of its genre may help to explain some of the confusion in the structure of the poem. Anyone reading *Piers Plowman* for the first time must be struck by the bewildering plunges into and out of scenes, the unannounced and unexpected comings and goings of a multitude of new characters, the apparently unrelated sequence of events which seem to follow no cause-and-effect relationships. It could be argued that a dream vision would follow the logic of dream—of association and symbol rather than induction and deduction; this may be a partial answer. One could also say that the poem is not intended to be a narrative, which would follow a cause-and-effect pattern. It has, rather (like a sermon) a thematic unity. The Dreamer asks in the beginning, "What must I do to save my soul?"; and the theme which unites the poem is the answer to that question. Essentially, the unifying motif is the quest for the answer, a quest which becomes a pilgrimage of the individual to God. Significantly, Langland calls the divisions of his poem *passus*, or *steps*—each new incident is another step toward the goal of the quest.

Structurally, the poem is divided into two sections, the *Visio* and the *Vita*. The *Visio* section depicts the world as it is, introduces the main themes, and prepares the way for the search which follows in the *Vita*. The narrator, Will (a persona for William Langland, but also a personification of the human will), falls asleep and relates his dream of a "fair field full of folk"—the people of Middle Earth as they work out their lives between heaven (a Tower of Truth) and hell (a dark dungeon). The Holy Church appears to Will as a lady and discourses on the fall of Lucifer and on love as the way to Truth. When the Dreamer asks how he may recognize falsehood, he is shown a series of scenes involving Lady Meed and her proposed marriage, first to Falsehood, then to Conscience. Lady Meed is the representation of *cupiditas*, the opposite of love: she is the love of earthly reward, and when she is driven out by Conscience and Reason, it represents the possibility of man's controlling his desire for worldly wealth by following the dictates of reason and conscience. In Will's second dream, Reason gives a sermon inspiring the people to repent, and there follows Langland's noted portrayal of the confession of the seven deadly sins. The people then begin a pilgrimage in search of Truth; here Piers the Plowman makes his first appearance, offering to guide them to Truth. First, however, Piers must plow his half-acre. The implied moral is that the needs of the body must be taken care of, but that the will should desire no more than what is of material necessity.

The pilgrimage to Truth never takes place. Truth sends Piers a pardon, saying that those who do well will be saved. When a priest tells Piers that this is no pardon at all, Piers tears up the paper in anger. The point of this scene seems to be lost in obscurity. Robert Worth Frank considers the scene an attack on papal indulgences: the true "pardon" is God's command to do well. The priest, on the other hand, supports the idea of papal indulgences, which Piers angrily rejects by tearing the parchment, symbolically tearing up paper pardons from Rome. More recently, Denise N. Baker denies that Piers's pardon is a pardon at all. The scene, according to Baker, reflects the Nominalist-Augustinian controversy of the fourteenth century, which concerned man's ability to do good works. The Augustinian position was that man was unable to do good works without God's grace, and Piers's tearing up of the pardon is Langland's emblem of man's dependence on God's gift of grace. Whichever interpretation is correct, Piers decides to leave plowing and begin a life of prayer and penance in order to search for Do-Well.

The *Vita* section of the poem is divided into three parts: the lives of Do-Well, Do-Better, and Do-Best. With the abandonment of the people's search for Truth, it is apparent that society cannot be reformed corporately, but only on an individual basis. Will goes on an individual quest for the three degrees of doing well, for three grades of Christian perfection. The life of Do-Well is confusing: in the third dream, Will confronts his own faculties (Thought, Intelligence, Imagination), as well as guides such as Study, Clergy, and Scripture. In the meantime, Will has a dream within a dream wherein he follows Fortune for forty-five years. After he wakes, Will falls asleep again, and in a fifth vision, led by Patience and Conscience, he meets Haukyn, the Active Man, whose coat (his soul) is terribly stained with sin.

The sixth vision, the life of Do-Better, begins with Will's discourse with Anima, who rebukes Will for vainly seeking knowledge and extols the virtue of charity. Will falls into another, deeper, vision, in which he sees Piers Plowman as guardian of the Tree of Charity; sees Abraham, Moses, and the Good Samaritan as the personifications of Faith, Hope, and Charity; and learns about the Holy Trinity. In the eighth vision, the climax of the life of Do-Better and of the poem, the Dreamer witnesses the passion of Christ, sees Christ jousting in the arms of Piers Plowman, witnesses the Harrowing of Hell, a debate between the four daughters of God, and the resurrection.

The two final dreams present the life of Do-Best. Piers Plowman is now Christ's vicar on earth. The Holy Spirit descends, bestowing gifts on the Christian body, enabling Piers to plow the field of the world. Conscience, seeing the Antichrist preparing to attack, directs all Christians to build a fortress, the Church of Unity, but the Christians are unprepared for battle. In the final vision, the Antichrist attacks. Conscience makes the mistake of letting a Friar into Unity, whose easy confessions corrupt the Church, and the people lose all fear. Conscience then vows to become a pilgrim and search for Piers Plowman to help in the fight, and the quest begins anew as the Dreamer awakes.

The poem is unified by the repetition of various themes. Salter gives the example of the recurring themes of the nature and function of sin, which is introduced in the section on Lady Meed, expanded upon in the confession of the seven deadly sins, restated in the picture of Haukyn's coat, and returned to again as the sins assist the Antichrist in the final attack on Unity. Even so, the nature and function of love in the universe, as it pertains to personal salvation and the reform of society, is the chief theme of the poem; and that theme is inextricably linked with the chief unifying motif of the poem, Piers the Plowman in his many incarnations.

Deciding precisely what Piers signifies is part of the last and largest problem of the poem, that of interpretation. It is obvious that Langland's chief vehicle of expression in *Piers Plowman* is allegory, but it is unclear precisely how to read the allegory. Robert Worth Frank calls the kind of allegory which is typical of Langland "personification-allegory," which, he says, generally involves a single translation of the character's *name* (such as "Study," "Reason," "Scripture") into the abstract quality which it denotes. In this sense, the characters are "literal." It is a mistake to read more into the allegory than the form allows. In practice, however, this does not seem to work. "Sloth," for example, is simply sloth—one need inquire no further; but the more important characters, such as Do-Well, Do-Better, and Do-Best, are obviously much more complicated, and seem to have multiple meanings.

An alternative approach to the allegory is that of D. W. Robertson and Bernard Huppé, who, in applying medieval exegetical criticism to literary texts, see a fourfold interpretation of the allegory. In discussing the complex symbol of the Tree of Charity, for example, they say that it allegorically represents the just; anagogically, Christ on the cross; and tropologically, the individual Christian. The difficulty with this approach is its rigidity: some things are simply meant to be taken literally, while others may have multitudes of meanings far beyond these four.

A more beneficial approach to the meaning of these symbols is Salter's, which emphasizes a more open and flexible reading; here the reader is receptive to various sorts of significations, not necessarily in any exact order or category. The two most puzzling and multifaceted allegorical symbols are the three lives and Piers himself.

Do-Well, Do-Better, and Do-Best have been most often identified with the active, the contemplative, and the mixed lives. This may make more sense to modern readers if they realize, as T. P. Dunning notes, that the active life in the Middle Ages denotes, not manual labor, but rather the active practice of virtue, the works of prayer and devotion to which Piers devotes himself at the end of the *Visio*. This is the active life conceived of as the first stage of the spiritual life, and in the *Vita* it involves, first, the Dreamer's search through his own faculties, the emergence from intellectual error, and then, with the repentence of Haukyn, the rejection of moral disorder. Do-Better would then represent the contemplative life, in which the Dreamer actually experiences a kind of union with God in a firsthand vision of Christ's passion. Do-Best, however, represents the mixed life, in which the individual must return to life in the world and, with the assistance of the Holy Spirit, work for the reform of society: charity is not limited to love of the individual for God, but includes love for others as well.

At the same time, the three lives may suggest the mystical theme of the soul seeking God, where Do-Well represents the purgative state, and Do-Better the stage at which the mystic, like the Dreamer, achieves his illumination in a direct vision of God. For the mystic, however, there is no final unity in this world; he, like Conscience in the end, must continue the search and work toward another partial union. Do-Best reveals the practical results of illumination, which are in the service of others.

The three lives, then, suggest at least these things, and more, but Piers's meaning is more obscure. He appears in the poem only occasionally, but his presence dominates the action at crucial points. In the *Visio*, after the confession of the sins, Piers steps in, announcing that he is a friend and servant of Truth, and offering to lead all on a pilgrimage to Him. First, however, he must plow his half-acre, and he organizes all of the people to help with the work, thus establishing an ordered society in this world. At the end of the *Visio*, he receives the pardon from Truth for himself and his followers, which he tears up, pledging to leave his plow and search for Do-Well.

In the Do-Well section, Piers is mentioned by Clergy (Passus XIII) as one who preaches the primacy of love as opposed to learning. In Do-Better (Passus XV), Anima identifies Piers with Christ by means of a cryptic Latin comment about "Peter, that is Christ." In Passus XVI, Piers is warder of the Tree of Charity, which he explains to the Dreamer. The tree's fruit, identified as the patriarchs and prophets, is stolen by the devil, whom Piers chases, armed with a stave symbolizing Christ. Piers is then shown teaching Jesus the art of healing. At the climax, Christ fights for the souls of men, the fruit of Piers the Plowman, clad in Piers's arms.

In Do-Best, Piers returns to the poem. First the Dreamer sees a confused image in which Christ himself seems to be Piers, stained with blood and bearing a cross. The Holy Spirit then makes Piers the Plowman his vicar on earth, and Piers founds the Church, dispensing grace in the form of the eucharist, behaves like God in his charity to all, and then disappears.

All of this presents a confused figure who seems at times to be the symbol of moral integrity, at times Christ himself, and at the end perhaps the ideal pope whom conscience searches for to restore the corrupt and divided Church of the fourteenth century. Nevill Coghill thought that Piers personified Do-Well, Do-Better, and Do-Best successively. More recently, Barbara Raw has shown that Piers's career in the poem depicts the restoration of the divine image in man, somewhat distorted with the Fall but still present, and restored at Christ's incarnation. According to Augustine and Aquinas, the restoration of this image took place in three stages, which may parallel Do-Well, Do-Better and Do-Best. In Do-Better, Piers becomes the image of Christ because Christ has taken human form, Piers's arms. In Do-Best, Piers embodies the restored image of God in man: he has become like God. Salter sees Piers similarly: when Piers describes the way to Truth in Passus V, he declares that people will find Truth's dwelling in their own hearts. Piers represents this divine element in man, the Truth of God as it exists in man, and as the poem reaches its climax, it is revealed that God *is* to be found in man, as the man Piers becomes Godlike. This, then, is Langland's ultimate message, which in spite of all the problems with *Piers Plowman* can still be stated with some certainty: one bears the stamp of the image of God, and can, through Christ, achieve Do-Best with Piers the Plowman.

Bibliography

Baker, Denise N. "From Plowing to Penitence: *Piers Plowman* and Fourteenth-Century Theology," in *Speculum*. LV (October, 1980), pp. 715-725.

Bloomfield, Morton W. *Piers Plowman as a Fourteenth-Century Apocalypse*, 1962.

Burrow, J. A. "The Audience of *Piers Plowman*," in *Anglia*. LXXV (1957), pp. 373-384.

Chambers, R. W. *Man's Unconquerable Mind*, 1969.

Coghill, Nevill. "The Character of Piers Plowman Considered from the B Text," in *Medium Aevum*. II (1933), pp. 108-135.

Donaldson, E. Talbot. *Piers Plowman: The C-Text and Its Poet*, 1966.

Dunning, T. P., C. M. "Structure of the B Text of *Piers Plowman*," in *The Review of English Studies*. VII, n.s. (July, 1956), pp. 225-237.

Frank, Robert Worth, Jr. "The Art of Reading Medieval Personification-Allegory," in *Journal of English Literary History*. XX (1953), pp. 237-250.

——————. *Piers Plowman and the Scheme of Salvation: An Interpretation of Dowel, Dobet, and Dobest*, 1969.

Kane, George, ed. *Piers Plowman: The A Version*, 1960.

Kane, George, and E. Talbot Donaldson, eds. *Piers Plowman: The B Version*, 1975.

Lawlor, John. *Piers Plowman: An Essay in Criticism*, 1962.

Owst, G. R. *Literature and the Pulpit in Medieval England*, 1961.

Pearsall, Derek, ed. *Piers Plowman: An Edition of the C-Text*, 1967.

Raw, Barbara. "Piers and the Image of God in Man," in *Piers Plowman: Critical Approaches*, 1969.

Robertson, D. W., Jr., and Bernard Huppé. *Piers Plowman and Scriptural Tradition*, 1970.

Salter, Elizabeth. *Piers Plowman: An Introduction*, 1962.

Skeat, W. W., ed. *The Vision of William Concerning Piers the Plowman in Three Parallel Texts Together with Richard the Redeless by William Langland*, 1961.

Jay Ruud

SIDNEY LANIER

Born: Macon, Georgia; February 3, 1842
Died: Lynn, North Carolina; September 7, 1881

Principal collections
Poems, 1877; *Poems*, 1884 (Mary Day Lanier, editor).

Other literary forms
Although Sidney Lanier is remembered primarily as a poet, he wrote in a surprising variety of genres. His *The Science of English Verse* (1880) is a handbook of prosody which is still valuable as a discussion of poetic theory and technique, despite its overemphasis on the importance of sound. It was originally meant to be a textbook for Lanier's students at The Johns Hopkins University, and in fact his lecture notes were collected and published posthumously as *The English Novel* (1883) and *Shakspere* [sic] *and His Forerunners* (1902). Lanier's first book, however, was an autobiographical novel entitled *Tiger-Lilies* (1867), which drew upon his Civil War experiences and his reading in the German Romantics. His second published volume was *Florida: Its Scenery, Climate, and History* (1875), a travel book commissioned by the Atlantic Coast Line Railway and the standard guide to Florida for many years. Lanier was especially successful at revising classics, such as *The Boy's King Arthur* (1880) for juvenile audiences—a literary endeavor which appealed to his strong romantic sensibility while providing a welcome source of income. Finally, Lanier produced a remarkable number of essays, including "Retrospects and Prospects" (1871) and the four "Sketches of India" (1876), which were originally published in magazines. Lanier's writings are most readily available in the *Centennial Edition* (1945).

Achievements
Lanier was the first distinctively Southern poet to achieve a truly national recognition and acceptance. This is an honor usually accorded to Edgar Allan Poe (1809-1849); but unlike Poe, who was born in Boston, spent several of his formative years in Britain, and did much of his literary work in the Northeast, Lanier was a Georgian by birth who spent his entire life in the South. Nevertheless, by virtue of such works as "The Centennial Meditation of Columbia" and "Psalm of the West," Lanier came to be regarded as a spokesman for the American, rather than only the Southern, experience; yet, by one of those paradoxes of literary history, at the same time that he achieved this national status, Lanier won for Southern writers a degree of respect and credibility which was unprecedented in American literature and which is still evident today.

Lanier was one of the earliest American poets to use dialect in his verse, most notably the "Georgia cracker" speech utilized in "Thar's More in the Man Than Thar Is in the Land." In this regard, Lanier was an early practitioner of "local-color" writing, that literary movement which flourished at the end of the nineteenth century. Imbued with a strong social conscience, Lanier was noted for his poetic treatment of current economic difficulties. In poems such as "The Symphony," he pleaded that love and music be used as antidotes for the miseries generated by "Trade" (read "industry and commercialism"), and in "Corn" and "Thar's More in the Man Than Thar Is in the Land" he offered a practical solution to the economic problems of the postwar South: the cultivation of corn and grain instead of cotton. Lanier was also a tireless poetic experimenter. He is to be recognized for his ambitious attempts at metrical innovation (see "The Revenge of Hamish," an experiment in the use of logaoedic dactyls), as well as his attempts to achieve heightened musical effects in his verse (see, for example, "Song of the Chattahoochee"). He also is remembered for his *The Science of English Verse*, a textbook which is still interesting and perceptive, despite Lanier's unfortunate attempt to formulate a "science" of prosody which is analogous to musical notation.

Lanier is frequently cited as an example of a writer who could have achieved a great deal had he lived longer. There is no question that at the time of his death at age thirty-nine, his career was just getting under way. As Charles Anderson observes, Lanier wrote 164 poems; of these, 104 were written in two periods of intense creativity (1865-1868; 1874-1878), with the latter period producing his best work—fifty-eight major poems. At the time of his death Lanier had made plans for at least three more volumes of poetry, as is clear from the so-called "Poem Outlines" (see the *Centennial Edition*).

Biography

Sidney Clopton Lanier was born on February 3, 1842, in Macon, Georgia, a small city which was at the time the thriving center of the cotton industry. Both his parents were of good, long-established Virginia families who had settled comfortably into the urban, middle-class life-style of antebellum Macon. His father, Robert Sampson Lanier, was a graduate of Virginia's Randolph-Macon College and a practicing attorney; his mother, Mary Jane Anderson Lanier, was a devout Scottish Presbyterian who fostered in her children a deep appreciation for the writings of Sir Walter Scott. Sidney was the eldest child, with a sister Gertrude (born 1846), and a brother Clifford (born 1844) who occasionally collaborated with Sidney and who earned a minor literary reputation with the publication of his novel *Thorn-Fruit* (1867).

Lanier was a happy, bookish child noted for his good behavior and piety as well as for his love of literature, including works by Edward Bulwer-Lytton, John Keats, and the perennially popular Scott. He also demonstrated exceptional musical ability at a very early age and eventually became expert at playing the violin, guitar, organ, and flute. In certain respects, Lanier's musical talent was unfortunate: the distinctive musicality of his verse too often over-powers the meaning, and his desire to become a professional musician often diverted his time and energies away from his career as a poet. At any rate, music was an integral part of his formal education. Evidently, Macon had no public-supported schools during Lanier's youth, so he was educated at private academies run by local clergymen. It is unclear how solid an education he received in this fashion, but at a time when only one out of thirteen adult white Southerners could read or write, it was certainly adequate to gain him admittance into a relatively new Presbyterian college, Oglethorpe University. Lanier matriculated at the age of fifteen: he was a good student, being espe-cially adept at mathematics, and was named covaledictorian of his class. He returned to Oglethorpe in the fall after his graduation to serve as a tutor, a position secured for him by Professor James Woodrow. Woodrow (the uncle of Woodrow Wilson) possessed a degree of open-mindedness and cosmo-politanism which was unusual for Oglethorpe and something of a revelation for Lanier.

Before Lanier could explore the new worlds opened to him by Woodrow, however, the Civil War broke out. Lanier joined the Confederate Army in June, 1861, serving first as a private with the Macon Volunteers and later in the Mounted Signal Service. In 1864, while on signal duty on a blockade-runner, Lanier was captured and sent to a prison camp at Point Lookout, Maryland. Although Lanier was able to solace himself by playing his flute (which he had smuggled into prison inside his sleeve) and translating German poetry, the months spent at Point Lookout in 1864 and 1865 activated the latent tuberculosis which eventually killed him.

In 1867, Lanier married Mary Day, whom he had met while on furlough in 1863. It was not love at first sight: Lanier, a ladies' man of sorts, did not seem to notice Day until after his current sweetheart, one Gussie Lamar, jilted him. Day, an invalid, reportedly was advised by her physician that a marriage would improve her health (apparently it did: she outlived her hus-band by half a century, dying in 1931 at the age of eighty-seven). Despite the inauspicious circumstances surrounding the wedding, the marriage was a good one, and Lanier spent much of their fourteen years together attempting simultaneously to support his growing family (four sons), to satisfy his creative urges, and to find relief from his tuberculosis. From 1868 to 1873, he read law and clerked in his father's law office, an occupation for which he was temperamentally ill-suited, and which was all the more intolerable because of his worsening health and the frustration of having no time to write. He spent the winter and spring of 1872 to 1873 in Texas, and the trip which had been undertaken because of his health proved beneficial in another way. The Germans who played such a prominent role in San Antonio's cultural life encouraged him to pursue a career in music.

In 1873, with financial assistance from his brother Clifford, Lanier began his career as first flautist with the Peabody Orchestra of Baltimore. An extraordinarily talented player, Lanier was able to maintain his position with the orchestra intermittently for the next seven years. When his musical engagements were completed in the spring of 1874, he went to Sunnyside, Georgia, to spend a few months, and there he was deeply impressed with the region's cornfields. This led to the composition of "Corn," and his career as a poet began in earnest. "Corn," published in *Lippincott's Magazine* in 1875 after a devastating rejection by the *Atlantic Monthly*, was so successful that it resulted in commissioned work (including the guidebook *Florida*) and the opportunity to meet the writer-diplomat Bayard Taylor and Gibson Peacock, the editor of the Philadelphia *Evening Bulletin*, both of whom helped to further Lanier's career. In the first half of 1876, Lanier worked on two long poems: "The Centennial Meditation of Columbia," an assignment for the Philadelphia Centennial Exhibition, secured through the influence of Taylor, and "Psalm of the West," commissioned by the editor of *Lippincott's Magazine*. They are not among his best works ("The Centennial Meditation of Columbia" in particular was roundly criticized for its obscurity), but they did gain Lanier national attention.

In the summer of 1876, the exhausted Lanier moved with his family to a farm in West Chester, Pennsylvania, where he wrote a series of pot-boiling essays. That fall his health broke completely, and the generous Peacock financed a three-month vacation for Lanier in Tampa. While in Florida, Lanier felt sufficiently well to write eleven poems, including "The Stirrup-Cup"; but, homesick for Georgia, he left Tampa in April, 1877. Unsuccessful in his bid for a position in the U.S. Treasury, Lanier attempted to support his wife and children by borrowing from his brother and selling the family silver. He was fortunate enough, however, to be able to resume his position with the Peabody Orchestra. A few months later, in March, 1878, he began an intensive study of English literature at the Peabody Library in Baltimore in the hope that it would lead to a teaching position at The Johns Hopkins University. For once his hope was realized, and in the fall of 1879, he began to teach poetry and the English novel at the new Baltimore university.

The last few years of his life (from approximately 1877 to 1881) were remarkably full and productive. In addition to his research and teaching, Lanier was writing his best-known poems (including "Song of the Chattahoochee" in November, 1877, and "The Marshes of Glynn" in 1878), *The Science of English Verse*, and the series of books for children known as "The Boy's Library of Legend and Chivalry." He also had published in 1877 his first and only book of verse, *Poems*, a slim volume (ninety-four pages; ten poems) issued by *Lippincott's Magazine*. The attempt to compress a lifetime's work into a few months was, however, ultimately self-defeating: Lanier's final bout with tuberculosis began late in 1880, and he died in the mountains of North Carolina in September, 1881.

Analysis

Although literary historians are correct in maintaining that Sidney Lanier had only minimal influence on other writers, that influence is most apparent in the post-Civil War interest in the recording of regional dialects. Perhaps taking his cue either from James Russell Lowell's satirical, *The Biglow Papers* (1848, 1867) or Augustus Longstreet's humorous *Georgia Scenes* (1835), Lanier wrote several propagandistic poems in Southern dialect, in which humor was incidental rather than integral. Works written in dialect yet serious in intent were an innovation in American literature, and one of the first such works was Lanier's "Thar's More in the Man Than Thar Is in the Land." Written sometime between 1869 and 1871, the poem was originally published in the Macon *Telegraph and Messenger* on February 7, 1871, and thereafter in newspapers throughout the South and Midwest. Lanier reworked a local story into a serious statement of what he personally felt was the soundest strategy for the survival of the postwar South: resist the temptation to emigrate, and diversify crops. The poem itself (despite the challenges of the dialect) is unusually straightforward for a work by Lanier, not only because of the paucity of imagery, but also and more important, because of Lanier's uncharacteristic avoidance of sentimentality. Written in ten sestets, it recounts how a man named Jones (appropriately enough a resident of Jones County, Georgia) was a failure as a farmer. Jones sold his farm to a man named Brown for $1.50 an acre and moved to Texas where ostensibly "cotton would sprout/ By the time you could plant it in the land." The redoubtable Brown "rolled up his breeches and bared his arm" and within five years had become a prosperous farmer, "so fat that he wouldn't weigh." One day while Brown was sitting down to "the bulliest dinner you ever see," Jones showed up, having literally walked back to Georgia to try to find work. Brown fed him and provided the moral of the poem: "'whether men's land was rich or poor/ Thar was more in the *man* than thar was in the *land*.'"

In a region of the United States which was still suffering from a deep depression fully five years after the war, Lanier's little parable must have been a breath of hope and encouragement. The poem, however, is far more than a paean to the advantages of working hard and staying in Georgia. It is the emphatic statement of an economic reality: instead of continuing to raise "yallerish cotton" like Jones, one must grow corn and wheat. Thanks to crop diversification, Brown avoided the economic stranglehold which the Northern markets had on King Cotton (and, consequently, on the entire South), while enjoying the self-reliance that comes with raising a crop which one could literally consume. Whether or not the Southern audience noticed the poem's horticultural/economic message, they certainly admired "Thar's More in the Man Than Thar Is in the Land," and its immense popularity was due in part to its qualities as a poem. By virtue of its sing-songy rhythm, the familiar dialect, the predictable rhyme (generally aabbbc; the *c* invariably was the word "land"), and the surprisingly subtle humor (such as the broken rhyme "hum-/ Ble in stanza nine), it was ideally suited to essentially rural, semiliterate readers who were accustomed to a rich oral tradition and who frequently found themselves in situations comparable to that of the unfortunate Jones.

Even the most cursory glance at his letters, poems, and essays reveals that Lanier sincerely regarded poetry as a noble calling, and he resisted the temptation to write broadly popular, potentially remunerative verse. He preferred producing poems which appealed to the finer aspects of individual, regional, or national character, or which expressed his personal views on economic or political matters. There was no affectation inherent in these twin didactic conceptions of poetry, and they were at least partly responsible for the cool reception which his poems often received in his lifetime. Still, Lanier's poems occasionally did manage to achieve some popularity, and only a few years after the regional success of "Thar's More in the Man Than Thar Is in the Land," Lanier received his first national attention with "Corn."

"Corn" is a reiteration of the ideas presented in "Thar's More in the Man Than Thar Is in the Land," but the two poems are handled in strikingly different ways. Lanier apparently began the composition of "Corn" in July, 1874, while he was staying in the hamlet of Sunnyside, Georgia. Evidently he was especially impressed by the extensive corn fields and the terrain. Unlike "Thar's More in the Man Than Thar Is in the Land," this poem was definitely not intended for a semiliterate, rural Southern audience. In format, it is a sterling example of a Cowleyan ode. Unlike the technically rigid "Thar's More in the Man Than Thar Is in the Land," "Corn" is irregular in stanza length, line length, and rhythm. It is so heavily enjambed that at first one may not even be conscious of the extraordinary degree to which Lanier relies on rhyme to give his poem coherence. The rhyming couplets and tercets, the eye rhyme ("hardihood"/"food"), and the leonine rhyme ("Thou lustrous stalk, that ne'er mayst walk nor talk") are testimonies to Lanier's fascination with sound—a fascination which, unfortunately, was largely responsible for the charges of obscurity, sentimentality, and even banality which have been leveled against Lanier's poetry throughout the last century.

One need not look beyond the first stanza of "Corn" to understand what these critics have in mind. The persona passes through some woods before he encounters the field of corn, but the little forest, as is typical of Lanier, has been personified and emotionalized to such an embarrassing degree that the first stanza sounds like a sentimentalized psychosexual dream. The leaves which brush the persona's cheek "caress/ Like women's hands"; the "little noises" sound "anon like beatings of a heart/ Anon like talk 'twixt lips not far apart"; and the persona clearly has abandoned himself to the pleasures of the sensuous forest.

The persona proceeds through the concupiscent forest until finally, in stanza three, he encounters the corn itself, which Lanier had intended to be the controlling image of the poem. In one of his more fortunate metaphors, Lanier likens the field of corn to an army; and although at times that metaphor is strained (one stalk functions as the "corn-captain"), what makes it especially appropriate is that there are in fact three "battles" going on in this poem: the corn stalks are competing for soil with the sassafras and brambles, the antebellum "King Cotton" economy is clashing with the new diversified crop system, and Lanier is positing life as a battle with The Poet as its hero and the "corn-captain" as his symbol. It is apparent, then, that Lanier is attempting to make the battle metaphor operate on at least three levels; although it is an interesting concept and Lanier makes a noble effort to realize it, in the final analysis it simply does not work. Instead of being mutually enriching, the various images result in a confusing clutter. This fundamental technical problem and a host of others are readily apparent to even the most sympathetic reader of "Corn."

In stanza four, the "fieldward-faring eyes" of the persona do not simply look at the corn, but harvest it in his heart. It is characteristic of Lanier that he favors the use of rather grotesque metaphors. What tends to make the metaphor a bit less dubious, however, is that Lanier is not as interested in the physical corn as he is in the abstract qualities which he believes the corn embodies. Much as people can learn industriousness from bees and contentment from cows, Lanier felt that the cornstalk could teach readers about virtuous living.

One may reasonably question how a technically and thematically weak poem such as "Corn" could possibly attract a national audience. Part of the answer lies in the very matter of technique: at the time he was writing, Lanier was sufficiently innovative to generate interest. The second part of the answer is more a matter of sociology than of poetics. During the Reconstruction period, and in particular during the 1870's when Centennial enthusiasm was running high, there was an impulse toward reconciliation in the United States—an impulse which frequently took the form of Northern readers responding enthusiastically to any piece of writing from, or about, the South. Even though Lanier initially had some difficulty finding Northern periodicals which would publish his work, the fact is that these journals were far more receptive to Southern writers after the Civil War than they were at any time before it. Lanier's career actually came during an ideal time, for he was clearly, insistently a Southern writer, and nowhere is his Southern influence more apparent, perhaps, than in his two best-known poems, "Song of the Chattahoochee" and "The Marshes of Glynn."

"Song of the Chattahoochee" was written in Baltimore at the end of November, 1877, and its first verifiable publication (December, 1883) was in the *Independent*, a New York-based weekly paper with a wide circulation. It became so popular that for decades it was a staple of elementary school reading books, the only poem by Lanier with which many people were even vaguely familiar. That distinction is a dubious one, for in fact, "Song of the Chattahoochee" is not one of Lanier's better efforts; and yet the very qualities which tend to weaken it were those responsible for its popularity. In typical Lanierian fashion, its most striking feature is its sound. Ostensibly the Chattahoochee River itself is speaking the poem (an earlier version reprinted by F. V. N. Painter in his *Poets of the South*, 1903, is in the third person), and this provides a golden opportunity for Lanier to utilize diction which conveys the sound of moving water. Words featuring liquid consonants and alliteration are so common that at times the poem reads like a tongue-twister: "The willful waterweeds held me thrall,/ The laving laurel turned my tide." This effect is compounded by Lanier's heavy reliance on repetition, not only of individual words but also of phrases: each of the five stanzas both begins and ends with some variation of the opening couplet, "Out of the hills of Habersham, Down the valleys of Hall." Clearly Lanier is seeking to depict moving water onomatopoeically, and to a certain extent he succeeds, but in such a short poem (fifty lines) one simply does not need the phrases "the hills of Habersham" and "the valleys of Hall" repeated ten times each. The effect of soothing musicality which Lanier was trying to create becomes monotonous. It is so overwhelming that the reader may very well fail to detect either the structure of the poem or the theme.

The "Song of the Chattahoochee" begins with the river explaining how it rises in Habersham County (in northeastern Georgia) and travels through Hall County on its way to "the plain." In stanza two, the speaker/river provides a catalog of the various small plants which attempt to delay it; stanza three is a catalog of the trees which seek to distract the river; stanza four reveals the rocks and minerals which try either to retard the flowing of the river or to dazzle it with their beauty. Then in stanza five, readers learn why the river resists these sensuous distractions: compelled by a strong sense of Duty (with a capital *d*), it must both make itself useful through "toil" and allow itself to "be mixed with the main." It is possible to infer that the personified river represents a human being whose life is purposefully active and who willingly acknowledges the "rightness" of death (here conveyed as the merging of one's identity with the vastness of the ocean—an idea explored more fully in "The Marshes of Glynn"); but if this analogy were central to Lanier's purpose, he certainly did not handle it well, and as a result the depiction of the river as "dutiful" seems to be nothing more than a romantic imposition on the part of Lanier.

Despite its didactic impulse, Lanier's poem retained its popularity in elementary schools for many years and, consequently, among several generations of Americans. Brief and strikingly musical, it is ideally suited to introducing poetry to youngsters. "Song of the Chattahoochee" also had the dubious but undeniable advantage of posthumous publication: to be frank, Lanier's career was never stronger than in the years immediately following his early death.

Even so, he did enjoy some nationwide popularity in his lifetime, most notably with "The Marshes of Glynn."

It is unclear when Lanier began the composition of "The Marshes of Glynn," although it is possible that it had been evolving over at least a three-year period before Lanier actually wrote it in the summer of 1878. The "Glynn" of the title is Glynn County, Georgia, noted for its salt marshes near the coastal village of Brunswick, a favorite haunt of the Lanier family for many years. As with "Corn," "The Marshes of Glynn" had its origins in Lanier's personal response to a specific element of the Georgia landscape, but it is notably more private and esoteric than that early effort. Both as an artist and a man, Lanier had changed significantly during the four years following the composition of "Corn." For one thing, he had discovered Walt Whitman. Although Lanier (despite the distinctive sensuality of his imagery), was singularly reticent about sexual matters, he nevertheless was deeply impressed with Whitman's work, even going so far as somehow to amass the requisite five dollars and order a copy of *Leaves of Grass* (1855) from the Good Gray Poet himself. In a letter to Bayard Taylor in February, 1878, Lanier described that book as a source of "real refreshment" to him, and likened its effect, significantly, to "rude salt spray in your face." It is probably no coincidence that Lanier made that comparison only a few months before the composition of "The Marshes of Glynn," for the poem can justifiably be termed Whitmanesque in its remarkable range and sweep.

Lanier also had changed as a result of his discovery of Ralph Waldo Emerson. During his stay in Tampa in the winter of 1877, Lanier apparently read Emerson in earnest, an undertaking at least partly attributable to the precarious state of his health. By the late 1870's, Lanier was finally beginning to admit to himself that the tuberculosis with which he had struggled for a decade would probably kill him within a very few years, as indeed it did. This admission of imminent death, coupled with his lack of orthodox religious faith, apparently generated his interest in Emerson and fostered significant changes in the themes and techniques of his poems. These changes are especially evident in "The Marshes of Glynn," which shows Lanier in far better control of his material than was the case in "Corn."

The two poems begin in a similar fashion with an extensive catalog of the elements one encounters while walking through a forest, but in "The Marshes of Glynn" Lanier has carefully pruned the embarrassingly overwritten sensual passages which are so striking in the opening of "Corn." True, he mentions "Virginal shy lights/ Wrought of the leaves to allure to the whispers of vows," but this is as purple a passage as one finds in the opening of "The Marshes of Glynn." Then with remarkable skill, the orientation is shifted from the association of the forest with love to that of religious faith, and from this point on, the rather long ode is devoted to spiritual matters. Unlike the irrelevant opening of "Corn," that of "The Marshes of Glynn" almost immediately presents Lanier's two concerns: the traditional belief that Nature is the great refresher of men's souls, and the contemporary Emersonian view that one may find the true God in the natural world. The intimate relationship between nature (specifically the forest) and the persona (transparently Lanier himself) is first overtly presented in line 20, and it is at this point that the reader realizes that the previous nineteen lines were actually an exceptionally elaborate apostrophe to the forest. The persona's love for the beauties and mysteries of the wood is palpable, and that love is conveyed through Lanier's characteristic compound adjectives ("myriad-cloven"), alliteration ("beautiful-braided"), and assonance ("oaks"/"woven").

It is made abundantly clear, however, that the forest experience represents merely a phase in the persona's life which has now passed, a phase which was associated with "the riotous noon-day sun." It is impossible to determine whether this represents a point in the persona's maturation (most likely his young manhood) or an earlier moment in his shifting orientation (when his concerns were more material or "earthly" than spiritual), or a combination of the two; but perhaps this is a moot point. What matters is that one phase of his existence (represented by the forest) is over, and that a new one (represented initially by the marshy beach) has begun. In keeping with the previous association of the forest with noon, the new locale is associated with the setting sun, whose "slant yellow beam" seems "Like a lane into heaven." That this sunset is to be associated with an overwhelming spiritual experience (most likely death) is clear from the persona's observation that "now, unafraid, I am fain to face/ The vast sweet visage of space"—a space which a few lines later is depicted, significantly, as the "terminal" sea. Although the persona finds himself "drawn" to "the edge of the wood . . ./ Where the gray beach glimmering runs," he willingly submits and soon finds himself "Free/ By a world of marsh that borders a world of sea."

There is nothing even remotely frightening about the beach: it is gray (reportedly Lanier's favorite color), and it forms the transitional zone between something the persona has voluntarily rejected and something which he deeply desires. The Emersonian element of the poem is most evident as the persona reacts to the new freedom of the beach. At this point, the persona conveys his reaction to his spiritual freedom through two similes. First, "As the marsh-hen secretly builds on the watery sod,/ Behold I will build me a nest on the greatness of God," and he also will fly as she does; second, "By so many roots as the marsh-grass sends in the sod/ I will heartily lay me a-hold on the greatness of God." The two metaphors are perfect in their appropriateness and simplicity, and they usher in the third movement of the poem: the shift from sunset to night, and from marshy beach to ocean. Much as the persona's identity was blurred with that of the beach as he likened himself to the bird and grass, the identity of the beach is blended with that of the ocean as the tide rises, until finally "the sea and the marsh are one" and "it is night." The poem has progressed so steadily to this climax that the final stanza sounds almost like a postscript.

It is unfortunate that Lanier did not live long enough to complete the series of projected "Hymns of the Marshes" of which "The Marshes of Glynn" was to be only a small part. Experimental in subject, scope, and technique (note the logaoedic dactyls and the long, loose Whitmanesque lines), "The Marshes of Glynn" is one of Lanier's best poems, revealing an intellectual maturity and a technical expertise which, had they been allowed to flower, might well have placed him among the foremost American poets of the nineteenth century.

Major publications other than poetry

NOVEL: *Tiger-Lilies*, 1867.

NONFICTION: "Retrospects and Prospects," 1871; *Florida: Its Scenery, Climate, and History*, 1875; "Sketches of India," 1876; *The Science of English Verse*, 1880; *The English Novel*, 1883; *Shakspere and His Forerunners*, 1902.

CHILDREN'S LITERATURE: *The Boy's King Arthur*, 1880.

Bibliography

Abel, Darrel. *American Literature: Literature of the Atlantic Culture*, 1963.

Mims, Edwin. *Sidney Lanier*, 1905.

Pearce, Roy Harvey. *The Continuity of American Poetry*, 1961.

Starke, Aubrey Harrison. *Sidney Lanier: A Biographical and Critical Study*, 1933.

Waggoner, Hyatt. *American Poets*, 1968.

Alice Hall Petry

PHILIP LARKIN

Born: Coventry, England; August 9, 1922

Principal collections

The North Ship, 1945, 1966; *The Less Deceived*, 1955; *The Whitsun Weddings*, 1964; *High Windows*, 1974.

Other literary forms

Although Philip Larkin is thought of today primarily as a poet, his first literary successes were novels: *Jill* (1946, 1964) and *A Girl in Winter* (1947). The two were widely acclaimed for their accomplished style, accurate dialogue, and subtle characterization. *Jill* was valued highly for its intimate look at wartime Oxford. The protagonist in each is an outsider who encounters great difficulty in attempting to fit into society, and the two novels explore themes of loneliness and alienation to which Larkin returns time and again in his later poetry. Larkin has written comparatively little about literature and has granted very few interviews. None of his literary essays has been collected. He has written extensively, however, on jazz, chiefly in his reviews for the *Daily Telegraph*, and a number of those pieces appear in the volume *All What Jazz* (1970). His opinions in those works are frequently instructive for the reader who wishes to understand his views on poetry, particularly his comments on what he sees as the "modernist" jazz of Charlie Parker, which, like all modernism, concentrates on technique while violating the truth of human existence. True to his precepts, Larkin has eschewed, throughout his career, technical fireworks in favor of a poetic that reflects the language of the people. He edited *New Poems, 1958*, with Louis MacNeice and Bonamy Dobrée, and he was chosen to bring out *The Oxford Book of Twentieth-Century English Verse* (1973).

Achievements

Few poets have succeeded as Larkin has in winning a large audience and critical respect for such a small body of poetry, and indeed his success may be attributable in part to the rate at which he writes poems. Because he brings out, according to his own estimate, only three to five poems a year, he can give each one the meticulous attention required to build extremely tight, masterful verse. As a result, each of his slim volumes contains numerous poems that immediately catch the reader's attention for their precise yet colloquial diction.

His chief contribution to British poetry may well be his sustained determination to work in conventional forms and colloquial, even vulgar and coarse, language. In this attempt, as in his ironic self-deprecation and his gloomy outlook, he resembles Robert Frost. Also like Frost, he is working consciously against the modernist poetics of Wallace Stevens, T. S. Eliot, Ezra Pound, and their heirs, the poetics of disjunction and image. Most of Larkin's poetry demonstrates a distrust of symbolic and metaphorical language, and a reliance instead of discursive verse. His insistence on plain language reflects a belief in the importance of tradition, a faith in the people who remain in touch with the land, and a suspicion of modern society, urban development, and technological advancement. Larkin stands as the chief example among his contemporaries of the line of counter-modernist poetry running not from William Butler Yeats and the Symbolists but from Thomas Hardy and Rudyard Kipling, for both of whom he has great admiration.

Larkin's popularity also results, in part, from his speaking not only as one of the people but for them as well. For all its bleakness and irony, or perhaps because of it, his poetry represents the attitudes of a segment of the British population that found itself with greatly diminished expectations following World War II; institutions were losing their traditional value and function, and the problems of empire (the crowning achievement of those institutions) were rushing home to roost. His poetry has been a search for meaning within the bewildering complexity of the twentieth century.

Biography

The Englishness of Philip Larkin's poetry is decidedly provincial; his England does not revolve around London, and in fact, there is a marked suspicion of the capital and the cosmopolitan urbanity it represents. From his diction to the frequency with which his speakers are seated in cars or trains traveling through the countryside, his poems reflect the provincialism of his life. Larkin was born August 9, 1922, in Coventry, where his father served as City Treasurer throughout his childhood. He has described his childhood as a bore and not worth mentioning, suggesting that no biography of him need begin before he turned twenty-one. Although he was not a particularly good student at the King Henry VII School in Coventry, he matriculated at St. John's College, Oxford, in 1940, hoping to get in a year of school before he was called into the military. As it eventually turned out, he failed his Army physical and stayed in college, graduating with first-class honors in 1943. His time at Oxford had a profound effect upon the youthful Larkin; in the Introduction to *Jill*, he suggests that the war radically diminished the students' grand view of themselves, and this sense of reduced importance has stuck with him in his poetry. Perhaps even more crucial to his development, though, were his friendships with budding writers Bruce Montgomery (Edmund Crispin) and Kingsley Amis. The Amis-Larkin friendship seems to have influenced both men, and their early writings share many attitudes and themes.

While at the university, Larkin published poems in the undergraduate magazines and in the anthology *Poetry in Wartime* (1942). (He had had one poem published in the *Listener* in 1940.) Fortune Press took notice and asked him to submit a collection; he did, and *The North Ship* was published in 1945. The poetry in that collection is heavily influenced by Yeats's work, to which he was introduced by the poet Vernon Watkins, who read and lectured at the English Club at Oxford and with whom Larkin subsequently developed a friendship.

After graduation, Larkin took a post as librarian in Wellington, Shropshire. He claims that while there he began to read Thomas Hardy's poetry seriously, which allowed him to throw off the Yeatsian influence. He has subsequently worked as a librarian in Leicester, in Belfast, and, since 1955, as head librarian at the University of Hull. His attitudes toward his work have vacillated, and that ambivalence is displayed in his poems, particularly in "Toads" and "Toads Revisited." Nevertheless, he has remained at his position as librarian and eschewed the life of poet-celebrity.

Analysis

If Rudyard Kipling's is the poetry of empire, then Philip Larkin's is the poetry of the aftermath of empire. Having lived through the divestiture of England's various colonial holdings, the economic impact of empire-building having finally come home, together with the ultimate travesty of imperial pretensions and the nightmare of Nazi and Soviet colonization in Europe, Larkin is wary of the expansiveness, the acquisitiveness, and the grandeur implicit in the imperial mentality. Many features of his poetry can be traced to that wariness: from the skepticism and irony, to the colloquial diction, to the formal precision of his poems.

Indeed, of all the writers who shared those ideals and techniques and who came to be known in the 1950's as The Movement, Larkin has most faithfully retained his original attitude and style. Those writers—Kingsley Amis, Donald Davie, John Wain, Elizabeth Jennings, Thom Gunn, among others—diverse though they were, shared attitudes that were essentially empirical, antimodernist, skeptical, and ironic. Most of those views can be understood as outgrowths of an elemental alienation from society and its traditional institutions. Amis' Jim Dixon is the outstanding fictional embodiment of these attitudes; although he desperately wants and needs to be accepted into university society and the traditional power structure it represents, his contempt for the institution and those in it, bred of his alienation, carries him into situations that border on both hilarity and disaster. *Lucky Jim* (1954) is *the* Movement novel.

Isolation and alienation figure prominently in both of Larkin's novels, as well; yet it is in his poems that they receive their fullest development. The speakers of his poems—and in the great majority of cases the speaker is the poet himself—seem alienated from their surroundings, cut off from both people and institutions. While that alienation normally shows itself as distance, as irony and wry humor, it can sometimes appear as smugness, complacence, even sneering judgment. Larkin turns his sense of isolation, of being an outsider or fringe observer, into a position of centrality, in which the world from which he is alienated seems to be moving tangentially to his own sphere. In his best poems, that distance works two ways, allowing the poet to observe the world in perspective, as if viewing it through the wrong end of a pair of binoculars, so that weighty matters seem less momentous, while at the same time reminding the poet that he, too, is a figure of little consequence. When his poems fail, the poet risks very little of his own ego as he sits back in safety, judging others across the frosty distance.

Larkin gains his perspective in large measure through his belief that nothing lies beyond this world, that this existence, however muddled it may be, is probably the only one. His skepticism is thoroughgoing and merciless; he rarely softens his tone. In some writers such belief might provoke terror or a compulsion to reform the world. In Larkin, it gives rise to irony. He examines the feeble inhabitants of this tiny planet surrounded by the void and asks if it can all be so important.

The resulting sense of human insignificance, including his own, leads him to several of the characteristic features of his work. He rejects "poetic" devices in favor of simpler, more mundane vehicles. His diction, for example, is nearly always colloquial, often coarse, vulgar, or profane. His distrust of a specialized diction or syntax for poetry reflects his distrust of institutions generally. Similarly, he shics away from the intense poetic moment—image, symbol, metaphor—in favor of a discursive, argumentative verse. While he will occasionally resolve a poem through use of an image or a metaphor, particularly in *High Windows*, he more commonly talks his way through the poem, relying on intellect rather than emotion or intuition.

This rejection of the stuff of poetry leads him to a problem: if overtly poetic language and poetic devices are eschewed, what can the poet use to identify his poems *as* poems? For Larkin the answer lies in the external form of the poems: scansion, rhyme schemes, stanzaic patterns. The tension and the power of a Larkin poem often result from the interplay of common, unexceptional language with rigorously formal precision. "The Building," from *High Windows*, is an example of such tension. The poet meditates upon the function of the hospital in modern society and the way in which it takes over some of the duties traditionally performed by the Church, all in very ordinary language. The poem, however, is stretched taut over not one but two sophisticated units: a seven-line stanza and an eight-line rhyme scheme (abcbdad). Rhyme pattern and stanzaic pattern come together at the end of the eighth stanza, but the poem does not end there; rather, the poet employs another rhyme unit, a stanza plus a line, as a means of resolving the poem. Even here Larkin's shrewd distrust of the intellectual viability of poetic forms displays itself: ending neatly on the fifty-sixth line would be too neat, too pat, and would violate the poem's ambivalence toward the place. Similarly, although his rhyme schemes are often very regular, the same cannot be said for the rhymes themselves: speech/touch, faint/went, home/welcome. If Larkin recognizes his need for traditional forms in his poems, he recognizes also the necessity of altering those forms into viable elements of *his* poetry.

Finally, there is in Larkin a sense of an ending, of oblivion. For all he says against the "new apocalypse crowd," many of his poems suggest something similar, although with a characteristic difference. Where the "crowd" may prophesy the end of the world and everything in it, he, working out of his alienation, more commonly seems to be watching the string run out, as if he were a spectator at the edge of oblivion.

Larkin's first volume of poetry, *The North Ship*, went virtually unnoticed at the time of its original publication and would be unnoticed still were it made to stand on its own merits. It has few. The poems are almost uniformly derivative Yeatsian juvenilia, laden with William Butler Yeats's imagery but shorn of its power or meaning; this is the verse of a young man who wants to become a poet by sounding like a known poet. No one has been more critical, moreover, of the volume than the poet himself, characterizing it as an anomaly, a mistake that happened when he did not know his own voice and thought, under the tutelage of Vernon Watkins, that he was someone else. That he allowed the republication of the work in 1966, with an introduction that is more than anything else a disclaimer, suggests a desire to distance the "real" poet from the confused adolescent.

Despite his objections, the book can be seen as representative of certain tendencies in his later verse, and it is enlightening to discern how many features of his mature work show themselves even when buried under someone else's style. A major difference between Larkin's poems and Yeats's lies in the use of objects: while the younger poet borrows Yeats's dancers, horses, candles, and moons, they remain dancers, horses, candles, and moons. They lack transcendant, symbolic value; objects remain mere objects.

There is also in these early poems a vagueness in the description of the phenomenal world. Perhaps that generality, that vagueness, could be explained as the result of the Yeatsian influence, but it is also a tendency of Larkin's later work. One often has the impression that a scene, particularly a human scene, is typical rather than specific.

One of the things clearly missing from this first work is a suspicion of the Yeatsian symbols, attitudes, and gestures, almost none of which the mature Larkin can abide. His assertion that it was his intense reading of Hardy's poetry that rescued him from the pernicious influence of Yeats may have validity; more probably, time heals youthful excess, and during the period when he was outgrowing the poetry of *The North Ship*, he began a salutary reading of Hardy.

A striking development in Larkin's second book of poems, *The Less*

Deceived, is his insistence on the mundane, the unexceptional, the common-place. In "Born Yesterday," a poem on the occasion of Sally Amis' birth, for example, he counters the usual wishes for beauty or brilliance with the attractive (for him) possibility of being utterly unextraordinary, of fitting in wholly by having nothing stand out. This wish he offers, he says, in case the others do not come true, but one almost has the sense that he wishes also that the others will not come true, that being average is much preferable to being exceptional.

He makes a similar case for the ordinary in the wickedly funny "I Remember, I Remember," which attacks the Romantic notions of the writer's child-hood as exemplified in D. H. Lawrence's *Sons and Lovers* (1913). In other places he has described his childhood as boring, not worthy of comment, and in this poem he pursues that idea vigorously. In the first two stanzas, he comes to the realization that he does not recognize the Coventry station into which the train has pulled, although he used it often as a child. When his traveling companion asks if Coventry is where he "has his roots," the poet responds in his mind with a catalog of all the things that never happened to him that supposedly happen to writers in their youth, "the splendid family/ I never ran to," "The bracken where I never sat trembling." Through the course of that list, he recognizes that the place looks so foreign now because it never gave him anything distinctive, that there is nothing that he carries with him that he can attribute to it. Then, in a remarkable about-face, he realizes that the location has very little to do with how his childhood was spent or misspent, that life is largely independent of place, that the alienation which he senses is something he carries with him, not a product of Coventry.

The poem at first seems to be an honest appraisal of his youth in contra-distinction to all those romanticized accounts in biographies and novels, but the reader is forced finally to conclude that the poet protests too much. There is no childhood in which *nothing* happens, and in insisting so strongly on the vacuum in which he grew up, Larkin develops something like the inverse of nostalgia. He turns his present disillusionment and alienation back against the past and views it from his ironic perspective. Larkin is often the victim of his own ironies, and in this poem his victim is memory.

His irony, in this poem as in so many, is used defensively; he wards off criticism by beating everyone to the punch. Irony is in some respects safer than laying oneself open for inspection. In many of his finest poems, however, he drops his guard and allows himself to think seriously about serious subjects. The foremost example in *The Less Deceived* is "Church Going." The title turns out to be marvelously ambiguous, appearing at first blush to be a mere reference to attending church, but then becoming, as the poem progresses, an elliptical, punning reference to churches going out of fashion.

The first two stanzas are curtly dismissive in a manner often encountered in Larkin, as he describes his stop from a bicycle trip at a church that is apparently Ulster Protestant. Neither he (since he stops for a reason he cannot name and acts guilty as he looks around) nor the church (since it is not at all out of the ordinary) seems worthy of attention. He leaves, thinking the church "not worth stopping for." In the third stanza, however, the poem shifts gears in a way typical of Larkin's finest work: the dismissive attitude toward mundane existence, the wry observations give way to serious contemplation. "Church Going," in fact, contains two such shifts.

In stanzas three through seven Larkin reflects on the fate of churches when people stop going altogether—whether they will become places which people will avoid or seek out because of superstition, or become museums, or be turned to some profane use—and wonders, as well, who will be the last person to come to the church and what his reasons will be. Larkin has a sense, conveyed in a number of poems, that he and his generation of skeptics will be the end of religion in England, and in this poem he wonders about the results of that doubting. The final stanza contains yet another shift, this one rather more subtle. As if the "serious house on serious earth" were forcing the poet to be more serious, he shifts away from his musings about its fate, which are after all only another kind of dismissal, and recognizes instead the importance of the place. He suggests, finally, that the shallowness and disbelief of modern man cannot eradicate the impulse to think seriously and seek wisdom that the Church, however outmoded its rituals, represents.

The two finest poems in Larkin's succeeding volume display similar movements of thought. In the title poem, "The Whitsun Weddings," the movement takes on further embellishment; not only does the poem move from dismissiveness to contemplation, but also the language of the poem moves from specificity toward generality in a way that mirrors the theme. The poem also contains one of Larkin's favorite devices: the use of a train ride (occasionally a car ride) to depict the movement of thought.

The poem opens with the concern for specificity of someone who, like the speaker, is late; when the train leaves the station at "one-twenty," it is "three-quarters-empty." He catches glimpses of scenery along the way, none of it very interesting, much of it squalid and polluted. Not until the third stanza (suggesting the incompleteness of his detailed observation) does he notice the wedding parties at each station. Even then, it is with the dismissive attitude of someone who, as a professional bachelor and alienated outsider, rather scorns the tackiness of the families gathered on the platforms to see the couples off, as well as that of the unreflective couples with whom he shares the coach. His ironical, detailed description takes up most of the next five stanzas.

Toward the end of stanza seven, however, he undergoes a change, has a moment of vision in which the postal districts of London appear as "squares of wheat." That image leads him, in the final stanza, to see the couples as symbols of fertility, so that finally the slowing train inspires in him an image of arrows beyond the scope of his vision, "somewhere becoming rain." That he loosens the reins of his vision, so that he can describe not merely what he sees but also what he can only envision, is a major development in his attitude from the beginning of the poem. It demonstrates a breaking down, however slight or momentary, of his alienation from the common run of existence and of his resistance to recognizing his own relationship with these others. The poem may ultimately be judged a failure because of the brevity of that breaking down, but the image it spawns of fertility and life just beginning is magnificent.

"Dockery and Son" displays a similar movement and is a stronger poem because the poet is forced to lower his defenses much earlier and reveal himself more fully during the course of his meditation. An offhand comment by the Dean that a fellow student now has a son at school sets the speaker's mind in motion. His first musings on the train home are again mundane, dismissive, of the "you-never-know-do-you" sort, and so boring that he falls asleep. On reconsideration, though, the poet experiences the shock of being brought up hard against the reality of having missed, irrevocably, what is for most men a major part of life—familial relations. Even this reflection remains thin and unsatisfactory, and he moves on to explore the nature of unquestioned and unquestioning belief and its source, deciding that it results not from wisdom or truth but from habit and style grown sclerotic. Yet those beliefs are what a man's life turns on, producing a son for Dockery and nothing for the poet.

At this point, very late in the poem, Larkin develops one of his marvelous reversals on the word "nothing." For most, it connotes an absence, a negation, a nonentity, but for Larkin "nothing" is a positive entity, a thing or force to be reckoned with, "Nothing with all a son's harsh patronage." The line suggests that the poet has had to wrestle with this "nothing" he has created even as a father, such as Dockery, has had to wrestle with the problems brought on by having a son. The similarity, however, does not stop there; the poet goes on to recognize the common fate that awaits not only Dockery and himself but everyone as well. Most commentators read the final phrase, "the only end of age," as meaning death, and certainly that meaning is there. Nevertheless, to understand it as *merely* meaning death is to lose some of the force it holds for the speaker. Rather, it must be read back through the stanza and the poem as a whole, so that the emphasis on nothingness informs that certain knowledge of death. That the poet not only knows he will die, but also that he has already tasted the nothingness he knows, as an unbeliever, that death entails, makes the experience of that knowledge the more poignant. As is so often true in Larkin's work, that poignancy, which could border on self-pity, is tempered by the understanding that he at least comprehends, and there lies behind the poem's ending an unstated irony aimed at those such as Dockery who engage life so fully as to obscure that reality.

Again, that constant strain of alienation insinuates its way into poem after poem. Throughout *The Whitsun Weddings* the poet feels himself cut off from his fellow humans, often struggling to retrieve a spirit of community with them, sometimes simply wondering why it is so. The volume, while it represents little change from its predecessor, renders a picture of a man in middle age who feels life passing him by, and who sees more and more clearly the inevitable. Settings are close, small; lives are petty, insignificant; society is filled with graffiti and pollution. In "The Importance of Elsewhere," he finds comfort in being a foreigner in Ireland, since at least he can explain his estrangement from his fellow inhabitants there. In England, ostensibly at home, he has no such excuse.

A number of the poems in *High Windows* display that estrangement, often in unsettlingly smug tones. "Afternoons," in the previous book, shows Larkin at his judgmental worst, picking out nasty little details of petty lives and common tastes. In this volume, "The Old Fools," a poem that is often praised for its unexpected ending, displays a similar attitude. After railing against the infirmity and senility of the elderly throughout the poem, the tag line of "Well, we shall find out" rings false, sounding too much like an attempt to dodge inevitable criticism.

"Going, Going" presents some of the same problems, yet it implicates the poet in his critique in a way that "The Old Fools" does not. What is going is England itself, and that entity, it turns out, is place, not people. People have ruined the landscape and the architecture, reducing everything to rubbish. The poem redeems itself through its linguistic implication of its creator. The piece remains polemical throughout, avoiding the impulse to resolve through metaphor, as if the misanthropic, gloomy sensibility demands a crabbed style distrustful of the richness of figurative language and, perhaps, mirroring the destruction of English literature: if "carved choirs," echoing as they do William Shakespeare's "bare ruined choirs where late the sweet birds sang," are ruined and replaced with "concrete and tyres," then this poem's language is the replacement for Shakespeare's. Everywhere the poet turns, he finds traditional institutions, including poetry, degraded into mundane modern forms.

A much finer expression of that discovery is to be found in "The Building," which brings together numerous themes and ideas from throughout Larkin's canon. Like "Dockery and Son," it is a meditation on the foretaste of death; like "Going, Going," a consideration of the degradation of institutions in the modern world; like "Church Going," a questioning of what man shall do without churches.

The first two stanzas examine the ways the building in which the speaker sits resembles so many other modern buildings—high-rise hotels, airport lounges—although there is something disturbingly unlike them, as well. Not until the end of the second stanza does he reveal that it is a hospital. What unites people here is the common knowledge of their own mortality; even if they are not to die immediately, they are forced by the place to confront the fact that they will die eventually. The inescapability of that knowledge tames and calms the people in the building, as once the knowledge of death and its aftermath quieted them in church.

The recognition of this similarity grows slowly but steadily throughout the poem. The words keep insinuating a connection: "confess," "congregations," a "locked church" outside. The reaction people have in the hospital also suggests a function similar to that of the Church; outside they can hide behind ignorance or refusal to face facts, while inside the hospital those illusions are stripped away and reality is brought into the clear, sharp light, the unambiguous clarity of hospital corridors. This growing realization culminates in a final understanding that unless the modern hospital is more powerful than the traditional cathedral (and Larkin, suspicious of all institutions, does not think it is), then nothing can stop the ineluctable fate that awaits humanity, although (and now the similarities are overwhelming) every night people bring offerings, in the form of flowers, as they would to church.

A remarkable poem such as "The Building" can overcome a score of "Afternoons," and what is more remarkable about it is the way Larkin overcomes his initial alienation to speak not only at, but also to and even for, his fellow humans and their very real suffering. His finest poems end, like this one, in benedictions that border on the "Shantih" of T. S. Eliot's *The Waste Land* (1922), giving the reader the sense that a troubling journey has reached a satisfying end.

Major publications other than poetry
NOVELS: *Jill*, 1946, 1964; *A Girl in Winter*, 1947.
ANTHOLOGY: *New Poems*, 1958 (edited with Louis MacNeice and Bonamy Dobrée).

Bibliography
Bedient, Calvin. *Eight Contemporary Poets*, 1974.
Brown, Merle. *Double Lyric: Divisiveness and Community in Recent English Poetry*, 1980.
Brownjohn, Alan. *Philip Larkin*, 1975.
King, P. R. *Nine Contemporary Poets: A Critical Introduction*, 1979.
Martin, Bruce. *Philip Larkin*, 1978.
Timms, David. *Philip Larkin*, 1974.

Thomas C. Foster

D. H. LAWRENCE

Born: Eastwood, Nottinghamshire, England; September 11, 1885
Died: Villa Robermond, Vence, France; March 2, 1930

Principal collections

Love Poems and Others, 1913; *Amores*, 1916; *Look! We Have Come Through!*, 1917; *New Poems*, 1918; *Bay*, 1919; *Tortoises*, 1921; *Birds, Beasts and Flowers*, 1923; *Collected Poems*, 1928; *Pansies*, 1929; *Nettles*, 1930; *The Triumph of the Machine*, 1931; *Last Poems*, 1932; *Fire and Other Poems*, 1940; *Phoenix Edition of Complete Poems*, 1957; *The Complete Poems*, 1964, 1971 (Vivian de Sola Pinto and Warren Roberts, editors).

Other literary forms

D. H. Lawrence's productions reflect his artistic range. Accompanying his considerable body of poetry, the eleven novels published during his lifetime include *Sons and Lovers* (1913), *The Rainbow* (1915), *Women in Love* (1920), *The Plumed Serpent* (1926), and *Lady Chatterley's Lover* (1928). He wrote almost continuously for literary periodicals in addition to publishing five volumes of plays, nine volumes of essays, and several short story collections including *The Prussian Officer and Other Stories* (1914), *England, My England* (1922), *The Ladybird* (1923), and *The Woman Who Rode Away and Other Stories* (1928). His final works, including *Apocalypse* and *Etruscan Places*, appeared between 1930 and 1933, and more poetry, essays, and drafts of fiction have since been collected in *Phoenix* (1936) and *Phoenix II* (1968). Several of Lawrence's works, as well as his biography, *The Priest of Love*, have been adapted for the screen. The *Phoenix Edition of D. H. Lawrence* was published in 1957; Viking has printed *The Complete Short Stories of D. H. Lawrence* (1961) and *The Complete Plays of D. H. Lawrence* (1965). The definitive *Cambridge Edition of the Letters and Works of D. H. Lawrence* began appearing in 1979.

Achievements

Lawrence's work has consistently appealed to the adventurous and the perceptive. Ford Madox Ford, editor of the progressive *English Review*, printed Lawrence's earliest poems and short stories there in 1911, recognizing beneath their conventional surfaces potent psychological and emotional undercurrents previously unexplored in British letters. Before Freud's theories were widely known, Lawrence's *Sons and Lovers* daringly probed the dangerous multilayered mother-son-lover triangle he had experienced in his own life. After his elopement, itself a scandal, Lawrence produced *The Rainbow*, seized by Scotland Yard in 1915 and publicly condemned for obscenity. Lawrence's subsequent self-exile from England and his growing artistic notoriety came to a climax in the censorship trials of *Lady Chatterley's Lover*. Behind the alleged pornography, however, critics soon grasped Lawrence's genuine ability to convey what T. S. Eliot called "fitful and profound insights" into human behavior. Lawrence's admirers also included Edward Garnett, John Middleton Murry, Richard Aldington, Amy Lowell, and Rainer Maria Rilke, although Virginia Woolf perhaps illustrated her generation's ambivalence toward Lawrence most pungently: "Mr. Lawrence has moments of greatness, but he has hours of something quite different." Lawrence's own critical studies, particularly his pseudonymous *Movements in European History* (1921), and *Studies in Classic American Literature* (1923), reveal a singular blend of historical perspective and instinctive understanding appreciated only after his death. Once the laudatory memoirs and abusive denunciations had died out, Lawrence's artistic reputation grew steadily, attributed generally to the craftsmanship of his short fiction and the uncompromisingly honest investigations of sexuality in his novels. As readers young in spirit increasingly observe, however, Lawrence's greatest gift, his affirmation of life, shines most brightly in his poetry.

Biography

David Herbert Richards Lawrence was born in Eastwood, Nottinghamshire, England, on September 11, 1885. His mother, Lydia Beardsall, had come from a fiercely religious middle class family reduced in circumstances since the depression of 1837. Lydia, "a superior soul," as her third son called her, had been a schoolteacher, sensitive and musical, six years younger than her husband, to whom she was distantly related by marriage. His family had also lost money and position, and Arthur Lawrence, the proud possessor of a fine physique and a musical soul, had gone down into the mines as a child to work. Lydia's disillusion with her marriage, her husband's alcoholic degeneration, and the continual marital strife that haunted her son's childhood provided much of the conflict at the heart of Lawrence's work.

Out of hatred for her husband and a desperate resolve that her children should not sink to his level, Lydia used them as weapons against him. Much later, Lawrence regretted and in part redressed the unfavorable portrait of his father in his autobiographical "colliery novel," *Sons and Lovers*, which exhibits his mother's domination and his own fragile opposition through his love for Jessie Chambers, the "Miriam" whom he loved and left in literature as well as life.

Obedient to his mother's demands, Lawrence took a teaching position at Croydon, near London, in 1908. He was devastated by the ugly realities of urban life, disgusted by his savage pupils, and frustrated by the young women in his life. His mother's lingering death from cancer in late 1910, not long after he had laid an early copy of his first novel, *The White Peacock*, in her hands, sent him into a "heavy, bitter year," from which he emerged physically shaken by near-fatal pneumonia, unable to progress with his writing, and bent on leaving England. In the spring of 1912 he became smitten with "the woman of a lifetime," his former language professor's wife, the Baroness Frieda von Richthofen. Upon their elopement that May, they left behind them Frieda's children and Lawrence's England, except for a few brief and mostly unhappy intervals, forever.

Lawrence then had to live by his pen, and he increased his output dramatically, pouring out not only fiction and poetry but also criticism and travel essays. After a painful stay in Cornwall during World War I, shunned because of Frieda's German connections and his own antiwar sentiments, Lawrence, shocked by British repression of *The Rainbow*, began the worldwide wandering which lasted the remainder of his life.

Lawrence almost realized his ambition of writing a major novel on each continent. After visiting Ceylon and Australia, he settled for a time with Frieda and a few friends near Taos, New Mexico, devoting himself to the idealization of primitivism as a vehicle for modern man's regeneration. Working on his novel *The Plumed Serpent* in Mexico in late 1924, he was struck simultaneously with harsh psychic and physical blows; he realized that his artistic position was untenable and went down "as if shot" with a combination of typhoid and the long-standing illness diagnosed then for the first time as tuberculosis.

Slowly recuperating on his ranch, Lawrence regained his creative equilibrium in a play, *David*, and a lovely fragmentary novel, "The Flying Fish," written, he said, "so near the borderline of death" that its spell could not be recaptured "in the cold light of day." There he proclaimed the belief in "regenerate man" to which he dedicated the rest of his short life. He returned in thought at least to England with *Lady Chatterly's Lover*, written on a sunny hill in Italy, a "novel of tenderness" that awakened violent protests and lawsuits, driving him even further into his metaphysical contemplation of human destiny. Very ill, holding to life through the strange bond of creativity alone, Lawrence worked out his conclusions on personal immortality in his *Last Poems*, until on March 2, 1930, in a sanatorium on the French Riviera aptly called "Ad Astra," "once dipped in dark oblivion/the soul ha[d] peace, inward and lovely peace."

Analysis

D. H. Lawrence had written poetry all of his creative life, but he did not set his poetic theory down until 1923. His poetry, as with nearly everything that he wrote, is uneven; and he knew it, distinguishing between his early self-conscious verse and the "real poems" that his "demon" shook out of him, poems he called "a biography of an emotional and inner life." In a preface to another man's poetry, Lawrence defined the process by which he himself transmuted "inner life," the core of his work, into art: "a bursting of bubbles of reality, and the pang of extinction that is also liberation into the roving, uncaring chaos which is all we shall ever know of God." Lawrence's poetry is thus best seen in the context of his life and through the painful paradox of his creativity, rooted in his most profound basic concept, the theory of human regeneration that he conveyed so often in the image of Paradise Regained.

As Richard Hoggart has observed, Lawrence's inner life spoke with both "the voice of a down-to-earth, tight, bright, witty Midlander" and "the voice of a seer with a majestic vision of God and life and earth." The Midlands voice first announced the major themes that Lawrence never abandoned: class, religion, and love. Lawrence very early felt the strictures of a workingman's life and the humiliation of poverty as keenly as he felt the happiness he shared at the Chambers' farm, among birds, beasts, and flowers threatened by encroaching industrialism. His *Rhyming Poems* also reflect his youthful love, quivering between the extremes of idealistic "spirituality" pressed upon him by his mother and Jessie Chambers, so fatally alike, and a powerful sexual drive crying out for satisfaction. At sixteen he abandoned his mother's harsh Congregationalism, though the "hymns of a man's life" never lost their appeal for him, and from 1906 to 1908 he was affected deeply by his experience of Arthur Schopenhauer's "Metaphysics of Sexual Love," which places sex at the center of the phenomenal universe, and Friedrich Wilhelm Nietzsche's works, probably including *The Birth of Tragedy*, which sees Greek tragedy as the result of creative tension between Apollonian rationalism and Dionysian ecstasy. Lawrence's prophetic voice had begun to whisper.

While his mother's slow death gradually disengaged him from her domination, Lawrence tried to weave his early concerns of class, love, and religion into an organic whole. Once he recovered from his own severe illness late in 1911, he looked toward new physical and creative horizons, and after his elopement with Frieda he at last was able to complete *Sons and Lovers* in a new affirmation of life. There were, however, characteristic growing pains. Frieda's aristocratic connections in Germany afforded him the social position that he, like his mother, had always envied while decrying its values, and he delighted in using his wife's baronial stationary at the same time that he was undergoing inevitable agonies at her cavalier disregard for sexual fidelity. The first book of Lawrence's *Unrhyming Poems, Look! We Have Come Through!*, records the resolution of his complicated marital relationship in a form completely liberated from Georgian poetic convention. During World War I, Lawrence tried to locate man's vital meaning in a balance of power between love and friendship, replacing the God he had lost with the human values promised by his *The Rainbow* and the four-part sexual harmony of *Women in Love*.

After the debacle of *The Rainbow*, Lawrence's social message became more strident. From 1917 to 1925, rapt in his dream of human regeneration—now fixed upon the figure of a patriarchal political leader—Lawrence went to the ends of the civilized earth. The fiction that he produced during that period urges progressively more primitivistic reorganizations of society, culminating in a faintly ridiculous neo-Aztec pantheon imposed upon Mexico in *The Plumed Serpent*, a novel embedding Lawrence's highest hopes in stubbornly incantatory verse and sometimes turgid prose.

At the midpoint of his career, a substantial conflict was brewing between Lawrence's urge for social reform and his prophetic sense of responsibility. The religious voice was clear in the poems of *Birds, Beasts and Flowers*, where, as Vivian de Sola Pinto has observed, "the common experience is transformed and invested with mythical grandeur." Such a stirring transmutation proved incompatible with the "down-to-earth Midlands voice" calling for political answers to social questions. By 1923, possibly with memories of Nietzsche and Schopenhauer, Lawrence had defined his "simple trinity" as "the emotions, the mind, and then the children of this venerable pair, ideas." Lawrence also insisted that God's traditional position relative to man had changed, so that Christ could no longer serve as the pathway to the Father; the Holy Ghost would have to lead men to a "new living relation," nothing less than the spiritual regeneration that Lawrence hoped to bring to mankind from the wreckage of modern Western civilization.

When Lawrence collapsed upon completing *The Plumed Serpent*, he was forced to abandon his old dream of social rebirth through politically enforced primitivism. In the poetic "The Flying Fish" he announced that the Indian's "primeval day" and the white man's mechanism "nullified each other." Now, as de Sola Pinto remarked, Lawrence's "ecstasy controlled by the rational imagination" produced memorable poetry in *Birds, Beasts and Flowers*, foreshadowing the affirmation of life eternal that Lawrence finally was to achieve.

Lawrence's irritation with Western materialism erupted once more late in his life in the angry little poems that he called his *Pansies* and *Nettles*, glimpses of man's stupidity, conceit, and boorishness encapsulated in stinging doggerel. Hardly his finest poetic achievement, these poems nevertheless represent more than a sick man's impatience with human frailty. They also demonstrate a quality of Lawrence's insight that he called "quickness," "the breath of the moment, and one eternal moment easily contradicting the next eternal moment."

By 1928, already gravely ill, Lawrence had turned almost completely to examining "the pang of extinction that is also liberation," the paradox, as he saw it, of physical death. His prophetic voice far outstripped the satiric note as he painted and wrote in the familiar archetypes of the Garden of Eden, regained, he felt now, through the apocalypse of death. His three original themes had coalesced into a great hymn of man's essential renewal, the "religion of wonder" that he had glimpsed in the Etruscans: "The whole universe lived; and the business of man was himself to live amid it all." Lawrence paid a heavy price for restoring man to Paradise, the unification of his Midlands voice and his prophetic voice in the acceptance of death as life's necessary other half. At last he was able to create a convincing myth as he had created all his work, from the ideas born of his own mind and emotions. Lawrence's *Last Poems*, like Rainer Maria Rilke's terrible and beautiful angels, burst the bubbles of reality, and Lawrence closed his poems, like his life, upon the noble vision of resurrection.

Lawrence's "biography of an emotional and inner life" begins with his *Rhyming Poems*, written between 1904 and 1912. Those he called "imaginative or fictional" he reworked twenty years later, mostly in his Midlands voice, "to say the real say," because "sometimes the hand of commonplace youth had been laid on the mouth of the demon." The subjective poems of his early years, "with the demon fuming in them smokily," were unchangeable.

One of the lessons that Lawrence had had to learn as a young poet was when to leave his "demon" alone. "Discord in Childhood," a pain-filled record of the elder Lawrences' marital combat, had originally been a long poem, and, he said, a better one. Frightened by his own creativity, Lawrence burned the first poem as a young man, although he later worked the scene into *Sons and Lovers*. Characteristically, even the preserved version connects violent human emotion with nature and its forces: "Outside the house an ash-tree hung its terrible whips," while within, "a male thong" drowned "a slender lash whistling she-delirious rage" in a "silence of blood."

A similar sensuous absorption in brutal natural forces appears in the "Miriam" poems, darkening the mood of "Renascence," which celebrates "The warm, dumb wisdom" that Lawrence learned from his "Eve." Woman was to provide his pathway to creativity, the means to his apprehension of nature, and in much of his work the viewpoint of sensitivity, but for now Lawrence only received "Strange throbs" through her, as when "the sow was grabbing her litter/ With snarling red jaws"; and, as in "Virgin Youth," "We cry in the wilderness."

Later, when he lived in Croydon, Lawrence saw violent urban deformation of nature, and it nearly shattered him; in "Transformations," beauty spills continuously into decay before him as men, "feet of the rainbow," are "twisted in grief like crumpling beech-leaves," and Lawrence is left to wonder at humanity's destiny: "What are you, oh multiform?"

Soon enough, he began to sense an answer looming in the growing recognition of his prophetic mission. In the poem "Prophet," he proposed "the shrouded mother of a new idea . . . as she seeks her procreant groom," using familiar biblical symbolism to stress the religious aspect of his utterance. Before the "shrouded mother," "men hide their faces," the fear bred of artificial social pressures forcing them to deny the powerful enriching role of sexuality in their lives. At last, in "Dreams Old and Nascent," Lawrence called for violent social action: "to escape the foul dream of having and getting and owning." For the first time, he attempted to define his affirmation of the vital impulse: "What is life, but the swelling and shaping the dream in the flesh?"

Lawrence shaped the dream of his own "crisis of manhood, when he marrie[d] and [came] into himself" in the cycle *Look! We Have Come Through!*, attempting in these highly personal poems a crucial connection between the lives of the flesh and the spirit. Greeting physical love in intimate Imagist lyrics like "Gloire de Dijon," he passed through "the strait gate of passion" in "Paradise Re-entered," in which his typically fierce human love must be "Burned clean by remorseless hate." His religious sense, too, had already departed materially from orthodox Christianity. In the same poem, he abandoned both God and Satan "on Eternity's level/ Field," and announced, "Back beyond good and evil/ Return we," with a distinctly Nietzschean echo suggesting his burgeoning preoccupation with spiritual evolution.

From the same nontraditional quarter came the promise that Lawrence incorporated into "Song of a Man Who Has Come Through," one of the closing poems of this cycle. Lawrence willingly yielded himself up to "the wind that blows through me," "a fine wind . . . blowing the new direction of Time." The wind of his prophetic aspect, to prove at times tempestuous, was the vehicle that Lawrence hoped to use "to come at the wonder" he sensed in the act of being, and with it he fashioned the personal experiences recorded in this set of poems into *The Rainbow* and *Women in Love*.

The major poetic work of Lawrence's middle years was *Birds, Beasts and Flowers*, which R. P. Blackmur called "a religious apprehension" and de Sola Pinto has described as an "exploration of what may be called the divine otherness of non-human life." The social criticism that Lawrence vented in this volume is chiefly directed at America, "lurking among the undergrowth/ of Many-stemmed machines." Lawrence plainly confirmed his simultaneous fascination with and repulsion for "Modern, unissued, uncanny America" in "The Evening Land": "And I, who am half in love with you,/ What am I in love with?" Although Lawrence distrusted the American reliance on the machine, he saw "Dark, aboriginal eyes" in the American "idealistic skull," a "New throb," which, like his dramatic character David, he finally concluded was "the false dawn that precedes the real." The aspect of humanity that had always most repelled him, inflexible will, was even less acceptable to him in America than it had been in Europe, as he noted in "Turkey-Cock," "A raw American will, that has never been tempered by life." In several pieces of fiction, including "The Woman Who Rode Away" and *The Plumed Serpent*, he attempted to subdue that will by sheer force of primitive emotion and even compulsive self-sacrifice. Reversing that position in "Eagle in New Mexico," Lawrence candidly acknowledged the necessity of opposition to bloodthirsty will, negating his own proposal of primitivism as a remedy for modern civilization: "Even the sun in heaven can be curbed . . ./ By the life in the hearts of men." Finally, Lawrence unleashed considerable venom at "The American Eagle," which he had come to consider the symbol of civilization's disaster, "The new Proud Republic/ Based on the mystery of pride." Contradicting the very concept of political dominance by an "aristocracy of the spirit" that he had advocated for so long, Lawrence denounced the "bird of men that are masters,/ Or are you the goose that lays the . . . addled golden egg?"

None of the rancor of Lawrence's American-directed diatribes is present in the finest poetry of *Birds, Beasts and Flowers* in which de Sola Pinto finds "an affirmation of the grandeur and mystery of the life of nature." Working from a mundane incident, a visit by a poisonous Sicilian snake to his water trough on "a hot, hot day," "Snake" illustrates Lawrence the poet at his most capable, commanding a deceptively simple style, ordinary speech, and a consummate adaptation of rhythm to meaning. The resulting interior monologue evokes a passionate mythopoeic response. The snake "had come like a guest in quiet," and Lawrence described himself as "afraid," but "honoured still more/ That he should seek my hospitality." In one of Lawrence's flashes of intuitive perception, the snake "looked around like a god" before retreating through a cranny in the wall. Lawrence's "voices . . . of accursed human education" impelled him to toss a log at the creature, a petty act that he shortly regretted profoundly: "And so, I missed my chance with one of the lords of life." "Snake" realizes a striking balance between mind and emotion, penetrating the mystery of civilized man's destruction of nature and eclipsing the conventional Christian symbolism of Evil Incarnate. In the snake's deathly potential, too, is the premonition that "the lords of life are the masters of death," an insight not developed fully until Lawrence had returned to Europe.

Still closer than "Snake" to expressing man's most archetypal need, the yearning after life renewed, Lawrence's "Almond Blossom" opens "a heart of delicate super-faith/ [in] . . . The rusty swords of almond-trees." Much of Lawrence's poetry has been assailed for supposed incoherence of utterance and Whitmanesque repetitiousness, but in "Almond Blossom," de Sola Pinto notes, Lawrence is "thinking in images." Lawrence's old Christian path to God, "The Gethsemane blood," bursts now into "tenderness of bud," a splendid annunciation of "A naked tree of blossom, like a bridegroom bathing in dew." The "new living relation" of man with God which Lawrence was proclaiming in his philosophical essays now assumed fulfillment in an emboldened image that merged social consciousness, love, and religion: "Think, to stand there in full-unfolded nudity, smiling,/ With all the snow-wind, and the sunglare, and the dog-star baying epithalamion."

There is a marked shift in tone from *Birds, Beasts and Flowers* to the following volumes of poems, *Pansies* and *Nettles*. In *Pansies*, Lawrence was immediately accused of obscenity for using "the *old* words [Lawrence's italics], that belong to the body below the navel." Those who knew him intimately, like Frieda, often referred to him as a puritan in sexual matters, and a purpose far different from obscenity motivated both his *Pansies* and *Nettles*; he had a stern, almost Calvinistic urge to destroy what he considered genuine pornography, "the impudent and dirty mind[s]" that had condemned *Lady Chatterley's Lover*. Lawrence had never been a patient man, and his Introduction to *Pansies* is one of his most savage jeremiads: "In the name of piety and purity, what a mass of disgusting insanity is spoken and written." Such social "insanity" was his greatest enemy, and he fought the mob "in order to keep sane and to keep society sane." His chief weapon was a hard-edged Swiftian wit that did not shrink from the scatological to make a point. In *Pansies* Lawrence assailed most of the sacred cows of his time: censorship, "heavy breathing of the dead men"; "our bald-headed consciousness"; "narrow-gutted superiority"; the "Oxford cuckoos"; "ego-perverted love"; even "elderly discontented women."

His short series of *Nettles* must have stung his detractors even more viciously. In "13,000 People," a poem on the public reaction to the brief exhibition of his paintings abruptly terminated by British police, he flailed the "lunatics looking . . . where a fig-leaf might have been, but was not." He even figuratively neutered his "little Critics": "brought up by their Aunties/ who . . . had them fixed to save them from undesirable associations."

Despite his ferocity when assaulting social "insanity," the unhealthy forces of repression and censorship, Lawrence was still approaching a positive solution for modern man's woes in both *Pansies* and *Nettles*. In the little poem "God" in *Pansies*, he declared: "Where sanity is/ there God is," linking his own beliefs to the Supreme Being. He also dedicated several of the longer *Pansies* (*pensées*, or even heartsease, he had suggested in the Introduction) to the Risen Lord, the new subjective path to God by which man could serve as his own Savior: "A sun will rise in me,/ I shall slowly resurrect." In "More Pansies," a still later group, Lawrence came even nearer the mystery of man's being, identifying the Holy Ghost as "the deepest part of our own consciousness/ wherein . . . we know our dependence on the creative beyond." Finally, as Lawrence struggled both in his poems and in his philosophic essays with the immensity of his apocalyptic vision, his satiric voice became only an overtone of the religious message he was attempting to enunciate. That message sprang from his "strange joy/ in a great [new] . . . adventure."

None of the poetry that Lawrence wrote during his life became him more than the *Last Poems*, which he wrote while leaving it. In his final prose work, *Apocalypse*, he was still clinging to the physical life he had celebrated so long and so rapturously, but in the *Last Poems* Lawrence was setting out gladly into a new country whose borders he had glimpsed in *Etruscan Places*, his vivid sense of place even capturing the paradoxical "delight of the underworld" in ancient tombs, "deep and sincere honour rendered to the dead and to the mysteries."

In "Bavarian Gentians," Lawrence powerfully enlarged the mythic role of nature's archetypes of resurrection as he descended into the "new adventure": "Reach me a gentian, bring me a torch!" Previously concentrating on Eve as man's mediatrix with Paradise Regained, Lawrence now saw woman as symbolic Persephone, "a voice . . . pierced with the passions of dense gloom." The image of biblical mystical marriage could satisfy him no longer, and

Lawrence now looked toward the mythic "splendour of torches of darkness, shedding darkness on the lost bride and her groom."

With the relatively minor exceptions of poems dealing with the symbols of his *Apocalypse* and a few more prickly observations on man's social vicissitudes, *Last Poems* represents the birthpangs of Lawrence's incomplete poetic masterpiece, "The Ship of Death." He had seen a little model ship in an Etruscan tomb and it had carried his imagination toward the possibility of one long poetic testament, where, as Richard Aldington suggests, "suffering and the agony of departure are turned into music and reconciliation." The extant fragments of Lawrence's radiant vision center on a new concept in his stormy artistry, the peace of a soul fulfilled at last in its greatest adventure: "the long and painful death/ that lies between the old self and the new." Lawrence's long struggles with the nightmares of man's collective insanity were finally over, and he had "come through" his early preoccupations with the stresses of class and love and even religion, finding again within himself the possibility of a new dimension of human perception. At last body and mind, life and death had become one for him, "filling the heart with peace."

Lawrence's poetic development from conventional Georgian verse to mythopoeic vision spanned only the first thirty years of this century, yet his ultimate vision approaches the universal. In his "moments of greatness," far from a willfully obscene *Weltbild*, he opens a breathtaking vista of the potential of the human condition in its entirety, not only body, not merely soul, but a creativity as vital as the Greek tragedy that Nietzsche had earlier proclaimed as the result of Apollonian-Dionysian tension. Lawrence's occasional Midlands lapses from literary propriety seem a small enough price to pay for the validity and vitality of his finest poetry, described best in the tenderly honest words of his fellow poet Rainer Maria Rilke: "act[s] of reverence toward life."

Major publications other than poetry

NOVELS: *The White Peacock*, 1911; *The Trespasser*, 1912; *Sons and Lovers*, 1913; *The Rainbow*, 1915; *Women in Love*, 1920; *The Lost Girl*, 1920; *Aaron's Rod*, 1922; *Kangaroo*, 1923; *The Boy in the Bush*, 1924 (with M. L. Skinner); *The Plumed Serpent*, 1926; *Lady Chatterley's Lover*, 1928; *The Virgin and the Gipsy*, 1930; *Lady Chatterley's Lover*, 1932 (abridged); *The First Lady Chatterley*, 1944; *John Thomas and Lady Jane*, 1972 (second draft of *Lady Chatterley's Lover*).

SHORT FICTION: *The Prussian Officer and Other Stories*, 1914; *England, My England*, 1922; *The Ladybird*, 1923 (in America, *The Captain's Doll*); *St. Mawr*, with *The Princess*, 1925; *The Woman Who Rode Away*, 1928; *The Escaped Cock*, 1929 (later *The Man Who Died*); *Love Among the Haystacks*, 1930; *The Lovely Lady and Other Stories*, 1933; *The Tales*, 1933; *A Modern Lover*, 1934; *The Complete Short Stories of D. H. Lawrence*, 1961; *The Escaped Cock*, 1973 (with new material).

PLAYS: *The Widowing of Mrs. Holroyd*, 1914; *Touch and Go*, 1920; *David*, 1926; *The Plays*, 1933; *A Collier's Friday Night*, 1934; *The Complete Plays of D. H. Lawrence*, 1965.

NONFICTION: *Twilight in Italy*, 1916; *Movements in European History*, 1921; *Psychoanalysis and the Unconscious*, 1921; *Sea and Sardinia*, 1921; *Fantasia of the Unconscious*, 1922; *Studies in Classic American Literature*, 1923; *Reflections on the Death of a Porcupine and Other Essays*, 1925; *Mornings in Mexico*, 1927; *Pornography and Obscenity*, 1929; *Assorted Articles*, 1930; *A Propos of Lady Chatterley's Lover*, 1930; *Apocalypse*, 1931; *Etruscan Places*, 1932; *Phoenix: The Posthumous Papers*, 1936 (Edward McDonald, editor); *The Collected Letters*, 1962 (Harry T. Moore, editor); *Phoenix II: Uncollected, Unpublished and Other Prose Works*, 1968 (Harry T. Moore and Warren Roberts, editors); *The Cambridge Edition of the Letters and Works of D. H. Lawrence*, 1979 and continuing.

Bibliography

Alvarez, Alfred. *Stewards of Excellence*, 1971.
Delanvy, Paul. *D. H. Lawrence's Nightmare*, 1978.
Delavaney, Emile. *D. H. Lawrence: The Man and His Work*, 1972.
Gilbert, Sandra. *Acts of Attention*, 1972.
Moore, Harry T. *The Priest of Love: A Life of D. H. Lawrence*, 1974.
Nehls, Edward. *D. H. Lawrence: A Composite Biography*, 1957-1959.
Sagar, Keith. *D. H. Lawrence: A Calendar of His Works*, 1979.
Tiverton, Father William (Martin Jarrett-Kerr). *D. H. Lawrence and Human Existence*, 1951.

Mitzi M. Brunsdale

LAYAMON

Born: Unknown. Flourished, probably in North Worcestershire, England; c. 1200
Died: Unknown

Principal poem
Brut, c. 1205.

Other literary forms
Layamon is known only as the author of the partially translated poetic chronicle known as Layamon's *Brut*.

Achievements
Layamon's *Brut*, which J. S. P. Tatlock describes as "the nearest thing we have to a traditional racial Epic," is the first major literary work in Middle English, and the first version in English of the stories of King Arthur and of King Lear. Assessing Layamon's achievement is difficult because his *Brut* is a much expanded translation of Wace's *Roman de Brut* (c. 1155), itself an Anglo-Norman translation and expansion of Geoffrey of Monmouth's *Historia Regum Britanniae* (c. 1136, *History of the Kings of Britain*). Consequently, it is necessary first to briefly describe these earlier versions and the influence they are known to have exerted.

Geoffrey of Monmouth, writing in Latin in about 1136, constructed a pseudohistory of the British (as opposed to the Anglo-Saxon) kings of England, beginning with the legendary Brutus (a grandson of Aeneas), continuing through the celebrated reign of King Arthur, and ending with the last British kings in the seventh century. The primary effect of Geoffrey's *History of the Kings of Britain* was to stimulate international interest in the legends of Arthur, which previously had been well-known only to the Welsh and Breton peoples. Geoffrey's *History of the Kings of Britain* and the *Prophecies of Merlin* which make up its seventh book were translated in places as far away as Iceland. Centuries later, in Elizabethan times, Geoffrey's *History of the Kings of Britain* would be rediscovered by the Tudor kings, who wished to stress their ancient Welsh claims to the throne. As part of this new interest, the *History of the Kings of Britain* would provide subject matter for Edmund Spenser and William Shakespeare. Spenser devotes a canto of *The Faerie Queene* (1590-1596, Book II, Canto X) to a "Chronicle of British Kings," based on Geoffrey and derivative histories, such as Raphael Holinshed's *Chronicles* (1577). For his tragedy of *King Lear* (1605), Shakespeare consulted both Holinshed's and Spenser's versions. There he found the basic plot outline, including the opening love test, Lear's progressive humiliation by Goneril and Regan, and his eventual redemption (restoration in Geoffrey's *History of the Kings of Britain*) by Cordelia and the duke of France. To these elements Shakespeare added the parallel subplots of Gloucester, Kent, and the Fool, and he rearranged the ending in a masterful fashion typical of his treatment of source materials.

The influence of Geoffrey's *History of the Kings of Britain* on medieval Arthurian literature was primarily by way of the Anglo-Norman translation by Wace. Wace's courtly version in octosyllabic couplets motivated and stylistically influenced his immediate successors, Chrétien de Troyes, Marie de France, and Thomas of Britain. More substantial use of his subject matter was made by fourteenth century prose romancers, in the Vulgate *Merlin* and the *Morte Arthure*. The latter work was a major source for Thomas Malory's *Le Morte d'Arthur* (c. 1469), and thus one can trace a circuitous route from the first to the last of the great Middle English Arthurians. Malory also made use of the alliterative *Morte Arthure*, perhaps the Arthurian work closest in spirit and substance to Layamon's *Brut*. Even this product of the alliterative revival, however, is thought to be based not on Layamon but on Wace, or perhaps on the fourteenth century translation of Wace by Robert Mannyng of Brunne. Among medieval works, only Robert of Gloucester's chronicle (in its later recension, c. 1340) can confidently be said to have made direct use of Layamon's *Brut*.

Even though his chronicle, which survives in only two manuscripts, represented something of a dead end in the development of Arthurian legend, Layamon has been rediscovered in the nineteenth and twentieth centuries. Both Alfred, Lord Tennyson and Ezra Pound made demonstrable use of Layamon's poetic style. Linguists continue to study the *Brut*'s early, more highly inflected dialect, and stylistic critics remain fascinated by its poetic form, which lies somewhere between the formulaic, alliterative meter of Anglo-Saxon poetry and the developing meter of the Middle English rhymed romances. This century's major contribution to Layamon scholarship, however, is the new edition by G. L. Brook and R. F. Leslie. Interested readers would be well advised to consult the Introduction and notes to this edition when the third and final volume appears.

Biography

All the known details concerning Layamon's life are derived from the opening section of his *Brut*, the first five lines of which read as follows (in Madden's translation, which includes the significant manuscript variants):

> There was a priest on earth, (or in the land,) who was named Layamon; he was son of Leovenath (Leuca),—may the Lord be gracious to him!—he dwelt at Ernley, at a noble church (with the good knight,) upon Severns bank (Severn),—good (pleasant) it there seemed to him—near Radestone, where he books read.

The author's name, which has been spelled in a number of ways, is Scandi-

navian in origin, and is cognate with modern English "Lawman." The recorded
variant spellings of his father's name are less confusing when one realizes that
the scribe often writes "u" for "v"; "Levca" can then be seen as a shortened
form of "Leovenath." Tatlock hypothesizes, in light of the familiarity with
Ireland that Layamon exhibits in his poem, that perhaps Leovenath went to
Ireland with the Norman invading force, married a Scandinavian Irishwoman
(there having been a sizable Viking population in Ireland at that time), and
later returned to England with his son. In any case, the only residence Layamon himself mentions is a church at "Ernley" on the banks of the Severn
near "Radestone." These details accord well with a village variously referred
to as Lower Areley, Areley Kings, and Areley Regis, not far from Worcester
and the Welsh border. The books that Layamon mentions as having read
(line 5) have usually been taken to be service books that he used in his role
as a priest. Despite attempts to find the man behind these few details, however,
Layamon remains little more than a name, an occupation (priest and translator), and a place-name. Even the time in which he "flourished" is derived
from the supposed date of composition of the *Brut*, which is itself undergoing
a reevaluation.

Analysis

In order to analyze Layamon's *Brut*, it is first necessary to continue the
discussion of his sources. As mentioned above, Layamon's main source was
Wace's *Roman de Brut*, which in the edition that Madden consulted consisted
of 15,300 lines, as opposed to the 32,350 lines in his edition of Layamon's
Brut. Granted that Madden's lines (now termed half-lines) are shorter than
the lines in Wace, it is still apparent that Layamon considerably expanded his
main source. It has been suggested that Layamon may have used an already
expanded version of Wace, which had been conflated with an earlier chronicle
(now lost) by Gaimar. As this suggestion cannot be verified, however, most
critics have looked elsewhere for supplementary sources. One recent modi-
fication in this matter of primary sources is the discovery that some of the
material previously considered original in Wace derives instead from an extant
"variant version" of Geoffrey. Furthermore, additions occurring in a Welsh
version of Geoffrey are paralleled in Layamon.

Layamon in his Preface mentions two works in addition to Wace: "the
English book that Saint Bede made," and another book "in Latin, that Saint
Albin made, and the fair Austin." Bede's best-known work, and the work
potentially of the most use to Layamon, is his *Historia Ecclesiastica Genta
Anglorum* (c. 732, *Ecclesiastical History of the English Peoples*), written in
Latin and later translated into Anglo-Saxon. Albinus (d. 732) reportedly
helped Bede to gather source materials, and so a number of critics have
assumed that Layamon erroneously attributed the Old English translation to
Bede, and Bede's Latin original to Albius (and to the great apostle to the

English, "Austin" or Augustine of Canterbury, d. 604). Layamon claims both to have "compressed" these three books (including Wace) into one and to have used the latter two books "as a model." This second statement is closer to the truth, for Layamon did not in fact make any incontestable use of Bede. He was probably acting in a tradition of vague citation to a previous authority; Geoffrey before him had claimed access to a certain "most ancient" source book. Nor can Layamon be shown conclusively to have drawn upon Geoffrey in the original Latin, upon classical authors, upon French Arthurians (besides Wace), or upon Welsh records. Recent evidence does suggest, however, that he was familiar with late Anglo-Saxon homiletic literature, and may even have read classical Anglo-Saxon verse in manuscript.

Presumably the forthcoming notes to Brook's edition will supplant Madden in indicating where Layamon drew neither on Wace nor on any known source; it is in these passages that one would then look for Layamon's most original work. This is not to say that these are the only passages of interest, for there is much in Layamon's retelling that adds quite a different tone to the material in Wace; such considerations will be reserved for the discussion of style, below.

The best known of Layamon's additions are those that contribute new material to Arthurian legend. Wace had made the first recorded reference to the Round Table, to which Layamon adds an account of the quarrels over precedence which led to its institution (11360ff.) To Arthur's biography, Layamon adds an account of the elvish gifts at his birth (9608ff.), a premonetory dream of his final misfortunes in the battle with Molred (13982ff.), and an expanded version of Arthur's mysterious departure to Avalon (14277ff.) Arthur as a character seems less a romance hero than a stern and successful king, feared and respected by all the kings and great knights of Europe. (Perhaps it should be noted that the better-known exploits of some of Arthur's knights, such as the Lancelot affair and the quest for the Holy Grail, do not appear in Geoffrey, Wace, or Layamon.) As for Merlin, Layamon reports more of his prophecies than Wace had done, and adds an account of his stay in the wilderness (9878ff.) that can be compared with the Welsh tales of Merlin Silvestris. A long list of Layamon's minor Arthurian additions can be found in R. H. Fletcher, *The Arthurian Material in the Chronicles* (1906).

C. Friedlander discusses additions from other parts of Layamon's *Brut* in her examination of five of its longer episodes: those of Leir, Belin and Brennes, Vortiger, Colgrim and Childric, and Penda. Here Layamon invents dialogue (as Wace had also done), adds characters and scenes, interjects comments, introduces stylistic devices, and manifests what according to Friedlander is a predominant theme: a concern with reversal in personal and national fortunes. Of the Leir episode, for example, Friedlander remarks, "The demonstration of Leir's folly and gradual enlightenment, the emphasis on materialistic values, and the pervasive consciousness of reversals in human fortune are all Layamon's contributions." Friedlander's basic contention is that the theme of reversal, the focus on a few major episodes, and the repeated use of stylistic formulas all contribute to lend to the *Brut* a greater sense of structure than is usual for the chronicle genre.

C. S. Lewis characterized Layamon as "more archaic and less sophisticated" than Wace, adding that "Wace's characters are knights and courtiers; those of the *Brut*, heroes and thanes." As an illustration he cites an interesting Arthurian passage, in which Wace's knights ascend a tower and joke gaily about the relative merits of wartime and peace. Layamon, on the other hand, first characterizes the "ancient stonework" of the tower (12419), in a motif that recalls the older Anglo-Saxon elegies. The gay debate becomes a tense exchange or "flit" (12459) that recalls the "flytings" of Anglo-Saxon and Old Icelandic narrative verse. Another "Saxon echo" frequently alluded to is found in the description of Loch Ness (10848ff.), which is populated with the same sea-creatures ("nicors") mentioned in *Beowulf* (c. 1000).

Lewis also finds Layamon "fiercer but kinder" than Wace; Tatlock comments on a pervasive delight in crushing enemies, and sees therein echoes of Irish saga literature. Also suggestive of Irish influence is Layamon's greater emphasis on the marvelous and on appearances from the world of "faery." Layamon's additions concerning Arthur's weapons and the elvish smith who forged them evoke equally Anglo-Saxon and Irish legends. Finally, Tatlock also mentions Layamon's technical familiarity with matters of seamanship, which, together with other details from medieval life, contributes to the personal stamp that Layamon puts on his material.

Layamon achieves a further degree of originality simply by virtue of the poetic form he employs. Geoffrey's *History of the Kings of Britain* is in prose, and Wace's *Roman de Brut* is in octosyllabic couplets; Layamon's *Brut* is written in a combination of alliterating and rhyming half-lines. The presence of alliteration suggests an inheritance from Anglo-Saxon verse, though not without some attendant changes. Metrically, Layamon's lines favor an iambic-trochaic rhythm rather than the predominantly trochaic rhythm of Anglo-Saxon verse. This change leads to a greater proliferation of unstressed syllables at either end of the half-line. Furthermore, alliteration seems to be more an ornament than a strictly regulated requirement in Layamon's verse.

In these aspects of form, Layamon's *Brut* resembles a few other Early Middle English poems, including some late poetic entries in the Anglo-Saxon chronicle, the "Worcester fragments," "The Grave," and "The Proverbs of Alfred." Tatlock remarks how these poems also all lack the understatement, parenthesis, and periphrasis that characterized Anglo-Saxon verse. To account for these developments, scholars have hypothesized that a less strict, more popular form of alliterative verse may have existed alongside the more refined Anglo-Saxon compositions, such as *Beowulf*, which were committed to manuscript. It may be that the tradition degenerated (partially as a result of changes in the language itself), or, again, it may be that Layamon and the others, perhaps additionally influenced by the "rhythmic alliteration" of Anglo-Saxon prose, imperfectly revived the old forms. Such a revival (variously explained) did occur in the later Middle Ages, yielding, for example, the alliterative *Morte Arthure* mentioned above.

Another feature that Layamon's *Brut* shares with the earlier Anglo-Saxon poetry is the presence of repeated lines and half-lines called *formulas*. Examples have been collected by Tatlock and Herbert Pilch, who also lists formulas that the *Brut* shares with Anglo-Saxon verse and with roughly contemporary verse. Formulas are present in much of the world's traditional narrative poetry, the recurrent epithets in Homer perhaps being the best-known examples. Earlier in this century, the Homeric scholar Milman Parry, supplementing his research with fieldwork on contemporary Yugoslavian oral epic, developed what is known as oral-formulaic theory to account for this widespread appearance of formulas. According to Parry and his student Albert Lord, formulas are learned by apprentice poets as a means whereby they may improvise long oral narratives. This theory has since been applied to Old English and some Middle English verse, even though many of Parry's original statements have had to be modified considerably. For example, Layamon as a translator is not improvising but rather working in close conjunction with a written text (even if he probably worked more "in his head" than modern poets tend to do). Why, then, would he have a need for ready-made formulas? He may instead have been using formulas ornamentally, in imitation of the earlier models, or there may have been other factors at work which made formulas desirable. Layamon seems to have been constrained to avoid ending his sentence units with the first half-line (as had often been the case in the earlier poetry). Formulas, which are more frequent in his second half-lines, may have represented a useful way to "pad out" the whole line, acting somewhat like the "rhyme tags" in metrical romances. Layamon's use of formulas differs in other ways from Anglo-Saxon practice. Fixed epithets, such as "athelest kingen" for Arthur, are more common, as are formulas that recur in similar situations, such as "wind stod an willen," often used in sea voyage descriptions.

Rhyme was likewise employed ornamentally in the Early Middle English poems mentioned above, prompting some scholars to hypothesize that rhyme was developing independently in England, probably under influence from Latin hymns. Surely the example of Wace strengthened this tendency toward the couplet, which would become the norm in rhymed romances. There may also be an Irish influence at work in Layamon's unusual rhyming by consonant classes and on contrasting stresses. Here are some sample rhyme-pairs, modernized from the episode of Arthur's final dream (13971ff.): bestride/ride; tiding/king; son/welcome; fair knight/fare tonight. The first rhyme is exact; the second example rhymes an unstressed with a stressed syllable as does the third; yet here the consonants *m* and *n* do not match, but are related instead by way of a shared phonological class ("nasals"). The last example ingeniously interweaves homonyms and rhymes.

One final stylistic element distinguishing Layamon from his Anglo-Saxon predecessors is his use of the extended simile. Arthur's pursuit of Colgrim, for example, is compared (for eight lines, 10629ff.) to a wolf hunting down a mountain goat. Most of Layamon's extended similes, in fact, occur in this part of the Arthurian section, leading scholars to suppose that a single source may be responsible for this stylistic feature. Here, as elsewhere, however, the question of sources should not be allowed to overshadow Layamon's unique achievement. The *Brut* can and should be read for its own merits, as a poem and not simply as "Arthurian matter" divorced from its particular form.

Bibliography
Brook, G. L. *Selections from Layamon's Brut*, 1963.
Brook, G. L., and R. F. Leslie. *Layamon: Brut*, 1963, 1978.
Fletcher, R. H. *The Arthurian Material in the Chronicles*, 1906.
Friedlander, C. "The Structures and Themes of Layamon's *Brut*," 1973 (dissertation).
Hall, Joseph, ed. *Layamon's Brut*, 1924.
Madden, F. *Layamon's Brut*, 1847.
Mason, Eugene, tr. *Arthurian Chronicles: Wace and Layamon*, 1962.
Pilch, Herbert. *Layamon's Brut*, 1960.
Tatlock, J. S. P. "Epic Formulas, Especially in Layamon," in *PMLA*. XXXVIII (1923), pp. 494-529.
_____ . "Layamon's Poetic Style and Its Relations," in *Manly Anniversary Studies*, 1923.
_____ . *The Legendary History of Britain*, 1950.

Paul Acker

EDWARD LEAR

Born: Holloway, England; May 12, 1812
Died: San Remo, Italy; January 29, 1888

Principal collections

A Book of Nonsense, 1846, 1861; *Nonsense Songs, Stories, Botany and Alphabets*, 1871; *More Nonsense, Pictures, Rhymes, Botany, etc.*, 1872; *Laughable Lyrics: A Fourth Book of Nonsense Poems, Songs, Botany, Music, etc.*, 1877; *Nonsense Songs and Stories*, 1894; *Queery Leary Nonsense*, 1911 (Lady Strachey, editor); *The Complete Nonsense of Edward Lear*, 1947 (Holbrook Jackson, editor); *Teapots and Quails*, 1953 (Angus Davidson and Philip Hofer, editors).

Other literary forms

Edward Lear's verse collections include three prose stories and three prose recipes called "Nonsense Cookery." A few of his fanciful botanical drawings are accompanied by whimsical texts. Like his poems, these pieces show Lear at play with language, blithely disregarding common sense.

Two volumes of letters, most of them to Chichester Fortescue, were published in 1907 and 1911. Enlivened by riddles, cartoons, and bits of verse, they demonstrate Lear's fascination with the sound and meaning of words. He uses puns and creative phonetic spellings; he coins words and humorously distorts existing ones. A cold January day in Corfu is so "icicular" that it "elicits the ordibble murmurs of the cantankerous Corcyreans." He complains of the proliferation of tourists, especially "Germen, Gerwomen, and Gerchildren," around his property in San Remo. Although he often revealed his loneliness and depression, Lear characteristically found something to laugh about—if not in his situation, then in his response to it: he called himself "savage and black as 90,000 bears," and wished he were "an egg and was going to be hatched." In 1883 he wrote, "I sometimes wish that I myself were a bit of gleaming granite or pomegranite or a poodle or a pumkin"; at seventy-one and in ill health, Lear's imperishable delight in wordplay pulled him out of self-pity.

He kept journals of his painting excursions; these were later published with his own illustrations. Lacking the warmth and spontaneity of the letters, these topographical and travel books are valuable to readers who relish pictorial description and wish to know the conditions of travel in the last century.

Achievements

Lear thought of himself as a topographical landscape painter, but he is best known for the verses and cartoons he created to entertain children. He popularized the form which came to be known as the limerick. His innovative comic drawings have influenced many artists, notably James Thurber. Lear's ornithological drawings are highly regarded, and students of nineteenth century painting also admire his watercolor drawings—pen or pencil sketches executed out-of-doors and later elaborated and colored. Even so, his reputation as an author has overshadowed his painting. Known as the father of nonsense literature, Lear has never been surpassed in that genre. Charles L. Dodgson (Lewis Carroll) had the opportunity to learn from Lear, and Lear may have learned from him; however, Carroll's nonsense verse is much different: funnier, more intellectual, and less musical. Lear was a true poet, keenly sensitive to the sounds and "colors" of words. His poems have lasted not only because they are amusing and melodious but also because they express the innocence, melancholy, and exuberance of Lear himself.

Biography

Edward Lear was the twentieth of twenty-one children born to Jeremiah and Ann (Skerrett) Lear. Financial difficulties led to the dispersal of the family; although the Lears were later reunited, from 1816 Edward was looked after by his oldest sister, Ann. She was devoted to him and encouraged his interest in reading and painting, but the near-sighted, homely, rather morbid child brooded over being rejected, as he saw it, by his mother. His diary alludes mysteriously to another early trauma, perhaps a homosexual assault. His inclination to isolate himself grew after the onset of epilepsy (he called it his "demon") when he was five years old. He always felt that he was not like other people.

At fifteen he was earning his own living as a draftsman. Within five years, his skill in drawing birds brought him to the attention of Lord Stanley (later the thirteenth Earl of Derby), who invited him to Knowsley to make drawings of his private menagerie. There he made acquaintances who would become lifelong patrons and began to create comical verses and drawings to amuse his host's children.

In 1837, the Earl sent him to Italy to recover his health and to study landscape painting. From that time England was no longer his permanent home. Lear traveled throughout the Mediterranean world and lived in several places, explaining his wandering by saying that his health required a temperate climate, that he needed to make sketches as "studies" for his oil paintings, and that he must support himself by making his work available to wealthy tourists. His restlessness also suggests that he was searching for, and perhaps trying to avoid, something: an all-consuming interest.

Amazingly industrious even by Victorian standards, Lear generally spent most of his day sketching or painting; in leisure hours he read widely and taught himself a half-dozen languages. Hard work seemed to help ward off depression and epileptic attacks but did not prevent his being lonely. For thirty years his only constant companion was his Albanian servant, Giorgio

Kokali, to whom Lear showed extraordinary kindness and loyalty. While busily preparing one set of illustrations for a travel book and another for a volume of natural history, he decided to publish the series of limericks he had begun at Knowsley. His painting gave him less satisfaction than his non-sense verse, which he wrote for the children of friends and for other youngsters he met in hotels and aboard ships. His verse became a vehicle for self-expression, while painting all too often meant drudgery and frustration. Upon receiving a legacy at the age of thirty-seven, he studied for a time at the Royal Academy, as if hoping to win recognition as a serious artist. Lear apparently had small regard for the watercolor drawings he produced by the hundreds: they were "pot-boilers" and "tyrants" that required much time yet brought little money. Although he sometimes sold large landscapes in oil and received modest sums for his books, he often worried about his finances and had to rely on the patronage of wealthy friends.

Lear tried to be independent, but he constantly suffered from loneliness. He maintained a voluminous correspondence with scores of friends, some-times rising early to write as many as thirty-five letters before breakfast. Occasionally he expressed wonder that "this child," an odd, moody fellow, should have so many friends. He confided in a few—Chichester Fortescue, Franklin Lushington, and Emily Tennyson (his ideal woman)—but even to them he could not reveal his dark memories or speak of his "demon." More than once he considered marriage but could never bring himself to propose, despite evidence that Augusta Bethell would have accepted him. Terrified of rejection, this charming and lovable man told himself and his confidants that he was too crotchety, ugly, poor, and sickly to be a good husband. Another impediment of which he may have been conscious was his tendency to homo-sexuality. His response to Lushington, a kind but undemonstrative person, can only be called passionate; for several years he fretted over Lushington's inability to give and receive affection. Emotional and spiritual intimacy were what he most craved, however, and his relationship with Lushington even-tually became mutually satisfying. Throughout his adult years, Lear seems to have been happiest in the company of children.

Haunted by a sense of failure and determined to put an end to his wan-dering, in 1871 he moved into a house he had built in San Remo. Yet he traveled to India after his sixtieth birthday, making hundreds of drawings, and talked of going a second time. His last years were darkened by loneliness, illness, and a series of disappointments. He finally lost the will to work when his eyesight failed and he was near collapse. None of his friends was with him when he died.

Analysis

According to Edward Lear himself, he adopted the form for his limericks— or "nonsense rhymes," as he called them—from "There was a sick man of

Tobago," published in *Anecdotes and Adventures of Fifteen Gentlemen* (c. 1822). Most of them begin with this formula: "There was an Old Man [or Old Person, Young Lady] of [place name]." The last line is nearly the same as the first, with Lear typically using an adjective (sometimes appropriate, sometimes whimsical) before the character's designation. Each limerick is accompanied by a cartoon of its main character in action—riding a goose, sitting in a tree, refusing to respond sensibly to a sensible question. More than three-quarters of the limericks concern old people; even some of those called "young" in the texts appear elderly in the drawings. Most of Lear's folk are eccentrics. One old man runs through town carrying squealing pigs; another will eat nothing but roots. Physical oddities such as very long legs or huge eyes are common. Several characters with noses even more prodigious than Lear's deal variously with that handicap: one hires an old woman to carry it, another allows birds to roost on it, while a third adamantly denies that his nose is long. Lear's intended audience, children of the Victorian age, were surely amused not just by his characters' oddness but also by the fact that these laughable people were supposed to be "grown-ups."

Lear often found humor in incongruity and arbitrariness. An old man of Dunrose, "melancholy" because his nose has been "seized" by a parrot half as large as himself, is said to be "soothed" upon learning that the bird's name is Polly. A few characters suffer terrible ends—drowning, suicide, choking on food, death from despair, being baked in a cake. Yet even their situations are amusing; either the text indicates that these people somehow deserve their fate, or the poem or cartoon indicates that they are not distressed by it. For example, the "courageous" Young Lady of Norway, flattened by a door, asks, "What of that?"

Lear's avowed purpose was to write "nonsense pure and absolute" for the amusement of "little folks." Consciously or not, he also dramatized the conflict between the individual and society. Even children must have noticed how often the limericks' heroes and heroines were at odds with the people around them. In Brill, Melrose, Parma, Buda, Columbia, and Thermopylae, and other real-world settings specified by Lear, "they"—representatives of Respectable Society—stare, turn aside, express disapproval, offer unwanted advice, and punish. A man who "dance[s] a quadrille with a Raven" is "smashed" by his countrymen; so is the fellow who constantly plays his gong. A fat man is stoned by the children of Chester. The reader is not surprised that one old man has "purchased a steed, which he rode at full speed,/ And escaped from the people of Basing." Aldous Huxley called Lear a "profound social philosopher" for his portrayal of the consequences of nonconformity (*On the Margin*, 1928). Lear's touch, however, was always light; even the limericks containing violence or death are not sad or horrific.

The eccentrics are more likely to be friendly with animals than with other human beings. They live with birds, ride bears, play music for pigs, and try to teach fishes to walk—but they can also be attacked by insects, bulls, and dogs (Lear was terrified of dogs). Apparently, being truly alive is a lonely, risky affair. Accidents, physical and mental afflictions, and rejection by others, all in the nature of things, seem especially likely for the person who is different from his neighbors. Yet, unpredictably, "they" are sometimes solicitous and considerate, inquiring about the comfort of some irascible characters, warning others of imminent danger. "They" treat a depressed man by feeding him salad and singing to him; "they" glue together a hapless fellow "split quite in two" by a fall from a horse. Lear's society, then, is committed to maintaining order and the general well-being—if necessary, at the expense of people who behave in ways "they" do not approve and cannot understand. This is the world we know. Without the preachiness of much contemporary children's literature—or rather, literature written for the edification of children—the limericks convey that civil, mannerly behavior is expected. From Lear's perspective, as from the child's, adult judgments appear arbitrary. For some reason, or no reason, "they" are delighted with a girl named Opsibeena who rides a pig; "they" seem less likely to appreciate innovation than to encourage decorum, however meaningless: one man ingratiates himself with his neighbors by sitting in his cellar under an umbrella.

The nonsense songs are set in an imagined world in which animals and objects talk, sing, and dance with one another. Some of these characters are heroes; others are bored and lonely misfits. Like Lear, an early admirer of Lord Byron, they seek happiness in love, companionship, and travel. Odd friendships and courtships, mysterious events, and unexpected reversals abound. Lear has created a world in which anything wonderful may happen. The rules of decorum do not apply, do not exist. An owl marries a pussycat, and the Poker woos the Shovel. The title characters in "The Daddy Long-Legs and the Fly," unwelcome in polite society, sail away to "the great Gromboolian Plain," where they spend their days at "battlecock and shuttledoor." Disgusted with idleness, a Nutcracker and a Sugar-tongs ride off on stolen ponies, never to return—ignoring the protests of their household companions. Less adventurous, a perambulating table and chair ask some friendly animals to lead them safely home. Most successful in their quest are the Jumblies of the green heads and blue hands. Despite the warnings of "all their friends" (akin to the limericks' "they"), the Jumblies go to sea in a sieve, discover "the Lakes, and the Torrible Zone,/ and the hills of the Chankly Bore," and return home after twenty years to be lionized by their neighbors. Unlike most of Lear's songs, "The Jumblies" has no undercurrent of melancholy or dread.

A wanderer for most of his life, Lear often wished for (but doubted that he really wanted) a home with a wife and children. His "laughable lyrics," which sometimes poke fun at the conventional sex roles, courtship rituals, and marriage, reveal that he was ambivalent about committing himself to a woman. As George Orwell remarked in his essay "Nonsense Poetry," "It is easy to guess that there was something seriously wrong in [Lear's] sex life" (*Shooting an Elephant and Other Essays*, 1950). More recent critics, reading nonsense literature as a manifestation of the author's repressed emotions, have noted that it is the pussycat, not the owl, who proposes matrimony; judging by Lear's cartoon, the owl is somewhat afraid of his bride. Again, a duck (a cigar-smoking female) talks a rather effeminate kangaroo into letting her ride around the world on his tail. Deserted by the girl he loves, the sorrowful title character in "The Dong with a Luminous Nose" wanders in lonely frustration; at night his great red nose, illuminated by a lamp "All fenced about/ With a bandage stout," is visible for miles. In pre-Freudian times this poem was surely "laughable" in a simpler way than it is now. The hero of "The Courtship of the Yonghy-Bonghy-Bò" proposes to a married woman; when she regretfully refuses him, he flees to "the sunset isles of Boshen" to live alone. Remaining in Coromandel, "where the early pumpkins blow," the lady "weeps, and daily moans." So romantic and comical an ending would have been impossible if the Bò had offered himself to a woman who was free to marry him. "The Courtship of the Yonghy-Bonghy-Bò," one of the songs for which Lear composed a piano accompaniment, uses the verbal music of repetition, assonance, and alliteration. Indeed, in this and other songs he achieves a lyricism reminiscent of the Romantic poets. Parodying the Romantic manner as he made verse out of personal concerns and fantasies, he was looking for a way to deal with his emotions. He once burst into tears while singing the song, written while he struggled to make up his mind about marrying "Gussie" Bethell.

To the Nutcrackers and Sugar-tongs, domesticity—perhaps the most sacred of Victorian ideals—is a "stupid existence." Home is sweet only to the timorous table and chair, the phobia-ridden Discobboloses, and the cautious Spikky Sparrows. Mr. and Mrs. Sparrow don human clothing, ostensibly to protect themselves from catching cold but actually, it seems, to "look like other people." Lear does portray some happy and admirable couples. In "The Pelican Chorus," King and Queen Pelican sing of their present joys and recall their daughter's courtship by the King of the Cranes. They are content, even though they realize that they will probably never see Daughter Dell again. A less skillful poet would have allowed the song to become maudlin or merely ridiculous, but Lear maintains a balance of melancholy, nostalgia, and humor. He reveals the singers' pride in their "lovely leathery throats and chins" and pleasure in the "flumpy sound" their feet make as they dance. (This kind of music is impossible for the crane who, it is whispered, "has got no webs between his toes.") They complacently visualize Dell's "waddling form so fair,/ With a wreath of shrimps in her short white hair." The old pelicans' confusion—or fusion—of past and present is at once amusing and poignant; each stanza ends with this refrain:

Ploffskin, Pluffskin, Pelican jee,

We think no Birds so happy as we!
Plumpskin, Ploshkin, Pelican jill,
We think so then, and we thought so still!

"Mr. and Mrs. Discobbolos," another poem about a family, ends with what must be described as an entertaining catastrophe. For twenty years this couple lives in peaceful isolation atop a wall—because they are afraid of falling off. Then, quite suddenly, the wife begins to fret because their "six fine boys" and "six sweet girls" are missing the pleasures and opportunities of social intercourse. Disgusted, perhaps driven mad, Mr. Discobbolos slides to the ground and dynamites home and family "into thousands of bits to the sky so blue." One feels that he has done the right thing, even though his action is surprising and mysterious. Possibly he cannot endure mixing once again with conventional society or thinking that any of his children may marry such a "runcible goose" as his wife. Perhaps the poet is once again exploding the myth of the happy home. The attempt to make sense out of exquisite nonsense is part of the pleasure of reading Lear.

No doubt he exposed more of his hopes and fears than he intended. Some of the songs, especially those written late in his life, involve the emotions in a way that the limericks do not. Since the poet sympathizes with the pain and joy of these creatures of fantasy, so does the reader. Two works published posthumously are clearly autobiographical. Lear's last ballad, "Incidents in the Life of My Uncle Arly," is a formal imitation of "The Lady of Shalott" which tells of the wanderings and death of a poor and lonely man. At last "they" bury him with a railway ticket (representing Lear's freedom and root-lessness) and his sole companion, a "pea-green Cricket" (symbolic, perhaps, of the poet's inspiration to make music of his own experience). Lear, the "Adopty Duncle" of many children, states four times that the hero's shoes are "far too tight." Among the many afflictions of the poet's last years were swollen feet. Arly's tight shoes may represent any of the constraints on the poet's happiness. Thomas Byrom has pointed out that Lear, like UncLE ARly, was a homeless traveler for more than forty years before building a villa in Italy (*Nonsense and Wonder*, 1977). Sad without being pessimistic, the poem characterizes a man whose life was lonely yet rich in experience.

Lear's "Eclogue" is the product of his capacity for making fun of his sorrows and his tendency to self-pity and grumbling. In this parody of a classical genre, the singing contest between shepherds, Lear and John Addington Symonds catalog their woes; the latter's wife, Catherine, finally judges whose miseries are greater. The "Eclogue" is laughable, but the reader of Lear's correspondence sees how truly it reflects his assessment of himself and his career; but *A Book of Nonsense* saw thirty editions in his lifetime.

Lear's pleasure in his verse is expressed most clearly in "The Quangle Wangle's Hat." Wearing a beaver hat one hundred and two feet wide, the title character sits sadly in a Crumpetty Tree, wishing (like Lear in San Remo) that someone would come to visit. Then he is approached by a series of exotic animals, some of them (like the Quangle Wangle himself) familiar from Lear's other writings. When they ask for permission to live on his hat, the hero welcomes each one. Enjoying a simple yet profound comradeship, an assembly of Lear's creatures blissfully dances "by the light of the Mulberry moon"— "and all [are] as happy as happy could be." Here in microcosm is Lear's imagined world, singularly free of conflict. The real world is not like this, but Lear persuades readers to imagine that it might be. Friendship and sharing of oneself offer the best hope of contentment in the fantasy world, as in the real one. The Quangle Wangle is Edward Lear.

Major publications other than poetry
   NONFICTION: *Illustrations of the Family of Psittacidae: Or, Parrots*, 1832; *Views in Rome and Its Environs*, 1841; *Illustrated Excursions in Italy*, 1846; *Journals of a Landscape Painter in Greece and Albania*, 1851; *Journals of a Landscape Painter in Southern Calabria and the Kingdom of Naples*, 1852; *Views in the Seven Ionian Islands*, 1863; *Journal of a Landscape Painter in Corsica*, 1870; *Lear in Sicily*, 1938; *Edward Lear's Indian Journal*, 1953 (Ray Murphy, editor); *Edward Lear in Southern Italy*, 1964.

Bibliography
Bowra, C. M. *The Romantic Imagination*, 1961.
Brockway, J. T. "Edward Lear, Poet," in *Fortnightly Review*. CLXVII, n. s. (1950), pp. 334-339.
Hark, Ina Rae. "Edward Lear: Eccentricity and Victorian *Angst*," in *Victorian Poetry*. XVI (1978), pp. 112-122.
Jackson, Holbrook, ed. *The Complete Nonsense of Edward Lear*, 1947.
Noakes, Vivien. *Edward Lear: The Life of a Wanderer*, 1969.
Richardson, Joanna. "Edward Lear: Man of Letters," in *Ariel*. I (1970), pp. 18-28.

                                                                    Mary De Jong

DENISE LEVERTOV

Born: Ilford, England; October 24, 1923

Principal collections

The Double Image, 1946; *Here and Now*, 1957; *Overland to the Islands*, 1958; *5 Poems*, 1958; *With Eyes at the Back of Our Heads*, 1960; *The Jacob's Ladder*, 1961; *O Taste and See*, 1964; *City Psalm*, 1964; *Psalm Concerning the Castle*, 1966; *The Sorrow Dance*, 1967; *Penguin Modern Poets 9*, 1967 (with Kenneth Rexroth and William Carlos Williams); *In Praise of Krishna: Songs from the Bengali*, 1967 (translated with Edward C. Dimock, Jr.); *Three Poems*, 1968; *A Tree Telling of Orpheus*, 1968; *The Cold Spring and Other Poems*, 1968; *A Marigold from North Vietnam*, 1968; *Embroideries*, 1969; *Selected Poems of Guillevic*, 1969 (translation); *Relearning the Alphabet*, 1970; *Summer Poems/ 1969*, 1970; *A New Year's Garland for My Students, MIT 1969-70*, 1970; *To Stay Alive*, 1971; *Footprints: Poems*, 1972; *The Freeing of the Dust*, 1975; *Chekhov on the West Heath*, 1977; *Life in the Forest*, 1978; *Collected Earlier Poems: 1940-1960*, 1979.

Other literary forms

Denise Levertov's essays, reviews, talks, workshop lectures, and short stories have been collected in *The Poet in the World* (1973), *Conversations in Moscow* (1973), and *Light Up the Cave* (1981). Another short story was published by Albondocani Press in 1968. She is recorded with other poets on *Today's Poets 3* (Folkways). She has translated *Selected Poems of Guillevic* (1969), translated and edited *In Praise of Krishna: Songs from the Bengali* with Edward C. Dimock, Jr. (1967), and edited *Out of the War Shadow: The Peace Calendar of 1968* for the War Resisters League. She is a major figure in the peace movement today, protesting both in person and in poems against war and the threat of nuclear devastation.

Achievements

Levertov's unique poetic voice results from the formal fusion of her English literary and religious background with the American imagist-objectivist practice of William Carlos Williams and the allied theories of projectivist verse enunciated by Charles Olson and Robert Creeley. Kenneth Rexroth and Robert Duncan also influenced her early career. Her poetry is distinguished by a commitment to the authentic particulars of her experience as well as to a large vision of the human world. New Directions has published her books since 1960, and her poems have appeared in innumerable "little" magazines. She has been Poetry Editor of *The Nation*, Honorary Scholar at the Radcliffe Institute for Independent Study, and recipient of the Bess Hokin Prize, the

Harriet Monroe Memorial Prize, the Inez Boulton Prize, the Morton Dauwen Zabel Prize, the Longview Award, and the Lenore Marshall Prize. She has had two grants from the National Institute of Arts and Letters and a Guggenheim Fellowship. Colby College and the University of Cincinnati have awarded her the degree of D. Litt. She has taught at many colleges and universities and is popular among students for her activism. Not an "ivory tower" poet, Levertov interweaves the public with the private, the political with the personal in her poems. Her technical strength—an excellent example for young writers—comes from her use of the accurate image in a spare, energetic, musically formed line. Her craft, her commitment, and the extent of her oeuvre make her one of America's most important living poets.

Biography

Denise Levertov was born in Ilford, Essex, outside London, in 1923, the daughter of the Reverend Phillip Paul Levertoff, an Anglican clergyman, Jewish by birth, who was descended from Schneour Zalman, a noted early nineteenth century mystic called "The Rav of Northern White Russia," and Beatrice Spooner-Jones, whose great-grandfather was the Welsh tailor and mystic, Angell Jones of Mold. Denise had a sister, Olga, nine years older than she. Both daughters were educated at home by their mother, by educational BBC broadcasts, and by reading in their father's library. Levertov's only formal education was a period spent at a ballet school immediately before World War II. She served as a nurse during the war, published her first book of poems, *The Double Image*, in 1946, and then met and married the young American novelist Mitchell Goodman in 1947. After traveling in Europe, they came to America in 1948. Their son Nikolai was born in 1949.

They returned to Europe in 1950 on the G.I. Bill and lived for two years in Provence, France. Robert Creeley and his family lived nearby. Levertov began to read American poets extensively, especially Williams, and to discuss contemporary poetry with Creeley. Her second book, *Here and Now*, was published by City Lights in San Francisco in 1957 and was highly praised by Kenneth Rexroth. Her name then became associated with Allen Ginsberg and the "Beats," who were also published by City Lights. Although she never taught at Black Mountain College, her poems were published in *The Black Mountain Review* and by Cid Corman in *Origin*, so her name also became linked with the Black Mountain poets. Established as a poet of stature, she has written prolifically, adhering to the use of the direct image in the tradition of Ezra Pound and Williams but also pressing toward clarification of what is ineffable, "beyond," through invocations of memory, dream, and the "inscape" of natural objects expressed in language both colloquially modern and resonant of the Bible and classical English literature.

Levertov and her family lived in Mexico for a while in the 1960's. From 1964 on, she began to teach. She taught at the YM-YWHA Poetry Center in

New York in 1964, at the City College of New York in 1965, and at Vassar College in 1966-1967. During this period, she became active in the anti-Vietnam War movement. In 1967, her husband was indicted, along with Benjamin Spock and others, for allegedly illegal antiwar activity. She was teaching at the University of California, Berkeley, during the People's Park protests of 1968-1969 and sided actively with the protesters. In 1970, she traveled to Moscow and, in 1972, visited Hanoi with the poet Muriel Rukeyser. She was divorced from Mitchell Goodman in the mid-1970's. At present (1982), she continues to teach and to be active in the anti-nuclear war movement.

Analysis

Denise Levertov's poetic career can be roughly divided into three phases: a period of maturation from the 1940's to the mid-1960's; an anti-Vietnam War period from approximately 1964 to 1974; and the most recent period—postwar, post-marriage—from around 1975 to the present. From the beginning her poems manifested a sense of sanity and an appreciation of the world, sensitively uniting meticulous craft with large human concerns in a balanced poetic order. The horrors of the Vietnam War wrenched her out of that balance into a raw, pained poetic mode in which attention to craft was sometimes supplanted by her anger at torture and injustice and by her longing for revolutionary change. After the end of the war (and after her divorce), her poems resume composure and deepen in reflectiveness, and her political passion is interwoven with renewed attention to her perennial poetic motifs: love, commitment to art, woman's experience, life as journey, dreams, the mystical, and throughout all, a grappling with the fact of death.

When she began as a lyric poet in England in the 1940's, hardly out of her teens, Levertov almost inevitably had to be concerned with love in the Christian sense of *agapé*, *caritas* as well as individual and romantic love. In the earliest poems, the word "love" (as well as "dream," "life," and "time") is rather too often summoned as an abstract counter to provide a climactic ending. After she married, moved to America, and came under the influence of William Carlos Williams' objectivist technique, she used the word "love" more sparingly, but employed images to evoke the sense of tender joy in her husband, family, and domestic life. Erotic love is often expressed in images of the natural world—trees, flowers, water—which invest it with a Garden-of-Eden innocence and link the erotic with the poet's pleasure in everyday objects, a pleasure which stems from her insight into their power to make explicit the meaning implicit in themselves.

This attention to objects as revelatory comes from Williams' dictum "No ideas but in things" and forms the backbone of her craft, a strong reliance on the specific visual image. The art of poetry is thus seen as integrally related to clear seeing, to sight as prior and essential to insight. The poems opening her volume *With Eyes at the Back of Our Heads* may almost be read as a sequence exploring the relationship of the quotidian "thing" to the unseen or ineffable vision which haunts the poet and leads her on, an almost religious vision of ultimate meaning in ultimate beauty.

This volume begins with a translation of a Toltec poem, "The Artist," as her manifesto of commitment in poetry to the union of the emotional, the intellectual, the aesthetic, and the moral. In her life in Mexico at this time, her artistic Toltec "ancestor" has revivified the "line taut" between herself and her ancestors, the mystics Schneour Zalman and Angell Jones of Mold, described in the poem "Illustrious Ancestors" in *Overland to the Islands*. The actual mountain is seen with mystical eyes ("at the back of our heads") and so sets everyday experience in a meaningful perspective. A dress on a washline in the rain reminds her of her fear that she might forget her passion and vision, become "limp and clean, an empty dress," inundated by daily life ("The Five-Day Rain"). A lost cat suggests lost imagination to her;. she begs it to "come back, spring poems out of the whole/ cloth of silence." Silence (lack of poems) is an analogue of death, but quietness is not at all deathlike. The quiet surface of a lagoon is a reminder of what lies beneath the surface, the mind's depths where imagination swims like a fish. The poem "Pleasures" in like manner celebrates what lies beneath the surface, but the hidden itself is concrete and visual—the bone within the flesh of squid, the seed in the fruit *mamey*, the yellow glow in the throat of the blue morning glory.

This creative tension of polarities—cool and hot, hard and soft, sharp and yielding, seen and unseen—is the result of submitting to the stringencies of one's craft. In the poem "Art" (after Théophile Gautier), the poet is advised, in the metaphor of sculpture, to "Pit yourself against granite" and not to fall into easy rhythms, "Wear shoes that fit." It is important to "see again" and "break through" until the urge to live collaborates "as a mason" with art. In poetry, dream has to be made solid in substance; that is, in sensuous images and tight lines. Levertov sees this effort as a spiritual one, almost a secular religion for an age in which "the gods die every day," but "sovereign poems" live and have power. The fact of this power enables her to bear the return to the United States, to the "ashcan city," from Mexico, whose mountains had presented a more spiritual vision. Yet she never forgets that our minds and histories are not left behind in any place but are always with us in a "world indivisible."

Levertov's capacity to explore and tentatively harmonize contradictory emotions—the mature climax of this period—is revealed in the beautiful and moving "Olga Poems" of 1964 in *The Sorrow Dance*. These poems constitute one unified sequence mourning her sister Olga Levertoff, nine years her senior, also a poet and artist, who lived and died in extreme pain. The "Olga Poems" are Levertov's effort to "see again" with compassion the truth of her sister's life, and the "seeing" has to be done through the writing of the poem.

Levertov thinks of the poet as both "seer" and "maker," as she noted in a statement of her poetic for *The New American Poetry* (1960). The seer must also "communicate what he sees, that they who cannot see may see, since we are 'members one of another.'" The phrase "members one of another" from Romans 12:1 encapsulates Levertov's view of the interrelatedness and mutual responsibility of all members of society, but it also takes on a particular personal meaning in relation to her sister's death, since one's sister is like a "limb" or "member" of one's own body. Physical death is frightening, but even more terrifying is the "unlived life, of which one can die." The phrase is Rainer Maria Rilke's, repeated by Levertov in "From a Notebook" (1968) and in an essay "Dying and Living." Fear of the "unlived life" haunts the poet herself as she reenters in memory and dream her links with her sister's fate.

Poem I, the opening section of the "Olga Poems," is a graphic memory of the seven-year-old Denise, lying in bed, supposedly asleep but watching her sister, sixteen, undress. A sense of Olga's extremism is already hinted at through the sensuous extremes of firelight and darkness, Olga's olive skin scorched red but her nipples dark, a contrast of red and black symbolic as well as literal. Curiosity about adult status, sexuality, and an awed sense of identity all testify to abundant life in the child, who, now grown, painfully realizes that her sister's body at this moment lies rotting in the earth.

In Poem II, the emphasis switches from visual to aural, from the young woman's body to her later unpleasant nagging voice when she has become "ridden, ridden." The contrasting attitudes of the sisters emerges: Denise responds aesthetically to the Ley Street houses which Olga responds to only with moral rage as "slum." Repetitions form an elegiac thread throughout the poem, creating a liturgical effect. "Black one, black one," says the poet to her sister, referring not only to her coloring but also to her "black" mood of rage which is related to the deadliness of the "unlived life." The repetition has a tender effect as well, as the poet says there was compassion, "a white candle," burning in her sister's heart.

"*Everything flows*," a phrase, reminiscent of Heraclitus, repeated by Olga, forms a *leitmotiv* in Poem III, where the poet remembers her sister directing the theatricals and turning the actors, her friends, into "alien semblances," as she becomes alien to her family. To bridge the gap between herself and this disturbing alter ego, the child Denise remembers a line they both loved from the hymnbook, "Time like an ever-rolling stream/ bears all its sons away." The theme of impermanence is embodied in the image of water, time flowing like a river toward death.

The river of time is gentle, however, in comparison to the "rolling dark oncoming river" of dread which began to flow over Olga at this time. A religious fear or sense of sin infected Olga's normality, and at the end of this poem, dark and light again are metaphors for Olga's extremism. They are metaphysical, and ironic too, since Olga considers ordinary life as "dark" and her own mad "rage for order" as a new "light" which will save the world. The third subsection of Poem III, the midpoint of the sequence if one thinks of it as written in nine sections, embodies a dream which is parallel to and close to being a parody of the lovely simple memory of Poem I. Here "black one" describes a vision of Olga as "incubus," used in its full religious meaning of the Devil disguised as a human being. The dream—the poet's projection— reveals an ugly, warped person whose self-ravaging attitudes have made her dye her hair blonde, an allusion both to Olga's involvement in theater and to her destructively reversed value system. Levertov has always set store by dreams, often incorporating them in poems; the power of this dream, there- fore, brings the poet back into her sister's skin, to a human identification with her, so that, in Poem IV, which details Olga's final illness, the key repeated word is "love," creating a buried subtext, as if the poet were saying over and over, "I love you." As Olga lies dying, "pain and drugs/ quarrelled like sisters" in her, revealing the antipathy mingled with love between them. The past, however, is "burned out," leaving only that "kind candle" of compassion. The hymnbook line named here invokes God as compassionate, holding out his "everlasting arms," and as in the writing of this poem the poet is also holding out her arms in reconciliation, leading to a vision of apotheosis in Poem VI.

Here Olga is seen as a pagan goddess carved in olivewood; the artist's eye has made her shapely and comely. The word "eyes" is repeated like a litany, underlining the poet's urgent desire to *see* her sister in the form of her true self, not the mad self. She cannot forget her sister's brown eyes. Gone are the extremes of black and white, replaced by gold and golden brown. The metaphors of time's river and the Heraclitean flow are subsumed in the image of the actual river Roding of their childhood home, whose bridge also connects past and present through memory. Her sister's life and death were mysterious, but the poet hopes that behind the eyes of the goddess lies a vision of "festive goodness" which would amount to a pagan resurrection from the double death of a denied life and a pain-filled dying. In the "Olga Poems," the sense of organic connection between form and content rises from the intersubjective power of the relationship between the sisters and provides the bond between polarities which makes the poem one of Levertov's strongest.

Her capacity to balance extremes, however, is shaken and sometimes lost in the poems from the mid-1960's to the early 1970's, in the volumes *Relearning the Alphabet, To Stay Alive,* and *Footprints,* written under the pressure of the worsening Vietnam War and the heightening of protests against it. In "The Cold Spring," she speaks of an "amnesia of the heart" and appears to repudiate prior poems on minutely observed natural phenomena: the "Swing of the/ birch catkins" is "not enough." She wonders what she will do "if my poem is deathsongs," the strange use of the singular verb with the plural "songs" implying that the "poem" is her life. The sequence-poem "From a Notebook: October '68—May '69" is raw and blunt, ironically revealing an anger close to that which afflicted her sister. "Unlived life" haunts her; she is reminded of "Goldengrove unleaving" as autumn leaves fall, and (as Sr. Bernetta Quinn has pointed out) she, like the Margaret of Gerard Manley Hopkins' poem, is mourning for herself. The problem of death looms so large that writing poetry becomes small. Undigested prose is lumped into the "Notebook" almost as if shaping a poem were an antirevolutionary act. Once such a dichotomy between art and life has been established, the reader, of course, like the poet, chooses life. One feels a loss, however, despite admiration for Levertov's honesty. Despair and lack of concern for language or art is in itself a capitulation to the ugliness and inhumanity of prevailing attitudes.

With the ending of the Vietnam War, however, some easing of mind appears in Levertov's poems, although a number of poems in her 1975 volume *The Freeing of the Dust* date from her Hanoi visit of 1972 and express the enormous impact of her direct contact with the war victims. An old theme reappears: appreciation of solitude. She does not forget the war victims, but she is not guilt-ridden, either. In solitude, she discovers that some happiness comes each day, rising from "the heart's/ peat-bog darkness."

After the end of her marriage, solitude also gives her space to think and to find strength in herself, as attested to in the lovely three-poem sequence "Living Alone." Here, ordinary objects take on mysterious sheen in "the silvery now of living alone." Memories of childhood's sense of new beginnings, evoking "childhood's song" in her, restore her innate gentleness and equilibrium. Not every day, however, seems to offer song; some days offer only silence, as the tree near her window which might offer leaves seems to have no buds. The simple natural fact stated here, as in classical Chinese poems, without comment, carries symbolic weight. In the third poem, magic enters. She said the tree had no buds, and now, two days later, it is "flying on green wings," so she asks herself "What magic denial/ shall my life utter/ to bring itself forth?" Words *have* the gift of life. She has begun to shake off her bondage to "the fine art of unhappiness."

Her most recent book, *Life in the Forest*, continues her reaffirmation of the power of art. The long sequence-poem "Metamorphic Journal" can be seen as a parallel to the "Olga Poems," although in it the effort of writing is undertaken in order to resolve the grief of losing a lover. Childhood memories open Part I—December: how she hugged trees as a child and always put her feet in water, which is described in images reminiscent of Olga's Roding as well as of the lagoon in Mexico. Water is the image she uses for this slippery lover, "never at a standstill"; the metamorphoses of the river provide metaphors for aspects of the relationship. While she has always wanted to "fall into" the water, she also admits, in Part II—February, that the stream might be shallow, unable to bear her; she swears, however, that she will follow to where it is deep, as she is always looking "for the sea." Part III takes up the tree image again, and asks how the "trees" (beings) to which she felt drawn in the past are like the present "tree," thinking of tree both as lover and as the immovable core of self. "Sapling," however, is the too self-effacing word that she uses for herself, skirting recognition of the fact that she is not weak, although the relationship is.

Levertov elevates the lover mythically through dreaming of him and by picturing him as a prehistoric hunter in some Lascaux cavern; but elegance of language, strength of desire, and mastery of technique cannot mask the fact that the poet's imagination has invented the lover. The "Olga Poems" were informed by knowledge and depth of shared experience with which this transitory love affair cannot compete, no matter how beautifully it is described. The poet is stronger than her subject in life, and that is the strength of her poems. The "Olga Poems" are powerful because Olga Levertoff, her life and death, were no merely verbal invention; yet without her sister's words no meaning could be assigned to them.

The title of Levertov's most recent volume, *Candles in Babylon*, explicitly revives the motif of the "candle of compassion," which was introduced in the Olga poems. That candle is burning in everyone, but it is in danger of being extinguished in a world of nuclear madness. Fear and rage at death informs these latest poems as it has earlier ones, sometimes distorting them; the poet's strength of concrete imagery is sometimes lost. The poem "Unresolved" opens with an appropriate expression of confusion: is the life-destroying force in the world dominant over the life-giving force? Yet, this doubt is not sustained enough to prevent overstatements such as "Fools and criminals rule the world" and the poem's refrain: "We know no synthesis." All human beings live a synthesis of life and death; poetry—language beyond concept—is what sustains the human mind and heart in this painfully uncertain state. Levertov's poems are therefore best when they deal with doubt, as in the stately poem "Mass for the Day of St. Thomas Didymus," the saint known as "Doubting Thomas." By using the six sections of the traditional mass, Levertov releases herself into a wide range of feelings and questionings of the strength of the Christian God, Jesus the savior. He is a "dim star"; humans must shield *him*, a "spark/ of remote light." This spark is the little light of compassion that must be treasured and encouraged in the human world. It is the one tiny hope that Levertov experiences in the midst of desolation, sadness, and increasing human depravity.

Not every poem in this volume draws on the public arena; several continue an earlier style of Levertov's and are based on dreams, whose specific images give them strength, but even the beautiful dream of her mother, "Visitant," does not dispel her grief. In the personal realm also, her sense of herself takes on a somewhat negative though also humorous cast in the sequence "Pig

Dreams," another consequence of her preoccupation with the degradation of the world from which she cannot personally escape.

Although Levertov has become a mourner, sometimes gentle and sometimes infuriated, death-haunted and sometimes blinded by anger, her intensity and commitment remain inspiring. This poet need not fear that her life is unlived. She lives intensely, both as seer and maker, continuing to attempt to balance those recalcitrant yet interdependent extremes, language and reality.

Major publications other than poetry

MISCELLANEOUS: *The Poet of the World*, 1973; *Conversations in Moscow*, 1973; *Light Up the Cave*, 1981.

Bibliography

Mersmann, James. *Out of the Vietnam Vortex*, 1974.

Mills, Ralph J. *Contemporary American Poets*, 1966.

Rexroth, Kenneth. *Assays*, 1961.

_____ . *American Poetry in the Twentieth Century*, 1971.

Wagner, Linda W. *Denise Levertov*, 1967.

Wilson, Robert A. *A Bibliography of Denise Levertov*, 1972.

Jane Augustine

PHILIP LEVINE

Born: Detroit, Michigan; January 10, 1928

Principal collections

On the Edge, 1963; *Not This Pig*, 1968; *Thistles*, 1970; *5 Detroits*, 1970; *Pili's Wall*, 1971; *Red Dust*, 1971; *They Feed, They Lion*, 1972; *1933*, 1974; *On the Edge and Over*, 1976; *The Names of the Lost*, 1976; *Ashes: Poems Old and New*, 1979; *7 Years from Somewhere*, 1979; *One for the Rose*, 1981.

Other literary forms

Philip Levine has published a collection of interviews, *Don't Ask* (1981), in the University of Michigan's "Poets on Poetry" series.

Achievements

Levine's most important achievements are the two books of poetry *Not This Pig* and *They Feed, They Lion*. In the best poems of these two books, he reflects the influence of the surrealist and political poets of Spain and South America and takes on the subject of the city with a remarkable vitality. Along with James Wright, Allen Ginsberg, Denise Levertov, and Robert Bly, Levine has managed to incorporate politics into his poetry, going far beyond the immediate protest reaction to the Vietnam War. He writes about the working poor without condescension and with an empathy that puts him clearly in the tradition of Walt Whitman and William Carlos Williams; these poems are often about survivors, people who have suffered, but who are courageous and do not quit.

Biography

Philip Levine was born in Detroit of Russian-Jewish immigrant parents; his experiences of the Depression and World War II in that city play a central role in his poetry. In an interview Levine has said that he spent most of his childhood fighting against people who attacked him because he was a Jew. His father died when he was young (apparently in 1933, according to the poem entitled "1933"), and both his parents often appear in his many poems that explore the past. According to Levine, the workers he knew as a child and as a young man had a great effect on him, and various immigrant anarchists had a lasting effect on his politics. He married Frances Artley in 1954, and they have three sons, Mark, John, and Theodore.

Since Levine often writes from personal experience, it is possible to draw a picture of him and his relationship from his poems. There are many poems about his grandparents, parents, brother, sister, wife, and each of his three sons. Not all of the "facts" in his work, however, may necessarily be true.

The poems do reveal much about the writer, but the poet's tendency to fictionalize must be kept in mind.

After a number of jobs, including working in a foundry, Levine attended Wayne State University, where he studied under John Berryman, receiving a B.A. degree in 1950 and an M.A. in 1955. He refused to serve in the Korean War, and although this was clearly a political protest on his part, he was declared 4-F for psychological reasons. He received a Master of Fine Arts in Creative Writing from the University of Iowa in 1957 and won a fellowship to attend Stanford University. He has taught at California State University, Fresno, since 1958. He has won a number of awards for teaching. He has given readings of his poetry throughout the United States, often revealing a comic side of his character that is not obvious in his poetry. He has won a number of poetry awards, most significantly the Lenore Marshall Award for *The Names of the Lost*, the National Book Critics Circle Award for *Ashes* and *7 Years from Somewhere*, and the American Book Award for *Ashes*.

He was actively opposed to the Vietnam War, and his first trip to live in Spain in the late 1960's was taken, in part, to escape from America. In Spain the Levines lived near the Catalan city of Barcelona, the stronghold of the anarchists during the Civil War, a city that Levine has said reminds him of the Detroit of his childhood. He has had an interest in the Spanish Civil War for many years, sympathizing with the losing Republicans but identifying with the anarchists rather than the Communists or Socialists, and he has made Spain and that war the subject of some of his most memorable poems.

Analysis

When Philip Levine issued a new version of his first book *On The Edge*, he added to the title the words *and over*, declaring the direction of his dark and fierce poetry. His poems examine a world of evil, loneliness, and loss, where a poem entitled "Hymn to God in My Sickness" can only be a cry of unbelief. Paradoxically, there is a strong faith in human nature running throughout Levine's work. His is a poetry of community that at times holds out some distant but powerful dream of a better society. Often this is dramatized in the lives of the anarchists of the Spanish Civil War, celebrating their nobility and courage. His work expresses admiration for those who suffer but do not give in, those who fight against prejudice and pain. Many of his poems employ a second-person voice, and although they often have specific addresses, they are also addressed to the reader as a brother or sister to say "Your life is mine."

Levine is one of the most overtly urban poets in America today. His hometown of Detroit—its factories and foundries, its dead-end jobs, its dirt and smoke, its dying lives—plays a central part in his imagination. It is the city he escaped from—or tried to—to Fresno, California, a place often depicted by him as lonely and sad, a silent place where "each has his life/ private and sealed." Then there is the third city—Barcelona, Spain, where Levine often seems most at home, where he feels a greater sense of community and history, even though he carries what he sees as the political burden of America with him.

The second poem in Levine's first book, *On the Edge*, "Night Thoughts over a Sick Child," sets off a central image and theme of his work, presenting the speaker helpless before the boy's suffering, with no faith in the efficacy of prayer. He finds the situation intolerable and refuses to justify it in any way:

> If it were mine by one word
> I would not save any man,
> myself or the universe
> at such cost: reality.

There is nothing for him to do but to face "the frail dignity/ of surrender." The mixture of suffering and helplessness, anger and sadness, points toward many of Levine's later poems.

In this early volume Levine is writing rather formal poetry, metrical or syllabic, with rhymes or off-rhymes. In poems about World War II and the Algerian War, he shows his concern for the public causes of suffering. In "Gangrene" he draws an ugly picture of torture, "the circus of excrement," and ends with a self-righteous address to the reader as being secretively thrilled by these descriptions of torture even though he fakes boredom. In later volumes Levine achieves a more satisfactory tone of identification with suffering of this kind.

Probably the best poem in *On the Edge* is "For Fran," a picture of the poet's wife as gardener, an image that appears also in later poems. She is seen preparing the flower beds for winter, and she becomes for the poet the person who bears the promise of the future: "Out of whatever we have been/ We will make something for the dark." These final lines can be taken as a kind of motto for Levine's later poetry, his attempt to make something in the face of the dominant darkness.

Levine's second volume, *Not This Pig*, is the key work in his development as a poet. There are some poems that are like the tightly ordered style of *On the Edge*, but a number of them indicate a new direction—more open, riskier, and more original. The fact that he is moving away from syllabics and rhyme— as did most poets of his generation in the 1960's—is not the main source of this originality; but a more daring language is in evidence, opening his work to a wider and deeper range.

His poem "The Midget," drawing on his experiences in Spain, is a fine example of this new range. In a café where the anarchists planned the burning of the bishop of Zaragoza, the speaker sits on a December day—off-season, no tourists—amidst the factory workers and other laborers. A midget in the bar begins to sing of how he came from southern Spain "to this terrible/ Barcelona," telling them all that he is "big in the heart, and big down/ here, big where it really counts." The midget confronts the speaker with talk of his sexual prowess and insists that he "feel this and you'll believe." The speaker tries to turn away from him, buy him off with a drink, but the midget insists, tugging at him and grabbing his hand. The midget ends up sitting in his lap, singing of "Americas/ of those who never left." The others in the bar turn away in disgust, and then the drunken speaker begins to sing to the midget. In the final section, the poem goes beyond anecdote, stepping off into an eerie, mysterious world where the midget and the speaker merge in their opposition. They are both singers, old world and new, both strangers and outcasts. They come together in the brotherhood of freaks, the pain of being human.

The title of this volume comes from a brilliant tour de force "Animals Are Passing from Our Lives," a poem told from the point of view of a pig. At first the pig seems complacent, going off to market "suffering children, suffering flies,/ suffering the consumers." He has no intention, however, of giving in, playing the human fool as the boy who drives him along believes he will. He will not "turn like a beast/ cleverly to hook his teeth/ with my teeth. No. Not this pig." This can be taken as a kind of slogan for the entire book, Levine's "Don't tread on me." In a somewhat similar vein is the poem "Baby Villon," about a 116-pound fighter who was robbed in Bangkok because he was white, in London because he was black; he does not give in—not this pig—he fights back. Different as they are, the poet and Villon become one: "My imaginary brother, my cousin,/ Myself made otherwise by all his pain."

Levine identifies with these tough losers, even though he admits that their pains are greater than his, their toughness surpassing his. His attitude toward suffering can be summed up in his often-anthologized poem, "To a Child Trapped in a Barbershop." In mock seriousness he tells the six-year-old that his case is hopeless, advising him not to drink the Lucky Tiger because "that makes it a crime/ against property and the state." "We've all been here before," he informs the boy: we have all suffered the fears of the barbershop and the sharp instruments, but "we stopped crying." The boy should do the same; that is, welcome the world of experience, its difficulties, fears, and pains.

In his next full-length volume, *They Feed, They Lion,* and in the chapbooks *Red Dust* and *Pili's Wall,* Levine pushes further the discoveries that were made in poems such as "The Midget." As he said in his statement in *Contemporary Poets of the English Language,* he was influenced by the surrealistic Spanish and South American poets Miguel Hernández, Rafael Alberti, Pablo Neruda, and César Vallejo. These poets, as well as showing the way to a greater freedom of language, were political poets, all of them affected deeply by the Spanish Civil War. Possibly, though, the greatest reason for the renewed vigor of Levine's work is the discovery of his hometown, Detroit, as a subject for his poetry. This city is at the heart of *They Feed, They Lion*, and it provides the starting point for some of the finest of Levine's poems.

When Levine returns to the city in 1968 in the poem "Coming Home," he finds it an affront to nature, a riot-torn city with "the eyes boarded up," the auto factories' dirt and smoke dominate the hellish landscape: "We burn this city every day." In "The Angels of Detroit" sequence, however, the poet again and again expresses his sympathy for the workers, people such as Bernard:

> His brothers are factories and
> bowling teams, his mother is the
> power to blight, his father
> moves in all men like a threat,
> a closing of hands, an unkept
> promise to return.

Out of such beaten lives comes Levine's most remarkable poem, the title poem, "They Feed, They Lion." As that title illustrates, the poem breaks away from conventional language and syntax. It is a chant celebrating the workers who come "out of burlap sacks, out of bearing butter . . . out of creosote, gasoline, drive shafts, wooden dollies." "They lion grow," the refrain proclaims, "From 'Bow Down' come 'Rise Up.'" It is a cry of and for the workers, in praise of their resiliency and courage.

In the poem "Salami" Levine draws on his Spanish experience to praise the sausage and the culture it comes from. The poet draws a picture of a Spanish man rebuilding an old church all by himself, caring for his retarded child, and praying each night with "the overwhelming incense/ of salami." Then the poem returns to the speaker—so different from the old man— waking from a nightmare, full of guilt, fear, and chaos. He discovers his son sleeping peacefully, feeling that each breath of the boy carries a prayer for him, "the true and earthly prayer/ of salami." The salami gathers the figures of the poem into a community and draws from Levine an expression of reverence. It is an "earthly prayer," a praise of life in all its harshness and the beauty that, at times, comes from it.

After Levine had established his distinctive voice, he continued in a series of volumes—five in seven years—to mine the ore he had discovered in *They Feed, They Lion*. None of these later volumes have quite the excitement and explosiveness of the earlier ones, yet all of them contain excellent poems. During this period, Levine often moves back and forth between personal and political poems, although sometimes the personal and political merge.

Despite the difficulties of his life, despite encounters with prejudice and brutality, he often looks back with pleasure to the child who thought he could be happy. Now he knows that the earth will "let the same children die day/

after day." There is nothing one can do except "howl your name into the wind/ and it will blow it into dust." Everything is ashes and the best wish a man can make is to become "a fine flake of dust that moves/ at evening like smoke at great height/ above the earth and sees it all."

In the meantime, the poet seems to say, one can travel, looking for land-scapes of greater beauty and intensity than the bombed-out cities of America. In the poem "7 Years from Somewhere," Levine speaks of an experience, apparently in Morocco, where he was lost and a group of laughing Berber shepherds came to help him, even though they did not share a common language. One of the shepherds took his hand in an effort to communicate with him. After traveling on to "Fez, Meknes, Tetuan, Ceuta, Spain, Paris, here," he awakens to a world where no one takes his hand, and he remembers the shepherd's gesture:

> as one holds a blue egg
> found in tall grasses
> and smile and say something
> that means nothing, that
> means you are, you
> are, and you are home.

Human touch represents the hope that resides at the heart of many of Levine's best poems, and these poems show the way toward his directly political poetry. The poet Robert Bly, in "Leaping Up into Political Poetry," the Introduction to *Forty Poems Touching on Recent American History* (1970), argues that one has to be an inward poet to write about outward events successfully, that "the writing of political poetry is like the writing of personal poetry, a sudden drive by the poet inward." Levine fits this notion of political poetry better than any other American poet writing today, often exploring his own life while at the same time exploring the lives of the Spanish anarchists of the Civil War. He admits that someone else "who has suffered/ and died for his sister the earth" might have more to say than he, yet he feels the necessity to speak for those who have no other spokesman.

In "For the Fallen" Levine visits the graves in Barcelona of the leading anarchists who were executed during the war. After describing the sight of the graves amidst the noise of the city, he remembers himself as a schoolboy in Detroit going on with his own life at the same time that the heroes were killed. The boy and others trudging home from their dreary jobs knew, in some mysterious way, that there was an important relationship between them and the men in Barcelona. After all these years the feeling the poet has for these men can "shiver these two stiff/ and darkening hands."

A few reviewers have criticized Levine's later poetry for slipping into a kind of formula writing. The most negative criticism has come from Helen Vendler, who feels that in *One for the Rose*, Levine is controlled by a limited notion of realism and that the endings of many of his poems are sentimental. It is true that some of his recent memory poems follow an anecdotal pattern, familiar from earlier volumes, and that his critical success might have led him to write too much and too casually in recent years, yet he remains one of the most vivid poets writing today. No other contemporary poet in America has more imaginatively merged public and private emotions; no other poet today speaks more strongly of the mysteries of the lives of ordinary men and women.

Major publication other than poetry
NONFICTION: *Don't Ask*, 1981.

Bibliography
Mills, Ralph J., Jr. *Cry of the Human*, 1975.
Vendler, Helen. "All Too Real," in *The New York Review of Books*. XXVIII (December 17, 1981), pp. 32-36.
Yenser, Stephen. "Bringing It Home," in *Parnassus*. VI (Fall-Winter, 1977), pp. 101-117.

Michael Paul Novak

VACHEL LINDSAY

Born: Springfield, Illinois; November 10, 1879
Died: Springfield, Illinois; December 5, 1931

Principal collections

The Tramp's Excuse and Other Poems, 1909; *Rhymes to Be Traded for Bread*, 1912; *General William Booth Enters into Heaven and Other Poems*, 1913; *The Congo and Other Poems*, 1914; *The Chinese Nightingale and Other Poems*, 1917; *The Golden Whales of California and Other Rhymes in the American Language*, 1920; *The Daniel Jazz and Other Poems*, 1920; *Collected Poems of Vachel Lindsay*, 1923; *Going-to-the-Sun*, 1923; *Going-to-the-Stars*, 1926; *The Candle in the Cabin*, 1926; *Johnny Appleseed and Other Poems*, 1928; *Every Soul Is a Circus*, 1929; *Selected Poems of Vachel Lindsay*, 1931 (Hazelton Spencer, editor); *Selected Poems of Vachel Lindsay*, 1963 (Mark Harris, editor).

Other literary forms

Adventures While Preaching the Gospel of Beauty (1914) and *A Handy Guide for Beggars* (1916) are autobiographical accounts of Vachel Lindsay's walking tours, narratives that simultaneously articulate the populist ideals of his life and identify the sources for much of his poetry, the themes and characters that preoccupied him in the years before his great success. These and other prose works and designs are collected in *Adventures: Rhymes and Designs* (1968, Robert Sayre, editor); *Letters of Vachel Lindsay* (1979, Marc Chénetier, editor) offers a fair sampling of Lindsay's correspondence with the literary community after his fame was established. Lindsay produced quantities of broadsides and pamphlets on topics ranging from workers' rights in the mines, to racial injustice, to his own peculiarly passionate brand of Christianity. These, frequently set in frames of hieroglyphs of his own design, or scrawled sketches vaguely in the style of *art nouveau*, suggest both his wide-ranging ambition and his lack of focus, his mercurial temperament.

Achievements

Lindsay's achievements have always been measured by the size, enthusiasm, and attention of his audiences. The great recitals of the "higher vaudeville" poems of the 1910's aroused such enthusiasm that good critics responded with varying assessments: John Masefield, after meeting him in Indianapolis in 1916 and hearing him read in England in 1920, said flatly that Lindsay was "the best American poet"; whereas Ezra Pound, polite at first, finally dismissed Lindsay with the observation that one could write such stuff "as fast as one scribbles." Poets as various as William Butler Yeats, Robert Graves, Stephen Vincent Benét, and Theodore Roethke all saw Lindsay's work as

Masefield did, whereas Amy Lowell, Conrad Aiken, and many others not so politely scorned him. The difference of opinion, finally, has less to do with Lindsay's style than with the two basic ways of perceiving poetry: hearing and reading. Lindsay's accomplishment was that he could write good poetry that could be read aloud well. The language, themes, and implications of his verse were profoundly American; they canvassed American culture clearly, affectionately, and critically. He built his poetry on his "tramps" through the land as well as in the city, "tramps" which taught him to see, as Walt Whitman, Robert Frost, and Carl Sandburg did, the particulars of American life that defied sentimentality and generalization. When he invoked the gods, they were American heroes, the names that the folk he met knew and revered, both successes and failures: Abraham Lincoln, John Peter Altgeld, William Jennings Bryan, and John Chapman (Johnny Appleseed). Just as important, however, his poetry sang; it moved those who sounded it and those who heard it. His British audiences in 1920 heard the unfamiliar cadences of American speech in song and were astounded. His American audiences heard the rhythms and voices of their own culture, normally absent from the esoteric world of the "New Poetry." This balance of theme and song, of creed in distinctive rhythm, is Lindsay's most durable accomplishment. With it he achieves what Whitman seemed to predict for the twentieth century American poet. Masterpieces like "General William Booth Enters into Heaven," "Santa Fe Trail," "Chinese Nightingale," "Flower-fed Buffaloes," and others will remain among the classics of twentieth century American poetry, for they perfectly express the sounds and concerns of a complex moment in American history.

Biography

Nicholas Vachel Lindsay was born and died in his father's house next to the Governor's Mansion in Springfield, Illinois. His father, Dr. Vachel Thomas Lindsay, was a general practitioner whose home and financial stability made possible his son's slow progress toward a self-sustaining career as a poet. His mother, Esther Catharine Frazee Lindsay, a college mathematics teacher and instructor of painting before she married Dr. Lindsay, had the spirit and endurance to continue hopefully to support their son as he ambivalently moved from college (leaving Hiram College in June of 1900 without a degree after three years), to the Art Institute in Chicago, and on to New York to try to market his skills as an artist. His father may have hoped that his son would join his practice and settle down, but both parents were trampers and travelers in their own way. They had courted each other in the art galleries of Europe in the summer of 1875, and had taken the family to Europe in the summer of 1906, immediately after Lindsay's first American walking tour. In the spring of 1906, Lindsay had walked from Florida back north through the Okefenokee swamp to Atlanta, lecturing (on the Pre-Raphaelites), singing his poems ("The Tree of the Laughing Bells"), all the way to Grassy Springs, Kentucky and the home of relatives. The immediate leap to Europe, the Louvre, and the tomb of Napoleon was in some ways shocking, but Lindsay was comfortable in both milieux, marking the range of his experience, the talents and interests of his parents, and the end of the era of art and design as his principal interests.

His next "tramp" (in 1912) led directly to publication. He had tried "poem-peddling" in New York in the spring of 1905 without success, but now set out to trade rhymes for bread as he walked from Illinois to California. He caught the Santa Fe trail in Kansas and felt charged with poetic material and enthusiasm. That the trip was hard was undeniable; there was less room for self-delusion or self-indulgence than in any other episode of his life. When he "gave up" and took the train from Wagon Mound, New Mexico, to Los Angeles, he felt defeated; but here, after gloom and despair, came the inspiration for "General William Booth Enters into Heaven." Booth of the Salvation Army had died almost a month earlier, but as Lindsay walked the city at night, the poem flashed into being.

"General William Booth Enters into Heaven" was his making, and, because it was such a showpiece to read, perhaps his unmaking as well. Lindsay's career has been divided into sections of composition and recital, with the transitional stage between the publication of *General William Booth Enters into Heaven and Other Poems* by Kennerley in 1913 and *The Chinese Nightingale and Other Poems* by Macmillan in 1917. After this period, regardless of his own interests and enthusiasms, he was seen as a reciter of his own verse, a performer, an actor. His livelihood depended on the income generated from such recitals, and the verse he wrote later (with several notable exceptions) does not match the standard of the poetry of the 1910's.

It is important to note that Lindsay saw his public readings as the best way to reach the largest audience of American readers of poetry. If they all wanted to hear "The Congo," he would read it, repeatedly, even though he knew it was not representative of his best work. "I have tried to fight off all jazz," he said. He knew that it was he (as much as his verse, or more) who charmed or conjured his audiences; *he* had to read his work to have it go. He termed his reciting style and material a "higher vaudeville" and knew that in reaching new audiences he would have to alienate older or more traditional ones. In his day, however, academe did not scorn him: Yale, Wellesley, Oxford, Cambridge, all invited him to read, and they sat spellbound. Robert Graves, who introduced him to the circle of Oxford dons and students with the notion of showing off an American curiosity, was astonished at Lindsay's success. It is hard to reconstruct the experience: it depended on the power of Lindsay's delivery, but he asserted that the energy was there in the lines. In his passionate, reverent attention to his audience, his desire for its conversion, he poured himself out. Thus, in his reciting tours, Lindsay saw himself as no less than the Christian-democratic poet, a man who could, by the power of his poetry and personality, revive the artistic and moral sensibility of the nation.

Lindsay seemed more showman than troubadour, a performer, not a poet, primarily because he was more interested in speaking to America than to literary critics. The poets who supplanted him in American poetry anthologies consciously and particularly addressed themselves to the scholar-reader, the literary elite, the would-be student of literature. There is more to the contrast than this: Lindsay may have felt that he could not impress that literary elite beyond the first shock of amazement and delight at his readings: he may have doubted his staying power, his ability to follow "General William Booth Enters into Heaven" and "The Chinese Nightingale" with more of the same. Although Dr. Paul Wakefield (his brother-in-law) finally got him to the Mayo Foundation in Rochester, Minnesota, in June, 1924, for a diagnosis of his nervous condition, Lindsay must have feared the worsening of his serious physical and nervous disorder all his adult life. The word "epilepsy" was not mentioned until Eleanor Ruggles' biography (1938), but the severe seizures were public knowledge. Even now the Mayo diagnosis is unpublished. Celibate and unmarried until his mid-forties, but in love with a series of remarkable women who rejected his proposals, he married Elizabeth Conner on May 19, 1925 without revealing the secret of his seizures until after the ceremony. Paranoia, "morbid fancies," as Ruggles painfully documents them, insulting and insane accusations of family and stranger alike: these multiplied in the late 1920's, and gave Lindsay's career a kind of lurid richness that tempts readers to consider the pathological case and not the poet. Lindsay drank a bottle of Lysol at home, upstairs, early in the morning of December 5, 1931, killing himself quickly but painfully. In the past decade he had read triumphantly in England, married a young, bright, determined wife, and was known internationally for poems many could recite from memory, but fear of the increased frequency of epileptic attack, financial anxieties, anger with critics who wanted "more of the same," and despair that he was tied to the task of reading to audiences that would not read him—these concerns, and doubtless others, resulted in suicide.

Analysis

Music and message, rhythm and truth, Vachel Lindsay's best poetry offers extraordinary examples of the absolute interdependence of sound and sense. Lindsay finds ways of presenting on the page effects as various as the thump, whistle, and wheeze of a calliope ("The Kallyope Yell"), the staggered, percussive rattle of native dancing ("The Congo"), the smooth, mournful music of prairie birds singing in counterpoint to highway traffic ("The Santa Fe Trail"), and the unexpected brevity of a tall tale's punch line ("The Daniel Jazz"). Masterful as these effects are in themselves, they also illustrate Lindsay's affection for the details and the personality of his Midwestern world.

The gaudy steam calliope which blasted the fairgrounds with its din, the communities of blacks moving north to Illinois with their brand-new tempos of jazz music, the individual note of a bird called the Rachel Jane, the black servant's power in the household ("The Daniel Jazz") are all hard facts in his verse, keeping the dreams and generalizations, the hopes and fears of his populist idealism, rooted in the actual.

When, for example, Lindsay plucks General Booth out of his British setting for a tribute in a dream vision, marching deadbeats cruise around the courthouse in downtown Springfield. Here Lindsay harnesses the melting-pot theory of American meliorism to serve an evangelical cause, and where better to link the two powerful processes of social equality and salvation than on the courthouse steps that Abraham Lincoln climbed? The courthouse still dominates countless Midwestern town squares, a kind of secular temple: Lindsay recognized its power as a symbol. The paradoxical quality of the courthouse is carried on in the paradox of "Booth the Soldier," the tension derived from the "salvation" army, almost oxymoronic, however Pauline and familiar, from Protestant hymns. Again secular power and spiritual grace unite in a specific figure.

Lindsay revered the ideals of the courthouse and the Salvation Army, but the poem really celebrates the transformation of the "blear review." When all are made new, the "blind eyes" which are opened are not specifically identified as Booth's, because *all* gaze on "a new, sweet world." Lindsay's concern for a mass of people is evident in this poem; the variety of their disabilities, their instruments, their crimes, all fascinate him. Their energy is captured in the way the lines begin—trochees and spondees abound and alliteration provides speed and percussion. The principal accents are often just two, forcing the reading voice to pace on as it makes sense of the line.

In "General William Booth Enters into Heaven," Lindsay's technical genius can be appreciated; his belief in the new life of grace is given authority by the rippling power of the verse. In the first stanza, the alliteration and repeated stress at the start and finish of the first line exemplify Booth's confidence; the fact that he was blind makes this parade all the more bravely led. The undercurrent of the parenthesis "(Are you washed in the blood of the Lamb?)" changes the meter with its anapestic feet, implying the smooth confidence of the saint's question, but also slowing or interrupting the raucous motion of the parade. The couplet rhymes are remarkably appropriate as an organizing frame for this disorderly procession, but "the blood of the Lamb" never has its rhyme completed. Even in the last line of the poem, when the question is stripped of parentheses and quotation marks, when it comes straight to the reader/hearer, it has no echo, for it is Lindsay's unanswered, unanswerable question.

In the second stanza ("Every slum had sent . . .") Lindsay continues to move the reader/hearer through contradictory feelings: delight with the visual splendor of the scene (banners blooming and "transcendent dyes" in "the golden air") and awe or apprehension at the human forms that are here collected ("Bull-necked convicts," "Loons with trumpets"). The diction suggests salvation ("bloomed with glory," "transcendent," "upward thro' the golden air") while the subjects are clearly fallen, and likely to remain so.

The poem almost halts, therefore, caught by this paradox of evangelistic passion in fallen men, in the opening accounts of the third stanza with its three slow beats: "Booth died blind. . . ." Lindsay picks up the rhythm with uncharacteristic iambs: "and still by faith he trod," thus metrically emphasizing the miracle—dying blind but walking on. Lindsay hides the actual moment of transition here, as he does when the "blear review" is "in an instant" made new. In the middle of the stanza, with no italicized directions for music, Lindsay seems to lose the moment of salvation, and emphasizes instead the continuation of the parade of the purified host as it accompanies Booth to heaven.

Lindsay balances the familiar with the mystical perfectly. The parade of deadbeats playing musical instruments as they circle the town square becomes Booth's contribution to his world of slum victims, a metaphoric representation of his collected good works, and a fantastic vision of the heavenly scene.

It is easy to see that the italicized passages of advice ("Sweet flute music") are meant to invite the reader/hearer to change attitude, to prepare for a new meter, to modulate tone. Lindsay's stage directions are meant to aid readers, not to stage shows or revise the verse. Lindsay structured his verse with care, setting lines on the page in groups indented or flush, with headnotes or numerical demarcation, always trying to slow the reader's headlong rush through a poem.

Much more sober and conventional but no less successful is the trio of poems united under the title "The Gospel of Beauty." Lindsay sang the sections of this poem on his walking tours, and it is not hard to imagine the farmers of the plains listening with some pleasure to this celebration of their past and future. Once again, Lindsay's characteristic concerns emerge from the lines, although there is little of the jazzy movement of the Booth poem in these thoughtful stanzas. "The Proud Farmer" (the title of the first segment) was Lindsay's mother's father, whose town, church, fields, and cemetery he knew well. The poet sees the heroic accomplishments of the rural life and the failure of the town to grow and prosper according to his grandfather's design: "They sleep with him beneath the ragged grass . . ./ The village withers, by his voice unstirred." The poet, "a sturdy grandchild," is empowered by the meditation, this time admiring the characteristic American pioneer hero, the man who worked by day, read by night, preached the word, and sired a family to spread to the ends of the earth. Frazee, like Booth, was a hero, capable of converting and saving, and Lindsay feels his inheritance and expresses it in the run-ons of the last stanza. The inversions ("furtive souls and tame") and archaisms ("he preached and plowed and wrought") are not meant to ape the formal diction of poetic recollection; they are gestures of respect to a man of an earlier age, whose language was formed by biblical study.

The second section, "The Illinois Village," reminds the reader of Lindsay's preoccupation with Springfield as a holy and aesthetically charged place. *The Golden Book of Springfield* (1920) and *The Village Magazines* (which he published several times at his own expense) were documents of his vision of Springfield as a site for political and spiritual rebirth, a new American life to start in the fields of Illinois. The three parts of "The Gospel of Beauty" move from one man on the land, to a village with promise, to a visionary city of the ideal future. "The Illinois Village" is Springfield in its youth, with the "village church by night" the image of "Spirit-power." Commerce is deemphasized in favor of artful decoration ("fountain-frieze" and painters and poets); the church is the moral and cultural center. Lindsay's image of the church in moonlight and veiled by trees at dusty noon again places the fact between mere observation and fantasy, like the courthouse in "General William Booth Enters into Heaven": "The trees that watch at dusty noon/ Breaking its sharpest lines, veil not/ The whiteness it reflects from God."

"On the Building of Springfield" closes the work, its prophetic tone sharply in contrast to the meditative observations of the first two sections. Lindsay's dream here is like that of any booster of an "All-American city"; he wishes his city to claim its place with Athens, Oxford, and Florence. But his terms and rhythms are unique and defy casual description. "The Proud Farmer" saw the house of God and the farm to be one; in "The Illinois Village," the church organizes a square of town land, wreathed by trees; now a city is laid out in aisles, not streets, "where Music grows and Beauty is unchained." The renaissance of Springfield is larger than a religious conversion or a chamber of commerce scheme; it demands aesthetic appreciation, a vision beyond the practical payoff. Lindsay sees the danger of boosterism and calls Springfield "Ninevah" and "Babylon" unless it heeds his call, the proud farmer's heritage. Nature returns to assert its power when "Maple, Elm and Oak" are capitalized to suggest both the trees and the streets (as they are named in Springfield and almost every other American town); the trees again are the images of germinating genius in a town which tends to ignore the power of its own symbols. "Attics" are places to store rummage, not "sacred tears," as Attics of Athens might have shed. The curious choice of the verb form in the repeated line ("A city is not builded in a day.") reminds the reader/hearer of the process of the action, not its completeness: the open end of the trochee suggests both the incompleteness of the building and the hope for more.

Thus Lindsay continues to combine vision and fact, myth and reality, all set in a form whose sound and meter supports and explains the message. This pattern is still evident, on a larger scale, in "The Chinese Nightingale," a poem with its roots in the great tradition of nightingale poetry (Ovid, Samuel

Taylor Coleridge, John Keats, Thomas Hardy, William Butler Yeats) and in the fairy tale (Hans Christian Andersen's tale of the bird and the emperor). Typically, Lindsay starts with a metrical and literary joke: the "How, how," of Chang is the musical salutation in Chinese which the reader/hearer understands only in English. Lindsay's sister and brother-in-law in China provided accurate images and diction for this poem. The question in reply to "How?" reminds the reader/hearer of William Wordsworth's silly questions to the leech gatherer, but instead of a lament over lost greatness and present drudgery, the artful objects that surround Chang conjure up the beauty of a civilization gone, like Yeats's piece of lapis lazuli. The nightingale, the joss, and the lady all sing with appropriate imagery and rhythm, to create the tapestry of sound that makes up the poem. The introduction of the lady's song, for example, is effected with a couplet of lifting iambs, ending with a double-rhyme with an unaccented final syllable, a feminine ending: ("aflower . . . bower"), while Chang is solid in iambs at the lines' ends (his "countenance carved of stone/ ironed and ironed, all alone"). The living figure petrifies as the icons come alive: Keats would have approved, and Yeats did. The repetitions in the lady's song are mesmerizing, with their alterations ("bright bronze breast" and "bronze-brown wing") suggesting her accuracy, an accuracy which deteriorates in Chang's responses to short-line generalizations and visions of his San Francisco world. The Chinese laundryman is, like Keats, called back to his sole self after the nightingale's voice is stilled, but his memory of the dialogue between lady and joss whispers, hinting at evocative details, the remains of inspiration.

The tones of the song are distinct: the nightingale is the medium, the muse, whose brief invitation and occasional punctuation of the tale are done with almost nonsensical repetition. The lady sings gently, with fewer explosive consonants and more iambs at line-starts, dotting her lines with more anapestic feet ("I had a silvery name") than the "great gray joss" whose tone is more belligerent and stylized:

> Hear the howl of the silver seas,
> Hear the thunder.
> Hear the gongs of holy China
> How the waves and tunes combine
> in a rhythmic clashing wonder, . . .

A comparison of the speaking voices here with Yeats's later "Byzantium" poems will reveal how many of the images are shared, and how differently the poems sound. Lindsay's details are, literally, taken from the laundryman's shelf, as Yeats's stone in "Lapis Lazuli" was from his own desk, but the integrity of the speaking voices and the metrical effects are pure Lindsay.

Whether Lindsay impersonates a joss or a calliope, or celebrates heroes like Pocahontas, Altgeld, Bryan, or Lincoln, the theme is frequently one of measured loss, hopes unrealized, populist dreams evaporating, death before accomplishment. In this regard, "General William Booth Enters into Heaven" and "The Daniel Jazz" is a jolly retelling of a familiar tale. The "Kallyope" runs out of steam and will not, finally, convert the proud, but it *has* insisted on the equation of "the gutter dream" and "the golden dream." The senseless notes that it sounds at the poem's close are invitations to enjoy pure body rhythm, which cannot succeed on the page or with the ear. Lindsay was fascinated by the loss of the dream and the bittersweet recollections of the promise once imagined. From "The Last Song of Lucifer," which he worked on in college, to "The Flower-fed Buffaloes," published in *Going-to-the-Stars* in 1926, Lindsay seems to understand and accept the cycle of creation and destruction, hope and despair. This last poem, fifteen short lines, perfectly embodies the cycle in its music and diction.

The poem opens with the title's descriptive phrase, evoking the perfect pastoral, then quickly turns to the song of the locomotive in the third line. Like Henry David Thoreau, Lindsay did not see the railroad as an evil force; both poets allowed their trains to sing. Still, the flowers that sustained the buffalo "lie low" under the ties, just as the "perfumed grass" gives way to the wheat. Although flowers and grass have been replaced by railroad tracks and wheat farms, the spring "still is sweet"; Lindsay is not cheaply nostalgic or willing to falsify his experience. Nevertheless, something is gone, not just the buffalo, but the tribes that fed on the species. Lindsay surprises the reader/ hearer with the intrusion of the Blackfeet and the Pawnees "lying low, lying low." The savagery of the past age is captured in the diction describing the buffaloes' behavior ("They gore . . . they bellow . . . they trundle . . .") and the reader suddenly glimpses the vigor and violence of that age. Perfect pastoral? Not at all, but assuredly gone. The sibilant *s*'s, the aspirate *f*'s and *wh*'s and the lingering *l*'s create a mood that the bellowing and goring only briefly interrupt, for the spring *is* sweet, and the wheels of the harvesting machines and the railroad cars sweep through the prairie contentedly. Lindsay's point is to note the transition and loss and savor the memory, but not to hope for restoration.

Lindsay was an optimist, aware of history as creator as well as destroyer. His poetry urges the reader/hearer to hear and read: to know how we sound, where we came from, and "what to make of a diminished thing," that is, our future. When Frost used that phrase in "Oven Bird," he preceded it with "the highway dust is over all"; Frost, too, had "tramped" the American countryside in isolation and even despair. Frost and Lindsay represent different views of American culture, Frost so subtle and indirect, Lindsay so brassy; Frost so New England, Lindsay so plain; Frost so academically ironic, Lindsay so insistently proletarian. Lindsay exercised his power by singing, Frost by reflecting, but the two believed in a moral life, in which the poet's power to distinguish between what appears to be and what is was supremely important.

Major publications other than poetry

SHORT FICTION: *The Golden Book of Springfield*, 1920.

NONFICTION: *Adventures While Preaching the Gospel of Beauty*, 1914; *The Art of the Moving Picture*, 1915; *A Handy Guide for Beggars*, 1916; *The Litany of Washington Street*, 1929; *Letters of Vachel Lindsay*, 1979 (Marc Chénetier, editor).

MISCELLANEOUS: *Adventures: Rhymes and Designs*, 1968 (Robert Sayre, editor).

Bibliography

Flanagan, John T., ed. *Profile of Vachel Lindsay*, 1970.

Harris, Mark. *City of Discontent*, 1952.

Massa, Ann. *Vachel Lindsay: Fieldworker for the American Dream*, 1970.

Masters, Edgar Lee. *Vachel Lindsay, a Poet in America*, 1935.

Monroe, Harriet. *A Poet's Life*, 1938.

Ruggles, Eleanor. *The West-going Heart: A Life of Vachel Lindsay*, 1958.

John Chapman Ward

THOMAS LODGE

Born: London (?), England; 1558(?)
Died: London, England; September, 1625

Principal collections

Scillaes Metamorphosis, 1589; *Phillis*, 1593; *A Fig for Momus*, 1595; *The Works of Thomas Lodge*, 1875-1888 (Sir Edmund Gosse, editor, 4 volumes).

Other literary forms

Thomas Lodge wrote widely in genres other than poetry. His first prose work was *A Reply to Gosson* (1580), an answer to Stephen Gosson's *School of Abuse*. His prose romances include *The Delectable Historie of Forbonius and Prisceria* (1584), *Rosalynde* (1590), *Euphues Shadow* (1592), and *A Margarite of America* (1595). Other prose works encompass miscellaneous subject matter: a biography, *The Famous, True, and Historicall Life of Robert Second Duke of Normandy* (1591); an invective in dialogue form, *Catharos* (1591); and a historical narrative, *The Life and Death of William Longbeard* (1593). *An Alarum Against Usurers* (1584), an exposé of contemporary money lenders, has the strong moral message of *A Looking Glasse for London and England* (1594), the play that Lodge wrote with Robert Greene. In 1594 *The Wounds of Civil War*, another play he had written, was produced. His pamphlets on philosophical and religious topics include *The Diuel Coniured* (1596), *Prosopopeia* (1596), and *Wits Miserie and Worlds Madnesse* (1596). His later works are translations (*The Flowers of Lodowicke of Granada*, 1601, *The Famous and Memorable Workes of Josephus*, 1602, *The Workes, both Morrall and Natural, of Lucius Annaeus Seneca*, 1614, *A Learned Summary upon the Famous Poeme of William of Saluste, lord of Bartas*, 1625) and medical works (*A Treatise of the Plague*, 1603, *The Poore Mans Talentt*, 1621).

Achievements

Lodge's poetry displays a facility in versification that, by itself, would mark him as a poetic talent. His experiments with verse forms—quatrains and couplets in *Scillaes Metamorphosis*; sonnets of ten to thirty-two lines ranging from tetrameters to hexameters in the poems appended to *Scillaes Metamorphosis*; poems mixing long and short lines in the miscellanies; and iambic pentameter couplets in the satires—show him to be much concerned with the craft of poetry, even when his experiments are not successful. He shows the same eagerness in trying new types of poems and subject matter, and his works range from sonnets to verse epistles, complaints, satires, eclogues, lyrics, and Ovidian narrative. His debt to the Romans in his verse epistles, satires, and Ovidian narrative is one that later writers also incurred, and Lodge to a great extent introduced these literary forms into English. Not all of his works are equally successful and his facility at versification and image-making sometimes produces trivial or precious poems; nevertheless, he did point the way to later poetic development in English literature.

Biography

Thomas Lodge's biography is sketchy. The existing evidence prompted early biographers to portray him as a dissolute rake—disinherited by his family and jailed for debts—but more recent writers have been kinder. While his mother was apparently worried about Lodge's stability, she also favored him in her will above her other sons. Furthermore, even though there are ample records of suits and countersuits involving Lodge and various creditors, some of his problems seem to have been caused by naïveté, such as neglecting to get receipts and then being sued for ostensibly unpaid debts.

Lodge was born probably in 1558, since on taking his bachelor's degree in 1577 he would most likely have been eighteen or nineteen. Moreover, in a lawsuit with his brother William in 1594, he lists his age as being about thirty-six. In *A Treatise on the Plague*, he talks about London as if it were his birthplace, and presumably it was. His father was a prosperous grocer who became city alderman and, in 1562, Lord Mayor of London. As a child, Thomas Lodge may have been a page in the household of Henry Stanley, fourth Earl of Derby: *A Fig for Momus* opens with a dedication to Stanley's son, William, and reminds him of the time his "noble father in mine infancie . . . incorporated me into your house." If this reference is to a lengthy period of time spent in Stanley's household, he surely would have met the famous people of his day and acquired the attributes—and education—of a gentleman.

Lodge's affluence, however, was not to continue. By the time his father had finished his term as Lord Mayor he declared bankruptcy, a victim of financial problems caused by England's war with France and the 1563 outbreak of the plague. When Thomas Lodge entered the Merchant Taylor's School in 1571, he was one of a group of students who were admitted as the sons of poor men, paying reduced tuition. In 1573, Lodge entered Trinity College, Oxford. After taking his degree, he entered the Inns of Court in 1578.

His relationship with his parents at this period is problematical. When his father died in 1584, Thomas Lodge was not mentioned in his will. By this time Lodge was writing pamphlets—his *A Reply to Gosson*—and perhaps had converted to Catholicism. Trinity College, which had been founded during Mary's reign, still reflected strong Catholic influences, and Lincoln's Inn also had strong Catholic affinities, numbering among its members many recusants. In 1581, Lodge had been called before the Privy Council to answer charges, perhaps stemming from his religion. His literary activity and new religion might have displeased his father enough to cause him to disinherit his son; on the other hand, his mother's will, made in 1579, had already left him a large estate, which perhaps accounts for his father's reluctance to leave him any more. Yet even his mother's intentions are open to speculation. She stipulated that Lodge was not to receive his bequest until he was twenty-five, prompting some biographers to believe that she doubted her son's stability. She also included a proviso that Lodge would receive a yearly allowance only if he stayed at Lincoln's Inn and conducted himself "as a good student ought to do." If his behavior displeased her executors, they were to distribute his bequest among her other sons; Lady Anne seems to have felt the need to exercise special control over this particular son. Early biographers tended to see Lodge at this period as a profligate and debt-ridden young man. This view, however, is based partly on Gosson's attack on Lodge's character, which is hardly a credible source. Lodge's youthful degeneracy seems to have been exaggerated in early accounts of his life.

Sometime between 1585 and 1588, Lodge made a sea voyage, a venture he was to repeat in 1591 with Sir Thomas Cavendish. This latter voyage shows the perils to which the Elizabethan sense of adventure could lead: the expedition was plagued with bad weather, a mutinous crew, and widespread disease. Throughout his life, Lodge had published regularly, no matter what he did on a day-to-day basis; in 1597, however, he turned to the study of medicine and from then on produced only translations or works on medicine. He took his medical degree from the University of Avignon and probably practiced for a while in Belgium. He later returned to England and, in 1602, had his degree from Avignon registered at Oxford, a formality that would, perhaps, have attracted English clients. During the plague of 1603, Lodge worked tirelessly, even publishing a treatise on the disease with the intent of discrediting quack doctors who were profiting from people's fear and ignorance.

In 1604 Lodge married the widow of an Elizabethan spy who had formerly been a Catholic working for the Pope. Although this man eventually became an atheist, his wife remained loyal to her religion, receiving a pension from Gregory XIII. Lodge's marriage to her—along with his own earlier conversion—apparently brought him under suspicion by the government, and the Royal College of Physicians denied him permission to practice in London. By 1605, Lodge was again practicing in Belgium. Finally, with the help of the English ambassador to France, he was allowed to return to England and, in 1610, entered the Royal College of Physicians. The plague again swept through London in 1625 and Lodge was made plague-surgeon. He died in 1625, presumably a victim of that disease.

In many ways Lodge's life exemplifies the variety of experience that a Renaissance man might have. While born to wealth, he was often involved in litigation over debts, whether incurred through real want or only through carelessness. A writer of delicate sonnets, he was also an adventurer who undertook two sea voyages. Although he was not persecuted for his religion as actively as some, his fortunes still rose and fell as his beliefs changed.

Finally, the rather heedless young man acquired over the years a moral depth that caused him to work assiduously as a doctor throughout the plague years while others were fleeing London.

Analysis

Perhaps Thomas Lodge's most famous work is the prose romance *Rosalynde*, the source for William Shakespeare's *As You Like It* (1590-1600) and a lively piece of writing by itself. While the prose narrative of *Rosalynde* lies outside the bounds of this analysis, it does contain lyrical poems that, for their excellence, rival the best of Lodge's work. Their beauty was appreciated by Lodge's contemporaries, and many reappeared in *England's Helicon* (1600). Containing simple and even homely images and language, they explore the paradoxes of the Petrarchan lover without being excessive; as usual, Lodge is a master of metrics and many of these lyrics are presented as songs. "Rosalynds Madrigal" is an especially good example of Lodge's success as a lyricist. The poem alternates long and short lines in the first quatrain of each stanza; the stanzas close with four consecutive rhyming lines and a final line which may or may not rhyme with one of the lines in the first or second quatrain. Lodge's craftsmanship is evident in the way he can alternate long and short lines and use intermittently rhyming final stanza lines to achieve a musical effect. The homely images—love builds a "neast" in Rosalynd's eyes—also give the poem a certain lightness of tone. Many of the poems he wrote for the miscellanies show the same light touch and metrical skill:

> My bonnie Lasse thine eie,
> So slie,
> Hath made me sorrow so:
> Thy Crimsen cheekes my deere,
> So cleere,
> Hath so much wrought my woe.

When Lodge's lyrics fail they do so because they lack lightness and are not really profound enough to carry their serious, heavy tone; often they simply catalog the complaints of the Petrarchan lover and use balanced euphuistic lines to achieve a stately emphasis. Such emphasis seems misplaced, however, since the situations Lodge describes are often derivative. The sonnets in *Phillis* vary in quality. Some of them have the light touch of *Rosalynde*, although even in these Lodge is not consistent. Sonnet XIII opens by comparing Cupid to a bee:"If I approch he forward skippes,/ And if I kisse he stingeth me." The images describing love become more conventional as he goes along—tears, fire—and the poem ends with a conventional statement of constancy: "But if thou do not loue, Ile trulye serue hir,/ In spight of thee, by firme faith deserue hir." Sonnet XXXVII, containing heavy hexameter lines, lacks even the intermittently light tone of Sonnet XIII.

The *Phillis* sequence closes with a long medieval complaint, "The Complaint of Elstred." While hardly an inspired poem, it does show Lodge's affinities with pre-Renaissance verse. "Truth's Complaint over England" is also medieval in feeling and recounts Truth's lament over the condition of Lodge's England. Lodge's concept of satire seems mixed in his early works. "Truth's Complaint over England" achieves its social criticism through moralizing sentiments reminiscent of medieval complaint; Lodge's *A Reply to Gosson*, however, seems to show an awareness of different satiric possibilities. Confusing the etymology of *satire* and *satyr*—as most Renaissance writers did—Lodge gives a history of drama in which he asserts that tragedy evolved from satyr plays. The widely accepted Renaissance belief was that these plays allowed the playwright to scourge his audiences for their vices by having a satyr denounce them. In this way English writers came to think of satire as a harsh, uncouth form: Juvenal as opposed to the more urbane Horace. Lodge himself follows *Scillaes Metamorphosis* by a poem entitled "The Discontented Satyr," a paean to discontent, the best emotion one can feel in a corrupt age.

By the time he wrote *A Fig for Momus*, Lodge seems to have adopted this harsher Juvenalian mode of satire. This series of poems opens with a satire of flatterers and hypocrites, and Lodge is at his best in the imaginary characters and situations he evokes. Meeting an innkeeper with "a silken night-cap on his hed," the narrator is told that the man has had "An ague this two months." The narrator comments sardonically that "I let him passe: and laught to heare his skuce:/ For I knew well, he had the poxe by Luce." Lodge's second satire—incorrectly labeled the third—urges parents to set good examples for their children. The piece owes a special debt to Juvenal's Satire XIV on the same subject, and, if much of it seems simply moral preaching, the sheer number of vices which he catalogs keeps the poem moving. Perhaps Lodge's fourth satire offers his most memorable and bitter character study: a miser, old and decrepit, but still concerned with amassing a greater fortune. The gruesomely realistic description of the man shows Lodge at his best. His fifth satire opens with a paraphrase of Juvenal's Satire X, although his debt to Horace is also apparent in his description of the contented life. If this satire is less bitter and harsh than his others, it is perhaps because of the influence of Horace. In addition to introducing Juvenal into English literature, Lodge made one other lasting contribution to English satire: he was the first to use the epigrammatic pentameter couplet.

If *A Fig for Momus* does not seem, as a whole, the bitter invective that the satiric elements might lead one to expect, it is because Lodge has interspersed other genres: eclogues and verse epistles. His eclogues offer little new to English literature—Alexander Barclay, Barnabe Googe, Edmund Spenser, and Michael Drayton had already worked in this form—and their general theme of human corruption is not developed in an interesting way. Furthermore, their poetry, compared to Spenser's masterpiece in this genre, is noticeably deficient. Lodge's verse epistles, however, were the first to appear in English and, although they are uneven, the best of them have a lightness and wit that are typical of Lodge. The epistle "To his Mistress A. L." opens with a buildup in the first two lines which the following ones humorously deflate: "In that same month wherein the spring begins,/ And on that day when Phoebe left the twinnes/ (Which was on Saturday, the Twelfth of March)/ Your servant brought a letter seal'd with starch." The letter turns out to be a request for information on how to lose weight and the epistle cites various learned authorities on the subject, concluding that it is better to be "fat, slicke, faire, and full" than "leane, lancke, spare, and full." The epistle "In praise of his Mistris dogge" opens wittily enough with a request that his mistress "for a night . . . grant me Pretties place" and then proceeds to a canine history, ending with a pun: "Thus for your dog, my doggerell rime hath runne."

If Lodge introduced the verse epistle into English, he was also one of the first to write Ovidian narrative, a literary type that would later appear in Christopher Marlowe's *Hero and Leander* (1598), Shakespeare's *Venus and Adonis* (1593), Drayton's *Endimion and Phoebe* (1595), and John Marston's *The Metamorphosis of Pygmalion's Image and Certain Satires* (1598). Ovid had, of course, been known before Lodge: Arthur Golding's translation of the *Metamorphosis* (1567) was a standard Elizabethan treatment of the Roman poet. Yet Golding allegorizes Ovid to make his eroticism acceptable; Lodge is far from finding any allegory in his source. *Scillaes Metamorphosis* is noteworthy for its elaborate images and conceits: Lodge has taken Ovid's 143 lines and expanded them to nearly eight hundred. To the original story of Glaucus' love for the disdainful Scilla, Lodge adds an opening frame story in which the narrator, also a rejected lover, walks along the shore "Weeping my wants, and wailing scant reliefe." Finally he meets Glaucus, the sea god, and hears his story. As Glaucus recounts Scilla's disdain to a group of nymphs, Venus appears with Cupid. Cupid cures Glaucus' lovesickness with an arrow and then shoots Scilla, who immediately falls in love with Glaucus, who now rejects her. Knowing her case to be hopeless, Scilla finally curses all men, whereupon she is beset by the personifications *Furie*, *Rage*, *Wan-hope*, *Dispair*, and *Woe*, who transform her into a flinty isle.

If one could sum up Lodge's handling of Ovid in one word, it would be *embroidery*. Whenever he can stop for a lengthy and sensuous description, he does. Some of these are very successful, such as the description of Venus after she has found the wounded Adonis: it ends with Lodge's touching lines "How on his senseless corpes she lay a crying,/ As if the boy were then but new a dying." The story of Venus and Adonis itself shows Lodge's leisurely narrative pace, since it is interpolated in the main story of Glaucus. Glaucus' description of Scilla is also leisurely and sensuous. Ovid simply says that she was *sine vestibus* when Glaucus saw her; Lodge's Glaucus minutely recounts her physical beauty, dwelling on her hair, cheeks, nose, lips, neck, breasts, and arms.

The flaws in Lodge's poem—and it is by no means of uniform quality—have to do in part with this massing of description and detail. Lodge does not seem to have any awareness that his poem cannot sustain the same high pitch stanza after stanza: Glaucus' laments, for example, all begin to sound alike. Lodge has partially dealt with this problem in the frame story at the beginning of the poem, the very place where the reader is unlikely to need a rest from the high pitch of the poem. Nevertheless, Lodge does offer an interesting double perspective on Glaucus that the rest of the poem might have done well to develop. After the narrator spends four stanzas crying and groaning over an unrequited love, Glaucus appears and berates the narrator's love-sickness in stanzas that almost bristle with moral advice. After counseling the narrator, however, Glaucus falls into exactly the same error and even faints while describing his own hopeless love. This humorous contradiction between Glaucus' words and actions lends an ironic perspective to the story which the rest of the poem does not explore. Indeed, the personifications from medieval allegory who transform Scilla seem totally out of place in Lodge's poem, as if he had not really decided what the dominant tone of Ovidian narrative should be.

His verse form is also ill-chosen, although he does the best he can with it. Composed of stanzas consisting of a quatrain (abab) and a couplet (cc), the poem has difficulty moving forward: the couplets are always stopping the flow of action. In one sense this hardly matters, since Lodge is more concerned with leisurely description than with fast-paced narrative action. The poem, nevertheless, is a narrative, however leisurely, and the recurring couplets do present a problem. Lodge almost seems to feel that this is so and usually manages to begin a new clause as the couplet begins, avoiding at least the awkwardness of the self-contained couplet having to continue the lines before it.

Hardly any of Lodge's long poems are unqualified successes, although they all have striking passages and show much facility of versification. That he was an experimenter is evident in the number of new poetic forms he introduced into English; experimenters cannot always produce perfect products. Nevertheless, music and lightness of tone mark many of Lodge's best works and make him a considerable figure in the development of Renaissance poetry.

Major publications other than poetry

FICTION: *The Delectable Historie of Forbonius and Prisceria*, 1584; *Rosalynde*, 1590; *Euphues Shadow*, 1592; *A Margarite of America*, 1595.

PLAYS: *A Looking Glasse for London and England*, 1594 (with Robert Greene); *The Wounds of Civil War*, 1594.

NONFICTION: *A Reply to Gosson*, 1580; *An Alarum Against Usurers*, 1584;

The Famous, True, and Historicall Life of Robert Second Duke of Normandy (1591; *Catharos*, 1591; *The Life and Death of William Longbeard*, 1593; *The Diuel Coniured*, 1596; *Prosopopeia*, 1596; *Wits Miserie and Worlds Madnesse*, 1596; *The Flowers of Lodowicke of Granada*, 1601 (translation); *The Famous and Memorable Workes of Josephus*, 1602 (translation); *A Treatise of the Plague*, 1603; *The Workes, both Morrall and Natural, of Lucius Annaeus Seneca*, 1614 (translation); *The Poore Mans Talentt*, 1621; *A Learned Summary upon the Famous Poeme of William of Saluste, Lord of Bartas*, 1625 (translation).

Bibliography

Paradise, N. Burton. *Thomas Lodge, The History of an Elizabethan*, 1931.
Rae, Wesley D. *Thomas Lodge*, 1967.
Sisson, Charles. *Thomas Lodge and Other Elizabethans*, 1933.
Tannenbaum, Samuel A. *Thomas Lodge: A Concise Bibliography*, 1940.

Carole Moses

JOHN LOGAN

Born: Red Oak, Iowa; January 23, 1923

Principal collections

Cycle for Mother Cabrini, 1955; *Ghosts of the Heart*, 1960; *Spring of the Thief*, 1963; *The Zig-Zag Walk*, 1969; *The Anonymous Lover*, 1973; *Poem in Progress*, 1975; *John Logan: Poems/Aaron Siskind: Photographs*, 1976; *The Bridge of Change*, 1981; *Selected Poems: Only the Dreamer Can Change the Dream*, 1981.

Other literary forms

Because John Logan's reputation stems from his poetry, his fiction has, for the most part, been overlooked. In addition to several uncollected short stories in magazines such as *The New Yorker*, the *Chicago Review*, and the *Kenyon Review*, Logan's most sustained attempt at fiction, *The House That Jack Built* (1974), a volume of poetically rich autobiographical prose, celebrates the discovery and sheer joy of language. Concerned with the poet's young life, the book offers childhood experiences, relationships, and images which reveal the intellectual and emotional development of Logan's poetic sensibility. Also a teacher and critic, Logan has contributed essays, interviews, forewords, and reviews to numerous magazines and books, most of which are collected in *A Ballet for the Ear* (1982, Al Poulin, Jr., editor). This volume demonstrates Logan's wide-ranging scholarship and his dedication to the life of the poet. He explores with enthusiasm and keen insight such contrasting figures as Herman Melville and E. E. Cummings, and he develops provocative explanations for his own writing, his personal poetics, and the work and poetics of many contemporary writers. The passion of Logan's literary life, however, is best understood after hearing the poet read; his performances are often described as "spellbinding." Logan reads from his own work on a recording from the Watershed Foundation entitled *Only the Dreamer Can Change the Dream*.

Achievements

Often and incorrectly described as a confessional poet (a misnomer in Logan's vocabulary since good confessional poetry confesses the reader), Logan is one of the few truly personal poets to come to prominence in the twentieth century. James Wright tells an anecdote which best summarizes Logan's influence:

> I once stopped a fistfight between two of the best living poets I know, and I did it by reading aloud to them a poem by John Logan. . . . He is a genius of love in my lifetime, and, to my mind, one of the three or four masters we have to give to the world.

James Dickey places Logan's work alongside the poetry of Robert Lowell, and Robert Bly writes that "John Logan is one of the five or six finest poets to emerge in the United States in the last decades." Logan's reputation as a teacher equals his reputation as a poet, and some of his noteworthy students, including Marvin Bell, have written at length about Logan's "humanistic" workshops. Logan received the Miles Modern Poetry Prize from Wayne State University in 1967, a Rockefeller Foundation grant in 1969, the Morton Dauwen Zabel Award from the National Institute of Arts and Letters in 1973, a Guggenheim Fellowship in 1979, a grant from the National Endowment for the Arts in 1980, and the Robert Hazel Ferguson Award from the Friends of Literature, Chicago, 1982. He served as poetry editor for both the *Nation* and the *Critic*, and he was also the founder and editor of *Choice*, a magazine of poetry and photography.

Despite winning critical acclaim and the respect of his peers, Logan has never enjoyed a wide readership. The reasons are many, but most important is the fact that, like Walt Whitman, Logan is an intensely personal poet who demands an ultimate commitment from his reader. Logan's poetry transcends the ordinary form of things, and transforms those things into something more real, more useful, than conventional reality. Consequently, the reader of a Logan poem cannot in any way remain passive; instead, he must confront the shadow or inarticulate counterself that exists within. Logan's commitment to this type of self-searching is absolute, and while such intensity may alienate some readers, his insistent demands lend power, depth, and psychological complexity to the poems. At his best, Logan explores the inner self without moral judgment, conceit, sentimentalism, or self-pity. Instead, he uncovers what at first seems threatening and perhaps grotesque in order to reveal what is finally beautiful in all living things.

Biography

The speaker in John Burton Logan's poetry is a wanderer, due, in part, to Logan's belief that poets are constant, spiritual travelers, but also because of the fact that Logan's life cannot be identified, at least since his childhood in Iowa, with any one particular place. The outward search for home, a place of rest, combined with Logan's inward search, gives the poems their universal appeal.

Logan graduated *magna cum laude* from Coe College in 1943 with a B.A. in biology. In 1945, he married; it was a union that produced nine children but that finally ended in divorce. He received his M.A. in English in 1949 from the State University of Iowa, and in the years following, he did occasional graduate work in philosophy at Georgetown University and the University of Notre Dame. Beginning in 1947 and proceeding chronologically, Logan taught at St. John's College in Maryland, Notre Dame, St. Mary's College in California, the University of Washington, San Francisco State College, and, since 1966, the State University of New York at Buffalo. Logan has been and continues to be the resident writer for countless poetry workshops and colonies, and because of his popular and distinctive reading style, he maintains a busy schedule of public appearances.

Logan was reared as a Protestant but converted to Catholicism after his marriage. His early work reflects a clear and strong religious orientation that takes the Christian God very seriously. After the early books, however, religious allusions eventually disappear, and only in a few recent poems does Logan return to religious themes. Logan's meticulous cataloging of objects and artifacts in his poems probably stems from his early training as a scientist. His imagery comes from the world that surrounds him, a result of careful and rigorous observation. Knowledge of the body, not to mention nature's biological systems, provides the foundation upon which Logan constructs his metaphors for the soul. Robert Bly points out that Logan's "language is being used to build something, rather than to reflect something."

Readers, of course, have long understood the house imagery that is central to Logan's poetry—a partial reaction to his lack of home and a key component of Logan's grand design. Each poem, like a building block, and each book, like a separate and unique room, combines, with all the others, to finally form a complete and infinitely complex structure. Writing about Logan's first collection, *Cycle for Mother Cabrini*, Dan Murray observes: "Logan's recurrent themes are here like a skeleton of an incipient skyscraper or a diagram of a looming metaphorical structure." Logan's search has been long and often lonely, so he has built his own refuge, a house of poetry.

Analysis

Poets and critics often agree that John Logan has written more memorable lines than any of his contemporaries, yet the reasons for this claim are not at once apparent. It may be that, unlike most of his generation, Logan is not afraid of the God in his closet (see "On Poets and Poetry Today," *A Ballet for the Ear*); but certainly as one of the few personal poets writing in America, Logan confronts the day-to-day nightmares, fears, anxieties, and insecurities that most people only hope to escape. Fortunately, solutions exist, although they are transient in a Logan poem; or, more to the point, readers seek and take the poetry's spiritual strength. Logan writes from the world around him, from the self, building a personal poetry from his own obsessions: grace, the search for more than anonymous love, the friend or lover as rescuer, the father-son relationship, death, and poetry as rebirth.

Logan's recent work continues his established themes and, as if newly discovered, these recurring preoccupations show new recesses and an inexhaustible freshness. "Poem for My Brother" dramatizes the classic desire for acceptance and reconciliation between brothers that have grown apart. The younger of the two feels intimidated—or at least awkward—around his more athletic elder sibling and wants desperately to identify with him. This sense of physical and emotional alienation pervades Logan's poetry, paralleling a similar alienation in Logan's career as a writer. As a personal poet and descendant of Walt Whitman, Logan has stayed outside the mainstream of poetic schools, movements, and other such literary phenomena. He has been primarily a "loner," but he admits, while still criticizing the notion of poetic schools, that he misses the identity and support that a writing collective engaged in common philosophies and goals can offer its members (see "On Poets and Poetry Today"). Consequently, Logan seeks and waits for reconciliation with his brother poets. Although he constantly reasserts his individuality, a side of Logan not often seen desires a wider acceptance and a broader base of support.

In "Poem for My Brother," Logan explains the many differences between the poet and his elder brother, but always with a desire for identification. The contrasts between the two remain sharp (as illustrated by the brothers' colors, blue and brown), and this is what gives the poem its natural power. A capsulized history of the color blue included in the poem explains that many societies still do not have a word other than "dark" for this "last of the primary colors to be named." "It's associated with black. . . ." Blue, for Logan, represents the *other*, the society of *other lovers* to which Logan seeks admission— a place where, were he to gain access, he could not stay. Logan realizes that the redemption and grace of being accepted and forgiven is only temporary since any person soon finds himself alone again as he began, arguing only with himself, and being accountable, in the final analysis, only to himself. The tension between desire for the *other* and the knowledge that the consequent redemption is only temporary fuels much of Logan's poetry.

Grace, in Logan's own words, is the escape from anxiety through supernatural means—the sacraments and divine redemption—or through natural means: art and love. Logan's need for forgiveness and its subsequent grace motivates his outward and inward search, and his poems often show that such rare and precious gifts are not easily won. Indeed, implicit in Logan's poetry is the necessity for taking risks. Even in the early *Cycle for Mother Cabrini*, Logan charges his poems with a nervous energy that thrives on the anticipation of danger. In contrast, the volume overflows with classical allusions, establishing Logan as an extension of the poetic tradition that he so keenly feels. He carries on "The Lives of the Poet," the first poem in *Ghosts of the Heart*, both figuratively and literally; that is, the book begins a tradition of poems celebrating the lives of other poets, Arthur Rimbaud and Lord Byron, that continues with E. E. Cummings, John Keats, James Joyce, and Dylan Thomas, to name only a few, through several of the other books. These homages, tributes, and elegies not only reassert the presence of literary figures in the reader's consciousness, but they often reveal a great deal about Logan's own feelings and position as a poet.

Spring of the Thief deals primarily with the need for spiritual and physical change through imagination or uncanny transformation: the dread of stagnation suddenly transformed by new realization. This theme, however, does not fully mature until *The Zig-Zag Walk*. Although rich with translations of Georg Trakl and Tibor Tollas, the tone of *The Zig-Zag Walk* is more informal and the poetry less academic. Logan frees himself to explore personal relationships without the encumbrance of a superimposed poetic structure. Love becomes the central meaning of life, and it is love that saves the poet from his own self-destruction: ". . . as you reached for me/ . . . it was my self you hauled/ back from my despair." These lines from "The Rescue" resonate with lines from several poems, including the recent "Medicine Bow," in which the poet, shaking and losing his energy, is shocked back into life when he brings a handful of snow to his mouth. Such rescues always occur when the poet is on the edge, and, by their somber moods and continuing recurrence, the reader understands the transience of both rescue and relief.

Not until *The Anonymous Lover* is there any realization that the poet is also responsible for himself, that he is capable of self-rescue (as dramatized in "Medicine Bow"), and that he, indeed, must find or build his own refuge. In *Poem in Progress* (first published as a chapbook and then reprinted in *The Bridge of Change*), Logan manages to transcend many of the limitations that his younger obsessions seem to embody. He takes up with authority the wealth he has learned and constructs the world of his imagination (his fear of death and the desire for rebirth) around an in-depth study of the father-son relationship.

Throughout *Poem in Progress*, the poet appears variously as friend, brother, son, father (teacher), and lover, recapitulating many of the roles already established in Logan's poetry. (When Logan shifts his role, companions also change their position. In "Lines for Michael in the Picture" from *The Zig-Zag Walk*: ". . . that transforming island fire/ that seems to fade in your eyes in the picture./ It makes you brother, friend, son, father.") From the poet's shifting viewpoint, *Poem in Progress* explores a series of personal relationships which, to some degree, originate in erotic attraction creating homoerotic overtones and suggesting incestual fantasies. Some critics have made much of the text's "atmosphere" and have dwelled unnecessarily on what appear to be unfulfilled homoerotic confrontations. The characters in any one situation are of no importance to the total effect of the poem since love is fulfillment, even redemption, and love is not preferential about partners: "love in Plato's 'Phaedrus' is not thus: the need of man/ for woman, or of man for man, woman for woman;/ instead, it is the love that will be felt as fulfill-/ ment." Love that relieves human anxiety cannot be limited by predetermined judgments and prejudices. It must be accepted when offered and appreciated, for, as Logan knows all too well, its effects will not last.

Here, as in most of Logan's work, the poet is on an endless journey or search for the means to achieve grace. The poet is obviously still looking;

therefore, nothing he has found has been permanent. The moments of love and acceptance have been brief respites from the continuing frustration of grace that eludes. For example, the poet in "IV Rescue in Florida: The Friend," feeling insecure and childlike before a reading, takes strength from a stranger sitting in the audience. This unknown person will soon receive the poet's love, and so, for that moment, the poet is not isolated or *anonymous*. The stranger, again, performs a temporary rescue.

The word *anonymous* recurs several times in *Poem in Progress*, and working at the center of this one-word refrain is Pablo Neruda's idea ("V Interlude. The Colombian Statue: Archetype") that poetry is "an exchange between strangers," a token of thanks, perhaps, for what is given unknowingly. For example, the young lovers in section five give the poet a wooden figurine in thanks for what his poetry has given them. This gesture is unexpected and the poet as traveler identifies with the figure of the old Colombian man, sack over his back, with "fifty-year-old-hands." Yet, more than merely identification, the gesture of the gift returns to the poet some of what he has given: ". . . the breath/ he has breathed into it—or it has blown inside him—/ is given back again." Once more, Logan dramatizes the respite from the search, the rest in the middle of the journey.

In a new poem, Logan writes: "Poetry's form always brings a temporary peace,/ brings a natural form of grace." Notice that the key word here, again, is *temporary*. Art, like love, offers a temporary rest, and the friends, sons, brothers, students, and lovers that rescue Logan from time to time on his journey cannot offer what the poet ultimately searches for—a permanent state of grace. Although various religions offer contrary views, Logan seems to say that permanent bliss will come only with death. Regardless of where it can be found, the poet's grace has been brief and transient. Otherwise, Logan, like Edgar Allan Poe, is constantly undergoing a certain vertigo: just as Poe feared chaos and entropy, feared falling into the maelstrom or being sucked into the whirlpool, Logan fears the ultimate falling away of his gifts and powers. Acceleration toward the vulnerability of old age and consequent impotence is the vertigo that Logan faces except when hauled back from the edge or given a safe, although temporary, ledge where for a moment he can forget the fall. These preoccupations are forever present in Logan's images of his youthful sons and friends—godlike and indestructible—and the poet's own admissions, even guilt, over his slowly diminishing powers: "(. . . but my Greek is no longer sure)." In a new poem, the speaker asks: "Beloved student, what makes you think I can still teach?" What saves Logan's poetry at this level is that the narrator is not morose about his insecurities and fears. His offhand comments about his slipping abilities and his celebration of youth and confidence come as the natural components of Logan's total embrace. *Poem in Progress* portrays the lost, searching, sometimes fragile poet at odds with the various roles thrust upon him, but a poet still reveling in a sea of anonymous lovers provided by the Mardi Gras where the heat of the sculptor's kiln consumes the outer coverings of both the poet and his friends leaving them ". . . stark naked there as for making love or art."

"Believe It," the last poem in *The Bridge of Change*, is all at once a celebration of life's diversity and absurdity, an acknowledgement of fear concerning the loss of power and ability, the reassertion of the poet as a lifelong and constant traveler, and, finally, the reaffirmation of life and giving—the invitation to all the anonymous lovers that they are free to come and partake of the poet's joys. The lumps that are growing in Logan ("Each link or each lump in me is an offense against love") have been felt before (". . . and there is something vague that grows in me/ like a dead child"), at least since *The Zig-Zag Walk*. Still, for all their staying power, these lumps have not been able to destroy the poet's passion, his love of life, his celebrations of the flesh. At a deeper level, the poem challenges the notion of the "death of the lyric poet." In "Poem Slow to Come on the Death of Cummings," the poet says: "I wish I had not died when I was so young." With this exclamation, Logan acknowledges his deep-seated fear— that time will reveal a loss of ability, of power, and of mind. Logan fears the death of the lyric poet in himself, and yet, to the joy of his readers, this preoccupation remains only a fear and not a reality.

Bibliography

Altieri, Charles. "Poetry as Resurrection: John Logan's Structure of Metaphysical Solace," in *Modern Poetry Studies*. III (1973), pp. 193-224.

Bly, Robert. "John Logan's Field of Force," in *Voyages*. IV (Spring, 1972), pp. 29-36.

Chaplin, William. "Identity and Spirit in the Recent Poetry of John Logan," in *American Poetry Review*. May-June, 1973, pp. 19-24.

Dickey, James. *Babel to Byzantium: Poets and Poetry Now*, 1968.

Mazzaro, Jerome. "The Poetry of John Logan," in *Salmagundi*. II (Fall, 1968), pp. 78-95.

Thompson, Phyllis. "Journey to the New Waters of Brother, Sister," in *Modern Poetry Studies*. IX (1979), pp. 197-210.

Joseph Coulson

HENRY WADSWORTH LONGFELLOW

Born: Portland, Maine; February 27, 1807
Died: Cambridge, Massachusetts; March 24, 1882

Principal poems and collections

Voices of the Night, 1839; *Ballads and Other Poems*, 1841; *Poems on Slavery*, 1842; *The Belfry of Bruges and Other Poems*, 1845; *Evangeline*, 1847; *The Seaside and the Fireside*, 1850; *The Golden Legend*, 1851; *The Song of Hiawatha*, 1855; *The Courtship of Miles Standish*, 1858; *Tales of a Wayside Inn*, 1863; *Flower-de-Luce*, 1866; *The Divine Comedy of Dante Alighieri*, 1867-1869 (translation); *The New England Tragedies*, 1868; *The Divine Tragedy*, 1871; *Three Books of Song*, 1872; *Christus, A Mystery*, 1872; *Aftermath*, 1873; *The Hanging of the Crane*, 1874; *The Masque of Pandora and Other Poems*, 1875; *Kéramos and Other Poems*, 1878; *Ultima Thule*, 1880; *In the Harbor*, 1882; *Michael Angelo*, 1883.

Other literary forms

Besides his poetry, Henry Wadsworth Longfellow produced a variety of works, most of them connected with his scholarly duties as Professor of Modern Languages and Literature at Bowdoin College (1829-1835) and at Harvard College (1837-1854). He created his own grammars: *Elements of French Grammar* (1830) and *Manuel de Proverbes Dramatiques* (1830). He wrote a series of scholarly articles in linguistics and literature for *The North American Review*, most of them being reprinted in his collection, *Drift-Wood* (1857), and several other prose works. *Outre-Mer: A Pilgrimage Beyond the Sea* (1833-1834) was an account of his first European tour; *Hyperion* (1839) was an account of his second, highlighted by an autobiographical reshaping of his romance with Fanny Appleton, whom he married three years later. *Kavanagh: A Tale* (1849) was his only attempt at writing a novel. He edited four anthologies of poetry: *The Poets and Poetry of Europe* (1845) contained selections from four hundred poets from ten different countries; *The Waif: A Collection of Poems* (1845) and *The Estray: A Collection of Poems* (1847) gathered together antislavery verses; and the thirty-one volumes of *Poems of Places* (1876-1879) remains the largest anthology of poetry ever assembled. As the leading American poet of his age, Longfellow carried on a voluminous correspondence, writing more than five thousand letters, many of which have recently been published as *The Letters of Henry Wadsworth Longfellow* by Harvard University Press. George T. Little reissued twenty-seven poems written during Longfellow's college days in an edition entitled *Longfellow's Boyhood Poems* (1925).

Achievements

Longfellow was the most popular English-language poet of the nineteenth century. In both England and the United States, volumes of his poetry outsold all other verse and most fiction for nearly fifty years. When he died, more than a million copies of his poetry had been sold. He was granted private audiences with Queen Victoria, honorary degrees from Oxford and Cambridge, and a memorial in the Poets' Corner of Westminster Abbey, a distinction hitherto reserved for only the greatest of England's own poets. In America, a national holiday was proclaimed to celebrate his seventy-fifth birthday. From the late nineteenth century to the mid-twentieth, nearly every school-age child in the United States and most of those in Britain were required to read some of his lines. Apparently, few poets of any age had shown themselves better able to articulate the values, beliefs, and aspirations of their readership. The body of Longfellow's work can be seen as an index to some of the newly industrialized world's deepest self-images. Contemporaries praised "the sentiments of tenderness" in *Hyperion*, admired the "unexaggerated truthfulness" of *Evangeline*, and the "accuracy" of *The Song of Hiawatha*. They extolled the way he "obeyed the highest humanity of the poet's calling" in *The Golden Legend* and repeatedly singled out the universal appeal of his voice: "force of thought" for the old, "melody" for the young, "piety" for the serious, and a "slight touch of mysticism" for the imaginative.

Longfellow was decidedly the most popular of a concentrated group of American poets that helped shape one another's stylistic response to the demands of such an audience. The group included James Russell Lowell, John Greenleaf Whittier, and William Cullen Bryant, all of whom catered primarily to a mass readership. They have frequently been called "Fireside Poets," meaning that they wrote not by but rather for the family hearth. They specialized in polite, sentimental, and traditional homilies for readers trying desperately to reaffirm some of their oldest and most cherished values during a period of unsettling and apparently chaotic change. Longfellow specifically imagined that each of his lines would be read aloud after dinner around the family circle, with young and old profiting by his every word. For them, he tried to picture a world where an omniscient God was still in control, where the human soul was still immortal, where death remained only "a beginning, not an end," where noble and courageous acts could still affect the outcome of a crisis, where the first duty of men was to sustain their spirituality by concentrating on the good, the beautiful, and the true, and where the duty of poets was to help their readers in this concentration on the sublime.

Longfellow was lionized for supporting these pieties in the nineteenth century and has been largely ignored because of them during much of the twentieth. A literate, scholarly, and compassionate man, Longfellow's verses probably merit neither critical extreme. At his worst, he could write prosaic and long-winded verse which seemed to aim principally at giving his audience the sentimentality they came to demand of him. At his best, he could struggle with his own and his age's doubts forthrightly; he could write movingly of the passing of traditional agrarian society and Christian ideals. Stronger minds than Longfellow's were puzzled by the abrupt changes which industrialization, urbanization, and political revolution had brought to their world. If he remained unsure of the qualities which the new world needed, he articulated with precision those qualities from the old which had been lost. There was an elegiac suppleness in his affirmations which created a tone of frailty and a sense of transience that often contradicted the superficial optimism which his readers demanded of him.

Biography

Henry Wadsworth Longfellow, the second of eight children, was born into an old and distinguished New England family. Stephen Longfellow, his father, was a prominent lawyer who had served as a representative in Congress and who could count among his ancestors New England patriarchs such as Samuel Sewell. His mother, Zilpah, could trace the Wadsworth name back through a Revolutionary War general to seventeenth century Plymouth Puritans such as John Alden. Schooled at the Portland Academy and Bowdoin College, Longfellow finished his formal education in 1825, graduating in a class which included Nathaniel Hawthorne. From the beginning, he had been expected to carry on the traditions of his two family groups: "You must adopt a profession which will afford you subsistence as well as reputation," his father had counseled him just before graduation. During his collegiate years, Longfellow had shown so much aptitude for foreign languages that Bowdoin actually offered him a newly established professorship in modern languages. The trustees of the college, however, insisted that their new professor travel to Europe at his own expense to round out his language training.

Accepting the offer, Longfellow toured Europe from 1826 to 1829, dividing his time between France, Spain, Italy, and Germany. By August 11, 1829, he was back at Bowdoin, preparing lecture notes and writing his own grammars and study texts. For the next six years, his scholarly duties at the college and his academic writing in linguistics and literature occupied most of his professional life. He did, however, find time to renew an interest in creative writing. His only book during the stay at Bowdoin, *Outre-Mer: A Pilgrimage Beyond the Sea*, was a prose account of his European travels, modeled on Washington Irving's *The Sketch Book of Geoffrey Crayon, Gent.* (1819-1820). Settling more comfortably into academic life, Longfellow married Mary Storer Potter on September 14, 1831, and devoted himself to extending his reputation by publishing literary criticism. Three years later, Harvard College had been impressed enough with the quality of his academic writing to offer him the Smith Professorship of French and Spanish Languages, again contingent on his willingness to travel to Europe for further study.

He and his wife, Mary, sailed in April, 1835, to visit England, Denmark, Sweden, and Holland. In October, tragedy overtook the couple; Mary lost the child she was carrying and, in November, died from complications from the miscarriage. It took a year of grieving, studying, and falling in love again—this time with Fanny Appleton, the daughter of a prominent Boston family whom he had met in Switzerland—for Longfellow to recuperate fully from the loss. By the fall of 1836, he had returned to Harvard to continue his scholarly writing. By 1842, he had also finished *Hyperion*, a highly autobiographical account of his unrequited love for Fanny, and three volumes of original poetry. By 1843, he had apparently achieved enough recognition for Fanny to consent to marriage. The stay at Harvard marked the beginning of the most productive period of Longfellow's career, and his home life, with six children, was apparently a happy one. His creative writing blossomed: he issued three more volumes of poetry. His scholarly endeavors continued to absorb him, and he added to his academic bibliography two major collections of verse. By 1854, his poetry had gained so much recognition that he could afford to resign his professorship and devote himself to writing full-time. In the next seven years, he produced his most popular works: *The Seaside and the Fireside*, *The Golden Legend*, *The Song of Hiawatha*, *The Courtship of Miles Standish*, and *Tales of a Wayside Inn*. The flowering of Longfellow's productivity was again interrupted by personal tragedy: the death of his second wife in 1861. While sealing some letters with hot wax, Fanny set herself on fire and burned to death in the family living room. Longfellow himself was badly burned trying to rescue her. He never completely recovered from the loss, although he tried to lose himself in an ambitious verse translation of Dante's *The Divine Comedy* (c. 1320), in some passionate and realistic poems about the horrors of the Civil War, and in a dramatic narrative of the life of Christ.

Throughout the next decade, Longfellow devoted most of his flagging energies to reissuing previously published poetry, writing sequels to previously successful poems, and experimenting with a few new forms which he did not intend for publication during his lifetime. Much of his mature thought and many of his penetrating personal reflections were invested in an uncompleted drama about the life of Michelangelo. His health began to fail before the work was completed and he died from peritonitis after a short illness on March 24, 1882, less than a month after his seventy-fifth birthday had been celebrated all over America.

Analysis

Henry Wadsworth Longfellow worked in two entirely different poetic forms: short lyrical sketches which tried to point out similarities between passing, subjective emotions and lasting, objective settings or locations and long historical narratives which aimed at celebrating inspirational events. Like other Fireside Poets, Longfellow tailored both kinds of verse to an audience which, he envisioned, would read them aloud in front of the family hearth.

He once defined the persona for most of these public works as "no unwelcomed guest," who, he "hoped, would have [his] place reserved among the rest" at "your warm fireside." Appropriately, his subjects were often chosen so that young and old might be elevated by his treatment of traditional values. They stressed home, family, romantic love, dutiful children, quiet acceptance of suffering and death, and the appreciation of nature, God, and country. He wrote in traditional metrical patterns which would be easy for his readers to follow. He selected a solemn, sometimes archaic, diction which might add a devotional tone to the after-dinner recitations. He characteristically kept his symbols and images simple, so that even his youngest listeners might understand his homilies at first hearing. After the shocking death of his second wife, it became more difficult for Longfellow to confine himself to the expectations of such an audience and to such a rigid series of poetic restrictions. Yet the progress of his work showed a single-minded commitment to continue fulfilling the dictates of this public role, long after he himself had outgrown them. Increasingly, Longfellow's later lyrics and narratives showed a quiet subversion of the subjects and styles which his adoring audience expected of their laureate. The later poems proposed the same simple formulas in the same simple intonations as the earlier works had, but they seemed to waver, often undercutting themselves with a quiet pessimism which directly contradicted their superficial cheeriness.

In the last lyric he wrote, "The Bells of San Blas," Longfellow seemed to reevaluate his poetic career and to dismiss it as belonging to a "dreamer of dreams" to "whom what is and what seems" were frequently "the same." Like the bells of the decaying Catholic Church, he claimed that the voice of his public persona had tried "to bring us back once more" to the "vanished days of yore," when the world was still "filled with faith, with zeal." But like many a nineteenth century artist, Longfellow concluded that such sounds were probably "in vain": the past could not successfully be called back again. The struggle to affirm publicly traditional values while privately doubting their efficacy provided the central tension in much of his poetry. Even the twenty-seven short poems he composed during his college days and published in a variety of little magazines and academic journals were prophetic of the difficulties that Longfellow would encounter whenever he attempted to bring together the spirituality of the past with the progress of the present. Like "The Bells of San Blas," they were tinged with a solemn, mournful sense of desperation, rueful that the traditions, values, and wisdom painfully accumulated over mankind's previous three thousand years of history no longer offered much guidance to the present. The young Longfellow examined the deaths of a variety of heroic Indians, stoic ship captains, and brave infantrymen who had given their lives for some noble cause. He concluded sadly that such nobility produced little lasting effect: theirs had been moments of brightness darkened by an unappreciative and uncaring present. In *Voices of the*

Night (1839), a slim collection of nine short poems, Longfellow amplified the melancholy and focused it through a spokesman who was both confused and troubled by "life's deep storm." While striving to balance his images of life's forms, which could bring both "sorrow and delight," and life's sounds, which could both "soothe or affright," the collection kept straying to the darker, more negative pole.

Each of the nine major collections of lyrics which followed these tentative beginnings sustained his sense of confusion and foreboding. In *Ballads and Other Poems*, Longfellow examined the traditional life-styles of a Viking warrior, a New England sea captain, and a simple village blacksmith with the same effusive sentimentality he had employed on a similar grouping during his undergraduate years. He characterized these simple lives as an accumulation of "toiling and rejoicing and sorrowing," emphasizing heavily "the sorrowing," and dismissed them as incapable of providing workable models for surviving the modern world. The tone of the collection was established by the resignation inherent in "The Goblet of Life," whose brim, Longfellow concluded, tended too often to overflow "with bitter drops of woe." The best anyone could hope for, given such pessimism, was the "strength to bear a portion of the care" which "crushes one half of humanity with despair."

This pessimism was repeated throughout *The Belfry of Bruges and Other Poems* whose title piece forced a tenuous metaphorical comparison between the "sweet sonorous clangor" of a city's bell tower and the poet's own "airy chimes," anticipating the image he would execute with greater skill in "The Bells of San Blas" almost forty years later. In 1845, Longfellow could only claim that the sounds from "the belfry of his brain" were, like the city's bells themselves, "scattered downward, though in vain" to a world no longer moved by "the hollow sound of brass." He complained that producing such irrelevant music might only "overburden his brain" and fill him with a sense of weariness and pain. He ended the collection with a downtrodden portrait of a morose poet, despondent because his book was "completed and closed." Painfully, he sensed that "dim" would "grow its fantasies," soon "forgotten" they would "lie, like coals in the ashes, they darken and die." Such self-abjection, Longfellow suggested, could only partially be relieved with a night which grew "darker and darker" as the "black shadows fall" and with the troubled observation that shortly "sleep and oblivion will reign over all."

Longfellow was never exactly sure which names or shapes to give the fears which haunted his early lyrics. It is true that the undifferentiated anxiety seldom paraded itself in his more frequently read historical narratives, but the fears had much to do with his sense that traditional solutions were failing to answer modern questions. In *The Seaside and the Fireside*, he conjured up a slightly paranoid image of a fisherman's daughter staring dumbly "out into the night" from behind the window of her family's cottage, hoping to see "some form arise." The child remained incapable of discerning what "tales the roaring ocean and the night wind, bleak and wild" might have to tell. But at the poem's end, those projected fears could beat "at the heart" of the child's mother and "drive the color from her cheek." It was more than a child's fascination mingled with fear of night mysteries which colored much of Longfellow's lyricism, it was a vague but omnipresent fear that something was dreadfully wrong with the direction of modern civilization. Keener minds than Longfellow's remained similarly mystified, unable to articulate the questions which by the twentieth century would evolve into a systematic pattern of *Angst*.

The "Birds of Passage" sequence, which he distributed throughout many of the later collections of lyrics, confronted these fears as directly as Longfellow could. The poems purported to reproduce the sounds of modern life, "murmurs of delight or woe" and the "murmurs of pleasures and pains and wrongs" which comprised his polarized judgment. Like his earlier efforts, however, these dwelt on the negative side, frequently echoing "the only sound we can discern," the "sound of lament." Even these, "all this toiling for human culture," he worried, might prove to be "unavailing." The sequence showed Longfellow at his best: his lines filled with sophisticated internal rhymes, with sometimes startling end rhymes ("Flanders" and "commanders," "unafraid" and "cannonade," "mountbanks" and "tan and planks"), with easy musical rhythms.

The "Birds of Passage" sequence was representative of Longfellow at the height of his powers, groping sometimes toward a Whitmanesque mysticism which might redeem his early fears and negativities. "All the houses where men have lived and died are haunted houses," he offered as the cornerstone of his belief-system in one poem in the sequence: "The spirit world around this world of sense floats like an atmosphere." In the lyrics which transcended his sense of despair, Longfellow began to avow his own personal, haphazard mixture of New England mysticism, Bostonian New Thought, spiritualism, numerology, astrology, and staid Unitarianism, hoping to offer some redemptive spirituality to a world which frequently defined itself as a "dark abyss." "To the dark problems, there is no other solution possible," he wrote to James Russell Lowell, "except the one word, Providence."

The last collections of lyrics wavered between the knowledge of how darkly a people tended to live their lives and the hope of how brightly those lives could be lived. The poems tended to deal more directly with the paradoxical ambiguities which had provided many of the tensions in the "Birds of Passage" sequence. They turned on life and death, daylight and moonlight, the heart of man, "blithe as the air is, and as free" and the heart of man so burdened "by the cares of yesterday" that "each today" was "heavier still." A view of the world in which defeats frequently turned out to be victories in disguise and the lowest ebbs were often only "the turn of tides" bound together his *Masque of Pandora and Other Poems*, his *Kéramos and Other Poems*, and his *Ultima Thule*. These collections suggested a more peaceful and accepting stance toward the dynamic balance of opposites which, Longfellow believed, characterized all of life.

In the later poems, the destructive forces which men could unleash were being quieted by the vaguely meditative and heartfelt notion that "God is All." His last lyrics, though never completely shaking the sense of despair, transience, and futility which had dogged his poetic vision, showed a Longfellow who was coming to terms with evil and who was growing surer with hope. In the complex polarities of "Victor and Vanquished," Longfellow seemed to suggest that even the worst of life could lead to the best. The victim, harried into a corner and confronted with certain death, could still stand unmoved and unafraid, taunting the victor with the chivalric challenge, "Do with me what thou wilt." Such spirit, Longfellow insisted, could make even "the vanquished here," the "victor of the field." Whenever "a noble deed is wrought" or "spoken is a noble thought," Longfellow articulated his redemptive code of hope: "our hearts, in glad surprise to higher levels rise." In *Ultima Thule*, he was explaining the presence of evil with the time-honored formula that "noble souls" inevitably "rise from disaster and defeat, the stronger." The effort would make them more conscious of "the divine with them." For these traditional platitudes, Longfellow could, at his best, often find fresh and moving imagery.

The collections of late lyrics were probably his most enduring works. They chronicled a troubled soul, torn with the doubts of his age, groping to artic-ulate a sense of mystery, awe, and spirituality which might bring hope to a culture too concerned with its own certitudes and material advances. It was not these lyrics, however, but rather his long historical narratives which had brought him acclaim from his contemporaries. Neither the profound doubts nor the genuine hopes which animated his lyrics could be found in these more saccharine celebrations of traditional values. At their worst, *The Spanish Student* (1843), *Evangeline*, *The Song of Hiawatha*, *The Courtship of Miles Standish*, *The Divine Tragedy*, *The Golden Legend*, and *The New England Tragedies* were dull prosaic narratives which have done much to discourage modern readers from discovering the strengths of Longfellow's talents. *The Spanish Student* was an infelicitous three-act verse comedy intended for the stage. It found no one willing to venture the capital necessary for producing it. *Evangeline* was the work which first won a mass audience for Longfellow. It was a simple tale, first spun by the clergyman, H. L. Conolly, while he dined with Longfellow and Nathaniel Hawthorne. Longfellow seized the story line, picked a formal, though not always formally kept, dactylic hexameter metrical pattern for it, and composed a long tale of the French Arcadienne, Evangeline, as she wandered through the forests of eighteenth century New England looking for her kidnaped lover. It was a cliché-ridden effort whose descriptive powers ran to portrayals of Evangeline as "living at peace with

God and the World," to summaries of her relationship with her betrothed as "their two hearts, tender and true," and to a plot which described her quest for him as searches "in want and cheerless discomfort, bleeding, barefooted, over the shards and thorns of existence." When at the poem's and her own life's end Evangeline finally located her long-lost fiancé, the best Longfellow could fashion for an ending was to have her "meekly bow" her head and "murmur, 'Father, I thank Thee'" just before she died. The popularity of the poem probably revealed more about the tastes of Longfellow's readers than about his own talents.

The same audience responded even more enthusiastically to *The Song of Hiawatha*. With its two-footed lines vaguely resembling the alliterative verse of traditional northern European epics like the Finnish *Kalevala*, with its heavy borrowings from Henry Rowe Schoolcraft's two volumes on North American Indians, and with its upbeat ending, the appeal of *The Song of Hiawatha* was quick and widespread. The tale borrowed the grandiose proportions of the European epic, picturing a Hiawatha whose every stride measured "a Mile," whose canoe needed no paddles "for his thoughts as paddles served," whose father was "the west wind," and whose true love was Minnehaha, daughter of the god of arrow makers. The poem's rhythmic devices could sometimes be interesting. Especially when read aloud, the Indian material could lend a freshness to the overworked conventions of the epic, and Longfellow's battle scenes, pitting Hiawatha against a variety of mythic creatures, were frequently well-paced. All this technical virtuosity, however, could not hold together the disconnected elements of the plot or prepare the reader for the arbitrarily imposed ending in which Hiawatha vacates his native village so that his fellow Indians might be more inclined to listen to the redeeming gospel of Christianity brought to them by European missionaries. The same muddle of values and formlessness of plot marred *The Courtship of Miles Standish*. The poem returned to the dactylic hexameters of *Evangeline* and to the romantic love angle shared between two recognizably human historical figures. Set in seventeenth century Puritan New England, *The Courtship of Miles Standish* wavered between sustaining a heroic view of the Plymouth Colony and a lighthearted glance at the foibles of its founders. Longfellow could never quite make up his mind whether to emphasize the "strong hearts and true" of the pilgrims or to satirize the quirky leader who could lock himself in his room and cheer himself with passages from Julius Caesar: "Better be first, he said, in a little Iberian village/ Than be second in Rome, and I think he was right when he said it."

With *The Divine Tragedy*, an epic about the life of Christ, *The Golden Legend*, a retelling of the Faust story, and *The New England Tragedies*, an unfinished grouping about Christianity in the New World, Longfellow began to lose the mass audience he had so carefully cultivated. These works marked the same kind of transition to a tentative but serious spirituality which had characterized his later collections of lyrics. These poems, far more earnest than his early narratives, constituted reevaluations of two thousand years of Western religious thought through which Longfellow hoped to sift beliefs which might still have meaning to his contemporaries. He originally planned a chronicle of the triumph of religious progress in the ancient, medieval, and modern worlds. But his own lack of conviction in doctrinaire Christianity and his own unshakable doubts led him to undercut the tales of triumph by dwelling on those moments in which the purity of the original doctrines were perverted by fallible man. *The Divine Tragedy* set out to recapture the original message, but neither Longfellow's limited talents nor his scattered theology lent themselves to a subject of Miltonic proportions. His Christ blandly mouthed excerpts from the King James Bible; his apostles turned out to be featureless; his plot was a pastiche of New Testament incidents only vaguely related to one another; and his ending was an inconclusive recitation of the Apostles' Creed, with each of the twelve taking turns uttering the lines. "Poor sad humanity," St. John says, summarizing the effort, "turns back with bleeding feet by the weary road it came." With Longfellow's growing need to explain the tragedies which had befallen him, the turning back took the form of *The Golden Legend* and *The New England Tragedies*. Both sought to examine the storehouse of Western religious traditions and decide which "messages" from the "world of the spirits" could still animate contemporary man. "Death is the chilliness that precedes the dawn," he would declare in *Michael Angelo*, "then, we awake in the broad sunshine of the other life."

In *The Golden Legend*, Longfellow used the character of Prince Henry to examine how that belief in the other life came to be abandoned. His reshaping of both medieval and modern Christianity questioned, not the validity of the original doctrines, but the applications through which their adherents distorted them. His Faust figure in *The Golden Legend* was tempted by a sophisticated and worldly Lucifer, often disguised as a village priest, who counseled his charge not toward sin but toward a more modern point of view. Prince Henry was led to accept the belief in progress, materialism, the priority of the senses, and the certainty of the here and now. Lucifer eased his conscience. His temptations ran not to rejecting formal Christianity, but to ignoring its underlying sense of the mystical. In *The New England Tragedies*, this temptation was accepted with fewer questions. "O silent, sombre, and deserted streets," says a forlorn John Endicott, noting the emphasis on progress instead of spirituality: "To me, ye're peopled with a sad procession and echo only to the voice of sorrow." Where Prince Henry had placed too much faith in the powers of the intellect, the New Englanders had overemphasized the social mission of Calvinism. Both, Longfellow maintained, had lost sight of the underlying mystery and awe evident in the original testament espoused in *The Divine Tragedy*. Late in his last two narratives, Longfellow came to recommend the same kind of inchoate spirituality which had displayed redemptive powers in the most hopeful of his lyric poems. He was not enough of a theologian to formulate a systematic creed, nor enough of a zealot to recommend one path over another; and he was too much of a symbolist not to believe that all religious systems were only rough approximations of the same underlying unity. Nevertheless, a direct, experiential contact with the mysticism in man and the mysticism in nature could, Longfellow felt, explain much of the darkness of life.

Major publications other than poetry
NOVEL: *Kavanagh: A Tale*, 1849.
PLAY: *The Spanish Student*, 1843.
NONFICTION: *Elements of French Grammar*, 1830 (translation); *Manuel de Proverbes Dramatiques*, 1830; *Outre-Mer: A Pilgrimage Beyond the Sea*, 1833-1834; *Hyperion*, 1839; *Drift-Wood*, 1857; *The Letters of Henry Wadsworth Longfellow*, 1966-1974 (Andrew Hilen, editor, 5 volumes).
ANTHOLOGIES: *The Poets and Poetry of Europe*, 1845; *The Waif: A Collection of Poems*, 1845; *The Estray: A Collection of Poems*, 1847; *Poems of Places*, 1876-1879.

Bibliography
Arms, George T. "Longfellow," in *The Fields Were Green*, 1948.
Arvin, Newton. *Longfellow: His Life and Work*, 1963.
Austin, George L. *Henry Wadsworth Longfellow: His Life, His Works, His Friendships*, 1883.
Gorman, Herbert. *A Victorian American, Henry Wadsworth Longfellow*, 1926.
Hatsfield, James T. *New Light on Longfellow, with Special Reference to His Relations with Germany*, 1933.
Higginson, Thomas W. *Henry Wadsworth Longfellow*, 1902.
Hilen, Andrew. *Longfellow and Scandinavia*, 1947.
Hirsch, Edward L. *Henry Wadsworth Longfellow*, 1966.
Johnson, Carl L. *Professor Longfellow of Harvard*, 1944.
Longfellow, Samuel. *Final Memorials of Henry Wadsworth Longfellow*, 1887.
_____ . *Life of Henry Wadsworth Longfellow*, 1886.
Scudder, Horace E. "Longfellow and His Art," in *Men and Books*, 1887.
Thompson, Lawrance. *Young Longfellow, 1807-1843*, 1938.
Wagenknecht, Edward. *Longfellow: A Full-Length Portrait*, 1955.
Williams, Cecil B. *Henry Wadsworth Longfellow*, 1964.
Williams, Stanley T. "Longfellow," in *The Spanish Background of American Literature*, 1955.

Philip Woodard

RICHARD LOVELACE

Born: Woolwich, England, or Holland; 1618
Died: London, England; 1656 or 1657

Principal collections

Lucasta: Epodes, Odes, Sonnets, Songs, &c. to Which Is Added Aramantha, a Pastoral, 1649; *Lucasta: Posthume Poems of Richard Lovelace, Esq.*, 1659; *The Poems of Richard Lovelace*, 1925 (C. H. Wilkinson, editor, 2 volumes).

Other literary forms

Apart from the lyrics published in the two volumes of his poetry, Richard Lovelace wrote two plays, neither of which appears to be extant. The youthful *The Scholar* or *The Scholars*, a comedy, may have been produced at Gloucester Hall, Oxford, in 1636, and repeated later at Whitefriars, Salisbury Court, London. The prologue and epilogue appear in *Lucasta* (1649). A second play, a tragedy entitled *The Soldier* (1640), was written during the second Scottish expedition in 1640 but was never produced, according to Anthony à Wood, because of the closing of the theaters. Lovelace also wrote commendatory verses for a number of volumes published by friends or associates, versions of which appear in the collected editions of his poems. In addition, he wrote some lines, engraved under the portrait of Vincent Voiture, prefixed to the translation of the *Letters* by John Davies in 1657.

Achievements

Although chiefly remembered for a handful of exquisite lyrics celebrating what Douglas Bush called the Cavalier trinity of beauty, love, and honor, Lovelace has gradually risen to critical attention. Written for the most part against the somber landscape of England during the Civil War and Interregnum, Lovelace's poetry asserts more complex concerns and more authentic attitudes than those usually attributed to that "mob of gentlemen who wrote with ease." Decidedly a literary amateur in the Renaissance tradition of the courtier, Lovelace's sensibilities were deepened and roughened by the calamities that befell him, his cause, and his king. "To Althea, from Prison," and "To Lucasta, going to the wars," are justly admired along with a few other frequently anthologized pieces, but the achievement is considerably larger than their slight number and scope might suggest. In his ode "The Grasshopper," for example, written to his friend Charles Cotton, Lovelace fashions from an emblematic examination of the fate of that "poor verdant fool" an affirmation of human friendship that transcends particular circumstance and achieves an authentic tragic tone. In the lines written "To my worthy friend Mr. Peter Lely, on that excellent picture of his Majesty and the Duke of York, drawn by him at Hampton Court," Lovelace evokes the "clouded majesty" of King Charles the First, transforming a typical genre piece describing a painting into a somber elegiac on human dignity and courage in the face of adversity.

Like most of his fellow Cavalier poets, Lovelace was indebted to the poetry of Ben Jonson and John Donne. To Jonson he owed what graciousness and form he achieved, especially in the choice of classical models. To Donne he owed some degree of intellectual toughness and delight in what ingenious conceits he could master. To the limitations of both, in different ways, he was indebted for those infelicities of style that came with too much striving and too much care. Among his immediate contemporaries he was, no doubt, influenced by his relative, the translator Thomas Stanley, who may have helped him in more substantial matters than verse. Other poets with whom Lovelace shared stylistic affinities and thematic concerns were Robert Herrick, Sir John Suckling, and Andrew Marvell.

Biography

The broad outlines of Richard Lovelace's life are easy enough to sketch; but when it comes to filling in the details, much remains conjectural. Born in 1618 either at the family manor of Bethersden, Woolwich, Kent, or in Holland, Lovelace was the eldest son of Sir William Lovelace and his wife Anne (Barne). (The Woolwich church register does not commence until 1663.) His mother spent some time in Holland, where his father served under Sir Horace Vere and was later killed at the siege of Groll in 1627. Her references to her son Richard in her will make it seem likely that he was born while she was with her husband in the Low Countries.

Richard had four brothers, Thomas, Francis, William, and Dudley (the last of whom was responsible for seeing *Lucasta: Posthume Poems* through the press after his brother's death), and three sisters, Anne, Elizabeth, and Johanna. There are no records of Lovelace's childhood. In January, 1630, Lady Lovelace married Jonathan Brown or Browne of London, Doctor of Laws, and it may be presumed that the family's fortunes were enhanced as a result. The poet was educated at Charterhouse and entered Gloucester Hall, now Worcester College, Oxford, as a gentleman commoner in 1634.

By all accounts, the young scholar was handsome and amiable. In his second year, according to Anthony à Wood, a not very reliable authority in the case of Lovelace, he attracted the attention of an eminent Lady of the Queen, who prevailed upon the Archbishop of Canterbury, then Chancellor of the University, to have him awarded a Master of Arts, though he was only of two years' standing. The following year Lovelace was at Cambridge University, where he met several young men then in residence who were to contribute commendatory verses to *Lucasta* twelve years later; among them was Andrew Marvell.

Upon leaving the university, Lovelace joined the court, where he attracted the attention of George, Lord Goring, later Earl of Norwich, and was sent by him as an ensign in the first expedition against the Scots in 1639, under the Earl of Northumberland. During the second of these ineffectual campaigns, he was commissioned captain. Although he apparently wrote the tragedy entitled *The Soldier* during the second campaign, the only direct reference to the Scottish campaigns is the drinking song "To General Goring, after the pacification of Berwick." Among those who rode northward with Lovelace was the poet Sir John Suckling, whose "Ballad upon a Wedding" is traditionally thought to address Lovelace, although there is little, if any, substantive evidence for the attribution.

Following the Scottish campaigns, Lovelace returned to Kent and took possession of the family estates. In late April, 1642, he helped deliver the Kentish Petition to the House of Commons, for which he was confined in prison for perhaps as long as two months. The petitioners could not have hoped for any response less severe, especially as a similar petition of the previous month on behalf of the bishops and the liturgy had been ordered burned by the common hangman. In June, Lovelace was released on bail from his confinement, provided he remain in close communication with the Speaker of the House. Although he was forbidden to take an active role in the struggle between the King and Parliament, he outfitted his brothers Francis and William with men and money to aid the Royalist cause and arranged for his younger brother, Dudley, to study tactics and fortification in Holland.

Lovelace probably spent the greater part of the years 1643-1646 in Holland and France. His departure may have occasioned the lyric "To Lucasta, going beyond the seas." In Holland he presumably learned the language and acquired an appreciation of the world of art then flourishing with Rembrandt at the height of his powers. Lovelace was present at the siege of Dunkirk in 1646, where he was wounded. A year later he was back in London and was admitted with the Dutch-born portraitist Peter Lely to the Freedom of the Painters' Company. In 1648 he and his brother were taken as prisoners to Peterhouse in London, possibly as a precautionary measure because of their past activities and the turbulent state of affairs in Kent at the time. It was during this second confinement, apparently, that he prepared his lyrics for publication in 1649. He was discharged on April 10, 1649, some ten months after his incarceration. During the year Lovelace sold what remained of his family estates, including the family portraits, among which was one of himself by an unknown artist. These later came to Dulwich College.

Virtually nothing is known of Lovelace's activities in the years preceding his death, which occurred sometime before October, 1657, the date of the publication of Eldred Revett's *Poems*, which contained an elegy on Lovelace. Wood provides an account of Lovelace's last days and death. It has achieved popularity as suiting the legend of the man, but that Lovelace died a miserable death in utter poverty seems less than likely. Fifteen months prior to his death he wrote "The Triumphs of Philamore and Amoret" for the celebration of the marriage of his friend Charles Cotton. The poem, itself, may account for Wood's version of Lovelace's wretched end. Its references to Cotton's aid, however, "when in mine obscure cave/ (Shut up almost close prisoner in a grave)/ Your beams could reach me through this vault of night," would seem not to call for Wood's exaggerated description of the event. That Lovelace's fortune and fortunes were gravely reduced by the end seems clear. He would hardly have been alone in facing such hardships. There were friends to help, and it is unlikely that such abject poverty would not have been hinted at, had it occurred, in the various elegies occasioned by the publication in 1659 of *Lucasta: Posthume Poems*. The community of lettered friends was closely knit and evidence exists that discounts the implications of Wood's narrative. The poet Thomas Stanley, Lovelace's kinsman, had helped several needy and deserving poets and royalists, among them Sir Edward Sherburne, John Hall, and Robert Herrick. Cotton clearly assisted Lovelace in his time of need, and it is well known that Marvell tirelessly aided Milton in the early years of the Restoration. These are examples of the kind of support that surely would have been available to such an important gentleman and poet. Lovelace's place of burial, in Wood's account, was "at the west end of the Church of Saint Bride, alias Bridget, in London, near to the body of his kinsman William." The church was completely destroyed in the Great Fire along with any records that could verify the place of burial.

Analysis

Richard Lovelace's name has epitomized the supposed values of the world he inhabited, while its later link with Samuel Richardson's villain in *Clarissa* (1747-1748) has added guilt by association. The poet was, however, neither villain nor fop. Whatever glitter or romance touched his poems was incidental to a career dominated by darkness and despair, against which he strove with considerable stoicism. Indeed, although the themes of love, friendship, and retirement appear frequently in his poems (along with an informed and highly cultivated notion of the role of the arts of music, painting, and literature in relation to the good life), a pervasive sense of disillusionment and tragic isolation gives the best of them a keen edge. More than one critic has noted a claustrophobic sense of entrapment that is never far from the surface of his work. The traditional themes of what Earl Miner calls the "social mode of cavalier poetry" celebrate the good life, the ruins and remedies of time, the ordering process of art set against the disorder of the age, and the special values of love and friendship in the face of loss. Yet the cavaliers were forced increasingly to survive in a winter world, like that characterized by Lovelace in "The Grasshopper," a poem which has received considerable critical attention in recent years.

In this poem, as in "The Snail," "The Ant," and "A Fly Caught in a

Cobweb," Lovelace turns to the emblems of nature for lessons that bespeak the necessary fortitude of all life faced with the inevitable process of mutability. He shares his desire to fashion ethical and political statements of an allegorical kind by means of a microscopic examination of the natural world with other poets of his time, particularly Andrew Marvell, although the Anacreontic strain was most fully exploited by the royalist writers Thomas Stanley, Robert Herrick, and Abraham Cowley. Of the various reasons for examining the tiny creatures of the natural world, foremost was the wish to draw comparisons with the world of affairs amounting to little more than thinly veiled subversive propaganda. Although Lovelace and his fellow royalists were fascinated by the delicate craftsmanship that art shared with nature, "The Grasshopper" emerges as both a political and an ethical warning, as well as a pattern for refined artistry. The dual impulses in the poem, indeed, threaten its unity. In the end, it is only by recourse to paradox that Lovelace holds the disparate elements together.

In their enterprise to reinforce the royalist position by examples drawn from the world of nature, Lovelace and his fellow poets could not claim a monopoly on the material. Rebellion employed its own arguments from nature in support of human rights. When all else failed, the royalists found that their best alternative was a return to the nature found on what country estates were left to them, where they accepted a life of enforced retirement with whatever solace they could find. For Lovelace this last refuge from the political realities was no longer available.

The best known of Lovelace's lyrics are those that celebrate love, honor, and truth, especially "To Lucasta, going to the wars" and "To Althea, from prison," the latter set by John Wilson for John Playford's *Select Airs and Dialogues* (1659). It is one of a number of royalist dungeon pieces which may be indebted to Vincent Voiture's *Dans la prison*, although prison philosophy was certainly something of a Cavalier convention. For all of Lovelace's asseverations that "iron bars do not a prison make," a sense of lost conviction lingers about the poem like Althea's whispering to her loved one "at the grates." While the poet extravagantly claims his right to lie "tangled" in his mistress' hair and "fettered to her eye," a feeling of suffocating doom weighs heavily on the poem. In comparison, the joyous, almost Elizabethan "Gratiana, dancing and singing," creates a world of exuberance, excitement, and courtly fascination, defining an atmosphere that exists, like Izaak Walton's trout-filled streams, in a world forever vanished. The theme of mutability sparkles through the verse like the golden tresses of Amarantha, that flower of another poem, which when loosened and shaken out will "scatter day."

In truth, for Lovelace it is sorrow that scatters his days, along with the realization that "joys so ripe, so little keep." Though the popular lyric "The Scrutiny" flaunted that brand of cynicism and masculine arrogance learned from John Donne through Thomas Carew and Sir John Suckling, the richer imaginative strain is the note that sounds touching true worth irretrievably lost. The general slightness of Lovelace's lyrics is, in one sense, a measure of what has vanished; and the brief attention span that shows itself in many of the poems, such as "Gratiana, dancing and singing," which disintegrates after the brilliance of the opening four stanzas, may be as much the result of distracted or shattered sensibilities as it is of limited poetic skills. The lyrics frequently end in fragments of broken vision or imaginative exhaustion. There are debts, as well, to the courtier poet Thomas Wyatt, whose verse, like Lovelace's own, was often crabbed and tortured but could rise to take the measure of a tawdry world.

Perhaps because he was an amateur poet and a connoisseur of art, Lovelace saw very clearly the value of restoring the ruins of time. Like many of his contemporaries, particularly Stanley, an indefatigable translator, Lovelace went to continental as well as classical models for his verse, including that fantastic lyricist of the previous generation, Giambattista Marino. It may be assumed that the Petrarchan themes employed by Marino and his followers fascinated the royalist imagination, both by their sensuousness and by the brilliance of their metaphorical transformations. If poetry could change things, such linguistic strategies as the Marinisti presented in search of the marvelous might be enlisted by the Cavaliers in support of the royalist vision. After all, in the King they were accustomed to see poetically and politically the divinely linked agent of the miraculous. Beyond this, translation became for the poets of the time a means both to enrich their own meager gifts and to reinforce the realm of humane letters that was, they believed, the special preserve of the royalist writers.

From Marino, Lovelace borrowed the ideas and images for a number of his better poems. In "Elinda's Glove," working from Marino's *Il Guanto*, "Gli occhi di foco e'l sen di ghiaccio armata," Lovelace developed the images of sexual passion and feminine cruelty into an emblem that combined its sexuality with a social statement, transforming the intensely private into the mode of social convention and sophisticated tolerance, with tinges of mockery. Lovelace's "Song: To Amarantha, that she would dishevel her hair" develops one of Marino's favorite themes, while the complimentary verses "Gratiana, singing and dancing" paraphrases the sonnet of Giovanni Leone Sempronio, "La bella ballerina," and Lovelace's lyric "The Fair Beggar" employs a motif developed in the poem "Bellissima Mendica" by the Marinisti Claudio Achillini.

While much of his poetry written to celebrate friends and fellow artists was mere compliment, Lovelace often struck a note of sincerity that swept aside cant and allied human dignity with the longer life of art. On occasion these poems may owe something to models drawn from Marino's *La Galeria* (1619), but mere ingenuity gives way to the demands of authentic history and personal tragedy. In this regard, his poems written to Lely deserve a place in any appraisal of his accomplishments as a poet. In "Painture" (1659) he displays a fairly comprehensive understanding of painting and its particular fate in England, where the indifference of the average Englishman to anything but family portraits had troubled painters from Holbein on. With Lely, Lovelace shares a sense of the importance of painting and seeks, by that bond, to establish an alliance against philistinism: "Now, my best Lely, let's walk hand in hand,/ And smile at this un-understanding land," where men adore merely their "own dull counterfeits."

Like his "Fly Caught in a Cobweb," as a poet and courtier Lovelace may seem to be a "small type of great ones, that do hum/ Within this whole world's narrow room." His vision as a minor poet, however, may display more clearly the age that produced him than do the more majestic tones of genius that rise above the humble chorus of voices from the land. In his "Advice to my best brother, Colonel Francis Lovelace," he counsels that "to rear an edifice by art so high/ That envy should not reach it," one must inevitably "build low." The lessons of humanity lie close to the surface of his poetry, more visible than the treasures of his wit. In the analysis of his poetry, that shallow part has satisfied most inquirers. Many have failed even to look that closely.

In his own day Lovelace's poetry achieved little serious recognition. A few poems were known and recognized, but he did not enjoy a reputation such as Suckling did, for example. By the eighteenth century he seems to have been almost forgotten. Had it not been for Bishop Thomas Percy, who reprinted his two most famous lyrics in his *Relics of Ancient English Poetry* (1765), he might easily have completely faded from sight. From his friend and benefactor Cotton he received a suitable estimate in an elegy written for *Lucasta: Posthume Poems*:

> In fortune humble, constant in mischance,
> Expert in both, and both served to advance
> Thy name by various trials of thy spirit
> And give the testimony of thy merit;
> Valiant to envy of the bravest men
> And learned to an undisputed pen.

Major publications other than poetry
PLAYS: *The Scholar(s)*, 1636(?); *The Soldier*, 1640.

Bibliography
Bush, Douglas. *English Literature of the Earlier Seventeenth Century*, 1945.
Hartman, C. H. *The Cavalier Spirit and its Influence on the Life and Work of Richard Lovelace*, 1925.
Miner, Earl. *The Cavalier Mode from Jonson to Cotton*, 1971.
Judkins, David C. "Recent Studies in the Cavalier Poets: Thomas Carew,

Richard Lovelace, Sir John Suckling, and Edmund Waller," in *English Literary Renaissance*. VII (1977), pp. 243-258.
Weidhorn, Manfred. *Richard Lovelace*, 1970.

Galbraith M. Crump

AMY LOWELL

Born: Brookline, Massachusetts; February 9, 1874
Died: Brookline, Massachusetts; May 12, 1925

Principal collections

A Dome of Many-Coloured Glass, 1912; *Sword Blades and Poppy Seed,* 1914; *Men, Women and Ghosts,* 1916; *Can Grande's Castle,* 1918; *Pictures of the Floating World,* 1919; *Legends,* 1921; *Fir-Flower Tablets,* 1921 (translation with Florence Ayscough); *A Critical Fable,* 1922; *What's O'Clock,* 1925; *East Wind,* 1926; *Ballads for Sale,* 1927; *Selected Poems of Amy Lowell,* 1928 (John Livingston Lowes, editor); *The Complete Poetical Works of Amy Lowell,* 1955 (Louis Untermeyer, editor); *A Shard of Silence: Selected Poems of Amy Lowell,* 1957 (G. R. Ruihley, editor).

Other literary forms

In addition to the above collections, Amy Lowell published translations, criticism, and a literary biography. Her output was prodigious, fourteen of her books being published within a thirteen-year span. In addition, she wrote numerous essays and reviews and kept up an active correspondence, much of it concerning literature. Lowell edited three anthologies of Imagist poetry: *Some Imagist Poets* (1915); *Some Imagist Poets,* Vol. II (1916); and *Some Imagist Poets,* Vol. III (1917). Her three critical works were *Six French Poets* (1915), essays drawn from her lectures on the postsymbolist poets; *Tendencies in Modern American Poetry* (1917), essays also drawn from lectures on contemporary poetry and six poets in particular, including two Imagists; and *Poetry and Poets* (1930), essays compiled from her lectures and published posthumously. Although she did other translations (of operettas and verse dramas), Lowell's only published translations, with the exception of those in the appendix to *Six French Poets,* were those in *Fir-Flower Tablets* (1921), a collection of ancient Chinese poetry done in collaboration with Florence Ayscough. Lowell's monumental two-volume biography, *John Keats,* appeared in 1925, shortly before her death. A sampling of Lowell's letters can be found in *Florence Ayscough and Amy Lowell: Correspondence of a Friendship* (1946).

Achievements

During her lifetime, Lowell was one of the best-known modern American poets. This reputation had as much to do with Lowell the person and literary spokesperson as with Lowell the poet, though her work was certainly esteemed. Today her place in literary history as a whole is still to be determined, but her importance in the limited field of early twentieth century American letters is undisputed.

In her day, as F. Cudworth Flint has said, both Lowell and poetry were "news." Between 1914 and 1925, she spoke out for Imagism, free verse, and the "New Poetry" more frequently, energetically, and combatively than any of its other promoters or practitioners. She took on all comers in Boston, New York, Chicago, and any other city where she was invited to speak. "Poetry Society" meetings were often the best show in town when Lowell was on the platform.

Lowell's art probably suffered as a result of her taking on the role of promoter as well as producer of the new poetry, but she unquestionably helped to open the way for younger poets among her contemporaries and for free expression and experimentation in poetic form and theme. T. S. Eliot's *The Waste Land* (1922), which Lowell did not admire, might not have had such an immediate impact on the development of modern poetry had Lowell not helped to prepare for its reception.

Critical opinion on Lowell's own poetry is divided. Her detractors argue that she lacks passion and feeling; that she is concerned only with the surfaces of things; that she is imitative, an assimilator without any original creative force. Some even say that she never really understood the new poetry she so tirelessly advocated, that she was temperamentally grounded in the conservatism and sentimentality of the nineteenth century.

Her supporters, on the other hand, cite the enormous variety of her subject matter; the breadth of forms she employed and the extent to which she developed rhythmical variation in her polyphonic prose; the freshness and vitality of many of her lyrics, particularly her poetry dealing with love; her brilliant and vivid sensory perceptions; the intelligence that complemented emotion in her poetry; and the range of emotions that her verse expressed. Contemporary feminist critics, in particular, in their revisionist readings of Lowell, have found her worthy of greater prominence than literary criticism has generally accorded her.

What most critics would probably agree on is that Lowell wrote at least a handful of excellent poems worthy of inclusion in any anthology of American poetry. There would also be general agreement that she played a paramount role in the poetic renaissance of the early twentieth century.

Biography

Amy Lowell was born in the family home (named "Sevenels" after her birth because there were then seven Lowells) in Brookline, Massachusetts, just outside Boston. Both of her parents were from distinguished and wealthy Massachusetts families. Her father, Augustus Lowell, was a member of the wealthiest branch of the Lowells, the prominent family who had come to America in 1639 and later had become a major force in the intellectual and industrial history of Massachusetts. The mill town of Lowell, Massachusetts, was named for the family. Lowell's mother, Katherine Bigelow Lawrence, was the daughter of Abbot Lawrence. The Lawrences were also an old American family, and another Massachusetts mill town was named for them.

Although the Lowells also owned a town house for the winter months, most of Lowell's childhood was spent at Sevenels, and she continued to live there, with the exception of summers in New Hampshire and abroad, until her death. After her parents' deaths, her mother's in 1895 and her father's in 1899, Lowell settled into Sevenels and made it her own, remodeling and refurnishing it extensively. The gardens there were the source of much of Lowell's imagery.

Lowell had two brothers and two sisters. Both brothers distinguished themselves, each in a different area. The elder, Percival, after ten years in the Orient and the publication of two books on the Far East, went to Flagstaff, Arizona, where he founded the Lowell Observatory and made discoveries concerning Mars. The younger brother, Abbott Lawrence, became president of Harvard University in 1909.

Lowell's formal education was limited. She was a mischievous pupil who was easily bored and a challenge to her teachers. Although she received a private school education, she did not attend college. Her own comment on her formal education was that "it really did not amount to a hill of beans." Most of her real education came from her avid reading in her father's library and in the Boston Athenaeum, a building she later wrote about and saved from razing. Her future profession was foreshadowed when she discovered Leigh Hunt's *Imagination and Fancy* and read it through and through. She was particularly taken with John Keats, about whom she later wrote a biography. Hunt's ideas about poetry were those of an earlier time, however, and were responsible, in part, for Lowell's unsuccessful first volume of rather old-fashioned poetry.

Because of a glandular condition, the five-foot-tall Lowell became obese in her adolescence and remained so, eventually weighing about 250 pounds. In spite of such corpulence, she was a successful debutante, having some sixty dinners given for her. Suitors, however, were few. Those who did appear were interested chiefly in her family connections. Lowell rejected two proposals of marriage and then accepted a third, only to be rejected later by her fiancé.

Eventually reconciled to spinsterhood, though not without much suffering, including a nervous breakdown requiring several years of convalescence, Lowell finally turned to poetry as a focus for her life. It also seemed to serve as a substitute for the orthodox Christian faith of her childhood, which she had rejected. Lowell had always been fascinated by the theater and was a creditable performer. Many thought that had she not been heavy, she would have become a professional actress. Her interest in theater, and indeed in all of the arts, continued throughout her life. Perhaps not so coincidentally, then, it was an actress, the great Eleanor Duse, who inspired Lowell to become a poet. It was 1902, the third time that she had seen Duse perform. Lowell later said that watching her "loosed a bolt in my brain and I knew where my true function lay." Having little training in poetry, Lowell began a long period of study and writing, with Hunt as her primary tutor. It was eight years before she published her first poems and ten before her first book appeared. During those years, she gradually withdrew from her many civic activities in order to concentrate on poetry. She received much support and encouragement throughout this period from Carl Engel, a young composer who also introduced her to new music.

On March 12, 1912, she met the person who was later to become her companion, critic, supporter, and confidante for life, Ada Dwyer Russell, an actress whom Lowell eventually coaxed into retirement. Many of Lowell's poems were inspired by, or written for, Mrs. Russell.

On October 12, 1912, her first collection of poems, *A Dome of Many-Coloured Glass*, was published to uniformly bad reviews, including one by Louis Untermeyer, who was later to become her friend and eventually to edit her collected poems. The year 1912 was an important one in American poetry. Harriet Monroe launched her new magazine *Poetry* in that year, a journal to which Lowell contributed both money and poems. The early issues of *Poetry* alerted Lowell to a group of poets in England who called themselves Les Imagistes and who were led by Ezra Pound and T. E. Hulme. Recognizing her own poetic tendencies in what she read, Lowell sailed for England, in the summer of 1913, to meet with Pound and the other poets and learn more about Imagism. She returned enthusiastic about what she had learned and about her own future. Within a year, Pound was in the center of a new movement, Vorticism, though he had recently edited a small anthology called *Des Imagistes*. Lowell traveled to England again in 1914, meeting, among others, D. H. Lawrence, who was to become a close friend and whose talent Lowell immediately recognized. During that summer, Lowell and Pound parted in disagreement over the editorial policy of the next edition of *Des Imagistes*, and Lowell, with many of the poets on her side, took over the editorship of the anthology. She also took over the leadership of the Imagist movement and of the battle in America for the new poetic forms. Pound later dubbed the American movement "Amygism."

Lowell had learned much in two years, and *Sword Blades and Poppy Seed* was published in 1914 to great success, although only about a fourth of the poems were actually written in free verse. Lowell herself, in a short preface to the volume, used the term "unrhymed cadence." Three of the poems were written in what she called "polyphonic prose," a technique that she explained in the preface to a later book, *Can Grande's Castle*.

In 1915, 1916, and 1917, Lowell published the three volumes called *Some Imagist Poets*, picking up where Pound's *Des Imagistes* had left off and presenting seven to ten poems by each poet. Also in 1915, she published the successful *Six French Poets*, a book that brought her numerous speaking and reading engagements. From 1915 to 1918, Lowell was indefatigable. She gave countless lectures and readings, often traveling long distances on behalf of her own verse and of the New Poetry. She also wrote essays and reviews and produced several books. Always she was a friend to good writing and good writers, crusading tirelessly for others as well as for herself.

Men, Women and Ghosts, her next collection of poems, followed her French study. Next came another critical work, *Tendencies in Modern American Poetry*, followed by another volume of verse, *Can Grande's Castle*, her virtuoso production in polyphonic prose.

In 1916, Lowell injured herself lifting a carriage out of a ditch, causing the hernia which would eventually necessitate four operations and contribute to her death.

Her next publications were *Pictures of a Floating World*, reflecting her long study of the Orient, *Legends*, and *Fir-Flower Tablets*, translations of Chinese poetry done in collaboration with Florence Ayscough. *A Critical Fable* followed, and then Lowell began work on the book that was to be the culmination of a lifetime devotion to a single poet, John Keats. *John Keats* appeared in 1925; Lowell, driving herself to accomplish the task, became physically weaker and weaker during the course of its writing.

On May 12, 1925, she saw the side of her face droop while looking in a mirror, and in that moment, according to Damon, she "recognized her death." She died less than two hours later.

On August 25, *What's O'Clock* was published, and the following spring it won the Pulitzer Prize for Poetry.

Analysis

In its entirety, Amy Lowell's work is, as Flint has observed, a history of the poetry of her time. Born in the 1870's, she died just three years after the publication of *The Waste Land*.

Although her first published work owed much, in both theme and form, to the Romantics and the Victorians, by her second book Lowell was planted more firmly in the twentieth century and, more specifically, in what has come to be known as the Poetic Renaissance. She herself used this term in her critical work, *Tendencies in Modern American Poetry*. It was a time of experimentation in all of the arts, in America as well as abroad. Lowell took control in America of the movement to revolutionize and modernize poetic forms and, by the end of her life at fifty-one, she was largely responsible for the acceptance in America of the "New Poetry." Poetry was popular in Lowell's day, and Lowell made it even more so. Though both her poetry and her ideas about it often enraged her audience, they never failed to elicit responses, and Lowell was such a dynamic saleswoman that she usually had the final word. Not a highly original thinker or writer, Lowell was able, nevertheless, to absorb the best of what was going on around her and build on it.

Lowell's work, though often faulted for being focused on externalities and devoid of emotion, is psychologically revealing, both of her own emotional states and, in some poems, of the ideas of Sigmund Freud and modern psychology. Many of her poems reveal her own experiences and emotions, and much of her imagery derives from her own life. Lowell's childhood at Sevenels, at least into adolescence, when she became very heavy, was largely a happy one, and one of her greatest joys was her father's garden, later to become hers. Her knowledge and love of flowers, gardens, and birds permeates her work. The imagery is not all joyful, however, for Lowell lived out her life at Sevenels and her life also had its great disappointments and pain. Her obesity was probably responsible for her failure to marry and have a family, and, in disillusionment, she embraced poetry, almost as a spouse. Disillusionment about her work also occurs in the poems. In all, there is a tremendous amount of psychological as well as intellectual energy in her poems, partly a result of Lowell's driving need to achieve and compensate for what she had lost or never had. There is also peace in many of the poems, inspired by the security and contentment she found during the last eleven years of her life with Mrs. Russell. Many of the poems centering on love and devotion were inspired by Mrs. Russell.

Lowell's poetic subjects were wide-ranging. She wrote narratives on subjects as disparate as the frustration of a violinist's wife and the attempted rape of the moon by a fox. She wrote lyrics on such traditional subjects as love, disillusionment, artistic inspiration, and gardens, but she also wrote poems on buildings, cities, and wars. She wrote quasiepics that encompassed different centuries and countries, and dialect tales set in rural New England.

Glenn Richard Ruihley finds these diverse subjects unified by Lowell's transcendentalism, her search for the "Numinous or Divine" residing in all people and things. It was, according to Ruihley, the possibility of transcendence that she recognized that night while watching Duse act.

Her technical virtuosity was as great as her thematic range. Her use of metaphors and symbols was extensive. According to Ruihley, the only way to understand much of Lowell's work is through a study of "her chosen symbols." Though an outspoken advocate of poetic experimentation, she wrote in traditional forms as well as in free verse and polyphonic prose, often ranging through several forms in a single poem. Her virtuosity was unquestioned, but, like most virtuosity, it was exhausting as well as dazzling. She exhausted not through sheer variety of poetic forms but through a prolixity, particularly in much of her polyphonic prose, that left the reader drugged with sheer sensation and unable to absorb more.

Though she professed to be an Imagist, at least in her early work, and was the movement's leader in America, Lowell was never contained or restrained enough in her work to be truly Imagistic in the sense that the movement is usually defined. She was too expansive. In many of her poems, however, sometimes only in individual groups of lines, she did achieve what is usually thought of as Imagistic expression.

One of the recurring themes in Lowell's poetry is her disillusionment, self-doubt, and even despair. A representative poem in this vein is "On Looking at a Copy of Alice Meynell's Poems: Given Me Years Ago by a Friend" (*Ballads for Sale*). When Lowell learned of Meynell's death in November, 1922, she turned again to the volume of Meynell's poems given to her twenty-five years earlier by Frances Dabney. In that year, 1897, Lowell had had her marriage engagement broken off by her young Bostonian suitor. Hoping to alleviate her grief, Dabney had given her the poems. In rereading the poems on Meynell's death, Lowell found little to admire, but the poems did renew her feelings of despair and bitterness.

Written in a rhyming, metered, and regular stanzaic form, the poem records Lowell's present and past reflections on Meynell's book. She evaluates it both as a gift and as a work of art. As she reads again the "whispered greeting" inscribed by Dabney, the memories surface, "dim as pictures on a winking wall," but vivid enough in the illumination of the moment to revive her emotions. Dabney's gift, intended "to ease the smart," was instead a painful "mirror," reflecting Lowell's own tragic lack of fulfillment, yet Lowell remembers how she once "loved to quote" these lines.

From her present perspective, Lowell wonders at both her own and Dabney's judgment. She distances herself from her memories as she contemplates the changes brought by time. Both Dabney and Meynell are dead, and the verses that once seemed so brilliant now seem merely "well-made." Lowell has "lived the almanac" since that time and still has "so much to do." Though Meynell's and Lowell's old griefs seem insignificant now and Lowell refuses to linger any longer with them, she is still sympathetic to the pain, a sympathy tempered, however, by her awareness of old age and death and the ultimate futility of fame and happiness. These feelings are briefly captured in the magnificent and poignant third-from-the-last stanza: "So cried her heart, a feverish thing./ But clay is still, and clay is cold,/ And I was young, and I am old,/ And in December what birds sing!" Lowell cannot allow herself to remain in this mood, and in the final two stanzas, she returns the book to its shelf where "dust" will again cover the pain. For Ruihley, "Lowell's incompleteness" and "longing for wider satisfactions" are shared in some measure by everyone, albeit for varying reasons and in varying degrees. Her poem, then, transcends her own experience in its applicability and appeal.

A second theme running throughout Lowell's work, and one that is suggested rather than directly stated, is the relationship between human beings and material forms. Lowell's pictorialism is brilliant and abundant, but rather than representing only surface effects as it was often unfairly accused of doing, it has its origin in sympathetic feeling and reveals a passionate heart. A beautiful example of this theme (and the poem which was most often requested at Lowell's frequent readings) is "Lilacs" (*What's O'Clock*).

"Lilacs" expresses clearly the relationship between things or places and people, a relationship indivisible and full of emotion. The poem expansively chronicles the spatial and temporal domain of the lilac. It is a list that finally incorporates the poet herself until she and New England and history and time and the lilac are one. Throughout the poem, the lilac is an active participant in its settings, playing many roles—conversing, watching, settling, staggering, tapping, running, standing, persuading, flaunting, charging, and calling. Having originated in the East, the lilac beckons to those who sail in from China, but it has become most fully itself in the soil of New England. The flower is both in its settings and of its settings, and finally it becomes its settings as it mingles with places and lives and takes on a significance far beyond that of any of its individual manifestations:

> You are the great flood of our souls
> Bursting above the leaf-shapes of our hearts,
> You are the smell of all Summers,
> The love of wives and children,
> The recollection of the gardens of little children,
> You are State Houses and Charters. . . .

In the last stanza, Lowell identifies herself directly with the lilac as it embodies her own soil, New England ("Lilac in me because I am New England"). Her litany of reasons for such a union, underscored by repetitive structures, serves to emphasize the force and passion of her feelings.

Another example of the emotional import of material forms in Lowell's work is the popular "Meeting-House Hill." The scene portrayed is a simple one. The poet, from the eminence of "a squalid hill-top," observes a quiet scene: "the curve of a blue bay beyond a railroad track" and "a white church above thin trees in a city square." The scene itself is unremarkable except as it affects the poet, who suggests that she must be "mad, or very tired." The bay seems to sing to her and the church "amazes . . . as though it were the Parthenon." The imagination and emotion of the poet give movement to the scene until it is transformed into the final arresting image, which occupies ten of the poem's twenty-five lines. The spire of the church becomes the mast of a ship just returned from Canton. As the ship enters the bay carrying "green and blue porcelain," the poet sees a "Chinese coolie leaning over the rail/ Gazing at the white spire." It is a vivid scene and the reader moves within the imagination of the poet so that the reader too feels the emotion of the moment and sees the transformation.

The "coolie" is both of the spire (the mast of his ship) and gazing at it, both passive object of contemplation and active contemplator, so that the two worlds of reality and imagination merge fully. This is far from a mere portrayal of the surfaces of things. Objects, landscapes, flowers, and birds are emblems in Lowell's work and are always portrayed with feeling.

A third dominant theme in Lowell's poetry is that of love and devotion. It is "love in its combined physical and spiritual totality," as Jean Gould points out, that is celebrated in Lowell's work. Poems on this theme take many forms and honor many subjects, but the greatest are those inspired by Eleanor Duse and Mrs. Russell. Among those written for Russell are several of Lowell's most popular and enduring lyrics: "Madonna of the Evening Flowers," "Venus Transiens," "A Sprig of Rosemary," and "A Decade," all from *Pictures of a Floating World*; "In Excelsis" (What's O'Clock); and "The Taxi" (*Sword Blades and Poppy Seed*).

The scene in "Madonna of the Evening Flowers" is again simple. Lowell, tired from her day's work, calls for Russell. She is answered only by the wind and the sun shining on the remnants of her companion's recent activity—her books and her sewing implements. Though Lowell impatiently continues the search for her friend, the scene above has foreshadowed for the reader the simple domestic setting in which Russell will eventually be found. When finally spotted, Russell is "Standing under a spire of pale blue larkspur,/ With a basket of roses on [her] arm." The rest of the poem records Russell's practical responses to Lowell and Lowell's concomitant reflections. Lowell's attitude is worshipful, in contrast with the secularity of Russell's concerns, and the natural and human scene merges with the divine as Lowell hears the imagined "*Te Deums* of the Canterbury Bells."

"In Excelsis" again strikes a worshipful note and one full of rapture. In it, Lowell sees Russell as both the creator of the natural world and the embodiment of it. It is Russell whose movements control the processes of nature and Russell who is herself the "air—earth—heaven" of Lowell's universe. As in "Madonna of the Evening Flowers," the poet's impulse is to kneel before such glory, but she restrains herself from excesses: "Heaven" is not a "boon deserving thanks." She will accept the life that Russell brings to her; her poems will be her thanks, "rubies" set in "stone."

"The Taxi" has a different tone. Probably written during one of Lowell's separations from Russell, the poem speaks of the pain of separation. The images are vivid and startling, hauntingly modern in their metaphors. In the loved one's absence, the world turns hostile to the poet. The streets "wedge" Russell away from Lowell, and the city lights "prick" Lowell's eyes. The night has "sharp edges" that "wound."

Other love poems are more tranquil, projecting neither the rapturous adoration of "Madonna of the Evening Flowers" and "In Excelsis," nor the fearful tension of "The Taxi." The poet is often at peace in her love, admiring the beauty of her friend as if she were Botticelli's Venus ("Venus Transiens"), reflecting on the restfulness of her hands and voice ("A Sprig of Rosemary"), and savoring the simple nourishment of her presence ("A Decade").

Lowell's importance as a force in American literary history is undisputed. Her crusading efforts on behalf of modern poetry and poets had a formative influence on the development of American poetry in the twentieth century. The place of her own poetry is not as solidly determined. An untiring experimenter in verse forms, she was not a great poet, but she did write a few enduring poems which, it seems likely, will find a permanent place in the literary canon of her time.

Major publications other than poetry

NONFICTION: *Six French Poets*, 1915; *Tendencies in Modern American Poetry*, 1917; *John Keats*, 1925; *Poetry and Poets*, 1930; *Florence Ayscough and Amy Lowell: Correspondence of a Friendship*, 1946.
ANTHOLOGIES: *Some Imagist Poets*, Vols. I-III, 1915-1917.

Bibliography

Coffman, Stanley K. *Imagism: A Chapter for the History of Modern Poetry*, 1951.
Damon, S. Foster. *Amy Lowell*, 1935.
Flint, F. Cudworth. *Amy Lowell*, 1969 (University of Minnesota Pamphlets on American Writers).
Gould, Jean. *Amy: The World of Amy Lowell and the Imagist Movement*, 1975.
Heymann, C. David. *American Aristocracy: The Lives and Times of James Russell, Amy and Robert Lowell*, 1980.
Hughes, Glenn. *Imagism and the Imagists*, 1931.
Ruihley, Glenn Richard. *The Thorn of a Rose: Amy Lowell Reconsidered*, 1975.
Scott, Winfield Townley. *Exiles and Fabrications*, 1961.

Elaine Gardiner

JAMES RUSSELL LOWELL

Born: Cambridge, Massachusetts, February 22, 1819
Died: Cambridge, Massachusetts, August 12, 1891

Principal poems and collections

A Year's Life, 1841; *Poems*, 1844; *Poems: Second Series*, 1848; A Fable for Critics, 1848; *The Biglow Papers*, 1848; *The Vision of Sir Launfal*, 1848; *The Ode Recited at the Harvard Commemoration*, 1865; *The Biglow Papers: Second Series*, 1867; *Under the Willows and Other Poems*, 1869; *The Cathedral*, 1870; *Three Memorial Poems*, 1877; *Heartsease and Rue*, 1888; *Last Poems*, 1895.

Other literary forms

Besides thirteen volumes of poetry, James Russell Lowell published during his lifetime ten collections of essays, most of which had already been printed in periodicals. The ten collections centered themselves on literary criticism, arising from his scholarly duties as Professor of Modern Languages and Literature at Harvard University (1855-1886), and political theory, arising from his contact with the Republican party and his role as American ambassador to Spain (1877-1880) and England (1880-1887). The criticism—*Conversations on Some of the Old Poets* (1845), *Among My Books* (1870), *My Study Windows*, (1871), *Among My Books: Second Series* (1876), *The English Poets: Lessing, Rousseau* (1888), *Latest Literary Essays and Addresses* (1891), and *The Old English Dramatists* (1892)—shows a fluid, informal style grounded on few theoretical principles. The early works tend toward a vaguely Romantic approach, emphasizing the authors whom Lowell found inspirational. The later volumes are more conservative, based on more formal aesthetic principles. The same movement can be detected in Lowell's political theory. In *Fireside Travels* (1864) Lowell collected informal, chatty essays on Italy, Maine, and Cambridge. His *Democracy and Other Addresses* (1887) and *Political Essays* (1888) display a much more systematic approach to cultural commentary.

Since most of the thirteen volumes of poetry and ten volumes of prose were first printed in magazines and newspapers, Lowell's primary audience was found among periodical readers and editors. He helped to shape many of the major American magazines of the nineteenth century. He was a contributing editor to short-lived literary magazines such as *The Pioneer* and *The Dial*, to abolitionist magazines such as the *Pennsylvania Freeman* and the *National Anti-Slavery Standard*, and to major publications such as the *Atlantic Monthly* and the *North American Review*. Much of the work that he did for these publications was reprinted in *Early Prose Writings* (1902) and *Anti-Slavery Papers* (1902). Lowell saved some of his best prose for his personal friends, and the two-volume edition of his *Letters of James Russell Lowell* (1894, Charles Eliot Norton, editor) deserves to be more widely read.

Achievements

For Lowell, writing poetry was but one of several careers that he managed to sustain successfully and simultaneously. His first volume of poetry was composed during 1840 and 1841 while he was also trying to open his own law practice. His second was written while he was helping to launch a new magazine, *Pioneer: A Literary and Critical Journal*. After the magazine failed in 1843, Lowell threw himself into writing propaganda for the antislavery movement, accepting the post of editorial writer for the Philadelphia *The Freeman* and *Anti-Slavery Standard* simultaneously. From 1845 to 1848 he was also supplementing his meager income by writing literary criticism for *Graham's Magazine*. Despite the demands and prestige of the three assignments, he also found time to write three of his longest and best poems—*The Fable for Critics*, *The Biglow Papers*, and *The Vision of Sir Launfal*—all by 1848.

Lowell sustained such division of energy and interest throughout his career. In the 1850's, he mixed the publication of scholarly criticism, teaching at Harvard, and editing the newly founded *Atlantic Monthly* with his poetry. For good measure, he also started a novel. In the 1860's, he tried to edit the *North American Review*, keep his post at Harvard, issue collections of his prose works, and still write poetry. In the 1870's, he added a political career to his publishing, academic, and creative endeavors, campaigning to reform the Republican party and accepting appointments as the nation's ambassador to Spain in 1877 and to Great Britain in 1880. He broadened the base of his readership and reputation by publishing a great deal of political commentary as well. In addition to being a poet, he was, said one of his admirers, "our acknowledged, foremost man of letters." Diplomat, journalist, critic, academic, and poet, Lowell's life was divided among a variety of interests, none of which seemed capable of holding his attention for very long.

This multiplicity of interests proved to be both the greatest strength and the greatest weakness of his literary career. It injected into the corpus of his poetry a fresh stream of ideas, moving them from stilted and derivative lyrics to bitter abolitionist verse, biting satire, political commentary, cultural meditation, and warm-hearted regional description. The division of his energies, however, also robbed his poetry of the singularity of voice and consistency of tone that frequently mark poets of the first rank. Technically facile and frequently erudite, Lowell's poetry too often seemed to flow or ebb with the vagaries of his employment or the shifts in popular taste. His contemporaries thought that his poetry—which eventually filled 650 double-columned pages in the memorial edition of his work—was among the best their era had produced. He was generally acknowledged to be one of the two or three major American poets of the century. Twentieth century readers have not been so receptive, branding his ideas as commonplace, his style as derivative, and his voice as inconsistent. Lowell's poetry lacked the intensity to merit the praise it was given in the nineteenth century, but it deserves a more careful reading than it has been given by most twentieth century readers. With his range of tone, the fluidity of his cadences, the breadth of his intellect, the wit of his satire, and the accuracy of his depictions of nineteenth century American thought, Lowell's poetry remains much more than a historical curiosity.

Biography

James Russell Lowell was born into an important New England family that had been playing a prominent role in Massachusetts history ever since a wealthy merchant from Bristol, Percival Lowell, had helped to found the town of Newbury. Lowell's grandfather was a lawyer, a leading member of the Continental Congress. The poet's uncle, Francis Cabot Lowell, was one of the leading industrialists of the age, having given the family name to a factory town on the banks of the Merrimac River. His cousin was founder of Boston's Lowell Institute, and descendants of these Lowells, the poets Amy and Robert, have kept the family name before readers well into the twentieth century. To be born into such a family meant that Lowell was outfitted for success from birth. His parents had him reading before he was four, translating French before he was ten, studying Latin and Greek in the small classical school run by William Wells, and gaining admission to Harvard by the time he was fifteen.

The youngest of six children, Lowell never quite outgrew the advantages his family so willingly bestowed on him. As it turned out, he lived and died in the same familial mansion, Elmwood, in which he was born. His father helped to subsidize his first three volumes of poetry. In 1854, his cousin helped to launch his academic career by paying him to deliver a series of lectures at the Lowell Institute. The lectures turned out well enough to convince a close family friend, Henry Wadsworth Longfellow, to campaign to have him appointed to a professorship at Harvard the following year. Another cousin, James Elliot Cabot, as well as Longfellow and Ralph Waldo Emerson, recommended him for the editorship of the newly established *Atlantic Monthly* in 1867. The Lowell name and fortune, together with the conservative political commentary that he wrote for the *Atlantic Monthly* and the *North American Review*, proved to be influential enough to launch him eventually on a diplomatic career. By 1877, his support of President Hayes had netted him an appointment as the American ambassador to Spain. By 1880, he had moved up to become the country's ambassador to England.

From the start, Lowell abetted these advantages with his own hard work, his serious commitment to the craft of writing, and his enviable record for accomplishing nearly everything he set out to do. The Lowell name may have opened for him many a door, but his own steady performance guaranteed that he would be offered positions of increasing importance and influence. Yet the same hard work and the responsiveness to the traditions and duties of his family kept him from finding the real James Russell Lowell. From the time when his Harvard classmates elected him to write and read their class poem during the 1839 Commencement to the posthumous publication of his *Last Poems* in 1895, Lowell could be counted on to write what was expected of him rather than what he expected of himself. To gain the approval of his fellow graduates, Lowell could satirize the militancy and zeal of the abolitionist movement. To gain the approval, five years later, of his fiancée—Maria White was a protégé of Margaret Fuller and a militant abolitionist—he could turn his talents to editing the same abolitionist journals he had poked fun at in his Commencement poem. When she died in 1853, Lowell lost either his interest in or sense of duty toward the abolitionist movement. Yet another family commitment, a contract to deliver thirteen lectures on the English poets for his cousin's Lowell Institute, moved him from his bent toward satire, his involvement in reform, and his formal lyric poetry to a career as a literary critic.

Lowell spent nearly fifty years as an apologist for institutional America, articulating clearly and sometimes passionately the principal social, aesthetic, and political beliefs of the educated upper class of America's Atlantic seaboard. It was a community of readers for whom his family, his friends, his training, and his temperament had made him a perfect spokesman. Beneath the public success, however, Lowell privately grew more despondent about spending his life as a publicist for the country's most influential periodicals, prestigious universities, and reputable literary circles. "I feel that my life has been mainly wasted," he complained only a few years before his death: "that I have thrown away more than most men ever had." His confession that he was "never quite pleased with what I do," that he had "spent most of my life" pursuing "the muse, without ever catching up to her," hinted at an underlying frustration. Lowell invested so much of his energy in meeting the obligations of his station that he never quite settled on who he wanted to be or what he wanted to write. Retired from his diplomatic appointments, Lowell spent the last two years of his life at Elmwood, living with his daughter and grandchildren, rearranging and rewriting his volumes for a "collected" edition of his works, and lamenting occasionally that his poetry seemed "to me, just like all the verses I read in the papers." He died at home on August 12, 1891.

Analysis

Much of James Russell Lowell's poetry does not deserve as harsh a judgment as he himself accorded it. Partially, Lowell's sense of failure came from his inability to settle on what kind of verse he was most suited to write. He could pose as a lyric poet who was facile in dressing up contemporary ideas in traditional verse forms with appropriately suitable diction in the manner of the Fireside School. He could pose as a writer of light verse who could supply the periodical audience with historical romances such as *The Vision of Sir Launfal* or warmhearted, local-color sketches of New England eccentrics. He could pose as a satiric poet who could capture the foibles of the political and academic establishments. He could pose as a philosophical poet in the manner of William Wordsworth or Samual Taylor Coleridge. Yet none of his four most frequently employed poetic stances seemed to be the genuine voice of James Russell Lowell. His regret that he had never "really caught up" to his muse was a complaint that many of his severest critics would echo. "In Mr. Lowell's prose works," a reviewer pointed out in 1848, "we have before observed a certain disjointedness." With his new *A Fable for Critics*, the "looseness," the "rambling plot," the "want of artistic finish," the "lack of polish" characteristic of his criticism had spilled over into his approach to poetry, the critic continued. In 1952, one of Lowell's ablest biographers branded his work as lacking the kind of "coherent personality" that could make his words endure.

Unable to find a voice of his own, too distracted by the various employment opportunities that came his way to spend much time rewriting or repressing the worst of his poetry, and betrayed by his own prodigious talents, which enabled him to dash off verses quickly and fluently, Lowell had produced by the end of his life much undistinguished poetry. In each of his four characteristic modes, however, individual poems can be found that display a high degree of craftsmanship, a quick wit, a sharp eye for detail, an easy, natural cadence, and a steady and thoughtful mind.

Six of Lowell's thirteen collections of verse were anchored by traditional odes, sonnets, and lyrics dressed up in a style that one of Lowell's contemporaries praised as a "masterful" blend of all "the chords of a lyre," sounding in "loud, but harmonious concert." In *A Year's Life*, the 1844 and the 1848 editions of *Poems*, *Under the Willows and Other Poems*, *Heartsease and Rue*, and *Last Poems*, Lowell struggled with the poetic conventions of his day. Frequently, he lost. Imitating alternately the voices of John Keats, Wordsworth, Longfellow, and Alfred, Lord Tennyson, Lowell created a series of random reflections that stitched together pat phrases, formulistic ideas, long Latinate constructions, and overly generalized descriptions. These were the least successful of his four stylistic poses. They reworked well-worn subject matter: his love for Maria White in the earlier volumes and his awe of the New England countryside in the later ones. Frequently, they were derived not from his actual life experiences but from secondary reactions to some other art form: a review of "The Mona Lisa" or "On Hearing a Sonata of Beethoven Played in the Next Room" or his sonnet sequences to Keats or Wordsworth. Many of these poems managed to sound "poetic" without displaying much originality or passion. They could offhandedly summarize Keats's poetry as "serene and pure, like gushing joy of light." They could describe Lowell's fiancée as a "maiden whose birth could command the morning-stars their ancient music make." They could explain the duty of the poet as "his nobleness should be God like high" so "that his least deed is perfect as a star."

On occasion, however, he could infuse even these traditional forms with a freshness of diction, a naturalness of rhythm, a precision of image, and an economy of language showing that when he found the time to write, he could write very well indeed. In *Under the Willows and Other Poems* and *Heartsease and Rue*, Lowell's facility at turning a phrase could frequently redeem his conventional material by unconventional animation. His skies could be "sweet as a psalm." A scorned lover, "walking alone where we walked together," could discover "in the grey autumnal weather" that "the leaves fade, inconstant as you." His philosophy of life could be compressed into the pithy "not failure, but low aim, is the crime."

When Lowell aimed his poetry lower, however, he frequently achieved greater success. His conventional lyrics, which were aimed at a cultivated audience who demanded conventional ideas in a conventional style, frequently deadened Lowell's enthusiasms. When he wrote down to a less educated readership with the aim of persuading, delighting, or entertaining, he often gave his natural wit full reign and created a series of lighthearted poems having the suppleness, spontaneity, and mischieviousness of Mark Twain's prose or Ogden Nash's verse. His first three volumes contained few of these newspaper or magazine pieces, but *Under the Willows and Other Poems* and *Heartsease and Rue* were in the main collections of periodical pieces first printed in the *Atlantic Monthly*, the *Century Illustrated Monthly Magazine*, *The Nation*, and the *New York Ledger*.

"The Unhappy Lot of Mr. Knott," which first appeared in *Graham's Magazine* in 1851, typified this happier Lowell with its sharp-edged portrait of the more shallow aspirations of New England's middle classes. His description of Knott's daughter's wedding, complete with its digressive and gratuitous advertisement, was characteristic of the stylistic pyrotechnics he sustained throughout the thousand-line cultural portrait:

> Accordingly, this artless maid
> Her father's ordinance obeyed,
> And, all in whitest crape arrayed,
> (Miss Pulsifer the dresses made
> And wishes here the fact displayed
> That she still carries on the trade,
> The third door south from Bagg's Arcade.)

His control of rhyme, rhythm, and narrative showed a technical virtuosity that he seldom duplicated in his more serious poetry. His *Fitz Adam's Story*, published in the *Atlantic Monthly* in 1867, displayed several additional devices in his arsenal of skills. Primary was Lowell's command of regional dialect. Ezra Weeks, the proprietor of the country inn where Fitz Adams was staying could summarize his approach to cooking game birds this way:

> Wal, them's real nice uns, an'll eat A 1,
> Ef I can stop their bein' overdone;
> Nothin' riles me (I pledge my fastin' word)
> Like cookin' out the natur' of a bird . . .
> Jes scare 'em with the coals,—thet's my idee.

Lowell also exhibited a keen eye for detail and an even keener mind for universalizing the details he found. Above Weeks's mantel was this portrait of his parents:

> Mister and Mistress W. in their youth,—
> New England youth, that seems a sort of pill . . .
> Bitter to swallow, and which leaves a trace
> Of Calvinistic colic on the face.

Its breezy, iambic pentameter rhythm, accented with rhyming couplets, showed a playfulness and an experimental approach to metrics that kept the poem's cadences fresh for almost all of its 632 lines. In "The Flying Dutchman" and "The Voyage to Vinland," Lowell discovered that he could make the same informal approach to purely historical subjects. In his light verse, he seemed to find the freedom to overcome the deadening conventions that marred his more serious poetry. Yet his own sense of self-worth and his traditional attitudes toward what poetry should be prevented him from writing much verse in this, his happiest of styles. He had frequently proven that he was good at the pose, but he never quite let himself believe that the pose was good enough for him.

On occasion, Lowell could turn the warmhearted humor of his lighter verses into cool, even bitter, invective. Some of his satiric poetry managed to be as biting as some of Jonathan Swift's best prose and as angry as Alexander Pope's least charitable couplets. The most famous of his satires, and the most often anthologized, was his *A Fable for Critics*, which first appeared in 1848. It was a long, loosely structured narrative that gave Lowell the opportunity to demean most of the major and many of the minor writers in America. To a gathering of the gods on Olympus is summoned a critic who "bolts every book that comes out of the press/ Without the least question of larger or less." He was asked to review the careers of his fellow writers and find among them, "a rose." After ripping apart Bronson Alcott, Orestes Brownson, Theodore Parker, William Cullen Bryant, John Greenleaf Whittier, Richard Henry Dana, Edgar Allan Poe, and James Fenimore Cooper, the critic concluded that the best American has to offer Greece was but a thistle. If Lowell's critical summaries of rival authors tended toward brutality, he managed to leaven the tone of the whole by using the same playfulness he would later use in *Fitz Adams' Story*. He filled *A Fable for Critics* with puns, condemning, for example, prophets who "got their name of augurs, because they were bores." He tightroped his way around the downright silly with an array of surprising rhymes. In one breathless sequence, he strung twelve feminine rhymes together: rely on, scion, ply on, try on, eye one, zion, buy one, fie on, lion, spy on, wry on, and die on.

What *A Fable for Critics* did for American letters, the two series of *The Biglow Papers* did for American politics. Prompted by Lowell's conservative reaction against the imperialism of the Mexican-American War, the first series of satires appeared in 1848 along with *A Fable for Critics*. The papers consisted of a series of letters, essays, poems, and commentaries supposedly written by a variety of New England eccentrics. They indicted recruiters (with "twenty rooster tails stuck onto their hats and eenamost enuf brass a bobbin' up and down"), soldiering ("Ninepence a day for killin' folks comes kind o' low for murder"), American conformity ("for one might imagine America to have been colonized by a tribe of those nondescript African animals the Aye-Ayes, so difficult a word is 'No' to us all"), jingoistic politicians in general, General Winfield Scott and Senator John Calhoun in particular, and hawkish newspaper editors ("the name 'editor' is [derived] not so much from *edo*, to publish, as from *edo*, to eat. . . . They blow up the flames of political discord to boil their own pots"). Lowell's satires could be telling displays of a lifetime accumulation of stored anger: at writers who did not take themselves as seriously as he did, at politicians more swayed by popularity than by principle, at the general thickheadedness of the American public, and especially, perhaps, at his own failures to confront these concerns in his own serious writing.

On the few occasions when Lowell allowed himself to tackle serious thought with what he took to be serious verse, he produced a group of uneven reflections, sometimes brilliant, sometimes banal. In *Under the Willows and Other Poems*, *The Cathedral*, "The Ode for the 100th Anniversary of the Fight at Concord Bridge," "The Ode for the Fourth of July, 1876," "Agassiz," and *Ode Recited at the Harvard Commemoration*, Lowell tried to compress a lifetime of thought. Together, these poems shows his growing conservatism, a rigidity of mind and form that bears little resemblance to the inventiveness of his lighter verse. In *Under the Willows and Other Poems*, he moodily reflects on the glories of nature without garnering much glory for his subject or for his treatment of it. Its nearly four hundred lines do little more than recommend being gentle on and with New England's best June days. In *The Cathedral*, probably his best philosophical poem, he centers on a visit to Chartres and explores with precision, depth, and compassion some of the material only briefly touched on in "Under the Willows." Man's relationship with nature, so fuzzily treated in the early poem, is amplified in *The Cathedral* as a mixture of the objective and the subjective. Whether inspecting willows on a hot June day or building a monument, "graceful, grotesque, with ever new surprize," man seeks always, Lowell claims, some sort of synthesis between his interior consciousness and his exterior environment. For him, the cathedral becomes "Imagination's very self in stone." Like many a nineteenth century author, Lowell's visit occasioned a regret-filled commentary on the lack of the spiritual and the mystical in contemporary life. Whether in communing with nature or constructing edifices to religious aspirations, "this is no age to get Cathedrals built." Instead, modern man seems more likely to demean the efforts of the past, asking questions such as: "Did Faith build this wonder? Or did Fear, that makes a fetish and misnames it God?" In blotting "out life with questions marks," in unduly relying on "secular conclusions," in its own hyperconsciousness of "earth's comedy," modern civilization has failed to realize, he claims, that "each age must worship its own thought of God." His own age has been unable to find a satisfactory image of this transcendental impulse and thus remains a world of "incompleteness" where "sorrow" is "swift, consolation a laggard." The sense of faith and purposefulness, displayed so extravagantly at Chartres, suggests answers of a sort desperately needed by modern man. Lowell tries to end the rumination optimistically: "Faith and wonder and the primal earth," he asserts, "are born into the world with every child." As much as Emerson or Walt Whitman, Lowell believed that the godly was still available to contemporary man; he was simply less sure than his forebears how it should be attained.

Lowell vaguely recognized that his culture seemed to lack the sense of idealism that had driven previous civilizations. His was an era content with pat answers from the past and blind optimism regarding the future. This awareness filled his satiric poetry with hard-edged bitterness, but in his philosophical poetry Lowell never quite found the right voice to articulate his concerns, nor the courage to betray the commitments of his public voice.

Major publications other than poetry

NONFICTION: *Conversations on Some of the Old Poets*, 1845; *Fireside Travels*, 1864; *Among My Books*, 1870; *My Study Windows*, 1871; *Among My Books: Second Series*, 1876; *Democracy and Other Addresses*, 1887; *Political Essays*, 1888; *The English Poets: Lessing, Rousseau*, 1888; *Latest Literary Essays and Addresses*, 1891; *The Old English Dramatists*, 1892; *Letters of James Russell Lowell*, 1894 (Charles Eliot Norton, editor); *Early Prose Writings*, 1902; *Anti-Slavery Papers*, 1902.

Bibliography

Arms, George. *The Fields Were Green: A New View of Bryant, Whittier, Holmes, Lowell, and Longfellow*, 1953.
Beatty, R. C. *James Russell Lowell*, 1942.

Duberman, Martin. *James Russell Lowell*, 1966.

Hale, Edward Everett. *James Russell Lowell and His Friends*, 1899.

Howard, Leon. *Victorian Knight-Errant: A Study of the Early Literary Career of James Russell Lowell*, 1952.

Scudder, Horace E. *James Russell Lowell*, 1901.

Stewart, Charles Oran. *Lowell and France*, 1951.

Wagenknecht, Edward. *James Russell Lowell: Portrait of a Many-Sided Man*, 1951.

Philip Woodard

ROBERT LOWELL

Born: Boston, Massachusetts; March 1, 1917
Died: New York, New York; September 12, 1977

Principal collections

Land of Unlikeness, 1944; *Lord Weary's Castle*, 1946; *Poems 1938-1949*, 1950; *The Mills of the Kavanaughs*, 1951; *Life Studies*, 1959; *Imitations*, 1961; *For the Union Dead*, 1964; *Near the Ocean*, 1967; *Notebook 1967-68*, 1969; *Notebook*, 1970; *The Dolphin*, 1973; *History*, 1973; *For Lizzie and Harriet*, 1973; *Selected Poems*, 1976, 1977; *Day by Day*, 1977.

Other literary forms

Besides his free translations or rewritings of poems by writers from Homer to Boris Pasternak that constitute *Imitations* and the similar translations of Roman poems in *Near the Ocean*, Robert Lowell translated Jean Baptiste Racine's *Phaedra* (published in 1961, premiered at Wesleyan University in 1965), and *The Oresteia* of Aeschylus, which was published posthumously in 1979. *The Old Glory*, a trilogy of plays ("Endecott and the Red Cross," "My Kinsman, Major Molineux," and "Benito Cereno"), based on stories by Nathaniel Hawthorne and Herman Melville, was originally published in 1964, in which year the latter two plays premiered at the American Place Theater, winning Lowell an Obie Award; a revised edition, with an expanded version of "Endecott and the Red Cross" was issued in 1968, and "Endecott and the Red Cross" had its first performance at the American Place Theater in the same year. *Prometheus Bound*, Lowell's only other dramatic work, was presented at Yale in 1967 and published in 1969. Lowell also published a number of reviews and appreciations of writers.

Achievements

Lowell's poetry gives uniquely full expression to the painful experience of living in modern America; he speaks personally of his own experience as son, husband, lover, father, and mentally troubled individual human being; and publicly of American policy and society as a morally and spiritually troubled inheritor of Western cultural and Christian spiritual values. All the diverse kinds of poetry that Lowell wrote over a career in which he repeatedly transformed his art—religious, confessional, public—share a high degree of formal interest, whether written in traditional metrical forms or in free verse. Indeed, it was Lowell's ceaseless formal invention that enabled him to articulate, in so many different voices, the experience of modernity.

Biography

Robert Traill Spence Lowell, Jr., the only child of Commander Robert

Traill Spence Lowell, a naval officer, and Charlotte Winslow Lowell, was joined by birth to a number of figures variously prominent in the early history of Massachusetts Bay and in the cultural life of Boston. On his mother's side he was descended from Edward Winslow, who came to America on the Mayflower in 1620. His Lowell ancestors included a Harvard president, A. Lawrence Lowell, and the astronomer, Percival Lowell, as well as the poets James Russell Lowell and Amy Lowell. His ancestors' prominent roles in the early history of Massachusetts and its culture made him feel implicated in the shames of that history—such as the massacre of the native Indians—and the failings of the Puritan culture that became the ground out of which a money-centered American industrial society grew. His sense of his family's direct involvement in the shaping of American history and culture was conducive to the conflation of the personal and the public that is one of the distinguishing features of his poetry.

The poet had a childhood of outward gentility and inner turmoil. He had his schooling at Brimmer School in Boston and St. Mark's Boarding School in Southborough, Massachusetts. His parents had limited means relative to their inherited social position, and his ineffectual father and domineering mother filled the home with their contention. Richard Eberhart, then at the beginning of his poetic career, was one of Lowell's English teachers at St. Mark's and at Eberhart's encouragement he began to write poetry, some of which was published in the school magazine. In 1935 Lowell entered Harvard, intent on preparing himself for a career as a poet. He was disheartened by the approach to poetry of his Harvard professors, however, and frustrated in his search for a mentor. He was at a nadir of confidence, thrashing about for direction and desperate for encouragement, when an invitation to visit Ford Madox Ford, whom he had met at a cocktail party at the Tennessee home of Allen Tate, brought him to Tate's poetry and to Tate himself, who was to be a formative influence. Lowell was then torn between traditional metrical forms and free verse, and Tate brought him down, for the time being, on the side of the former. What Tate advocated was not bland mechanics but rather an intense struggle to apprehend and concentrate experience within the confines of form, depersonalizing and universalizing experience and revitalizing traditional forms.

His intimacy with Tate led to Lowell's immersion in the world and values of the traditionalist Southern agrarian poets who constituted the Fugitive group. After spending the summer of 1937 at the Tates' home, Lowell transferred from Harvard to Kenyon College to study with John Crowe Ransom, who had just been hired at Kenyon, which he would turn into a center of the New Criticism. At Kenyon, Lowell met Randall Jarrell, with whom he began a personal and literary friendship that ended only with Jarrell's suicide in 1965. While apprenticing himself as a poet, Lowell studied Classics, graduating *summa cum laude* in 1940.

Also in that year, he married the young Catholic novelist Jean Stafford and converted to Roman Catholicism. He did a year's graduate work in English at Louisiana State University, studying under Cleanth Brooks and Robert Penn Warren, and then worked as an editorial assistant at Sheed and Ward, a Catholic publishing house in New York City. Then he and his wife spent a year with the Tates, a year in which Lowell and Allen Tate both did a great deal of writing under each other's inspiration. For Lowell, the year's output became the poems of his first book, *Land of Unlikeness* (1944), about half of which were subsequently revised and included in *Lord Weary's Castle* (1946), the book that launched his poetic career, winning him the Pulitzer Prize. Also during this period Lowell, having earlier tried to enlist, refused to serve in the army in protest against Allied bombing of civilian populations and served time in prison for this failure to comply with the Selective Service Act. In 1948, Lowell's marraige to Jean Stafford ended in divorce, and the following year he married the essayist and fiction-writer Elizabeth Hardwick.

The late 1940's saw the reemergence of Lowell's respect for William Carlos Williams' free verse. Lowell admired the unpoetical language of Williams' "American idiom," and developed a close friendship with the older poet, who succeeded Tate as his mentor. The impact of Williams' work and ideas is reflected in the free verse form of the poems in the last of the four sections of *Life Studies* (1959). From 1950 to 1953, Lowell and his wife were in Europe. Returning to the United States in 1953, he taught at the University of Iowa, where one of his students was W. D. Snodgrass; the younger poet, along with the older Williams, helped Lowell to develop the "confessional" mode pioneered in *Life Studies* and in Snodgrass' *Heart's Needle* (1959). Lowell's mother died in February, 1954, in Italy; "Sailing Home from Rapallo" (*Life Studies*) tells of his trip bringing her coffin, on which "Lowell" had been misspelled "LOVELL," back for her burial in the Winslow-Stark graveyard in Dunbarton, New Hampshire. From 1954 to the end of the decade, Lowell and his wife lived on Marlborough Street in Back Bay, Boston, while he taught at Boston University. His students included Sylvia Plath and Anne Sexton. His daughter Harriet was born in 1957. In 1959, *Life Studies* won Lowell the National Book Award for poetry, while Snodgrass' *Heart's Needle* took the Pulitzer Prize.

In 1960, Lowell moved with his wife and daughter to New York City. *Life Studies* was followed in 1961 by a volume of *Imitations* of European poets, translations intended to represent what the poets might have written had they been alive in contemporary America, and arranged not chronologically but in an expressive sequence of Lowell's own. From 1963 to 1977 he taught at Harvard. During the 1960's Lowell became active in the movement against American involvement in Vietnam. In June, 1965, in an open letter to President Lyndon Johnson, published in *The New York Times*, he refused an invitation to participate in the White House Festival of the Arts in protest

against American foreign policy. He participated in the Pentagon March protesting American bombing and troop activities in Vietnam in October, 1967,
and was active in Eugene McCarthy's campaign for the Democratic nomination for the Presidency in 1967-1968, becoming a warm personal friend of
McCarthy. His political experiences are recorded in *Notebook 1967-68* and
the subsequent revisions of that book.

At the beginning of the 1970's, Lowell moved to England. He was a Visiting
Fellow at All Soul's College, Oxford, in 1970, and taught at Essex University
from 1970 to 1972. His book *The Dolphin* records the breakdown of his
marriage of more than twenty years to Elizabeth Hardwick and his developing
relationship with the English novelist Caroline Blackwood. While the emotional realities—entangled passion, fear, and joy in the relationship with
Caroline, a period of mental breakdown, the pull of his old life and wife and
their daughter Harriet—are vividly represented in the poetry, the events,
except for the birth of Lowell's son to Caroline, are not always clear. In 1972
he was divorced from Elizabeth Hardwick and married to Caroline
Blackwood.

By the late 1970's, Lowell was commuting back and forth between Ireland,
where he and Caroline had a house, and America, where he was teaching a
term each year at Harvard. His experience at that time, including the trouble
into which his third marriage was falling and the experience of having a son
late in life, is rendered in the poems of *Day by Day*, the title of which reflects
its closeness to the recordings and reflections of journal-writing. In the spring
of the last year of his life, he took a trip to Russia. In September, he died
of a heart attack in a taxicab in New York City, shortly after he had returned
from Ireland.

Analysis

American and European history and historical figures—military, political,
and religious—and other writers and their works were very much present in
Robert Lowell's consciousness. This influence is reflected in all of his poetry,
although the learning is worn more lightly after *The Mills of the Kavanaughs*.
As evident in his poetry, as his historical sense and awareness of literary
tradition, is the intensity of his mental and emotional life, expressed indirectly
through the vehicles of historical and fictional personae in his early poetry,
and in undisguised, if more or less fictionalized, autobiography, beginning
with *Life Studies*. Lowell's is a poetry in the symbolist tradition; its symbols,
whether used to convey religious significance (as in his first two books) or to
express psychological realities (as in his subsequent works) are remarkable
for their irreducible ambiguity. Ambiguity is indeed an essential feature of
Lowell's mature vision. Symbolic resonance is accompanied in his work by
a wealth of named particulars of the represented world; Norman Mailer has
aptly described Lowell's language as "particular, with a wicked sense of names,

details, places." His craftsmanship in prosody is remarkable in his early metrical verse, with its complex stanzaic forms and tension between the syntactical and the metrical structures. It is equally remarkable, albeit less flamboyant, in his later poetry, whether metrical or free verse. A gristly texture, partly the product of heavy alliteration, is characteristic of the sound of Lowell's verse. Also contributing to this characteristic choppiness is a syntax in which the subject-verb-adjunct sequence is frequently deferred or interrupted, especially by strings of adjectives, or broken off, leaving fragments interspersing the sentences.

Lowell's poetic career is remarkable for the number of times and the extent to which he transformed his art and for the frequency with which he revised his poems in public, publishing successive versions of a poem or different treatments of a single subject in successive volumes or incorporating passages from earlier pieces in new ones.

Lowell's voice in *Lord Weary's Castle* is that of a Catholic convert raging against the spiritual depravity of the Protestant and secular culture of New England, of which his own family was so much a part, and that of a conscientious objector decrying the waging of war. A note reveals that the book's title comes from an old ballad that tells of "Lambkin," a good mason who "built Lord Weary's castle" but was never paid for his work; in Lowell's poems, the mason Lambkin becomes a figure for Christ and Lord Weary for the people who wrong God in their lives. The verse of this early collection is in strict metrical forms, which are strained by features in tension with the metrical pattern, such as terminal caesura followed by violent enjambment. Prominently heavy alliteration also helps to weave its characteristically rough texture.

Of the poems in this book, "The Quaker Graveyard in Nantucket," an elegy for Lowell's cousin Warren Winslow, whose ship had disappeared at sea in the war, has been the most frequently anthologized and extensively discussed. The poem is in seven parts, all in rhymed iambic pentameter verse, varied, except in parts II and V, by occasional trimeter lines. Part I is a dramatic account, with much vivid and grotesque physical detail, of the recovery and sea burial of the drowned sailor's body, derived not from actual experience (Lowell's cousin's body was apparently never found), but, as Hugh Staples has shown, from Henry David Thoreau's *Cape Cod* (1865). It presents the sea as implacable in its power and the loss of life as irrevocable. Parts II to IV elaborate on the power of the sea and view the newly dead sailor as joining dead generations of Quaker whalers who foolishly dared the sea's and the whale's might; Lowell takes his imagery from Herman Melville's *Moby Dick* (1851) and associates the fatal presumption of the Quaker sailors with Ahab's obsessive and fatal quest of the white whale. The whale in whose pursuit the earlier generations of sailors lost their lives is multivalent in its symbolic associations—at once the wrathful, inscrutable Jehovah of the Old

Testament and the merciful Christ of the New. In Part III, "only bones abide/ There . . . where their boats were tossed/ Sky-high, where mariners had fabled news/ of IS, the whited monster" alludes, Staples suggests, both to such a biblical passage as Exodus 3:14—("And God said unto Moses, I AM THAT I AM: and he said, Thus shalt thou say unto the children of Israel, I AM hath sent me to you"—and to Christ under the epithet "*Iesus Salvator*." Lowell's dead cousin, who joins the whalers in their "graveyard," is implicated in their guilt, together with the war-waging society of which he was a member. Part IV closes with the question, "Who will dance/ The mast-lashed master of Leviathans/ Up from this field of Quakers in their unstoned graves?"— ambiguously alluding at once to Ahab and to the Christ whom the whalers are seen as having crucified again in their slaughter of the whale, as the contemporary soldier/sailors do in their killing in war. Part V presents a horrific scene of whale-butchering as a sort of vision of apocalypse; drawing on the exegetical tradition that sees Jonah as a prefiguration of Christ, Lowell concludes this section with a prayer to the hacked, ripped whale, in the richness of its symbolic associations, "Hide,/ Our steel, Jonas Messias, in Thy side." The scene then switches abruptly from the violence of the sea to the pastoral serenity of the Catholic shrine of Our Lady of Walsingham in England, destroyed in the Reformation but recently restored. Yet, while the first of Part VI's two stanzas presents an attractive landscape, the Virgin Mother in the second stanza offers no accessible comfort: "There's no come-liness/ At all or charm in that expressionless/ Face . . ./ This face, . . ./ Expressionless, expresses God." The final part returns the reader to the death-dealing sea, closing with a vision of Creation in which, even as "the Lord God formed man from the sea's slime," "blue-lung'd combers lumbered to the kill." After this formulation of the implacability and inscrutability of God's will, the poem closes with the line, "The Lord survives the rainbow of His will," offering, despite its recollection of the covenant at the end of the flood, no reassurance to the individual human creature who sins and dies, but only an assertion of an ultimate abiding that may or may not prove gracious to him.

The inscrutability and violence of God's ways in "The Quaker Graveyard in Nantucket" as well as the crassness and violence of the ways of men are typical of *Lord Weary's Castle*. This poem is also representative as a family elegy, a subgenre that was to become one of Lowell's most characteristic and successful. "At the Indian Killer's Grave" is another poem in which the poet confronts his dead ancestors, again censoriously. The cenotaph of his ancestors John and Mary Winslow is mentioned as one of the monuments in the grave-yard behind King's Chapel, where the poet's persona meditates amid "baroque/ And prodigal embellishments," that are in vain against the grime and noise of the impinging city (a subway "Blacker than these black stones" lies beneath the graveyard, and its train "grinds . . ./ And screeches").

Unmentioned by name, but part of the public history to which the poem makes reference, is another ancestor, Josiah Winslow, who was noted as an Indian fighter and served as Governor of Plymouth during the war against the Indian leader King Philip. The conquered Indian was beheaded and his head set on a pole in Plymouth. In Lowell's poem, King Philip's head "Grins on a platter" and delivers a jeremiad to his and his people's buried killers, the poet's ancestors, evoking "nature and the land/ That fed the hunter's gashed and green perfection" in implicit contrast to the urban scene that has been sketched earlier in the poem, mocking the Puritans' notions of election as of no avail to save them. In the last of the poem's five rather long verse-paragraphs, the persona of the poet "ponder[s] on the railing" of the grave-yard, wondering who the remote ancestor was "Who sowed so ill for his descent." The poem closes with paradise-garden imagery to answer the image at the beginning of the poem of the cemetery as fallen garden, and, in accord with Lowell's Catholic belief of the time, with an image of Mary conceiving Christ by the divine "Bridegroom," presumably suggesting divine mercy for both victims and victors.

Lowell's next significant collection, *The Mills of the Kavanaughs*, marks a sharp departure from the style and the outlook of *Lord Weary's Castle*. The long title poem and the other six poems of this volume are all at least partially dramatic monologue, and they deal mostly with situations of extremity—incest, madness, death—in the personal lives of their characters. They seem to follow from "Between the Porch and the Altar," a multipart poem of adulterous love in *Lord Weary's Castle*, with a third-person narrative section and a section of dramatic monologue by a woman, "Katherine's Dream." The Catholicism of the earlier book is gone, however; neither Christ nor Mary comes to offer the people of these poems a way to transcend the ills of their worlds. While *Lord Weary's Castle* is densely interlarded with biblical allu-sions, *The Mills of the Kavanaughs* draws heavily on classical literature. The allusions here are significantly different in their operation from those in the earlier book: while the apparatus of Catholic symbols was imposed on events by the poet in his interpretation of them, the myth of Persephone is very much a part of Anne Kavanaugh's consciousness and, as Richard Fein has pointed out, enters into her own efforts to interpret her situation, and the *Aeneid* (c. 29-19 B.C.) is similarly familiar to the old man in "Falling Asleep over the Aeneid," who assimilates his personal life to his literary experience. Randall Jarrell has remarked that the title poem is an unremitting succession of nightmares and nightmarish visions all at the same high level of intensity, and several reviewers of the book objected to its monotonous violence. With hindsight, subsequent critics have seen the characters of the poems here as vehicles for Lowell to convey experiences of his own, including that of mad-ness, that he would speak of straightforwardly in the first person in *Life Studies*. Certainly one acquainted with the poet's life will recognize autobiographical elements—in "The Mills of the Kavanaughs," the morally problematic heritage and the declining vitality and fortunes of an eminent family (the Kavanaugh family emblem, "Cut down we flourish," is that of the Winslows), Lowell's father's failed military career, and his own mental illness. Anne Kavanaugh seems to combine elements of Lowell's mother and of his wives. One of the remarkable features of the poem, indeed, is the extent to which it sympathetically conveys a woman's experience of a man who fails her; in this it is heralded by "Katherine's Dream" and anticipates "'To Speak of Woe That Is in Marriage'" in *Life Studies*, the poems given to painfully moving quotations of Elizabeth Hardwick's letters in *The Dolphin*, and many other later poems.

After an eight-year silence, Lowell published *Life Studies*. The book is in four parts: the first consists of four poems close in form and mode (two are dramatic monologues) to Lowell's previous work, although the poem that opens the book, "Beyond the Alps," definitely announces a change of stance from the Catholicism of *Lord Weary's Castle*; the second is an autobiographical prose piece on the poet's childhood; the third consists of four poems on writers who influenced Lowell (Ford Madox Ford, George Santayana, Delmore Schwartz, and Hart Crane); and the fourth, which gives the book its title, "Life Studies," contains the poems that drew the epithet "confessional."

"Beyond the Alps" is actually a sequence of three sonnets, each with a different complex rhyme scheme. The speaker is on the train going from Rome to Paris in 1950, the year the Pope proclaimed the dogma of Mary's bodily assumption. At the end of the octet of the first sonnet, the speaker says, "Much against my will/ I left the City of God where it belongs"; in the sestet he characterizes the figure who has ruled there in his time, Benito Mussolini, as "one of us/ only, pure prose." The central sonnet treats the proclamation of Mary's Assumption as dogma, undercutting it by a description of the Pope listening to the crowds in St. Peter's Square that implies he too is "pure prose": "His electric razor purred,/ his pet canary chirped on his left hand." In the final sonnet, the "mountain-climbing train had come to earth," and the speaker somewhat ruefully owns that "There were no tickets for that altitude/ once held by Hellas."

In the third and fourth parts of this volume Lowell turns from the accentual-syllabic metrics of his previous poetry to free verse rhythms much closer to those of conversation and, especially after the first part, from the relative impersonality and obliqueness of the earlier poetry to the confessional mode that *Life Studies* helped to pioneer. If the artifice is no longer obtrusive and the verse relatively transparent in Part IV, however, the poetry is no less artful in its construction: rhyme and half-rhyme, used occasionally rather than systematically, help to make the lines perceptible as units and to bind together stanzas; and alliteration continues to give the language a gristly texture. In imagery as well as in sound, these poems—sequences as well as individual poems—are unified.

The poems in the first section of Part IV, arranged in order of the chronology of their events in the poet's life, focus successively on Lowell's grandfather (the first three), his father (the next three), his mother (a further three), and an adult mental breakdown of his own (the final two). The last two in the first section take place in the world of Lowell's adult married life, and there is a continuity between their imagery of place and that of the poems in the second section, which focus on the writer's present, even if that present is preoccupied with memories (in "Memories of West Street and Lepke"). In "Man and Wife" and "To Speak of Woe That Is in Marriage" in the second section, Lowell's marriage, in the background in "Waking in the Blue" and "Home After Three Months Away" at the end of the first section, comes into the foreground. The particulars of decor, attire, and gesture with which these poems are richly furnished serve not to invoke an anagogic level of meaning, but at once to create a sense of actual experience in all its centrifugal detail and to convey character and psychological fate.

"Skunk Hour," the poem that closes the book, while highly particular in its dramatized situation, nevertheless has, more than any of the rest of these confessional pieces, a degree of independence from temporal succession, which, besides its power, has probably been a factor in the frequency with which it has been chosen to represent Lowell in anthologies. The eight six-line stanzas of "Skunk Hour" carry the speaker from detached, amusingly sharp observations of the foibles and failings of fellow residents of his New England summer resort town and the "illness" of its season to direct, mordantly sharp confession of his own neurotic behavior and his mind's and spirit's illness, to the richly ambiguous image of vitality and survival in the face of the town's enervation, the season's fading, and the speaker's despair that concludes *Life Studies*. The first four stanzas are devoted to social observation—of "Nautilus Island's hermit/ heiress" who is "in her dotage" and "buys up all/ the eyesores facing her shore,/ and lets them fall"; of the disappearance of the "summer millionaire,/ who seemed to leap from an L. L. Bean/ catalogue," and the sale of his yacht; of the "fairy/ decorator [who] brightens his shop for fall," but finds "no money in his work," would "rather marry." Significantly, where the first person pronoun appears, it is in the plural ("**our** summer millionaire," "**our** fairy decorator"); the poet speaks as a townsman, one of a community (albeit a derelict one). By the fifth stanza, however, he has ceased to be one of the people; now, apart from them, he tells the reader that he "climbed the hill's skull," where "I watched for love-cars." In a scene of anguished isolation suggestive of St. John of the Cross's "dark night of the soul," he declares, "My mind's not right." By the end of the sixth stanza, his voice has come to echo that of Milton's Satan: "I myself am hell;/ nobody's here." From this nadir, his attention swings to be arrested, in the final two stanzas, by "a mother skunk with her column of kittens" that "march[es] . . .

up Main Street," "swills the garbage pail . . ./ and will not scare." Where the man of sensibility has skulked and shrunk, the animal swaggers and holds her ground; if her crassness is appalling, her vitality is indeed a "rich air" against the town's stale atmosphere and the speaker's close self-constructed cell. The significance of the image is as intractable in its ambiguity as its subject is stubborn in her determination to feed on the sour cream in the garbage.

In *For the Union Dead*, Lowell's poetry continues to speak in the personal voice that emerged in *Life Studies*. Poems such as "Eye and Tooth" and "Myopia: A Night" are of the eye turned inward, focused on the "I," its tormenting memories and self-hatred. Others, notably "The Old Flame," "The Scream," "The Public Garden," and "Returning," revisit scenes of the poet's past as child or lover; interestingly, both "The Old Flame" and "The Public Garden" incorporate passages from poems in *The Mills of the Kavanaughs*, where the experiences in question were ascribed to dramatic characters rather than to the poet's self. A difference from the "Life Studies" poems is that these are separate lyrics and do not fit together into sequences. The theme of the cultural heritage of New England, treated in *Lord Weary's Castle*, is again treated here in a poem that speaks of Nathaniel Hawthorne and one that addresses Jonathan Edwards in intimate tones and with great sympathy. (A similar intimacy and sympathy inform the poem addressed to Caligula, by whose name Lowell had been called by his classmates at St. Mark's.) There is, besides, a new element in this book: the poet deals with contemporary society and politics, not, as he had in *Lord Weary's Castle*, in Christian terms, as features of a world for which apocalypse was imminent, but with the same keen, painful observation and moral concern he had, since *Life Studies*, been bringing to bear on his personal life; he deals with them, indeed, as part and parcel of his personal experience.

The title poem, "For the Union Dead," revisits the old Boston Aquarium that the poet had gone to as a child, even as "The Public Garden" revisits that old "stamping ground" of Lowell and his wife. The difference is that while in the latter "[t]he city and its cruising cars surround" a private failure to "catch fire," in "For the Union Dead" the Aquarium is presented not as part of a personal landscape only, but, closed, its fish replaced by "giant finned cars," as emblematic of the course of Boston's, New England's, and America's culture. The other complex emblem in the poem is the monument to Colonel Shaw, friend and in-law to the poet's Lowell ancestors, who led the first regiment of free blacks in an attack on a fort defending Charleston harbor, in which he and about half of his black soldiers were killed. The poem is in a sense another of Lowell's family elegies, but it opens beyond family history to national history. As the Aquarium's fish have been replaced by finned cars, the monument to the Civil War hero is now "propped by a plank splint" as support against the "earthquake" produced by excavation for a parking garage, and it has come to "stick like a fishbone/ in the city's throat."

In a city of giant cars and parking garages, the martyred leader, "lean/ as a compass-needle," who "seems to wince at pleasure," is "out of bounds"; such firm sense of direction and such asceticism are no longer virtues the populace is comfortable contemplating or moved to emulate.

The poem is not, however, a sentimental one of pure nostalgia for an earlier period of the society's life or of the poet's, for the heroism of war before the World Wars or for the lost Aquarium and the child's pleasure in it. The fish that lived in the Aquarium tanks are described as "cowed, compliant," and the child's eagerness was "to burst the bubbles/ drifting from their noses." Colonel Shaw is said to have enjoyed "man's lovely,/ peculiar power to choose life and die"—hardly an unequivocal good, albeit preferable to the power to choose "a Mosler Safe, the 'Rock of Ages'/ that survived the blast" at Hiroshima to safeguard one's material wealth. Nor is the contemporary landscape presented as wholly desert; the steamshovels that excavate for the parking garages are "yellow dinosaur steamshovels . . . grunting/ as they cropped up tons of mush and grass," creatures not without appeal. Indeed, the attractiveness of martyrdom, as Lowell presents it, may not be that far removed from the appeal of fish behind glass or steamshovels behind barbed wire: "I often sigh still," says the poem's speaker, "for the dark downward and vegetating kingdom/ of the fish and reptile." There is, finally, an irreducible ambiguity in the poem's treatment of past and present, Aquarium and garage, Union soldier and contemporary Bostonian.

The title sequence of *Near the Ocean* consists of five numbered poems. The first two of these ("Waking Early Sunday Morning" and "Fourth of July in Maine") and the last ("Near the Ocean") are composed in rhymed couplets of iambic tetrameter lines, arranged in eight-line stanzas. This is the stanza form of Andrew Marvell's "The Garden" and *Upon Appleton House*, a formal resemblance that may be taken to link Lowell's efforts to mediate between the private and the public realms of experience with the similar achievement of his seventeenth century predecessor. Of the remaining poems in the sequence, the third ("The Opposite House") is in nine-line stanzas of unrhymed short-line free verse; the fourth ("Central Park") is in iambic tetrameter couplets grouped in verse paragraphs. One cannot help being struck at the relative traditional formality of this verse after the free verse of *Life Studies* and *For the Union Dead*. Also very striking in the stanzaic verse is the fact that every one of the long stanzas is closed, giving each a tendency toward autonomy and setting the poem trembling with centrifugal forces. The blockiness and relative independence of these individual stanzas that yet for the most part do not stand quite free anticipates the fourteen-line blank verse units that will constitute *Notebook*.

Another striking feature of *Near the Ocean*—speaking, now, of the whole book—is that it consists partly of original poems, partly of translations (of Horace, Juvenal, and Dante). Lowell said in an interview that his translation enabled him to bring into English something that he would not dare write in English himself although he wished he could; thus, even where the translations are close, they are, to an important extent, expressions of Lowell's sensibility. If the translations are, thus, more of Lowell himself than one might at first take them to be, the original poems turn out to engage his poetic predecessors as significantly as do the translations. "Waking Early Sunday Morning" has its meaning in relation to Wallace Stevens' "Sunday Morning"; "Central Park" similarly evokes and responds to the "Sunday in the Park" section of William Carlos Williams' *Paterson* (1946-1958). The title poem of the sequence can be interpreted as a sort of Lowellian "Dover Beach."

While the poet of "Sunday Morning" was content that earth should turn out to "Seem all of paradise that we shall know," the poet of "Waking Early Sunday Morning" finds no "heavenly fellowship/ Of men that perish and of summer morn" (Stevens) to supersede the failed fellowship of "the Faithful at Church," where the Bible is "chopped and crucified/ in hymns we hear but do not read." Lowell finds instead that "Only man thinning out his kind/ sounds through the Sabbath noon," and instead of the vision of earth as a paradisal garden with deer, whistling quail, ripening berries, and flocks of pigeons that closes Stevens' poem, Lowell sees the planet as a joyless "ghost/ orbiting forever lost," its people "fall[ing]/ in small war on the heels of small/ war." The world of Lowell's poem is a more complicated one than that of Stevens' in that it has a political aspect; the state with its monstrous militarism and the vulgarity of its leader, which is seen as "this Sunday morning, free to chaff/ his own thoughts with his bear-cuffed staff,/ swimming nude, unbuttoned, sick/ of his ghost-written rhetoric," is part of what the speaker here must assimilate. Furthermore the spiritual yearning of the speaker in Lowell's poem is more complex than Stevens'. The poem opens with his cry, "O to break loose," but not simply "to break loose"; rather "to break loose like the chinook/ salmon" that overcomes the current to reach its river birthplace "alive enough to spawn and die." The release longed for is the release of suicide. This is not all, though. Further on, the speaker voices an exclamation: "O that the spirit could remain/ tinged but untarnished by its strain!" This cry is preceded by a passage describing a glass of water fuzzed with condensation that looks silvery in the light of the sky; when it is seen from a shifted perspective, with brown wood behind it, the wood comes "to darken it, but not to stain." Salmon and glass of water, like key images in other Lowell poems, are profoundly ambiguous; there is no claim for objectivity in the anatomy of his world by a speaker who looks upon it through the dark glass of his own psychology—which is itself part of the world that the poem presents.

In his next book, *Notebook 1967-68*, Lowell again effects a striking formal transformation. The fourteen-line pieces in blank verse that Lowell used to register his various preoccupations—his marriage, wife and daughter, love affairs; his dreams; the Vietnam War, the Pentagon March, Eugene McCarthy's campaign for the Democratic presidential nomination, other political events by which he was affected or in which he was involved; other writers, both his friends among contemporaries and the predecessors who contributed to the literary tradition that he inherited; figures of history—were, he said in his "Afterthought" to *Notebook 1967-68*, "written as one poem." The organization of the pieces is partially according to Lowell's order of composition/ experience, partially according to subject, setting, or season. Individual poems do, however, resist being subsumed in the whole book, either the original or the expanded edition of *Notebook*, in part because they are sonnetlike in more than number of lines and meter. In particular, Lowell's tendency to epigrammatic conclusions helps endow individual poems with an autonomy stronger than the centripetal force exerted by a loosely seasonal organization.

Despite the frequency of the memorable concluding line or couplet, however, and despite the fact that these poems often embrace what Lowell called "the themes and gigantism of the sonnet," they do not have the sort of logical structure characteristic of the traditional sonnet. Their movement is typically associative, sometimes obscurely so; their phrases frequently do not join into complete sentences. The first poem in the section called "October and November" in *Notebook 1967-68*, "Che Guevara," can be taken as representative in its technique and in the spheres of reference—contemporary public affairs, the poet's personal life, the historical past—that it telescopes. Beginning with the notation, "Week of Che Guevara," it sketches Che's assassination and conveys Lowell's attitude toward it (as an instance at once of violence begetting violence and of a spirit having a certain grandeur being done in by meaner ones) in a series of participles and absolute constructions taking the first five lines. The scene then switches, by the mere transition of an "as" (which disappears in subsequent revision) indicating temporal simultaneity, to the poet's autumn in Manhattan, presented first through features indicating the season and evoking a mood—still-green leaves "burn to frittered reds," an oak tree "swells with goiters"—then through ones adumbrating the socioeconomic realities of the city—its "high white stone buildings over-/ shadow the poor"—then sliding through progressive subordination to the personal—"where our clasped, illicit hands/ pulse." Abruptly the final couplet first returns readers to the public event with which the poem began; then, taking up an association of the mentioned oak tree, the final couplet throws it into historical perspective, in a resonant, memorable conclusion: "Rest for the outlaw . . . kings once hid in oaks,/ with prices on their heads, and watched for game."

Both the heterogeneity of material treated as readers move from poem to poem, section to section, and the quick shifts within individual poems that are characteristic of their style (Lowell at one point makes explicit reference to this stylistic trait, saying, in the second poem of the "Harvard" section,

"My mind can't hold the focus for a minute./ A sentence? A paragraph? . . ./ Flash-visions . . ."), create the impression of a mind besieged by an unremitting succession of disparate experiences that cannot be checked in their passing. When, in the second poem of *Notebook 1967-68*, the poet, killing a fly that has been "wham[ming] back and forth across" his daughter's bed, says "another instant's added/ to the horrifying mortmain of/ ephemera," he strikes a keynote for the whole book.

The succession of experiences do not, of course, all come from external events, but also from Lowell's reading and memory. The order in which subjects appear from poem to poem reflects his mental associations and the tensions in his thought as much as the flux of events in his life. In two poems on the Pentagon March, Lowell expresses his ambivalence toward pacificism and military valor. In the first, he compares the marchers he is among to "green Union Army recruits/ for the first Bull Run" and characterizes the soldiers who face them by a series of images, "the Martian, the ape, the hero,/ his new-fangled rifle, his green new steel helmet," conveying a profound ambivalence, confounding the two groups even as he distinguishes them and simultaneously both exalting and deflating each of them. The second poem on the March, which closes with Lowell helped staggering to his feet to "flee" the soldiers, is followed by an elegy on his ancestor Charles Russell Lowell, a "Union martyr," a cavalry officer who, struck and dying, "had himself strapped to the saddle . . . bound to death." It all seems to add up to the coexistence in Lowell's mind of pacifist convictions and an admiration for military heroism, which, Richard Fein has remarked, could not be more tellingly displayed.

"Obit," the poem that Lowell uses to end his book, looks toward the ending of the flux of experience in death, toward "the eternal return of earth's fairer children" (that has been adumbrated in the seasonal basis of the book's structure and in its attention to the poet's growing daughter), and back toward the onset and passage of moments of consciousness, as lovers' "unconquered flux, insensate oneness, their painful 'it was. . . .'" The question that constitutes the final couplet is not the typical rhetorical question. "After loving you so much, can I forget/ you for eternity, and have no other choice?" asks Lowell, while the accumulated context of this poem and of the whole book that precedes it indicate that his intellect would answer yes, his inclination, no.

Lowell did not stay satisfied with either the pieces or the whole of *Notebook 1967-68*. First, he revised poems and added to sections to produce the expanded *Notebook*; then, he separated the poems dealing with his marital life into *For Lizzie and Harriet* and rearranged the rest into a sequence following the chronology of history, filling in gaps with new poems and sometimes turning what began as autobiographical poems into poems associating the same attitudes or experiences with historical or mythological figures; this revised sequence constitutes the volume Lowell entitled *History*.

While the arrangement of *History*, as contrasted with that of *Notebook*, might at first seem superficial, the book has a thematic focus for which the ordering of poems in accord with the dates of their subject is appropriate. Stephen Yenser has pointed to the section called "The Powerful" in *Notebook*, an expanded version of that called "Power" in *Notebook 1967-68*, as the germ of *History*'s structure and theme. The poem that originally ended the chronological sequence of poems on historical figures in this section becomes, slightly revised, the conclusion of the whole book. It is a summational poem that articulates the relationship among the book's principal subjects—the mythical and legendary heroes and villains, the historical political and military leaders, the writers, and Lowell himself as writer and as a citizen and public man. Originally entitled "New Year's 1968," it is, significantly, retitled "End of a Year." In a book dominated by the elegiac mode, it is an elegy of elegies. From an opening couplet that declares, "These conquered kings pass furiously away/ gods die in flesh and spirit and live in print," it moves to qualify that continued "life" in print as one of misquotation, then to look at the poet's writing of a run-out year "in bad, straightforward, unscanning sentences," the year's "hero" the poet himself, of unsound mind (*"demens"*), his story, given in the imagery of the stories of "conquered kings," one of running his ship on the rocks. From the image of the foundering ship, the text slides to the scene present to the poet, where slush-ice in the Hudson "is rose-heather in the New York sunset"; then, dispensing with the requirements of complete clauses, the poem concludes abruptly and hauntingly with a juxtaposition of images of the landscape before the poet and the carbon that inks copies of his typescript (earlier in the poem compared to a Rosetta Stone): "bright sky, bright sky, carbon scarred with ciphers."

The thread of personal life that was drawn out of the weave of *Notebook* to constitute *For Lizzie and Harriet* is continued in *The Dolphin*, a slim volume which continues the use of the fourteen-line blank verse form. A feature that significantly differentiates *The Dolphin* from those others is the use of a central symbol, accreting in complexity and ambiguity over the course of the book. The dolphin, with variants (mermaid, "baby killer whale") and in its various attractive and fearsome aspects (graceful, playful swimmer; powerful predator), is associated with Caroline, and the contradictory connotations of Lowell's symbol reflect his ambivalence toward her. In the course of the book, Caroline is progressively mythicized and becomes a gigantic, ambiguous, and disturbing character set forth in the image of the dolphin, while Elizabeth, the wife Lowell is waveringly leaving, becomes an ever clearer, ever more human voice, presented principally through quotation from her letters.

"Fishnet" and "The Dolphin," respectively the opening and closing poems of the book and serving as its frame, have become the best-known pieces of this collection. "Fishnet" begins with one of the series of nominals detached from any predication common in Lowell's poems of the *Notebook* form: "Any clear thing that blinds us with surprise,/ your wandering silences and bright trouvailles,/ dolphin let loose to catch the flashing fish." Already in its initial appearance, the dolphin symbol is ambiguous, associated with the appealing image of the "bright trouvailles," but presented as catching "the flashing fish" rather than as a flashing fish itself. In other poems the reader will find dolphin-Caroline presented both as a fish that the poet angles for and as a creature that may devour him. After its opening catalog of images, this first poem turns to reflect on the fates of poets: they "die adolescents, their beat embalms them." After several years of writing in the same verse form, Lowell was conscious that it was risky to continue with it any longer. (In a 1971 interview, he said of the form, "I mustn't tempt it.") The conclusion of the poem is affirmative in some of its diction, but ambivalent in its imagery. The poet presents his activity as a writer as "knotting, undoing a fishnet of tarred rope," the "undoing" presumably being a reference to his habitual revising and recasting of his previous work. In the closing couplet the product of this work is presented as surviving, but hardly in the manner in which, say, Elizabethan sonneteers spoke of their poetry as surviving: "the net will hang on the wall when the fish are eaten,/ nailed like illegible bronze on the futureless future." It seems that Lowell foresees a time when his poetry will have ceased not only to be part of a life being lived, but even to be intelligible.

The final poem addresses "My Dolphin" as a guide, guiding "by surprise," "surprise" being conspicuous as the last word of the first line in each of the "frame" poems. The language in which the dolphin's activity is described is again ambivalent: she "made for my body/ caught in its hangman's-knot of sinking lines," the fishnet of the opening poem turned against its maker, become at once noose and weight. Focusing on his own making, the poet indicates that in his use of his life in his art, both in what he has altered and in what he has told as it was, he has done injury to others and to himself, and he calls the book that is ending "an eelnet made by man for the eel fighting," the ambiguity of "for" pointed up by the inversion of normal word order in the participial phrase. Ambiguity of reference is particularly insistent in the final line, "my eyes have seen what my hand did," which points at once to the poet's registering of his life in his poems and to his awareness of what his writings have done with and to his life. Such ambiguity is appropriate to the complexities of experience and of language.

In his last book of poems, *Day by Day*, Lowell left the fourteen-line blank verse form in which he had been working for nearly a decade to write poems in a free verse more transparent and less marked with features such as sound repetition than that of *Life Studies* or *For the Union Dead*. The syntax has the looseness of the poems of *Notebook* and its progeny, without the tightness of their metrical form to resist its centrifugal pressures. Although lacking a single central symbol such as that of *The Dolphin*, this book has a central and insistent theme: age, the fear of aging and pain, the prospect of death. This theme is introduced in the first poem, "Ulysses and Circe"; in Lowell's interpretation of Ulysses' story, the old veteran of the Trojan wars, leaving a troubled affair with the young Circe, returns to Ithaca to find his wife "well-furnished with her entourage" and himself superfluous. Humiliated, cuckolded, his infuriated mind is set on the murder of Penelope's lovers. The situation of the aged lover and husband, here presented through the retelling of a much-retold tale, is presented through autobiographical poetry in the rest of the book.

The bulk of the book, its third part, bearing the title of the book, stays exceedingly close to a journal's day-by-day record of events and emotions. This final part is itself divided into three sections. The first covers a summer in England with Caroline, her daughters, and Lowell's son whom she bore. There is a measure of detachment and a certain urbanity in the reflections on the fate of England's great houses in poems such as "Domesday Book" and "*Milgate*." These poems of summer's fullness are all haunted, however, by intimations of coming emptiness; every subject becomes an occasion for meditation on infirmity and mortality. Most poignant, perhaps, is the edge given to the poet's sense of his age and apprehension of his death by his observation of his young son; a poem named for him, "Sheridan," finds its way to that ancient image of death, the scythe, presented, as is usual in Lowell's poetry, as a particular in the represented scene: "High-hung/ the period scythe silvers in the sun,/ a cutting edge, a bounding line,/ between the child's world and the earth." The second section of "Day by Day" covers a stay in Boston without Caroline, framed by poems of Caroline's departure and her return. This interlude is one for reencounter with figures and events of the past: a poem "To Mother" ends, "It has taken me the time since you died/ to discover you are as human as I am . . ./ if I am"; there is an imaginary dialogue with his father; his grandfather looms in two poems. A terrible memory from his St. Mark's days is told—being taunted to tears by his classmates and possibly having deserved it, having made a habit of harping on the defects of other boys to their friends; Lowell comes to a harsh self-judgment that "even now/ my callous unconscious drives me/ to torture my closest friend."

The third and final section, the most wrenching, records living with Caroline, ill from an old spinal injury and a mental breakdown and then recovery. Lowell envisions himself and Caroline bound together as "seesaw inseparables," always "one up, the other down," represents her as experiencing "my sickness only as desertion." In sickness, his fear of sickness and expectance of death evoke nostalgia for his lost Catholic faith: "The Queen of Heaven, I miss her,/ we were divorced." Voices and memories crowd upon Lowell in this section, which begins, in "Turtle," with an invocation to memory. In that poem, a memory of hunting snapping turtles turns into a nightmare of death. In "Unwanted," words from an article on John Berryman, remembered words from a family psychiatrist with an ambiguous relation to his mother, and remembered words of his mother, converge on his consciousness to bring home the recognition of his having been an unwanted child and of the impact of that on his psychological development—"to give my simple autobiography a plot," as the poet says wryly. The last three poems bring the book to a gentle conclusion. "The Downlook" turns back with nostalgia to the previous year in Lowell's and Caroline's love; evoked in pastoral imagery as a time when "nothing dared impede/ the flow of the body's thousand rivulets of welcome"; such turning back in memory is a consolation in "days of the downlook." The penultimate poem is a "Thanks for Recovery"; the last, an "Epilogue" that is an apologia, in which the poet regrets that "Those blessed structures, plot and rhyme," have been no help to him in this book, complains that his writings seem to him snapshots, neither fully true to life nor truly imaginary, but concludes by accepting and justifying his work as a response to the fact of mortality, giving "each figure in the photograph,/ his living name."

Major publications other than poetry
PLAYS: *The Old Glory*, 1964 ("Endecott and the Red Cross," "My Kinsman, Major Molineux," and "Benito Cereno"); *Prometheus Bound*, 1967, 1969 (published).

Bibliography
Axelrod, Steven Gould. *Robert Lowell: Life and Art*, 1978.
Cooper, Philip. *The Autobiographical Myth of Robert Lowell*, 1971.
Fein, Richard. *Robert Lowell*, 1970.
Kalstone, David. *Five Temperaments: Elizabeth Bishop, Robert Lowell, James Merrill, Adrienne Rich, John Ashbery*, 1977.
London, Michael, and Robert Boyers, eds. *Robert Lowell: A Portrait of the Artist in His Time*, 1970.
Mazzaro, Jerome. *The Poetic Themes of Robert Lowell*, 1975.
Oberg, Arthur. *Modern American Lyric: Lowell, Berryman, Creeley, and Plath*, 1978.
Parkinson, Thomas, ed. *Robert Lowell: A Collection of Critical Essays*, 1968.
Perloff, Marjorie. *The Poetic Art of Robert Lowell*, 1973.
Vendler, Helen. *Part of Nature, Part of Us: Modern American Poets*, 1980.
Williamson, Alan. *Pity the Monsters: The Political Vision of Robert Lowell*, 1974.
Yenser, Stephen. *Circle to Circle: The Poetry of Robert Lowell*, 1975.

Eleanor von Auw Berry

JOHN LYDGATE

Born: Lydgate, England; 1370(?)
Died: Bury St. Edmunds, England; 1451(?)

Principal poems

Translation of Aesop; *Complaint of the Black Knight*, c. 1400; *The Life of Our Lady*, c. 1409; *The Pilgrimage of Man*, c. 1424; *Guy of Warwick*, c. 1426; *Dance of Death*, c. 1426; *Ballade at the Reverence of Our Lady, Qwene of Mercy*, c. 1430; *The Lives of St. Edmund and St. Fremund*, c. 1433; *The Life of St. Albon and St. Amphibal*, 1439; *Margaret's Entry into London*, c. 1445; *Testament*, 1448-?; *The Secrees of Olde Philosoffres*, c. 1451; *Falls of Princes*, 1494; *The Story of Thebes*, c. 1500; *Troy Book*, 1513.

Other literary forms

John Lydgate wrote only one significant piece of prose, *The Serpent of Division*. Scholars are uncertain as to its exact date of composition, but Walter Schirmer, in his *John Lydgate: A Study in the Culture of the Fifteenth Century* (1961), suggests the year 1422. Drawing on Lucan's *Pharsalia* (c. A.D. 80) and Vincent of Beauvais' *Speculum Historiale*, Lydgate here presents the first comprehensive account of the rise and fall of Julius Caesar ever written in English. As he does in so many of his other writings, Lydgate uses this story as an *exemplum*, a story used to teach morality. Here Lydgate's lesson had to do with civil war.

Certain of Lydgate's poems are very intimately connected with later English dramatic forms, especially the *masque*. His "mummings" were meant to accompany short pantomimes or the presentation of *tableaux vivantes*. For example, in 1424 *Mumming at Bishopswood* was presented at an outdoor gathering of London's civic officials. A narrator presented the verses while, at the same time, a dancer portrayed the Goddess of Spring with various gestures and dance steps. The lesson of the poem is conveyed through allegory, where immaterial entities are personified. Here Spring represents civil concord, and Lydgate argues that just as the joy, freshness, and prosperity of Spring replace the heaviness and trouble of winter, so too the various estates, the nobles, the clergy, and the commoners, should throw off their discord and work together in their God-given roles. Success in these "mummings" probably helped prepare Lydgate for his part in the preparation of the public celebrations for the coronation of Henry VI in 1429, and for the triumphant entry into London of the same king with his new queen, Margaret, in 1445.

Achievements

Lydgate was one of the most prolific writers in English, with 145,000 lines of verse to his credit. To match this, one would have to write eight lines a day, every day, for about fifty years. Further, almost every known medieval poetic genre is represented in the Lydgate canon.

Once the uncrowned Poet Laureate of England, Lydgate was appreciated by kings, princes, and nobility. Today, however, he is unknown to the general English-speaking public and often disparaged by literary scholars. Critics have charged that his poetry is dull, long-winded, and poorly wrought. Not all of these charges will stand scrutiny, however, and one could argue that Lydgate's fall is due primarily to a shifting of tastes in poetry rather than to poor craftsmanship on his part.

It is true that Lydgate's poetry consistently frustrates the modern reader, who expects poetry to be compressed and concise; Lydgate's poems are generally voluminous. Instead of irony or ambiguity, Lydgate usually assumes a rather prosaic straightforwardness. On the other hand, instead of ordinary words in their natural order, Lydgate uses obscure terms in complicated syntax. Far from writing "art for art's sake," Lydgate consistently insists on teaching sound doctrine and morality. Finally, in place of a uniquely personal vision and style, Lydgate always writes as a conventional public poet.

If one reads Lydgate through "medieval spectacles," however, these characteristics seem not only normal but praiseworthy as well. Lydgate saw himself as a rhetorician and thus felt it necessary to be both "sweet and useful" in his writing. Poetical art, to the medieval mind, was the application of rhetorical know-how to traditional themes and stories. Thus, he was first a craftsman, not a prophet or seer. He would not have considered his personal emotions or insights worthy of remembrance.

It is ironic, therefore, that Lydgate the careful craftsman has developed the reputation of being a poor versifier. If one assumes that his lines were supposed to be strictly iambic pentameter, this opinion may be justified. Fortunately, beginning with C. S. Lewis in 1939, certain scholars have suggested that Lydgate's line was based on a slightly different model, one which blends the French tradition of decasyllabic verse with the native tradition of balanced half-lines, thus allowing a variable number of stresses and syllables. In the light of these scholarly studies, Lydgate's verse seems consistently good.

Some critics, such as Schirmer (in *John Lydgate*) and Alain Renoir (in *The Poetry of John Lydgate*, 1967), argue that Lydgate is important as a poet of transition, since they find the seeds of Renaissance humanism in some of his work. While it would be foolish to discount their insights completely, however, the more traditional reading, expressed by Derek Pearsall in his *John Lydgate* (1970), still seems more satisfactory: "Looking for signs of humanism in Lydgate is an unrewarding task, because the whole direction of his mind is medieval." Lydgate will best be understood, therefore, if read as a medieval poet *par excellence*.

In any case, for hundreds of years the English literary public regarded Lydgate's achievement as equal to that of Geoffrey Chaucer or John Gower.

Indeed, the three writers were generally grouped together into a conventional triad of outstanding English poets. George Ashby's praise in 1470 is typical:

> Maisters Gower, Chaucer & Lydgate,
> Primier poetes of this nacion,
> Embelysshing oure Englisshe tendure algate
> Firste finders to oure consolacion.

Further, Lydgate was the glass through which his contemporaries understood and appreciated Chaucer, whom they considered a rhetorician, not a realist, the writer who finally formed English into a suitable vehicle for poetry, philosophy, and learning. In the end, perhaps Lydgate's greatest achievement was to consolidate this new status for his native tongue.

Biography

John Lydgate was born into turbulent times. His life spanned seventy years of the Hundred Years' War with France, and, when he died, the Wars of the Roses were about to begin. In 1381, he witnessed the Peasants' Revolt; in 1399, he saw Richard II deposed. The earlier years of his life were those of the Great Western Schism, with popes in both Avignon and Rome. At the same time the anticlerical Lollards were stirring up trouble for the Church in England. Even nature seemed to conspire against the peace, for, beginning in 1349, the plague struck regularly, killing large portions of the English population.

Born of peasant stock, Lydgate was reared in the quiet village of Lydgate, far from the civil turmoil which raged elsewhere. He must have had a fairly normal childhood, for he later wrote: "Loth to lerne [I] loved no besyness,/ Save pley/ or merth . . . Folowyng alle appetytes longyng to childhede" (*Testament*, 11). His serious side prevailed, however, and perhaps as early as 1385 he joined the Benedictine monastery at Bury St. Edmunds, about sixty-five miles northeast of London. Bury St. Edmunds was one of the richest of England's monasteries, with eighty monks, twenty-one chaplains, and 111 servants. Here Lydgate received much of his formal education, although it is likely that he also spent a few years at Oxford, where he may have begun his literary career by writing his *Translation of Aesop*, the first book of fables written in Middle English. If Oxford was a good place to begin writing, however, the magnificent library of Bury St. Edmunds was just the place to nourish such a career, for it is thought to have contained about two thousand volumes, at the time making it one of the finest in England.

By the time he was ordained a priest in 1397, Lydgate probably had begun building a modest literary reputation. Indeed, John Bale, a sixteenth century biographer, suggests that Lydgate had already started a school of rhetoric for the sons of noblemen. Although some scholars are dubious about this, it is certain that Lydgate at this time began to make friends among the aristocracy, many of whom were later to become his literary patrons.

As a matter of fact, Lydgate soon came to the attention of Prince Hal, later Henry V, who in 1409 charged him with writing a life of the Blessed Virgin Mary. Thus Lydgate wrote his first saint's legend, *The Life of Our Lady*. This was to be the start of a long and fruitful relationship between Lydgate and the Lancastrian dynasty, a dynasty which both the poet and his brother monks saw as a strong bulwark of Catholic orthodoxy against the Lollards.

Henry V was more interested in battle, conquest, and deeds of chivalry than in piety, however, and by October, 1412, he conceived a different sort of project for Lydgate's talent: a retelling of the popular story of Troy. It took Lydgate eight years, relying mostly on Guido delle Colonne's *Historia Troiana* (c. 1285), to construct this long epic of thirty thousand lines. His taste for versifying history, however, was hardly sated by this massive work, for very soon after completing *Troy Book* (1513), Lydgate set out on another long poem: *The Story of Thebes* (c. 1500). He found the frame for this tale in Chaucer's works; he presents the work as a continuation of *The Canterbury Tales* (1387-1400). Thus the pilgrim "Daun John" Lydgate himself tells the Thebes story—at length. In the Prologue Lydgate shows his sense of humor, ironically contrasting his own appearance, "so pale, al devoyde of blode," to that of Chaucer's strong, lusty monk.

Lydgate's admiration for his master, Chaucer, knew no bounds; for Lydgate, Chaucer was the "lodesterre" of English letters. Although he probably never met the older poet, Lydgate was a very close acquaintance of Chaucer's son, Thomas, who was a wealthy country gentleman in Oxfordshire. A glimpse of the closeness of this relationship is seen in Lydgate's *Ballad to Thomas Chaucer* (1417).

In 1423, Lydgate moved closer to the circles of power at Windsor; he was given charge of the priory at Hatfield in Essex, a post which he retained, at least nominally, until 1434, when he was granted a *dimissio*, or formal written permission to return to Bury St. Edmunds "to seek the fruit of a better life." In fact, Lydgate probably resided at Hatfield only until 1426. It seems that in that year Lydgate was sent to Paris to take up a senior post on the staff of John of Lancaster, Duke of Bedford. Here, among other things, he wrote *Guy of Warwick*, an adaptation of an old epic poem glorifying a mythical English hero who saves England from the Danes by overcoming their champion, Colbrand.

While in France Lydgate met Thomas de Montacute, the fourth Earl of Salisbury, who was the second husband of Alice Chaucer, the granddaughter of the poet. Montacute had a great interest in letters and commissioned Lydgate's translation of Guilliam de Deguileville's popular *Pèlerinage de la vie humaine* (1330-1331), a long allegorical romance concerning the "pilgrimage" of man through this earthly existence.

It can be assumed that in Paris Lydgate mixed with people of the highest tastes and education, both English and French, for these years were productive ones for him, during which he wrote many of his satires and religious poems. He was inspired, for example, by one of the most popular themes of fifteenth century art, the *Danse macabre*. Both in painting and in verse, this motif portrays the skeletons of men and women of all social classes dancing together as equals—in death. Lydgate's *Dance of Death* is a fairly close translation of verses which he discovered written on the colonnade surrounding the cemetery of the Église des Innocents in Paris.

In 1429, Lydgate returned to London for the coronation of the seven-year-old Henry VI. By this time, he was the premier poet of England, and thus he was commissioned to write an official *Roundel for the Coronation*, setting forth Henry's hereditary claim to the throne. Lydgate also had a hand in the planning of the official public celebrations for the event. He did the same in 1432 when Henry triumphantly returned to London from his coronation in Paris as King of France.

Falls of Princes (1494), Lydgate's most important work, was commissioned in May, 1431, by Henry V's brother, Humphrey, Duke of Gloucester, then Warden of England. In some thirty-six thousand lines the poet chronicles the continual movement of the Wheel of Fortune, raising up and then casting down men and women of power and wealth. The work took the poet eight years to complete, a period in which he increasingly felt his powers being drained away by age.

In 1433, the King spent four months at Bury St. Edmunds and in commemoration of the event Lydgate was asked to write a life of the monastery's patron, St. Edmund, for presentation to the monarch. Later, in 1439, Lydgate wrote his final piece of hagiography, *The Life of St. Albon and St. Amphibal*.

Lydgate received a lifelong pension from the King in 1439, but he was not left in peace at Bury St. Edmunds to enjoy it. In 1445, he was again given responsibilities for the planning of a public celebration, this time for the arrival in London of Henry VI's new queen, Margaret, daughter of King Rene of Anjou. For this occasion he wrote *Margaret's Entry into London*, a work that no longer exists in its entirety.

In 1448, the poet, suspecting that his life was almost over, began his versified *Testament*, perhaps his most intensely personal poem. In it he denounces, somewhat conventionally, the levity of his youth, but he later proclaims in very moving terms his personal devotion to the name of Jesus. The tone and range of subject matter in Lydgate's *Testament* are much different from those of the more famous *Testament* written less than a decade later by François Villon.

Lydgate must have passed his last few years with some sadness over his country's fortunes. The Hundred Years' War was winding down, but not in England's favor. Further, the internal political turmoil which would eventually lead to the Wars of the Roses was growing in England. Lydgate's final work, which he left unfinished, is another attempt to offer wise counsel to the country's leaders. *The Secrees of Olde Philosoffres* is a translation of the *Secreta Secretorum*, supposedly written by Aristotle for his pupil Alexander. Benedict Burgh, who completed the work, relates that just after Lydgate wrote verse 1,491, "deth al consumyth," the pen dropped from his hand, and the much-honored poet passed into history.

Analysis

Much of what can be said about John Lydgate's art in the *Complaint of the Black Knight* can be applied very readily to the bulk of his writings, so it is a fitting piece with which to begin. The poem, written about 1400, is a conventional Love Complaint, a very popular genre of the age, of ninety-seven Chaucerian stanzas (stanzas of seven pentameter lines rhyming ababbcc). It begins with the poet, sick at heart, journeying out into the May morning to find some succor for his pain. He encounters birds singing, beautiful trees and flowers, a clear river, and a fountain which provides him water to refresh his spirits. All of a sudden, the poet discovers an arbor in which a handsome knight, dressed in black, sits moaning as if sick. After hiding, the poet discreetly listens to the lover's complaint.

The centerpiece of this poem is the highly artificial soliloquy which follows. Here the knight first confesses that he is tortured with overwhelming love; second, protests that his lady, because of false rumors about his conduct, disdains him; third, remonstrates with the God of Love, who, he claims, is unfair to honest lovers and rewards only the false; and fourth, offers his life to his lady: "My hert I send, and my spirit also,/ What so-ever she list with hem to do." Moved to tears by this complaint, the poet prays to the rising Venus, asking that she will have pity on this true lover. He then prays that all lovers will be true and that they will enjoy one another's embraces. Finally, he sends his poem off to his princess, hoping that this "little book" will speak eloquently of his pain in love.

The whole poem, in Derek Pearsall's words, is "a tissue of borrowings," not only from Geoffrey Chaucer's *The Book of the Duchess* (1370), Lydgate's main source, but also from many of the poems of the French allegorical school. Borrowing, however, is normal procedure for medieval poets, for, as Robert Payne has shown in his *The Key of Remembrance* (1963), they considered their primary task to be not poetic invention but rather the reordering and the embellishment of traditional truths or literary works. Lydgate here is true to his times, and he works as a craftsman, not a seer. His main talent, then, lies squarely within the confines of rhetoric.

The landscape in the *Complaint of the Black Knight*, for example, is not constructed from personal observation or experience, but is taken directly from conventional descriptions of nature which Lydgate found in "old books." He tries to construct a *locus amoenus*, an idealized natural site fit for idealized lovers, both successful and frustrated. Thus, he uses all the details, the May morning, the flowers, the birds, the clear stream, that the sources stipulated. Moreover, Lydgate borrows not only descriptions of nature but also many other traditional themes, images, and literary postures, making the poem entirely conventional.

After selecting his genre, his themes, and his sources, Lydgate, working methodically, amplifying, contracting, or rearranging parts according to his own tastes, next fashions a fitting structure for them. Finally, he adds the embellishment, the literary "colors," such as alliteration, antithesis, chiasmus, echoing, exclamation, parallelism, or repetition. Thus, in lines 232 to 233 the Knight describes his woes with an elaborate chiasmus, reminiscent of Chaucer's *Troilus and Criseyde* (1382), I, 420: "Now hote as fire, now colde as asshes dede,/ Now hote for colde, now colde for hete ageyn." In lines 400 to 403, Lydgate adapts an exclamation from *Troilus and Criseyde*, V, 1828-1832:

> Lo her the fyne of loveres servise!
> Lo how that Love can his servantis quyte!
> Lo how he can his feythful men dispise,
> To sle the trwe men, and fals to respite!

Lydgate regularly protests that he has no literary "colors," but this too is a conventional literary pose. On the contrary, one finds "colors" used carefully and continuously throughout the Lydgate corpus.

In fact, Lydgate is so much interested in the surface decoration of his poetry that he sometimes seems to neglect its deeper significance. The elaborate descriptions of nature in the literature of courtly love, for example, were meant to have a purpose beyond that of mere ornamentation; they were supposed to carry allegorical meaning. In Chaucer's *The Romance of the Rose* (c. 1370), from which Lydgate borrowed some of his landscape, the fountain of Narcissus represents the Lady's eyes, the garden represents the life at court, and the rose-plot is the mind of the lady wherein personified fears and hopes do battle. C. S. Lewis discusses these allegorical meanings at length in *The Allegory of Love* (1936), but he could not do the same for Lydgate's version of the garden, for here the long description of the garden is not integrated with the rest of the poem. Once the Knight begins his soliloquy, Lydgate seemingly forgets the garden, whose description is thus solely a piece of rhetorical virtuosity. Indeed, that which is of most value in the poem is the part which is most intrinsically rhetorical: the formal complaint of the Knight. In Lewis' words, "The slow building up and decoration, niche by niche, of a rhetorical structure, brings out what is best in the poet."

In this context Lydgate's famous predilection for florid Latinate diction makes sense. The poet himself coined the term *aureate* to describe both a highly wrought style and an elevated diction. In *Falls of Princes* he describes his task in the following way: "Writyng of old, with lettres aureat,/ Labour of poetis doth hihli magnefie." The medium here fits the message, for Lydgate cannot resist twisting normal English word order. Moreover, the influence of Lydgate's style upon his successors was great indeed, for the use of "aureat lettres" came to dominate fifteenth century verse. It was not until the nineteenth century, when William Wordsworth began to attack "poetic diction," that "aureate" came to have pejorative connotations.

Lydgate, however, felt that, just as the host of the Holy Communion was encased in a highly decorated monstrance for public adoration, so too religious matter should be placed in a suitably ornate poetic vehicle. His invocations to Mary in the *Ballade at the Reverence of Our Lady, Qwene of Mercy*, are often cited as prime examples of this suitably ornate diction. After invoking the "aureat licour of Clyo" to enliven his dull wit, Lydgate compares Mary to the stars, precious jewels, various birds, a red rose, and to many other things in a riot of exotic images expressed in extravagant terminology. Lines 36 through 39 are a good example:

> O closid gardeyn al void of weedes wicke,
> Cristallyn welle of clennesse cler consigned,
> Fructifying olyve of foilys faire and thicke,
> And redolent cedyr most derworthly ydyned.

These images certainly were not original with Lydgate; they are doubtless echoes of the *Song of Songs*, but Lydgate has presented them in fittingly sonorous language, filled with alliteration. Ian Robinson, in *Chaucer's Prosody: A Study of the Middle English Verse Tradition* (1971), summarizes the matter well when he remarks: "Material enters the Lydgate factory mud and leaves it terracotta.

Not surprisingly, a great body of Lydgate's verse is explicitly religious, and nowhere is he more representative of his times than when he writes his saints' lives. Christian saints were the heroes of the medieval Catholic Church, and there was a great thirst on all levels of society for knowledge about them. Very early in the Christian era short narratives about the deaths of martyrs, *passiones*, or about the lives of confessors, *vitae*, began to be composed. These were meant to be read during the liturgy or the Divine Office. In the High Middle Ages, vernacular legends began to be written for the common folk, and, especially with the advent of the friars, these were used for public preaching. The legends, however, were viewed primarily as a literature of edification rather than as objective history or biography. Thus, "successful" structures, incidents, and even historical details were exchanged freely among the various legends. Generally speaking, then, medieval legend can be considered a type of popular formulaic literature.

In honor of the visit, in 1433, of Henry VI to Bury St. Edmunds, Abbott William Curteys commissioned Lydgate, who had written a number of *vitae* earlier, to write *the Lives of St. Edmund and St. Fremund* for presentation to the King. Lydgate's response was an "epic legend", in which the life of Edmund, the former king of East Anglia (d. 870) is retold in a suitably long (3,693 lines) narrative.

The work is divided into three sections. Books I and II recount the life, death, and burial of Edmund; Book III treats the life of Fremund, the King's nephew and avenger; and, finally, an appendix records several of Edmund's posthumous miracles. Most of the work is in Chaucerian stanzas.

Lydgate, using the Latin *Vita et Passio cum Miraculis Sancti Edmundi*, Bodlian Ms. 240, as his primary source, incorporates many of the standard characteristics of the *passio*. Thus, Edmund's birth is miraculously foretold by a strange widow when Alkmund, his Saxon father, is on a pilgrimage in Rome. In his youth, Edmund is pious and mature well beyond his years, so much so that his distant relative, Offa, chooses him as his successor to the East Anglian throne. After Offa dies, Edmund governs wisely and moderately, but despite his ability as a warrior, he comes to realize that bloodshed is hateful in the sight of God and repudiates warfare. Therefore, to protect his people from the marauding Danes, he offers his own life in return for their safety. When brought before the violent Hyngwar, leader of the Danes, Edmund refuses apostasy in the standard interrogation. Hyngwar loses self-control, as is typical of "evil judges," at Edmund's aggressive retorts and orders the King's execution. After undergoing a sustained round of tortures with superhuman endurance, Edmund is finally beheaded, but not before he sings out a long panegyric to God in which he asks to die as God's "true knight." The head of the slain king, although hidden, is miraculously protected by a wolf until it is found by Edmund's subjects. Other miracles follow before Fremund is introduced in Book III.

In this legend Lydgate uses his sources freely, carefully choosing incidents that serve his own purposes. The posthumous miracles, for example, are chosen to illustrate his theme that tyrants and other prideful people are eventually punished by God. His arrangement of those miracles indicates concern for symmetry, balance, and artistic control. In short, Lydgate's contribution to the history of the Edmund legend is that of a masterful rhetorician who fitted the legend into an elegant structure, added rhetorical flourishes such as prologues, prayers, and epilogues, and finished the surface with the appropriate sonorous diction.

The literary cousin to the saint is the fallen prince, for one can fashion an *exemplum* from each. If medieval audiences could be edified by the courage of the former, they could be taught detachment and humility from the life of the latter: for example, from the lives of Priam and Saul, Alexander and Caesar, Arthur and King John of France.

The theme of the world's transitoriness was another medieval commonplace, but Giovanni Boccaccio's *De Casibus Illustrium Virorum* (1358) treated the theme in a systematic and comprehensive way for the first time. In this work, all of the kings just mentioned, and many more besides, pass before the Italian poet and complain of their downfalls. Boccaccio's work became extremely popular and was translated into French in 1409 by Laurent de Premierfait. In 1431, Duke Humphrey of Gloucester commissioned Lydgate to translate it into English, and this free translation was entitled *Falls of Princes*. The task took Lydgate eight years.

Working from the French translation, Lydgate expands Boccaccio's work even more, filling in abbreviated stories, adding missing ones, inserting exhortations, and writing envoys for the end of each chapter. The result is a massive medieval history book (36,365 lines), a mirror for princes, an encyclopedia of world biography. Lydgate follows his medieval penchant for inclusion rather than concision, and thus the sheer bulk of the work is both a positive attribute—it contributes to an impression of weight and solemnity—and a fault—Boccaccio's fine structure seems completely lost.

Falls of Princes may be called a book of tragedies, for the medieval definition of tragedy was much simpler than Aristotle's: "For tragedie, as poetes spesephie,/ Gynneth with ioie, eendith with adversite:/ From hih estate [Men] caste in low degre." Lydgate follows both Boccaccio and Laurent in deprecating the blind goddess Fortune, a personification blamed as the fickle distributor of both tragedy and good luck. In the Prologue to Book I, Lydgate describes her as "transitory of condicioun," "hasty & sodeyne," since "Whan men most truste, than is she most chaungable." One often encounters medieval representations of the Wheel of Fortune, where one sees the blindfolded goddess spinning a wheel to which various men are attached. Those on the top, the rulers, enjoy the favors of good fortune, whereas those on the bottom, paupers or prisoners, are in misery. Figures on either side, however, the rising courtier or the falling prince, emphasize that the wheel is never static, and that both kingdoms and rulers pass away.

There were several common reactions to these lessons in mutability. First of all, they inspired sorrow over time's passing. Thus the *Ubi sunt?* (Where are they?) theme is found in much of medieval poetry, from the Anglo-Saxon *Wanderer* to the "ballade des dames du temps jadis" ("Ballad of the Ladies of Bygone Times") of Villon. Poets using this theme complain that everything beautiful, noble, or great in this world eventually passes away, leaving very little behind. As might be expected, Lydgate repeats this theme often and at length in *Falls of Princes*. In the Envoy to Book II, Lydgate ponders the fate of Rome. "Where be thyn Emperours, most sovereign of renown?" he asks. "Where is now Cesar"; where "Tullius?" His answer is not as poetic as Villon's "But where are the snows of bygone years?" for he states directly that "Off alle echon the odious ravyne of time/ Hath be processe the brought to ruyne."

If, on one hand, time brings everything to an end and princes are brought low by Fortune's variability, on the other hand, a good Christian ought to see

God's Providence working through Fortune, punishing pride or arrogance. Thus, by pondering tragedy, men of power can learn meekness, detachment, and humility, and place the highest value on spiritual things. "Ley doun thi pride," cries Lydgate; "Cri God merci, thi trespacis repentyng!" For the Romans, of course, it is too late, but it is not too late for Lydgate's contemporaries.

One wonders how many medieval princes read completely through all nine books of Lydgate's *exempla*. Even the Knight from Chaucer's *The Canterbury Tales*, for example, could stand only so many of the similar tragedies told by Chaucer's Monk: "good sire, namoore of this!" he cries, for "litel hevyness/ Is right ynough to muche folke" (*Prologue to the Nun's Priest's Tale*). Even Lydgate himself grew tired of his forced march through the ruins of history, for he complains about his fatigue in the Prologue to Book VIII. Moreover, Lydgate expanded on his sources less and less with each succeeding book.

All this has led Pearsall to speculate that perhaps the best way to read *Falls of Princes* would be to read only extracts of the best passages, which "are too good to miss." The structure of the work is basically inorganic and encyclopedic, since Lydgate, again being true to the aesthetics of his age, seems to have expanded on his sources to include in his work all "useful knowledge" rather than critically selecting and editing his material to allow an organic structure to emerge. Moreover, Pearsall remarks that probably Lydgate's contemporaries more often read the poem in extracts than as a whole, since parts of the work often appear detached from the rest in surviving manuscripts. Practicality supports this view, for there is much repetition and dull elaboration in the poem which most people would rather avoid; but, on the other hand, more detailed work needs be done on the poem's structure before it can be said that here Lydgate completely lacked structural control.

The versifying in *Falls of Princes*, as in most of Lydgate's work, has traditionally given critics problems. Although most of his lines can be scanned as rather regular iambic pentameter, a large number cannot, and these have in the past led certain writers to call Lydgate a bungling versifier. Recent critics have been fairer to the poet, however, and for good reason. First, medieval scribes were notoriously free in "correcting" their copy, adding or deleting words or changing spelling according to regional pronunciations. Especially with regard to the final -e, the sounding of which had probably ceased by the fifteenth century, scribal practices varied widely. Second, for all the current philological sophistication, medievalists are still not sure how Lydgate's contemporaries would have pronounced their native tongue. In short, all scansion of Lydgate's poetry is tentative at best.

The best approach to Lydgate's line seems to be that of Ian Robinson. He claims that Lydgate wrote a "balanced pentameter" line, a line which was meant to work both in half-lines and as a full line of five metrical feet. The English metrical line was in transition at the time, and this means that there were two sometimes conflicting traditions competing not only in the art of Lydgate but also of Chaucer. The first was the rather recently adopted French decasyllabic line, later to evolve into the English iambic pentameter of William Shakespeare. The oldest English tradition of verse, however, revived in the thirteenth and fourteenth centuries, constructed lines based on stress and alliteration rather than on syllable count. Thus the opening lines of *The Vision of William Concerning Piers the Plowman*, a poem of the fourteenth century Alliterative Revival, run as follows: In a sómer séson // whan sóft was the sónne/ I shópe me in shróudes // as I a shépe wére." Although one generally finds four stressed syllables per line (the first three of which were usually alliterated), the total number of syllables per line, stressed and unstressed, varied widely. That is why it makes no difference, metrically speaking, whether the final unstressed syllables italicized above were pronounced or not. In either case these lines are good alliterative verse since both read smoothly in rhythmic half-lines.

So too with Lydgate. If his verse is read with a strong medial caesura, letting the stresses, whether two or three per half-line, fall where they are most natural, the lines hardly every seem awkward. On the contrary, they are generally easy to scan. Some lines, especially the "broken-backed" variety—lines with only four stressed syllables—seem to fit the English side of the tradition a bit more, whereas others, being to the modern sensibility more "regular," favor the French side. Line 4,465 from Book II, for example, "Off sláuhtre, móordre // & outráious róbbyng," even offers a hint of alliteration in the stressed syllables. On the other hand, lines such as "Thi bíldyng gán // off fáls discéncioun" can be seen as favoring the French side of the tradition, although it still breaks easily into two smooth half-lines.

In the end, one must rightly conclude that Lydgate, wholehearted monk, sometime administrator, and laureate versifier for kings and princes, wrote poetry representative of his times and proper for someone of his position: sometimes prolix, often dull, but everywhere sincere, decorous, well-crafted, and worthy of remembrance.

Major publication other than poetry
NONFICTION: *The Serpent of Division*, 1422(?).

Bibliography
Brewer, Derek, ed. *Chaucer and Chaucerians*, 1966.
Lewis, C. S. *The Allegory of Love*, 1936.
_____ . "The Fifteenth-Century Heroic Line," in *Essays and Studies of the English Association*. XXIV (1938), pp. 28-42.
Miller, James I. "Lydgate the Hagiographer as Literary Artist," in *Harvard English Studies*. V (1974), pp. 279-290.

Pearsall, Derek. *John Lydgate*, 1970.

Renoir, Alain. *The Poetry of John Lydgate*, 1967.

—————— , and C. David Benson. "John Lydgate," in *A Manual of the Writings in Middle English, 1050-1500*, 1967.

Robinson, Ian. *Chaucer's Prosody: A Study of the Middle English Verse Tradition*, 1971.

Schirmer, Walter. *John Lydgate: A Study in the Culture of the Fifteenth Century*, 1979. Translated by Ann E. Keep.

Gregory M. Sadlek

JOHN LYLY

Born: Canterbury(?), England; c. 1554
Died: London, England; November, 1606

Principal collection

The Complete Works of John Lyly, 1902 (R. Warwick Bond, editor, 3 volumes, poetry and prose).

Other literary forms

John Lyly remains important both as a writer of prose fiction and as a dramatist. In *Euphues, the Anatomy of Wit* (1579), he forged a prose style which became an Elizabethan obsession. Characterized by the heavy use of balance, antithesis, elaborate similes based on fanciful natural history, and classical mythology, "euphuism," as the style became known, marked an attempt to adapt eloquent English to a narrative purpose. Much imitated by some contemporaries, greatly despised by others, euphuism is parodied in a speech by Falstaff in William Shakespeare's *Henry IV*, Part I (Act II, Scene iv):

> For though the camomile, the more it is trodden, the faster it grows, yet youth, the more it is wasted, the sooner it wears. . . . For, Harry, now I do not speak to thee in drink, but in tears; not in pleasure, but in passion: not in words only, but in woes also.

The plot of *Euphues, the Anatomy of Wit* is easily summarized: two young Europeans meet, become friends, fall in love with the same woman, contend, and finally—after she rejects them both in favor of a third suitor—reestablish their friendship. The work exemplifies the Renaissance courtesy book, which depicts the qualities of a gentleman or courtier, often in dialogue, though not usually in narrative form. Lyly's youthful effort became a model in two senses: a representation (of behavior) and a standard (of rhetorical prose).

A year later Lyly issued a sequel, *Euphues and His England* (1580), in which he sends his hero, together with his friend, to England for more social adventures at the court of Queen Elizabeth. Like its predecessor, this book combined romance and moralizing in a way congenial to readers of Lyly's time, who, it became evident, also enjoyed learning of those intrigues and glories of the court which only the privileged could experience firsthand. By taking romance out of remote Arcadian settings, Lyly demonstrated prose fiction's potential for depicting the morals and manners of society—though this potential remained mostly undeveloped until the eighteenth century.

Turning his attention to the stage, Lyly next wrote a series of plays for boys' theatrical companies. Beginning with *Campaspe* and *Sapho and Phao*, both performed at court early in 1584, and continuing with *Galathea* (c. 1585), *Endymion* (1588), *Love's Metamorphosis* (c. 1589), and *Midas* (1589), Lyly crafted comedies that mediate between earlier Elizabethan court plays and the comedies of the public theater, soon afterward to reach maturity in the works of Shakespeare and Ben Jonson. Euphuism lingers in *Campaspe*, but Lyly possessed sufficient theatrical sense to recognize that the elaborate rhetoric of his fiction could not survive translation to the stage. In his essay "The Prose Style of John Lyly" (*English Literary History*, 1956), Jonas A. Barish claims that Lyly "invented, virtually single-handed, a viable comic prose for the English stage." Two later Lyly plays are *Mother Bombie* (c. 1589), which does not seem to have been performed at court, and *The Woman in the Moon* (c. 1593), which was, although most likely by adult actors.

Achievements

Although Lyly gained a reputation as a comic dramatist and prose stylist while still in his twenties, any discussion of Lyly the poet must commence with the odd fact that aside from the blank verse of his late play *The Woman in the Moon* and a few Latin verses, no single poem can be assigned to him with absolute confidence. Because the songs found in his plays do not appear until Edward Blount collected the plays in 1632, some scholars have questioned Lyly's authorship of these often delightful lyrics. Readers who wish to review the pros and cons of Lyly's authorship may consult G. K. Hunter, *John Lyly: The Humanist as Courtier* (1962), the best modern book on Lyly, the appendix of which discusses the matter judiciously.

The Woman in the Moon, published in 1597 but written perhaps as early as 1593, qualifies as one of the relatively early blank verse plays of the Elizabethan age. The verse, while not "mighty" like Christopher Marlowe's, is euphonious and appropriate to a mythological comedy. It may be that Lyly found the verse drama uncongenial, but his verse is never less than serviceable.

Twenty-three surviving songs from the plays exhibit versatility and, in a few cases, a universal appeal that such songs often do not possess outside their dramatic contexts. One of the conjectural poems in Bond's edition, an allegorical complaint called "The Bee," may well be Lyly's, although it is often credited to Robert Devereux, Second Earl of Essex. Most of the doubtful poems, even if authenticated, would not add materially to Lyly's fame.

It is entirely likely that poems by Lyly have vanished or repose among the numerous anonymous poems of his age. Lyly himself, in a prefatory letter to Thomas Watson's *Hecatompathia* (1582), seems to claim a body of poetry which he might be prevailed upon to publish. Blount referred to him on the title page of *Six Court Comedies* as a "rare poet," and later in the seventeenth century the Oxford antiquarian Anthony à Wood finds him "naturally bent to the pleasant paths of poetry." There may be more to Lyly the poet than it is now possible to determine.

Biography

William Lyly, the grandfather of John, was one of England's early humanist scholars, the first headmaster of St. Paul's School in London, and coauthor of an influential Latin grammar. The grandson carried into his generation a similar respect for learning and language as vehicles of personal and social improvement. The younger Lyly earned degrees from both universities (B.A., 1573, M.A., 1575, Oxford; and M.A., 1579, Cambridge) and in the following decade earned a literary reputation, along with such writers as Robert Greene, Thomas Nashe, George Peele, and Thomas Lodge, as one of the "University Wits."

His first published works, *Euphues, the Anatomy of Wit* (1578) and *Euphues and His England* (1580), earned him fame but neither fortune nor the preferment at court that he sought, although he did gain employment, possibly as secretary, with the Earl of Oxford, to whom the second of these books was dedicated. In 1583, Lyly married Beatrice Browne, whose connections with several prominent families, including that of Queen Elizabeth's Secretary of State, Lord Burghley, probably intensified his ambitions.

In the early 1580's, Lyly associated himself with William Hunnis, Master of the Children of the Chapel Royal, and others at the Blackfriars Theatre in productions intended for court performance. After the performance of several of Lyly's own comedies, the Queen encouraged him to hope for eventual appointment as her Master of Revels, but, like many others, Lyly was kept dangling for years. He continued writing plays for the boys' companies of the Chapel Royal and St. Paul's until the dissolution of the latter group in 1590, and he took part in the "Martin Marprelate" controversy of the late 1580's on the side of the Anglican bishops against their Puritan antagonists.

His Euphues books make it clear that Lyly's ambitions reflected the influence of Baldassare Castiglione's *The Courtier* (1528) and other courtesy books of the sixteenth century, which stressed not only the courtiers' means to success at court but also the need of princes for the learning and eloquence of courtiers in such capacities as counselors, diplomats, and—in the case of a man like Lyly—resident influencers of court life. Lyly served in parliament four times between 1589 and 1601 but never gained the position that he coveted at court. In 1592 he and his family withdrew to Mexborough, home of his wife's family; in 1596, however, they were back in London, living in the tenement complex fashioned from the monastery of St. Bartholomew's. Lyly continued to petition the Queen until the year of her death, 1603, alleging long unrewarded service and proclaiming—perhaps exaggerating—his family's poverty. Otherwise, his later years were quiet ones. His funeral was held from St. Bartholomew's on November 30, 1606.

Analysis

The love of songs and singing was deeply ingrained in Englishmen well before John Lyly's time. Sir Thomas Wyatt, the best English poet in the time of Queen Elizabeth's father, Henry VIII, wrote songs for the entertainment of Henry's court; Wyatt also wrote other poems complaining of its corruption and its neglect of the meritorious. From the middle of the sixteenth century on, song lyrics were collected with other poems in anthologies called "miscellanies." Songs punctuated the plays and romances of the time, and late in Elizabeth's reign, song books, containing both words and music, went through sufficient printings to confirm that people did not merely listen to songs but sang them regularly in their homes.

Aside from the ballads and folk songs that had long been springing up apart from professional musicianship, two main classes of Elizabethan song may be distinguished: madrigals and airs. The former were unaccompanied, polyphonic songs for from three to six or even more voices. Poems settable as madrigals usually contained only one stanza, but the music was very elaborate and required skill and practice for successful performance. Elizabethans did not shrink from the challenge, however, and from the time the form was imported from Italy in the early 1580's it developed a distinctively English character. Madrigals were essentially "do it yourself" songs; the performers were their own listeners. Sung for enjoyment, madrigals were also read for enjoyment; the recollection of having sung or heard a madrigal enhances the pleasure of reading one considerably.

The air, on the other hand, was a solo song with an accompaniment by lute or other stringed instrument. In Lyly's play *Midas*, Pan, who is a piper, envies Apollo's ability to play the lute and sing at the same time, whereas he can only play and sing in succession. Lute songs might contain several stanzas, which could be set to existing melodies or music devised for the occasion. The apparent irregularities in airs, on closer inspection, usually turn out to be repeated at the corresponding places in the other stanzas. The limitations imposed by the musical phrases challenged poets to create variety within rather narrow limits. The words of the air, unlike those of the madrigal, go forward with fewer repetitions, and those are confined to obvious places, such as at the end of a stanza. Thus the air strikes a balance between words and music, as well as between feeling and the restraint of form.

Some songs in Elizabethan plays show madrigal influence, but for several reasons the madrigal does not accommodate itself to the theater as well as the air does. First of all, it is a "sing along" medium rather than one associated with performance before a substantial audience. In addition, the madrigal has little capacity for dramatic mood and movement. Then again, it is difficult to hear the words distinctly. Attentive as Elizabethans were to language and adept as they were in distinguishing the various independent voices of the madrigal, the balance between words and music characteristically tipped in favor of the latter. In a medium that emphasizes words and action, a predominantly musical interest is obviously impractical.

The music for Lyly's lyrics, as well as that for most other Elizabethan songs, has not survived, but the reader notices more air than madrigal traits. Several of Lyly's lyrics are part songs in which a group of characters—often three—sing successive verses and then join in a chorus. Such a song is the well-known "O for a bowl of fat Canary" in *Campaspe*. In *Galathea*, three of Diana's nymphs sing a verse each of vengeance against Cupid, betrayer of maidens; at the end of each verse they join in something like a refrain. In *Midas*, a page sings about his toothache in concert with another page and the barber to whom he has applied for relief from his pain. In songs such as these, however, it is doubtful that more than one voice was heard at a time.

One Lyly song which may be a madrigal, or at least madrigal-influenced, is "Sing to Apollo, god of day," which closes *Midas*. Indicated as a song for a chorus, it has two stanzas, and the rhyming is in couplets—a scheme preferred by Lyly and by writers of airs generally, but it could have been sung contrapuntally. Its subject matter and its position at the end permit the lengthy and intricate development characteristic of the madrigal.

More often, though, Lyly's songs are suited to the single voice, and the sound effects are those of a poet rather than of a musician. An example is the frequently anthologized song from *Campaspe*: "Cupid and my Campaspe played/ At cards for kisses, Cupid paid." Not only obvious alliteration on *c*, but also the reiteration of *p*, *d*, and *m* sounds, along with the pattern of *u*, *i*, and *a* vowels, knit the couplet together, as does the enjambment, while the strong caesura in the second line accentuates the outcome of the game. The poem exhibits not only technical proficiency but wit as well, for it explains Cupid's blindness as a result of having lost his eyes to the same girl. The singer ends: "O Love! has she done this to thee?/ What shall (alas!) become of me?" The emphasis, falling on the pronouns at the end of the lines, brings the plight of the lover into focus. Wit, which Lyly had anatomized in his stories of Euphues, is traditionally equated with intelligence; in the Renaissance it came to signify the use of the intelligence to surprise and delight the listener or reader.

Wit also marks the competition between Pan and Apollo in *Midas*. Apollo's song, "My Daphne's hair is twisted gold," typifies the idealized praise of many Elizabethan lyrics. It is lovely, disarming, but rather simple. Pan's song about Syrinx, a girl transformed into the reed from which Pan's pipe was subsequently fashioned, enables him to conclude that, although he misses her, nevertheless, any time he plays "still my Syrinx' lips I kiss." Asked to judge the competition, Midas prefers Pan's song, avowedly because the "shrillness" of Pan's pipe delights him more than the "nice tickling" of Apollo's accompanying lute. Affronted by the rebuff, Apollo confers a pair of asses' ears on Midas, who presumably deserves them for preferring shrillness to soft music and a rude satyr to a true Olympian. It may be part of Lyly's wit to suggest that in dealing with the great, wit must yield to the audience's normal expectations.

Witty and comical songs dot most of Lyly's plays. In *Sapho and Phao*, Vulcan, while making arrows for Venus—who, except for work orders, has been neglecting him—sings to his "shag-hair Cyclops" about the haplessness of the lovers who will be struck down by the arrows. In *Endymion* three servants sing to the sleeping Sir Tophas:

> That amorous ass,
> Who loves Dipsas,
> With face so sweet,
> Nose and chin meet.

In the same play a troop of fairies sing over another sleeping lover, Corsites: "Pinch him, pinch him, black and blue." Even at a potentially romantic spot in his comedy, Lyly is likely to particularize, not the splendor of love, but its folly and discomfort.

Some of the songs, of course, take passion seriously, such as Pipenetta's lament in *Midas*: "'Las! How long shall I/ And my maidenhead lie/ In a cold bed all night long?" and Sappho's in *Sapho and Phao*: "O cruel love! on thee I lay/ My curse." The feeling in these songs is relatively restrained, however, as might be expected in airs written for boy performers and designed for court performance. Lyly exercised his lyrical powers more often when, as in *The Woman in the Moon*, he was writing for adult actors.

In this play, Nature creates a woman, Pandora, as companion for four Utopian shepherds. Under alternate influences of the Seven Planets, Pandora first encourages, then discourages, each of the perplexed shepherds. They do not sing, but they speak in songlike tones: "Sweet is the night when every creature sleeps./ Come night, come gentle night, for thee I stay." Furthermore, they can present their cases in very respectable pastoral: "I'll give thee streams whose pebble shall be pearl,/ Love birds whose feathers shall be beaten gold" (and much more of the same). Sweet poesy does not, however, facilitate true love; Pandora winds up stationed in the moon with Stesias (he of the pearl and gold) as her slave, although, as the shepherd most thoroughly disabused of his folly, he must be cautioned by nature at the end of the play: "I charge thee follow her, but hurt her not." Nowhere can Lyly be confused with a romantic.

Of the seventy-three doubtful poems in Bond's edition of Lyly's works, one seems more interesting and less doubtful than most of the others. A popular poem in its day, it survives in many manuscripts; in some it is anonymous, in others it is attributed to the Earl of Essex, in only one is it ascribed to John Lyly. The poem can be conveniently referred to as "The Bee." Its association with Essex, a great favorite of Queen Elizabeth and later the victim of her wrath, virtually ensured its popularity at the end of the sixteenth century. In fifteen six-line stanzas with a closing Latin couplet, the poem gives a first-person account of a bee whom the king bee has "cast down." The bee's devotion to the hive having gained him only ill-usage, he withdraws, feeds on nettles, endures the taunts of the other bees, and finally decides to fly off to a place where tobacco grows, since "all the world's but smoke" anyway. Ten years of "slumber" elapse, the narcotic being not tobacco fumes but unfulfilled hopes; then the bee awakens.

Essex was known to be a poet, and he knew how it felt to be rejected—eventually to be condemned to death—by his sovereign. He even wrote poems expressing the disappointments of a life dependent on royal favor. On the other hand, the allegorical mode, while common enough in Lyly's plays, does not seem to have been Essex's usual one, which is characteristically more simple and direct: "She was false—bid her adieu;/ She was best, but yet untrue." While it is easy enough, therefore, to understand its ascription to Essex—poems were often attributed uncritically to another conspicuous Elizabethan courtier-poet, Sir Walter Raleigh, also—the evidence for his authorship seems far from conclusive.

Two scraps of internal evidence point obliquely—it would have been imprudent to point directly—toward Lyly. First, his editor points out that two contemporaries, Thomas Nashe and Ben Jonson, describe Lyly as addicted to tobacco. Second, it is possible that in one line Lyly was swelling the ranks of English Renaissance poets—Shakespeare, Sir Philip Sidney, and John Donne included—who made puns on their own names: "Once did I see by flying in the field/ Foul beasts to browse upon the lily fair." Puns were not low humor; they were a device of wit suitable for serious contexts.

A more important link between Lyly and "The Bee" is the frequency of the bee image in Lyly's known work. In *Euphues and His England*, an old man named Fidus, whom Euphues and his friend Philautus encounter "as busy as a bee among his bees" in a garden in Canterbury, gives the two an extended description of the social and "political" life of bees. The wise Fidus delights in the order of the hive and the good management of its king. "I have wished oftentimes," he tells them, "rather be a bee, than not be as I should be." Euphues readily accepts the validity of Fidus' assessment of bees.

The poem "The Bee" begins with the lines "It was a time when silly bees could speak,/ And in that time I was a silly bee," a considerably different attitude, to be sure, but one that may be explained by the passage of time itself, for the man who wrote *Euphues and His England* was in his mid-twenties and envisioned the court as an attainable goal, while the author of "The Bee" had known years of frustration. The author of the poem, for whom the honey for the court had turned sour, was time-obsessed; the word "time" appears no fewer than twelve times in the first four stanzas, while in the final stanza he counts the "five years twice" of his patience.

The reader of Lyly's extant letters to Queen Elizabeth discovers a similar preoccupation with time. In one—undated but presumably written about 1595—Lyly "fears to commit the error I discommend—tediousness; like him that vowing to search out what time was, spent all his time and knew it not." Like the bee, he reminds his monarch of the "ten years I have attended with unwearied patience" and concludes that "after ten years' tempest I must at court suffer shipwreck of my time." In a letter of 1598, counting himself "thirteen years your Highness' servant," Lyly begins his plea: "Time cannot work my petitions, nor my petitions the time." The Queen's answer, if she bothered to reply, must have satisfied him no more than that of the king bee in the poem: "Thou art born to serve the time, the time not thee." It goes without saying that Essex—no patient drone he—suffered no long years of neglect. To read autobiography into Elizabethan poems is always a dangerous occupation, but the mood of "The Bee" reflects that of the patient commoner rather than the mercurial nobleman.

If "The Bee" is Lyly's and dates from, say, 1595, the rest, except for beseeching letters to court, is silence. Baffled in his quest of Revels—where one of his jobs would have been the censorship of plays—and unable or unwilling to write the kind of plays then in fashion, Lyly had perhaps little more to say and no ready medium for saying it. In his songs, as in his euphuistic and dramatic prose, he had written cool, witty, detached English. The generation after him—Ben Jonson's generation—was learning to employ wit in satire, a direction in which Lyly's interests never traveled. Another possibility for a late Elizabethan poet was the uniting of wit with the kind of emotional density that Lyly displays only in his letters to court and, perhaps, in "The Bee." G. K. Hunter devotes the last chapter of his study of Lyly to his influence on the man who, by creating characters in whom wit and genuine emotion could coexist, achieved a synthesis impossible for Lyly. That man was William Shakespeare.

Major publications other than poetry

NOVELS: *Euphues, the Anatomy of Wit*, 1579; *Euphues and His England*, 1580.

PLAYS: *Campaspe*, 1584; *Sapho and Phao*, 1584; *Galathea*, c. 1585; *Endymion*, 1588; *Midas*, 1589; *Mother Bombie*, c. 1589; *Love's Metamorphosis*, c. 1589; *The Woman in the Moon*, c. 1593.

Bibliography

Hunter, G. K. *John Lyly: The Humanist as Courtier*, 1962.
Ing, Catherine. *Elizabethan Lyrics*, 1969.
Pattison, Bruce. *Music and Poetry of the English Renaissance*, 1970.
Smith, Hallett. *Elizabethan Poetry*, 1968.

Robert P. Ellis

THOMAS BABINGTON MACAULAY

Born: Rothley Temple, England; October 25, 1800
Died: Campden Hill, London, England; December 28, 1859

Principal collection
Lays of Ancient Rome, 1842.

Other literary forms

Thomas Babington Macaulay was a well-known writer of history and essays. His major work was the *History of England from the Accession of James II*, of which he completed five volumes, published in 1848, 1855, and posthumously in 1861. His essays include literary criticism, biographies, political arguments, book reviews, and encyclopedia articles. Much of his prose work originally appeared in the *Edinburgh Review*. There are many correspondences between Macaulay's historical, political, and critical works and his poetry. Both his poetry and his literary criticism tended to be historical.

In his historical writings, he conceived of history as a series of changes made by human beings, and he was scrupulously fair in dealing with different factions. In his famous essay on John Milton, which appeared in the *Edinburgh Review* in 1825, he defended the Puritans against facile satirical judgment, but he likewise found the Cavaliers honest in their convictions. This even-handedness is also evident in his historical narrative poetry.

His remarks about history are also relevant to his historical poetry. He stated in his essay on "History" in the *Edinburgh Review* of May, 1828, that to be a great historian is perhaps the rarest intellectual distinction; the historian must have a great imagination, he averred, but must keep it under control. History is "philosophy teaching by examples," and the historian manages the perspective of history, considering the foreground and the background, diminishing some events and giving others importance. Thus the talent required for writing history is comparable to the talent of a great dramatist.

His remarks about poetry in his essays also give the reader some idea of what he was trying to do in his own verse. In his review of *Letters and Journals of Lord Byron: With Notices of His Life*, by Thomas Moore, which appeared in the *Edinburgh Review*, June, 1831, he found no necessary antithesis between correctness and creative power in poetry, provided that correctness means conformity to rules founded in reality rather than conformity to arbitrary rules. Homer, Dante, William Shakespeare, and Milton are the most correct of poets, and William Wordsworth is more correct than Alexander Pope. He termed irrational the rule concerning dramatic unities of time and place, and he condemned the "pathetic fallacy" as invalid. He declared that while poetry cannot represent realities as vividly as painting, sculpture, and acting, the range of poetry is broader than that of any other imitative art.

Achievements

Macaulay was a renowned writer in his own time. His *History of England from the Accession of James II* and his *Lays of Ancient Rome* sold very well, and he was awarded many honors as a man of letters. He became Rector of Glasgow University and was offered the Cambridge Professorship of Modern History. He was a member of the famous Literary Club. He had an active political as well as literary career. In 1857 he was raised to the peerage as Baron Macaulay of Rothley, a title which was granted in recognition of his literary accomplishments.

He is less popular today, and is ranked lower critically. While Victorian scholars and critics tended to reject him, modern critics have largely ignored him. Literary historians have described him as superficial, and his reputation has fallen more drastically than that of most other writers of his period. He is often regarded as smug, because of his optimism about the future, and shallow, because he strove for clarity. Yet his narrative genius has never been denied. He wrote verse throughout his life but published only one small volume, the *Lays of Ancient Rome* (1842). His historical subject-matter make his *Lays of Ancient Rome* difficult for the modern reader, who often has little background in ancient history. His clear and straightforward style runs counter to the modern taste for intriguing obscurity, and the patriotism and courage he so often wrote about are no longer universally popular themes.

In his poetry, he was a learned and dramatic storyteller, and he composed lines that are so simply and correctly constructed that they are easily memorized.

Biography

Thomas Babington Macaulay was born on October 25, 1800, at Rothley Temple, Leicestershire. One of nine children, his childhood was spent among the Clapham Sect, a group of well-to-do Church of England activists that included his father, Zachary, who edited *The Christian Observer*, the organ of the abolitionists. When he was eight years old, he wrote an epic as well as a *Compendium of Universal History*. He entered Trinity College, Cambridge, when he was eighteen and loved Cambridge dearly although he hated the required mathematics courses. He won gold medals for poetry, a prize for Latin declamation, a scholarship and then a fellowship, and was graduated in 1822, remaining there as a Fellow until 1825.

While at Trinity College, he gained the Chancellor's gold medal for a poem entitled "Pompeii" and recited it in public in July, 1819, in a black silk waist-coat he had ordered for the occasion. He wrote poetry of various kinds while in college, and one piece was published in the *Morning Post*. He did not have to work hard to do well in college, as he seemed to have had a photographic memory. He said that he could reproduce the whole of *Paradise Lost* (1667) or *The Pilgrim's Progress* (1678, 1684). He did not like the idea of going away to college, and advocated the idea of what today would be called a commuter college, since he was very attached to his family. He studied for the mathematical tripos exams, which were necessary to pass in order to obtain an honors degree from Cambridge; he failed, however, withdrawing soon after entering the examination room. He wrote for *Knight's Quarterly* magazine, under the pseudonym "Tristram Merton," critical essays, poems, book reviews, dramatic reconstructions of historical scenes, and allegories.

Macaulay was admitted to the Bar in 1826 but continued to write light verses and political and literary pieces for magazines, including the *Edinburgh Review*. He became Commissioner in Bankruptcy, and in 1830 he became Member of Parliament for the Whig Lord Lansdowe's "pocket" borough of Calne in Wiltshire. He spoke in support of the Whig Reform bills. Money became a personal problem, since his father's firm had suffered financial reverses, but after Earl Grey's government came into power, Macaulay became a member of the Indian Board of Control. In 1834 he became a member of the Supreme Council of India. He had no desire to go to India, but went for the sake of his family's financial security, one of his sisters accompanying him. From India, he helped to abolish press censorship and persuaded the government not to allow English residents to bring civil appeals before the Calcutta Supreme Court (thus making native Indians and English citizens legally equal). He had little respect for Indian learning, and as President of the Committee of Public Instruction in India, he implemented the Governor General's edict promoting European literature and science. He wrote a criminal law code that was adopted for India. He left India in 1838, but not before he had begun writing the *Lays of Ancient Rome*.

Macaulay was elected a Member of Parliament again in 1839 for Edinburgh, and in 1840 he was made Secretary of War. He began working on the *History of England from the Accession of James II* in 1842, the year that his *Lays of Ancient Rome* was published, to general acclaim. Macaulay never married, but enjoyed playing the uncle to his nephews and nieces. The first two volumes of his *History of England from the Accession of James II* were published in 1848; they were highly praised, the first printing selling out in ten days.

In 1849 Macaulay was elected Rector of Glasgow University. He became ill with a heart condition in 1852 and suffered from breathing difficulties after that time. The third and fourth volumes of his history of England appeared in 1855. He died December 28, 1859, in Campden Hill, and was buried in the Poets' Corner of Westminster Abbey. The last of the five volumes of his history that he completed was published posthumously.

Analysis

Much of Thomas Babington Macaulay's best poetry is about the personal courage shown by individuals in trying to prevent loss of freedom or death. To Macaulay, history was "philosophy teaching by examples," and the courage, stoicism, self-sacrifice, and patriotism displayed by the heroes of his historical narrative poems were qualities to be emulated by all.

Death was the subject of one of his earlier nonnarrative poems, "Sermon in a Churchyard" (1825). The poem begins satirically, with a description of Damon, the minister, taking his seat in church with mincing step, scented handkerchief, and jeweled hand, while the young ladies in the congregation "Admire his doctrines, and his hair," a surprising and amusing shift from the metaphysical to the physical that is reminiscent of Alexander Pope. The minister explains what is most clear until it seems most difficult, but the speaker of the poem stays instead in the churchyard and reads his sermon on skulls and bones.

The rest of the poem is melancholy and philosophical, graveyard poetry a century after the graveyard school. The speaker admonishes those who have unsuccessfully sought fame to look at these graves. He speaks directly and intimately to the reader, and compares the graveyard to a school from which one learns greater stoicism than Zeno's. In the latter part of the poem, Macaulay uses game and toy imagery to indicate the insubstantiality of so much in human life. The plots and intrigues of life make it seem like a game of chess, and it is not important whether the pieces are real or not. Griefs and joys are like the toys of children. Even science is "a blind man's guess," an allusion to the children's game of blind man's buff, and history is "a nurse's tale." Everything the reader loves and hates ends in the grave. This early poem on the subject of death exemplifies Macaulay's effective use of figures of speech. The next year (1826) he translated the Latin Judgment Day hymn, *Dies Irae*, into English.

In his *Lays of Ancient Rome*, Macaulay puts aside the *memento mori* theme and portrays the risk of death as a dramatic crisis in human life. Macaulay was apparently fascinated with the idea, identified with the German historian Barthold Niebuhr and others, that the early histories were based on early ballad verse, and most of his general introduction to the *Lays of Ancient Rome* argues that there were such metrical ballads in Latin, long since lost, which became history. He says that the object of his work is to reverse the process, transforming history back into something like the original poetry. The speakers of the lays are to be ancient minstrels who know only what someone of their time would have known, and who have their time's prejudices and enthusiasms. He acknowledges his indebtedness to the English ballads, Sir Walter Scott, and the *Iliad* (c. 800 B.C.). He decides not to include notes, he says, because the learned reader would find them unnecessary, and the unlearned reader would not be interested.

The first and best-known of the *Lays of Ancient Rome* is "Horatius." Macaulay, in his Preface to the work, speaks of several ancient versions of the story, stating his belief that it was originally in verse. He notes that Polybius used the tale as an example of a narrative recited at a funeral, in this case a funeral of some official descended from the Horatian patricians. In Polybius, Horatius defends the bridge alone and drowns. According to Livy and Dionysius, he had two companions, swam to shore, and was greatly honored. Macaulay adopts Niebuhr's idea that each of the three defenders represents one of the three patrician tribes.

For this story and the other lays, Macaulay uses a verse form which he calls the Saturnian measure, used by very early Roman poets such as Naevius, consisting of a catalectic dimeter iambic part, followed by a second part composed of three trochees. In the general Introduction to the *Lays of Ancient Rome*, he notes that a similar verse form for ballads was used in many different countries. In the Preface to "Horatius," he discusses the length of the syllables in the name "Porsena," which seems to indicate that he was taking quantitative metrical values into account in the meter in the classical manner.

The poem begins with the date of its composition, supposedly between 360 and 394 B.C. The first stanza is in the past tense, while the second stanza is in the present tense. The point of view is first that of the Etruscans, who are invading Rome from the north. The Tarquins, the Etruscan dynasty, are villains, and the rape of the Roman matron Lucretia by the Tarquin prince Sextus is referred to a number of times in the poem, but here at the beginning of the work the reader is on the side of the Etruscans. Their great leader Lars Porsena of Clunium swears that the great house of Tarquin should no longer be in exile from Rome, and gathers his forces from a great many places that are named in the poem. The thirty professional prophets advise him to go forth to glory. Mamilius, Prince of the Latines from Tusculum, joins the muster.

The reader is then transported to Rome, surrounded by blazing villages. The Fathers of the City, or senators, decide in council to pull down the bridge in order to keep the enemy from the city, but a scout informs them that Lars Porsena is already approaching, in an ivory car with Mamilius and Sextus beside him. The Consul fears that their vanguard will get in before the bridge can be destroyed. The reader's sympathy is now very much with the Romans. There are several long stanzas throughout the poem in which the army is described.

Horatius, the Captain of the Gate, speaks in a philosophical way, noting that death will come to all sooner or later, "And how can man die better/ Than facing fearful odds,/ For the ashes of his fathers/ And the temples of his Gods." They will die protecting their mothers, their wives, and the vestal virgins from Sextus. Horatius' words are both simple and memorable. He tells the Consul to hew down the bridge while he and two volunteers, Spurius Lartius and Herminius, hold back the army. The bard exhorts his listeners to remember the past, when people were for the state rather than a faction, and showed brotherly love.

The encounters with the Etruscan army are described. At first the Etruscans laugh at them, but they grow serious as their men are defeated or killed. The great Etruscan Astur, the Lord of Luna, comes forth scornfully, and manages to wound Horatius, who has to rest for a moment against Herminius. Horatius then manages to kill Astur; his death is compared to the falling of a giant oak tree in a storm. The prophets previously mentioned mutter and become pale, a dramatic reversal, and the army of the Etruscans shrinks like boys who are ringing the woods to start a hare and come to a dark lair where they see a growling bear who "Lies amid bones and blood." This is a very effective Homeric simile. When the Fathers of the City warn the three to go back before the bridge collapses, the other two manage to get back, but Horatius stands fast. Alone and facing a multitude, he does not surrender but turns to the city, prays to Father Tiber, the river, and plunges into the water with his armor. When he manages to swim to the city through the swollen river, even the Etruscans can hardly forbear to cheer, and he is much honored by the Romans.

In the next lay, "The Battle of the Lake Regillus," supposedly about ninety years later, the Etruscans are once more invading Rome, hoping to put Etruscan kings back on the throne. In response to a message that the Tarquins should be allowed to return, Consul Aulus replies with the parable of how the jays sent a message to the eagle to yield his eyrie to the kite, but when the eagle looked angry, the jay and the kite fled. Aulus is appointed temporary Dictator and the war commences, described in a series of single combats. At one point Mamilius and Herminius, one of the defenders of the bridge, do battle, both of them familiar to the reader from the "Horatius." Mamilius vows that one of them will never go home. "I will lay on for Tusculum,/ And lay thou on for Rome!" They wound and kill each other. At last two princes enter the fray on white steeds; they say that they are called by many names. They are the twin gods Castor and Pollux, who fight for Rome and then bring news of the victory back to the city. Livy omitted this supernatural intervention, but Macaulay included it. Both Manilius and Herminius are brave in battle, and the bard cites Manilius' memorable words.

In the third lay, "Virginia," the image of courage is not a man facing death in battle, but a man who kills his daughter rather than have her dishonored and made a slave. In the fourth lay, "The Prophecy of Capys," the sightless prophet Capys recognizes Romulus and predicts that he will build a glorious city. Romulus was exposed to die but nursed by a she-wolf, and Capys warns that the nurse of Romulus has no master and bears no load, and woe to them who shear or goad her. When she is surrounded by a pack of baying dogs, "She dies in silence, biting hard,/ Amidst the dying hounds." The theme of fighting bravely to prevent death or loss of freedom is here magnificently exemplified in the image of the wolf. Romulus had Mars for his father and the she-wolf for his nurse, and thus bravery becomes characteristic of the Romans. The passage is only a small part of the whole poem, but it is most striking.

Critical judgments about the quality of the lays have varied widely. Matthew Arnold, in *On Translating Homer* (1861-1862), states that a reader's ability to detect falseness in the *Lays of Ancient Rome* is a good measure of his ability as a critic. George Saintsbury, on the other hand, argued that while the work is poetry for the crowd, those who do not recognize its quality have a deficient poetical thermometer. Noting that Queen Victoria had been on the throne only four years when the *Lays of Ancient Rome* was published, and that she was still unpopular and had been the object of three assassination attempts, Gilbert Highet tried to link the theme of freedom and democracy in the *Lays of Ancient Rome* to ideas of abolishing the monarchy.

Macaulay wrote a number of poems about English history, including two ballads on the English revolution, one Royalist ("The Cavalier's March to London") and one Puritan ("The Battle of Naseby"). It is impossible to tell from them which side he preferred, which indicates how tenuous is an argument for a contemporary political purpose on Macaulay's part. John Clive has noted that some of Macaulay's most moving occasional poems are sympathetic to causes which he did not endorse. One of Macaulay's very short poems, "Epitaph on a Jacobite" (1845 or 1847), is haunting in its simplicity, symbolizing in one emigre the pain of many other emigres from that period who left England to avoid loss of freedom or death for religious and political beliefs. The epitaph presents the dead man's own words to the observer. He declares that he offered courage and faith to his true king, but mourns that his sacrifice was in vain because he lost everything. He had been haunted by images of his homeland, until God finally gave him the rest of an early grave. He tells the observer from England looking at his nameless tombstone to "forget all feuds" and to shed a tear over English dust where his broken heart lies.

Major publications other than poetry

NONFICTION: *Critical and Historical Essays, Contributed to the Edinburgh Review*, 1843 (3 volumes); *History of England from the Accession of James II*, 1849, 1855, 1861 (5 volumes); *Speeches of the Right Honourable T. B. Macaulay, M. P., Corrected by Himself*, 1854.

MISCELLANEOUS: *The Works of Lord Macaulay*, 1866 (Lady Trevelyan, editor).

Bibliography

Clive, John. *Macaulay: The Shaping of the Historian*, 1973.
Cruikshank, Margaret. *Thomas Babington Macaulay*, 1977.
Griffin, John R. *The Intellectual Milieu of Lord Macaulay*, 1964.

Highet, Gilbert. "Lays of Ancient Rome, Propaganda and Poetry," in *The Powers of Poetry*, 1960.

Magoun, Francis P. "Lord Macaulay, a Singer of Tales," *Neuphilologische Mitteilungen*. LXXIII (1972), pp. 686-689.

Mill, J. S. "Macaulay's *Lays of Ancient Rome*," in *Westminster Review*. XXXIX (1843), pp. 55-59.

Millgate, Jane. *Macaulay*, 1973.

Young, Kenneth. *Macaulay*, 1976. Edited by Ian Scott-Kilvert.

Rosemary Ascherl

GEORGE MACBETH

Born: Shotts, Scotland; January 19, 1932

Principal collections

The Broken Places, 1963; *A Doomsday Book*, 1967; *The Colour of Blood*, 1967, 1969; *The Night of Stones*, 1968; *A War Quartet*, 1969; *The Burning Cone*, 1970; *The Orlando Poems*, 1971; *Collected Poems: 1958-1970*, 1971; *Shrapnel and a Poet's Year*, 1973, 1974; *In the Hours Waiting for the Blood to Come*, 1975; *Buying a Heart*, 1978; *Poems of Love and Death*, 1980; *Published Collections*, 1982.

Other literary forms

In addition to his numerous volumes of poetry, George MacBeth has published a great many poetry pamphlets, chapbooks, and limited edition books since the early 1960's. Although these have usually been printed in small numbers and reached only a limited audience, many of them have become parts of larger books and been incorporated into the mainstream of MacBeth's work. Apart from poetry, MacBeth has also published two children's books, four novels, an autobiography, and has edited five volumes of poetry, including *The Penguin Book of Sick Verse* (1963), *Poetry 1900-1965* (1967), and *The Falling Splendour* (1970), a selection of Alfred, Lord Tennyson's poetry. The sheer volume of MacBeth's production reveals his almost obsessive dedication to writing and the breadth of his interests. Among his publications other than poetry, the autobiography *My Scotland* (1973) probably holds the greatest interest for the reader of his poetry because of the insights it offers into his background and development. MacBeth himself has described the book as a nonlogical, nonnarrative, massive jigsaw of autobiographical bits, a collection of about two hundred short prose pieces about being Scottish.

Achievements

MacBeth is arguably the most prolific poet writing in England today and, in fact, in terms of his total output, he has few rivals in the United States. Naturally, volume alone has not made him a significant poet; rather, he has gained stature because of the diversity of his writing. MacBeth is, in the best sense of the word, an "experimental" poet. He seems absolutely fearless in his willingness to attempt new forms and take on unusual subjects, and yet at the same time he is fascinated by traditional meter and rhyme, as well as by material that has fueled the imagination of poets for centuries. One of his most recent books, *Poems of Love and Death*, contains poems ranging from the dangerously romantic "The Truth," with its didactic final stanza which includes the lines "Happiness is a state of mind,/ And grief is something frail and small," to the satiric "The Flame of Love, By Laura Stargleam," which mocks the dime novel plot-line that it exploits. MacBeth is as likely to write about a missile commander as about evening primroses, and the reader familiar with his writing is not at all surprised to find these disparate topics dealt with in a single book, in this case *Buying a Heart*. In fact, it is the sense of discovery and the vitality of MacBeth's imagination that attract a great many readers.

Biography

Born in Scotland near Glasgow, George Mann MacBeth has lived the greater part of his life in England. This circumstance has had a substantial impact on his poetry, because it has led him to view himself as something of an exile. Although he feels comfortable in England, he does not regard himself as English and has remarked on the sensation of detachment, of living and working in a foreign country. The Scotland he left as a child remains in his mind as a lost world, a kind of Eden which can never be regained, and his sense of loss has helped to make him, in his own evaluation, "a very retrospective, backward-looking poet." Perhaps more significantly, his detachment, or rootlessness, has enabled him to embrace a larger part of the world than is available to most writers. Attached to Scotland only in his imagination and not physically, MacBeth is free to range abroad. This may well account for his eclectic approach to poetry; he is free to encompass everything, to absorb all influences.

Another significant element of MacBeth's life was his long-term association with the British Broadcasting Corporation, where he worked as a producer of poetry programs. This position brought him into contact with the leading poets in England and around the world and exposed him to everything that was happening in poetry. MacBeth himself has acknowledged that his close work with a broad variety of poets over the years influenced his writing, particularly in the areas of technique and structure. Always careful not to become too involved in purely "English" writing, he has consciously tried to keep in touch with poetic developments in the world at large, and his accomplishments as a poet can be measured most accurately if they are considered in the context of this endeavor.

Analysis

George MacBeth has remarked that he considers the word "experimental," which is often used to describe his work, to be a term of praise. While he acknowledges the possibility of failing in some of his excursions into new forms and new subjects, he obviously feels that the risk is justified. His strongest impulse as a writer is to test the bounds of poetry and, wherever possible, to extend them. This daring push toward the very limits of his craft is nowhere better revealed than in the fourth section of his *Collected Poems:*

1958-1970, where MacBeth employs his no-holds-barred approach and enjoys doing it. Indeed, the sense of pleasure that MacBeth manages to communicate, his pure delight in the shape of language on the page, is essential to the reader because it helps to carry him through poems which at first glance may repel rather than attract.

Two such forbidding poems which challenge the analytical mind in satiric fashion are "Two Experiments" and "LDMN Analysis of Thomas Nashe's 'Song.'" The first of these poems, divided into two sections, presents a "Vowel Analysis of 'Babylonian Poem' from the German of Friederike Mayröcker" and a "Numerical Analysis of 'Brazilian Poem' from the German of Friederike Mayröcker." If the ponderous and unlikely subtitles are not enough to warn the reader not to be too serious, the actual text should be sufficiently illuminating. The first section is a listing of vowels, ostensibly from the Mayröcker poem, presented in the following fashion: "U EE-EI A I AE-IIE-EIE UE EOE U EI; E." Thus runs the first line, and the second section begins in the following way: "(. .2 2 6 2 3 5: 2 3 3-6 3 8: 3." Clearly, these representations are meaningless, but they do make a point, not a very positive point, about the analytical approach to poetry: that critical analyses of poetry may make no more sense than these vowel and number analyses. A similar statement is made in "LDMN Analysis of Thomas Nashe's 'Song,'" which offers an arrangement of *L*'s, *D*'s, *M*'s, and *N*'s, presumably as they might be extracted from the Nashe poem.

As might be expected, the response to such experimentation has not been universally positive, and a number of readers have questioned whether such strategies can properly be called poetry. Ironically, this may be the very question that MacBeth wants the reader to ask, the ultimate critic's question: "What is poetry?" MacBeth himself is as sincere as any reader in his search for an answer, for he offers no dogmatic views of his own; he merely tosses out experiments in an effort to determine where the boundaries lie.

Other poems that are somewhat less eccentric but nevertheless experimental are "The Ski Murders" and "Fin du Globe." The first is an "encyclopaedia-poem" consisting of twenty-six individual entries, one for each letter of the alphabet. The entries themselves are written in a prose style that might have been taken from a spy novel, and the reader is invited to construct his own story by piecing the vignettes together in whatever fashion he wishes. The second poem is presented as a game containing fifty-two "postcards" and four "*fin du globe*" cards. The players (the readers) are instructed to deal out the cards as in an ordinary deck and to read, in turn, the brief postcard message printed on each. When a *fin du globe* card is turned up, the game is over. Again, the question arises—Is this poetry?—and once again MacBeth is challenging the reader while exploring the limits of his craft and trying to extend his artistic territory. Even the most skeptical reader can, if he allows himself, find pleasure in these and similar experiments, for they are clever and entertaining, and one can sense the pleasure that MacBeth himself must have experienced in giving free rein to his imagination.

Among MacBeth's most successful comic poems is "A Poet's Life," which first appeared in *In the Hours Waiting for the Blood to Come* and has since developed into a kind of serial poem published in various installments. In its original form, the poem consists of twelve episodes focusing on various aspects of the poet's life. The point of view is third person, to permit MacBeth as much distance as possible from his subject, himself. The result is a poem, which avoids the gloomy seriousness of typical introspection and yet focuses on some serious themes, showing the poet to be as human as anyone else. The first section of the poem is representative of MacBeth's technique; it shows the poet at home, trying to write and jotting down the following lines: "today I got up at eight, felt cold, shaved,/ washed, had breakfast, and dressed." The banality here reflects a larger tedium in the poet's life, for nothing much happens to him, except in his imagination. It is not surprising, then, when his efforts to write lead nowhere and he turns to the television for an episode of the *Avengers*, a purely escapist adventure show.

Viewed almost as a specimen or as a caged animal might be viewed, the poet is an amusing creature, sipping his "peppermint cream" and sucking distractedly on his pencil; and yet he is also pitiable. There is, in fact, something of the fool about the poet, something reminiscent of Charlie Chaplin's little tramp, for although he evokes laughter or a bemused smile there is something fundamentally sad about him. The poignancy comes from the realization that the poet, no matter how hard he tries to blend into the common crowd, must always remain isolated. It is the nature of his craft; writing poetry sets him apart. Consequently, when he goes to the supermarket, dressed in "green wranglers" to make himself inconspicuous, he still stands out among the old women, the babies, and the old men. He is "looking/ at life for his poems, is helping/ his wife, is a normal considerate man," and yet his role as poet inevitably removes him from the other shoppers and from the world at large.

Technically, "A Poet's Life" is rather simple and straightforward, but several significant devices work subtly to make the poem successful. The objective point of view enables MacBeth to combine the comic and the pathetic without becoming maudlin or self-pitying; this slightly detached tone is complemented by MacBeth's freewheeling, modernized version of the *Don Juan* stanza. It is typical of MacBeth to turn to traditional forms for inspiration, to borrow them and make them new.

Not a poet to break the rules without first understanding what the rules are, MacBeth is fascinated by traditional forms as well as by those that are new and experimental. It is a measure of his poetic temperament that he is able to take a traditional form and incorporate it into his general experimentation. The reader often encounters regular rhyme and meter in Mac-

Beth's work and occasionally recognizes something like a sonnet or sestina. Invariably, though, the standard form is modified to conform to MacBeth's urge to experiment. "How to Eat an Orange" is as nearly a sonnet as it can possibly be without actually being one. It has fourteen lines and a Shakespearean rhyme scheme, including the final couplet; but it lacks the iambic pentameter. In fact, it has no regular meter at all, although the iambic does surface from time to time like a theme played in the background. Form, then, is not an end in itself but a means to an end, and MacBeth employs whatever forms he finds useful, including the traditional, in communicating his ideas.

MacBeth's attitude toward form is captured most provocatively in a poem entitled "What Metre Is." A tour de force of technique, this poem stands as the poet's manifesto. The controlling idea is that the poem itself will provide examples of various poetic devices while they are being discussed. For example, when alliteration is mentioned, it appears in the context of the following passage: "leaping/ long lean and allusive/ through low lines." The uses of prose are considered in this fashion: "Prose is another possibility. There could be three/ sentences in the stanza. This would be an example of/ that." Other aspects of metrics discussed and illustrated in the poem are syllabics, free verse, word and interval counting, internal rhyming, rhythm, assonance, and finally, typography, "its mos/ t irrit/ ating (perhaps) manif/ estation." Irritating and mechanical it may be, representing the voice of the typewriter and the "abdic/ ation of insp/ iration," but still the poet feels compelled to say "I li/ ke it." He likes it because it is "the logica/ l exp/ ression o/ f itsel/ f." Having gone through his paces, the way a musician might play the scale or some well-known traditional piece just to prove he can, MacBeth turns finally to the experimental, which, despite its flaws, holds some irresistible attraction for him. He can manage traditional metrics, and he illustrates this ability in the poem, but he can also handle the riskier, less traditional devices. This poem, then, embodies on a small scale the range of poetic techniques one is likely to encounter in MacBeth's poetry: the traditional, often with modifications, and the experimental, always with MacBeth's own particular daring.

If MacBeth takes chances with the form of his poems, he also takes considerable risks with the content. Many of his poems are violent or sexually explicit, and some readers have found his subject matter objectionable. Perhaps the chief characteristic of the content of his poetry is a fascination with fear and violence, which MacBeth feels can be traced to his childhood. As a boy during World War II, MacBeth lost his father and experienced the bombing of his house. He collected shrapnel in the streets after air raids, spent night after night in the shelters, and grew up surrounded by physical violence and the threat of death. This kind of environment affected him strongly, and MacBeth feels that it led ultimately to a kind of obsession with violence that finds an outlet through his poetry.

The connection between his childhood experience of the war and such poems as "The Sirens," "The War," and "The Passing Ones" is obvious because these poems are explicitly about that experience, about "those bombed houses where/ I echoed in/ The empty rooms." Other poems, such as "Driving West," with its apocalyptic vision of a nuclear war, are less concerned with the actual experiences of World War II than with the nightmare vision it instilled. MacBeth's childhood fear of bombs has been translated into an adult's vision of the end of the world: "There was nothing left,/ Only a world of scrap. Dark metal bruised,/ Flung soup of blood, anchors and driven screws." This is the inheritance of Hiroshima and Nagasaki, a vision of the potential that man has to destroy himself and the entire planet.

The same influences are operating, though less obviously, in "The Burning Poem," which ends with the following passage: "Burning, burning,/ and nothing left to burn:/ only the ashes/ in a little urn." Here the violence has been freed of its war context with only a passing reference to suggest the connection: "rice paper, cartridge-paper,/ it was all the same." The merging of art, as represented by the rice paper, and war, represented by the cartridge paper, suggests the relationship between MacBeth's experiences of the war and his poetry. He is, in effect, "Spilling petrol/ on the bare pages." There is a sense in which many of MacBeth's poems are burning with the effects of remembered violence.

Inevitably, the violence loses its war context entirely and becomes associated with other things, just as it must have been absorbed into MacBeth's life. In "A Confession," for example, the topic is abortion, and the woman who has chosen to abort her child remembers the procedure as "the hard cold inrush of its killer,/ Saw-teeth, threshing fins, cascading water,/ And the soul spat like a bubble out of its head." The act was not clinical or antiseptic but personal and highly violent. The woman, in the course of her dramatic monologue, reveals an obsessive guilt and an inability to deal with what she has done. She wonders, finally, what her punishment might be "For crucifying someone in my womb." In this case MacBeth is somewhat removed from the poem because he uses the persona of the woman, but in "In the Hours Waiting for the Blood to Come" and "Two Days After" he approaches the topic of a lost or aborted child in a much more personal way, considering the impact of the death on the people involved in the relationship. In "Two Days After" the couple make love but the act has less to do with love than with guilt and a kind of spent violence.

Often, MacBeth's images seem designed specifically to shock the reader, to jolt him out of complacency. It is important, however, to realize that MacBeth employs violent and sexually explicit passages for more than merely sensational purposes. He wants to consider the darker side of human nature; violence and fear are alive in the world, and acknowledging their existence is a first step toward coming to terms with them.

It would be a mistake to regard MacBeth as merely a poet of sex and violence, for he has more dimensions than those. MacBeth himself seems bothered by the attention that has been given to the more sensational aspects of his poetry to the exclusion of other elements, and has remarked that he does not find his poetry any more violent than anyone else's. In terms of his total body of work, he is right, but the shocking and explicit poems inevitably call more attention to themselves than those that are more subdued in tone and subject matter, especially the very fine children's poems and MacBeth's engaging forays into the fantastic or surreal.

"The Red Herring" is a good illustration of MacBeth's poetry for children. The elements of the poem are a dried red herring, a bare wall, a ladder, and a man with a hammer, a nail, and a long piece of string. After the man has tied the red herring to the string suspended from the nail in the top of the wall and gone away, the poet addresses the question of why he would bother to make up such a simple story: "I did it just to annoy people./ Serious people. And perhaps also/ to amuse children. Small children." Undoubtedly, a child could take pleasure in this poem, but it is not entirely limited to the child in its appeal. The adult who is able to put off his seriousness for a moment or two will find himself smiling at the poem because of its saucy tone and at himself because he was probably gullible enough to enter the poem with a serious mind, even though the title itself warned him that things were not what they seemed. The playfulness here is characteristic of MacBeth's sense of humor, and, as usual, it is designed to make a serious point as well as to please.

Related to the children's poems are MacBeth's trips into the fantastic, as reflected in "Scissor-Man." The speaker, a pair of scissors used to cut bacon rind, contemplates his position in life, grousing about being kept under the draining-board rather than in the sink unit. Further, he worries about what might be going on between the nutcrackers and the carrot grater and vows that if he should "catch him rubbing/ those tin nipples of hers/ in the bread-bin" he will "have his/ washer off." Clearly, this is not meant to be children's poetry, but it is, perhaps, a kind of children's poetry for adults, for it engages the imagination in the same way that nursery rhymes and fairy tales do. In this case, MacBeth's humor seems designed to be an end in itself, an escape into the purely fanciful.

If one were to compile a list of adjectives to describe MacBeth's poetry, he would include at least the following: experimental, traditional, humorous, serious, violent, compassionate. The fact that these adjectives seem to cancel one another is significant, for MacBeth is possessed of a vital desire to encompass everything. In all his diversity, MacBeth is an original and important contemporary poet, a risk-taker who is continually trying to extend the boundaries of his art.

Major publications other than poetry

NOVELS: *The Transformation*, 1975; *The Samurai*, 1975; *The Survivor*, 1977; *The Seven Witches*, 1978.

NONFICTION: *My Scotland*, 1973.

ANTHOLOGIES: *The Penguin Book of Sick Verse*, 1963; *Penguin Modern Poets VI*, 1964 (with J. Clemo and E. Lucie-Smith); *The Penguin Book of Animal Verse*, 1965; *Poetry 1900-1965*, 1967; *The Penguin Book of Victorian Verse*, 1968; *The Falling Splendour*, 1970.

CHILDREN'S LITERATURE: *Noah's Journey*, 1966; *Jonah and the Lord*, 1969.

Bibliography

Black, D. M. "The Poetry of George MacBeth," in *Scottish International*, 1968.

Garfitt, Roger. "The Group," in *British Poetry Since 1960*, 1972. Edited by Michael Schmidt and Grevel Lindop.

Rosenthal, M. L. *The New Poets: American and British Poetry Since World War II*, 1967.

Neal Bowers

CLAUDE MCKAY

Born: Sunny Ville, Jamaica; September 15, 1889
Died: Chicago, Illinois; May 22, 1948

Principal collections
Songs of Jamaica, 1912; *Constab Ballads*, 1912; *Spring in New Hampshire and Other Poems*, 1920; *Harlem Shadows*, 1922; *Selected Poems of Claude McKay*, 1953.

Other literary forms
Even though he is probably best known as a poet, Claude McKay's verse makes up a relatively small portion of his literary output. While his novels, *Home to Harlem* (1928), *Banjo* (1929), and *Banana Bottom* (1933), do not place him at the forefront of American novelists, they were remarkable at the time for their frankness and slice-of-life realism. *Home to Harlem* was the first best-selling novel of the Harlem Renaissance, yet it was condemned by the majority of black critics, who felt that the black American art and literature emerging in the 1920's and 1930's should present an uplifting image of the Afro-American. McKay, however, went on in his next two novels to express his admiration for the earthy ways of uneducated lower-class blacks, somewhat at the expense of black intellectuals. The remainder of McKay's published fiction appears in *Gingertown* (1932), a volume of short stories.

McKay produced, as well, a substantial body of literary and social criticism, a revealing selection of which appears, along with a number of his letters and selections from his fiction and poetry, in *The Passion of Claude McKay: Selected Poetry and Prose, 1912-1948* (1973), edited by Wayne F. Cooper. An autobiography, *A Long Way from Home* (1937), and an important social history, *Harlem: Negro Metropolis* (1940), round out the list of his principal works.

Achievements
McKay's contribution to American poetry cannot be measured in awards and citations, nor in visiting professorships and foundation grants. His peculiar pilgrimage took him from Jamaica to Moscow, from Communism to Catholicism, from Harlem to Marseilles. He lived and worked among common laborers most of his life, and developed a respect for them worthy of Walt Whitman. He rejected the critical pronouncements of his black contemporaries and, as Melvin Tolson points out, he "was unaffected by the New Poetry and Criticism." His singular blend of modern political and social radicalism with the timeworn cadences of the sonnet won for him, at best, mixed reviews from many critics, black and white. In any attempt to calculate his poetic achievement, however, one must realize that, with the exception of his early

Jamaican dialect verse (certainly an important contribution in its own right to the little-studied literature of the British West Indies) and some rather disappointing poetry composed late in his life, his poetic career spanned little more than a decade. At the publication in 1922 of *Harlem Shadows*, the furthest extent of his poetic development, he was only thirty-three. McKay should be read as a poet on the way up, who turned his attention almost exclusively to prose after his initial success in verse.

Surely there is no more ludicrous task than to criticize a writer on the basis of his potential, and so one should take McKay as one finds him, and indeed, in those terms, he does not fare badly. His was the first notable voice of anger in modern black American poetry. Writing when he did, he had to struggle against the enormous pressure, not of white censure, but of a racial responsibility that was his whether he wanted it or not. He could not be merely a poet—he had to be a "black poet," had to speak, to some extent, for countless others; such a position is difficult for any poet. Through it all, however, he strove for individuality, and fought to keep from being bought by any interest, black or white, right- or left-wing.

Largely through the work of McKay, and of such Harlem Renaissance contemporaries as Countée Cullen and Langston Hughes, the task of being a black poet in America was made easier. *Harlem Shadows* marked a decisive beginning toward improving the predicament so concisely recorded by Cullen, who wondered aloud in the sonnet "Yet Do I Marvel" how a well-intentioned God could in his wisdom do "this curious thing:/ To make a poet black and bid him sing."

Biography

Claude McKay was born in 1889 on a small farm in Clarendon Parish, Jamaica. His parents were well-respected members of the community and of the local Baptist church. He received his early education from his older brother, a schoolteacher near Montego Bay. In 1907, he was apprenticed to a wheelwright and cabinetmaker in Brown's Town; this apprenticeship was short-lived, but it was in Brown's Town that McKay entered into a far more fruitful apprenticeship of another sort. Walter Jekyll, an English aristocrat and student of Jamaican culture, came to know young Claude and undertook the boy's literary education. As McKay recalled years later in his autobiography, *A Long Way from Home*, Jekyll opened a whole new world to him:

> I read poetry: *Childe Harold*, *The Duncaid*, *Essay on Man*, *Paradise Lost*, the Elizabethan lyrics, *Leaves of Grass*, the lyrics of Shelley and Keats and of the late Victorian poets, and . . . we read together pieces out of Dante, Leopardi, and Goethe, Villon and Baudelaire.

It was Jekyll who first recognized and nurtured McKay's gift for writing poetry, and who encouraged him to put that gift to work in the service of his own

Jamaican dialect. The result was the publication of *Songs of Jamaica* and *Constab Ballads*. The first is a celebration of peasant life, somewhat after the manner of Robert Burns; *Constab Ballads* is more like Rudyard Kipling, drawing as it does upon McKay's brief stint as a constable in Kingston, Jamaica.

Kingston gave McKay his first taste of city life, and his first real taste of racism. The contempt of the city's white and mulatto upper classes for rural and lower-class blacks was an unpleasant revelation. The most blatant racism that McKay witnessed in Kingston, however, was not Jamaican in origin—it was imported in the form of American tourists. He would come to know this brand of racism much more intimately in the next few years, for, after only eight months in the Kingston constabulary, he resigned his post and left for the United States. In 1912 he enrolled, first at Tuskegee Institute, then at Kansas State College, to study agronomy. His plan was to return to Jamaica to help modernize the island's agriculture. The plan might have succeeded but for a gift of several thousand dollars from an unidentified patron—most likely Walter Jekyll—that paid McKay's way to New York, where he invested his money in a restaurant and married Eulalie Imelda Edwards, an old Jamaican sweetheart. Neither marriage nor restaurant survived long, but McKay found a certain consolation in the bustle and energy of the city. One part of town in particular seemed to reach out to him: Harlem.

In the next five years or so he worked at a variety of jobs—barboy, long-shoreman, fireman, and finally porter, then waiter, on the Pennsylvania Railroad. This was yet another apprenticeship, one in which he further developed the sympathy for the working class that remained with him all his life. Since his youth he had leaned politically toward socialism, and his years among the proletariat solidified his beliefs. His race consciousness developed hand-in-hand with his class consciousness. During this period of apprenticeship and developing awareness, he wrote. In 1918, he began a long association with Max Eastman, editor of the Communist magazine, *The Liberator*. McKay began publishing poems and essays in this revolutionary journal, and eventually became an associate editor. In 1919, in response to that year's bloody postwar race riots, McKay published in *The Liberator* what would become his most famous poem, "If We Must Die." The defiant tone, the open outrage of the poem caught the attention of the black community, and practically overnight McKay was at the forefront of black American poets.

Then came another of the abrupt turns that were so much a part of McKay's life and work. Before his newly won reputation had a chance to flourish, he left for England where he stayed for more than a year, writing and editing for a Communist newspaper, *Workers' Dreadnought*, and, in 1920, publishing his first book of poetry since the Jamaican volumes, *Spring in New Hampshire and Other Poems*. He returned to New York early in 1921 and spent the next two years with *The Liberator*, publishing a good bit of prose and verse and working on his principal book of poems, *Harlem Shadows*. Upon its publication in 1922, observes Wayne Cooper, McKay "was immediately acclaimed the best Negro poet since Paul Laurence Dunbar." Once again, however, he did not linger long over success. He was tired and in need of a change, especially after a chance meeting with his former wife reopened old wounds. Late in 1922, he traveled to Moscow for the Fourth Congress of the Third International. He quickly became a great favorite with Muscovites, and was allowed to address the Congress on the plight of American blacks and on the problem of racism within the Communist Party. As McKay described it, he was greeted "like a black ikon in the flesh." He was, it seemed, on the verge of a promising career as a political activist; but despite his successes in Russia, he still saw himself primarily as a writer. When he left Russia, he was "eager to resume what he considered the modern writer's proper function—namely, to record as best he could the truths of his own experience."

The 1920's were the decade of the Expatriate Artist, but though he spent most of his time in France until settling in Tangiers in 1931, McKay had very little to do with such writers as Ernest Hemingway and F. Scott Fitzgerald; his exile was too different from theirs. During his stay in Europe and North Africa, McKay published all his major fiction, along with a number of magazine articles. His first two novels, *Home to Harlem* and *Banjo*, were financially successful, in spite of the outraged reaction they drew from most black American critics. *Gingertown*, a collection of short stories, was not nearly so successful, and McKay's third novel, *Banana Bottom*, was a critical and financial disaster. Financially ruined, McKay was forced to end his expatriate existence.

With the help of some American friends, McKay returned to New York in 1934. He hoped to be of service to the black community, but upon his return, observes Wayne Cooper, "he found a wrecked economy, almost universal black poverty, and little sense of unity among those black writers and intellectuals he had hoped to work with in years ahead." As for his literary ambitions, the Harlem Renaissance was finished; black writers were no longer in vogue. Not only could he not find a publisher, he was unable to find any sort of a job, and wound up in Camp Greycourt, a government welfare camp outside New York City. Fortunately, Max Eastman was able to rescue him from the camp, and help him to get a job with the Federal Writers' Project. In 1937 he was able to publish his autobiography, *A Long Way from Home*. Once again, he was publishing articles in magazines, but his views isolated him from the mainstream black leaders; he felt, again in Cooper's words, that "their single-minded opposition to racial segregation was detrimental to any effective black community organization and to the development of a positive group spirit among blacks." McKay's thought at this time also shows a drift away from Communism, and a growing disillusionment with the fate of the "Grand Experiment" at the hands of the Soviets.

A Long Way from Home was neither a critical nor a financial success. Neither was his next and last book, *Harlem: Negro Metropolis*, a historical study published in 1940. By then, in spite of the steady work provided him by the Federal Writers' Project, his literary reputation was declining steadily. Despite his final acceptance of American citizenship in 1940, he could still not bring himself to regard America as home. His exile from both the black leadership and the left-wing establishment was becoming more and more total; worse still, his health began to deteriorate rapidly. Once again, like Walter Jekyll and Max Eastman in earlier years, a friend offered a hand. Ellen Terry, a Catholic writer, rescued McKay from a Harlem rooming house, and McKay's life took one last unexpected turn. As a young man he had rejected the fundamentalist Christianity of his father, and during his varied career had had little use for religion. Through his friendship with Terry, and later with the progressive Chicago bishop, Bernard Scheil, McKay experienced a change of mind and heart. In the spring of 1944 he moved to Chicago, and by fall of that year he was baptized into the Roman Catholic Church.

At last he seemed to have found a refuge, though his letters reveal a lingering bitterness over his lot. With his newfound faith, however, came a satisfying involvement in Chicago's Catholic Youth Organization and the opportunity to go on writing. His health continued to decline, and on May 22, 1948, McKay died of heart failure. He had recently finished preparing his *Selected Poems of Claude McKay* for publication. It is probably just as well that the volume appeared posthumously, as it took five years to find a publisher; at the time of his death, all of his works were out of print.

After a requiem mass in Chicago, McKay was brought back to Harlem for a memorial service. He was buried in Queens, "a long way from home."

Analysis

At the conclusion of his essay "The Renaissance Re-Examined," which appears as the final chapter of Arna Bontemps' 1972 book, *The Harlem Renaissance Remembered*, Warrington Hudlin insists that any true appreciation of the Harlem Renaissance hinges on the realization that this celebrated literary phenomenon "'opened the door' for the black writing of today. The Renaissance will always be remembered for this reason. It will be valued for its merits. It will come again to importance because of its idea." The poetry of Claude McKay must be read in much the same light. Though it is easy enough to find fault with much of his verse, he did help to "open the door" for those who would follow; as such, he deserves to be valued for his merits, judged by his strengths.

Though progressive enough in thought, McKay never felt compelled to experiment much with the form of his poetry. In content he is a black man of the twentieth century; in form he is more an English lyricist of the nineteenth, with, here and there, Miltonic echoes. The effect is, at times, a little peculiar, as in "Invocation," a sonnet in which the poet beseeches his muse to

> Let fall the light upon my sable face
> That once gleamed upon the Ethiopian's art;
> Lift me to thee out of this alien place
> So I may be, thine exiled counterpart,
> The worthy singer of my world and race.

Archaic trappings aside, there is a kind of majesty here, not bad work for a young man in his twenties. The Miltonic ring is probably no accident; McKay, it must be remembered, received something of an English gentleman's education. As the work of a black man pursuing what had been to that time primarily a white man's vocation, McKay's "Invocation" bears comparison with John Milton's "Hail native Language." One of the young Milton's ambitions was to vindicate English as poetic language, deserving of the same respect as Homer's Greek, Vergil's Latin, or Dante's Italian. McKay found himself in the position of vindicating a black man's experience of a white culture as a worthy subject for poetry.

Not all of McKay's verse concerns itself specifically with the theme of interracial tension. Among his poems are love lyrics, idyllic songs of country life, and harsher poems of the city, where "the old milk carts go rumbling by,/ Under the same old stars," where "Out of the tenements, cold as stone,/ Dark figures start for work." A recurring theme in McKay's work is the yearning for the lost world of childhood, which for him meant memories of Jamaica. This sense of loss is the occasion for one of his finest poems, "The Tropics in New York":

> Bananas ripe and green, and ginger-root,
> Cocoa in pods and alligator pears,
> And tangerines and mangoes and grape fruit,
> Fit for the highest prize at parish fairs.

The diction here is simple; one can almost hear Hemingway in the loving list of fruits. The speaker's memory stirs at the sight of a shop window. In the midst of the city his thoughts turn to images of "fruit-trees laden by low-singing rills,/ And dewy dawns, and mystical blue skies/ In benediction over nun-like hills." Here, in three straightforward quatrains, is the mechanism of nostalgia. From a physical reality placed by chance before him, the observer turns his eyes inward, visualizing a happy scene of which he is no longer a part. In the final stanza his eyes are still involved in the experience, only now they have grown dim, "and I could no more gaze;/ A wave of longing through my body swept." All of the narrator's senses tune themselves to grief as the quickening of smell and taste turns to a poignant hunger for "the old, familiar ways." Finally, the poem closes on a line as classically simple and tersely musical as anything in the poems of A. E. Housman: "I turned aside and bowed my head and wept."

Indeed, the poem is reminiscent of "Poem XL" in A. E. Housman's *A Shropshire Lad* (1896):

> Into my heart an air that kills
> From yon far country blows:
> What are those blue remembered hills,
> What spires, what farms are those?

It is a long way, to be sure, from Shropshire to Clarendon Parish, Jamaica, but the issue here is the long road back to lost experience, to that "land of lost content" that shines so plain, "The happy highways where I went/ And cannot come again." Any fair assessment of McKay's verse must affirm that he knew that land, those highways, all too well.

That same fair assessment, however, must give a prominent place to those poems upon which McKay's reputation was made—his poems of protest. McKay, in the estimation of Arna Bontemps, was black poetry's "strongest voice since [Paul Laurence] Dunbar." Dunbar's "racial" verse is a good indication of the point to which black American poetry had progressed by World War I. His plantation-style dialect verse tries, with a certain ironic cheerfulness, to make the best of a bad situation. At their best, these poems exhibit a stinging wit. At their worst, they are about as dignified as a minstrel show. In his poems in literary English, Dunbar is more assertive of his racial pride, but with an emphasis on suffering and forbearance, as in "We Wear the Mask." This poem, which could be read in retrospect as an answer to those critics and poets who would later disown Dunbar for not being "black" enough, speaks of the great cost at which pain and anger are contained:

> We smile, but O great Christ, our cries
> To Thee from tortured souls arise.
> We sing, but oh, the clay is vile
> Beneath our feet, and long the mile;
> But let the world dream otherwise,
> We wear the mask.

The anguish is plain enough, yet the poem, couched in a prayer, seems to view this "wearing of the mask" as an ennobling act, as a virtuous sacrifice. McKay was not inclined to view things in quite that way.

From the spring through the fall of 1919, numerous American cities were wracked by bloody race conflicts, the worst of which was a July riot in Chicago that left dozens dead and hundreds injured or homeless. While he was never the object of such violence, McKay and his fellow railroad waiters and porters walked to and from their trains with loaded revolvers in their pockets. Not unexpectedly, his reaction to the riots was far from mild; his concern was not with turning the other cheek, but with returning the offending slap. When the sonnet "If We Must Die" appeared in *The Liberator* it marked the emergence of a new rage in black American poetry:

> If we must die, let it not be like hogs,
> Hunted and penned in an inglorious spot,
> While round us bark the mad and hungry dogs,
> Making their mock at our accursed lot.

Again, the form is of another century, the language dated, even by late nineteenth century standards—"O kinsmen! We must meet the common foe! . . . What though before us lies the open grave?" The message, however, is ageless, avoiding as the poem does any direct reference to race.

On the heels of much-publicized violence against black neighborhoods, the implications were clear enough, but the universality of the poem became more obvious with time. A Jewish friend of McKay's wrote him in 1939, "proclaiming that . . . ["If We Must Die"] must have been written about the European Jews persecuted by Hitler." In a more celebrated instance, Winston Churchill read the poem before the House of Commons, as if, in the words of black poet and critic, Melvin Tolson, "it were the talismanic uniform of His Majesty's field marshal." The message reaches back to Thermopylae and Masada, and forward to Warsaw, Bastogne, and beyond. In its coverage of the bloodbath at the New York State Prison at Attica, *Time* (September 27, 1971) quoted the first four lines of McKay's sonnet as the "would-be heroic" effort of an anonymous, rebellious inmate. McKay might not have minded; he stated in his autobiography that "If We Must Die" was "the only poem I ever read to the members of my [railroad] crew." A poem that touches prisoners, railroad workers, and prime ministers alike must be termed a considerable success, despite any technical flaws it may exhibit.

Even so, one must not altogether avoid the question of just how successful McKay's poems are as poems. James Giles, in his 1976 study, *Claude McKay*, remarks on the disparity "between McKay's passionate resentment of racist oppression and his Victorianism in form and diction," finding in this conflict "a unique kind of tension in many of his poems, which weakens their ultimate success." Giles is probably correct to a point. In many cases McKay's art might have found fuller expression had he experimented more, let content more often shape form; he had shown abilities in this direction in his early Jamaican poems, and he was certainly open to experimentation in his later prose. The simple fact, however, is that he consistently chose to use traditional forms, and it would be unfair to say that it was a wholly unsuccessful strategy.

Indeed, the very civility of his favorite form, the sonnet, sometimes adds an ironic tension that heightens, rather than diminishes, the effect of the poem. For example, one could imagine any number of grisly, graphic effects to be achieved in a *vers libre*, expressionistic poem about a lynching. In

McKay's "The Lynching," though, one cannot help feeling the pull of an understated horror at seeing the act translated to quatrains and couplets: "and little lads, lynchers that were to be,/ Danced round the dreadful thing in fiendish glee." No further description of the "dreadful thing" is necessary. When McKay uses his poems to focus on real or imagined experience—a lynching, a cornered fight to the death, an unexpected remembrance of things past—his formal restraint probably works most often in his favor.

In poems that set out to convey a self-conscious message, however, he tends to be less successful, not so much because the form does not fit the content as because poetry and causes are dangerous bedfellows. Some of McKay's other angry sonnets—"The White House," "To the White Fiends," "Baptism"—may leave readers disappointed because they preach too much. McKay's specifically sociological, political, and, later, religious views receive better expression elsewhere, in his prose. Perhaps that is why he did not devote so much of his time to poetry after the publication of *Harlem Shadows*. In any case, his position in black American poetry is secure. Perhaps he should be judged more by that which was new in his poems, and that which inspired other black writers to carry on the task, as later generations have judged the Harlem Renaissance—as a bold and determined beginning, a rolling up of the sleeves for the hard work ahead.

Major publications other than poetry

NOVELS: *Home to Harlem*, 1928; *Banjo*, 1929; *Banana Bottom*, 1933.
SHORT FICTION: *Gingertown*, 1932.
NONFICTION: *A Long Way from Home*, 1937 (autobiography); *Harlem: Negro Metropolis*, 1940.
MISCELLANEOUS: *The Passion of Claude McKay: Selected Poetry and Prose, 1912-1948*, 1973 (Wayne F. Cooper editor; contains social and literary criticism, letters, prose, fiction, and poetry).

Bibliography

Bronz, Stephen H. *Roots of Negro Racial Consciousness: The 1920's, Three Harlem Renaissance Authors*, 1964
Cooper, Wayne F. "Claude McKay and the New Negro of the 1920's," in *Phylon*. XXV (1964), pp. 297-306.
Giles, James R. *Claude McKay*, 1976.
Smith, Robert A. "Claude McKay: An Essay in Criticism," in *Phylon*. IX (1948), pp. 270-273.
Tolson, Melvin B. "Claude McKay's Art," in *Poetry*. LXXXIII (February, 1954), pp. 287-290.

Richard A. Eichwald